W9-AOI-087

IN CONFLICT AND ORDER

Understanding Society

Thirteenth Edition

D. Stanley Eitzen
Colorado State University

Maxine Baca Zinn
Michigan State University

Kelly Eitzen Smith
University of Arizona

PEARSON

Boston   Columbus   Indianapolis   New York   San Francisco   Upper Saddle River
Amsterdam   Cape Town   Dubai   London   Madrid   Milan   Munich   Paris   Montreal   Toronto
Delhi   Mexico City   Sao Paulo   Sydney   Hong Kong   Seoul   Singapore   Taipei   Tokyo

Editorial Director: Craig Campanella
Editor in Chief: Dickson Musslewhite
Senior Executive Acquisition Editor: Brita Mess
Assistant Editor: Seanna Breen
Editorial Assistant: Zoe Lubitz
Executive Marketing Manager: Kelly May
Marketing Assistant: Frank Alarcon
Production Manager: Fran Russello
Media Editor: Rachel Comerford
Art Director: Anne Nieglos

Creative Director: Jayne Conte
Cover Designer: Suzanne Behnke
Cover Art: "Untitled" from Society Series #8 by D. Stanley Eitzen
Full-Service Project Management: Sudip Sinha, PreMediaGlobal
Printer/Binder: Edwards Brothers Malloy
Cover Printer: Lehigh Phoenix, Hagerstown, MD
Text Font: *Photina MT Std*

Credits and acknowledgments borrowed from other sources and reproduced, with permission, in this textbook appear on page 465.

Library of Congress Cataloging-in-Publication Data
Eitzen, D. Stanley.
  In conflict and order : understanding society / D. Stanley Eitzen, Maxine Baca Zinn, Kelly Eltzen Smith. — Thirteenth ed.
     p. cm.
  Includes bibliographical references and index.
  ISBN-13: 978-0-205-85441-7
  ISBN-10: 0-205-85441-9
  1. Sociology.   2. Social structure.   3. Social psychology.   4. United States—Social conditions.
I. Zinn, Maxine Baca, 1942-   II. Smith, Kelly Eitzen.   III. Title.

HM51.E334 2013
301—dc23

                                          2012012844

10 9 8 7 6 5 4 3 2 1

Student Edition
ISBN 10: 0-205-85441-9
ISBN 13: 978-0-205-85441-7

Instructor's Review Copy
ISBN 10: 0-205-85440-0
ISBN 13: 978-0-205-85440-0

Ála Carte
ISBN 10: 0-205-85816-3
ISBN 13: 978-0-205-85816-3

PEARSON

Why Do You Need This New Edition?

If you're wondering why you should buy this new edition of *In Conflict and Order,* here are six good reasons:

1. New Globalization panels include an international view on gay marriage, a look inside the mind of a suicide bomber, globalization's affect on disease, the stock market, pollution, and job insecurity, and more.

2. More information about the changing economy, including extensive coverage of the rise of multinational corporations, outsourcing and offshoring jobs, the decrease in work benefits, the increasing gap between the wealthy and everyone else, the hidden welfare system that supports big business, and "the best democracy money can buy."

3. New coverage of popular contemporary topics, including the causes and consequences of the Great Recession, especially the legacy of this difficult time in our history, the fragmentation of society, the widening inequality gap, the downward pressure on wages, "benefits insecurity," poverty level employment, work-related injuries by race, the decline of unions, and the 2010 Supreme Court decision giving organizations the right to give unlimited amounts to political campaigns.

4. A new set of panels, "Technology and Society," are found throughout. Some of the topics considered are: the social media and the invasion of privacy; computer technology and middle-class job loss; race and computer technology; the Internet's private eye; family life in the digital age; helicopter parenting and GPS devices; and gender and social networking.

5. Updated statistics reflect rapid changes in society and the intransigence of many social problems.

6. Incisive cartoons.

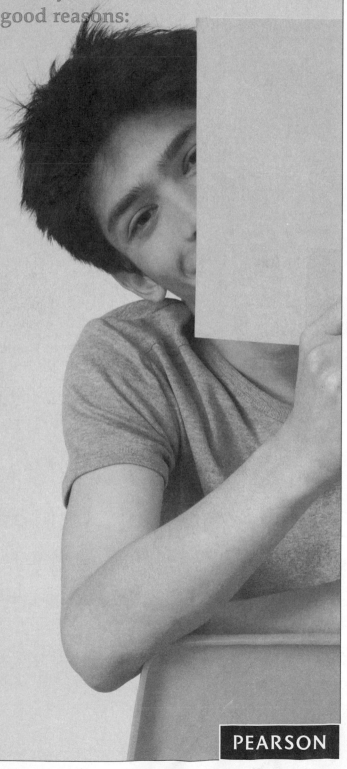

PEARSON

CONTENTS

Preface   xiii

PART ONE   The Sociological Approach

1   The Sociological Perspective   3

Sociology   4
Assumptions of the Sociological Perspective   4
The Sociological Imagination   7
Problems with the Sociological Perspective   7
The Historical Development of Sociology   9
    Auguste Comte (1798–1857): The Science of Society   10   •   Emile Durkheim
    (1858–1917): Social Facts and the Social Bond   10   •   Karl Marx (1818–1883):
    Economic Determinism   10   •   Max Weber (1864–1920): A Response to Marx   11
Sociological Methods: The Craft of Sociology   11
    Sociological Questions   11   •   Problems in Collecting Data   12
A CLOSER LOOK: Thinking Like a Sociologist   13
RESEARCH METHODS: Standards for Objectivity and Integrity in Social Research   16
    Sources of Data   18

2   The Structure of Social Groups   23

The Micro Level   23
    Social Organization   23
TECHNOLOGY AND SOCIETY: The Isolating Effects of E-mail   26
    Norms   27   •   Status and Role   27   •   Social Control   30   •
    Primary and Secondary Groups   31
A CLOSER LOOK: The Declining Significance of Family   31
    Bureaucracy: The Ultimate Secondary Group   32   •   Power of the Social Group   33
The Societal or Macro Level   37
    Society as a Social System   37   •   The Culture of Society   38   •
    Social Classes   38   •   Social Institutions   38
DIVERSITY: Gay Marriage?   39

3   The Duality of Social Life: Order and Conflict   43

Social Systems: Order and Conflict   44
    The Order Model   44
RESEARCH METHODS: Social Scientists and Values: Taking Sides   44
    The Conflict Model   45   •   The Duality of Social Life   46
Synthesis of the Order and Conflict Models   48

v

The Fragmentation of Social Life: Deepening Divides in U.S. Society   50
  Increasing Polarization   *50*   •   Declining Trust in Societal Institutions   *51*   •
  The Widening Inequality Gap   *52*   •   The Deepening Divides over Diversity   *52*
  Violence and the Myth of Peaceful Progress   *53*
A CLOSER LOOK: Violence and Division in India   *54*
The Integrative Forces in Society   57
A CLOSER LOOK: Twinkies, Pencils, and Functional Integration   *58*
DIVERSITY: The Media's Selective Perception of Race and Class   *60*
The Use of the Order and Conflict Models in This Book   61

PART TWO   The Individual in Society: Society in the Individual

 Culture   65

Culture: The Knowledge That People Share   66
  Characteristics of Culture   *66*
A CLOSER LOOK: Ethnocentrism in U.S. Schools   *68*
  Types of Shared Knowledge   *69*
TECHNOLOGY AND SOCIETY: Test Your Emoticon Knowledge   *69*
  The Social Construction of Reality   *72*
The Globalization of Culture   74
Values   76
  Values as Sources of Societal Integration and Social Problems   *77*
A CLOSER LOOK: Competition in the Era of Reality Television   *80*
  Values and Behavior   *83*   •   Cultural Diversity   *83*
DIVERSITY: Life in a Religious Sect   *85*
Values from the Order and Conflict Perspectives   86

 Socialization   89

The Personality as a Social Product   91
  Theories   *92*
A CLOSER LOOK: The Looking-Glass Self and Body Image   *93*
  Society's Socialization Agents   *95*
TECHNOLOGY AND SOCIETY: Helicopter Parenting and GPS Devices   *96*
Socialization in a Changing Social Landscape   99
  Changing Family Forms   *99*   •   Trends in Schooling   *100*   •
  Changing Racial Landscape   *101*   •   Changing Generation
  Cohorts   *101*   •   Changing Images in the Media   *101*   •
  Changing Gender Roles   *103*
Socialization from the Order and Conflict Perspectives   103

 Social Control   107

Agents of Ideological Social Control   108
  Family   *108*   •   Education   *109*   •   Religion   *109*
DIVERSITY: The Amish and Social Control   *110*
  Sport   *110*   •   Media   *111*   •   Government   *113*
Agents of Direct Social Control   113
  Social Welfare   *113*   •   Science and Medicine   *114*   •   Government   *116*

A CLOSER LOOK: Singapore: The Iron Fist in the Land of Order   *117*
A CLOSER LOOK: Homeland Security on Campus   *122*
Social Control in the Private Sector: Implications for Contemporary Social Life   *124*
TECHNOLOGY AND SOCIETY: The Internet's Private Eye   *124*
Social Control from the Order and Conflict Perspectives   *126*

 7   Deviance   129

The Characteristics of Deviance   *129*
TECHNOLOGY AND SOCIETY: Shame Sites   *131*
Traditional Theories for the Causes of Deviance   *133*
   The Individual as the Source of Deviance   *133*   •   Society as the Source of
   Deviance   *138*
DIVERSITY: The Criminal Justice System: Unreasonable Stops and Searches by Race   *139*
HUMAN AGENCY: Civil Disobedience   *144*
Deviance from the Order and Conflict Perspectives   *147*

PART THREE   The Study of Society

 **8   Structural Sources of Social Change: Economic
and Demographic   151**

Globalization and the Structural Transformation of the Economy   *151*
   Globalization   *152*
GLOBALIZATION: Sending U.S. Jobs Overseas   *153*
   Structural Transformation of the Economy   *154*
A CLOSER LOOK: Capitalism's Changing Job Market: A Process of Creative Destruction   *155*
TECHNOLOGY AND SOCIETY: Computer Technology and Middle-Class Job Loss   *156*
The New Immigration and the Changing Racial Landscape   *160*
   Immigration Patterns   *160*
DIVERSITY: Popular Surnames in the United States Are No Longer Exclusively Anglo   *161*
   Immigration and Increasing Diversity   *162*   •   Consequences of the New
   Immigration   *163*
GLOBALIZATION: Yes, Global Free Market Mobility for Corporations; No, Global Free Market
   Mobility for Workers George H. Sage   *165*
   Immigration and Agency   *167*
The Aging Society   *169*
   Demographic Trends   *169*   •   Demographic Portrait of the Current Elderly
   Population   *171*   •   Problems of an Aging Society   *174*   •   Responses by
   the Elderly: Human Agency   *177*   •   The Three Structural Transformations of
   Society   *178*

 9   Social Stratification   183

A CLOSER LOOK: Birth as Destiny: India's Caste System   *184*
GLOBALIZATION: Inequality among Nations   *185*
Major Concepts   *185*
   Class   *187*   •   Race and Ethnicity   *187*   •   Gender   *188*   •
   The Intersection of Class, Race, and Gender   *188*
Order and Conflict Theories of Stratification   *189*
   Order Theory   *189*   •   Conflict Theory   *189*

Deficiency Theories   *190*

  Biological Inferiority   *190*   •   Cultural Inferiority   *193*

Structural Theories   *195*

  Institutional Discrimination   *195*   •   The Political Economy of Society   *196*

DIVERSITY: Who Benefits from Poverty?   *197*

10   Class   201

Dimensions of Inequality   *202*

  Wealth   *202*   •   Income   *203*   •   Education   *204*   •
  Occupation   *206*   •   The Consequences of Increasing Inequality for Society   *207*

A CLOSER LOOK: The Widening Inequality Gap   *208*

Social Classes   *209*

  The Order Model's Conception of Social Class   *209*

DIVERSITY: The Near Poor: The Missing Class   *210*

  The Conflict Model's Conception of Social Class   *211*   •   Summary: Class from the
  Order and Conflict Perspectives   *213*

The Consequences of Social Class Positions   *214*

  Physical Health   *214*   •   Family Instability   *216*   •   Fighting the Nation's
  Wars   *216*   •   Justice   *217*   •   Education   *217*

Social Mobility   *218*

  Education and Social Mobility   *219*

Poverty in the United States   *221*

HUMAN AGENCY: Coping Strategies among the Poor   *222*

  Racial Minorities   *222*   •   Nativity   *223*   •   Gender   *223*   •
  Children   *223*   •   The Elderly   *223*   •   The Geography of Poverty   *224*   •
  The Severely Poor   *225*

Myths about Poverty   *226*

  Refusal to Work   *226*   •   Welfare Dependency   *226*   •   The Poor Get Special
  Advantages   *228*   •   Welfare Is an African American and Latino Program   *229*

11   Racial Inequality   233

How to Think about Racial and Ethnic Inequality   *233*

Racial and Ethnic Minorities   *234*

  Racial Categories   *235*   •   Ethnic Groups and Their Differences   *236*   •
  Racial-Ethnic Groups in the United States   *237*

Explanations of Racial and Ethnic Inequality   *240*

  Deficiency Theories   *240*   •   Bias Theories   *241*

A CLOSER LOOK: Culture and Structure in Today's Poverty Debates   *242*

  Structural Discrimination Theories   *243*   •   Racial Stratification from the Order
  and Conflict Perspectives   *244*

Discrimination against Blacks and Hispanics: Continuity and Change   *245*

  Income   *246*   •   Education   *248*   •   Unemployment   *249*   •
  Type of Employment   *249*   •   Health   *250*

Contemporary Trends and Issues in U.S. Racial and Ethnic Relations   *251*

  Growing Racial Strife   *251*   •   More Racially Based Groups and Activities   *252*

TECHNOLOGY AND SOCIETY: Race and Computer Technology   *253*

  Social and Economic Isolation in U.S. Cities   *253*   •
  Racial Policies in the New Century   *254*

12 Gender Inequality 259

Women and Men Are Differentiated and Ranked *259*
    Is Gender Biological or Social? *260* • Gender and Power *262*
Gender Stratification from the Order and Conflict Perspectives *262*
    The Order Perspective *262* • The Conflict Perspective *263* •
    The Implications of the Order and Conflict Perspectives *263*
Learning Gender *264*
    Children at Home *264* • Children at Play *266* •
    Formal Education *267* • Socialization as Blaming the Victim *269*
Reinforcing Male Dominance *269*
    Language *270* • Interpersonal Behavior *270* • Mass Media *270*
TECHNOLOGY AND SOCIETY: Gender and Social Networking *271*
    Religion *272* • The Law *273* • Politics *274*
Structured Gender Inequality in the Workplace *275*
    Occupational Distribution *275* • The Earnings Gap *278*
HUMAN AGENCY: Take Control: How to Negotiate Your Salary *279*
    Intersection of Race and Gender in the Workplace *279* • How Workplace
    Inequality Operates *279* • Gender in the Global Economy *281*
GLOBALIZATION: Trafficking Sex for a Globalized Market *282*
The Costs and Consequences of Sexism *282*
    Who Benefits? *282* • The Social and Individual Costs *283*
Fighting the System *283*
    Feminist Movements in the United States *283* • Women's Struggles in the
    Twenty-First Century *284*

PART FOUR   Social Institutions

 The Economy 287

Capitalism and Socialism *287*
    Capitalism *288* • Socialism *289*
The Corporation-Dominated Economy *290*
    Monopolistic Capitalism *291* • Transnational Corporations *292*
Capitalism and Inequality *293*
    Concentration of Corporate Wealth *293* • Concentration of Private Wealth and
    Income *293* • Concentration of Want and Misery *294*
Work in U.S. Society *294*
    The Problems of Work *295*
GLOBALIZATION: Modern Day Slavery in the United States *299*
    Discrimination in the Workplace: The Perpetuation of Inequality *301* •
    Unemployment *303*
Capitalism in Crisis *305*
    The Great Recession (2007–2010) *305*
A CLOSER LOOK: The Subprime Crisis for African Americans and Latinos *306*
A CLOSER LOOK: The Effects of the Great Recession on Recent College Graduates *310*
    The Negative Consequences of Private Profitability over Social Need *311* •
    Declining Wages, Jobs, Consumerism, and Profits *312* • The Lack of Economic
    Planning *313*

14 Power and Politics 317

Models of the National Power Structure 318
Pluralist Models *318*
A CLOSER LOOK: Structural Barriers to Democracy 319
A CLOSER LOOK: The Best Democracy Money Can Buy 322
A CLOSER LOOK: Is the United States a Plutocracy? Some Warnings 323
Elitist Models *324*
A CLOSER LOOK: The Dark Side of Lobbying 331
The Consequences of Concentrated Power 333
TECHNOLOGY AND SOCIETY: Facebook Lobbies Washington 334
Subsidies to Big Business *335* • Trickle-Down Solutions *336* •
The Powerless Bear the Burden *337*
A CLOSER LOOK: Guns or Butter? Who's Paying for the War? 338
Foreign Policy for Corporate Benefit *339*
The Order and Conflict Perspectives on the Distribution of Power 339

15 Families 343

The Mythical Family in the United States 343
U.S. Families in Historical Perspective 344
The Family in Capitalism *344* • Stratification and Family Life: Unequal Life
Chances *345* • Economic Transformation and Family Life *348* •
Today's Diverse Family Forms *349*
Changes in Marriage and Family Roles 351
The Social and Individual Benefits of Marriage *352* • The Benefits of
Marriage Reconsidered *353* • Same-Sex Marriage *353* • Divorce and
Remarriage *354* • Work and Family Roles *355*
RESEARCH METHODS: Researching Families: How Sociologist Arlie Hochschild Interviewed
Couples about the Demands of Work and Family *356*
Children and Adolescents *357*
TECHNOLOGY AND SOCIETY: Family Life in the Digital Age 360
The Aged *360*
Violence in Families 360
The Modern Family from the Order and Conflict Perspectives 362
Families of the Future 363

16 Education 367

The Characteristics of U.S. Education 367
Education as a Conserving Force *367* • Mass Education *368* • The
Preoccupation with Order and Control *368* • A Fragmented Education
System *369* • Local Control of Education *369* • A Lack of
Curriculum Standardization *371* • The Competitive Nature of U.S.
Education *372* • The Sifting and Sorting Function of Schools *372*
A CLOSER LOOK: Leaving Boys Behind? 373
Education and Inequality 373
DIVERSITY: The Tiger Mom Controversy 375
Financing Public Education *376* • Family Economic Resources *377* • Higher
Education and Stratification *379* • Minorities and Higher Education *380* •
Curriculum *380* • Segregation *380* • Tracking and Teachers' Expectations *381*
Education from the Order and Conflict Perspectives 383

17 Religion 387

GLOBALIZATION: The Global Reach of the World's Major Religions   390

Classical Sociology's Differing Interpretations of Religion   *391*

Religion from the Order Perspective of Emile Durkheim   *391*   •   Religion from the Conflict Perspective of Karl Marx   *391*   •   Max Weber's View of Religion and Social Change   *392*

Some Distinctive Features of U.S. Religion   *392*

Civil Religion   *392*   •   The Variety of Religious Beliefs in the United States   *394*

DIVERSITY: Islam in the United States   395

GLOBALIZATION: Outsourcing Prayer   396

Religious Organization   *396*

Class, Race, Gender, Sexuality, and Religion   *399*

The Relationship between Social Class and Religion   *399*   •   Religion and Race: The Case of African Americans   *400*   •   Religion and Ethnicity: The Case of Recent Immigrants   *401*   •   Religion and Gender   *401*

DIVERSITY: Religion and Patriarchy   402

Religion and Sexuality   *402*

Religious Trends   *404*

The Decline of the Mainline Denominations   *405*   •   The Rise of Christian Fundamentalism   *406*   •   The Spread of the Evangelical Message via Savvy Marketing   *407*

Contemporary Christianity and Politics   *408*

The Religious Right   *408*   •   The Role of Mainline Churches: Comfort or Challenge?   *410*

Religion from the Order and Conflict Perspectives   *411*

PART FIVE   Human Agency

18 Human Agency: Individuals and Groups in Society Changing Social Structures 415

The Sociological Paradox: Social Structure and Agency   *415*

Social Movements   *416*

Types of Social Movements   *416*   •   The Life Course of Social Movements   *417*

HUMAN AGENCY: The Political Muscle of Americans with Disabilities   *418*

GLOBALIZATION: Students against Sweatshops   *419*

Agency: Social Change from the Bottom Up   *420*

The Civil Rights Movement   *420*   •   Gender Equity in Sports   *423*   •   Is There Hope for a People's Social Movement Now?   *426*

A CLOSER LOOK: The Paradox of Social Progress and Economic Reaction   *428*

Conclusion   *429*

Glossary   **433**

References   **441**

Photo Credits   **465**

Name Index   **467**

Subject Index   **477**

M any introductory students will be exposed to sociology in only one course. They should leave that course with a new and meaningful way of understanding themselves, other people, their society, and other societies. The most fundamental goal of this book, then, is to help the student develop a sociological perspective.

This goal is emphasized explicitly in the first chapter and implicitly throughout *In Conflict and Order: Understanding Society*, thirteenth edition. The sociological perspective focuses on the social sources of behavior. It requires shedding existing myths and ideologies by questioning all social arrangements. One of the most persistent questions of the sociologist is, Who benefits from the existing customs and social order, and who does not? Because social groups are created by people, they are not sacred. Is there a better way?

Although there will be disagreement on the answers to these questions, the answers are less important, sociologically, than is the willingness to call into question existing social arrangements that many people consider sacred. This is the beginning of the sociological perspective. But being critical is not enough. The sociologist must have a coherent way to make sense of the social world, and this leads us to the second goal of this edition of *In Conflict and Order*—the elaboration of a consistent framework from which to understand and interpret social life. *In Conflict and Order*, thirteenth edition, is guided by the assumption that there is an inherent duality in all societies. The realistic analysis of any one society must include both the integrating and stabilizing forces, on one hand, and the forces that are conducive to malintegration and change, on the other. Society in the United States is characterized by harmony and conflict, integration and division, stability and change. This synthesis is crucial if the intricacies of social structure, the mechanisms of social change, and the sources of social problems are to be understood fully.

This objective of achieving balance between the order and the conflict perspectives is not fully realized in this book, however. Although both perspectives are incorporated into each chapter, the scales are tipped toward the conflict perspective. This imbalance is the conscious product of how the authors, as sociologists and teachers, view the structure and mechanisms of society. In addition to presenting what we believe is a realistic analysis of society, this imbalance counters the prevailing view of the order perspective, with its implicit sanctification of the status quo. Such a stance is untenable to us, given the spate of social problems that persist in U.S. society. The emphasis on the conflict approach, on the other hand, questions existing social arrangements, viewing them as sources of social problems, a position with which we agree. Implicit in such a position is the goal of restructuring society along more humane lines.

That we stress the conflict approach over the order model does not suggest that *In Conflict and Order* is a polemic. On the contrary, the social structure is also examined from a sympathetic view. The existing arrangements do provide for the stability and maintenance of the system. But the point is that, by including a relatively large dose of the conflict perspective, the discussion is a realistic appraisal of the system rather than a look through rose-colored glasses.

This duality theme is evident primarily at the societal level in this book. But even though the societal level is the focus of our inquiry, the small-group and individual levels are not ignored. The principles that apply to societies are also appropriate for the small social organizations to which we belong, such as families, work groups, athletic teams, religious organizations, and clubs. Just as important, the sociological perspective shows how the individual is affected by groups of all sizes. Moreover, it shows how the individual's identity is shaped by social forces and how in many important ways the individual's thoughts and actions are determined by group memberships. The linkage of the individual to social groups is shown throughout *In Conflict and Order*. The relationship of the individual to the larger society is illustrated in special panels that examine societal changes and forces impinging on individuals and the choices available to us as we attempt to cope with these societal trends.

Organization of the Book

The book is divided into five parts. Part One (Chapters 1 through 3) introduces the reader to the sociological perspective, the fundamental concepts of the discipline, and the duality of social life. These chapters set the stage for an analysis of the structure (organization) and process (change) of U.S. society. The emphasis is on the characteristics of societies in general and of the United States in particular.

Part Two (Chapters 4 through 7) describes the way in which human beings are shaped by society. The topics include the values that direct our choices, the social bases of social identity and personality, the mechanisms that control individual and group behavior, and the violation of social expectations—deviance. Throughout these chapters we examine both the forces that work to make all of us living in the United States similar, and those that make us different.

Part Three (Chapters 8 through 12) focuses on social change and social inequality. This section begins with a chapter showing how three major social forces (globalization, the new immigration, and the aging of the population) affect human behavior and social life. Among other things, these structural changes affect social stratification by class and race. These are the topics of the remaining chapters in this section. We look at how societies rank people in hierarchies. We also examine the mechanisms that ensure that some people have a greater share of wealth, power, and prestige than do others, and the positive and negative consequences of such an arrangement. Other chapters focus on the specific hierarchies of stratification: class, race, and gender.

Part Four (Chapters 13 through 17) discusses another characteristic of all societies: the presence of social institutions. Every society historically has developed a fairly consistent way of meeting its survival needs and the needs of its members. The organization of society into families, for example, ensures the regular input of new members, provides for the stable care and protection of the young, and regulates sexual activity. In addition to discussions of the family, chapters in Part Four are devoted to education, the economy, the polity, and religion. The understanding of institutions is vital to the understanding of society because these social arrangements are part of its structure, resist change, and have a profound impact on the public and private lives of people.

Part Five (Chapter 18) examines social changes that occur from the bottom up. The goal of this chapter is to combat the strong structural determinism bias of the earlier chapters by focusing on how human beings, individually and collectively, change social structures.

Themes of the Book

As in previous editions, *In Conflict and Order*, thirteenth edition incorporates four themes: diversity, the struggle by the powerless to achieve social justice, the changing economy, and globalization. First, although there are separate chapters on race, class, and gender, these fundamental sources of differences are infused throughout the book and in the photographs. This emphasis is important to an understanding of the diversity in society as well as the structural sources of inequality and injustice. Second, the tendency toward structural determinism is countered by Chapter 18 and various examples of human agency throughout the book: the powerless organizing to achieve power and positive social changes (for example, civil rights, gay rights, rights for people with disabilities, and gender equity in sports and the workplace). Third, the sources and consequences of the structural transformation of the economy are examined. This is a pivotal shift in the U.S. economy with significant implications for individuals, communities, the society, and the global economy. And, fourth, the focus is often shifted away from the United States to other societies through descriptions, panels, and tables. This global perspective is important for at least two reasons: to illustrate the universality of sociological concepts and to help us understand how the world is becoming ever more interdependent.

These four themes—diversity, the struggle by the powerless to achieve social justice, the changing economy, and globalization—are important concepts to consider sociologically. We see that social problems are structural in origin and that the pace of social change is accelerating, yet society's institutions are slow to change and meet the challenges. The problems of U.S. society are of great magnitude, and solutions must be found. But understanding must precede action, and that is one goal of *In Conflict and Order.*

The analysis of U.S. society is a challenging task. It is frustrating because of the heterogeneity of the population and the complexity of the forces impinging on U.S. social life. It is also frustrating because the diversity within the United States leads to many inconsistencies and paradoxes. Furthermore, it is difficult, if not impossible, for people in the United States to be objective and consistently rational about their society. Nevertheless, the sociological study of U.S. society is fascinating and rewarding. It becomes absorbing as people gain insights into their own actions and into the behavior of other people. Understanding the intricate complex of forces leading to a particular type of social structure or social problem can be liberating and can lead to collective efforts to bring about social change. This book attempts to give the reader just such a sociological perspective.

Finally, we are unabashedly proud of being sociologists. Our hope is that you will capture our enthusiasm for exploring and understanding the intricacies and mysteries of social life.

Features

To help students develop and foster their sociological perspective, we integrate the following features throughout the book.

- **Human Agency** panels show how individuals and groups can become empowered to achieve positive social change.
- **Globalization** panels present examples of the interconnections among the world's peoples.
- **Diversity** panels address tolerance and understanding of a wide range of groups, institutions, choices, and behaviors.
- **A Closer Look** panels elaborate on specific topics in detail.
- **Research Methods** panels explore different stages and facets of the research process in the social sciences.
- **New to this edition are Technology and Society** panels to examine how technological innovations such as the Internet and social media like Facebook affect social life.
- **End-of-chapter-pedagogy** includes Chapter Reviews, Key Terms, and Study Questions.

New to This Edition

This thirteenth edition of *In Conflict and Order*, while retaining the structure of the earlier editions, is different and improved in the following ways:

- **New Globalization panels** include an international view on gay marriage, a look inside the mind of a suicide bomber, globalization's affect on disease, the stock market, pollution, and job insecurity, and more.

- **More information about the changing economy,** including extensive coverage of the rise of multinational corporations, outsourcing and offshoring jobs, the decrease in work benefits, the increasing gap between the wealthy and everyone else, the hidden welfare system that supports big business, and "the best democracy money can buy."
- **New coverage of popular contemporary topics,** including the causes and consequences of the Great Recession, especially the legacy of this difficult time in our history, the fragmentation of society, the widening inequality gap, the downward pressure on wages, "benefits insecurity," poverty level employment, work-related injuries by race, the decline of unions, and the 2010 Supreme Court decision giving organizations the right to give unlimited amounts to political campaigns.
- **A new set of panels,** "Technology and Society," are found throughout. Some of the topics considered are: the social media and the invasion of privacy; computer technology and middle-class job loss; churches use of social networking to sell their product, and social interaction through social media; race and computer technology; the Internet's private eye; helicopter parenting and GPS devices; and gender and social networking.
- **Updated statistics** reflect rapid changes in society and the intransigence of many social problems.
- **Incisive cartoons.**

Acknowledgments

We want to thank the following reviewers for their critiques of the thirteenth edition: Dr. Daniel M. Harrison, Lander University; Mary Ann Maher, Paradise Valley Community College; Daniel Schwartz, University of New Mexico; and Russell E. Ward, Jr., Francis Marion University.

We especially thank Paula Miller of Michigan State University for research assistance on this edition.

D. Stanley Eitzen
Maxine Baca Zinn
Kelly Eitzen Smith

IN CONFLICT AND ORDER

Understanding Society

CHAPTER 1

The Sociological Perspective

Life appears to be a series of choices for each of us. We decide how much schooling is important and what field to major in. We choose a job, a mate, and a lifestyle. But how free are we? Have you ever felt trapped by events and conditions beyond your control? Your religious beliefs may make you feel guilty for some behaviors. Your patriotism may cost you your life—even willingly. These ideological traps are powerful, so powerful that we usually do not even see them as traps. Have you ever felt trapped in a social relationship? Have you ever continued a relationship with a friend, a group of friends, a lover, or a spouse when you were convinced that this relationship was wrong for you? Have you ever participated in an act, which later seemed absolutely ridiculous, even immoral, because of peer pressure? Most likely your answers to these questions are in the affirmative, because the people closest to us effectively command our conformity.

At another level, have you ever felt that because of your race, gender, age, ethnicity, or social class, certain opportunities were closed to you? For example, if you are a woman, you may want to try certain sports or jobs, but to do so would be to call your femininity into question. Or you may seek a leadership position in your church but you are denied because of that church's beliefs.

Even more remotely, each of us is controlled by decisions made in corporate boardrooms, in government bureaus, and in foreign capitals. Whether we retain employment may not be the consequence of our work behavior but rather the result of corporate decisions to move a plant overseas, or to outsource the work offshore, or to buy equipment that replaces human labor.

Similarly, the actions of investment bankers and hedge fund managers can cause a worldwide financial crisis as occurred in the last months of 2007. When their too risky investments cratered, the stock market plunged and some major banks and brokerage houses went bankrupt while others were rescued by the government. Panic ensued and fortunes were lost. Millions of Americans lost as much as half of the value of their savings as their stock portfolios and the value of their homes plummeted.

The weather in China and Russia or the actions of speculators affects grain prices in the United States, meaning bankruptcy or prosperity for individual farmers and high or low prices for individual consumers. So, too, do soaring inflation rates in a country, as occurred in 1999 when Brazil, which grows 10 percent of the world's soybean crop, devalued its currency, causing a rapid decline in the world price of soybeans and a decline of 10 percent or more in the price for U.S. farmers.

Finally, we are also trapped by our culture. We do not decide what is right or wrong, moral or immoral. We do not decide what is beautiful and what is not. Even the decision on what is important and what is not is a cultural bias decided for us and incorporated and embedded deep inside each one of us.

Sociology

Sociology is the discipline that attempts to understand these social forces—the forces outside us that shape our lives, interests, and personalities. In John Walton's words, "Sociology explores the determinants of individual and collective behavior that are not given in our psychic or biological makeup, but fashioned in the broader arena of social interaction" (Walton, 1990:5). As the science of society and social behavior, sociology is interesting, insightful, and important. This is so because sociology explores and analyzes the ultimate issues of our personal lives, of society, and of the world. At the personal level, sociology investigates the causes and consequences of such phenomena as romantic love, violence, identity, conformity, deviance, personality, and interpersonal power. At the societal level, sociology examines and explains poverty, crime rates, racism, sexism, homophobia, pollution, and political power. At the global level, sociology researches such phenomena as societal inequality, war, conflict resolution, immigration patterns, global warming, and population growth. Other disciplines are also helpful in understanding these social phenomena, but sociology makes a unique contribution. The insights of sociology are important for individuals because they help us understand why we behave as we do. This understanding is not only liberating but a necessary precondition for meaningful social action to bring about social change. As a scholarly discipline, sociology is important because it complements and in some cases supersedes other disciplines concerned with understanding and explaining social behavior.

"I'm a social scientist, Michael. That means I can't explain electricity or anything like that, but if you ever want to know about people I'm your man."

Assumptions of the Sociological Perspective

To discover the underlying order of social life and the principles that explain human behavior, scientists have focused on different levels of phenomena. The result of this division of labor has been the creation of scholarly disciplines, each concentrating on a relatively narrow sphere of phenomena. Biologists interested in social phenomena have focused on organic bases for behavior such as DNA, brain chemistry, and hormone balance. Psychological explanations assume that the source of human behavior lies in the psyches of individuals causing guilt, aggression, phobias, lack of motivation, and low self-esteem.

The understanding of human behavior benefits from the emphases of the various disciplines. Each discipline makes important contributions to knowledge. Of the three major disciplines focusing on human behavior, sociology is commonly the least understood. The explicit goal of this book is to remedy this fault by introducing the reader to the sociological ways of perceiving and interpreting the social world. Let us begin by considering the assumptions of the sociological approach that provide the foundation for this unique, exciting, and insightful way of viewing and understanding the social world.

Individuals Are, by Their Nature, Social Beings. There are two fundamental reasons for this assumption. First, human babies enter the world totally dependent on other people for their survival. This initial period of dependence means, in effect, that each of us has been immersed in social groups from birth. A second basis for the social nature of human beings is that throughout history people have found it to their advantage to cooperate with other people (for defense, for material comforts, to overcome the perils of nature, and to improve technology).

Individuals Are, for the Most Part, Socially Determined. This essential assumption stems from the first assumption, that people are social beings. Individuals are products of their social environments for several reasons. During infancy, the child is at the mercy of adults, especially parents. These people shape the infant in an infinite variety of ways, depending on their proclivities and those of their society. The parents have a profound impact on the child's ways of thinking about himself or herself and about other people. The parents transmit religious views, political attitudes, and attitudes toward the evaluation of others. The child is punished for certain behaviors and rewarded for others. Whether that child becomes a bigot or integrationist, traditionalist or innovator, saint or sinner depends in large measure on the parents, peers, and other people who interact with her or him.

The parents may transmit to their offspring some idiosyncratic beliefs and behaviors, but most significantly they act as cultural agents, transferring the ways of the society to their children. Thus, the child is born into a family and also into a society. This society into which individuals are born shapes their personalities and perceptions. Sociologist Peter Berger has summarized the impact of society:

> Society not only controls our movements, but shapes our identity, our thoughts and our emotions. The structures of society become the structures of our own consciousness. Society does not stop at the surface of our skins. Society penetrates us as much as it envelops us. (Berger, 1963:121)

The individual's identity is socially bestowed. Who we are, how we feel about ourselves, and how other people treat us are usually consequences of our social location, "the corners in life that people occupy because of where they are located in a society" (Henslin, 2008:4), corners such as social class, race/ethnicity, gender, and sexuality. Individuals' personalities are also shaped by the way they are accepted, rejected, and defined by other people. Whether an individual is attractive or plain, witty or dull, worthy or unworthy depends on the values of society and the groups in which the individual is immersed. Although genes determine one's physiology and potential, the social environment determines how those characteristics will be evaluated. Suggesting that human beings are socially determined is another way of saying that they are similar to puppets. They are dependent on and manipulated by social forces. A major function of sociology is to identify the social forces that affect us so greatly. Freedom, as Reece McGee has pointed out, can come only from a recognition of these unseen forces:

> Freedom consists in knowing what these forces are and how they work so that we have the option of saying no to the impact of their operation. For example, if we grow up in a racist society, we will be racists unless we learn what racism is and how it works and then choose to refuse its impact. In order to do so, however, we must recognize that it is there in the first place. People often are puppets, blindly danced by strings of which they are unaware and over which they are not free to exercise control. A major function of sociology is that it permits us to recognize the forces operative on us and to untie the puppet strings which bind us, thereby giving us the option to be free. (McGee, 1975:3)

Thus, one task of sociology is to learn, among other things, what racism is and to determine how it works. This is often difficult because we typically do not recognize its existence—because we have been puppets, socialized to believe and behave in particular ways. To say that we are puppets is too strong, however. This assumption is not meant to imply a total

social determinism (the assumption that human behavior is explained exclusively by social factors).* The puppet metaphor is used to convey the idea that much of who we are and what we do is a product of our social environment. But there are nonconformists, deviants, and innovators. Society is not a rigid, static entity composed of robots. While the members of society are shaped by their social environment, they also change that environment. Human beings are the shapers of society as well as the shapees. This is the third assumption of the sociological approach.

Individuals Create, Sustain, and Change the Social Forms within Which They Conduct Their Lives. Even though individuals are largely puppets of society, they are also puppeteers. Chapter 2 describes this process of how people in interaction are the architects of society. In brief, the argument is that social groups of all sizes and types (families, peer groups, work groups, corporations, communities, and societies) are constructed by people. Interacting people create a social structure that becomes a source of control over those individuals (that is, they become puppets of their own creation). But the continuous interaction of the group's members also changes the group.

Successful social movements usually require a leader with extraordinary personal attributes (charisma) to challenge and inspire followers to join in a common quest to change society.

There are four important implications of this assumption that groups are human-made. First, these social forms that are created have a certain momentum of their own that defies change. The ways of doing and thinking common to the group are viewed as natural and right. Although human-made, the group's expectations and structures take on a sacred quality—the sanctity of tradition—that constrains behavior in the socially prescribed ways.

A second implication is that social organizations, because they are created and sustained by people, are imperfect. Slavery benefited some segments of society by taking advantage of other segments. A free enterprise system creates winners and losers. The wonders of technology make worldwide transportation and communication easy and relatively inexpensive but create pollution and waste natural resources. These examples show that there are positive and negative consequences of the way people have organized themselves.

The third implication is that through collective action, individuals are capable of changing the structure of society and even the course of history. Consider, for example, the social movement in India led by Mahatma Gandhi that ended colonial rule by Great Britain, or the civil rights movement in the South led by Martin Luther King, Jr., that ended segregationist laws, or the failure of the attempted coup by Communist hardliners in the summer of 1991 because of the refusal of Soviet citizens and soldiers to accept it.

The final significance of this assumption is that individuals are not passive. Rather, they actively shape social life by adapting to, negotiating with, and changing social structures. This process is called **human agency**. A discussion devoted to this meaningful interaction between social actors and their social environment, bringing about social change, is reserved for the final chapter. Human agency provides the crucial vantage point and insights from the bottom up, and whereas most of this book examines social life from the top down, occasional panels will highlight human agency throughout the text.

---

*Advocates of social determinism are guilty of oversimplifying complex phenomena, just as are genetic determinists, psychological determinists, geographical determinists, and economic determinists.

The Sociological Imagination

C. Wright Mills (1916–1962), in his classic *The Sociological Imagination* (1959), wrote that the task of sociology was to realize that individual circumstances are inextricably linked to the structure of society. The **sociological imagination** involves several related components (Eitzen and Smith, 2003):

- The sociological imagination is stimulated by a willingness to view the social world from the perspective of others.
- It involves moving away from thinking in terms of the individual and her or his problem, focusing rather on the social, economic, and historical circumstances that produce the problem. Put another way, the sociological imagination is the ability to see the societal patterns that influence individuals, families, groups, and organizations.
- Possessing a sociological imagination, one can shift from the examination of a single family to national budgets, from a low-income person to national welfare policies, from an unemployed person to the societal shift from manufacturing to a service/knowledge economy, from a single mother with a sick child to the high cost of health care for the uninsured, and from a homeless family to the lack of affordable housing.
- To develop a sociological imagination requires a detachment from the taken-for-granted assumptions about social life and establishing a critical distance (Andersen and Taylor, 2000:10–11). In other words, one must be willing to question the structural arrangements that shape social behavior.
- When we have this imagination, we begin to see the solutions to social problems not in terms of changing problem people but in changing the structure of society.

The sociological imagination requires that we look beyond an individual unemployed person and look rather at the social, economic, and historical circumstances that produce the problem of unemployment.

Problems with the Sociological Perspective

Sociology is not a comfortable discipline and therefore will not appeal to everyone. To look behind the closed doors of social life is fraught with danger. Sociology frightens some people because it questions what they normally take for granted. Sociologists ask such questions as: How does society really work? Who really has power? Who benefits under the existing social arrangements, and who does not? To ask such questions means that the inquirer is interested in looking beyond the commonly accepted official definitions. As Peter Berger has put it, the "sociological perspective involves a process of 'seeing through' the facades of social structures" (Berger, 1963:31). The underlying assumption of the sociologist is that things are not as they seem. Is the mayor of your town the most powerful person in the community? Is the system of justice truly just? Are professional sports free of racism? Is the United States a meritocratic society in which talent and effort combine to stratify people fairly? To make such queries calls into question existing myths, stereotypes, and official dogma. The critical examination of society will demystify and demythologize. It sensitizes the individual to the inconsistencies present in society. Clearly, that will result if you ask: Why does the United States, in the name of freedom, protect dictatorships around the world? Why do we encourage subsidies to the affluent, but resent those directed to the poor? How high would George W. Bush have risen politically if his surname was Hernandez and his parents had been migrant workers? Why are people who have killed Whites more likely to be sentenced to death than people who have killed African Americans? Why are many women opposed to the Equal Rights Amendment? Why, in a democracy such as the United States, are there so few truly democratic organizations?

The sociological assumption that provides the basis for this critical stance is that the social world is human-made—and therefore not sacred. Belief systems, the economic system, the law, the way power is distributed—all are created and sustained by people. They can, as a result, be changed by people. But if the change is to correct imperfections, then we must understand how social phenomena work. The central task of this book is to aid in such an understanding of U.S. society.

The sociological perspective is also discomforting for many people because an understanding of society's constraints is liberating. Traditional sex roles, for example, are no longer sacred for many people. But while this understanding is liberating from the constraints of tradition, it is also freedom from the protection that custom provides. The acceptance of tradition is comfortable because it frees us from choice (and therefore blame) and from ambiguity. Thus, the understanding of society is a two-edged sword—freeing us, but also increasing the probability of frustration, anger, and alienation.

Sociology is also uncomfortable because the behavior of the subjects is not always certain. Prediction is not always accurate, because people can choose among options or be persuaded by irrational factors. The result is that if sociologists know the social conditions, they can predict, but in terms of probabilities. In chemistry, on the other hand, scientists know exactly what will occur if a certain measure of sodium is mixed with a precise amount of chlorine in a test tube. Civil engineers armed with the knowledge of rock formations, rainfall patterns, types of soils, wind currents, and temperature extremes know exactly what specifications are needed when building a dam in a certain place. They could not know these, however, if the foundation and building materials kept shifting. That is the problem—and the source of excitement—for the sociologist.

The political proclivities of people in the United States during the past few decades offer a good example of shifting attitudes. In 1964, the Republican candidate for president, Barry Goldwater, was soundly defeated, and many observers predicted the demise of the Republican Party. But in 1968, Richard Nixon, the Republican, won. He won again in 1972 by a record-setting margin, leading to the prognostication that the Democratic Party would no longer be viable. Two years later, however, Nixon resigned in disgrace, and in 1976 the Democratic candidate, Jimmy Carter, was the victor. In 1980, President Carter was defeated by Ronald Reagan, and a number of liberal senators were defeated by conservatives. These wide swings seemed to stop as Reagan was reelected in 1984, and he was succeeded four years later by his loyal vice president, George H. W. Bush. But Bush was defeated by Democrat Bill Clinton in 1992, leading some observers to predict the end of the Republican era. Then Clinton's first two years in office, and the timidity of the Democratic majorities in the House and Senate, led to the Republicans winning majorities in the House and Senate in 1994 and ushered in what appeared to be a new era of conservatism. By 1996, however, the Republican blueprint (the "Contract with America") was no longer viable. President Clinton was reelected, although the Republicans held majorities in the House and Senate. In 1998, when Clinton was a lame duck president and involved in a serious scandal, it seemed obvious that Republicans would increase their majorities in the House and Senate. Actually, they lost seats in the House and stayed even in the Senate. Later, Clinton was impeached by the House but acquitted by the Senate, and President Clinton's approval ratings by the public stood at 70 percent. Then in the election of 2000, Al Gore, Clinton's vice president, won the popular vote but was narrowly defeated in the electoral college (and, dare we say it, in the Supreme Court). George W. Bush began his presidency without a popular mandate, but given the events of September 11, 2001, and the military actions afterward, Bush's approval rating soared to over 80 percent. In Bush's second term, however, his approval ratings plummeted below 30 percent. He and the Republican majorities in the House and Senate overreached on several issues, leading to Democratic majorities in both houses in Congress after the 2006 election. The 2008 election appeared to usher in a new era with the election of a Democratic president, Barack Obama, and an increase in the Democratic majorities in both houses of Congress. Was this the beginning of the demise of the Republican Party power in national politics? Not according to the 2010 midterm election, when a high unemployment rate and the Great Recession resulted in the Republicans retaking the majority in the House of Representatives and gaining six seats in the Senate. Moreover, Obama's approval rating was less than 50 percent. Was this now the beginning of the end of the Democrats? If history is any guide, the answer is no.

What does the future hold? History reveals that as long as human beings are not robots, their behaviors will be somewhat unpredictable. International events, economic cycles, scandals, natural disasters, and other occurrences will lead to shifts in political opinions and shifts in the prevailing political ideology.

In sum, "sociology excites a unique set of reactions—it bores some and frightens others. ... Sociology is extraordinary because it can be regarded as both trivial and threatening" (Walton, 1990:4). Students tend to react to sociology in either of these ways. One reaction is that sociology is the trivial and tedious examination of the obvious. Sociology for them is boring. After all, they have lived in families, communities, and society. They know social life. To them, we argue, immersion in social life does not equate with understanding social life. As Zygmunt Bauman has written: "Deeply immersed in our daily routines, though, we hardly ever pause to think about the meaning of what we have gone through; even less often have we the opportunity to compare our private experience with the fate of others, to see the social in the individual, the general in the particular; this is precisely what sociologists can do for us" (Bauman, 1990:10).

To be sure, we are all sociologists of sorts because we know how to behave socially, we intuitively understand social distance, and we have "street smarts." Many go through life knowing how to behave socially, but they do so unconsciously, without being analytical about things social. Most go through life accepting social boundaries of class, race, gender, and sexuality without understanding that they are social constructions. And many are manipulated by advertising, the media, charlatans, preachers, and politicians.

To understand social life requires more than social experiences. It requires a perspective—the sociological perspective—that leads to sociological questions and analysis. With this perspective, students will find excitement and engagement in looking behind the facades of social life and finding patterns in human behaviors (seeing the general in the particular).

A second common reaction by students to sociology is that they find this inquiry threatening. Sociology is subversive—that is, sociology undermines our foundations because it questions all social arrangements, whether religious, political, economic, or familial. Even though this critical approach may be uncomfortable for some people, it is necessary for understanding human social arrangements and for finding solutions to social problems. Thus, we ask that you think sociologically. The process may be scary at first, but the results will bring enlightenment, and interest and excitement in all things social.

The Historical Development of Sociology

Sociology emerged in Western Europe in the late eighteenth century during the Enlightenment (also known as the Age of Reason). Spurred by dramatic social changes such as the Industrial Revolution, the French Revolution, urbanization, and capitalism, intellectuals during this period promoted the ideals of progress, democracy, freedom, individualism, and the scientific method. These ideas replaced those of the old medieval order, in which religious dogma and unquestioned obedience to royal authorities dominated. The new intellectuals believed that human beings could solve their social problems. They also believed that society itself could be analyzed rationally. Out of this intellectual mix, several key theorists laid the foundation for contemporary sociological thought. We focus briefly on the contributions of four: Auguste Comte, Emile Durkheim, Karl Marx, and Max Weber. We further elaborate on the sociological explanations of Marx, Durkheim, and Weber throughout this book.

Auguste Comte (1798–1857): The Science of Society

The founder of sociology was a Frenchman, Auguste Comte, who coined the word *sociology*—from the Latin *socius* ("companion," "with others") and the Greek *logos* ("study of")—for the science of society and group life. Comte sought to establish sociology as a science (his initial name for the discipline was "social physics") free of religious arguments about society and human nature using the Enlightenment's emphasis on **positivism** (knowledge based on systematic observation, experiment, and comparison). Comte was convinced that, using scientific principles, sociologists could solve social problems such as poverty, crime, and war.

Emile Durkheim (1858–1917): Social Facts and the Social Bond

Durkheim provided the rationale for sociology by emphasizing social facts. His classic work *Suicide* (Durkheim, 1951, first published in 1897) demonstrates how social factors explain individual behavior (see Chapter 2). Durkheim focused on **social facts**—social factors that exist external to individuals such as tradition, values, laws, religious ideology, and population density. The key for Durkheim was that these factors affect the behaviors of people, thus allowing for sociological explanations rather than biological and psychological reasoning.

Durkheim was also interested in social integration—what holds groups and society together. His works show how belief systems bind people together; how public ceremonies and rituals promote solidarity; how labeling some people as deviant reaffirms what society deems to be right; and how similarities (shared traditions, values, ideology) provide the societal glue in traditional societies, while differences (division of labor) provide the social bond in complex societies.

Durkheim made invaluable contributions to such core sociological concepts as social roles, socialization, anomie, deviant behavior, social control, and the social bond. In particular, Durkheim's works provide the foundation for the order model that is found throughout this book (see Chapter 3).

Karl Marx (1818–1883): Economic Determinism

Karl Marx devoted his life to analyzing and criticizing the society he observed. He was especially concerned with the gap between the people at the bottom of society and the elite, between the powerless and the powerful, the dominated and the dominant. Marx reasoned that the type of economy found in a society provides its basic structure (system of stratification, unequal distribution of resources, the bias of the law, and ideology). Thus, he was vitally interested in how the economic system of his day—capitalism—shaped society. The owners of capital exploited their workers to extract maximum profits. They used their economic power to keep the less powerful in their place and to benefit unequally from the educational system, the law, and other institutional arrangements in society. These owners of capital (the ruling class) also determined the prevailing ideas in society because they controlled the political system, religion, and media outlets. In this way, members of the working class accept the prevailing ideology. Marx called this **false consciousness** (believing in ideas that are not in a group's objective interests but rather in the best interests of the capitalist class). Social change occurs when the contradictions inherent in capitalism (see Chapter 13) cause the working class to recognize their oppression and develop **class consciousness** (recognizing their class interests, common oppression, and an understanding of who the oppressors are), resulting in a revolt against the system. Thus, **class conflict** is the engine of social change.

Marx made extraordinary contributions to such core sociological concepts as systems of inequality, social class, power, alienation, and social movements. Marx's view of the world is the foundation of the conflict perspective, which is infused throughout this book.

Max Weber (1864–1920): A Response to Marx

Although it is an oversimplification, it helps to think of Weber's thought as a reaction to the writings of Marx. In Weber's view, Marx was too narrowly deterministic. In response, Weber showed that the basic structure of society comes from three sources: the political, economic, and cultural spheres, not just the economic, as Marx argued. Similarly, social class is not determined just by economic resources, but also includes status (prestige) and power dimensions. Political power does not stem just from economic resources, as Marx argued, but also from the expressive qualities of individual leaders (**charisma**). But power can also reside in organizations (not individuals), as Weber showed in his extensive analysis of bureaucracy (see Chapter 2). Weber countered Marx's emphasis on material economic concerns by showing how ideology shapes the economy. Arguably his most important work, *The Protestant Ethic and the Spirit of Capitalism* (Weber, 1958, first published in 1904) demonstrates how a particular type of religious thought (the protestant belief system) made capitalism possible. In sum, Weber's importance to sociology is seen in his mighty contributions to such core concepts as power, ideology, charisma, bureaucracy, and social change.

Sociological Methods: The Craft of Sociology

Sociology is dependent on reliable data and logical reasoning. These necessities are possible, but there are problems that must be acknowledged. Before we describe how sociologists gather reliable data and make valid conclusions, let us examine the kinds of questions sociologists ask and the two major obstacles sociologists face in obtaining answers to these questions.

Sociological Questions

To begin, sociologists try to ascertain the facts. For example, let's assume that we want to assess the degree to which the public education system provides equal educational opportunities for all youngsters. To determine this, we need to do an empirical investigation to find the facts concerning such items as the amount spent per pupil by school districts within each state and by each state. Within school districts, we need to know the facts concerning the distribution of monies by neighborhood schools. Are these monies appropriated equally, regardless of the social class or racial composition of the school? Are curriculum offerings the same for girls and boys within a school? Are extra fees charged for participation in extracurricular activities, and does this affect the participation of children by social class?

Sociologists also may ask comparative questions—that is, how does the situation in one social context compare with that in another? Most commonly, these questions involve the comparison of one society with another. Examples here might be the comparisons among industrialized nations on infant mortality, murder, leisure time, or the mathematics scores of sixteen-year-olds.

A third type of question that a sociologist may ask is historical. Sociologists are interested in trends. What are the facts now concerning divorce, crime, and political participation, for example, and how have these patterns changed over time? Figure 1.1 provides an example of trends over time by examining the divorce rate in the United States from 1860 to 2008.

The three types of sociologist questions considered so far determine the way things are. But these types of questions are not enough. Sociologists go beyond the factual to ask why. Why have real wages (controlling for inflation) declined since 1973 in the United States? Why are the poor poor? Why do birth rates decline with industrialization? Why is the United States the most violent (as measured by murder, rape, and assault rates) industrialized society? (See the Closer Look panel titled "Thinking Like a Sociologist" for an example of sociological questions applied to a particular social occurrence.)

A **sociological theory** is a set of ideas that explains a range of human behavior and a variety of social and societal events. "A sociological theory designates those parts of the social world that are especially important, and offers ideas about how the social world works" (Kammeyer, Ritzer, and Yetman, 1997:21).

Chapter 3 provides two competing theories that guide many sociologists. In that chapter there is a quote from Michael Harrington: "The data of society are, for all practical purposes, infinite. You need criteria that will provisionally permit you to bring some order into that chaos of data and to distinguish between relevant and irrelevant factors" (Harrington, 1985:1). Thus, theory not only helps us to explain social phenomena, it also guides research.

Problems in Collecting Data

A fundamental problem with the sociological perspective is that bane of the social sciences—objectivity. We are all guilty of harboring stereotyped conceptions of such social categories as Muslims, hard hats, professors, gays and lesbians, fundamentalists, business tycoons,

---

FIGURE 1.1

Annual Divorce
Rates, United
States, 1860–2008
(divorces per
thousand married
women age 15
and over)

Sources: Andrew J.
Cherlin, *Marriage,
Divorce, Remarriage,*
Cambridge, MA;
Harvard University
Press, 1981, p. 22: Sar
A. Levitan, Richard S.
Belous and Frank Gallo,
*What's Happening to the
American Family?* Rev.
ed. Baltimore: Johns
Hopkins University
Press, 1988, p. 27; and
current U.S. Census
Bureau documents.

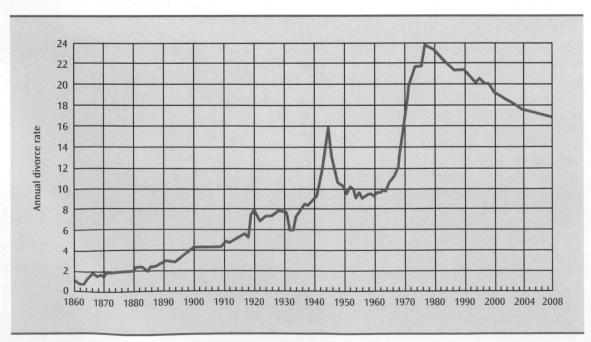

Thinking Like a Sociologist

An article in the *New York Times* (Henneberger and Marriott, 1993) reported a disturbing social trend—male teenagers, apparently to demonstrate their manhood, were abusing or showing disrespect to girls in ever greater numbers. These incidents included verbal abuse, such as yelling explicit propositions, and physical abuse, such as fondling girls and other sexual assaults. This story also reported a nationwide survey of junior high and high school students, which found that more than two-thirds of the girls and 42 percent of the boys reported being touched, grabbed, or pinched on school grounds.

A sociologist interested in adolescence, courtship patterns, or gender might wish to research this apparent trend. The particular research questions of the sociologist depend on his or her interests and theoretical orientation. For our purposes, though, some likely questions might be the following.

Factual Questions

Is sexually oriented abuse aimed at females by adolescent males common today? The authors of the *New York Times* article interviewed only fifty adolescents. If it is common, is it more an urban phenomenon or is it found in the suburbs and rural areas as well? Is it more concentrated in the Northeast or is it found throughout the United States? Is this behavior pattern more prevalent among the youth in some racial and ethnic groups than others? Is it related to social class? And, if the reported incidents occur most often among the disadvantaged in society, is this an accurate measure or the result of the bias of the criminal justice system?

Comparative Questions

Is this trend limited to the United States or is it found in other societies as well? If so, are these societies similar to the United States in affluence, religious heritage, and economic activities?

Historical Questions

How do the current adolescent behaviors compare with those behaviors at other times in the United States? Have there been times in U.S. history when adolescent gendered behavior was less abusive and more courtly? If so, have the changes become gradually more abusive or has sexual abuse among teenagers varied according to some social condition such as the level of economic affluence or gender inequality?

Theoretical Questions

Assuming that the facts indicate that male teenagers are especially abusive to females now, the important question is, Why? Sociologists persuaded by the theoretical perspective of the order model (which is discussed in Chapter 3) might ask questions such as: How have the socialization patterns of youth changed from an earlier, more genteel time? Is the loosening of family ties (higher rates of separation/divorce/remarriage) the reason? Are these behavioral changes congruent with the changes in values? Are changing gender roles invoking this hostile response by males? Is this type of violence the result of a culture of poverty that idealizes a tough "macho" image? Conflict theorists, on the other hand, would ask quite different questions: Are patterns of male aggression toward females correlated with poverty rates, unemployment rates, and low wage rates? Is this form of violence related to a changing economy in which opportunities are becoming more limited because of technology and global competition? Does male abuse of females increase as the degree of inequality in a society increases?

---

socialists, the rich, the poor, and jocks. Moreover, we interpret events, material objects, and people's behavior through the perceptual filter of our religious and political beliefs. When fundamentalists oppose the use of certain books in school, when abortion is approved by a legislature, when the president advocates cutting billions from the federal budget by eliminating social services, or when the Supreme Court denies private schools the right to exclude certain racial groups, most of us rather easily take a position in the ensuing debate.

Sociologists are caught in a dilemma. On the one hand, they are members of society with beliefs, feelings, and biases. On the other hand, though, their professional task is to study society in a disciplined (scientific) way. This latter requirement is that scientist-scholars be dispassionate, objective observers. In short, if they take sides, they lose their status as scientists.

This ideal of **value neutrality** (to be absolutely free of bias in research) can be attacked from three positions. The first is that scientists should not be morally indifferent to the implications of their research. Sociologist Alvin Gouldner has argued that science has the potential to be constructive and destructive. Scientists and their students should not be oblivious to the difference (Gouldner, 1962:212).

Or, put another way, this time by historian Howard Zinn, explaining his style of class-room teaching:

> I would start off my classes explaining to my students—because I didn't want to deceive them—that I would be taking stands on everything. They would hear my point of view in this course, that this would not be a neutral course. My point to them was that in fact it was impossible to be neutral. *You Can't Be Neutral on a Moving Train* [the title of Zinn's memoir] means that the world is already moving in certain directions. Things are already happening. Wars are taking place. Children are going hungry. In a world like this—already moving in certain, often terrible directions—to be neutral or to stand by is to collaborate with what is happening. (Quoted in Barsamian, 1997:37–38)

The second argument against the purely neutral position is that such a stance is impossible. Howard Becker, among others, has argued that there is no dilemma—because it is impossible to do research that is uncontaminated by personal and political sympathies (Becker, 1967; see also Gould, 1998:19). This argument is based on several related assumptions. One is that the values of the scholar-researcher enter into the choices of what questions will be asked. For example, in the study of poverty, a critical decision involves the object of the study—the poor or the system that tends to perpetuate poverty among a certain segment of society. Or, in the study of the problems of youth, we can ask either of these questions: Why are some youths troublesome for adults? Or, Why do adults make so much trouble for youths? In both illustrations, quite different questions will yield very different results.

Similarly, our values lead us to decide from which vantage point we will gain access to information about a particular social organization. If researchers want to understand how a prison operates, they must determine whether they want a description from the inmates, from the guards, from the prison administrators, or from the state board of corrections. Each view provides useful insights about a prison, but obviously a biased one. If they obtain data from more than one of these levels, researchers are faced with making assessments as to which is the more accurate view, clearly another place in the research process where the values of the observers have an impact.

Perhaps the most important reason why the study of social phenomena cannot be value-free is that the types of problems researched and the strategies used tend either to support the existing societal arrangements or to undermine them. Seen in this way, social research of both types is political. Ironically, however, there is a strong tendency to label only the research aimed at changing the system as political. By the same token, whenever the research sides with the powerless, the implication is that the hierarchical system is being questioned—thus, the charge that this type of research is biased (Becker, 1967:240,242).

In summary, bias is inevitable in the study and analysis of social problems. The choice of a research problem, the perspective from which one analyzes the problems, and the solutions proposed all reflect a bias that either supports the existing social arrangements or does not. Moreover, unlike biologists, who can dispassionately observe the behavior of sperm and the egg at conception,[*] sociologists are participants in the social life they seek to study and understand. As they study homelessness, poor children, or urban blight, sociologists cannot escape from their own feelings and values. They must, however, not let their feelings and values render their analysis invalid. In other words, research and reports of research must reflect reality, not as the researcher might want it to be. Sociologists must display scientific integrity, which requires

---

[*]Scientists are subject to the political, cultural, and social influences of the times and places in which they live. Thus, even the seeming objectivity of biologists watching and interpreting the behavior of sperm and egg at conception is questionable. Biologists have long assumed that sperm are the more active participants in conception while the egg is passive (which fits, of course, with the patriarchal model). But new research shows that rather than being forceful swimmers, sperm flounder around, meandering sideways and even moving away from the egg. The egg, on the other hand, has now been found to actively grab the sperm. Also, we now know that rather than the genes in the sperm activating the development program in the passive egg, the genetic material in the egg alone guides development in the first few hours after fertilization. These new findings have been known since 1964 "but research indicating an active role for the egg 'just sat there,' says anthropologist Emily Martin of Princeton University. 'No one knew what to do with it' " (Begley, 1997:56).

recognizing biases in such a way that these biases do not invalidate the findings (Berger, 1963:5). When research is properly done in this spirit, an atheist can study a religious sect, a pacifist can study the military-industrial complex, a divorced person can study marriage, and a person who abhors the beliefs of the Ku Klux Klan can study that organization and its members.

In addition to bias, people gather data and make generalizations about social phenomena in a number of faulty ways. In a sense, everyone is a scientist seeking to find valid generalizations to guide behavior and make sense of the world. But most people are, in fact, very unscientific about the social world. The first problem, as we have noted, is the problem of bias. The second is that people tend to generalize from their experience. Not only is one's interpretation of things that happen to him or her subjective, but there also is a basic problem of sampling. The chances are that one's experience will be too idiosyncratic to allow for an accurate generalization. For example, if you and your friends agree that abortion is appropriate, that does not mean that other people in the society, even those of your age, will agree with you. Very likely, your friends are quite similar to you on such dimensions as socioeconomic status, race, religion, and geographic location.

Another instance of faulty sampling leading to faulty generalizations is when we make assumptions from a single case. An individual may argue that African Americans can succeed economically in this country as easily as Whites because he or she knows a wealthy African American. Similarly, you might argue that all Latinos are dumb because the one you know is in the slowest track in high school. This type of reasoning is especially fallacious because it blames the victim (Ryan, 1976). The cause of poverty or crime or dropping out of school or scoring low on an IQ test is seen as a result of the flaw in the individual, ignoring the substantial impact of the economy or school.

Another typical way that we explain social behavior is to use some authority other than our senses. The Bible, for example, has been used by many people to support or condemn activities such as slavery, capital punishment, war, homosexuality, or monogamy. The media provide other sources of authority for individuals. The media, however, are not always reliable sources of facts. Stories are often selected because they are unusually dramatic, giving the faulty impression of, for example, a crime wave or questionable air safety (see the Research Methods panel titled "Standards for Objectivity and Integrity in Social Research").

Our judgments and interpretations are also affected by prevailing myths and stereotypes. We just "know" certain things to be true, when, actually, they may be contradicted by scientific evidence. As examples, six common beliefs about the poor and racial minorities are presented and discussed.

1. *Most homeless people are disabled by drugs, mental disease, or physical afflictions.* The facts show, however, that the homeless, for the most part, are not "deficient and defective" but rather not much different from the nonhomeless. People are not homeless because of their individual flaws but because of structural arrangements and trends that result in extreme impoverishment and a shortage of affordable housing (Timmer, Eitzen, and Talley, 1994).

2. *African American and Latino youth are more likely than White youth to use illicit drugs.* The data show consistently that this is false. In 2008, for example, 4 percent of White eighth-graders used illicit drugs, compared with 2 percent of Black eighth-grade students; in twelfth grade, only 3 percent of Black students used illicit drugs other than marijuana, compared with 10 percent of their White peers (Child Trends, 2011).

3. *Welfare is given more generously to the poor than to the nonpoor.* Farm subsidies, tax deductibility for taxes and interest on homes, low-interest loans to students and victims of disasters, and pork-barrel projects are examples of government welfare and even the dependency of nonpoor people on government largesse. Most important, these government handouts to the nonpoor are significantly greater than the amounts given to the poor (see Chapters 10 and 14).

4. *African Americans are similar in their behaviors.* Blacks are not a monolithic group, with members acting more or less alike. A study by the Rand Corporation, for example, found that about 1 in 100 young, high-ability, affluent Black women from homes with two parents

Standards for Objectivity and Integrity in Social Research

Social scientists must contend with the essential problem of credibility of their research. How is objectivity possible, though, when they cannot escape their personal values, biases, and opinions? The answer lies in the norms of science.

Sociologists share with other scientists norms for conducting research that minimize personal bias. Their research must reflect the standards of science before it is accepted in scholarly journals. These journals function as gatekeepers for a discipline. What they accept for publication is assumed by their readers to be scientific. The editors of scholarly journals send manuscripts to referees who are unaware of the identity of the authors. This system of anonymity allows the referees to make objective judgments about the credibility of the studies. They review, among other things, the methods used to assess validity and reliability. Validity is the degree to which a study actually measures what it purports to measure. Reliability is the degree to which another study repeating the same methods would yield the same results.

To guide sociologists, their professional association, the American Sociological Association, has a code of ethics, which includes a number of standards for objectivity and integrity in sociological research.

1. "Sociologists adhere to the highest possible technical standards that are reasonable and responsible in their research, teaching, practice, and service activities. They rely on scientifically and professionally derived knowledge; act with honesty and integrity; and avoid untrue, deceptive, or undocumented statements in undertaking work-related functions or activities."

2. "Sociologists conduct research, teach, practice, and provide service only within the boundaries of their competence, based on their education, training, supervised experience, or appropriate professional experience."

3. "In research, teaching, practice, service, or other situations where sociologists render professional judgments or present their expertise, they accurately and fairly represent their areas and degrees of expertise."

4. "Sociologists maintain the highest degree of integrity in their professional work and avoid conflicts of interest and the appearance of conflict."

5. "Irrespective of their personal or financial interests or those of their employers or clients, sociologists adhere to professional and scientific standards in (1) the collection, analysis, or interpretation of data; (2) the reporting of research; (3) the teaching, professional presentation, or public dissemination of sociological knowledge; and (4) the identification of implementation of appropriate contractual, consulting, or service activities."

Source: American Sociological Association, 1997. "Code of Ethics." Washington, DC: *American Sociological Association*, pp. 4–7.

become single, teenage mothers (for White women in this category, the chances were 1 in 1,000, explained, in part, by the much greater willingness to use abortion). In contrast, a poor Black teenager from a female-headed household who scores low on standardized tests has a 1 in 4 probability of becoming an unwed teenage mother (for White women in this category, the odds were 1 in 12) (cited in Luker, 1991:76–77). In the words of Kristin Luker, "Unwed motherhood thus reflects the intersecting influences of race, class, and gender; race and class each has a distinct impact on the life histories of young women" (Luker, 1991:77).

5. *Unmarried women have babies to increase their welfare payments.* Three facts show that this belief of political conservatives is a myth (Carville, 1996:23–24; Males, 1996): (a) From 1972 to 1996, the value of the average Aid to Families with Dependent Children check declined by 40 percent, yet the ratio of out-of-wedlock births rose in the same period by 140 percent; (b) states that have lower welfare benefits usually have more out-of-wedlock births than states with higher benefits; and (c) the teen out-of-wedlock birth rate in the United States is much higher than the rate in countries where welfare benefits are much more generous.

6. *Violence along the border with Mexico is spiraling out of control.* In 2010, twelve members of Congress argued for stricter border security because the level of violence is escalating. This seems logical because of the drug violence in Mexico especially in Mexican cities near the border and the continued trek across the border by illegal migrants. The facts, however, do not support this claim. FBI crime reports reveal that violent crimes in Southwest border counties have dropped more than 30 percent in the past twenty years. Moreover, the nation's four safest big cities are San Diego, Phoenix, El Paso, and Austin—all in border states (reported in *USA Today*, 2010:7A).

7. *Children from low-income families in the United States have a greater chance of earning high incomes as adults than comparable children in Britain, France, Germany, Canada, and the Scandinavian countries.* The belief in the American Dream, that men and women born in poverty can achieve wealth and success through hard work is less likely to occur in the United States than in other wealthy countries (Sawhill and McLanahan, 2006).

8. *Food stamps are limited to relatively few Americans.* Actually half of U.S. children will reside in a household that uses food stamps at some point during childhood (Rank, 2011).

Conventional wisdom is not always wrong, but when it is it can lead to faulty generalizations and bad public policy. Therefore, it is imperative to know the facts, rather than accept myths as reality.

A similar problem occurs when we use aphorisms to explain social occurrences. The problem with this common tactic is that society supplies us with ready explanations that fit contradictory situations and are therefore useless. For instance, if we know a couple who are alike in religion, race, socioeconomic status, and political attitudes, that makes sense to us because "birds of a feather flock together." But the opposite situation also makes sense. If partners in a relationship are very different on a number of dimensions, we can explain this by the obvious explanation: Opposites attract. We use a number of other proverbs to explain behavior. The problem is that there is often a proverb or aphorism to explain the other extreme:

- Absence makes the heart grow fonder.
  Out of sight, out of mind.
- Look before you leap.
  He who hesitates is lost.
- Familiarity breeds contempt.
  To know her is to love her.
- Women are unpredictable.
  Isn't that just like a woman?
- You can't teach an old dog new tricks.
  It's never too late to learn.
- Above all, to thine own self be true.
  When in Rome, do as the Romans do.
- Variety is the spice of life.
  Never change horses in the middle of the stream.
- Two heads are better than one.
  If you want something done right, do it yourself.
- You can't tell a book by its cover.
  Clothes make the man.
- Many hands make light work.
  Too many cooks spoil the broth.
- Better safe than sorry.
  Nothing ventured, nothing gained.
- Haste makes waste.
  Strike while the iron is hot.
- Work, for the night is coming.
  Eat, drink, and be merry for tomorrow you may die.
- There's no place like home.
  The grass is always greener on the other side of the fence.

These contradictory explanations are commonly used and, of course, explain nothing. The job of the sociologist is to specify under what conditions certain rates of social behaviors occur.

Sources of Data

Sociologists do not use aphorisms to explain behavior, nor do they speculate based on faulty samples or authorities. Because we are part of the world that is to be explained, sociologists must obtain evidence that is beyond reproach. In addition to observing scrupulously the canons of science, there are four basic sources of data that yield valid results for sociologists: survey research, experiments, observation, and existing data. We describe these techniques only briefly here.

Survey Research. Sociologists are interested in obtaining information about people with certain social attributes. They may want to know how political beliefs and behaviors are influenced by differences in sex, race, ethnicity, religion, and social class. Or sociologists may wish to know whether religious attitudes are related to racial antipathy. They may want to determine whether poor people have different values from other people in society, the answer to which will have a tremendous impact on the ultimate solution to poverty. Or they may want to know whether voting patterns, work behaviors, or marital relationships vary by income level, educational attainment, or religious affiliation.

To answer these and similar questions, the sociologist may use personal interviews or written questionnaires to gather the data. The researcher may obtain information from all possible subjects or from a selected **sample** (a representative part of a population). Because the former method is often impractical, a random sample of subjects is selected from the larger population. If the sample is selected scientifically, a relatively small proportion can yield satisfactory results—that is, the inferences made from the sample will be reliable about the entire population. For example, a probability sample of only 2,000 from a total population of 1 million can provide data very close to what would be discovered if a survey were taken of the entire 1 million.

Sociologists use personal interviews from a number of people to determine if they vary in behaviors and/or beliefs by age, sex, race, ethnicity, religion, social class, or region.

Typically with survey research, sociologists use sophisticated statistical techniques to control the contaminating effects of confounding variables to determine whether the findings could have occurred by chance, to determine whether variables are related, and to see whether such a relationship is a causal one. A **variable** is an attitude, behavior, or condition that can vary in magnitude and significance from case to case.

A special type of survey research, **longitudinal surveys**, holds special promise. This type of research collects information about the same persons over many years and in doing so has "given the social sciences their Hubble telescope. Both allow the observing researcher to look back in time and record the antecedents of current events and transitions" (Butz and Torrey, 2006:1898). For example, the Panel Study of Income Dynamics at the University of Michigan has followed the same people for forty years, "documenting the importance of accumulated life experience in causing transitions from health to infirmity; from work to unemployment or retirement; and across the states of marriage, family structure, and wealth" (Butz and Torrey, 2006:1898).

Experiments. To understand the cause-and-effect relationship among a few variables, sociologists use controlled experiments. Let us assume, for example, that we want to test whether White students in interracial classrooms have more positive attitudes toward African Americans than Whites in segregated classrooms have toward them. Using the experimental method, the researcher would take a number of White students previously unexposed to Blacks in school and randomly assign a subset to an integrated classroom situation. Before actual contact with the Blacks, however, all the White students would be given a test of their racial attitudes. This pretest establishes a benchmark from which to measure any changes in attitudes. One group, the control group, continues school in segregated classrooms. (The **control group** is a group of subjects not exposed to the independent variable.) The other group, the experimental group, now has Blacks as classmates. (The **experimental group** is a group of subjects who are exposed to the independent variable.) Otherwise, the two groups are the same. Following a suitable period of time, the Whites in both groups are tested again for their racial attitudes. If this posttest reveals that the experimental group differs from the control group in racial attitudes (the **dependent variable**), then it is assumed that interracial contact (the **independent variable**) is the source of the change. (The dependent variable is a variable that is influenced by the effect of another variable. The independent variable is a variable that affects another variable.) As an example of a less contrived experiment, a researcher can test the results of two different treatments on the subsequent behavior of juvenile delinquents. Delinquent boys who had been adjudicated by the courts can be randomly assigned to a boys' industrial school or a group home facility in the community. After release from incarceration, records are kept on the boys' subsequent behavior in school (grades, truancy, formal reprimands) and in the community (police contacts, work behavior). If the boys from the two groups differ appreciably, then we can say with assurance, because the boys were randomly assigned to each group, that the difference in treatment (the independent variable) was the source of the difference in behavior (the dependent variable).

Observation. The researcher, without intervention, can observe as accurately as possible what occurs in a community, group, or social event. This type of procedure is especially helpful in understanding such social phenomena as the decision-making process, the stages of a riot, the attraction of cults for their members, or the depersonalization of patients in a mental hospital. Case studies of entire communities have been very instrumental in the understanding of power structures (Dahl, 1961; Hunter, 1953) and the complex interaction patterns in cities (Whyte, 1988). Longtime participant observation studies of slum neighborhoods and gangs have been insightful in showing the social organization present in what the casual observer might think of as disorganized activity (Gans, 1962; Liebow, 1967; Whyte, 1956).

Existing Data. The sociologist can also use existing data to test theories. The most common sources of information are the various agencies of the government. Data are provided for the nation, regions, states, communities, and census tracts on births, deaths, income, education, unemployment, business activity, health delivery systems, prison populations, military spending, poverty, migration, and the like. Important information can also be obtained from such sources as business firms, athletic teams and leagues, unions, and professional associations. Statistical techniques can be used with these data to describe populations and the effects of social variables on various dependent variables.

1. Sociology is the science dealing with social forces—the forces outside us that shape our lives, interests, and personalities. Sociologists, then, work to discover the underlying order of social life and the principles regarding it that explain human behavior.

2. The assumptions of the sociological perspective are that (a) individuals are, by their nature, social beings; (b) individuals are socially determined; and (c) individuals create, sustain, and change the social forms within which they conduct their lives.

3. The sociological imagination involves (a) a willingness to view the social world from the perspective of others; (b) focusing on the social, economic, and historical circumstances that influence families, groups, and organizations; (c) questioning the structural arrangements that shape social behavior; and (d) seeing the solutions to social problems not in terms of changing problem people but in changing the structure of society.

4. Sociology is uncomfortable for many people because it looks behind the facades of social life. This requires a critical examination of society that questions the existing myths, stereotypes, and official dogma.

5. The basis for the critical stance of sociologists is that the social world is not sacred because it is made by human beings.

6. Sociological research involves four types of questions: factual, comparative, historical, and theoretical.

7. The development of sociology was dependent on four European intellectuals. Auguste Comte was the founder of sociology. His emphasis was on a rigorous use of the scientific method. Emile Durkheim emphasized social facts (sociological explanation for human behavior) and the social bond. Karl Marx wrote about the importance of economics in understanding social stratification, power, and ideology. Max Weber, in reaction to Marx, demonstrated that social life is multidimensional and that ideology shapes the economy.

8. Sociology depends on reliable data and logical reasoning. Although value neutrality is impossible in the social sciences, bias is minimized by the norms of science.

9. Survey research is a systematic means of gathering data to obtain information about people's behaviors, attitudes, and opinions.

10. Sociologists may use experiments to assess the effects of social factors on human behavior. One of two similar groups—the experimental group—is exposed to an independent variable. If this group later differs from the control group, then the independent variable is known to have produced the effect.

11. Observation is another technique for obtaining reliable information. Various social organizations such as prisons, hospitals, schools, churches, cults, families, communities, and corporations can be studied and understood through systematic observation.

12. Sociologists also use existing sources of data to test their theories.

13. Sociology is a science, and the rules of scientific research guide the efforts of sociologists to discover the principles of social organization and the sources of social constraints on human behavior.

KEY TERMS

Sociology	Class consciousness	Longitudinal surveys
Social determinism	Class conflict	Control group
Human agency	Charisma	Experimental group
Sociological imagination	Sociological theory	Dependent variable
Positivism	Value neutrality	Independent variable
Social facts	Sample	
False consciousness	Variable	

STUDY QUESTIONS

1. How would sociologists differ from psychologists in studying phenomena such as divorce and racism?
2. Peter Berger has said that "the sociological perspective involves a process of 'seeing through' the facades of social structure." What does this mean? Give examples.
3. To what extent are you shaped by your social environment? Provide examples of the social facts (Durkheim) that affect you.
4. Speculate (sociologically) on why sociology developed where and when it did.
5. Apply the sociological imagination to the social problem of poverty.
6. Are you comfortable or uncomfortable with the sociological perspective? Elaborate.
7. How do sociologists minimize bias in their research activities?

http://www.asanet.org/

The American Sociological Association is a nonprofit association "dedicated to advancing sociology as a scientific discipline and profession serving the public good."

http://socserv2.mcmaster.ca/w3virtsoclib/

WWW Virtual Library: Sociology contains links to many websites related to sociology. The links include information about online sociological journals, related fields, and work done by contributors to the emergence of sociology (Marx, Durkheim, and Weber).

http://www.sociologyonline.co.uk/

An interactive website that includes polls and quizzes on different topics, such as race, class, and gender. It also has a library with links to different sites on theory.

http://www.pscw.uva.nl/sociosite/

SocioSite has an extensive list of influential sociologists, with links to each, which contain information about their work and other pertinent information. The site also has other options, such as searching journals related to sociology.

http://ryoung001.homestead.com/index.html

Sociologist At Large "has been introducing students and non-students to the Sociological Perspective since 1999." It contains information in terms that are very accessible for those new to sociology.

http://trochim.human.cornell.edu/kb/qual.htm

This site offers information on the various types of qualitative methods of research that are used in sociology, such as participant observation and indepth interviewing.

http://odwin.ucsd.edu/glossary/

This is a glossary of social science computing and data terms, which can be searched for definitions relevant to research.

http://www.latrobe.edu.au/aqr/

The Association for Qualitative Research is an international organization for those with an interest in qualitative research. The site has a journal that can be downloaded.

http://ericae.net/ft/tamu/vpiques3.htm

This site offers a guide to developing questionnaires. It includes descriptions of problems that may arise and how to avoid them.

CHAPTER 2

The Structure of Social Groups

An experiment was conducted some years ago when twenty-four previously unacquainted boys, age twelve, were brought together at a summer camp (Sherif and Sherif, 1966). For three days the boys, who were unaware that they were part of an experiment, participated in campwide activities. During this period, the camp counselors (actually, they were research assistants) observed the friendship patterns that emerged naturally. The boys were then divided into two groups of twelve. The boys were deliberately separated in order to break up the previous friendship patterns. The groups were then isolated from each other for five days. During this period the boys were left alone by the counselors so that what occurred was the spontaneous result of the boys' behavior. The experimenters found that in both groups there developed (1) a division of labor; (2) a hierarchical structure of ranks— that is, differences among the boys in power, prestige, and rewards; (3) the creation of rules; (4) punishments for violations of the rules; (5) argot—that is, specialized language such as nicknames and group symbols that served as positive in group identifications; and (6) member cooperation to achieve group goals.

This experiment illustrates the process of social organization. The counselors did not insist that these phenomena occur in each group. They seemed to occur naturally. In fact, they happen universally (Liebow, 1967; Whyte, 1956). The goals of this chapter are to understand the components of social structure that emerge and how these components operate to constrain behavior. Although the process is generally the same regardless of group size, we examine it at two levels—the micro level and the societal level, also known as the *macro level*.

The Micro Level

Social Organization

Social organization refers to the ways in which human conduct becomes socially organized—that is, the observed regularities in the behavior of people that are due to the social conditions in which they find themselves rather than to their physiological or psychological characteristics as individuals (Blau and Scott, 1962:2). The social conditions that constrain behavior can be divided into two types: (1) **social structure**—the structure of behavior in groups and society and (2) **culture**—the shared beliefs of group members that unite them and guide their behavior.

Social Structure. Sociology is the study of the patterns that emerge when people interact over time. The emphasis is on the linkages and networks that emerge and that transform an aggregate of individuals into a group. (An **aggregate** is a collection of individuals who happen to be at the same place at the same time. A **group** is a collection of people who, because of sustained interaction, have evolved a common structure and culture.) We begin, then, with social interaction, the basic building block of groups. When the actions of one person affect another person, **social interaction** occurs. The most common method is communication through speech; the written word; or a symbolic act such as a wink, a facial expression, or gestures such as a wave of the hand or the raising of a finger (which finger is often crucial).

Behavior can also be altered by the mere presence of other people. The way we behave (from the way we eat to what we think) is affected by whether we are alone or with other people. Even physical reactions such as crying, laughing, or passing gas are controlled by the individual because of the fear of embarrassment. It could even be argued that, except in the most extreme cases, people's actions are always oriented toward other human beings whether other people are physically present or not. We, as individuals, are constantly concerned about the expected or actual reactions of other people. Even when alone, an individual may not act in certain ways because of having been taught that such actions are wrong.

Social interaction may be either transitory or enduring. Sociologists are interested in the latter type because only then does patterned behavior occur. A case of enduring social interaction is a **social relationship**. Relationships occur for a number of reasons: sexual attraction, familial ties, a common interest (for example, collecting coins or growing African violets), a common political or religious ideology, cooperation to produce or distribute a product, or propinquity (being neighbors). Regardless of the specific reasons, the members of a social relationship are united at least in some minimal way with the other members. Most important, the members of a social relationship behave quite differently from the way they would as participants in a fleeting interaction.

Once the interaction is perpetuated, the behavior of the participants is profoundly altered. An autonomous individual is similar to an element in chemistry. As soon as there is a chemical reaction between them, however, the two elements become parts of a new entity, as sociologist Marvin Olsen (1976) notes:

> The concepts of "elements" and "parts" are analogous to terms in chemistry. By themselves, chemical elements—sodium and chlorine, for instance—exhibit characteristics peculiarly their own, by which each can be separately identified. This condition holds true even if elements are mixed together, as long as there is no chemical reaction between them. Through a process of chemical interaction, however, the elements can join to form an entirely new substance—in this case, salt. The elements of sodium and chlorine have now both lost their individual identities and characteristics, and have instead become parts of a more inclusive chemical compound, which has properties not belonging to either of its component parts by themselves. In an emergent process such as this, the original elements are transformed into parts of a new entity. (37)

Olsen's description of a chemical reaction is also appropriate for what arises in a social relationship. Most sociologists assume that the whole is more than just the sum of its parts—that is, through the process of enduring interaction, something is created with properties different from the component parts.* The two groups of boys artificially formed at the summer camp, for example, developed similar structural properties regardless of the unique personalities of the boys in each group. Although groups may differ in size or purpose, they are similar in structure and in the processes that create the structure. In other words, one group may exist to knit quilts for charity while another may exist to commit terrorist bombings, but they will be alike in many important ways. Their social structure involves the patterns

---

*This assumption—the realist position—is one side of a fundamental philosophical debate. The nominalist position, on the other hand, argues that to know the parts is to know the whole. In sociology, the realist position is dominant and is found in the words of Emile Durkheim (1958) and in the classic work by Charles Warriner (1956). The minority nominalist position in sociology is represented most prominently by George Homans (1964).

of interaction that emerge, the division of labor, and the linking and hierarchy of positions. The social structure is an emergent phenomenon bringing order and predictability to social life within the group.

Social Interaction Through Social Media. Throughout human history, social interaction was face-to-face, with the occasional exception of smoke signals or the sound of drums or other instruments. In the past 150 years or so new innovations such as the telegraph and telephone made it possible to interact at great distances. But those technological wonders were nothing compared to the interaction potential from the new technologies in the past two decades. Instead of interacting through clicks and speech, we now can communicate with almost anyone of the planet through e-mails via the Internet. The interaction potential has been magnified many times in the last few years through the new social media such as Twitter, Facebook, MySpace, LinkedIn, and YouTube, interaction sites that did not exist in 2000. So, too, with technological advances such as iPhones, iPads, netbooks, and BlackBerrys. Consider these changes in the first decade of the twenty-first century: The number of Internet users worldwide increased from 360.1 million in December 31, 2000 to 1.97 billion on June 2010 (Internetstats.com, 2010). Daily e-mails have increased from 12 billion in 2000 to 247 billion in 2010 (the following statistics are from *Newsweek*, 2010; and McGrath, 2010). Daily text messages have gone from 400,000 to 4.5 billion (text was only a noun in 2000, now it is a noun and a verb). Facebook did not exist in 2000 (it began in 2004), yet it reached 900 million members worldwide by April 2012 and is adding 700,000 new members a day, thus making it the largest in the social network universe. Its members upload more than one billion pieces of content a day. If the recent growth rate continues, Facebook will have 1 billion users by August 2012 (Grossman, 2010/2011). Twitter was created in 2006 and by October 2010 it had 25.7 million unique monthly visitors and 186 million monthly visits (Compete.com, 2010).

These individuals are interacting electronically with others while ignoring those around them.

We are in the midst of a cultural shift. What does it mean when the interaction is in the form of tweets (text-based posts limited in length to 140 characters sent to one's followers)? What does it mean for relationships when we "increasingly connect with even our most intimate friends and family via instant messaging"? (Jackson, 2009:13). How connected are we when we share information about ourselves with our "friends" on Facebook? As Mark Vernon, author of *The Meaning of Friendship*, has said: Social connectivity is not the same as intimate friendship.

> While social networking sites and the like have grown exponentially, the element that is crucial and harder to investigate is the quality of the connections they nurture. ...
> A connection may only be a click away, but cultivating a good friendship takes more.
> It seems common sense to conclude that "friending" online nurtures shallow relationships.
> (Vernon, 2010:11A)

Facebook users share more than 30 billion pieces of information such as interests, complaints, likes, writing samples, and photos every month (Helft, 2010). A cover story in *Time* argues that "Facebook has changed our social DNA, making us more accustomed to openness" (Fletcher, 2010:33). Most important, what does this new realm of public exposure mean for social interaction and relationships? Do the multiplying friendships increase intimacy? While Facebook sends and receives data, does the exchange of data add to connecting with others or make the connections more superficial (Grossman, 2010/2011:68). The new social transparency may result in a much richer and more connected place than the more private lives of the past (Johnson, 2010). More likely, it will result in a society of "intimate strangers."

Sociologist Barry Wellman, writing in 2000 before Facebook and Twitter, said that in this new technological age we live in a society dominated by "networked individualism" (Wellman, 2000). We can connect with almost anyone and at any time, but the connection to that person is "largely to a slice of the person and not the whole" (quoted in Jackson, 2009:54). In this context, relations are more easily formed and abandoned. In other words, in this connected world, the bonds holding us together are weak.

A nationally representative survey in 1985 revealed that the modal (most common) response was to have three confidants (persons with whom they discussed important matters). This study was replicated in 2004. Among the findings, one fourth of the sample reported that they had no confidant. The average network of confidants had shrunk from 2.94 in 1985 to 2.08 in 2004 (an average loss of one confidant). The authors, three sociologists, express concern that these shrinking networks reflect an important social change in the United States (McPherson, Smith-Lovin, and Brashears, 2006). The data for this study were last collected in 2004, before the advent of Facebook and Twitter. If the question were asked now, would the results show that amid the dazzling new ways to connect, that we actually are more detached from others than earlier? (See the Technology and Society panel titled "The Isolating Effects of E-mail.")

Culture. The other component of social organization is culture—the shared beliefs of a group's members that serve to guide conduct. Through enduring social interaction, common expectations emerge about how people should act. These expectations are called norms.

TECHNOLOGY AND SOCIETY

The Isolating Effects of E-mail

Americans send many times more e-mail messages a day than they do first-class mail messages. However, some important elements go missing in the process. "As more and more of us go online, we become accustomed to e-mail's mix of intimacy and anonymity. … Gone are intonation, affect, facial expression; e-mail offers only bare words, without even the nuances of handwriting" (Sklaroff, 1999:55). Chat rooms on the Internet are something like coffeehouses where like-minded people share their interests. This allows scholars, for example, from around the world to regularly interact. This is good but it is quite different from the bonds that emerge from regular face-to-face interaction. As sociologist Philip Slater says, "A community life exists when one can go daily to a given location and see many of the people [one] knows" (quoted in Oldenburg, 1997:32).

John L. Locke, a professor of communications, argues in *The De-Voicing of Society: Why We Don't Talk to Each Other Anymore* (1998) that e-mail, voice mail, fax machines, beepers, and Internet chat rooms are robbing us of ordinary face-to-face talking. Talking, he says, like the grooming of apes and monkeys, is the way we build and maintain social relationships. Ironically,

these incredible communication devices that combine to connect us in so many dazzling ways also separate us from intimate relationships. Our connections are now superficial—even devoid, often, of human contact. A generation or two ago when people talked with someone it was face-to-face, giving the communicants messages in addition to the words, such as the tone of the voice, the intensity of feeling, and whether there was eye contact or not. Now with e-mails and the like, we miss these social feedback mechanisms, and thus there is the possibility for miscommunication as well as the weakened human connection (Locke, 1998:18–19).

The new forms of communication reduce face-to-face interaction in other ways. Some people now work out of their homes, communicating with colleagues and clients through faxes and e-mails rather than standing around the water cooler at work. Even when physically with other employees at work, more and more communication is done over the Internet. Virtual conferences now often take the place of meetings with business associates. Human contact is also reduced when we shop, invest, bank, pay bills, play games, and do research over the Internet.

Criteria for judging what is appropriate, correct, moral, and important also emerge. These criteria are the **values** of the group. Also part of the shared beliefs are the expectations that group members have of individuals occupying the various positions within the group. These are **social roles**. The elements of culture are described briefly here for the micro and macro levels and in detail in Chapter 4. To summarize, social organization refers to both culture and social structure. Blau and Scott describe how these operate to constrain human behavior:

> The prevailing cultural standards and the structure of social relations serve to organize human conduct in the collectivity. As people conform more or less closely to the expectations of their fellows, and as the degree of their conformity in turn influences their relations with others and their social status, and as their status in turn further affects the inclinations to adhere to social norms and their chances to achieve valued objectives, their patterns of behavior become socially organized. (Blau and Scott, 1962:4–5)

Norms

Our behaviors are governed by rules (**norms**). All social organizations have rules that specify appropriate and inappropriate behaviors. In essence, norms are the behavioral expectations that members of a particular group collectively share. They ensure that action within social organizations is generally predictable. There are some basic aspects for understanding social rules at the micro level. First, there are consequences for breaking rules. The severity of punishment for nonconformity to the rules depends on whether the rule in question is considered by the social organization as important or not. Minor rules, **folkways**, are not severely punished if violated. Folkways vary, of course, from group to group. A particular fraternity may expect its members to wear formal dress on certain occasions. In a church, wine may be consumed by the parishioners at the appropriate time—Communion. To bring one's own bottle of wine to Communion, however, would be a violation of the folkways of that church. (Could you imagine an announcement in your church bulletin that Communion will be next Sunday—B.Y.O.B.?) These examples show that folkways involve etiquette, customs, and regulations that, if violated, do not threaten the fabric of the social organization.

Violation of the group's mores, on the other hand, is considered important enough that it must be punished severely. (**Mores** are important norms, the violation of which results in severe punishment.) This type of norm involves morality—in fact, mores can be thought of as moral imperatives. In a sorority, for instance, examples of the violations of mores might be disloyalty, stealing from a sister, and conduct that brings shame to the organization, such as dealing drugs.

Second, rules may be formal or informal. That is, they may be laws and enforced by the leaders of the social organization. Social norms, on the other hand, are part of the culture of the organization. To violate these social norms may mean being ostracized by the group or ridiculed by one's fellow members. Individuals through socialization internalize these social norms resulting in their enforcement often being self-administered through guilt, shame, feeling awkward, and the like (Wright and Rogers, 2011:4).

Status and Role

One important aspect of social structure is composed of the positions of a social organization. If one determines which positions are present in an organization and how they are interrelated, then the analyst has a structural map of that social group. The existence of positions in organizations has an important consequence for individuals—the bestowing of a social identity. Each of us belongs to a number of organizations, and in each we occupy a position, or **status**. If you were asked, "Who are you?" chances are you would respond by listing your various statuses. An individual may at the same time be a student, sophomore, daughter, sister, friend, female, Baptist, Sunday school teacher, Democrat, sales clerk, U.S. citizen, and secretary-treasurer of the local chapter of Weight Watchers.

The individual's social identity, then, is a product of the particular matrix of statuses that she or he occupies. Another characteristic of statuses that has an important influence on social identity is that these positions in organizations tend to be differentially rewarded and esteemed. This element of **hierarchy** (the arrangement of people in order of importance) of status reinforces the positive or negative image individuals have of themselves depending on placement in various organizations. Some individuals consistently hold prestigious positions (bank president, deacon, chairman of United Fund), while others may hold only statuses that are negatively esteemed (welfare recipient, aged, Latino, janitor), and some people occupy mixed statuses (bus driver, thirty-second-degree Mason, union member, church trustee).

Group memberships are vital sources of our notion of our own identity. Similarly, when they know of our status in various organizations, other people assign a social identity to us. When we determine a person's age, race, religion, and occupation, we tend to stereotype that person—that is, we assume that the individual is a certain type. Stereotyping has the effect of conferring a social identity on that person, raising expectations for certain behaviors that, very often, result in a self-fulfilling prophecy. This phenomenon is heightened when considering an individual's **master status**, which is a status that has exceptional significance for social identity. The master status trumps all other statuses when a situation or an individual is evaluated by others. For most of us, occupation is a master status because it informs others of our educational attainment, skills, and income. But it may also be the status of African American, or athlete, or ex-convict, or having acquired immune deficiency syndrome (AIDS).

The mapping of statuses provides important clues about the social structure of an organization, but the most important aspect of status is the behavior expected of the occupant of a status. To determine that an individual occupies the status of father does not tell us much about what the group expects of a father. In some societies, for example, the biological father has no legal, monetary, or social responsibility for his children, who are cared for by the mother and her brother. In U.S. society, there are norms (legal and informal) that demand that the father be responsible for his children. Not only must he provide for them, but he must also, depending on the customs of the family, be a disciplinarian, buddy, teacher, Santa Claus, and tooth fairy.

The behavior expected of a person occupying a status in a group is that person's **role**[*] (the behavioral expectations and requirements attached to a position in a social organization). The norms of the social organization constrain the incumbents in a status to behave in prescribed and therefore predictable ways, regardless of their particular personalities. Society insists that we play our roles correctly. To do otherwise is to risk being judged by other people as abnormal, crazy, incompetent, and/or immature. These pressures to conform to role demands ensure that there is stability in social groups even though member turnover occurs. For example, ministers to a particular congregation come and go, but certain actions are predictable in particular incumbents because of the demands on their behavior. These demands come from the hierarchy of the denomination, from other ministers, and most assuredly from the members of the parish. The stability imposed by a role is also seen with other statuses, such as professor, janitor, police officer, student, and even president of the United States.

The expectations of behavior of members in the various statuses are not to make behavior totally predictable, however. Occupants of the statuses can vary their behavior within limits. There are at least three reasons for this.

- First, personality variables can account for variations in the behavior of people holding identical statuses. People can be conformist or unconventional, manipulated or manipulators, passive or aggressive, followers or inspirational leaders, cautious or impetuous, ambitious or lackadaisical. Personality traits can make obvious differences in the behavior of individuals, even though individuals may face identical group pressures.

---

[*]This section introduces the concept of role as it is appropriate to the context of social organization. We elaborate on it in Chapter 4.

- A second reason role does not make social actors robots is that the occupants of a status may not receive a clear, consistent message as to which behavior is expected. A minister, for example, may find within his or her congregation individuals and cliques that make conflicting demands. One group may insist that the minister be a social activist. Another may demand that the pastor be apolitical and spend time exclusively meeting the spiritual needs of the members.

- Another circumstance leading to conflicting expectations—and unpredictability of action—results from multiple group memberships. The statuses we occupy may have conflicting demands on our behavior. When an African American politician, for example, is elected as mayor of a large city, as has been the case in Los Angeles, Chicago, Detroit, Philadelphia, Baltimore, and Atlanta, he or she is faced with the constraints of the office on one hand, and the demands of the African American constituency on the other. Other illustrations of conflicting demands because of occupying two quite different statuses are daughter and lover, son and peer-group member, and businessperson and church deacon. Being the recipient of incompatible demands results in hypocrisy, secrecy, guilt, and, most important for our consideration, unpredictable behavior.

Although role performance may vary, stability within organizations remains. The stability is a consequence of the strong tendency of people in a social organization to conform. Let us look briefly at just how powerfully roles shape behavior. First, the power of role over personal behavior is seen dramatically as one moves from one status to another. Think about your own behavior at home, at church, at school, in the dorm, at a party, or in a parked car. In each of these instances you occupy multiple statuses and face conflicting role expectations, resulting in overall inconsistent behavior but likely behavior that is expected for each separate role.

The power of role to shape behavior is also demonstrated as one changes status within an organization. The Amish, for instance, select their minister by lot from among the male adults of the group. The eligible members each select a Bible. The one choosing the Bible with the special mark in it is the new pastor. His selection is assumed to be ordained by God. This individual now has a new status in the group—the leader with God's approval. Such an elevation in status will doubtless have a dramatic effect on that person's behavior. Without special training (the Amish rarely attend school beyond the eighth grade), the new minister will in all likelihood exhibit leadership, self-confidence, and wisdom. Less dramatically, but with similar results nonetheless, each of us undergoes shifts in status within the organizations to which we belong— from first-year student to senior, bench warmer to starter, assembly-line worker to supervisor, and adolescent to adult. These changes in status mean, of course, a concomitant shift in the expectations for behavior (role). Not only does our behavior change but so, too, do our attitudes, perceptions, and perhaps even our personalities.

The Amish make a conscious effort not to conform to the norms of modernity.

A dramatic example of the power of role over behavior is provided by an experiment conducted by Philip Zimbardo, who wanted to study the impact of prison life on guards and prisoners. Using student volunteers, Zimbardo (1972) randomly assigned some to be guards and others to be inmates. By using subjects who were not associated with a prison, the researcher could actually study the effects of social roles on behavior without the confounding variables of personality traits, character disorders, and the like.

Zimbardo constructed a mock prison in the basement of the psychology building at Stanford University. The students chosen as prisoners were arrested one night without warning, dressed in prison uniforms, and locked in the cells. The guards were instructed to maintain order. Zimbardo found that the college students assigned the roles of guard or inmate actually became guards and inmates in just a few days. The guards showed brutality and the prisoners became submissive, demonstrating that roles effectively shape behavior because they have the power to shape consciousness (thinking, feeling, and perceiving). Interestingly, Zimbardo, who is a psychologist, concluded that social factors superseded individual ones: "Individual behavior is largely under the control of social forces and environmental contingencies rather than personality traits, character, will power or other empirically unvalidated constructs" (Zimbardo, 1972:6).

Finally, roles protect individuals. The constraints on behavior implied in the role provide a blueprint that relieves the individual from the responsibility for action. Thus, the certainty provided by role makes us comfortable. Gay rights, to name one contemporary movement, is aimed at liberation from the constraints of narrowly prescribed sex and gender roles. But to be free of these constraints brings not only freedom but also problems. So, too, when one is freed from the constraints of a particular community, job, or marriage, the newfound liberty, independence, and excitement are countered by the frustrations involving ambiguity, choice, loneliness, and responsibility.

Social Control

Although they vary in the degree of tolerance for alternative behaviors, social groups universally demand conformity to some norms. In the absence of such demands, groups would not exist because of the resulting anarchy. The mechanisms of social control are varied. They can occur subtly in the socialization process (see Chapter 5) so that people feel guilty or proud, depending on their actions. They can occur in the form of rewards (medals, prizes, merit badges, gold stars, trophies, praise) by family members, peers, neighbors, fellow workers, employers, and the community to reinforce certain behaviors. Also common are negative sanctions such as fines, demerits, imprisonment, and excommunication, which are used to ensure conformity. More subtle techniques, such as gossip or ridicule, are also successful in securing conformity because of the common fear of humiliation before one's friends, classmates, coworkers, or neighbors. Gossip is especially interesting. "Gossip is how we establish cultural norms. Talking about others is our way to test the social boundaries— to learn what raises eyebrows, what is met by shrugs—without directly talking about ourselves" (Belkin, 2009:9).

An example of a particularly devastating and effective technique is the practice of shunning the sinner used by some of the Amish and Mennonite religious sects. No one in the religious community, not even the guilty party's spouse and children, is to recognize her or his existence. In one celebrated case, Robert Bear was the victim of shunning. He took the case to court on the grounds that this practice was unconstitutional because it was too severe. Since the shun had been invoked by church leaders, Bear's wife had not slept with him, his six children were alienated from him, and his farm operation was in ruin because no one would work for him or buy his produce. The courts ruled, however, that it was within the province of the church to punish its members for transgressions. The severity of the shun is an extremely effective social control device for the Amish community, guaranteeing, except in rare cases, conformity to the dictates of the group.

Whatever the mechanism used, social control efforts tend to be very effective, whether within a family, peer group, organization, community, or society. Most people, most of the time, conform to the norms of their groups and society. Otherwise, the majority of the poor would riot, most of the starving would steal, and more young men would refuse to fight in wars. The pressure to conform comes from within us (by internalizing the group's norms and values during the socialization process) and from outside us (from **sanctions**, or the threat of sanctions, which are social punishments for approved or disapproved behavior that may be lifted as a reward), and we obey. In fact, what we consider self-control is really the consequence of social control. These constraints are usually not oppressive to the individual. Indeed, we want to obey the rules.

Primary and Secondary Groups

A **social group** is an organization created through enduring and patterned interaction. It consists of people who have a common identity, share a common culture, and define themselves as a distinct social unit. Groups may be classified in a number of ways, the most significant of which involves the kind and quality of relationships that members have with each other. Sociologists have delineated two types of groups according to the degrees of intimacy and involvement among the members—primary and secondary.

Primary groups are groups whose members are most intimately involved with each other. These groups are small and display face-to-face interaction. They are informal in organization and long-lasting. The members have a strong identification, loyalty, and emotional attachment to the group and its members. Examples are the nuclear family, a child's play group, a teenage gang, and close friends. Primary groups are crucial to the individual because they provide members with a sense of belonging, identity, purpose, and security. Thus, they have the strongest influence on the attitudes and values of members (see the Closer Look panel titled "The Declining Significance of Family").

Secondary groups, in contrast to primary groups, are much larger and more impersonal. They are formally organized, task oriented, and relatively nonpermanent. The individual member is relatively unimportant. The members may vary considerably in beliefs, attitudes, and values. Americans are greatly affected by this type of group. The government at all levels deals with us impersonally. So, too, do our schools, where we are a number in a computer. We live in large dormitories, apartment buildings, or in neighborhoods where we are barely acquainted with people near us. We work in large organizations and belong to large religious organizations.

A CLOSER LOOK

The Declining Significance of Family

One's family is the ultimate primary group, providing physical and emotional care, intimacy, intense loyalty, and attachment. While this continues, there is change. For many, friends have supplanted blood ties as the new family (this panel draws heavily on Jayson, 2005). Several demographic (population) factors have diminished the influence of the family and increased that of friends. Whereas a generation or two ago families tended to be geographically near, getting together often, now they are typically geographically dispersed. Ours is a mobile society, with 20 percent of the population moving each year usually because of jobs. One's parents or adult children may be thousands of miles away. Also, more and more households (27.8 percent in 2008) are now composed of singles. This is because of a relatively high divorce rate, women and men marrying later, the increased economic independence of women, and many choosing a single lifestyle rather than marriage (Baca Zinn, Eitzen, and Wells, 2011:418–420). And, as society becomes more heterogeneous, people choose friends like themselves in occupation, income, values, and lifestyle preferences. Whereas family members may be judgmental of divorce, single parenthood, cohabitation, or gay/lesbian relationships, friends will be chosen for their support of these alternatives.

As a consequence, for many, close friends are replacing the family as the primary source of identity, emotional support, and help in time of need. Sociologist Pepper Schwartz says this: "I do think family—as being the center of one's universe—has weakened. It's hard to find three generations of the same family in the same town anymore. You have more in common with people who are approximal to you—friends, neighbors, colleagues. They know you in ways your family ceases to know you" (quoted in Jayson, 2005:D2).

Family, of course, is still a vital primary group. But our changing society has broadened the definition of family to include relatives as well as friends as either a substitute or an extension of the primary group.

In today's lesson, class, we explore the increasing isolation of the individual in society.

© Kirk Anderson. Reprinted by permission.

Secondary groups spawn the formation of primary groups. Primary groups emerge at school, at work, in an apartment complex, in a neighborhood, in a church, or in an army. In other words, intensely personal groups develop and are sustained by their members in largely impersonal settings.

The existence of primary groups within secondary groups is an important phenomenon that has ramifications for the goals of the secondary group. Two examples from military experience make this point. In World War II, the German army was organized to promote the formation of primary groups. The men were assigned to a unit for the duration of the war. They trained together, fought together, went on furloughs together, and were praised or punished as a group. This was a calculated organizational ploy to increase social solidarity in the small fighting units. This worked to increase morale, loyalty, and a willingness to die for the group. In fact, individuals often became more loyal to their fighting unit than to the nation (Shils and Janowitz, 1948).

In contrast, the U.S. Army in Vietnam was organized in such a way as to minimize the possibility of forming primary groups. Instead of being assigned to a single combat unit until the war was over, soldiers were given a twelve-month tour of duty in Vietnam. This rotation system meant that in any fighting unit, soldiers were continually entering and leaving. This constant rotation prevented the development of close relationships and a feeling of all for one and one for all. Because each soldier had his own departure date, his goal was not to win the war but to survive until he was eligible to go home. This individualism made morale difficult to maintain and loyalty to one's unit difficult if not impossible to achieve. It also made the goal of winning the war less attainable than would a system that fostered primary groups (Moskos, 1975).

Bureaucracy: The Ultimate Secondary Group

A **bureaucracy** is a hierarchical formal organization characterized by rationality and efficiency—that is, improved operating efficiency and more effective attainment of common goals. As an organization grows in size and complexity, there is a greater need for coordination if efficiency is to be maintained or improved. Organizational efficiency is maximized (ideally) under the following conditions (Weber, 1947:329–341):

- When the work is divided into small tasks performed by specialists.
- When there is a hierarchy of authority (chain of command), with each position in the chain having clearly defined duties and responsibilities.
- When behaviors are governed by standardized, written, and explicit rules.
- When all decisions are made on the basis of technical knowledge, not personal considerations.
- When the members are judged solely on the basis of proficiency, and discipline is impartially enforced.

In short, a bureaucracy is an organization designed to perform like a machine. The push toward increased bureaucratization pervades nearly all aspects of U.S. life, including government (at all levels), the church (for example, the Catholic Church and the Methodist Church), education (all school systems), sports (the National Collegiate Athletic Association [NCAA], athletic departments at big-time schools, professional teams), health care (hospitals, health maintenance organizations, Blue Cross/Blue Shield), corporations (General Motors, Microsoft), and even crime (the Mafia) and fast-food chains. The increasing bureaucratization in social life is

called **McDonaldization**, coined by sociologist George Ritzer. By this he means "the process by which the principles of the fast-food restaurant are coming to dominate more and more sectors of American society as well as the rest of the world" (Ritzer, 1996:1).

The benefits of bureaucracy include a division of labor that promotes efficiency, specific expectations of members, rewards based on achievement rather than favoritism, and expertise for specific tasks coordinated to accomplish complex goals.

There is also a significant downside to bureaucracy. Ironically, while created for efficiency, bureaucracies often foster the opposite result by having too many regulations—individuals evade responsibility by passing the buck, and creativity is stifled by rules. Blind obedience to rules and the unquestioned following of orders mean that new and unusual situations cannot be handled efficiently because the rules do not apply. Rigid adherence to the rules creates automatons. Robert Merton (1957) observes that "adherence to the rules, originally conceived as a means, becomes transformed into an end-in-itself" (199). Most significant, there is the danger that Max Weber feared from the **"iron cage" of rationality**; that is, bureaucracies can be dehumanizing since they would trap people in rational systems devoid of creativity (Ritzer, 1996:21).

Power of the Social Group

We have seen that primary and secondary groups structure the behavior of their members by providing rules, roles, and mechanisms of social control. The result is that most of us, most of the time, conform to the expectations of social groups. Let us examine some illustrations of the profound influence of social groups on individuals, beginning with Emile Durkheim's classic study of suicide.

The Group Affects the Probability of Suicide. One's attachment to social groups affects the probability of suicide. Suicide would appear on the surface to be one area that could strictly be left to psychological explanations. An individual is committing the ultimate individual act—ending one's own life—presumably because of excessive guilt, anxiety, and/or stress. Sociologists, however, are interested in this seemingly individual phenomenon because of the social factors that may produce the feelings of guilt or the undue psychological stress.

Sociologists are not interested, however, in the individual suicide case, as psychologists are, but in a number of people in the same social situation. Let us look at how sociologists would study suicide by examining in some detail the classic study by the nineteenth-century French sociologist Emile Durkheim (1951, first written in 1897). Durkheim was the consummate sociologist. He reacted to what he considered was the excessive psychologism of his day by examining suicide rates (the number of suicides per 100,000 people in a particular category) sociologically. Some of the interesting results of his study were that single people had higher rates than married people, childless married people had a higher rate than those with children, the rate of city dwellers exceeded that of rural people, and Protestants were more likely to be self-destructive than Catholics or Jews. Societal conditions were also correlated with suicide rates. As expected, rates were higher during economic depressions than in periods of economic stability, although surprisingly high rates were found during economic booms.

Durkheim went an important step beyond just noting that social factors were related to suicide rates. He developed a theory to explain these facts—a theory based on the individual's relationship to a social organization. Durkheim posited three types of suicide—the egoistic, altruistic, and anomic—to illustrate the effect of one's attachment to a group (society, religion, family) on self-preservation. **Egoistic suicide** occurs when an individual has minimal ties to a social group. The person is alone, lacking group goals and group supports. This explains why married people are less likely to commit suicide than are single people, and why married people with children are not as likely to kill themselves as are married people who are childless. Being an important part of a group gives meaning and purpose to life. This lack of group supports also explains why Protestants during Durkheim's day had a higher suicide rate than did Catholics. The Catholic religion provided believers with many group supports, including the belief in the authority of religious leaders to interpret the scriptures. Catholics also believed that through the confessional, sinners could be redeemed. Protestants, on the other hand, were expected to be their own priests, reading and interpreting God's word. When guilty of sin, Protestants again were alone. There was no confessional where a priest would assure one of forgiveness. The differences in theology left individual Protestants without religious authority and with a greater sense of uncertainty. This relatively greater isolation left Protestants without the group of believers and the authority of priests in times of stress.

Altruistic suicide occurs in a completely different type of group setting. When groups are highly cohesive, the individual member of such a collectivity tends to be group oriented. Such a group might expect its members to kill themselves for the good of the group under certain conditions. Soldiers may be expected to leave the relative safety of their foxholes and attack a strategic hill even though the odds are against them. The strong allegiance to one's group may force an act that would otherwise seem irrational. The kamikaze attacks by Japanese pilots during World War II were suicide missions in which the pilot guided his ammunition-laden plane into a target. These pilots gave their lives because of their ultimate allegiance to a social group—clearly an example of altruistic suicide. So, too, are the Muslim suicide bombers in the Middle East, young men (and occasionally women and children) who die for the cause of their group.

The third type of suicide—**anomic suicide**—is also related to the individual's attachment to a group. It differs from the other two types in that it refers especially to the condition in which the expectations of a group are ambiguous or they conflict with other sets of expectations. Typically, behavior is regulated by a clear set of rules (norms). But there are times when these rules lose their clarity and certainty for individuals. This is a condition of **anomie** (normlessness). Anomie usually occurs in a situation of rapid change. Examples of anomic situations are emigration from one society to another, movement from a rural area to an urban one, rapid loss of status, overnight wealth, widowhood, divorce, and drastic inflation or deflation. In all these cases, people are often not sure how to behave. They are not certain of their goals. Life may appear aimless. Whenever the constraints on behavior are suddenly lifted, the probability of suicide increases. The irony is that we tend to be comfortable under the tyranny of the group and that freedom from such constraints is often intolerable. The sexual freedom of married people in U.S. society, for example, is highly regulated. There is only one legitimate sex partner. The unmarried person is not limited. But even though married people might fantasize that such a life is nirvana, the replacement of regulated sexual behavior with such freedom is a condition of normlessness conducive to higher suicide rates.

The Group Affects Perceptions. The group may affect our perceptions. Apparently, our wish to conform is so great that we often give in to group pressure. Solomon Asch, a social psychologist, has tested this proposition by asking the subjects in an experiment to compare the length of lines on cards (Asch, 1958). The subjects were asked one at a time to identify verbally the longest line. All the subjects but one were confederates of the experimenter, coached to give the same wrong answer, placing the lone subject in the awkward position of having the evidence of her or his senses unanimously contradicted. Each experiment consisted of eighteen trials, with the confederates giving wrong responses on twelve and correct ones on six. For the fifty subjects going through this ordeal, the average number of times they went along with the majority with incorrect judgments was 3.84. Thirteen of the fifty were independent and gave responses in accord with their perceptions, but thirty-seven (74 percent) gave in to the group pressure at least once (twelve did eight or more times). In other experiments in which the confederates were not unanimous in their responses, the subjects were freed from the overwhelming group pressure and generally had confidence enough in their perceptions to give the correct answer.

Muzafer Sherif (1958) also conducted a series of experiments to determine the extent of conformity among individuals. An individual subject was placed in a dark room to observe a pinpoint of light. The subject was asked to describe how many inches the light moved (the light appears to move, even though it is stationary, because of what is called the autokinetic effect). In repeated experiments each subject tended to be consistent as to how far she or he felt the light had moved. When placed in a group, however, individuals modified their observations to make them more consistent with those of the other people in the room. After repeated exposures, the group arrived at a collective judgment. The important point about this experiment is that the group, unlike the one in the Asch experiment, was composed entirely of naive subjects. Therefore, the conclusion about group pressure on individual members is more valid, reflecting natural group processes.

The Group Affects Convictions. Sectarians with group support maintain their conviction despite contrary evidence. Leon Festinger and his associates Riecken and Schachter (1956) carefully studied a group that believed that in 1956 a great flood would submerge the West Coast from Seattle to Chile on December 21 of that year. On the eve of the predicted cataclysm the leader received a message that her group should be ready to leave at midnight in a flying saucer that had been dispatched to save them. The group waited expectantly at midnight for the arrival of the saucer. It did not appear, and finally at 4:45 A.M. the leader announced that she had received another communication. The message was that the world had been spared the disaster because of the force of good found among this small band of believers. Festinger was especially interested in how the group would handle this disconfirmation of prophecy. But this group, like other millennial groups of history, reacted to the disconfirmation by reaffirming their beliefs and doubling their efforts to win converts.

The Group Affects Health and Life. Membership in a group may have an effect on one's health and even on life itself. Rural Pakistan maintains the traditional caste system where children are destined to occupy the stratum of society into which they are born. Their occupation will be that of their parents with no questions asked. One of the lowest castes is that of beggar. Because the child of a beggar will be a beggar and because the most successful beggars are deformed, the child will be deformed by his or her family (usually by an uncle). Often the method is to break the child's back because the resulting deformity is so wretched. All parents wish success for their children, and the beggar family wishing the same is forced by the constraints of the rigid social system to physically disable their child for life.

Over the past twenty years or so, hundreds of children have died across the United States because their parents belonged to religious sects that do not believe in medical intervention. Eight of these deaths have occurred in Colorado within one sect, the Church of the First Born. One child died of meningitis; others died from pneumonia or other conditions that very likely could have been healed through traditional medical care. A three-year-old boy, for example, whose mother belonged to this sect died of diphtheria. The boy had never been immunized for this disease. Moreover, the mother refused medical treatment for her son after the illness had been diagnosed. The mother knew the consequences of her refusal of medical treatment because her nephew had died of diphtheria, but her faith and the faith of the other members kept her from saving her son's life. This is dramatic evidence for the power of the group to curb what we erroneously call maternal instinct.

Another example of a group demanding hazardous behavior of its members is found among some religious sects of Appalachia that encourage the handling of poisonous snakes (rattlesnakes, water moccasins, and copperheads) as part of worship. Members pick up handfuls of poisonous snakes, throw them on the ground, pick them up again, thrust them under their shirts and blouses, and even cover their heads with clusters of snakes. The ideology of the group thus encourages members literally to put their faith to the ultimate test—death. The ideology is especially interesting because it justifies both death by snakebite and being spared the bite or recovering if bitten. If the serpent-handler dies, this is a sign showing the scoffers how dangerous it is to obey God. If the serpent-handler survives the snake bite, this is proof of the Lord's power (Gerrard, 1968:23).

The Group Affects Behavior. The group can alter the behavior of members, even behaviors that involve basic human drives. Human beings are biologically programmed to eat, drink, sleep, and engage in sexual activity; but human groups significantly shape how these biological drives are met. How we eat, when we eat, and what we eat are all greatly influenced by social groups. Some groups have rigid rules that require periods of fasting. Others have festivals at which huge quantities of food and drink are consumed. Sexual behavior is also controlled. Although the sex drive is universal, mating is not a universal activity among adults. Some people, because of their group membership, take vows of chastity. Some people, because they have certain physical or mental traits, are often labeled by groups as undesirable and are therefore involuntarily chaste. Some societies are obsessed with sex; others are not. An example of the latter is the Dani tribe of New Guinea. Sexual intercourse is delayed between marriage partners until exactly two years after the ceremony. After the birth of a child there is a five-year period of abstinence.

These dramatic examples of the power of groups over individuals should not keep us from recognizing the everyday and continual constraints on behavior. Our everyday activities, our perceptions and interpretations, and our attitudes are the products of our group memberships. The constraints, however, are for the most part subtle and go unrecognized as such. In short, what we think of as autonomous behavior is generally not autonomous at all.

In summary, social groups undergo a universal process—the process of social organization. Through enduring social interaction, a matrix of social expectations emerges that guides behavior in prescribed channels, making social life patterned and therefore predictable. Thus, social organizations tend to be stable. But this is also a process, as Figure 2.1 indicates.

FIGURE 2.1

Process of Social
Organization

Source: This scheme
is adapted from that
developed by Marvin
E. Olsen, The Process
of Social Organization,
2nd ed. New York:
Holt, Rinehart and
Winston, 1976.

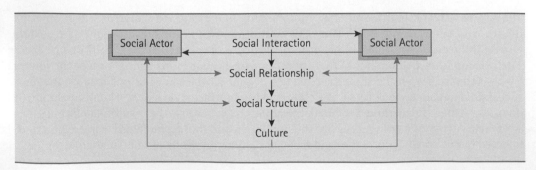

Interaction among the social actors in a social organization is constant and continuous, reinforcing stability but also bringing about change. Social organizations are never static. New ideas and new expectations emerge over time. Social change, however, is generally gradual. This is because, as shown in Figure 2.1, while social organizations are human-made, the creation, like Frankenstein's monster, to an important degree controls the creator. The culture that emerges takes on a sacred quality (the sanctity of tradition) that is difficult to question. This quality profoundly affects the attitudes and behaviors of the social actors in the social organization and the organization itself. As Wilbert Moore (1969), the distinguished sociologist, puts it,

> [M]an is an inevitably social animal, and one whose social behavior is scarcely guided by instinct. He learns social behavior, well or poorly of one sort or another. As a member of social groups he invents values for himself and his collectivities, rules for his conduct, knowledge to aid him in predicting and controlling his environment, gods to reward and punish him, and other ingenious elements of the human condition. ... Once [the products of this activity] are established in the human consciousness, they become, in turn, guides to behavior. (283)

The Societal or Macro Level

Primary and secondary groups illustrate nicely the process and the components of social organization. But each of these groups exists in a larger social setting—a context that is also structured with norms, statuses, roles, and mechanisms of social control. These are the components of social structure through which society affects our attitudes and behaviors regardless of our other group memberships.

A **society** is the largest social organization to which people owe their allegiance. It is an aggregate of people, united by a common culture, who are relatively autonomous and self-sufficient and who live in a definite geographical location. It is difficult to imagine a society undergoing the same processes as other, smaller, social organizations because societies are typically composed of so many different people and groups, none of whom was present at the beginning of the society. But the conceptual scheme for the process of social organization shown in Figure 2.1 is also applicable at the societal level. Continuing interaction among the members reinforces stability but also is a source of change. At any given time, the actors in the society are constrained by the norms, values, and roles that are the results of hundreds of years of evolution.

Society as a Social System

A society is a **social system**, composed of interdependent parts that are linked together into a boundary-maintaining whole. This concept of system implies that there is order and predictability within. Moreover, there are clear boundaries to a system in terms of membership and territory. Finally, the parts are independent.

The U.S. economy illustrates this interdependence nicely. There is a division of labor in society that provides a wide range of products and services meeting the needs of society's members. The presence of economic booms and depressions further illustrates the interdependence in society. For example, a depression comes about (in overly simplistic terms) when the flow of money is restricted by high taxes, high interest rates, high unemployment, and restricted buying practices by individuals. When large numbers of people delay buying items such as a new car or refrigerator because they are uncertain of the future, the sales of these items decline dramatically. This decrease itself is a source of further pessimism, thereby further dampening sales. The price of stocks in these companies will, of course, plummet under these conditions, causing further alarm. Moreover, many workers in these industries will be laid off. These newly unemployed people, in turn, will purchase only necessities, thereby throwing other industries into panic as their sales decline. A depression, then, is the result of actions by individual consumers, boards of directors of corporations, banks and savings and loan associations, individual and institutional investors, and the government. Additionally, the actions of the United States and the actions of other nations greatly affect the economic conditions of each other because nations, too, form an interdependent network.

The Culture of Society

Culture explains much individual and group behavior, as well as the persistence of most aspects of social life. Social scientists studying a society foreign to them must spend months, perhaps years, learning the culture of that group. They must learn the meanings for the symbols (written and spoken language, gestures, and rituals) used by the individuals in that society. They must know the feelings people share as to what is appropriate or inappropriate behavior. Additionally, they need to know the rules of the society: which activities are considered important, the skills members have in making and using tools, and the knowledge members need to exist in that society. In short, analysts must discover all the knowledge that people share—that is, they must know the culture. Culture and its transmission are discussed fully in Chapters 4 through 7.

Social Classes

A structural component of societies is **social stratification**, the hierarchical arrangement of people in terms of power, prestige, and resources. This universal phenomenon of social inequality is so important for the understanding of individual behavior and the structure of society that Chapters 9 through 12 are devoted to it. At the individual level, one's placement in the hierarchy directly affects self-perception, motivation, political attitudes, and the degree of advantage or disadvantage in school, in the economy, in the courts, and even in life itself. At the societal level, the extent of inequality affects the types and magnitude of social problems, societal stability, and economic growth.

Social Institutions

One distinguishing characteristic of societies is the existence of a set of institutions. The popular usages of this term are imprecise and omit some important sociological considerations. An institution is not anyone or any thing that is established and traditional (for example, a janitor who has worked at the same school for forty-five years). An institution is not limited to specific organizations, such as a school or a prison or a hospital. An institution is much broader in scope and importance than a person, a custom, or a social organization.

Institutions are social arrangements that channel behavior in prescribed ways in the important areas of social life. They are interrelated sets of normative elements—norms, values, and role expectations—that the people making up the society have devised and passed on to succeeding generations in order to provide permanent solutions to society's perpetually unfinished business. Institutions are cultural imperatives. They serve as regulatory agencies, channeling behavior in culturally prescribed ways. "Institutions provide procedures through which human conduct is patterned, compelled to go, in grooves deemed desirable by society. And this trick is performed by making the grooves appear to the individual as the only possible ones" (Berger, 1963:87).

For example, a society instills in its members predetermined channels for marriage. Instead of allowing the sexual partners a host of options, it is expected in U.S. society that the couple, composed of a man and a woman, will marry and set up a conjugal household. Although the actual options are many, the partners choose what society demands. In fact, they do not consider the other options as valid (for example, polygamy, polyandry, or group marriage). The result is a patterned arrangement that regulates sexual behavior and attempts to ensure a stable environment for the care of dependent children. The current demand by some state legislatures that gay partners should not be allowed to marry illustrates the strict institutional demands of society over individual behavior (see the Diversity panel titled "Gay Marriage?").

Institutions are, by definition, conservative. They are the answers of custom and tradition to questions of survival. Although absolutely necessary for unity and stability,

Gay Marriage?

At mid-2011 Argentina, Belgium, Canada, Iceland, the Netherlands, Norway, Portugal, South Africa, Spain, and Sweden were the only countries to legalize same-sex marriage. Eighteen other nations had granted same-sex couples rights equal to those of heterosexual couples. The response by politicians in the United States is different—much different. Same-sex marriage was illegal in forty-one states. Only Massachusetts, Iowa, Vermont, Connecticut, New Hampshire, New York, and the District of Columbia allowed same-sex marriages. Civil Unions or Domestic Partnerships were legal in California, Colorado, Hawaii, Maine, Maryland, Nevada, New Jersey, Oregon, Washington, and Wisconsin. These legal arrangements, while not called marriages, are explicitly defined as offering all or part of the rights and responsibilities of marriage under state law to same-sex couples.

In 1996, a conservative Congress and a centrist president signed the so-called Defense of Marriage Act, which allowed states to deny recognition to same-sex marriages that might be accorded full legal status in other states. This is in direct opposition to the "full faith and credit" clause of the Constitution, which requires that each state recognize "the public acts, records, and judicial proceedings of every other state" (Tribe, 1996:E11).

Public opinion in the United States is split on the legalization of same-sex marriage, with polls typically showing support from 48 percent to 52 percent. The support is increasing each year. Opposition to same-sex marriage is found mainly among conservative religious groups, older Americans, Republicans, and residents of the South and Midwest. Most Christian religious leaders and denominations resist homosexual marriage because they believe that it violates biblical commands for sex to be heterosexual and within marriages, with procreation as the goal. Conservative, pro-family advocates oppose gay marriage because it will change the family (Rotello, 1996). The institution of the family is by definition conservative, holding to the traditional demands of heterosexual unions only. Seen in this light, same-sex marriage is considered by some as subversive and therefore an intolerable idea that must be prohibited.

institutions in contemporary U.S. society are often outmoded, inefficient, and unresponsive to the incredibly swift changes brought about by technological advances, population shifts, and increasing worldwide interdependence.

Institutions arise from the uncoordinated actions of multitudes of individuals over time. These actions, procedures, and rules evolve into a set of expectations that appear to have a design, because the consequences of these expectations provide solutions that help maintain social stability. The design is accidental, however; it is a product of cultural evolution.

All societies face problems in common. Although the variety of solutions is almost infinite, there is a functional similarity in their consequences, which are stability and maintenance of the system. Table 2.1 cites a number of common societal problems and the resulting institutions. This partial list of institutions shows the types of societal problems for which solutions are continually sought. All societies, for instance, have some form of the family, education, polity, economy, and religion. The variations on each theme that are found in societies are almost beyond imagination. These variations, while most interesting, are beyond the scope of this book. By looking at the interrelated norms, values, and role expectations that provide pat solutions to fundamental societal problems, we can begin to understand U.S. society.

As we look at the institutions of U.S. society, we must not forget that institutions are made by people and can therefore be changed. We should be guided by the insight that even though institutions appear to have the quality of being sacred, they are not. They can be changed, but critical examination is imperative. Social scientists must look behind the facades. They must not accept the patterned ways as the only correct ways. This is in the U.S. heritage—as found in the Declaration of Independence. As Skolnick and Currie (1970) put it,

> Democratic conceptions of society have always held that institutions exist to serve man, and that, therefore, they must be accountable to men. Where they fail to meet the test imposed on them, democratic theory holds that they ought to be changed. Authoritarian governments, religious regimes, and reformatories, among other social systems, hold the opposite: in case of misalignment between individuals or groups and the "system," the individuals and groups are to be changed or otherwise made unproblematic. (15)

TABLE 2.1

Common Societal Problems and Their Institutions

Societal Problems	Institution
Sexual regulation; maintenance of stable units that ensure continued births and care of dependent children	Family
Socialization of the newcomers to the society	Education
Maintenance of order, the distribution of power	Polity
Production and distribution of goods and services; ownership of property	Economy
Understanding the transcendental; the search for meaning of life and death and the place of humankind in the world	Religion
Understanding the physical and social realms of nature	Science
Providing for physical and emotional health care	Medicine

CHAPTER REVIEW

1. Social organization refers to the observed regularities in the behavior of people that are due to social conditions rather than the physiology or psychology of individuals.

2. Social organization includes both social structure and culture. These emerge through enduring social interaction.

3. Social structure involves the linkages and networks that transform individuals into a group. It includes the patterns of interaction that emerge, the division of labor, and the links and hierarchy of positions.

4. Culture, the shared beliefs of a group's members, guides conduct. The elements of culture include the norms (rules), roles (behavioral expectations for the occupants of the various positions), and values (the criteria for judging people, things, and actions).

5. Norms are rules specifying appropriate and inappropriate behaviors. The important norms are called mores; the less important ones, folkways.

6. Each of us belongs to a number of social organizations, and in each we occupy a position (status). These statuses are a major source of identity for individuals.

7. The behavior expected of a person occupying a status in a social organization is the role. The pressures to conform to role demands ensure that there is stability and predictability in social groups even though member turnover occurs.

8. There are three reasons, however, that role expectations do not make behavior totally predictable: (a) personality differences, (b) inconsistent messages as to what behavior is expected, and (c) multiple group memberships resulting in conflicting demands.

9. Social organizations use positive sanctions (rewards) and negative sanctions (punishments) to enforce conformity to the norms, values, and roles of the group.

10. Two ways to classify social groups are on the basis of size and the quality of interaction. Primary groups are those whose members are involved in intimate, face-to-face interaction, with strong emotional attachments. The organization is informal and long-lasting. The members identify strongly with each other and with the group. In contrast, secondary groups are large, impersonal, and formally organized. The individual member is relatively unimportant.

11. Primary groups often emerge within secondary groups.

12. Bureaucracies are complex organizations designed to increase efficiency by dividing work into small tasks performed by specialists, by having a chain of command in which each position has clearly defined responsibilities, by making decisions based on technical knowledge, and by judging performance by proficiency.

13. Positively, bureaucracies accomplish coordination, reliability, efficiency, stability, and continuity. Negatively, they create inefficiency through blind obedience to the rules and authority, stifling creativity, and too many regulations. Also, bureaucracies can be dehumanizing (Weber's iron cage of rationality).

14. Social groups have enormous power over their members and affect their beliefs, behaviors, perceptions, and even health.

15. A society is the largest social organization to which people owe their allegiance. The society provides the social context for primary and secondary groups. Society places constraints on these groups and their members through its own norms, values, roles, and mechanisms for social control.

16. A society is a social system composed of interdependent parts that are linked together in a boundary-maintaining whole. There is order and predictability within. There is a division of labor providing for self-sufficiency.

17. A society, like other social organizations, has a culture involving norms, roles, values, symbols, and technical knowledge.

18. Unlike other social organizations, a society has a set of institutions. These are social arrangements that channel behavior in prescribed ways in the important areas of social life.

19. Institutions are conservative, providing the answers of custom and tradition to questions of social survival. Even though they are absolutely necessary for unity and stability, institutions can be outmoded, inefficient, and unresponsive to the swift changes of contemporary life.

KEY TERMS

Social organization
Social structure
Culture
Aggregate
Group
Social interaction
Social relationship
Values
Social roles
Norms
Folkways

Mores
Status
Hierarchy
Master status
Role
Sanctions
Social group
Primary groups
Secondary groups
Bureaucracy
McDonaldization

"Iron cage" of rationality
Egoistic suicide
Altruistic suicide
Anomic suicide
Anomie
Society
Social system
Social stratification
Institutions

STUDY QUESTIONS

1. What is meant by social organization? Describe the social organization of a group to which you belong, using the appropriate sociological concepts.
2. In 2010, thirty-three Chilean miners were trapped 2,300 feet beneath the surface in a copper mine for several months. Assume that one of these miners was actually a sociologist. What sociological insights would he likely have observed as these men organized for survival?
3. How has recent technology affected interaction patterns? Consider, for example, the effects of television, the Internet, cell phones, cyberspace games, Facebook, and Twitter, on the number and quality of interactions for children and adults.
4. Define the related concepts of status and role. What do they have to do with social organization?
5. Illustrate McDonaldization with some bureaucracy with which you are familiar.
6. Emile Durkheim made a sociological analysis of the most private of acts—suicide. Describe this sociological analysis. How would psychologists differ from sociologists in their explanations of this phenomenon?
7. What are social institutions? Explain the apparent anomaly that they are both sources of stability in society as well as sources of social problems.

WEB RESOURCES

http://www.mcdonaldization.com/main.shtml
This site provides information on the McDonaldization of society and the different dimensions of it outlined by sociologist George Ritzer, who coined the term.

http://www.uiowa.edu/~grpproc/
Part of the Sociology Department at the University of Iowa, the online Center for the Study of Group Processes contains an electronic journal with research related to the study of groups. Included in the group studies are formal organizations, political groups, families, intimates, social categories, and societies.

http://www.slis.lib.indiana.edu/CSI/
The Center for Social Informatics does research on the relationship between technology and social change. The site has information on papers, conferences, and other related resources.

http://sun.soci.niu.edu/~sssi/
The Society for the Study of Symbolic Interaction is an "international social science professional organization of scholars interested in qualitative, especially interactionist research."

We The
PeopLe..
We're Back
LESS FEDERAL
DO YOU
SORRY!
I can't
HEEEAR You!
IN GOD
MEMBER

CHAPTER 3

The Duality of Social Life:
Order and Conflict

What is violence? The answer depends on one's vantage point in the power structure, because violence is defined as such if the act threatens the power structure. Protesting in Pakistan in 2007, for example, was perceived by the government as violent, whereas the actions of the police to maintain order were seen as violent by the protestors. Similarly, in the spring of 1989, the students in Tiananmen Square in Beijing who demonstrated for increased freedoms were viewed by the Chinese government as a threat and were forcibly defeated. The students' actions were depicted on government television as being illegitimate (violent), whereas the actions to maintain order were defined as legitimate. From the perspective of the victimized group, however, the actions of the police were illegitimate and, therefore, amounted to police brutality.

Violence always refers to a disruption of some condition of order, but order, like violence, is also politically defined. Order itself can be destructive to some categories of people. Somehow, the term violence is not applied to high infant mortality and rates of preventable diseases that prevail among the poor and powerless in every society. Critics of this type of societal violence might call such harmful outcomes "institutional violence," to imply that the system itself injures and destroys (Skolnick, 1969:3–8).

Violence is also defined politically through the selection process. Some acts of force (to injure people or to destroy property) are not always forbidden or condemned in U.S. society. Property damaged during celebrations (winning the crucial football game, on Halloween, or during Mardi Gras) is often overlooked. Even thousands of drunken, noisy, and sometimes destructive college students on the Texas beaches of Padre Island during spring break are usually tolerated because they are just boisterous youth on a binge (and the money they spend helps the local economy). But if these same thousands of students were to destroy the same amount of property in a demonstration of which the goal was to change the system, then the acts would be defined as violent and the police would be called to restore order by force if necessary (which, of course, would not be defined as violence by the authorities). Thus, violence is condoned or condemned through political pressures and decisions. The basic criterion is whether the acts are in approved channels or are supportive of existing social and political arrangements. If not supportive, then the acts are, by definition, to be condemned and punished.

In sum, there is a relationship between the power structure and violence. The perception of how violence is defined provides insight toward a greater understanding of the role of conflict and order in society.

Social Systems: Order and Conflict

The analysis of society begins with a mental picture of its structure. This image (or model) influences what scientists look for, what they see, and how they explain the phenomena that occur within the society.

One of the characteristics of societies—the existence of segmentation—is the basis for the two prevailing models of society. Every society is composed of parts. This differentiation may result from differences in age, race, sex, physical prowess, wisdom, family background, wealth, organizational membership, type of work, or any other characteristic considered salient by the members. The fundamental question concerning differentiation is this: What is the basic relationship among the parts of society? The two contradictory answers to this question provide the rationale for the two models of society—order and conflict.

One answer is that the parts of society are in harmony. They cooperate because of similar or complementary interests and because they need each other to accomplish those things beneficial to all (examples are the production and distribution of goods and services and protection). Another answer is that the subunits of society are basically in competition with each other. This view is based on the assumption that the things people desire most (wealth, power, autonomy, resources, high status) are always in short supply; hence, competition and conflict are universal social phenomena. (See the Research Methods panel titled "Social Scientists and Values: Taking Sides.")

The Order Model

The **order model** (sometimes referred to as **functionalism**) attributes to societies the characteristics of cohesion, consensus, cooperation, reciprocity, stability, and persistence. Societies are viewed as social systems, composed of interdependent parts that are linked together creating order and stability. The parts of the system are basically in harmony with each other. If something disrupts this order, the parts will adjust to produce a new stable

RESEARCH METHODS

Social Scientists and Values: Taking Sides

Social scientists are not value neutral. Whether they admit it or not, they take sides by adopting a way of perceiving and interpreting the social world. This does not render social science useless, as the late Michael Harrington (1985), a highly esteemed social scientist and political activist, argues in the following excerpt:

> Truths about society can be discovered only if one takes sides. ... You must stand somewhere in order to see social reality, and where you stand will determine much of what you see and how you see it. The data of society are, for all practical purposes, infinite. You need criteria that will provisionally permit you to bring some order into that chaos of data and to distinguish between relevant and irrelevant factors or, for that matter, to establish that there are facts in the first place. These criteria cannot be based upon the data for they are the precondition of the data. They represent—and the connotations of the phrase should be savored—a "point

of view." That involves intuitive choices, a value-laden sense of what is meaningful and what is not. ...

> The poor, I suggest, see a different social world from the rich—and so do those who think, whether consciously or not, from the vantage point of the poor or the rich. I was born into and have lived my life in the middle class. But I have tried to write from the point of view of the poor and excluded, those in the United States and elsewhere. I am therefore a deeply biased man, a taker of sides; but that is not really distinctive at all. Everyone else is as biased as I am, including the most "objective" social scientist. The difference between us is that I am frank about my values while many other analysts fool both themselves and their audiences with the illusion that they have found an intellectual perch that is free of Earth's social field of gravity. (1–2)

Source: Taking Sides: The Education of a Militant Mind, by Michael Harrington. © 1985 by Michael Harrington. Reprinted by permission of Henry Holt and Company, LLC.

order. The high degree of cooperation (and societal integration) is accomplished because there is a high degree of consensus on societal goals and on cultural values. Moreover, the different parts of the system are assumed to need each other because of complementary interests. Because the primary social process is cooperation and the system is highly integrated, all social change is gradual, adjustive, and reforming. Societies are therefore basically stable units.

For order theorists, the central issue is: What is the nature of the social bond? What holds groups together? This was the focus of Emile Durkheim, the French social theorist of the early 1900s (see Chapter 1). The various forms of integration were used by Durkheim to explain differences in suicide rates (see Chapter 2), social change, and the universality of religion (Durkheim, 1951; 1960; 1965).

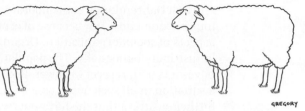

"Sure, I follow the herd—not out of brainless obedience, mind you, but out of a deep and abiding respect for the concept of community."

For Durkheim, there are two types of societies, based on the way the members are bonded. In smaller, less complex societies, solidarity among the members occurs through the collective holding of beliefs (ideologies, values, moral sentiments, traditions). Social integration, therefore, occurs because the members are alike. Modern, complex societies, in contrast, achieve social integration through differentiation. Society is based on the division of labor, in which the members involved in specialized tasks are united by their dependence on others.

One way to focus on integration is to determine the manifest and latent consequences of social structures, norms, and social activities. Do these consequences contribute to the integration (cohesion) of the social system? Durkheim, for example, noted that the punishment of crime has the **manifest consequence** (intended) of punishing and deterring the criminal. The **latent consequence** (unintended) of punishment, however, is the societal reaffirmation of what is to be considered moral. The society is thereby integrated through belief in the same rules (Durkheim, 1958).

Taking Durkheim's lead, sociologists of the order persuasion have made many penetrating and insightful analyses of various aspects of society. By focusing on all the consequences of social structures and activities—intended and unintended, as well as negative (malintegrative functions or dysfunctions)—we can see behind the facades and thereby understand more fully such disparate social arrangements and activities as ceremonials (from rain dances to sporting events), social stratification, fashion, propaganda, and even political machines.

The Conflict Model

The assumptions of the **conflict model** (the view of society that posits conflict as a normal feature of social life, influencing the distribution of power and the direction and magnitude of social change) are opposite from those of the order model. The basic form of interaction is not cooperation but competition, which often leads to conflict. Because the individuals and groups of society compete for advantage, the degree of social integration is minimal and tenuous. Social change results from the conflict among competing groups and therefore tends to be drastic and revolutionary. The ubiquitousness of conflict results from the dissimilar goals and interests of social groups. It is, moreover, a result of social organization itself. The most famous conflict theorist was Karl Marx. He theorized that there exists in every society (except in, Marx believed, the last historical stage of communism) a dynamic tension between two groups—those who own the means of production and those who work for the owners. Contrary to Durkheim, who saw modern industry and its required division of labor as promoting social solidarity, Marx viewed these groups as the sources of division and exploitation (Walton, 1990:20). Marx focused on inequality—the oppressors and the oppressed, the dominant and the dominated, the powerful and the powerless. For him, the powerful protect their privileges by supporting the status quo. The laws, religion, education, and the mass media all work for the advantage of the advantaged. The powerful use and abuse the powerless, thereby sowing the seeds of their own destruction. The destruction of the elite is accomplished when the dominated people unite and overthrow the dominants.

Ralf Dahrendorf, a contemporary conflict theorist, has also viewed conflict as a ubiquitous phenomenon, not because of economic factors as Marx believed, but because of other aspects of social organization. Organization means, among other things, that power will be distributed unequally. The population will therefore be separated into the haves and the have-nots with respect to power. Because organization also means constraint, there will be a situation in all societies in which the constraints are determined by the powerful, thereby further ensuring that the have-nots will be in conflict with the haves—thus, the important insight that conflict is endemic to social organization.*

One other emphasis of conflict theorists is that the unity present in society is superficial, because it results not from consensus but from coercion. The powerful, it is asserted, use force and fraud to keep society running smoothly, with benefits mostly accruing to those in power.

The Duality of Social Life

The basic duality of social life can be seen by summarizing the opposite ways in which order and conflict theorists view the nature of society. If asked, "What is the fundamental relationship among the parts of society?" the answers of order and conflict theorists would disagree. This disagreement leads to and is based on a number of related assumptions about society. These assumptions are summarized in Table 3.1.

One interesting but puzzling aspect of Table 3.1 is that these two models are held by different scientific observers of the same phenomenon. How can experts on society derive such different assumptions? The answer is that both models are partially correct. Each model focuses on reality—but on only part of that reality. Scientists have tended to accept one or the other of these models, thereby focusing on only part of social reality, for at least two reasons:

TABLE 3.1

Duality of Social Life: Assumptions of the Order and Conflict Models of Society

	Order Model	*Conflict Model*
Question: What is the fundamental relationship among the parts of society?		
Answer:	Harmony and cooperation.	Competition, conflict, domination, and subordination.
Why:	The parts have complementary interests. Basic consensus on societal norms and values.	The things people want are always in short supply. Basic dissent on societal norms and values.
Degree of integration:	Highly Integrated.	Loosely integrated. Whatever integration is achieved is the result of force and fraud.
Type of social change:	Gradual, adjustive, and reforming.	Abrupt and revolutionary.
Degree of stability:	Stable.	Unstable.

---

*This description is a very superficial account of a complex process that has been fully described by Ralf Dahrendorf (1959).

(1) one model or the other was in vogue at the time of the scientist's intellectual development or (2) one model or the other made the most sense for the analysis of the particular problems of interest—for example, the interest of Emile Durkheim, who devoted his intellectual energies to determining what holds society together, or the fundamental concern of Karl Marx, who explored the causes of revolutionary social change.

The analyses of sport and of social problems are two important areas in which sociologists have been influenced by the order and the conflict models. Let us turn to these contrary ways to view these two social phenomena before examining a synthesis of the two models.

Sport from the Order and Conflict Perspectives. Order theorists examining any aspect of society emphasize the contribution that aspect makes to the stability of society (this section is dependent on Coakley, 2007; Eitzen and Sage, 2009). Sport, from this perspective, preserves the existing social order in several ways. To begin, sport symbolizes the American way of life—competition, individualism, achievement, and fair play. Not only is sport compatible with basic U.S. values, but it also is a powerful mechanism for socializing youth to adopt desirable character traits, such as the acceptance of authority, obeying rules, and striving for excellence.

Sport also supports the status quo by promoting the unity of society's members through patriotism (for example, the national anthem, militaristic displays, and other nationalistic rituals accompanying sports events). Can you imagine, for example, a team that espouses anti-establishment values in its name, logo, mascot, and pageantry? Would Americans, for example, tolerate a major league team called the Atlanta Atheists? the Boston Bigamists? the Pittsburgh Pacifists? or the Sacramento Socialists? Finally, sport inspires us through the excellent and heroic achievements of athletes, the magical moments in sport when the seemingly impossible happens, and the feelings of unity in purpose and of loyalty of fans.

Sports support the status quo by promoting the unity of members through patriotic rituals and displays.

Clearly, then, sport from the order perspective is good. Sport socializes youth into proper channels; sport unites; and sport inspires. Thus, to challenge or to criticize sport is to challenge the foundation of our society's social order.

Conflict theorists argue that the social order reflects the interests of the powerful. Sport is organized at every level—youth, high school, college, professional, and Olympic—to exploit athletes and meet the goals of the powerful (for example, public relations, prestige, and profits).

Sport inhibits the potential for revolution by society's have-nots in three ways. First, sport validates the prevailing myths of capitalism, such as anyone can succeed if he or she works hard enough. If a person fails, it's his or her fault and not that of the system. Second, sport serves as an opiate of the masses by diverting attention away from the harsh realities of poverty, unemployment, and dismal life chances by giving them a "high" (Hoch, 1972). And third, sport gives false hope to oppressed members of society, because they see sport as a realistic avenue of upward social mobility. The high visibility of wealthy athletes provides proof that athletic ability translates into monetary success. The reality, of course, is that only an extremely small percentage of aspiring athletes ever achieve professional status. In basketball, for example, there are about 500,000 male high school players and about 4,000 college seniors playing in any one year, and only about fifty of them will play as rookies at the professional level. The chances of upward mobility for women through sport are even less (Eitzen, 2009).

Conflict theorists agree with order theorists on many of the facts concerning sport but differ significantly in interpretation. Both agree that sport socializes youth, but conflict theorists view this socialization negatively, because they see sport as a mechanism to get youth to follow orders, work hard, and fit into a system that is not necessarily beneficial to them. Both agree that sport maintains the status quo. But instead of this being interpreted as good, as the order theorists maintain, conflict theorists view this as bad because it reflects and reinforces the unequal distribution of power and resources in society.

Social Problems from the Order and Conflict Perspectives. **Social problems** are societally induced conditions that harm any segment of the population, or acts, or conditions that violate the norms and values of society (Eitzen, Baca Zinn, and Smith, 2011). Under this rubric fall phenomena such as poverty, homelessness, crime, gender inequality, and discrimination.

The order and conflict perspectives constrain their adherents to view the causes, consequences, and remedies of social problems in opposing ways. The order perspective focuses on deviants themselves. This approach (which has been the conventional way of studying social problems) asks, Who are the deviants? What are their social and psychological backgrounds? With whom do they associate? Deviants somehow do not conform to the standards of the dominant group; they are assumed to be out of phase with conventional behavior. This is believed to occur most often as a result of inadequate socialization. In other words, deviants have not internalized the norms and values of society because they either are brought up in an environment of conflicting value systems (as are children of immigrants or the poor in a middle-class school) or are under the influence of a deviant subculture such as a gang. Because the order theorist uses the prevailing standards to define and label deviants, the existing practices and structures of society are accepted implicitly. The remedy is to rehabilitate the deviants so that they conform to the societal norms.

The conflict theorist takes a different approach to social problems. The adherents of this perspective criticize order theorists for blaming the victim (Ryan, 1976). To focus on the individual deviant locates the symptom, not the disease. Deviants are a manifestation of a failure of society to meet the needs of individuals. The sources of crime, poverty, drug addiction, and racism are found in the laws, the customs, the quality of life, the distribution of wealth and power, and the accepted practices of schools, governmental units, and corporations. In this view, then, the schools are the problem, not the dropouts; the quality of life, not the mentally ill; the maldistribution of wealth, not the poor; the roadblocks to success for minority-group members, not apathy on their part. The established system, in this view, is not sacred. Because the system is the primary source of social problems, it, not the individual deviant, must be restructured.

Although most of this book attempts to strike a balance between the order and conflict perspectives, the conflict model is clearly favored when social problems are brought into focus. This is done explicitly for two reasons. The subject matter of sociology is not individuals, who are the special province of psychology, but society. If sociologists do not make a critical analysis of the social structure, who will? Also, we are convinced that the source of social problems is found within the institutional framework of society (Eitzen, Baca Zinn, and Smith, 2009). Thus, a recurrent theme of this book is that social problems are societal in origin and not the exclusive function of individual pathologies.

Synthesis of the Order and Conflict Models

The assumptions of both models are contradictory for each comparison shown in Table 3.1, and their contradictions highlight the duality of social life. Social interaction can be harmonious or acrimonious. Societies are integrated or divided, stable or unstable. Social change can be fast or slow, revolutionary or evolutionary.

Taken alone, each of these perspectives fosters a faulty perception and interpretation of society, but taken together, they complement each other and present a complete and realistic model. A synthesis that combines the best of each model would appear, therefore, to be the best perspective for understanding the structure and process of society (see Lenski, 1966; van den Berghe, 1967).

The initial assumption of a synthesis approach is that *the processes of stability and change are properties of all societies.* There is an essential paradox to human societies: They are always ordered; they are always changing. These two elemental properties of social life must be recognized by the observer of society. Within any society there are forces providing impetus for change, and there are forces insisting on rooted permanence. Allen Wheelis (1958) has labeled these two contrary tendencies as the instrumental process and the institutional process, respectively.

The **instrumental process** is based on the desire for technological change—to find new and more efficient techniques to achieve goals. The **institutional process**, on the other hand, designates all those activities that are dominated by the quest for certainty. We are bound in our activities, often by customs, traditions, myths, and religious beliefs. So, there are rites, taboos, and mores that people obey without thinking. There also are modern institutions such as monotheism, monogamy, private property, and the sovereign state, all of which are coercive because they limit freedom of choice, but they are assumed proper by almost all individuals in U.S. society.

These two processes constitute the **dialectic** (opposing forces) of society. As contrary tendencies, they generate tension because the instrumental forces are constantly prodding the institutions to change when it is not their nature to do so.

The second assumption is that *societies are organized, but the process of organization generates conflict.* Organization implies, among other things, the differential allocation of power. Inequalities in power are manifested in at least two conflict-generating ways: differentials in decision making and inequalities in the system of social stratification (social classes and minority groups). Scarce resources can never be distributed equally to all people and groups in society. The powerful are always differentially rewarded and make the key decisions as to the allocation of scarce resources.

A third basic assumption for a synthesis model is that *society is a social system.* The term *social system* has three important implications: (1) that there is not chaos but some semblance of order—that action within the unit is, in a general way, predictable; (2) that boundaries exist that may be in terms of geographical space or membership; and (3) that there are parts that are interdependent—thus conveying the reality of differentiation and unity. A society is a system made up of many subsystems (for example, groups, organizations, and communities). Although these subsystems are all related in some way, some are strongly linked to others, whereas others have only a remote linkage. The interdependence of the parts implies further that events and decisions in one sector may have a profound influence on the entire system. The terrorist attacks on the World Trade Center and the Pentagon in 2001, for example, had profound effects throughout U.S. society (for example, the airline and leisure industries suffered financial setbacks resulting in layoffs; airlines received government subsidies while workers put out of work were denied; the stock market declined; screening procedures in airports were elevated, causing long delays; and the Justice Department instituted new rules that invaded privacy). Some events, however, have little or no effect on all of U.S. society. Most important for the synthesis approach is the recognition that the parts of the system may have complementary interests with other parts but may also have exclusive, incompatible interests and goals. There is generally some degree of cooperation and harmony found in society because of consensus over common goals and because of similar interests (for example, defense against external threats). Some degree of competition and dissent is also present because of incompatible interests, scarcity of resources, and unequal rewards. Societies, then, are imperfect social systems.

A fourth assumption is that *societies are held together by complementary interests, by consensus on cultural values, and also by coercion.* Societies do cohere. There are forces that bind diverse groups together into a single entity. The emphasis of both order and conflict models provides twin bases for such integration—consensus and coercion.

Finally, *social change is a ubiquitous phenomenon in all societies*. It may be gradual or abrupt, reforming or revolutionary. All social systems change. Order theorists have tended to view change as a gradual phenomenon occurring either because of innovation or because of differentiation (for example, dividing units into subunits to separate activities and make the total operation more efficient). This view of change is partially correct. Change can also be abrupt; it can come about because of social movements, or it can result from forces outside the society (that is, as a reaction to events outside the system or an acceptance of the innovations of others).

To summarize, a synthesis of the order and the conflict models views society as having "two faces of equal reality—one of stability, harmony, and consensus and one of change, conflict, and constraint" (Dahrendorf, 1968:127).

The remainder of this chapter illustrates the duality of social life by examining the society of the United States from the perspectives of the conflict and order theorists. We consider the sources of disunity in the United States and the major instances of violence that have occurred throughout U.S. history. Despite the existence of division and violence, the United States is unified, at least minimally. We therefore also consider the factors that work to unify.

The Fragmentation of Social Life: Deepening Divides in U.S. Society

Societies are integrated, but disunity and disharmony also exist to some degree in all societies. It is especially important to examine the segmenting influences in U.S. society, for they aid in explaining contemporary conflict and social change.

President Obama began his State of the Union message in 2011 with these words: "We believe that in a country where every race and faith and point of view can be found, we are still bound together as one people." He ended the speech with: "the state of the union is strong." Are the bonds that link Americans strong? Does societal unity transcend the divides in society? (this section is taken from Eitzen, 2011). There are fissures that divide the nation. What are they? Are they capable of fracturing society into pieces? While there are many indicators of reduced societal cohesion, let's consider four—increasing polarization, declining trust in societal institutions, the widening inequality gap, and the deepening divides over diversity.

Increasing Polarization

Public voices, whether in the legislature or in the media have become more shrill, more demanding of ideological purity, and, consequently, more dividing than uniting. As the sides coalesce at the extremes, the possibility of consensus, compromise, and civility shrinks. There is a philosophical divide between the two major political parties. In Congress, for example, Republicans favor solutions that help business. Thus, they oppose unions and the government regulation of business. In seeking to revive the economy, they believe in the power of tax cuts, primarily for the wealthy, assuming that the benefits will trickle down. Republicans also oppose government welfare programs because they believe that subsidies encourage dependency rather than self-reliance and individual accountability. Lower taxes and reduced welfare reveal their wish to make government smaller. In their view, government is not the solution, it is the problem.

Democrats, in contrast, believe in strong government regulation to protect the environment, workers, and consumers. They support unions and a rising minimum wage. They work for a strong safety net for the disadvantaged. To stimulate an economic recovery Democrats believe in the financial powers of the government. In short, the Democrats are for Big Government (Madrick, 2009).

In the past, Republicans and Democrats in Congress debated these issues and often reached consensus. The discourse, for the most part, was civil. Recently, though, political partisans have sometimes demonized their opponents, using ridicule and threats to make their cases (*New York Times*, 2011). Most significant, compromise between Republicans and Democrats has become increasing rare.

An ever greater proportion of the public has become more polarized because of changes in the media. Thirty years ago, there were three broadcast networks. Regardless of the network chosen for the news, the message was essentially the same, that is, it was mainstream. Balance and objectivity were the norm. But now, with the advent of cable television, talk radio, political blogs, chat rooms, political magazines, and specialized websites consumers can choose messages that reinforce their beliefs. Liberals can read, watch, and listen to liberal outlets such as MSNBC while Conservatives can limit their exposure to conservative venues, such as FOX NEWS. According to Harvard Law Professor Cass Sunstein, when we hear only one side, or are with only like-minded people, soft views harden, becoming more dogmatic. This phenomenon is known as "group polarization" (Sunstein, 2009).

Declining Trust in Societal Institutions

An important ingredient in the glue that holds society together is trust in society's institutions. Trust in the business world, for example, unravels when corporations from time to time are caught in fraudulent actions such as deceptive advertising, bribery, and other scandals. Most notably, many millions of homeowners were brought to bankruptcy or foreclosure with the bursting of the housing bubble caused by unscrupulous actions by lending institutions and inadequate government oversight.

Religious institutions have been rocked by scandals, calling their legitimacy into question (Parenti, 2010). There have been televangelists implicated in financial malfeasance. There have been hypocritical preachers who, while damning gays and lesbians, were engaged in homosexual activities. There are guru-worshiping cults that sometimes have engaged in sexual abuse, forced confinement, and other nefarious practices. The child molestations by priests and the subsequent cover-up by the Catholic hierarchy have caused a great financial burden on the Church as well personal grief and doubts. These personal transgressions are not just the acts of flawed individuals, but they also reveal the corruption of religious organizations. As Michael Parenti states:

> These perpetrators and their organizations are corrupt and criminally hurtful of human life. They have operated with something close to impunity, using their sacred robes, elevated status, and moral authority to prey upon the vulnerable, while making the religious establishment their base of operation, a den of soul-damaging deeds. (Parenti, 2010:153)

The federal government also is mistrusted by millions of citizens. The Birthers are concerned that President Obama's holding office is not legitimate because they claim that he is not a natural-born citizen. Radical conservatives such as Glenn Beck rant that Obama is a socialist and that he is taking the country down a path to destruction of our way of life. When Obama became president in 2009 he faced fast rising unemployment, failed banks, and a crashing housing market. To counter these economic crises, the federal government spent many billions to bail out financial institutions and the automobile industry. This was viewed by conservatives as an unwarranted and, they aver, an unconstitutional government intrusion in the market place. Tea Partiers objected to this bailing out the economic elite while leaving common people adrift. Moreover, these actions added mightily to an already huge government debt.

With Obama in the White House, Republicans in the House and Senate, although in the minority, used a variety of tactics to stall efforts by the Democrats to pass progressive legislation. This resulted, for the most part, in gridlock. When legislation was passed, such as the health care plan, many objected because they felt it was an assault on individual freedoms. Add to all of this the role of money and questions of whose interests are served by the actions of government officials (see Chapter 14). The midterm election in 2010 reflected this serious unease with political institutions as many Congressional incumbents failed to be reelected, many Tea Partiers were elected, Republicans became the majority in the House, and the Democrat majority in the Senate was diminished.

In short, the actions in the business world, religion, and politics increase the cynicism in citizens and thereby diminish the trust required to make markets and society cohere.

The Widening Inequality Gap

Compared to other developed nations, the chasm between the rich and the poor in the United States is the widest, and steadily increasing. The share of the national income of the richest 20 percent of households in 2008 was 50 percent, while the bottom 20 percent received only 3.4 percent of the nation's income. In 2007, the Federal Reserve Board reported that the richest 1 percent of U.S. households owned 33.8 percent of the nation's private wealth (that is, more than the combined wealth of the bottom 90 percent) (Kennickell, 2009). The earnings gap, as measured by comparing the top 5 percent of the earnings distribution by the bottom 20 percent, is now the greatest since the Census Bureau began keeping track in 1947. In 2007, the average salary of the chief executive officers for the S&P 500 companies was 344 times the pay of the typical workers. In 1980, the difference was only forty-two times as much. At the bottom end of wealth and income, more than 14.3 percent (47 million) Americans were below the government's official poverty line in 2009 and 6.3 percent were in so-called deep poverty, earning less than half the official poverty threshold. The safety net for them is weak and getting weaker. Funds for Head Start are so inadequate that less than 40 percent of children who are eligible are enrolled in the program. The numbers of homeless and hungry are rising. It's not just the gap between the rich and the poor, but between the rich average workers.

The data on inequality show clearly that the United States is moving toward a two-tiered society. This has at least three implications for society. First, it divides people into the "deserving" and the "undeserving." This, in turn, justifies not providing a generous safety net. Third, the larger the gap, the more destabilized society becomes with increased crime and violence, the threat of violence increases, Former Secretary of Labor Robert Reich has put it this way: "Global terrorism now poses the largest threat to our survival. But the widening split between our have-mores and have-lessers poses the largest single threat to our strength as a society" (Reich, 2002:20).

The number of hate groups has risen sharply in the past decade fueled in large part by the riding numbers of illegal immigrants.

The Deepening Divides over Diversity

The civil rights gains of the previous generation are in jeopardy as U.S. society becomes more diverse. Currently, the racial composition in the United States is two-thirds White. In 2042, it will be 50 percent non-White. Many Whites fear becoming a numerical minority. They are especially concerned about the influx of Latino and Asian immigration, most notably undocumented immigrants. As a result, some twenty-two states have passed made English the official state language. In-state college tuition has been denied to noncitizens in some states. White Supremacy groups and other hate groups are growing in number. Vigilante groups have organized to watch the border. Former Congressman Tancredo sums up the fear that fuels these actions: "If we don't control immigration, legal and illegal, we will eventually reach the point where it won't be what kind of a nation we are, Balkanized or united; we will have to face the fact that we are no longer a nation at all" (quoted in Zeskind, 2005:A15). An indicator of fragmentation along racial lines is the "White flight" from high-immigration areas, which is leading to the "Balkanization of America." The trends toward gated neighborhoods, the rise of private schools, and home schooling are manifestations of exclusiveness rather than inclusiveness and are motivated by the increasing number of non-Whites in society.

Along with increasing racial and ethnic diversity, there is religious diversity with millions of Jews, Muslims, and other non-Christians, including Buddhists and Hindus, as well as atheists. Some groups, most notably Muslims, are often victims of hate crimes.

There is also widespread intolerance of and discrimination toward those whose sexual orientation differs from the majority. The behaviors of gay men and lesbian women are defined as deviant and stigmatized by many members of society.

In sum, our ever-increasing diversity is a fact of life in U.S. society. If we do not find ways to accept the differences among us, we will fragment into class, race, ethnic, and sexual enclaves. The challenge is to shift from building walls to building bridges.

All societies have the potential for cleavage and conflict because of the differential allocation of power. Concomitant with having power is the holding of other advantages (prestige, privilege, and economic benefits). People with advantage almost invariably wish to keep it, and those without typically want to change the reward system.

Coupled with the U.S. stratification system (the structured inequality of categories of people; see Chapter 9) are other aspects of social structure that increase the probability of conflict. The United States, perhaps more than any other society, is populated by a multitude of ethnic groups, racial groups, and religious groups. (For a similar situation in India, see the Closer Look panel titled "Violence and Division in India.") The diversity is further increased by the existence of regional differences and by a generation gap. Although assimilation has occurred to some degree, the different groups and categories have not blended into a homogeneous mass but continue to remain separate—often with a pride that makes assimilation unlikely and conflict inevitable.

Violence and the Myth of Peaceful Progress

Two beliefs held typically by U.S. Americans combine to make the **myth of peaceful progress**—the incorrect belief that throughout U.S. history disadvantaged groups have gained their share of power, prosperity, and respectability without violence (Graham and Gurr, 1969; Rubenstein, 1970; Skolnick, 1969). First, there is a widely held notion that the United States is made up of diverse groups that have learned to compromise differences in a peaceful manner. Second, there is the belief that any group in the United States can gain its share of power, prosperity, and respectability merely by playing the game according to the rules. Hence, there is no need for political violence in the United States because the system works for the advantage of all.

Because these beliefs are widely shared, most people in the United States do not understand dissent by minority groups. Their opinions are believed to be aberrations and are explained away by saying that they are communist-inspired, or that some groups are exceptions to the rule because they are basically immoral and irrational. Perhaps the most prevalent explanation locates the source of all violence in the individual psyches of the people involved.

These explanations are incomplete because they locate the blame outside the system itself. U.S. history shows that, with few exceptions, powerless and downtrodden groups seeking power have not achieved it without a struggle. U.S. institutions, Rubenstein notes, are better designed to facilitate the upward mobility of talented individuals than of oppressed groups. "Most groups which have engaged in mass violence have done so only after a long period of fruitless, relatively nonviolent struggle in which established procedures have been tried and found wanting" (Rubenstein, 1970:8). The problem is that the United States, like all other societies, has not allowed and does not allow for the nonviolent transfer of power.

Violence and Division in India

Although well known for a strong socioreligious tradition of nonviolence, India has been beset by many forms of collective violence stemming from the many divisions that characterize that society.

1. *Religious violence.* The formation of India and Pakistan in 1947 into predominantly Hindu and Muslim states, respectively, was accompanied by numerous riots between both communities and a bloody, massive exchange of population. In recent times, Hindu-Muslim riots have taken place centering on issues such as the conversion of lower-caste Hindus to Islam, processions on the holy days of each faith, and over mosques that some Hindus claim were built on the sites of preexisting temples and places holy to Hinduism. Religious connotations are also evident in the violence and terrorism that has wracked three states: Punjab (through much of the 1980s), based on demands by followers of the Sikh religion, as well as Kashmir and Gujarat (more recently), by and against Muslims.

2. *Caste violence.* Caste is a form of social stratification that determines one's position at birth and narrows one's choices with regard to occupation, marriage, and social interaction while rigidly controlling mobility. In an effort to do away with the resulting discriminatory and degrading treatment of the lower castes, government policies provide for preferential treatment in education and employment of some of these groups. Caste violence traditionally has been, and continues to be, a rural phenomenon pitting members of the upper castes against those of the lower castes. Such violence has also been seen in urban areas, often as a result of the opposition of upper castes to the extension of these preferential policies.

3. *Partisan violence.* For about thirty years following independence, the major political party in India was the Indian National Congress (known as the Congress). However, the dominance of the Congress has declined in parliament, where it is now an opposition party, and in some state legislatures, where it shares power with other regional parties or is in the opposition. Given the proliferation of parties with narrow and conflicting agendas, collective violence over political issues has taken place regularly. Demands for increased autonomy to particular areas, governmental assistance to certain groups and not others, subsidies, demarcation of state borders, disputes over water and other resources, and elections have all been issues that have generated political violence.

4. *Linguistic violence.* India has fifteen officially recognized languages (including Hindi, the "national" language) along with English, which is used for a number of official and business purposes. Recent censuses have enumerated thirty-three languages that are spoken by at least 100,000 people each. Although often unrecognized outside India, the language issue is a potent divisive factor in Indian life and complicates educational, media, and governmental policies. State borders in India were redrawn according to linguistic criteria in the late 1950s. This has enabled, for example, political parties in these "linguistic" states to be formed around and to claim to represent the interests of speakers of those languages. While the number of incidents of linguistic violence has dwindled, demands for and against the recognition of particular languages as "official" or as a medium of educational instruction crop up from time to time.

5. *Ethnic violence.* Race/ethnicity has not been considered a major factor in collective violence in India. Most of India's population represents an intermingling of various racial groups. However, perceived differences between the "Aryan"-dominated north and the "Dravidian"-dominated south resulted in a number of riots, primarily in the southern state of Tamil Nadu in the early 1960s. More recently, the northeastern states of India have witnessed separatist violence based on "pan-Mongolism," a professed identification with similar ethnic groups in Nagaland, Mizoram, Manipur (bordering states in India), and Myanmar (Burma), as well as among various tribal groups.

6. *Economic violence.* Two forms of collective violence, rural and urban, can be traced to the economic structure. Around 70 percent of India's population lives in rural areas, where caste norms still hold sway and economic violence in these settings are often confounded with inter-caste violence. Violent confrontations between peasants and landowners (or their hired thugs) on issues related to inadequate pay, debts, putative land ownership reforms and other work-related conditions typify rural economic violence. These result from the structured inequality of traditional village life in India.

Urban economic violence also revolves around a number of issues such as union strikes, lockouts, price rises, job terminations of fellow employees, or it is instigated by factional disputes. Nearly 30 percent of India's population lives below the official poverty line, which in 1990 was set at an annual income of $370. In terms of both absolute and relative deprivation, there is a large segment of the rural and urban population that has not shared in the fruits of economic development and more recent economic liberalization. This segment is consequently willing to engage in the violence of protest to highlight its members' conditions. This, in turn, provokes counterviolence from those whose interests are threatened.

Source: Reprinted with permission of N. Prabha Unnithan, Colorado State University.

Throughout the history of the United States, groups that were oppressed resorted to various legitimate and illegitimate means to secure rights and privileges that they believed to be rightfully theirs. Those in power typically reacted either by doing nothing or by further repressing the protesters—the choice depended on the degree to which the minority groups' actions were perceived as a real threat. The following discussion is a partial list of groups that at various times in U.S. history have resorted to violence to achieve social, economic, or political objectives.

Revolutionary Colonists. A notable case of violence by a minority in the New World was the American Revolutionary War. The United States was born through violence. The colonists first petitioned the king of England to redress grievances, and when this failed, they turned to acts of civil disobedience and finally to eight years of war. The Declaration of Independence, clearly a revolutionary document, provided the rationale for mass violence:

> We hold these truths to be self-evident, that all men are created equal, that they are endowed by their Creator with certain unalienable Rights, that among these are Life, Liberty, and the pursuit of Happiness. That to secure these rights, Governments are instituted among Men, deriving their just powers from the consent of the governed. That whenever any Form of Government becomes destructive of these ends, it is the Right of the People to alter or to abolish it, and to institute new Government, laying its foundation on such principles and organizing its powers in such form, as to them shall seem most likely to effect their Safety and Happiness. Prudence, indeed, will dictate that Governments long established should not be changed for light and transient causes; and accordingly all experiences hath shewn that mankind are more disposed to suffer, while evils are sufferable, than to right themselves by abolishing the forms to which they are accustomed. But when a long train of abuses and usurpations, pursuing invariably the same Object evinces a design to reduce them under absolute Despotism, it is their right, it is their duty, to throw off such Government, and to provide new Guards for their future security.

This document, a cornerstone of the heritage of the United States, legitimates the use of violence by oppressed peoples. It could have been written by a modern-day revolutionary. While still revered, its content is no longer taken literally by the bulk of U.S. citizenry.

Native Americans. Long before the Revolutionary War and continuing to the present day, Native Americans attempted to change the order established by Whites. When White settlers took their land, ruined their hunting, and imprisoned them on reservations, the Native Americans fought these occurrences and were systematically suppressed by the U.S. government (Brown, 1971). In recent years, Native Americans have occasionally boycotted, resorted to violence, or used legal offensives to regain former Indian lands. The last tactic has become especially popular. More than half of the 266 federally recognized tribes have claims in various federal courts.

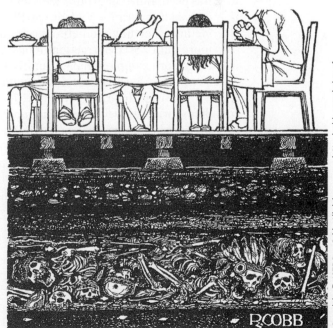

Exploited Farmers. Farmers have used violence on occasion to fight economic exploitation. Between the Revolutionary War and 1800, for example, three such revolts took place—Shays' Rebellion, the Whiskey Rebellion, and Fries' Rebellion. Protesting farmers have used various forms of violence (destruction of property, looting, and killing) throughout U.S. history. Some modern farmers have resorted to acts of violence to publicize their demands and to terrorize other farmers in order to present a united front against their opponents.

Slaveholders. Feeling the threat of the abolitionist movement, White Southerners beginning in about 1820 used violent means to preserve slavery. In the early stages this amounted to civil disobedience, and later it burst out into fighting in places like "bleeding Kansas." Eventually the South seceded, and the Civil War was waged—a classic example of a minority group using violence to force a change and being suppressed by the power of the majority.

WASP Supremacists. Following the Civil War and continuing to the present day, some Whites have engaged in guerrilla warfare, arson, terrorism, and lynching in order to maintain the subjugation of Blacks. From 1882 to 1903, for example, 1,985 Blacks were killed by southern lynch mobs (Cutler, 1905:177).

Riots, lynchings, and mob actions are not solely southern phenomena. Many people from other sections of the United States have used these techniques against various alien groups (usually Catholics and immigrants from non-Teutonic Europe) in order to maintain their superiority. U.S. history is rife with examples of this phenomenon: "native" Americans tore apart the Irish section of Philadelphia in 1844; a Roman Catholic Church and homes of Irish Catholics were destroyed in Boston in 1854; Chinese and Japanese immigrants were victims of both riots and discrimination, particularly on the West Coast; Japanese, even those who were U.S. citizens, were put in concentration camps during World War II because their patriotism was suspect; and Jews have been the objects of physical attack, boycotts, intimidation, and discrimination throughout U.S. history.

Contemporary examples of mob violence against intruders can be seen in some communities where an all-White neighborhood is faced with one or more Haitian or Vietnamese families moving in. Threats, burning crosses, ostracism, and occasional physical violence have occurred with alarming regularity where Blacks have moved into previously all-White areas. This is not a southern phenomenon, but one that is found throughout the United States. So, too, are incidents of violence directed at Muslims and their places of worship. Now Arab Americans and other Muslims are the victims of a growing number of violent incidents aimed at them.

Ethnic Minorities. Immigrant groups (that is, those groups most recently immigrant), as well as racial groups, because they have been the target of discrimination, threats, and physical violence, have themselves participated in violence. Sometimes gangs have attacked the groups responsible for their deprived condition. Most often, however, hostility by immigrants has been aimed at groups with less power, either toward Blacks or toward more recently arrived immigrants. Violence by Blacks has occurred throughout U.S. history. Always the victims, they have sometimes responded to violence in kind. During the years of slavery, more than 250 insurrections took place. Mass Black violence has occurred in many major cities (for example, Chicago and Washington, DC, in 1919; Detroit in 1943 and again in 1967; Los Angeles in 1965 and again in 1992; Newark in 1967; and Miami in 1987).

The rage that racial minorities feel against Whites has surfaced sporadically in small and diffuse ways as well. Most commonly, it has been manifested in individual crimes (murder, theft, and rape) or in gang assaults on Whites or in destruction of property owned by Whites.

Labor Disputants. Another relatively powerless group resorting to violence to achieve its aims has been organized labor. In the 1870s, workers attempted to organize for collective action against unfair policies of the industrialists. Unions formed, such as the Knights of Labor, American Federation of Labor, and the Industrial Workers of the World. Their primary tactic was the strike, which in itself is nonviolent. But strikers often used force to keep people from crossing the picket lines. Nor were the owners blameless. Their refusal to change existing wages, hours, and working conditions was the source of grievance. They sometimes turned to violence themselves to suppress the unions (for example, hiring people to physically break up picket lines). The intransigent refusal of the owners to change the awful conditions of nineteenth-century workers resulted in considerable violence in many industries, particularly in the coal-mining, steel, timber, and railroad industries. Labor violence, as in other cases mentioned previously, was ultimately effective. Working conditions, wages, and security of the workers improved. Legislation was passed providing for arbitration of differences and recognition of unions. Clearly, the use of force was necessary to gain advances for laboring men and women.

Given the evidence just cited, it is remarkable that people still believe in the myth of peaceful progress. Violence was necessary to give birth to the United States. Violence was used both to keep the Blacks in servitude and to free them. Violence was used to defeat rebellious Native Americans and to keep them on reservations. Additionally, violence has been a necessary means for many groups in the United States to achieve equality or something approaching parity in power and in the rights that all citizens and residents are supposed to enjoy.

The powerful have not been munificent in giving a break to the powerless. To the contrary, much effort has been expended by the powerful to keep the powerless in that condition. Many times in the history of the United States, violence has been the only catalyst for change. Relatively powerless groups in the United States (for example, African Americans, women, and farmers) have repeatedly gone outside existing law. To these groups, the use of force was justified because of the need to right insufferable wrongs—the reason the colonists gave for breaking from England.

We should note, however, that violence does not always work. The revolts of Native Americans were not beneficial in any way to their people. Moreover, some groups, such as the Jews, have advanced with comparatively little violence. Historically, however, violence is as "American" as apple pie. The Presidential Commissions on Civil Disorders and Violence have laid bare the inaccuracies of the "peaceful progress" idea held by so many people. The uniform remedy suggested by these commissions for minimizing violence is to eliminate the causes of social unrest and perceived injustice. It cannot be a surprise that minority groups occasionally use violence because they are reacting against a system that systematically disadvantages them with little hope for change through peaceful means.

The Integrative Forces in Society

Order theorists recognize that conflict, disharmony, and division occur within societies, particularly in complex, heterogeneous societies. They stress, however, the opposite societal characteristics of cooperation, harmony, and solidarity. They see U.S. society as "We the people of the United States" rather than as a conglomerate of sometimes hostile groups. In particular, order theorists focus on what holds society together. What are the forces that somehow keep anarchy from becoming a reality—or as the English philosopher Thomas Hobbes asked long ago, "Why is there not a war of all against all?" The answer to this fundamental question is found in the combined effects of a number of factors.

Functional Integration. Probably the most important unifying factor is the phenomenon of **functional integration** (the unity among divergent elements of society resulting from a specialized division of labor, noted by Durkheim). In a highly differentiated society such as the United States, with its specialized division of labor, interaction among different segments occurs with some regularity. Interdependence often results because no group is entirely self-sufficient. The farmer needs the miller, the processor, and retail agents, as well as the fertilizer manufacturer and the agricultural experimenters. Manufacturers need raw materials, on one hand, and customers, on the other. Management needs workers, and the workers need management.

These groups, because they need each other, because each gains from the interaction, work to perpetuate a social framework that maximizes benefits to both parties and minimizes conflict or the breaking of the relationship. Written and unwritten rules emerge to govern these relationships, usually leading to cooperation rather than either isolation or conflict and to linkages between different (and potentially conflicting) groups. See the Closer Look panel titled "Twinkies, Pencils, and Functional Integration."

Twinkies, Pencils, and Functional Integration

The products we eat and use are produced and manufactured from a number of sources. These materials are processed and shipped to a central place where the final product is put together. Then the product is packaged, advertised, and sent to retail outlets for sale. Order theorists view this complicated procedure as a number of parts fitting together in a system (differentiation produces unity).

Consider first the Twinkie—a delightful sponge cake snack (the following is from Ettlinger, 2007; Hunt, 2007). This product is made from thirty-nine ingredients originating from an international nexus of suppliers such as thiamine mononitrate from China, palm oil from Malaysia, colorants from Peru, and niacin from Switzerland. Domestic parts to the Twinkie come from a gypsum mine in Oklahoma, a tree farm in Arkansas, eggs, corn, and soybeans from farmers and their suppliers in the United States. These ingredients are then mixed, baked, and, voilà, we have millions of tasty snacks. The key is that the overall process is orchestrated formally and informally as many links in the chain work together to produce a product.

Then there is the making of a pencil (the following is from Roberts, 2009; Will, 2008). To make a Dixon Ticonderoga No. 2 pencil, for instance, loggers take down cedar trees in California; truckers haul them; and machines built by manufacturers cut the wood into five-sided portions to hold graphite mined in Sri Lanka, Mexico, China, and Brazil. Miners and smelters produce the aluminium that holds the rubber eraser, which comes from Malaysia. This is a marvel of orderly cooperation as George Will explains:

> The graphite miner in Sri Lanka doesn't realize he's cooperating with the cedar farmer in California to serve the pencil customer in Maine. The boss of the pencil factory does not boss very much: He does not decide the prices of the elements of his product—or of his product. No one decides. Everyone buying and selling things does so as prices steer resources hither and yon, harmonizing supplies and demands. (Will, 2008:80)

The result is the spontaneous emergence of social cooperation—a complex system of order that "emerges without anyone imposing it" (Will, 2008:80).

Consensus on Societal Values. A second basis for the unification of diverse groups in the United States is that almost all people hold certain fundamental values in common. Order theorists assume that commonly held values are like social glue binding otherwise diverse people in a cohesive societal unit. Unlike functional integration, unity is achieved here through similarity rather than through difference.

Erik Olin Wright and Joel Rogers, two contemporary sociologists, argue that most people in U. S. society affirm the following values (2011:5–6):

1. *Freedom.* This is the commonly held idea that people should be free from coercive restrictions imposed by others.

2. *Prosperity.* The belief that the economy should generate a good standard of living for most people, not just a privileged elite.

3. *Efficiency.* The idea that the economy should generate rational outcomes, maximizing the efficient use of resources.

4. *Fairness.* The notion that people should be treated justly, and they should have equal opportunity to succeed with unfair privileges and unfair disadvantages.

5. *Democracy.* This is the belief that public policy decisions should reflect the wish of the public, not just a powerful elite.

Many symbols epitomize the consensus of people in the United States with respect to basic values. One such unifying symbol is the national flag. Although a mere piece of cloth, the flag clearly symbolizes something approaching the sacred. Reverence for the flag is evidenced by the shock shown when it is defiled and by the punishment given to defilers. The choice of the flag as an object to spit on or burn is a calculated one by dissident groups. They choose to defile it precisely because of what it represents and because most citizens revere it so strongly. In 1989, the Supreme Court ruled that an individual who had desecrated the flag was guaranteed the right to do so because the Constitution protects the freedom of political expression. This decision outraged the majority of citizens, and politicians seized the opportunity to pass legislation making flag desecration an illegal act.

Similarly, such documents as the Declaration of Independence and the Constitution are held in high esteem and serve to unify citizens. The heritage of the United States is also revered through holidays such as Thanksgiving, Memorial Day, and Independence Day. Consensus is also achieved through the collective reverence for such leaders as George Washington, Abraham Lincoln, and John F. Kennedy.

The Social Order. A third factor that unifies people in the United States, at least minimally, is that they are all subject to similar influences and rules of the game. U.S. inhabitants are answerable to the same body of law (at the national level), and they are under the same government. Additionally, they use the same system of monetary exchange, the same standards for measurement, and so on. The order in society is evidenced by our taking for granted such assorted practices as obeying traffic lights, the use of credit, and the acceptance of checks in lieu of money.

Group Membership. A source of unity (as well as of cleavage) is group memberships. Some groups are exclusive because they limit membership to people of a particular race, ethnic group, income category, religion, or other characteristic. The existence of exclusive organizations creates tension if people are excluded who want to be included, because exclusiveness generally implies feelings of superiority. Country clubs, fraternities, some churches, and some neighborhoods are based on the twin foundations of exclusiveness and superiority. There are other groups, however, whose membership consists of people from varying backgrounds (that is, the membership includes rich and poor, or Black and White). Consequently, heterogeneous organizations such as political parties, religious denominations or churches, and veterans' organizations allow members the chance not only to interact with people unlike themselves but also to join together in a common cause.

Many, if not most, Americans who belong to several organizations belong to organizations with different compositions by race, religion, or other salient characteristics. To the extent that these cross-cutting memberships and allegiances exist, they tend to cancel out potential cleavages along social class, race, or other lines. Individuals belonging to several different organizations will probably feel some cross pressures (that is, pulls in opposite directions), thereby preventing polarization.

Additionally, most people belong to at least one organization such as a school, church, or civic group with norms that support those of the total society. These organizations support the government and what it stands for, and they expect their members to do the same.

International Competition and Conflict. External threats to the society's existence unify us. The advice Machiavelli gave his prince is a regrettable truth: "If the Prince is in trouble, he should promote a war." This was the advice that Secretary of State William Seward gave to President Lincoln prior to the Civil War. Although expedient advice from the standpoint of preserving unity, it was, Lincoln noted, only a short-term solution.

A real threat to security unifies those groups, no matter how diverse, that feel threatened. Thus, a reasonable explanation for the lack of unity in the U.S. involvement in an Indochinese war was that the Vietcong were not perceived by most Americans as a real threat to their security. The Soviet buildup in armaments in the 1980s, on the other hand, was perceived as a real threat, unifying many Americans in a willingness to sacrifice in order to catch up with and surpass the Soviets. Now that the Soviet Union has been dismantled and the Cold War is a thing of the past, we no longer are united by the possible attack by communists. The Persian Gulf War in 1991, however, was an instance when most Americans were unified against a dictator who threatened democracy and stability in the Middle East. Following the September 11, 2001, attacks by terrorists on the World Trade Center and the Pentagon, Americans of all types rallied behind their president in a sense of outrage and a common purpose in reducing as much as possible the threat of terrorism. The threat of terrorism has become the new source of unity from external sources.

The Mass Media. The world is in the midst of a communications revolution. Television, for example, has expanded to encompass virtually every home in the United States. This phenomenon—universal exposure to television—has been blamed, among other things, for rising juvenile delinquency, lower cultural tastes, declining test scores, general moral deterioration, and suppressed creativity. These criticisms are countered by order theorists, who see television and the other forms of mass media as performing several integrative functions. Government officials, for example, can use the media to shape public actions (for example, to unite against an enemy or to sacrifice by paying higher taxes). The media also reinforce the values and norms of society. Newspaper editorials extol certain people and events while decrying others. Soap operas are stories involving moral dilemmas, with virtue winning out. Newspaper and magazine stories under the caption "It Could Only Have Happened in America" abound. The media do not usually rock the boat. The heroes of the United States are praised and its enemies vilified. Our way of life is the right way; the ways of others are considered incorrect or downright immoral. For an example of how the media tend to ignore the realities of race and class, see the Diversity panel titled "The Media's Selective Perception of Race and Class."

DIVERSITY

The Media's Selective Perception of Race and Class

From the window that I wake at, most of my city is untouched. Houses stand stately after the 7.1 earthquake.

Everyone knows from watching television that earthquake damage in the Bay Area has been restricted to a relatively few neighborhoods. But not everyone may realize that considerations of race and class shaped the images that Americans saw on their TV screens.

The Marina district of San Francisco is a stately, upper-middle-class neighborhood. Homes sit alongside the Bay. People here lived well, and they faced tragedy with dignity after their neighborhood was devastated. Marina residents on TV were articulate, focused. No wonder television crews set up their cameras at this neighborhood's periphery and interviewed the residents who, even in anger and frustration, remained gentle.

But why have so few of the television crews chosen to go to the Moscone Center where those who lost homes in the city's low-income neighborhoods are now bedded down? Many of those who sleep at Moscone do not speak in tones modulated with good humor. Many of them possessed little to begin with, and they lost that little bit with the earthquake. Some had nothing and now have to redefine what nothing means.

Why were so few of the camera crews talking to people who live in West Oakland's projects, a stone's throw away from the Interstate 880 freeway that collapsed? These people now live under the same sort of stress that affects those of the Marina district.

Despite the fact that the stench of dead bodies permeates the air around the Cypress projects, help was slow in coming to those people. Not until I-880 was threatened with further collapse did the social service system that sheltered the Marina even reach out to those who lived in the midst of the Cypress deaths.

Why didn't Bryant Gumbel and Jane Pauley [NBC newscasters at the time] venture down to Watsonville, where the population is mostly Mexican and poor, where average family income is about $15,000 a year? Are the losses there less painful, the survival tales less moving?

Or do the media value White life over all by ignoring the fact that the lives of far too many people of color were also shattered by the earthquake?

TV's silence about the earthquake's impact on the non-White and the poor is reminiscent of the Depression, when aid was more available to Whites than to Blacks; when the employment expansion resulting from World War II included Blacks only after a march on Washington was threatened.

At every tragedy we are told to pull together and ignore our differences. We should not complain that the Marina was more televised than the Cypress neighborhoods because earthquake relief will finally assist both areas. We must not point out that Hispanics in Watsonville have been largely ignored because they, too, will gain from regional awareness.

But when the urgency abates, we become separate again: Black, White, yellow, brown. Some have the skills to lobby for press attention or emergency aid, while others merely have the fortitude to survive and pray for help.

This is not the time to speak of race and class, a friend of mine cautions. Our television anchors reflect this point with pithy clichés: "We are all in this together." Together or not, it rankles that some people's suffering generates more concern than that of others.

The fact is that the earth shrugged, concrete tumbled, and people lost their lives. But once again, race and class determined the focus of the news and our national concern.

Source: Julianne Malveaux, 1989. "Race and Class Shape TV Images of Earthquake." *Rocky Mountain News* (November 4):57.

Planned Integration. Charismatic figures or other people of influence may work to unite segmented parts of the system (conversely, they can promote division). Thus, a union leader or the archbishop of a Catholic diocese can, through personal exhortation or by example, persuade group members to cooperate rather than compete, or to open membership requirements rather than maintain exclusiveness.

Public officials on the local, state, and national levels can use their power to integrate the parts of society in three major ways: (1) by passing laws to eliminate barriers among groups, for example, the repeal by Congress in late 2010 of the military rule of "Don't Ask, Don't Tell," which had kept gays and lesbians hiding their sexual orientation; (2) by working to solve the problems that segment the society; and (3) by providing mediators to help negotiate settlements between such feuding groups as management and labor (Mott, 1965:283–284).

High officials such as the president use various means of integration. First, there is the technique of **co-optation** (appointing a member of a dissident group to a policy-making body to appease the dissenting group). Second, they can use their executive powers to enforce and interpret the laws in such a way as to unite groups within the society. Finally, the president and other high officials can use the media to persuade the people. The president, for example, can request television time on all networks during prime time, thereby reaching most of the adult population in order to use full presidential powers of persuasion to unite diverse groups.

False Consciousness. Most people in the United States do not feel oppressed. Even many people who do not have many material blessings tend to believe in the "American" creed that anyone can be upwardly mobile—if not themselves, then at least their children (Sennett and Cobb, 1973). According to Marxian theory, when oppressed people hold beliefs damaging to their interests, they have **false consciousness**.

Thus, contrary to Karl Marx's prediction more than a century ago that capitalism would be overthrown by an oppressed majority, most of us today consider ourselves as haves or as could-be haves rather than as have-nots. There has been little polarization along purely economic lines because of a relatively large middle class. This may be changing, however, as more and more of the middle class are moving downward (see Chapter 10).

The Use of the Order and Conflict Models in This Book

There are two contradictory models of society—the order and conflict models. The order model views society as basically cooperative, consensual, and stable. The system works. Any problems are the faults of people, not of society. At the other extreme, the adherents of the conflict model assume that society is fundamentally competitive, conflictual, coercive, and radically changing. Social problems are the faults of society, not of individuals, in this view.

The order and conflict models of society are both significant, and they are used in the remainder of this book. While each model, by itself, is important, a realistic analysis must include both. The order model must be included because there is integration, order, and stability; because the parts are more or less interdependent; and because most social change is gradual and adjustive. The conflict model is equally important because society is not always a harmonious unit. To the contrary, much of social life is based on competition. Societal integration is fragile; it is often based on subtle or blatant coercion.

A crucial difference between the two models is the implicit assumption of each as to the nature of the social structure (rules, customs, institutions, social stratification, and the distribution of power). The order perspective assumes that the social structure is basically right and proper because it serves the fundamental function of maintaining society. There is, therefore, an implicit acceptance of the status quo, assuming that the system works. As we examine the major institutions of society in this book, one task is to determine how each institution aids in societal integration.

Although order theorists also look for the dysfunctions of institutions, rules, organizations, and customs (**dysfunctions** refer to negative consequences), the critical examination of society is the primary thrust of conflict theorists. While this book describes the way the United States is structured and how this arrangement works for societal integration, a major consideration centers on the question of who benefits under these arrangements and who does not. Thus, the legitimacy of the system is always doubted.

CHAPTER REVIEW

1. Sociologists have a mental image (model) of how society is structured, how it changes, and what holds it together. Two prevailing models—order and conflict—provide contradictory images of society.

2. Order model theorists view society as ordered, stable, and harmonious, with a high degree of cooperation and consensus. Change is gradual, adjustive, and reforming. Social problems are seen as the result of problem individuals.

3. Conflict model theorists view society as competitive, fragmented, and unstable. Social integration is minimal and tenuous. Social change, which can be revolutionary, results from clashes among conflicting groups. Social problems are viewed as resulting from society's failure to meet the needs of individuals. Indeed, the structure of society is seen as the problem.

4. The order and conflict models present extreme views of society. Taken alone, each fosters a faulty perception and interpretation of society. A realistic model of society combines the strengths of both models. The assumptions of such a synthesis are that (a) the processes of stability and change are properties of all societies; (b) societies are organized, but the very process of organization generates conflict; (c) society is a social system, with the parts linked through common goals and similar interests, and is competitive because of scarce resources and inequities; (d) societies are held together both by consensus on values and by coercion; and (e) social change may be gradual or abrupt, reforming or revolutionary.

5. The divisive forces bringing about segmentation in U.S. society are diminished trust in societal institutions, increasing polarization, the widening inequality gap, and divides over diversity. Thus, society has the potential for cleavage and conflict.

6. There is a widespread belief in the myth of peaceful progress—that disadvantaged groups throughout history have gained prosperity and equality without violence. The evidence, however, is that oppressed groups have had to use force or the threat of force to achieve gains.

7. The integrative forces in the United States are functional integration, consensus on values, the social order, group memberships, threats from other societies, the mass media, planned integration, and false consciousness.

KEY TERMS

Order model (functionalism)
Manifest consequence
Latent consequence
Conflict model
Social problems

Instrumental process
Institutional process
Dialectic
Myth of peaceful progress
Functional integration

Co-optation
False consciousness
Dysfunctions

1. What is the order model of society? On what kinds of social phenomena does it focus? What social phenomena are neglected from this perspective?
2. What is the conflict model of society? On what kinds of social phenomena does it focus? What social phenomena are neglected from this perspective?
3. What are the potentially divisive forces in society?
4. Contrary to popular belief, throughout much of U.S. history, oppressed groups have used violence to achieve progress. What is the evidence to support this refutation of the myth of peaceful progress?
5. What are the integrative forces of society?
6. Pretend that you are in a revolving restaurant at the top of a skyscraper in a large city. Every hour the restaurant rotates to give a 360-degree panoramic view of the city. As you look at the city from this vantage point, sometimes with binoculars, what do you see that illustrates the order model? Do you see any evidence that supports the conflict model?

WEB RESOURCES

http://www.hewett.norfolk.sch.uk/curric/soc/theory.htm
This site offers a visually effective map of sociological theories. Included in the map are functionalism and conflict theory.

http://odur.let.rug.nl/~usa/usa.htm
Search this site to find out about U.S. history, including information on slaves and the taking of land from Native Americans.

http://www.journale.com/withoutsanctuary/
Without Sanctuary is a powerful site that contains photographs and postcards on lynchings.

http://www.tolerance.org/index.jsp
Tolerance.org has information on hate groups and encourages everyone to fight hate and promote tolerance.

CHAPTER 4

Culture

In 2009 Sony Pictures released the movie *2012*, a movie based on the fact that the Ancient Mayan long-count calendar ends on December 21, 2012. Some have taken this to mean that the world is going to end in 2012, and there are numerous websites dedicated to that idea. The movie depicts a global cataclysm that occurs on December 21 and destroys the world as we know it.

Along similar lines, much was made of the year 2000. It delineated the end of a thousand-year period and the beginning of another millennium. It is believed to mark the 2,000th year after the birth of Jesus. Some cults believed that this date would bring the apocalypse (the end of the present temporal world) because of their interpretation of two books in the Bible—Daniel in the Old Testament and Revelation in the New Testament. Obviously for them, the number 2,000 is of ultimate importance. But is it? Why is a calendar divided into thousand-year epochs meaningful? If it is important, then did the new millennium begin on January 1, 2000, or January 1, 2001? To begin, the calendar we use, beginning with the birth of Jesus, is off by as much as six years. A sixth-century monk, Dionysius Exiguus, computed the Christian calendar. Scholars now believe that Exiguus was wrong because Herod, ruler of Judea at the time of Jesus' birth, died in 4 B.C., and Jesus was probably born a year or two before that (Zelizer, 1999). So, was the year 2000 really 2005 or 2006?

When the West marked the year 2000, the Chinese celebrated the year 4698. For followers of Zoroastrianism in Iran, the year was 2390; for Muslims, it was 1421, for it had been that many years since the birth of the prophet Muhammad; and for Jews, it was the year 5760. Obviously, the starting date for calendars is an arbitrary decision on which societies differ. And yet, a calendar that is not universally accepted throughout the world and that is off by as much as six years and one that did not begin with zero was, nevertheless, used by most of the Western world to designate January 1, 2000, as the beginning of a new millennium. Because some people believed that chaos would ensue on this date, they stocked up on canned goods and other necessities, demonstrating that even though the notion of the beginning of a new millennium and when it occurred are social constructions, people attach meanings to these social constructions. These cultural meanings then become powerful determinants of human behavior.

An important focus of sociology is the social influences on human behavior. As people interact over time, two fundamental sources of constraints on individuals emerge—social structure and culture. As noted in Chapter 2, social structure refers to the linkages and networks among the members of a social organization. Culture, the subject of this chapter, is the knowledge that the members of a social organization share. Because this shared knowledge includes ideas about what is right, how one is to behave in various situations, religious beliefs, and communication, culture constrains not only behavior but, as demonstrated in the previous examples, how people think about and interpret their world.

This chapter is divided into two major sections. The first section describes the nature of culture and its importance for understanding human behavior. The second section focuses on one aspect of culture—values. This discussion is especially vital for understanding the organization and some of the problems of U.S. society. We conclude with a discussion of values from the order and conflict perspectives.

Culture: The Knowledge That People Share

Characteristics of Culture

Culture Is an Emergent Process. As individuals interact on any kind of sustained basis, they exchange ideas about all sorts of things. In time they develop common ideas, common ways of doing things, and common interpretations for certain actions. In so doing, the participants have created a culture. The emergent quality of culture is an ongoing process; it is built up slowly rather than being present at the beginnings of social organization. The culture of any group is constantly undergoing change because the members are in continuous interaction. Culture, then, is never completely static.

Culture Is Learned. Culture is not instinctive or innate in the human species; it is not part of the biological equipment of human beings. The biological equipment of humans, however, makes culture possible. That is, we are symbol-making creatures capable of attaching meaning to particular objects and actions and communicating these meanings to other people. When a person joins a new social organization, she or he must learn the culture of that group. This is true for the infant born into a society as well as for a college student joining a sorority or fraternity, a young man or woman joining the armed forces, or immigrants in a new country. This process of learning the culture, called **socialization**, is the subject of the next chapter. When we learn the culture of a society, or a group within society, we share with others a common understanding of words and symbols; we know the rules, what is appropriate and inappropriate, what is moral and immoral, and what is beautiful and what is ugly. Even the down-deep emotions of disgust, anger, and shame are related to the culture. A food that makes one gag in one society (insects, for example) may be considered a delicacy in another.

Culture Channels Human Behavior. Culture, because it emerges from social interaction, is an inevitable development of human society. More important, it is essential in the maintenance of any social system because it provides two crucial functions—predictability of action and stability. To accomplish these functions, however, culture must restrict human freedom (although, as we shall see, cultural constraints are not normally perceived as such).

How does culture work to constrain individuals? Or stated another way, how does culture become internalized in people so that their actions are controlled? Culture operates not only outside individuals but also inside them. Sigmund Freud recognized this process when he conceptualized the superego as the part of the personality structure that internalizes society's morals and thus inhibits people from committing acts considered wrong by their parents, a group, or the society.

The process of **internalization** (during which society's demands become part of the individual, acting to control her or his behavior) is accomplished mainly in three ways. First, culture becomes part of the human makeup through the belief system into which a child is born. This belief system, provided by parents and those people immediately in contact with youngsters, shapes their ideas about the surrounding world and also gives them certain ideas about themselves. A child in the United States, for example, may be taught to accept Christian beliefs without reservation. These beliefs are literally force-fed, since alternative belief systems are considered unacceptable. It is interesting to note that after the child internalizes Christian beliefs, they are often used as levers to keep the child in line.

Second, culture is internalized through psychological identification with the groups to which individuals belong (membership groups) or to which they want to belong (**reference groups**). Individuals want to belong; they want to be accepted by other people. Therefore, they tend to conform to the behavior of their immediate group as well as to the wishes of society at large. Research in childhood socialization has continually shown the importance of this process. The internalization of society's norms is reflected in the fact that children, from age five onward, show less and less liking for in-group members who do not conform to group norms (Nesdale, 2007:222).

Finally, culture is internalized by providing the individual with an identity. People's age, sex, race, religion, and social class affects the way others perceive them and the way they perceive themselves.

Culture, then, is not freedom but rather constraint. Of the entire range of possible behaviors (which probably are considered appropriate by some society somewhere), the person of a particular society chooses only from a narrow range of alternatives. Individuals do not see the prison-like qualities of culture because they have internalized the culture of their society. From birth, children are shaped by the culture of the society into which they are born. They retain some individuality because of the configuration of forces unique to their experience (gene structure, peers, parents' social class, religion, and race), but the behavioral alternatives deemed appropriate for them are narrow.

Culture even shapes thought and perception. What we see and how we interpret what we see are determined by culture. For example, every culture has different beliefs about what makes a person beautiful, what foods are good to eat, and what clothing is appropriate to wear. So one culture may perceive a man wearing a kilt as bizarre or ridiculous, where another may see a man wearing a kilt as perfectly acceptable.

For a dramatic illustrative case of the kind of mental closure that may be determined by culture, consider the following riddle about a father and son driving down a highway: "There is a terrible accident in which the father is killed, and the son, critically injured, is rushed to a hospital. There, the surgeon approaches the patient and suddenly cries, 'My God, that's my son!' " How is it possible that the critically injured boy is the son of the man in the accident as well as the son of the surgeon? Answers might involve the surgeon being a priest, or a stepfather, or even artificial insemination. The correct answer to this riddle is that the surgeon is the boy's mother. Some North Americans, male and female alike, have been socialized to think of the occupation of surgeon as a "male" occupation (or, likewise the occupation of nurse as a "female" occupation). If Russians were given this riddle, they would almost uniformly give the correct answer because approximately three-fourths of Russian physicians are women. Culture thus can be confining, not liberating. It constrains not only actions but also thinking.

Culture Maintains Boundaries. Culture not only limits the range of acceptable behavior and attitudes, but also instills in its adherents a sense of naturalness about the alternatives peculiar to a given society (or other social organization). Thus, there is a universal tendency to deprecate the ways of people from other societies as wrong, old-fashioned, inefficient, or immoral and to think of the ways of one's own group as superior (as the only right way). The concept for this phenomenon is **ethnocentrism**. The word combines the Greek word *ethnikos*, which means "nation" or "people," and the English word *center*. One's own race, religion, or society is the center of all and therefore superior to all.

Ethnocentrism is demonstrated in statements such as "My fraternity is the best," "We are God's chosen people," or "Polygamy is immoral." To call the playoff game between the American and National Leagues the "World Series" implies that baseball outside the United States (and Canada) is inferior. Religious missionaries provide a classic example of a group convinced that their own faith is the only correct one. Ethnocentrism is pervasive in many institutions. For examples of institutional ethnocentrism, see the Closer Look panel titled "Ethnocentrism in U.S. Schools."

Ethnocentrism in U.S. Schools

In 1994, the Lake County (Florida) school board enacted a new school policy for the 22,000 children in the district. The policy: Teachers will be required to teach their students that America's political system, its values, and its culture in general are superior to other cultures in every regard. Specifically, it stated:

> Any instruction about other cultures shall also include and instill in our students an appreciation of our American heritage and culture such as: our republican form of government, capitalism, a free enterprise system, patriotism, strong family values, freedom of religion and other basic values that are superior to other foreign or historic cultures. (cited in Buchanan, 1994:B7, emphasis added)

This school policy is clearly ethnocentric. Opponents of the board's decision argue that the blatant teaching of "We're Number One" masks our flaws, mistakes, and immoral acts. To believe in one's superiority is also to believe in the inferiority of others. This has racist overtones, it hinders cooperation among nations, and it fosters exclusionary policies.

Another example of ethnocentrism in schools comes from Arizona. In May 2010 Arizona Governor Jan Brewer signed a law prohibiting Arizona schools from offering classes that advocate ethnic solidarity, promote the overthrow of the U.S. government, or are designed for specific ethnic groups. In effect, the law dismantles the state's Mexican-American studies programs when Hispanic students fill nearly half the seats in Arizona's public schools (Calefati, 2010).

> By imposing a curriculum that forbids the exploration of divergent cultures while propping up the dominant one, there's another process at work here, what we might call *ethnonormativity*. This takes the teachings of one culture—the colonizer's—and makes it the standard version of history while literally banning other accounts, turning the master narrative into the "normal" one and further denigrating marginalized perspectives. (Amster, 2010:1)

In both the Florida and Arizona examples, the people in power used their influence to enforce ethnocentric policies that affect thousands of students (then 22,000 in Florida and 55,000 currently in Arizona). In Arizona, the ban will mean that students not only lose access to Mexican-American studies, but African American and Native American studies as well. This will deny many students the opportunity to explore their own heritage, or to learn about the history of other ethnic groups besides their own.

It is also ethnocentric to view other culture's food choices as weird or bizarre. For example, various websites on the Internet list the top "disgusting" foods around the world such as balut (fertilized duck egg) in the Philippines, or maggot cheese in Italy. The Travel Channel even has a show titled *Bizarre Foods*, where a host samples "bizarre" dishes from other countries.

Further examples of ethnocentrism from U.S. history are manifest destiny, exclusionary immigration laws such as the Oriental Exclusion Act, and Jim Crow segregation laws. A current illustration of ethnocentrism can be seen in the activities of the United States as it engages in exporting the so-called American way of life because it is believed that democracy and capitalism are necessities for the good life and therefore best for all peoples.

Ethnocentrism, because it implies feelings of superiority, leads to division and conflict among subgroups within a society and among societies, each of which feels superior. Ethnocentric ideas are real because they are believed and they influence perception and behavior. Analysts of U.S. society (whether they are Americans or not) must recognize their own ethnocentric attitudes and the way these attitudes affect their own objectivity.

To summarize, culture emerges from social interaction. The paradox is that although culture is human-made, it exerts a tremendous complex of forces that constrain the actions and thoughts of human beings. The analyst of any society must be cognizant of these two qualities of culture, for they combine to give a society its unique character. Culture explains social change as well as stability; culture explains existing social arrangements (including many social problems); culture explains a good deal of individual behavior because it is internalized by the individual members of society and therefore has an impact (substantial but not total) on their actions and personalities.

Types of Shared Knowledge

The concept of culture refers to knowledge that is shared by the members of a social organization. In analyzing any social organization and, in this case, any society, it is helpful to conceive of culture as combining six types of shared knowledge—symbols, technology, ideologies, societal norms, values, and roles.

Symbols. By definition, language refers to symbols that evoke similar meanings in different people. Communication is possible only if people attribute the same meaning to such stimuli as sounds, gestures, or objects. Language, then, can be written, spoken, or unspoken. A shrug of the shoulders, a pat on the back, the gesturing with a finger (which finger can be very significant), a wink, and a nod are examples of unspoken language and vary in meaning from society to society. Consider the varying meaning for two common gestures:

> When displayed by the Emperor, the upright-thumb gesture spared the lives of gladiators in the Roman Coliseum. Now favored by airline pilots, truck drivers and others who lean out of windows, it means "all right" in the United States and most of Western Europe. In other places, including Sardinia and Northern Greece, it is the insulting "up yours." [The "A-Okay" gesture with the thumb and forefinger making a circle means "everything is fine" in the United States but it] has very different meanings in parts of Europe. In Southern Italy, for instance, it means "you asshole" or signifies that you desire anal sex. It can mean "you're worth nothing" in France and Belgium. (Ekman, Friesen, and Bear, 1984:67–68)

Former president George H. W. Bush unknowingly used the wrong symbolic gesture while on a trip to Australia. While riding in his limousine, the president flashed a "V" sign with the back of his hand. In Australia, this does not mean victory—it is the equivalent of flashing the middle finger in the United States. (For a look at modern era symbols, see the Technology and Society panel titled "Test Your Emoticon Knowledge.")

Technology. Technology refers to the information, techniques, and tools used by people to satisfy their varied needs and desires. For analytic purposes, two types of technology can be distinguished—material and social. **Material technology** refers to knowledge of how to make and use things. It is important to note that the things produced are not part of the culture. They represent the knowledge that people share and that makes it possible to build and use the object. The knowledge is culture, not the object. For example, the knowledge of how to make and use a table is part of material technology.

TECHNOLOGY AND SOCIETY

Test Your Emoticon Knowledge

An **emoticon** is a sequence of computer keyboard characters that is meant to convey emotions or other messages. Most computer users in the Western world are familiar with "smileys," which are generally read horizontally from left to right. Increasingly, users are being exposed to Japanese emoticons, known as *kaomoji*, which are read vertically. Test your emoticon knowledge by identifying the symbols below:

1. m(_ _)m
2. (^_^;)
3. (ToT)
4. (^^;)
5. *_*
6. })i({
7. (_x_)
8. o_o
9. ==):-)=
10. *o*

Answers: 1) apology/bowing head (kaomoji); 2) troubled (kaomoji); 3) crying (kaomoji); 4) shy (kaomoji); 5) just woke up or hyper; 6) butterfly; 7) kiss my butt; 8) scared; 9) Abraham Lincoln; 10) hyper and screaming.

Sources: http://www.muller-godschalk.com; http://whatjapanthinks.com/2006/08/14/japans-top-thirty-emoticons

Social technology is the knowledge about how to establish, maintain, and operate the technical aspects of social organization. Examples of this are procedures for operating a university, a municipality, or a corporation, or the kind of specialized knowledge citizens must acquire to function in society (knowing the laws, how to complete income tax forms, how to vote in elections, how to use credit cards and banks).

Ideologies. Ideologies are shared beliefs about the physical, social, and metaphysical worlds. They may, for example, be statements about the existence of supernatural beings, the best form of government, or racial pride.

Ideologies help individuals interpret events. They also provide the rationale for particular forms of action. They can justify the status quo or demand revolution. A number of competing ideologies exist within U.S. society—for example, fundamentalism and atheism, capitalism and socialism, and republican and democrat. Clearly, ideology unites as well as divides and is therefore a powerful human-made cultural force within societies.

Societal Norms. Norms are societal prescriptions for how one is to act in given situations— for example, at a football game, party, concert, restaurant, church, park, or classroom. We also learn how to act with members of the opposite sex, with our elders, with social inferiors, and with equals. Thus, behavior is patterned. We know how to behave, and we can anticipate how other people will behave. This knowledge allows interaction to occur smoothly.

Ethnomethodology is a subdiscipline in sociology that is the scientific study of the commonplace activities of daily life. Its goals are to discover and understand the underpinnings of relationships (the shared meanings that implicitly guide social behavior). The assumption is that much of social life is scripted; that is, the players act according to society's rules (the script). Societal scripts determine the conduct in a family, in the department store between customer and salesperson, between doctor and patient, between boss and employee, between coach and player, and between teacher and student.

What happens when people do not play according to the common understandings (the script)? Examples of possible norm breaking include the following: (1) when answering the phone, you remain silent; (2) when selecting a seat in the audience, you ignore the empty seats and choose to sit next to a stranger (violating that person's privacy and space); (3) in an elevator, instead of facing the door you face the other person in the elevator; and (4) you bargain with clerks over the price of every item of food you wish to purchase. These behaviors violate the rules of interaction in our society. When the rules are violated, the other people in the situation do not know how to respond. Typically, they become confused, anxious, and angry. The breaking of norms is often the subject of humor on television shows. When a hidden camera captures a deliberate norm violation and the unknowing subject's reaction, the audience reacts with laughter. These behaviors buttress the notion that most of the time social life is very ordered and orderly. We behave in prescribed ways, and we anticipate that other people will do the same.

Body piercings and tattoos are becoming more and more acceptable, especially among the young and among college and professional athletes.

In addition to being necessary for the conduct of behavior in society, societal norms vary in importance, as we saw in our discussion of norms at the micro level. Norms that are less important (the **folkways**) are not severely punished if violated. Examples of folkways in U.S. society are the following: People should not wear curlers to the opera; a person does not wear a business suit with flip-flops; and people should not talk during another person's speech.

Violation of the **mores** (pronounced "more-rays") of society is considered important enough by society to merit severe punishment. This type of norm involves morality. Some examples of mores are the following: A person must have only one spouse at a time; thou shalt not kill (unless defending one's country); and one must be loyal to the United States.

There is a problem, however, for many Americans in deciding the degree of importance and the severity of punishment for some norms. Some behaviors are not important to the survival of society or the maintenance of its institutions yet they receive severe punishments (at least relative to the crime). For example, in 2007 the mayor of Delcambre, Louisiana signed an ordinance setting penalties of up to six months in jail and a $500 fine for wearing saggy pants that show undergarments or certain parts of the body (Associated Press, 2007). More recently, in 2010 teenager Constance McMillen was banned from her school prom for wearing a tuxedo and having a female date (Goldwert, 2010).

Both criteria used to delineate types of norms—degree of importance and severity of the punishments—are determined by the people in power. Consequently, activities that the powerful people perceive as being disruptive of the power structure or institutional arrangements that benefit some people and not others are viewed as illegitimate and punished severely. For example, if 10,000 young people protest against the political system with marches, speeches, and acts of civil disobedience, they are typically perceived as a threat and are jailed, beaten, gassed, and harassed by the police and the National Guard. Compare the treatment of these young people with another group of 10,000 on the beaches at Padre Island, Texas, during their annual college spring break. These people often drink to excess, are sexually promiscuous, and are destructive of property. Generally, the police consider these behaviors nonthreatening to the system and therefore treat them relatively lightly.

Norms are also situational. Behavior expected in one societal setting may be inappropriate for another. Several examples should make this point clear. One may ask for change from a clerk, but one would not put money in a church collection plate and remove change. Clearly, behavior considered acceptable by fans at a football game (yelling, booing authority figures, even destroying property) would be inexcusable behavior in a classroom. Behavior allowable in a bar probably would be frowned on in a bank. Or doctors may ask patients to disrobe in the examining room but not in the subway.

Finally, because they are properties of groups, norms vary from society to society and from group to group within societies. Thus, behavior appropriate in one group of society may be absolutely inappropriate in another. Some examples of this include the following:

- Couvade is a practice surprisingly common throughout the world but in sharp contrast to what occurs in the United States. This refers to the time when a woman is in childbirth. Instead of the wife suffering, the husband moans and groans and is waited on as though he were in greater pain. After his wife has had the baby, she will get up and bring her husband food and comfort. The husband is so incapacitated by the experience that in some societies he stays in bed for as many as forty days.
- In some Latin American countries, high-status males are expected to have a mistress. This practice is even encouraged by their wives because it implies high status (given the cost of maintaining two households). In the United States, such a practice is grounds for divorce.
- In Pakistan, one never reaches for food with his or her left hand. To do so would make the observers physically sick. The reason is that the left hand is used to clean oneself after a bowel movement. Hence, the right hand is symbolically the only hand worthy of accepting food.
- Unmarried Dinka men of the Sudan gorge themselves on as much as five gallons of milk blended with cow urine daily for more than three months (Davies, 1996). They do as little

activity as possible during this period to avoid burning calories, thus maximizing their weight gain. This is considered the way for them to make themselves attractive to women; by showing that their family's cattle herd is large enough to spare the extra milk.

- In the United States, in 2009 more than 10 million people underwent surgical and nonsurgical cosmetic procedures to enhance their looks according to the cultural ideal. For women, the top three procedures were breast augmentation, liposuction, and eyelid surgery. The top three procedures for men were liposuction, rhinoplasty, and eyelid surgery (American Society for Aesthetic Plastic Surgery, 2009).

Values. Another aspect of society's structure is its values, which are the bases for the norms. **Values** are the criteria used in evaluating objects, acts, feelings, or events as to their relative desirability, merit, or correctness (see Chapter 2). Values are extremely important, for they determine the direction of individual and group behavior, encouraging some activities and impeding others. For example, efforts to get people in the United States to conserve energy and other resources run counter to the long-held values of growth, progress, and individual freedom. Consequently, the prevailing values have thwarted the efforts of various presidents and other people to plan carefully about future needs and to restrict use and the rate of growth now. Values are discussed in greater detail later in this chapter.

Roles. Societies, like other social organizations, have social positions (statuses) and behavioral expectations for the people who occupy these positions (roles). There are family statuses (son, daughter, sibling, parent, husband, wife); age statuses (child, adolescent, adult, elderly); sex statuses (male, female); racial/ethnic statuses (African American, Asian American, Arab American, Latino, Native American, White); and socioeconomic statuses (poor, middle class, wealthy). For each of these statuses, there are societal constraints on behavior. To become sixty-five years old in U.S. society is a traumatic experience for many people. The expectations of society dramatically shift when one reaches this age. The aged are forced into a situation of dependence rather than independence. To be a male or female in U.S. society is to be constrained in a relatively rigid set of expectations. Similarly, African Americans, Latinos, and other minorities, because of their minority status, have been expected to occupy certain social roles. The person who occupies two relevant statuses—for example, the Black physician or the female airline pilot—best illustrates the power of the social role. Although each of these people is a qualified professional, both will doubtless encounter many situations in which other people will expect them to behave according to the dictates of the traditional role expectations of their **ascribed status** (race, sex, age, or other statuses over which the individual has no control) rather than of their **achieved status** (that is, their occupation).

The Social Construction of Reality

How are we to define what we see, feel, and hear? The important sociological insight is that meaning is not inherent in an object. Rather, people learn how to define reality from other people in interaction and by learning the culture. This process is called the **social construction of reality**.

Language, in particular, influences the ways in which the members of a society perceive reality. The idea that language shapes thought is called **linguistic relativity** and is most often associated with the classic writings of two linguists, Edward Sapir and Benjamin Whorf. Sapir and Whorf have demonstrated linguistic relativity by the way the Hopi and Anglos differ in the way they speak about time. The Hopi language has no verb tenses and no nouns for times, days, or years. Consequently, the Hopi think of time as continuous and without breaks. The English language, in sharp contrast, divides time into seconds, minutes, hours, days, weeks, months, years, decades, and centuries. The use of verb tenses in English clearly informs everyone whether an event occurred in the past, present, or future. Clearly, precision regarding time is important to English-speaking peoples, whereas it is unimportant to the Hopi.

There is an African tribe that has no word for the color gray. This implies that they do not see gray, even though we know that there is such a color and readily see it in the sky and in hair. The Navajo do not distinguish between blue and green, yet they have two words for different kinds of black.

The Aimore tribe in eastern Brazil has no word for two. The Yancos, an Amazon tribe, cannot count beyond poettarrarorincoaroac, their word for three. The Temiar people of West Malaysia also stop at three. Can you imagine how this lack of numbers beyond two or three affects how these people perceive reality?

"Now that we can tell time, I'd like to suggest that we begin imposing deadlines."

Combining ethnocentrism with social construction, the Western world refers to the Arab countries as in the "Middle East." This is "true" only if one views the world from England, which has been the norm for two hundred years or so. As sociologist Jay Coakley (2001) has said, "This is a trivial point to make unless one is concerned with how various forms of culturally constructed concepts and terminology have been used as a basis for assumed truth."

The social interpretation of reality is not limited to language. For example, some people believe that there is such a thing as holy water. There is no chemical difference between water and holy water, but some people believe that the differences in properties and potential are enormous. Similarly, consider the difference between saliva and spit (Brouillette and Turner, 1992). There is no chemical difference between them; the only difference is that in one case the substance is inside the mouth and in the other it is outside. We swallow saliva continuously and think nothing about it, yet one would not gather his or her spit in a container and then drink it. Saliva is defined positively and spit negatively, yet the only difference is a social definition. Our bodies produce fluids and substances continuously (urine, feces, mucus, phlegm, saliva, blood), and how individuals feel about these fluids varies from society to society. The standards also, typically, vary within society by age, social class, and gender. For example, in the United States, "[w]omen are held up to different standards in the realm of the disgusting. A woman picking her nose, a belching or a flatulent woman, a spitting woman—all qualify as rather more revolting than men happily engrossed in the same activities" (Epstein, 1997:80).

Cultural Relativity. This chapter has so far described a number of customs from around the world. They may seem to us to be weird, or strange. Anthropologists, though, have helped us to understand that in the cultural context of a given society, the practice may make considerable sense. For example, in his classic work on cultural relativism, anthropologist Marvin Harris (1974) has explained why sacred cattle are allowed to roam the countryside in India while the people may be starving. Outsiders see cow worship as the primary cause of India's hunger and poverty—cattle do not contribute meat, but they do eat crops that would otherwise go to human beings. Harris, however, argues that cattle must not be killed for food because they are the most efficient producers of fuel and food. To kill them would cause the economy to collapse. Cattle contribute to the Indian economy in a number of significant ways. They are the source of oxen, which are the principal traction animals for farming. Their milk helps to meet the nutritional needs of many poor families. India's cattle annually excrete 700 million tons of recoverable manure, half of which is used for fertilizer and the rest for fuel. Cow dung is also used as a household flooring material. If cows were slaughtered during times of famine, the economy would not recover in good times. To Western experts it looks as if Indians would rather starve to death than eat their cows. But as Harris argues, "They don't realize that the farmer would rather eat his cow than starve, but that he will starve if he does eat it" (Harris, 1974:21).

Muli men of Papua, New Guinea, wear mushroom-shaped wigs every day. They believe that hair is a symbol of health and strength for men, so they wear elaborate wigs made from their own hair to earn the respect of their tribe.

The practice of cow worship also allows for a crude redistribution of wealth. The cattle owned by the poor are allowed to roam freely. In this way, the poor are able to let their cows graze the crops of the rich and come home at night to be milked. As Harris concludes, "Practices and beliefs can be rational or irrational, but a society that fails to adapt to its environment is doomed to extinction" (Harris, 1978:36).

This extended example is used to convey the idea that the customs of a society should be evaluated in the light of the culture and their functions for that society. These customs should not be evaluated by our standards, but by theirs. This is called **cultural relativity**. The problem with cultural relativity, of course, is ethnocentrism—the tendency for the members of each society to assume the rightness of their own customs and practices and the inferiority, immorality, or irrationality of those found in other societies.

The Globalization of Culture

Using the conventional view of culture, there should be no global equivalencies to global myths, legends, and symbols that unite the world's people. However, Western culture, especially the commercialized culture of the United States, is marketed worldwide. As a consequence, the popular culture of the United States as manifested in rock music, film, television, video, advertising, fast food chains, sodas, and fashion is found in urban centers throughout the world. The English language has become the world's dominant language of commerce. The global economy is becoming more and more unified with multinational corporations organized in various countries to manufacture and sell goods usually compatible with a Western lifestyle. These organizations, regardless of geographical location, are structured along similar Western-style bureaucratic lines and their managers "spend as much time in the air criss-crossing the globe as they do at home, identifying with a global, cosmopolitan culture rather than that of their own nations" (Appelbaum and Chambliss, 1995:73). The Internet increases the likelihood of a global culture as people interact across political boundaries and have access to the same databases and other sources of information (Eitzen, Baca Zinn, and Smith, 2009).

This spread of one society's cultural characteristics to another is called **cultural diffusion**. This process has existed throughout human history, as people have been influenced by strangers from other societies because of trade, conquest, migration, and other forms of contact. This diffusion of cultures has been slow, but since World War II the process has increased rapidly. Where travel from Europe to the United States used to take months, it now takes less than a day. Today, many millions of people travel back and forth across political boundaries, some to stay permanently. Corporations move their business activities to societies where labor is cheap and regulations minimal (outsourcing). Because of computers and satellites, messages can be sent and money transferred instantaneously across national boundaries. Plagues, viruses, and

Western culture, especially the commercialized culture of the United States, is marketed worldwide.

organized crime (drugs, sex trade) spread across the globe. In short, national boundaries and traditional institutions are becoming increasingly obsolete, resulting in what we might call **global culture**.

While the forces of globalization are relentless, the opposite forces of localism and parochialism are also at work. Benjamin Barber (1995) calls these contradictory forces "Jihad vs. McDonaldization." He argues that the trivializing, commercialized McWorld ethos associated with the economic power and culture of the West (especially the United States) has led to an ethnic, religious, or nationalistic resurgence or jihad in various parts of the world (Kennedy, 2001:15). This ethnic resurgence is made even more prominent by growing anti-American sentiment. Perceptions of the United States abroad have gradually worsened since 2000 and intensified as a result of U.S. foreign policy and the U.S.-led invasion of Iraq (Oxford Analytica, 2007).

This resistance to globalization and nationalistic resurgence is found not only in the Islamic world but also among warring factions in places like the Sudan, Croatia, Macedonia, and the Philippines. At the same time that many women across the globe accept the fashions of the West, others willingly cover their bodies completely in public. When leaders attempt to negotiate compromise, others refuse to "water down" their principles, and sometimes they use force to make their case. While science and rationality dominate Western culture, many, including in the West, reject the findings of science in favor of ancient "truths."

Thus, while the world moves toward a secular Western culture, there are ethnic and religious enclaves that reject the secular modernity of the West. The driving force of division is fundamentalist religion, which is adamantly opposed to many of the most positive values of modern society. Fundamentalists have no time for democracy, pluralism, religious tolerance, peacekeeping, free speech, or the separation of church and state. Christian fundamentalists reject the discoveries of biology and physics about the origins of life and insist that the Book of Genesis is scientifically sound in every detail. At a time when many are throwing off the shackles of the past, Jewish fundamentalists observe their revealed Law more stringently than ever before, and Muslim women, repudiating the freedoms of Western women, shroud themselves in veils and chadors. Muslim and Jewish fundamentalists both interpret the Arab-Israeli conflict, which began as defiantly secularist, in an exclusively religious way.

Fundamentalism, moreover, is not confined to the great monotheisms. There are Buddhist, Hindu, and even Confucian fundamentalisms, which also cast aside many of the painfully acquired insights of liberal culture, which fight and kill in the name of religion and strive to bring the sacred into the realm of politics and national struggle (Armstrong, 2000:xi).

Thus, the world is faced with contradictory trends. One is toward convergence—toward a common language, acceptance of science and rationality, and a sense of pluralism and inclusion. But the processes of globalization trigger movements that create localized, cultural-specific identities (Kloos, 2000), emphasizing difference and exclusion. Local folk cultures remain a force in rural areas. At the same time that there is a move to diminish the importance of political boundaries, the importance of tribes is paramount for many. So, it is too facile to say that there is a global culture. As Cohen and Kennedy (2000) put it: "On occasions, some inhabitants of Lagos or Kuala Lumpur may drink Cokes, wear Levi 501 jeans and listen to Madonna records. But that does not mean they are about to abandon their customs, family and religious obligations or national identities wholesale even if they could afford to do so, which most cannot" (243).

Values

Because all the components of culture are essential for an understanding of the constraints on human behavior, perhaps the quickest way to reach this understanding is to focus on its values. These are the criteria the members of society use to evaluate objects, ideas, acts, feelings, or events as to their relative desirability, merit, or correctness.

Human beings are valuing beings. They continually evaluate themselves and other people. What objects are worth owning? What makes people successful? What activities are rewarding? What is beauty? Of course, different societies have distinctive criteria (values) for evaluating. People are considered successful in the United States, for example, if they accumulate many material things as a result of hard work. In other societies people are considered to be successful if they attain total mastery of their emotions or if they totally reject materialism.

One objective common to any social science course is the hope that students will become aware of the various aspects of social life in an analytical way. For people studying their own society, this means that while immersed in the subject matter, they also become participant observers. This implies an objective detachment (as much as possible) so that one may understand better the forces that in large measure affect human behavior, both individually and in groups.

The primary task for the participant observer interested in societal values is to determine what the values are. To begin, one might ask: Toward what do people most often direct their action? Is it, for example, contemplation and meditation, or physical fitness, or acquisition of material wealth? In other words, what gives individuals high status in the eyes of their fellows?

A second technique that might help delineate the values is to determine the choices that people make consistently. For example, how do individuals dispose of surplus wealth? Do they spend it for self-aggrandizement or for altruistic reasons? Is there a tendency to spend it for the pleasure of the present, to save it for security in the future, or to spend it on other people?

A third procedure is used typically by social scientists—to find out through interviews or written questionnaires what people say is good, bad, moral, immoral, desirable, or undesirable. A problem in the study of values exists because there are sometimes discrepancies between values and actual behavior. Even if there is a difference between what they write on a questionnaire or say in an interview and their actual behavior, people will probably say or write those responses they feel are appropriate, and this response by itself is a valid indicator of what the values of the society are.

One may also observe the reward–punishment system of the society. What behavior is rewarded with a medal, or a bonus, or public praise? Alternatively, what behavior brings condemnation, ridicule, public censure, or imprisonment? The greater the reward or the punishment received, the greater the likelihood that important societal values are involved. Consider, for example, the extraordinary punishment in the United States given to people who willfully destroy or steal the private property of others (for example, a thief, a looter, or an arsonist). Closely related to the reward–punishment system are the actions that cause individuals to feel guilt or shame (losing a job, living on welfare, declaring bankruptcy) or actions that bring about ego enhancement (getting a better-paying job, receiving an educational degree, owning a business). Individuals feel guilt or shame because they have internalized the norms and values of society. When values and behavior are not congruent, feelings of guilt are a typical response.

Another technique is to examine the principles that are held as part of the so-called American way of life. These principles are enunciated in historical documents such as the Constitution, the Declaration of Independence, and the Bible. Elected officials continually remind us of these principles in speeches; we are also reminded by editorials in the mass media, and from religious pulpits. The United States has gone to war to defend such principles as democracy, equality, freedom, and the free enterprise system. Therefore, one question the analyst of values should ask is, for what principles will the people fight? The remainder of this chapter describes the system of values prevalent in the United States. Understanding these values is essential to the analysis of society, for they provide the basis for this country's uniqueness as well as the source of many of its social problems.

Values as Sources of Societal Integration and Social Problems

U.S. society, while similar in some respects to other advanced industrial societies, is also fundamentally different. Given the combination of geographical, historical, and religious factors found in the United States, it is not surprising that the cultural values found there are unique. Geographically, the United States has remained relatively isolated from other societies for most of its history. The United States has also been blessed with an abundance of rich and varied resources (land, minerals, and water). Until only recently, the inhabitants of the United States were unconcerned with conservation and the careful use of resources (as many societies must be to survive) because there was no need. The country provided a vast storehouse of resources so rich that they were often used wastefully.

Historically, the United States was founded by a revolution that grew out of opposition to tyranny and aristocracy. Hence, people in the United States have verbally supported such principles as freedom, capitalism, democracy, equality, and impersonal justice. Another historical factor that has led to the particular nature of the culture in the United States is that the society has been peopled largely by immigrants. This has led, on one hand, to a blending of many cultural traits, such as language, dress, and customs, and on the other hand to the existence of ethnic enclaves that resist assimilation.

A final set of forces that have affected the culture of the United States stem from its religious heritage. First is the Judeo-Christian ethic that has prevailed throughout U.S. history. The strong emphases on humanitarianism, the inherent worth of all individuals, a morality based on the Ten Commandments, and even the biblical injunction to "have dominion over all living things" have had a profound effect on how Americans evaluate each other. Another aspect of religious heritage, the **Protestant ethic**, has been an important determinant of the values believed to typify most people in the United States (see Weber's classic work, *The Protestant Ethic and the Spirit of Capitalism*, 1958). The Protestant ethic is the religious belief emphasizing hard work and continual striving to prove that one is saved. The majority of early European settlers in the New World tended to believe in a particular set of religious beliefs that can be traced back to two individuals, Martin Luther and John Calvin. Luther's contribution was essentially twofold: Each person was considered to be his or her own priest (stressing the person's individuality and worth), and each person was to accept his or her work as a calling. To be called by God to do a job, no matter how humble, was to give dignity to the job and to the individual. It also encouraged everyone to work very hard to be successful in that job.

The contribution of John Calvin was based on his belief in predestination. God, because He is all knowing, knows who will be saved. Unfortunately, individuals do not know whether they are saved or not, and this is very anxiety producing. Calvinists came to believe that God would look with more favor on people who were preordained to be saved than on people who were not. Consequently, success in one's work became a sign that one was saved, and this was therefore anxiety reducing. Calvinists worked very hard to be successful. As they prospered, the capital they accumulated could be spent only on necessities, for to spend on luxuries was wasteful and therefore scorned by God. The surplus capital was therefore invested in the enterprise (purchasing more property or better machinery, or hiring a larger workforce, for example).

Luther's and Calvin's beliefs led to an ethic that flourished in the United States. This ethic stressed the traits of self-sacrifice, diligence, and hard work. It stressed achievement, and most important, it stressed a self-orientation rather than a collectivity orientation. Indirectly, this ethic emphasized private property, capitalism, rationality, and growth.

Thus, geography, religious heritage, and history have combined to provide a distinctive set of values for North Americans. However, before we describe these dominant values, several caveats should be mentioned. First, the tremendous diversity of the United States precludes any universal holding of values. The country has people and groups that reject the dominant values. Moreover, there are differences in emphasis for the dominant values by region, social class, age, race/ethnicity, and religion. Second, the system of U.S. values is not always consistent with behavior. Third, the values themselves are not always consistent. How does one reconcile the coexistence of individualism with conformity, or competition and cooperation?

To minimize the problem with inconsistencies, this section examines, in turn, only the most dominant of U.S. values.

Success (Individual Achievement). The highly valued individual in U.S. society is the self-made person, the person who has achieved money and status through personal efforts in a highly competitive system. Our cultural heroes are people like Abraham Lincoln, John D. Rockefeller, Sam Walton, Bill Gates, and Oprah Winfrey, each of whom rose from relatively humble origins to the top of her or his profession.

Success can be achieved, obviously, by outdoing all other people, but it is often difficult to know exactly the extent of one's success. Hence, economic success (one's income, personal wealth, and types of possessions) is the most commonly used measurement. Economic success, moreover, is often used to measure personal worth.

There is evidence that today's parents are putting more and more pressure on their children to succeed. Parents today are involving their children in much more structured activities to develop sport, musical, artistic, and cognitive skills than did parents in earlier generations. There are piano and ballet lessons, sessions with tutors, beauty pageants, sports practices and games, personal trainers, and specialized summer camps. And these activities are not cheap. Consider the following example of young hockey players in Jefferson Township, New Jersey:

> Everyone there knows that promising puck chasers have to join a competitive travel team ($3,500 a season), attend practice and games four to five times a week at a rink 45 minutes away ($150 a week for gas), and play a 55-game schedule with matches in Boston, Baltimore and Pennsylvania. Then there's the gear: $200 hockey sticks are standard, as are $400 skates with Kevlar-composite blades. (Kadet, 2008:1)

These families are pursuing the American dream. Their efforts can be characterized positively as dedicated and achievement-oriented or negatively as fanatical and one-dimensional. But they and countless others are bent on being successful.

While the push by parents toward structured activities for their children is due in part to both parents in the labor force and the need for adult supervision of their children outside of

Many parents feel pressured to sign up their children for competitive sports at a very young age. These players are part of the Orange County Youth Football League.

school, the other and more important reason is that parents want their children to find their niche and specialize early so that they can get a college scholarship and get on the narrow road to success in the ever more competitive society where corporate downsizing is common-place and wages are stagnant (see Chapter 8).

Competition. Competition is highly valued in U.S. society. Most people believe it is the one quality that has made the United States great because it motivates individuals and groups to be discontent with the status quo and with being second best. Motivated by the hope of being victorious in competition, or put another way, by fear of failure, Americans must not lose a war, or the Olympic Games, or be the second nation to land its citizens on the moon.

That competition and winning are highly valued in the United States can be seen in the extremely large number of awards shows celebrating entertainers. The Country Music Awards, the American Music Awards, the Video Music Awards, and the Grammy Awards celebrate success in music, while the Emmy Awards, the Golden Globe Awards, the Screen Actor's Guild Awards, and the Academy Awards celebrate success in film and television. In 2010, the Academy announced that they were changing the language that presenters use to give out the award. For twenty-two years, the presenters had used the more noncompetitive phrase "And the Oscar goes to ..." In 2010 the presenters went back to the old phrase "And the winner is ..." For a closer look at competition in the media, see the Closer Look panel titled "Competition in the Era of Reality Television."

Competition pervades almost all aspects of U.S. society. The work world, sports, court-ship, organizations such as the Cub Scouts, and schools all thrive on competition. The perva-siveness of competition in schools is seen in how athletic teams, cheerleading squads, debate

Competition in the Era of Reality Television

The reality show Toddlers and Tiaras reveals the highly competitive and often disturbing world of children's beauty pageants.

Since the year 2000, reality television shows have dominated the market. It began with the contest-based reality show *Survivor*. In the show, a group of strangers are stranded at a remote location, divided into "tribes," and made to perform challenges each week. Individuals form alliances with each other to strengthen their chances of surviving, because each episode someone gets voted off the island (often by those same people that they have formed alliances with). In the end, one person is left winning a million dollars. This highly rated and profitable show started a chain of other shows replicating the formula, like *The Biggest Loser*, *The Amazing Race*, *The Apprentice*, *Dancing with the Stars*, *Project Runway*, and *American Idol* (to name a few). While they vary between contestants being voted off by the public, by each other, or by celebrity judges, they have the same structure of competition and elimination.

What do these contest-based shows teach us about life? Here are a few lessons: (1) There is only one winner. Even though you may have made friends during the process, they are not really your friends in the end, and you must crush and/or betray them if necessary. (2) Success, fame, and winning are possible without an education. (3) Personality is more important than ability. In the world of reality television, what gets ratings are the controversial personalities that stir things up, not necessarily the most talented. In other words, bad behavior is rewarded. (4) Fame is its own reward. Often the losers from reality shows go on talk shows and receive other job offers due to their television exposure.

teams, choruses, bands, and casts are composed. Competition among classmates is used as the criterion for selection. Of course, the grading system is also often based on the competition of individuals.

The Cub Scouts, because of their reliance on competition, are an all-American organization. In the first place, the level one has achieved through the attainment of merit badges determines individual status in the den or pack. Although all boys can theoretically attain all merit badges, there is competition as the boys are pitted against each other to see who can obtain the most. Another example of how the Cub Scouts use competition is their annual event—the Pinewood Derby. Each boy in a Cub pack is given a small block of wood and four wheels that he is to shape into a racing car. The race is held at a pack meeting, and one boy eventually is the winner. The event is rarely questioned, even though nearly all the boys go home disappointed losers. Why is such a practice accepted and publicized? The answer is that it is symbolic of how things are done in virtually all aspects of American life.

An important consequence of this emphasis on the survival of the fittest is that some people take advantage of their fellows to compete successfully. In the business world, we find some people who use theft, fraud, interlocking directorates, and price fixing to get ahead dishonestly. A related problem, abuse of nature for profit, while not a form of cheating, nevertheless takes advantage of other people, while one person pursues economic success. The current ecology crisis is caused by individuals, corporations, and communities that find pollution solutions too expensive. Thus, in looking out for themselves, they ignore the short- and long-range effects on social and biological life. In other words, competition, while a constant spur for individuals and groups to succeed, is also the source of some illegal activities and hence of social problems in U.S. society.

Similar scandals are also found in the sports world. The most visible type of illegal activity in sports is illegal recruiting of athletes by colleges and universities. In the quest to succeed (that is, to win), some coaches have violated NCAA regulations by altering transcripts to ensure an athlete's eligibility, allowing substitutes to take admissions tests for athletes of marginal educational ability, paying athletes for nonexistent jobs, illegally using government work-study monies for athletes, and offering money, cars, and clothing to entice athletes to their schools (Eitzen and Sage, 2003). Another dark side to the extremely competitive nature of sports is the abuse of steroids and other performance-enhancing drugs. The 2007 Mitchell report to the Commissioner of Major League Baseball indicates widespread illegal use of these substances by players (Mitchell, 2007). Nationwide studies indicate that a number of high school students are turning to steroid use as well.

In sum, while competition can be motivating and have positive consequences, competition can also foster unhealthy behaviors and a "winning at all costs" attitude that can cause other societal problems.

Work. North Americans, from the early Puritans to the present day, have elevated people who were industrious and denigrated those who were not. Most North Americans, therefore, assume that poor people deserve to be poor because they are allegedly unwilling to work as hard as people in the middle and upper classes. This type of explanation places the blame on the victim rather than on the social system that systematically thwarts efforts by the poor. Their hopelessness, brought on by their lack of education, or by their being a racial minority, or by their lack of experience, is interpreted as their fault and not as a function of the economic system.

Progress. Societies differ in their emphasis on the past, the present, and the future. U.S. society, while giving some attention to each time dimension, stresses the future. North Americans neither make the past sacred nor are content with the present. They place a central value on progress—on a brighter tomorrow, a better job, a bigger home, a move to the suburbs, college education for their children, and self-improvement. People in the United States are not satisfied with the status quo; they want growth (new buildings, faster planes, bigger airports, more business moving into the community, larger profits, and new world records). They want to change and conquer nature (dam rivers, clear forests, re-channel rivers, seed clouds, and spray insecticides).

Although the implicit belief in progress is that change is good, some things are not to be changed, for they have a sacred quality (the political system, the economic system, U.S. values, and the nation-state). Thus, North Americans, while valuing technological change, do not favor changing the system (revolution).

The commonly held value of progress has also had a negative effect on contemporary life in the United States. Progress is typically defined to mean either growth or new technology. Every city wants to grow. Chambers of commerce want more industry and more people (and more consumers). No industry can afford to keep sales at last year's figures. Everyone agrees that the gross national product (GNP) must increase each year. If all these things are to grow as people wish, then concomitant with such growth must be increased population, more products turned out (using natural resources), more electricity, more highways, and more waste. Continued growth will inevitably throw the tight ecological system out of balance because there are limited supplies of air, water, and places to dump waste materials. Not only are these resources limited, but they also diminish as the population increases.

Progress also means faith in technology. Typically, North Americans believe that scientific knowledge will solve problems. Scientific breakthroughs and new technology have solved some problems and do aid in saving labor. But new technology often creates problems that were unanticipated. Sociologists call these phenomena **latent functions**, which mean, in effect, unintended consequences. The intended consequences of an activity or social arrangement are called **manifest functions**.

For example, although the automobile is of fantastic help to humankind, it has polluted the air, and each year it kills about 60,000 people in the United States in accidents. It is difficult to imagine life without electricity, but the creation of electricity pollutes the air and causes the thermal pollution of rivers. Insecticides and chemical fertilizers have performed miracles in agriculture, but they have also polluted food and streams.

Material Progress. A belief of people in the United States holds that work pays off. The payoff is not only success in one's profession but also in economic terms—income and the acquisition and consumption of goods and services that go beyond adequate nutrition, medical care, shelter, and transportation. The superfluous things that we accumulate or strive to accumulate, such as country club memberships, jewelry, stylish clothes, lavish homes, boats, second homes, pool tables, and season tickets to the games of our favorite teams or orchestras, are symbols of success in the competitive struggle. But these acquisitions have more than symbolic value because they are elements of what people in the United States consider the good life and, therefore, a right.

This emphasis on having things has long been a facet of U.S. life (Kulman, 2004). This country, the energy crisis notwithstanding, has always been a land of opportunity and abundance. Although many people are blocked from full participation in this abundance, the goal for most people is to accumulate things that bring status and that provide for a better way of life by saving labor or enhancing pleasure in our leisure.

Individual Freedom. North Americans value individualism. They believe that people should generally be free from government interference in their lives and businesses and free to make their own choices. Implied in this value is the responsibility of each individual for personal development. The focus on individualism places responsibility on the individual for his or her acts—not on society or its institutions. Being poor is blamed on the individual, not on the maldistribution of wealth and other socially perpetuated disadvantages that blight many families generation after generation. The aggressive behavior of minority youth is blamed on them, not on the limits placed on their social mobility by the social system. Dropping out of high school before graduation is blamed on individual students, not on the educational system that fails to meet their needs. This attitude helps explain the reluctance by people in authority to provide adequate welfare, health care, and compensatory programs to help the disadvantaged. This common tendency of individuals to focus on the deviant (blaming the victim) rather than on the system that produces deviants has also been true of U.S. social scientists analyzing social problems.

Individual freedom is, of course, related to capitalism and private property. The economy is supposed to be competitive. Individuals, through their own efforts, business acumen, and luck can (if successful) own property and build profits.

The belief that private property and capitalism are not to be restricted has led to several social problems: (1) unfair competition (monopolies, price fixing); (2) a philosophy held by many entrepreneurs of caveat emptor (let the buyer beware), whereby the aim is profit with total disregard for the welfare of the consumer; and (3) the current ecology crisis, which is due in great measure to the standard policy of many people and most corporations in the United States to do whatever is profitable—and thus neglect conservation of natural resources.

These practices have led the federal and state governments to enact and enforce regulatory controls. Clearly, Americans have always tended to abuse nature and their fellows in the name of profit. Freedom, if so abused, must be curtailed, and the government (albeit somewhat reluctantly, given the pressures from various interest groups) has done this.

The related values of capitalism, private property, and self-aggrandizement (individualism) have also led to an environmental crisis. Industries fouling the air and water with refuse and farmers spraying pesticides that kill weeds and harm animal and human life are two examples of how individuals and corporations look out for themselves with an almost total disregard for the short- and long-range consequences of their actions.

As long as people in the United States hold a narrow self-orientation rather than a collectivity orientation, this crisis will continue and steadily worsen. The use people make of the land (and the water on it or running through it and the air above it) has traditionally been theirs to decide because of the belief in private property. This belief in private property has meant, in effect, that individuals have had the right to pave a pasture for a parking lot, tear up a lemon grove for a housing development, put down artificial turf for a football field, and dump waste products into the air and water. Consequently, individual decisions have had the collective effect of taking millions of acres of arable land out of production permanently; polluting the air and water; and covering land where vegetation once grew with asphalt, concrete buildings, and Astroturf even though green plants are the only source of oxygen.

Values and Behavior

The discrepancy between values and behavior has probably always existed in the United States. For example, inconsistencies between the Christian ethic of love, brotherhood, and humanitarianism, on one hand, and the realities of religious bigotry, the maximization of self-interest, and property rights over human rights, on the other. The gap may be widening because of the tremendous rate of social change taking place (the rush toward urbanization and the increased bureaucratization in all spheres of social life). Values do not change as rapidly as do other elements of the culture. Although values often differ from behavior, they remain the criteria for evaluating objects, people, and events. It is important, however, to mention that when behaviors contradict values, this hypocrisy may lead to social protest or the development of countercultures (a topic that we discuss later in this chapter). Let us examine a few of these contradictions.

Equality vs. Injustice. North Americans have always placed high value on the equality of all people (in the courts or in getting a job). This value is impossible to reconcile with the racist, sexist, homophobic, and superiority theories held by some individuals and groups. It is also impossible to reconcile the value on equality with many of the formal and informal practices in workplaces, in the schools, in the lending procedures of banks, and in the courts.

Civil Liberties vs. Government Control. Related to the stated belief in equality are the other fundamental beliefs enunciated by the Founding Fathers: the freedoms guaranteed in the Bill of Rights and the Declaration of Independence. Ironically, although the United States was founded by a revolution, the same behavior (called for by the Declaration of Independence) by dissident groups is now squelched. As elaborated in Chapter 6, individual rights and freedoms have become more and more curtailed by the necessity of security following the September 11, 2001, terrorist attacks on the United States.

Individualism vs. Conformity. North Americans glorify individualism and self-reliance. These related traits, however, are not found in bureaucracies, where the watchword is that to get along you have to go along. Rather than individualism, the way to get ahead in corporations and other large bureaucracies is to be a team player and not rock the boat.

Not only is there an inconsistency between societal values and individual behavior, but there is also a lack of unity about some of the values themselves. This lack of unity can be traced back to the multicultural heritage of the United States and its increasingly diverse population.

Cultural Diversity

In the United States, people are far from unanimous on a number of public issues (for example, gun control, abortion, the death penalty, or prayer in schools). Despite inconsistencies and ambiguities, North Americans as a whole do tend to believe in certain things—for example, that democracy is the best form of government; that capitalism is the best economic system; that success can be defined in terms of hard work, initiative, and the amassing of wealth and property; and that there should be equality of opportunity and equal justice before the law. But even though the U.S. populace holds these values generally, there is never total agreement on any of them. The primary reason for this is the tremendous diversity found within the United States.

The United States is composed of many people who differ on important social dimensions: age, sex, race, region, social class, ethnicity, religion, geography, and so on. These variables suggest that groups and categories will differ in values and behavior because certain salient social characteristics imply differential experiences and expectations. These are noted often in the remainder of this book.

Let us examine a few differences held by various groups and categories to illustrate the lack of consistency among people in the United States. Values are the criteria used to determine, among other things, morality. Public opinion polls show that the vast majority accepts the legality of abortion, at least under certain circumstances. When these data are examined according to the age, income, and education of the respondents, we find systematic differences. The older the individual and the lower a person's income or education, the more likely the person is to be antiabortion.

Similarly, different age groups tend to feel differently about the topic of same-sex marriage. A 2009 Gallup poll shows that the younger generation (aged 18–29) is more in favor of same-sex marriage (59 percent in favor) than the older generation over age 65 (32 percent in favor) (Jones, 2009).

The rural–urban differences in U.S. society are well known. An interesting example is the probability that rural people are more humanitarian, yet more intolerant of deviance among their neighbors, than are urban dwellers. There also are variations among rural communities, as there are among urban places, on these and other differences.

Region of the country accounts for some variation in values held. But the generalizations made about Southerners, Easterners, and Midwesterners, while having some validity, gloss over many real differences. Within any one region there are differences among rural and urban people, among different religious groups, and among different ethnic groups.

The concept of **subculture** has been defined typically as a relatively cohesive cultural system that varies in form and substance from the dominant culture. Under the rubric subculture, then, there are ethnic groups, delinquent gangs, and religious sects. In 1962, Milton Yinger proposed that the concept of subculture be defined more precisely. He suggested that it be used for one type of group, and that counterculture be used for another type that had been previously called a subculture.

For Yinger, the concept of subculture should be limited to relatively cohesive cultural systems that differ from the dominant culture in such things as language, values, religion, and style of life. Typically, a group that is a subculture differs from the larger group because it has emigrated from another society and, because of physical or social isolation, has not been fully assimilated. The cultural differences, then, are usually based on ethnicity. Tradition keeps the culture of this group somewhat unique from the dominant culture. Examples of such subcultures in the United States include the Amish, some Orthodox Jewish sects, many Native American tribes, and Polish, Croatian, Hungarian, Italian, Greek, and Irish groups at one time or another in U.S. history. Recent immigrants often cluster together for mutual benefit but also to maintain their traditions.

A **counterculture**, as defined by Yinger, is a culturally homogeneous group that has developed values and norms that differ from the larger society because the group opposes the larger society. This type of group is in conflict with the dominant culture. The particular values and norms can be understood only by reference to the dominant group. (For an example of a counterculture see the Diversity panel titled "Life in a Religious Sect") The existence of numerous subcultures and countercultures within the United States explains much of the lack of consistency with respect to U.S. values.

Life in a Religious Sect

In April 2008, the world watched in fascination as over 400 children were taken into state custody from the 1,700 acre Yearning for Zion ranch near Eldorado, Texas. The ranch is run by the Fundamentalist Church of Jesus Christ of Latter-Day Saints (FLDS), a radical offshoot of the Mormon Church (the Mormon Church claims no affiliation with FLDS and does not consider them a Mormon faith group). The images captured by the media showed children and mothers dressed differently from the dominant culture. The women wore long, high-necked plain dresses, no makeup, and their hair in long braids. The state removed the children after receiving an anonymous call from a sixteen-year-old girl who claimed that she was being sexually and physically abused by her husband. The state removed *all* the children based on concerns about the sect's practices regarding the marriages of underage girls to older men and reports of sexual and physical abuse. In the media, the press interviewed FLDS mothers. In these interviews, they pleaded for their children to be returned, they refused to answer any questions about their husbands or about the marriages of young girls to older men, and they denied the allegations of abuse. Nearly a month after the children were taken into protective custody, the Texas Supreme Court ruled that the children must be returned to the Yearning for Zion ranch.

The FLDS sect is an excellent case study in the power of socialization. Girls and boys are taught from birth that girls are the servants of men: their fathers, their husbands, and their prophets. They are taught to accept the rulings of the prophet who will decide who marries whom and at what age. While a few women rebel, the majority of the women are fully indoctrinated in the culture and believe that their highest calling is to have as many children as possible. In her book *Escape*, Carolyn Jessop, a former FLDS member who escaped from the sect with her eight children, describes her life as the fourth wife of a fifty-year-old man whom she married when she was eighteen. She describes how children in the sect are viewed as property, and physical violence/abuse is not only tolerated but is an expected part of the socialization process.

The sect is also known for its beliefs regarding polygamy. According to Jessop, the more wives a man has, the more status and power he has within the community. Furthermore, in order to reach the highest realm of heaven, a man must have at least three wives. Girls are raised to believe that polygamy is a natural and privileged lifestyle, and the Prophet is the one who decides who will be joined in "spiritual marriage" and when. Once married, the women often collect welfare or hold jobs and turn over all of their earnings to their husband. Girls can refuse a marriage, but

Jessop claims that the pressures to do as the Prophet asks are so great that no one refuses. In this way, young girls are married off to much older men. In fact, some young girls in Jessop's book were married to men more than sixty years their senior. According to Jessop, wives compete among each other to become the favorite wife, because this will determine how she is treated by her husband, by the other wives, and by her stepchildren.

Obedience to one's husband is the key to a woman's success in FLDS. According to their belief system, men have the power to decide whether a woman will be his partner or his slave in the afterlife, so women must please their husband, and therefore please God.

Carolyn Jessop escaped FLDS in 2003, and her story demonstrates the enormous power of socialization. After leaving the sect, her children experienced Christmas and birthday parties for the first time and were able to go to school and live life like other children in the United States. From the perspective of those outside the sect, it is hard to imagine that her children were not happy with their newfound freedom. But in reality her oldest children were initially very angry with her for leaving FLDS. Her daughter Betty had a very hard time adjusting to life outside the sect, and returned to FLDS after she turned eighteen. "Generation after generation of believers have been conditioned to equate obedience with salvation. People who have never been taught or allowed to think for themselves don't suddenly change. Change is too frightening" (2007:410).

Values from the Order and Conflict Perspectives

Values are sources of both societal integration and social problems. Order theorists assume that sharing values solves the most fundamental problem of societal integration. The values are symbolic representations of the existing society and therefore promote unity and consensus among people in the United States. They must, therefore, be preserved.

Conflict theorists, on the other hand, view the mass acceptance of values as a form of cultural tyranny that promotes political conservatism, inhibits creativity, and gets people to accept their lot because they believe in the system, rather than joining with others to try to change it. Thus, conflict theorists believe that slavish devotion to society's values inhibits necessary social change. Moreover, conflict theorists assume that U.S. values are the actual source of social problems such as crime, conspicuous consumption, planned obsolescence, the energy crisis, pollution, and the artificial creation of winners and losers.

Regardless of which side one may take on the consequences of U.S. values, most people would agree that the traditional values of individual freedom, capitalism, competition, and progress have made the United States relatively affluent. The future, however, will probably be very different from the past, requiring a fundamental change in these values. As a result of the recent Great Recession, the future of slow growth or no growth, lower levels of affluence, and resource shortages will require that people adapt by adopting values that support cooperation rather than competition, group goals over individual goals, and a mode of making do rather than purchasing unnecessary products.

CHAPTER REVIEW

1. Culture, which is the knowledge that members of a society or other social organizations share, constrains behavior and how people think about and interpret their world.

2. Culture emerges as a result of continued social interaction.

3. Culture is learned behavior. The process of learning the culture is called socialization.

4. Through the socialization process, individuals internalize the culture. Thus, the control that culture has over individuals is seen as natural.

5. Culture channels behavior by providing the rules for behavior and the criteria for judging.

6. Culture is boundary-maintaining. One's own culture seems right and natural. Other cultures are considered inferior, wrong, or immoral. This tendency to consider the ways of one's own group superior is called ethnocentrism.

7. Six types of shared knowledge constitute the culture—symbols, technology, ideologies, norms, values, and roles.

8. Norms are divided into two types by degree of importance and severity of punishment for their violation. Folkways are less important. Mores are considered more vital and therefore are more severely punished if violated.

9. Roles are the behavioral expectations of people who occupy the statuses in a social organization.

10. Through language and other symbols, culture determines how the members of a society will interpret their environment. The important point is that through this construction of reality, the members of a society make sense out of a world that may have no inherent meaning.

11. The variety of customs found throughout the world is staggering. The members of one society sometimes view the customs found elsewhere as weird, cruel, and immoral. If we understand the cultural context of a given society, however, their practices generally make sense. This is called cultural relativity.

12. There are two contradictory forces at work in today's world. One is toward a global culture based on the customs and values of the West, especially the United States. At the same time, opposite forces of localism and parochialism are at work, fueled by resistance to the ways of the secular West and anti-American sentiment. These tribal identities openly oppose the new and reinforce tradition.

13. Knowing the values (the criteria for evaluation) of a society is an excellent way of understanding that society. To determine the dominant values of a society, one might ask: What gives individuals status in their society? What choices do people consistently make? One might also find out through interviews and questionnaires, or by observing the reward–punishment system in a society.

14. Values in the United States are the result of three major factors: (a) geographical isolation and being blessed with abundant resources; (b) founding of the nation in opposition to tyranny and aristocracy and supporting freedom, democracy, equality, and impersonal justice;

and (c) a religious heritage based on the Judeo-Christian ethic and the Protestant work ethic.

15. The dominant U.S. values are success through individual achievement, competition, hard work, progress through growth and new technology, material progress, and individual freedom.

16. Values are the sources of societal integration as well as social problems.

17. Despite the power of culture and U.S. values over individual conduct, the diversity present in U.S. society means that for many people there are inconsistencies between values and actual behavior. There are clear variations in how people feel on public issues based on their different social situations.

18. A major source of cultural variation in the United States is the existence of subcultures. Because of different religions and ethnicity, some groups retain a culture different from the dominant one. Other groups form a culture because they oppose the larger society. The latter are called countercultures.

19. Order theorists assume that sharing values promotes unity among the members of society. The values therefore must be preserved.

20. Conflict theorists view the mass acceptance of values as a form of cultural tyranny that promotes political conservatism, inhibits creativity, and encourages false consciousness.

KEY TERMS

Socialization
Internalization
Reference groups
Ethnocentrism
Material technology
Emoticon
Social technology
Ethnomethodology

Folkways
Mores
Values
Ascribed status
Achieved status
Social construction of reality
Linguistic relativity
Cultural relativity

Cultural diffusion
Global culture
Protestant ethic
Latent functions
Manifest Functions
Subculture
Counterculture

STUDY QUESTIONS

1. Explain the concept of ethnocentrism and give examples.
2. Is it possible for scientists to study other cultures in a truly objective manner? Use the idea of cultural relativity to explain your answer.
3. What is meant by the social construction of reality? Provide examples.

4. How are U.S. values sources of both societal integration and social problems?
5. How do order theorists and conflict theorists differ in their interpretation of values?

WEB RESOURCES

http://dmoz.org/Society/Subcultures/
This site provides a list of some common and some not-so-common subcultures. Each category offers links to sites related to the subculture.
http://www.americanpopularculture.com
This institute is dedicated to the study of American popular culture of the twentieth and twenty-first centuries. They publish *Americana: The Journal of American Popular Culture.*
http://www.h-net.org/~pcaaca/
The Popular Culture Association/American Culture Association encourages scholarly discussion of popular U.S. and world cultures.
http://www.culturalsurvival.org/newpage/index.cfm
Cultural Survival is a site "promoting the rights,

voices, and visions of indigenous peoples since 1972." The site offers links and information on different indigenous cultures in various parts of the world.
http://www.chcp.org/
The Chinese Historical and Cultural Project (CHCP) was founded in 1987. CHCP's goal is to promote and preserve Chinese American culture and history through community outreach activities.
http://www.jewishculture.org/
Founded by the Council of Jewish Federations, the Foundation for Jewish Culture invests in creative individuals in order to nurture a vibrant and enduring Jewish identity, culture, and community.

CHAPTER 5

Socialization

Northern Ireland is rigidly divided between pro-British Protestants and pro-Irish Catholics. The hatred between the members of these two groups is intense, as evidenced by the number of violent incidents. The elementary schoolchildren of Northern Ireland are educated in segregated schools. But even before these children go to school they have been taught to fear and loathe the other side.

Research conducted by the University of Ulster surveyed children at forty-four elementary schools and nurseries throughout Northern Ireland (reported in Pogatchnik, 2002). The children were shown pictures and objects such as Irish and British flags, Protestant and Catholic parades, and different soccer teams' uniforms. The research found that girls and boys from the British Protestant and Irish Catholic sides of Northern Ireland society absorbed their communities' prejudices by age five. They expressed preferences for the symbols that represented their side. And they made comments such as, "I like the people who are ours. I don't like those ones because they are Orangemen [Protestants]. They're bad people," and, "Catholics are the same as masked men. They smash windows."

Children are not born with prejudices; they learn them from their families and communities. In this chapter, we examine this learning process. How do children learn the dominant beliefs of their society? How do they learn what is expected of them? This process of learning cultural values, norms, and expectations is called **socialization**.

Socialization is a lifelong process from infancy to death, where at each stage of the life cycle individuals are continually socialized into different institutions and expected behaviors. For example, when an individual enters the institution of marriage, he or she must learn the expected behaviors as a married person in that culture. This includes norms regarding gender roles as well as society's rules regarding taxes and other laws. Even though socialization is a lifelong process, the focus of this chapter is on the most critical time of socialization—childhood.

Children are born with the limits and potential established by their unique genetic compositions. But even though children are biologically human, they do not have the instincts or the innate drives that will make them human. They acquire their humanness through social interaction. Their concepts of themselves, personality, love, freedom, justice, right and wrong, and reality are all products of social interaction. In other words, human beings are essentially the social creations of society.

Evidence for this assertion is found by examining the traits and behaviors of children raised without much human contact. There have been approximately one hundred documented cases of **feral children** throughout history—children alleged to have been raised by animals or raised in severe isolation. When found, they may look human but act like the animals with which they have had contact. One case involved a Tarzan-like child allegedly

The fictional Tarzan is the most well-known example of a feral child. Tarzan was raised by apes in the jungle with no human contact.

raised by monkeys in the jungles of central Africa. The boy was discovered in 1974 at about age six with a troop of gray monkeys. Two years later, after painstaking efforts to rehabilitate him, he remained more monkey than human. "He is unable to talk and communicates by 'monkey' grunts and chattering. He will eat only fruit and vegetables, and when excited or scared jumps up and down uttering threatening monkey cries" (Associated Press, 1976). If a child's personality were largely determined by biological heritage, this child would have been much more human than simian. But there is a consistent finding in all cases that feral children are not normal. They cannot talk and have great difficulty in learning human speech patterns. They do not walk or eat like human beings. They express anger differently. In essence, the behavior that arises in the absence of human contact is not what we associate with human beings.

While the reported cases of feral children should be viewed with considerable skepticism, the cases of children living in human settings but kept isolated from most human contact reveal much about the importance of human interaction in becoming human. The most famous case of a child who was raised with only minimal human contact was a girl named Anna (Davis, 1940; 1948). Anna was an illegitimate child. Her grandfather refused to acknowledge her existence, and to escape his ire, the mother put the child in an attic room and, except for minimal feeding, ignored her. Anna was discovered by a social worker at about age six, and she was placed in a special school. When found, Anna could not sit up or walk. She could not talk and was believed to be deaf. She was immobile and completely indifferent to the people around her. She did not laugh, show anger, or smile. Staff members worked with Anna (during one year, a single staff member had to receive medical attention more than a dozen times for bites she received from Anna). Eventually, Anna learned to take care of herself and to walk, talk, and play with other children:

> By the time Anna died of hemorrhagic jaundice approximately four and a half years [after she was found], she had made considerable progress as compared with her condition when found. She could follow directions, string beads, identify a few colors, build with blocks, and differentiate between attractive and unattractive pictures. She had a good sense of rhythm and loved a doll. She talked mainly in phrases but would repeat words and try to carry on a conversation. She was clean about clothing. She habitually washed her hands and brushed her teeth. She would try to help other children. She walked well and could run fairly well, though clumsily. Although easily excited, she had a pleasant disposition. Her involvement showed that socialization, even when started at the late age of six, could still do a great deal toward making her a person. Even though her development was no more than that of a normal child of two or three years, she had made noteworthy progress. (Davis, 1948:205)

The conclusion from observers of Anna and other cases of isolated children is that being deprived of social interaction during one's formative years deprives individuals of their humanness. Thanks to modern science and studies of the brain, we now know that in cases of extreme child neglect, the brains of these children are smaller than nonneglected children, with obvious atrophy (Perry, 2002). In other words, the very makeup of their brains is altered by lack of human contact.

In addition to social contact, the second essential requirement for socialization is language. Language is the vehicle through which socialization occurs. In Anna's case, what little human contact she had during her first six years was physical and not communicative interaction. As Kingsley Davis has noted, Anna's case illustrates "that communicative contact is the core of socialization" (Davis, 1948:205). Helen Keller also illustrates this principle. This remarkable person became deaf and blind as a result of illness during infancy. She was locked in her own world until her teacher, Anne Sullivan, was able to communicate to her that the symbols she traced on Helen's hand represented water. That was the beginning of language for Helen Keller and the beginning of her understanding of who she was and the meaning of the world and society in which she was immersed (Keller, 1954).

The language of a society has profound effects on how individuals think and perceive the world. In learning our cultural language, we discover the meaning of symbols not only for words but also for objects such as the cross, the flag, and traffic lights. Language symbolizes the values and norms of the society, thus enabling the user to label and evaluate objects, acts, individuals, and groups. Language is a very powerful labeling tool, clearly delineating who is in and who is out. For example, Nesdale (2007) points to the importance of social categories and labeling in his research on ethnic prejudice in young children. He notes:

> In sum, according to the present analysis, ethnic self-identification and ethnic preference tend to occur in all children, sooner or later. They reflect the child's growing understanding of the social structure in the community, the statuses of the different groups and their inter-relationships, and the language used to describe other group members. (225)

Language is used to attribute positive traits and characteristics to a child's in-group and negative traits and characteristics to the out-group, thus resulting in ethnic preference among most children, and even ethnic prejudice in some cases.

In addition to learning about racial and ethnic identity through language, children also learn about gender identity. Most societies have particular traits and behaviors that are associated with masculinity and femininity (for more on gender roles, see Chapter 12). In the United States, the stereotypes and language surrounding masculinity and femininity often indicate opposite traits; for example, aggressive/passive, independent/dependent, strong/weak, objective/subjective, provider/nurturer, rational/emotional, to name a few. Nilsen (2000) argues that language reveals much about society and gender expectations. She demonstrates this in a telling look at the military, noting:

> Once the [male] recruits are enlisted, they find themselves doing much of the work that has been traditionally thought of as "women's work." The solution to getting the work done and not insulting anyone's masculinity was to change the titles as shown below:

> | waitress | orderly |
> |---|---|
> | nurse | medic or corpsman |
> | secretary | clerk-typist |
> | assistant | adjutant |
> | dishwasher or kitchen helper | KP (kitchen police) (310) |

In sum, language is a powerful medium of socialization, and through language, children absorb subtle messages regarding societal expectations.

The Personality as a Social Product

Chapter 2 notes the dialectic character of society. Society is at once a product of social interaction, yet that product continuously acts back on its producers. Scientists have long argued as to what extent humans are the products of nature versus nurture. Bruce Perry (2002) writes:

> Are we born evil—natural born killers or the most creative and compassionate of all animals? Are we both? Does our best and our worst come from our genes or from our learning? Nature or nurture? ... We now know more about our genes and more about the influence of experience on shaping biological systems than ever before. What do these advances tell us about the nature or nurture debate? Simply, they tell us that this is a foolish argument. Humans are the product of nature and nurture. Genes and experience are interdependent. (1)

Matt Ridley, a zoologist and science writer, agrees. Ridley argues that genes are not just the carriers of heredity. They are constantly active, switching on and off as a response to one's environment (2003).

While it is clear that we are all products of nature and nurture, in this section the emphasis is on this second process—human beings as a product of society. In particular, we examine the emergence of the human personality as a social product.

We develop a sense of **self** (our personality) in interaction with other people. Newly born infants have no sense of self-awareness. They are unable to distinguish between themselves and their surroundings. They cry spontaneously when uncomfortable. They eventually become aware that crying can be controlled and that its use can bring a response from other people. In time, and especially with the use of language, the child begins to distinguish between "I" and "you" and "mine" and "yours"—signs of self-awareness. But this is just the beginning of the personality formation process. Let us examine several classical theories of how children develop personalities and how they learn what is expected of them in the community and society.

Theories

Charles H. Cooley (1864–1929): The Looking-Glass Self. Charles Cooley (1922) believed that children's conceptions of themselves arise through interaction with other people. He used the metaphor of a **looking-glass self** to convey the idea that all people understand themselves through the way in which other people act toward them. They judge themselves on how they think others judge them. Cooley believed that each of us imagines how we look to others and what their judgment of us is. Robert Bierstedt (1974) summarizes this process: "I am not what I think I am and I am not what you think I am. I am what I think you think I am" (197).

The critical process in Cooley's theory of personality development, then, is the feedback the individual receives from other people. Others behave in particular ways with regard to an individual. The individual interprets these behaviors positively or negatively. When the behaviors of other people are perceived as consistent, the individual accepts this definition of self, which in turn has consequences for her or his behavior. In sum, there is a self-fulfilling prophecy— the individual is as defined by other people. Suppose, for example, that whenever you entered a room and approached a small knot of people conversing with each other, they promptly melted away with lame excuses. This experience, repeated many times, would affect your feelings about yourself. Or if, wherever you appeared, a conversational group quickly formed around you, would not such attention tend to give you self-confidence and ego strength?

Cooley's insight that our self-concepts are a product of how other people react to us is important in understanding behavior. Why are some categories of people more likely to be school dropouts, deviants, or criminals, while others fit in? As we see in Chapter 7, deviance is the result of the successful application of a social label, a process akin to the looking-glass self. For more on the impact of the media and the looking-glass self, see the Closer Look panel, "The Looking-Glass Self and Body Image."

George Herbert Mead (1863–1931): Taking the Role of the Other. George Mead (1934) theorized about the relationship of self and society. In essence, he believed that children find out who they are as they learn about society and society's expectations. This occurs in several important stages, the first being the imitation stage. Infants learn to distinguish between themselves and others from the actions of their parents. By age two or so, children have become self-conscious. By this Mead meant that the children are able to react to themselves as others will react to them. For example, they will tell themselves "no-no," as they have been told many times by their parents, and not touch the hot stove. The importance of this stage is that the children have internalized the feelings of other people. What others expect has become a part of them. They have become conscious of themselves by incorporating the way other people are conscious of them.

The Looking-Glass Self and Body Image

According to Charles Cooley (1922), the looking-glass self involves three elements: the perception of one's appearance or behavior as seen by other persons; the perception of *their* judgment of that appearance or behavior; and the resulting feelings of pride or mortification. Where does this perception come from? In terms of body appearance, is it possible that the beauty ideals put forth in the media might have a profound impact on how we imagine others view or judge us? If that is indeed the case, what do we learn from the media?

Recent "reality" television has put average citizens in the spotlight, usually competing for some kind of monetary reward. Unfortunately, much of this programming involves transforming those individuals into people other than their normal selves. For example, shows like MTV's *I Want a Famous Face*, *America's Next Top Model*, *Extreme Makeover*, *Ambush Makeover*, *The Biggest Loser*, and *Sports Illustrated Swimsuit Model Search* all emphasize beauty and outward appearance. Shows like *The Swan* advocate the complete transformation of a person from head to toe, with painful cosmetic surgery required as part of the transformation from "ugly duckling" to beautiful swan. Along similar lines, in 2010 E! Television launched the show *Bridalplasty*, where twelve women compete to win a dream wedding and their choice of plastic surgery procedures.

While reality television is a more recent phenomenon, famous actors have always set the standards for beauty ideals. Media analysts argue that while the Miss Americas, Playboy models, Barbie dolls, and famous actresses have become increasingly thin over time, young boys are assaulted with an ever-muscular, increasingly larger male ideal. In *The Adonis Complex*, Pope et al. argue that men are becoming more affected by the muscular images they see in the media and are increasingly dissatisfied with their own bodies, leading to steroid abuse, eating disorders, weightlifting compulsion, and body obsession (2000).

Although it is impossible to make a direct causal argument between the media and behavior, many Americans are certainly concerned with their appearance. According to the American Society of Plastic Surgeons, over seven million surgical and nonsurgical cosmetic procedures were performed in 2010, an increase of 77 percent over 2000. Are the media to blame? Recall Cooley's looking-glass self: "I am not what I think I am, and I am not what you think I am. I am what I think you think I am" (Bierstedt, 1974:197).

The next stage is the play stage. Children from ages four to seven spend many hours a day in a world of play. Much of this time is spent in pretending to be mothers, teachers, doctors, police officers, and other roles. Mead called this form of play "taking the role of the other." As they play at a variety of social roles, children act out the behavior associated with these social positions and thus develop a rudimentary understanding of adult roles and why people in those positions act the way they do. They also see how people in these roles interact with children. Thus, children learn to look at themselves as other people see them. The play stage accomplishes two things. It provides further clues for children as to who they are, and it prepares them for later life. Furthermore, this stage is crucial to the development of gender roles. If the child sees the adult roles of "mommy" or "daddy" in a certain way, or if in playacting adult roles the child sees work occupations as masculine or feminine, this may affect the way that she or he learns gender.

The game stage, which occurs at about age eight, is the final stage of personality development in Mead's scheme. In the play stage, the children's activities are fluid and spontaneous. The game stage, in contrast, involves activities that are structured. There are rules that define, limit, and constrain the participants. Mead used baseball to illustrate what occurs in the game stage. In baseball, children must understand and abide by the rules. They must also understand the entire game—that is,

According to George Herbert Mead, during the play stage children spend much of their free time pretending to be mothers, fathers, teachers, police officers, and other types of adult roles. This is an important stage for their understanding of social positions and behavior.

when playing second base, what they and the other players must do if there is a player on first, one out, and the batter bunts down the first baseline. In other words, the various individuals in a game must know the roles of all the players and adjust their behavior to that of the others. The assessment of the entire situation is what Mead called the discovery of the "generalized other." In the play stage, children learn what is expected of them by **significant others** (parents, relatives, teachers). The game stage provides children with constraints from many other people, including people they do not know. In this way children incorporate and understand the pressures of society—what Mead called the **generalized other**. By passing through these stages, children have finally developed a social life from the expectations of parents, friends, and society. The important insight of Mead is that the self emerges as the result of social experience. Thus, the self does not exist at birth but is a social creation.

Albert Bandura (1925–): Social Cognitive Theory. According to social cognitive theorist Albert Bandura (1977; 1986), human behavior is the result of the continuous interaction between cognitive, behavioral, and environmental influences. In this way, people both produce and are produced by their environment. In its simplest form, children observe the behavior of others and the feedback (positive and/or negative) for such behavior. This then serves as a guide for their actions as they model after others. According to Bandura, children will use their cognitive skills to predict the outcomes of their behavior, and thus exercise personal control over their thoughts and actions. They will also adopt a behavior if it results in outcomes that they value.

These ideas are in fact the backbone of the advertising industry, where advertisers display products and the positive outcomes of using those products in the hopes that consumers will buy them. So, for example, consumers who desire the outcome of happiness will choose one particular brand of diet soda over another.

In terms of socialization, children then learn appropriate and inappropriate behavior by observing and modeling others in society. If, for example, a young boy never observes other boys playing with Barbie dolls and receives negative feedback from adults and peers by playing with them, he will be less likely to adopt such behavior. Instead, if he receives positive rewards for playing with trucks and army toys, he will be more likely to pursue them in order to receive the desirable outcome. In this way, he has learned the expectations of society for his gender.

Sigmund Freud (1856–1939): The Psychoanalytic View. While in recent years Sigmund Freud has fallen out of favor with many academics, it is impossible to overlook his significant contributions to the field of psychology. Freud (1946) emphasized the biological dimension along with social factors in personality development. For Freud, the infant's first years are totally egocentric, with all energies directed toward pleasure. This is an expression of a primitive biological force—the **id** that dominates the infant. The id, although a force throughout life, is gradually stifled by society. Parents, as the agents of society, hamper children's pleasure-seeking by imposing schedules for eating, punishing them for messy behavior and masturbation, forcing them to control their bowels, and the like.

The process of socialization is, in Freud's view, the process of society controlling the id. Through this process, children develop egos. The **ego** is the rational part of the personality that controls the id's basic urges, finding realistic ways of satisfying these biological cravings. The individual also develops a **superego** (conscience) (Chapter 4), which regulates both the id and ego. The superego is the consequence of the child's internalizing the parents' morals. A strong superego represses the id and channels behavior in socially acceptable ways. Freud saw the individual as being pulled by two contradictory forces—the natural impulses of biology and the constraints of society—resulting in the imperfection and discontent of human beings.

Two themes stand out in this section. First, the personality of the child is, to a large degree, socially created and sustained. Second, through the process of socialization, the child internalizes the norms and values of society. In a sense, the child learns a script for acting, feeling, and thinking that is in tune with the wishes of society. Before we leave this topic, let us look briefly at a few of society's socialization agents: the family, the schools, peers, and the media.

The Family. Aside from the obvious function of providing the child with the physical needs of food, clothing, and shelter, the family is the primary agent of socialization. The family indoctrinates the child in the ways of society. The parents equip the child with the information, etiquette, norms, and values necessary to be a functioning member of society. In blatant and subtle ways, parents emit messages of what is important, appropriate, moral, beautiful, and correct—and what is not.

According to Eleanor Maccoby's overview of socialization research (2007), socialization by the family has been viewed in different ways over time. In the mid-twentieth century the dominant view was that proper socialization was the teaching of good habits and desired behaviors.

> From the "socialization as habit building" point of view, a well-socialized child is one who has accumulated a large store of the habits needed for acceptable social behavior and acceptable level of skills, while not having acquired bad (antisocial or nonfunctional) habits. (Maccoby, 2007:15)

At the same time, proper socialization was seen as the way to teach children to regulate their unpredictable impulses. These earlier views placed a high priority on reinforcement for "good" behavior and impulse control, which led to arguments over whether authoritative or permissive parenting styles are more effective.

Socialization that occurs in the family goes well beyond just the learning of "good" behavior, however.

> Socialization involves the acceptance of values, standards, and customs of society as well as the ability to function in an adaptive way in the larger social context. These values, standards, and customs are not simply transmitted from one generation to the other but, to some extent at least, constructed by each generation. Thus parents are not so much purveyors of information as helpers in setting the stage for their children to become well-functioning members of the social group. Also, an important (but not the only) goal of socialization is that values and standards be internalized in the sense that members of the group behave in accord with them willingly, rather than out of fear of external consequences or hope of reward. (Grusec and Davidov, 2007:284)

Thus, the key to the socialization process is the **internalization** of society's values and norms, so that children will act according to parental expectations, even when no one is watching. This is an important step in the process of maturation and separation from parents that each child must go through. According to anthropologist Sherry Turkle, this process is fundamentally changing as children are increasingly "tethered" to their parents through technology like cell phones (2011). For a look at how technology is changing the way some parents monitor their children, see the Technology and Society panel "Helicopter Parenting and GPS devices."

The Schools. In contrast to families who may differ somewhat in their attitudes, interests, and emphases, schools provide a more uniform indoctrination of youth in culturally prescribed ways. The formal curriculum provides children with the education needed to take on adult roles: reading, math, science, and so on. In addition to the formal curriculum, young people are also exposed to the hidden curriculum—expectations about appropriate skills, character traits, and attitudes (such as patriotism) that pay off. In the United States, some valued character traits are competitiveness, ambition, and conformity.

Helicopter Parenting and GPS Devices

In 2009 television personality Joan Lunden and her husband invented the KinderKord, a leash that keeps a child within three feet of its parent. As children grow older, the cell phone has become the leash that keeps them connected to their parents and others.

Sometimes called "over-parenting" or "hyper-parenting," the term *helicopter parent* has come to represent the parent that hovers over his or her child at every stage of development. A helicopter parent is overprotective and overinvolved in every part of his or her child's life, ready to jump in and smooth the way when his or her child confronts a problem or conflict. Protecting their children from safety hazards as well as failure in school, helicopter parents shuttle their children from one activity to the next, complain to their children's teachers and coaches if they are not satisfied, and constantly monitor their children's activities (Gibbs, 2009).

Technology has taken helicopter parenting to a new level. Hovering has become simple with the popularity of the cell phone, sometimes called the "world's longest umbilical cord" (Graves, 2007). The cell phone allows a parent to be in almost constant communication with his or her child. If that is not enough, the helicopter parent can buy a cell phone with GPS (Global Positioning System) so that the parent always knows where his or her child is located. GPS remote tracking devices are also available and can be placed in a teenager's automobile or in a child's backpack. These remote devices can tell the distance traveled, the speed achieved, the addresses where stops were made, and the duration of those stops.

In Japan, new technology is being tested that builds on these existing tracking devices. The new gadgets actually monitor what a child is seeing, and even record the child's pulse rate (Nagano, 2010). If the child's heart rate increases, the device will snap a photo of the child's point of view and e-mail it to the child's parents.

Not everyone agrees that this type of technology is a good thing. One of the largest critics of helicopter parenting is Lenore Skenazy. A newspaper columnist for the *New York Sun*, in 2008 Skenazy dropped off her nine-year-old son at Bloomingdales in New York City and left him to find his way home alone on the subway (without a cell phone). She wrote an article about it in the paper (see Skenazy, 2008) and soon found herself on numerous television shows and radio programs defending her actions. This prompted her to write several books and start a blog called Free Range Kids. In one of her columns she writes about a GPS device called Traakit. She says, "with the Traakit, this mom can have the ILLUSION that she is keeping her child safe, which just happens to be the mass parental delusion of this century—that we can and should watch our kids every second of every day with whatever device we can afford (cell phones and nanny cams, anyone?) and that people who do not do this are putting their kids in dire peril" (2009:1). Skenazy believes in safety measures like seat belts and bike helmets, but also believes that children must have the freedom to explore and become independent without parents hovering every step of the way.

Writing about cell phones and independence, Sherry Turkle says, "the tethered child does not have the experience of being alone with only him- or herself to count on. For example, there used to be a point for an urban child, an important moment, when there was a first time to navigate the city alone. It was a rite of passage that communicated to children that they were on their own and responsible. If they were frightened, they had to experience those feelings. The cell phone buffers this moment" (2011: 173).

It is clear that cell phones and other technology have changed the way parents monitor and communicate with their children. What remains to be seen is what effect this will have on individual personalities and character development.

As we see in Chapter 16, the formal system of education is conservative; it transmits the attitudes, values, and training necessary for the maintenance of society. Thus, schools are preoccupied with order and control. This emphasis on order teaches the norms and prepares youth for the organizational life they are expected to experience as adults. Unlike the family, in which the child is part of a loving relationship, the school is impersonal. The rules are to be obeyed. Activities are regimented rather than spontaneous. Thus, the child learns how to function in the larger society by learning the formal prescriptions of society and by learning that to get along one must go along.

Peers. While the family may be the primary agent of socialization, a child's peer group becomes increasingly important as a transmitter of social norms and values.

> For many children and adolescents, peers are a nearly daily source of many forms of experience. Children find in their peers opportunities for companionship, help, amusement, intimacy, novelty, instruction, and alas, challenge, conflict, victimization, and rejection. Children who spend 7 or 8 hours each weekday in the peer-rich environment of day care or a school probably spend more time with their peers than with their parents except on weekends. And when students are at home at night, they often, maybe too often according to some parents, stay in touch with their friends via a range of terrestrial and wireless communication systems. (Bukowski et al., 2007:355–356)

Through a system of observation and constant feedback from peers, children learn ideas about in-groups and out-groups, cultural norms, and gender-appropriate behavior. Research has suggested that children, through same-sex play, develop gender-specific ways of relating to each other (Ladd, 2007). In addition, those children who veer away from the culturally prescribed expectations regarding gender find that their peers act as "gender police" to reel them back in. Such was the experience of Daniel Farr, who describes how peers treated his interests in nonmasculine activities such as a crochet project that he took to school.

> I was proud of that little project, so I took it to school for show-and-tell. This led to another magnified moment, in which I learned one of the harshest lessons of my gender socialization. My classmates picked on me endlessly. I was beginning to see that there were certain hobbies and activities that I might be interested in and had talent in doing, but which could never be shared with the kids at school. (Farr, 2007:140)

According to Ladd (2007), research has shown that negative experiences with peers can lead to a number of psychological problems such as anxiety and depression, as well as behavioral problems in youth. On the other hand, positive experiences with peers can boost a child's self-esteem and lead to a variety of positive outcomes. These kinds of negative and positive peer interactions are becoming more prevalent through faceless communication on social networking sites like MySpace, Twitter, and Facebook, and through cell phone texting. According to a 2010 Nielsen report, teenagers are in constant communication through texting. Teenagers between the ages of thirteen and seventeen send and receive an average of 3,339 texts per month (Nielsen, 2010). Clearly peers play a very important role in the socialization process.

The Media. The mass media, consisting of newspapers, magazines, movies, radio, the Internet, and television, also play a vital role in the socialization process.

> Given the sheer amount of time from infancy to adolescence that youth devote to media consumption, given the lack of parental awareness and control over that media exposure, and given the reduction in time that some children might spend on other socializing activities, one has to be concerned with the role of the mass media in socializing children. The very act of engaging with the mass media either alone or with peers provides learning opportunities that socialize children, and what children observe through the mass media's window on the world alters their beliefs, attitudes, and behaviors. (Dubow et al., 2007:408)

Critics point to the sexual and violent nature of movies, television, and music as a source of society's problems. What effect do the media have on youth? In their review of relevant research, Dubow et al. (2007) point to three possible long-term effects of the media: (1) Repeated media exposure can cause observational learning. "Through repeated observation of real-life models and models portrayed in the media, as well as by reflecting on the consequences of their own behaviors in social situations, children develop normative beliefs about what social behaviors are appropriate" (411). In essence, long-term exposure to the ideas promoted in the media can affect a child's beliefs and behaviors. (2) Children become increasingly desensitized to the violent and sexual images they see in the media. (3) The persuasive content of the media becomes incorporated into the child's consciousness without awareness. Subtle messages about race, ethnicity, gender, social class, and sexual orientation are promoted and then absorbed at a subconscious level.

The media, whatever the source, tend to present a similar message. This is because fewer and fewer corporations control the media. Consider the following:

- According to Freepress.net, six major corporations dominate the U.S. media landscape and control what we see, hear, and read. They are General Electric, TimeWarner, News Corp., Walt Disney, CBS, and Viacom (2009).
- Until the 1980s, one company could legally own no more than seven AM and seven FM radio stations. Today, Clear Channel Communications owns more than a thousand radio stations (Freepress.net, 2009). Critics of Clear Channel argue that the company uses its considerable power to squeeze recording companies and artists and contributes to the growing blandness of broadcast music (Krugman, 2003). In addition, Clear Channel has been accused of political bias in that many of the stations they own have participated in pro-war rallies, including the banning of music by country artists the Dixie Chicks after they criticized President George W. Bush.
- About 80 percent of the daily newspaper circulation in the United States belongs to a few giant chains (Gannett, Knight-Ridder, New York Times, Washington Post, and the Tribune Company).
- In 2011, the Federal Communications Commission approved the megamerger of Comcast and NBC, which means that one company will account for 20 percent of all network and cable television viewing hours (Saldana, 2011).

In 2010 Activision launched the popular video game Call of Duty: Black Ops, which surpassed $1 billion in sales in just 42 days after it became available. Like other popular games, killing or wounding an opponent is necessary to advance to the next level of the game. Some researchers argue that this encourages violence and aggression among youth.

This increasing concentration of the media in the hands of a few has several important consequences. First, it results in an ideological monopoly, that is, newspapers, magazines, television, and radio offer little variety in perspective and editorial policy, ranging from centrist to moderately conservative. There is an unquestioned acceptance of the foundations of society. Attorney and journalist Dave Saldana writes:

> When one company, motivated solely by profit, can choose what news to cover and how to cover it, you may not be getting the full story. When it can exclude competing ideas or perspectives, whether for political or economic reasons, you may be denied a full hearing on the issues. And that's bad for democracy. (2011:1)

A second consequence of the media consolidation is that, since the media conglomerates are profit-seeking organizations, they emphasize entertainment over news. This often results in broadcast dissemination that does not distinguish well between the trivial and the momentous, and thus the daily lives of Angelina Jolie and Brad Pitt become prime-time entertainment. The result, as one observer puts it, is that the media cartel "keeps us fully entertained and permanently half-informed" (Miller, 2002:18). Third, and related to the profit emphasis: "When a media outlet is a cog in a wheel that must help maximize corporate profits, not part of an information-gathering entity, then containing costs, not providing information, is a priority" (Malveaux, 2002:34). And, fourth, the decision makers in these conglomerates are located in the large urban centers of the United States and Europe. Thus, the focus is away from local issues and toward what is believed of interest to the widest audience nationwide.

The messages the public receives are consistent: We are bombarded with materialism and consumerism; with what it takes to be a success; with sex, violence, and the value of law and order. In short, the media have tremendous power to influence us all.

Socialization in a Changing Social Landscape

Each society has its own unique way of perceiving, interpreting, and evaluating reality. Members of society internalize this common culture through the process of socialization—thus, people are a product of their culture. It follows, then, that the members of a society will be similar in many fundamental respects (this is called a **modal personality** type). Although there are individual exceptions and subcultural variations, we can say that Americans differ fundamentally from Mexicans, Germans, Malaysians, the French, and others.

The individual growing up in the United States, with its set of values, tends to be individualistic, competitive, materialistic, and oriented toward work, progress, and the future. Even though this characterization is generally correct, there are some problems with the assumption that socialization into a culture is all-powerful. First, the power of socialization can vary by the type of society. Small, **homogeneous** societies like those of some Native American tribes provide the individual member of society with a consistent message, whereas in a large, **heterogeneous** society like the United States, individuals are confronted with a number of contradictory themes and expectations. Recall from Chapter 1 that the sociological perspective views individuals as both the puppet and the puppeteer of society. Thus, the socialization process is adaptive as times and conditions change. Let's examine some of the trends that influence the socialization process and result in a heterogeneous society.

Changing Family Forms

We have said that the family is the ultimate societal agency for socialization. Families teach their child the language, etiquette, and skills that enable the child to find her or his niche in society. But families differ in a variety of important ways (for example, in religion, political views, optimism, and affluence). The family may have little influence on the child if the

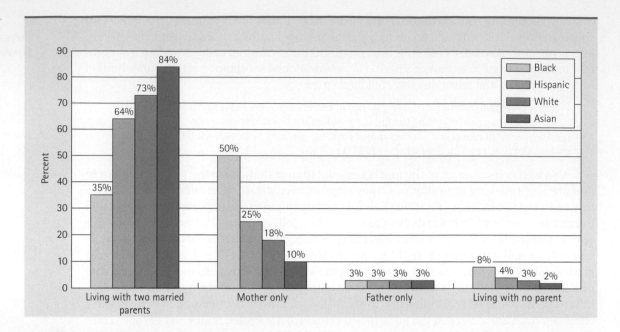

FIGURE 5.1

Living Arrangements of Children by Race/Ethnicity 2009

Source: Child Trends, 2010. http://www.childtrendsdatabank.org/alphalist?q=node/334

parents disagree on politics, religion, and/or values. Or, if they are consistent, the parents' views may be neutralized by contrary values held by friends. This neutralization process is facilitated by the decreasing amount of time that parents spend with their children compared to the time spent in previous generations. For example, since 1970, the percentage of children living in mother-only families has increased from 11 percent to 23 percent in 2009 (Child Trends, 2010). This percentage is also complicated by race, with Black children being significantly less likely to live with two married parents (see Figure 5.1). With changing family forms and the increasing need for dual incomes, parents spend less and less time raising and influencing their children while their youngsters are influenced more and more not only by their peers but also by day care centers, schools, the Internet, and television.

In sum, although children raised in the United States are affected by a common culture, family forms, experiences, and emphases can vary enough to result in behavioral and attitudinal differences. That children and families can be fundamentally different is seen in the occasional value conflicts between parents and school authorities on sex education, the use of certain literature, and on rules and the proper way to enforce those rules. But the schools themselves also vary, resulting in different products by type of school.

Trends in Schooling

U.S. schools, like schools in all societies, are conservative. But there are differences that have a substantial impact on students. According to the National Center for Education Statistics, U.S. Department of Education (2010), in 2007, 1.5 million U.S. children were home-schooled (up from 850,000 in 1999). In 2007–2008, charter schools saw 1.3 million children in attendance, and 5.9 million children attended a private elementary or secondary school, the majority of which were church related. These numbers represent significant increases over previous years, and the type of education received varies tremendously. In some schools, for example, the curriculum, schedule, and philosophy are very rigid. Children sit in straight rows, may talk only with permission, wear the prescribed clothing, and accept without question the authority of the teacher. In other schools, however, the curriculum, schedules, teachers, and rules are flexible. The products of these two types of schools are likely to differ in much the same way as do the children of autocratic or permissive homes.

Changing Racial Landscape

Each of us is located within society, not only geographically, but also socially. Depending on our wealth, occupation, education, ethnic or racial heritage, gender, and family background, we see ourselves (and other people see us) as being superior to some people and inferior to others. The United States is shifting from a predominantly Anglo-White society to a society with three large racial/ethnic minorities, each of them growing in size while the proportion of Whites declines (the following is taken from Eitzen, Baca Zinn, and Smith, 2011). Currently, about one third of the people in the United States are African American, Latino, Asian, or Native American, and four states have non-White majorities (California, Texas, New Mexico, and Hawaii). Furthermore, racial minorities are increasing faster than the majority population, with immigration now accounting for a large share of the nation's population growth. Our varying position in this racial/ethnic hierarchy affects our attitudes and perceptions. In particular, people who are highly placed tend to support the status quo, whereas those who are less advantaged are likely to be more antagonistic to the way things are and to desire changes beneficial to them. As the United States changes demographically, the chances of a modal personality type decreases in the face of heterogeneity.

Changing Generation Cohorts

An **age cohort** is a category of people of the same age. The life experiences of people typically vary depending on when they were born. In other words, people of the same age tend in a general way to be alike in behavior and attitudes, because they were influenced by the same major events such as the Great Depression, World War II, or the antiwar protests of the 1960s. Similarly, the members of age cohorts such as the **baby boomers** (born 1946–1964), the **post–baby boomers ("Generation X" born 1965–1976**), and the "**Millennial Generation**" (born 1977–1995, a generation larger than the baby boom generation) differ from each other because of differing opportunities, changing economic realities, and the circumstances of their parents. Generation Xers are often seen as individualistic, resistant to authority, and skeptical about politics. They are the first generation of "latch-key" children, whose mothers were more likely to work outside the home. The Millennial Generation is often characterized as affluent, protected, educated, and technologically savvy. They have also been called the "Look at Me" or "**Documentation Generation**." With reality television, films, and books, "they've been documented like no group before them, most especially by themselves: on their blogs, their MySpace, Facebook and Flickr pages, and on YouTube" (Yabroff, 2008:67). Researchers are just beginning to study the consequences that this type of documentation may have on this generation. In a world where private becomes public, how will this affect personal relationships?

This generation has grown up with highly structured lives and does not know a life without seatbelts, bike helmets, computer technology, and cable television. Overall, differences between the generation cohorts reflect larger societal changes and can cause conflict, disagreement, and misunderstanding between children and their parents and grandparents.

Changing Images in the Media

We have seen that youngsters may experience pulls in opposite directions from family, church, and school. Other sources of contradictory attractions are peer groups and the media. Parents may insist, for instance, that their children not fight. Yet, the children's peers might demand such behavior. Moreover, children are bombarded by violence (much of which is considered appropriate) in the movies, on television, and in video games. In their content analysis of programming from 1998 to 2002, the Parents Television Council (2008) found that television violence increased 134.4 percent in the 9:00 P.M. programming hour. Moreover, they argue that television violence has become steadily more graphic with the increasing use of guns and other weapons and with more depictions of blood and on-screen killings.

In the documentary *Tough Guise: Violence, Media, and the Crisis in Masculinity* (Jhally, 1999), narrator Jackson Katz argues that the increase in violence in action movies is apparent in that not only has the size of the gun or weapon used gotten bigger over time, but also the bodies of male action heroes have gotten much larger, eventually being seen as weapons themselves.

There has also been an increase in female action heroes who use violence and wield physical power. Films like *Girlfight*, *Lara Croft*, *Kill Bill*, and *Crouching Tiger, Hidden Dragon* all feature strong women who display a new type of feminine hero.

How are children to behave in everyday life, faced with opposing and powerful socialization messages? In addition to violence, teenagers are also bombarded with sexual images and themes in the media, but at the same time they are not given consistent sex education and healthy messages about sexual behavior. In many states they receive abstinence-only education, yet are assaulted by images of teenagers engaging in sexual activity on television and in movies. How are they to behave? Some will follow their parents' dictates or their religion; others will succumb to other pressures.

The images of male and female action heroes have significantly changed over time.

Gender roles provide another example of varying expectations depending on the individual, audience, and community. Traditional masculine and feminine roles are in flux. What precisely is expected of a man and woman as they enter a building? Does the man open the door for the woman? This was appropriate behavior in the past and it may be now, but one is never sure, for some women find such behavior offensive. What are the expectations of a newly married husband and wife? How will they divide the household chores? Who is to be the breadwinner? If a couple divorces, who will take the children? Twenty years ago, or even five years ago, the answers to these questions were much more certain and gender role socialization was much more uniform. Today, lesbians, gays, bisexuals, transgenders, inter-sexuals, and others are challenging the traditional gender boundaries and notions of gender role socialization.

To conclude, the emphasis of this chapter is on how the individual is shaped by powerful social forces, but we must remember that people are not utterly predictable. Moreover, human beings are actively involved in shaping the social landscape. In sum, the person is, as Kenneth Westhues (1982) says, "a two-sided being, at once created and creating, predictable and surprising" (viii).

Socialization from the Order and Conflict Perspectives

Both order and conflict theorists acknowledge the power of the socialization process. They differ, however, in their interpretation of this universal process. The order theorists view this process as necessary to promote stability and law-abiding citizens. Children must be social-ized into the values, morals, and expectations of society in order to keep balance and har-mony. Conflict theorists, on the other hand, view the process as one in which people are led to accept the customs, laws, and values of society uncritically and therefore become willing participants in a society that may be in need of change. In other words, the members of so-ciety are taught to accept the way things are, even though the social order benefits some people and disadvantages others. This process is so powerful that most of the powerless and disadvantaged in our society do not rebel because they actually believe in the system that systematically keeps them down. What is undeniable to both order and conflict theorists is that the socialization process is inevitable, powerful, and necessary.

CHAPTER REVIEW

1. Socialization is the process of learning the val-ues, norms, and expectations of a society. Children must learn the culture of the society in which they are born. So-cialization, however, is a lifelong process and occurs in all social groups.

2. Infants become human only through learning the culture they live in.

3. The socialization of youth requires social interaction.

4. Another essential to socialization is language, which has profound effects on how individuals think and perceive the world.

5. The personality emerges as a social product. We develop a sense of self only through interaction with other people.

6. One theory of how personality develops is Cool-ey's "looking-glass self." Through interaction, children define themselves according to how they interpret how other people think of them.

7. Mead's theory of self-development involves several stages. Through interaction with their parents, infants are able to distinguish between themselves and other people. By age two, they are able to react to them-selves as others react to them. In the play stage (from ages

four to seven), children pretend to be in a variety of adult roles (taking the role of the other). In the game stage (about age eight), children play at games with rigid rules. They begin to understand the structure of the entire game with the expectations for everyone involved. This understanding of the entire situation is called the "generalized other."

8. According to Bandura's social cognitive theory, children observe the behavior of others and the feedback (positive and/or negative) for such behavior. This then serves as a guide for their actions as they model after others.

9. According to Freud's theory, socialization is the process by which society controls the id (the biological needs for pleasure). Through this process, children develop egos (the control of the id by finding appropriate ways to satisfy biological urges). A superego also emerges, which is the internalization of the morals of the parents, further channeling behavior in socially acceptable ways.

10. Through interaction, children internalize the norms and values of society. Four major agents of socialization are the family, the schools, peers, and the media.

11. The key to the socialization process is the internalization of society's values and norms so that children will act according to parental expectations, even when no one is watching.

12. Six major corporations control television, radio, movies, books, magazines, and the Internet in the United States. This concentration of the media in the hands of a few results in: (a) an ideological monopoly that supports the status quo; (b) an emphasis on entertainment over news; (c) an emphasis on profit-making over information gathering; and (d) news of local interest being sacrificed for what the media moguls consider of interest to the widest audience nationwide.

13. The members of a society tend to be alike in fundamental ways (modal personality type). The smaller and more homogeneous the society, the more alike the members of that society will be.

14. Despite the tendency for the members to be alike, people, especially in large, heterogeneous societies, are not all similar. Different societal trends influence the socialization process and contribute to the heterogeneity of society. Some of those trends are changing family forms, trends in U.S. schooling, the changing racial/ethnic landscape, changing generation cohorts, changing media images, and changing gender role expectations.

15. Both order and conflict theorists acknowledge the power of the socialization process, but differ in their interpretation of it. Order theorists view socialization as necessary to promote stability and the development of law-abiding citizens. Conflict theorists, in contrast, view the process as one in which people are led to accept the customs, laws, and values of society uncritically. This process is so powerful that disadvantaged people may accept the system that disadvantages them (false consciousness).

KEY TERMS

Socialization
Feral children
Self
Looking-glass self
Significant others
Generalized other
Id

Ego
Superego
Internalization
Modal personality
Homogeneous
Heterogeneous
Age cohort

Baby boomers
Post–baby boomers
   ("Generation X" born 1965–1976)
Millennial generation
Documentation generation

STUDY QUESTIONS

1. How much of the personality is a social product versus a product of biology?
2. What is meant by the assertion that "human beings are social animals"?

3. How do order and conflict theorists differ in their evaluation and interpretation of the socialization process?
4. The forces that socialize us are powerful, but they are not totally deterministic. Why not?

http://media.pfeiffer.edu/lridener/courses/LKGLSSLF.HTML
This site is an excerpt from Charles Cooley's Human Nature and the Social Order, which talks about the looking-glass self.

http://www.honestreporting.com/
Honest Reporting is a media watch group that advocates honesty in news reporting and exposes dishonesty. The site has links to other media watch groups.

http://www.mediachannel.org
MediaChannel is concerned with the political, cultural, and social impacts of the media, large and small. MediaChannel exists to provide information and diverse perspectives and inspire debate, collaboration, action, and citizen engagement.

http://www.cyfc.umn.edu/
The Children, Youth, and Family Consortium is part of the University of Minnesota. It does studies on children, including those that have implications for socialization.

http://www.feralchildren.org/
This site documents the cases of feral children throughout history.

CHAPTER 6

Social Control

At 9:34 P.M. on July 13, 1977, the electricity went out in New York City and in some areas was not restored for twenty-five hours. Under the cover of darkness, many areas of the city were pillaged. More than 2,000 stores were wrecked or looted, over 1,000 fires were set, with property losses estimated at more than $1 billion. The plunderers were of all ages. They stole appliances, jewelry, shoes, groceries, clothes, furniture, liquor, and automobiles (fifty new Pontiacs from one dealer). The atmosphere was a mixture of revenge, greed, and festival. Observers characterized the looting binge as a carnival atmosphere in which the actors had no concept of morality. It was as if they were immune from the law and from guilt. All of society's constraints were removed, resulting in anarchy. When the lights went out, the social controls on behavior left as well for many people.

Social control is a central fact of social organization (Eitzen, 2000b). As Ray Cuzzort (1989) asserts: "A sociocultural system cannot rely on random individual responses to create the structure and the cohesiveness required of organized effort. A society cannot, in other words, rely on people simply 'doing their thing.' A society must, in effect, generate ways that ensure that what gets done is 'society's thing'" (179). Control, then, is essential for social order. Without it, social organizations—whether they are societies, communities, churches, prisons, hospitals, schools, corporations, athletic teams, or families—would be chaotic, fragmented, uncoordinated, unpredictable, and fragile.

All social groups have mechanisms to ensure conformity—mechanisms of **social control**. The socialization process is one of these ways by which individuals internalize the norms and values of the group. People are taught what is proper, moral, and appropriate. This process is generally so powerful that individuals conform, not out of fear of punishment, but because they want to. In other words, group demands that are out there become demands that are inside us. But socialization is never perfect—we are all not robots. As we will see in Chapter 7, people sometimes deviate from their group's expectations. To cope with this, social groups exert external control over their members. These two types of controls are the subject of this chapter.

The focus of this chapter is on social control at the societal level. The dominant modes of socialization vary by type of society. Small, homogeneous societies, for example, are dominated by tradition, whereas large, modern societies are less affected by the force of tradition. Traditional societies tend to have an overriding consensus on societal values; therefore, the family, religion, and community convey to each individual member a consistent message about which behaviors are appropriate and which ones are not. Although formal punishment of norm violators does occur in traditional societies, informal controls are usually quite effective and more typical.

In a complex society such as the United States, social control is more difficult to attain because of the existence of different groups with values that often compete. Therefore, social control tends to be more formal and appears more repressive (because it is more overt) than that found in traditional societies. It occurs in many forms and disguises. Social control is accomplished in the home and school and through various other institutions. It is attained through the overt and covert activities of political agencies, psychotherapists, and even genetic engineers. Efforts to manipulate the masses through various techniques of persuasion also keep deviance in check.

The remainder of this chapter is devoted to an extensive examination of the various agents of social control in U.S. society. These agents are divided into two types, by the means used to achieve social control: ideological control (belief systems, one of Peter Berger's eight sources of social control, listed in the next section) and direct intervention (the other seven sources). The former aims at control through manipulation of ideas and perceptions; the latter controls the actual behavior of individuals.

Agents of Ideological Social Control

All social groups have mechanisms to ensure conformity—mechanisms of social control. Peter Berger (1963:68–78) has identified eight sources of social control: (1) force, the use of violence or threats of violence; (2) economic rewards or punishments, the promise or denial of material rewards; (3) ridicule and gossip, fear of being belittled for outside group expectations; (4) ostracism, the threat or actual removal from the group; (5) fraud and deception, actions to manipulate (trick) others to conform; (6) belief systems, the use of ideology to induce individuals to conform; (7) the sphere of intimates, pressures from close friends, peers, and relatives to conform; and (8) the contract, actions controlled by the stipulations of a formal agreement.

Ideological social control (belief systems) is the attempt to manipulate the consciousness of citizens so that they accept the ruling ideology and refuse to be moved by competing ideologies. Other goals are to persuade the members of society to comply willingly with the law and to accept without question the existing distribution of societal power and rewards. These goals are accomplished in at least three ways. First, ideological social control is accomplished through the socialization of youth. Young people, for example, are taught the values of individualism, competition, patriotism, and respect for authority at home, in school, in scouting organizations, in sports, and through the media. The socialization process could be referred to as cultural control, because the individual is given authoritative definitions of what should and should not be done, which make it appear as if there were no choice (Stivers, 1975). Second, ideological conformity occurs by frontal attacks on competing ideologies by politicians, pastors, teachers, and other people in authority. Finally, there are propaganda efforts by political authorities to convince the public of which actions are moral, who the enemies are, and why certain courses of governmental action are required.

Ideological social control is more effective than overt social control measures because individuals impose controls upon themselves (Collins, 1992:63–85). Through the socialization process we learn not only the rules of a social organization but also the supporting ideology. The norms are internalized in this process. To the degree that this process works, individuals are not forced to conform; *they want to conform*. Let us examine this process by describing the agents of social control that are especially important in accomplishing the goal of ideological conformity.

Family

The primary responsibility of parents is to teach their children the attitudes, values, and behavior considered appropriate by the parents (and society). Parents universally want their children to succeed. Success is measured in terms of not only monetary achievement but also whether the child fits in society. Fitting in requires that the child learns to behave and think in the ways that are deemed proper. Although, as noted in Chapter 5, there is a wide latitude in the actual mode of socialization in the family, most children do behave in acceptable ways.

Education

The formal system of education is an important societal agent for conformity. The school insists that the behavioral standards of the community be maintained in speech, dress, and demeanor. More than this, the schools indoctrinate their pupils in the correct attitudes about work, respect for authority, and patriotism. The textbooks used in schools have typically not provided an accurate account of history, for example, but rather an account that is biased in the direction the authorities wish to perpetuate (Loewen, 1995). The treatment given to minorities in these texts is one indicator of the bias. Another indicator is the contrast between descriptions of the behavior of the United States and the behavior of its enemies in wars (see FitzGerald, 1979).

One critic of the schools is concerned with the problem of conformity, which taken to the extreme results in blind obedience to such malevolent authority figures as Adolf Hitler, Charles Manson, Osama bin Laden, and Saddam Hussein. Rather than turning out conformists, the schools should be turning out individuals with the ability to recognize false prophets and the courage to disobey them (McCarthy, 1979:34).

Religion

Religious groups are actively involved with social control. Most noticeably, they typically have guidelines for the behavior of members and punishments for disobedience. As an extreme example, see the Diversity panel titled "The Amish and Social Control."

Established religion in the United States tends to reinforce the status quo. Few clergy and their parishioners work actively to change the political and economic system. Instead, they preach sermons extolling the virtues of "the American way of life" and "giving unto Caesar the things which are Caesar's." Directly or indirectly, there has been a strong tendency for religious groups throughout U.S. history to accept existing government policies, whether they are slavery, war, or the conquest of Native Americans.

Religious groups also preserve the status quo by teaching that people should accept an imperfect society (poverty, racism, and war) because they are born sinners. In this way, religion, as Marx suggested, is an opiate of the masses because it persuades them to accept an unjust system rather than work to change it. The downtrodden are advised to accept their lot because they will be rewarded in the next life. Thus, they have no need to change the system from below. As Albert Szymanski (1978) argues:

> The doctrine of the omnipotence of God and total submission to His will pervades the general world views of religious people, and hence is sublimated as submission to political rulers and the upper class. Religion provides a consolation for the suffering of people on earth and a deflection of one's hopes into the future. Combined with its advocacy of the earthly status quo, religion thus typically serves as a powerful legitimatizing force for upper-class rule. Further, most religions, especially the religions of the working class and the poor—Baptism, Methodism, the Messianic sects, and Catholicism—in their sermons typically condemn radical political movements and preach instead either political abstention or submission to government authority. (253)

An important function of schools is to promote idealogical conformity.

The Amish and Social Control

The Amish are a religious sect found mainly in Pennsylvania, Indiana, and Kansas. They are farmers who resist modern technology. They forbid the use of motorcycles, automobiles, and electricity. They wear simple clothes of the nineteenth century. They believe that they are only temporary visitors on earth, and hence remain aloof from it. This explains why they insist on being different. Most important, the Amish insist on conformity within their community.

The Amish descend from Jacob Amman, a Mennonite preacher in Switzerland. The Mennonites and other Anabaptists of that day differed from mainstream Protestants because they believed in the separation of church and state, adult baptism, and refusal to bear arms and take oaths. Amman and his followers split away from the Mennonites in 1700 over an issue of church discipline—the Meidung. Amman felt that the Mennonites were too lax in their discipline of deviants and that the Meidung must be enforced in severe cases. The Meidung is one of the most potent of all social control mechanisms. The following is a description by William M. Kephart and William W. Zellner (1990):

> The ultimate sanction is imposition of the Meidung, also known as the "shunning" or "ban," but because of its severity, it is used only as a last resort. The followers of Jacob Amman have a strong religious orientation and a finely honed conscience—and the Amish community relies on this fact. Actions such as gossip, reprimand, and the employment of confession are usually sufficient to bring about conformity. The Meidung would be imposed only if a member were to leave the church, or marry an outsider, or break a major rule (such as buying an auto) without full repentance.
>
> Although the Meidung is imposed by the bishop, he will not act without the near unanimous vote of the congregation. Generally speaking, however, the ban is total. No one in the district is permitted to associate with the errant party, including members of his or her own family. Even normal marital relations are forbidden. Should any member of the community ignore the Meidung, that person would also be placed under the ban. In fact, the Meidung is honored by all Amish districts, including those that are not in full fellowship with the district in question. There is no doubt that the ban is a mighty weapon that Jacob Amman intended it to be.
>
> On the other hand, the ban is not irrevocable. If the shunned member admits the error of his or her ways—and asks forgiveness of the congregation—the Meidung will be lifted and the transgressor readmitted to the fold. No matter how serious the offense, the Amish never look upon someone under the ban as an enemy, but only as one who has erred. And while they are firm in their enforcement of the Meidung, the congregation will pray for the errant member to rectify her or his mistake.
>
> Although imposition of the ban is infrequent, it is far from rare. Males are involved much more often than females, the younger more frequently than the old. The Meidung would probably be imposed on young males more often were it not for the fact that baptism does not take place until the late teens. Prior to this time, young males are expected to be—and often are—somewhat on the wild side, and allowances are made for this fact.
>
> Baptism changes things, however, for this is the rite whereby the young person officially joins the church and makes the pledge of obedience. Once the pledge is made, the limits of tolerance are substantially reduced. More than one Amish youth has been subjected to the Meidung for behavior that, prior to his baptism, had been tolerated.

Source: From *Extraordinary Groups: An Examination of Unconventional Life-Styles,* 4th ed., by William Kephart and William Zellner, p. 25. © 1990 by St. Martin's Press. Used with permission of W. H. Freeman and Company/Worth Publishers.

Sport

School and professional sports work to reinforce conforming attitudes and behaviors in the populace in several ways (Eitzen, 2000b; 2009; Sage and Eitzen, 2012). First, there is the strong relationship between sport and nationalism. Success in international sports competition tends to trigger pride among that nation's citizens. The Olympic Games and other international games tend to promote an us-versus-them feeling among athletes, coaches, politicians, the press, and fans. It can be argued, then, that the Olympic Games are a political contest, a symbolic world war in which nations win or lose. Because this interpretation is commonly held, citizens of the nations involved unite behind their flag and their athletes.

The integral interrelationship of sport and nationalism is easily seen in the blatantly militaristic pageantry that surrounds sports contests. The playing of the national anthem, the presentation of the colors, the jet aircraft flyovers, and the band forming a flag or a liberty bell are all political acts supportive of the existing political system.

For whatever reason, sport competition and nationalism are closely intertwined. When U.S. athletes compete against athletes of another country, national unity is the result (for both sides, unless one's athletes do poorly). Citizens take pride in their representatives' accomplishments, viewing them as collective achievements. This identification with athletes and their cause of winning for the nation's glory tends to unite a nation's citizens regardless of social class, race, and regional differences. Thus, sport can be used by political leaders whose nations have problems with divisiveness.

As noted in Chapter 3, sport can serve as an opiate of the masses in several ways. Virtually all homes have television sets, making it possible for almost everyone to participate vicariously in and identify with local and national sports teams. Because of this, the minds and energies of the viewers are deflected away from the hunger and misery that are disproportionately the lot of the lower classes in U.S. society. The status quo is thereby preserved.

Sport also acts as an opiate by perpetuating the belief that people from the lowest classes can achieve upward mobility through success in sports. Clearly this is a myth; for every major leaguer who has come up from poverty, tens of thousands of poor people have not become professional athletes. The point, however, is that most people in the United States believe that sport is a mobility escalator and that it is merely a reflection of the opportunity structure of the society in general. Again, poor youth who might otherwise invest their energies in changing the system work instead on a jump shot. The potential for revolution is thus impeded by sport.

Another way that sport serves to control people ideologically is by reinforcing U.S. values among the participants. Sport is a vehicle by which the values of success in competition, hard work, perseverance, discipline, and order are transmitted. This is the explicit reason given for the existence of Little League programs for youngsters and the tremendous emphasis on sports in U.S. schools. Coaches commonly place signs in locker rooms to inspire certain traits in their athletes. Some examples include the following (Snyder, 1972):

- "The will to win is the will to work."
- "By failing to prepare yourself you are preparing to fail."
- "Winners never quit and quitters never win."
- "United we stand, divided we fall."

One explicit goal of sports is to build character. The assumption is that participation in sports from the Little Leagues through the Big Leagues (professional ranks) provides athletes with American values: achievement in competitive situations through hard work, materialism, progress, and respect for authority. As David Matza (1964b) puts it: "The substance of athletics contains within itself—in its rules, procedures, training, and sentiments—a paradigm of adult expectations regarding youth" (207). Schools want individuals to follow rules, to be disciplined, to work hard, and to fit in; sports accomplish these goals.

Not only do schools insist that athletes behave a certain way during practice and games, but they also strictly monitor the behavior of the athletes in other situations. The athletes must conform to the school's norms in dress, speech, demeanor, and grades if they want to continue to participate. In this way, school administrators use athletes as models of decorum. If other people in the school and community admire athletes, then athletes serve to preserve the community and school norms.

Media

The movies, television, newspapers, and magazines also serve to reinforce the system. There is clearly a conservative bias among the various corporations involved because their financial success depends on whether the public will buy their product and whether advertisers will use their vehicles. As Michael Parenti (1986) argues:

> [A]long with products, the corporations sell themselves. By the 1970s, for the first time since the Great Depression, the legitimacy of big business was being called into question by large sectors of the public. Enduring inflation, unemployment, and a decline in real wages, the American people became increasingly skeptical about the blessings of the corporate economy. In response, corporations intensified their efforts at the kind of "advocacy advertising," designed to sell the entire capitalist system rather than just one of its products....
> *Today, one-third of all corporate advertising is directed at influencing the public on political and ideological issues as opposed to pushing consumer goods.* (That portion is tax deductible as a "business expense," like all other advertising costs.) Led by the oil, chemical, and steel companies, big business fills the airwaves and printed media with celebrations of the "free market," and warnings of the baneful effects of government regulation. (67)

That the media reinforce the values and norms of society is seen in newspaper editorials that extol certain people and events while decrying others and in stories under the caption, "It Could Only Have Happened in America." Soap operas also accomplish this because they are stories involving moral dilemmas, with virtue winning out. Television, in particular, has had a significant impact on the values of people in the United States. The average two- to eleven-year-old child watches television twenty-five hours a week. What are the consistent messages that television emits?

Michael Parenti's book *Make-Believe Media: The Politics of Entertainment* (1992) demonstrates that films and television programs promote images and ideologies that support imperialism, capitalism, racism, sexism, militarism, authoritarian violence, vigilantism, and anti-working-class attitudes. More specifically, he argues that media dramas teach us the following:

- Individual effort is preferable to collective action.
- Free enterprise is the best economic system in the world.
- Private monetary gain is a central and worthy objective of life.
- Affluent professionals are more interesting than blue-collar or ordinary service workers.
- All U.S citizens are equal, but some (the underprivileged) must prove themselves worthy of equality.
- Women and ethnic minorities are not really as capable, effective, or interesting as White males.
- The police and everyone else should be given a freer hand in combating the large criminal element in the United States, using generous applications of force and violence without too much attention to constitutional rights.
- The ills of society are caused by individual malefactors and not by anything in the socio-economic system.
- There are some unworthy people in our established institutions, but they usually are dealt with and eventually are deprived of their positions of responsibility.
- U.S. military force is directed only toward laudable goals, although individuals in the military may sometimes abuse their power.
- Western industrial and military might, especially that of the United States, has been a civilizing force for the benefit of "backward" peoples throughout the Third World.
- The United States and the entire West have long been threatened from abroad by foreign aggressors, such as Russians, communist terrorists, and swarthy hordes of savages, and at home by un-American subversives and conspirators. These threats can be eradicated by vigilant counterintelligence and by sufficient doses of force and violence (Parenti, 1992:2–3).

In short, the media shape how we evaluate ourselves and other people. Just as important, they affect directly the way viewers or readers perceive and interpret events. The media, therefore, have tremendous power to influence us to accept or question the system. Although the media do investigative reporting and occasionally question the system, the overall impact of the media is supportive of it.

Government

Governmental leaders devote a great deal of energy toward ideological social control. One governmental effort is to convince the public that capitalism is good and socialism is bad. That the government (and schools) have been successful is seen in the powerful argument by noted theologian Harvey Cox that in the United States the market is believed to have the same characteristics as God—omnipotent (all-powerful), omniscient (all-knowing), and omnipresent (existing everywhere) (Cox, 1999).

Government ideological control occurs in political speeches, books, and legislation. Sometimes state legislatures have tried to control the ideological content in schools by requiring certain course content (patriotism, pro-capitalism, anticommunism). Another example of ideological control is seen in government agencies such as the Defense Department and the Departments of Agriculture, Commerce, and Education. Each department maintains active public relations programs that spend millions of dollars to convince the public of their views.

The public can also be manipulated by being convinced that their security is threatened by an enemy. The efforts by President George W. Bush and the members of his cabinet following the terrorist attack on September 11, 2001, to convince the public that we must come together against the terrorist threat, that we must spend more to enhance our security, and to inform us who the enemies were (Osama bin Laden and his al-Qaeda network, Saddam Hussein of Iraq, and more obliquely, the threat by rogue nations such as Iran and North Korea) were prime examples of this manipulation.

Perhaps the most obvious way that government officials attempt to shape public opinion is through speeches, especially on television. The president can request free prime-time television to speak to the public. These efforts are typically intended to unite the people against an enemy (inflation, the national debt, the energy crisis, global warming, al-Qaeda, Iran).

We have described how the various agents of ideological social control operate. Perhaps the best evidence that they are successful is that few of the downtrodden in U.S. society question the legitimacy of the political and economic system. Karl Marx theorized that the have-nots in a capitalist society (the poor, the minority-group members, the workers) would eventually feel their common oppression and unite to overthrow the owners of capital. That this has not happened in the United States on a large scale is due, mainly, to the success of the various agents of ideological social control (Parenti, 1978).

Agents of Direct Social Control

Direct social control refers to attempts to punish or neutralize (render powerless) organizations or individuals who deviate from society's norms. The deviant targets here are essentially four: the poor, the mentally ill, criminals, and political dissidents. This section is devoted to three agents of social control whose efforts are directed at these targets—social welfare, science and medicine, and the government.

Social Welfare

Piven and Cloward (1993), in their classic study of public welfare, argue that public assistance programs serve a social control function in times of mass unemployment by defusing social unrest. When large numbers of people are suddenly barred from their traditional occupations, the legitimacy of the system itself may be questioned. Crime, riots, looting, and social movements bent on changing the existing social and economic arrangements become more widespread. Under this threat, relief programs are initiated or expanded by the government. Piven and Cloward show how during the Great Depression, for example, the government remained aloof from the needs of the unemployed until there was a great surge of political disorder. The function

"So, does anyone else feel that their needs aren't being met?"

of social welfare, then, is to defuse social unrest through direct intervention of the government. Added proof for Piven and Cloward's thesis is the contraction or even abolishment of public assistance programs when political stability is restored.[*]

The conditions of the Great Recession and beyond should provide an interesting test of Piven and Cloward's theory. Current trends indicate that the middle class is shrinking, that the gap between the haves and the have-nots is increasing (see Chapters 10, 11, and 13), and the 1996 welfare legislation has caused a drastic shrinkage in those receiving welfare, leaving many poor people poorer than before. Moreover, the fiscal crisis at the federal and state levels has brought about a reduction of social programs to help the poor and the recently unemployed. As long as these increasing numbers of the deprived are docile, government programs to alleviate their suffering will be meager; but should the outrage of the oppressed be manifested in urban riots (for example, the 1992 Los Angeles riots), acts of terrorism by the disaffected (Church burnings, abuse of minorities), or in social movements aimed at political change, then, if Piven and Cloward are correct, government welfare programs to aid the poor will become more generous.

Science and Medicine

Practitioners and theoreticians in science and medicine (physicians, psychotherapists, geneticists, electrical engineers, and public health officials) have devised a number of techniques for shaping and controlling the behavior of nonconformists. In the words of Michael Parenti (1988):

> In their never-ending campaign to contain the class struggle and control behavior unacceptable to the existing order, authorities have moved beyond clubs, bullets, and eavesdropping devices and are resorting to such things as electroshock, mind-destroying drugs, and psychosurgery. Since the established powers presume that the present social

---

[*]The second function of welfare mentioned by Piven and Cloward is more subtle (and fits more logically as an agent of ideological social control). Even in good times some people must live on welfare (the disabled). By having a category of people on welfare who live in wretched conditions and who are continually degraded, work is legitimized. Thus, the poor on welfare serve as an object lesson—keeping even those who work for low wages relatively satisfied with their lot. As Piven and Cloward (1971) conclude: "In sum, market values and market incentives are weakest at the bottom of the social order. To buttress weak market controls and ensure the availability of marginal labor, an outcast class—the dependent poor—is created by the relief system. This class, whose members are of no productive use, is not treated with indifference but with contempt. Its degradation at the hands of relief officials serves to celebrate the virtue of all work and deters actual or potential workers from seeking aid" (52).

system is virtuous, then those who are prone to violent or disruptive behavior, or who show themselves to be manifestly disturbed about the conditions under which they live, must be suffering from inner malfunctions that can best be treated by various mind controls. Not only are political and social deviants defined as insane, but sanity itself has a political definition. The sane person is the obedient one who lives in peace and goes to war on cue from his leaders, is not too much troubled by the inhumanities committed against people, is capable of fitting into one of the mindless job slots of a profit-oriented hierarchical organization, and does not challenge the established rules and conventional wisdom. Since authorities accept the present politico-economic system as a good one, then anything that increases its ability to control dissident persons is also seen as good. (150–151)

Psychologists and psychotherapists are clearly agents of social control. Their goal is to aid people who do not follow the expectations of society. In other words, they attempt to treat people considered abnormal in order to make them normal. By focusing on the individual and his or her adjustment, mental health practitioners validate, enforce, and reinforce the established ways of society. The implicit assumption is that the individual is at fault and needs to change, not that society is the root cause of mental suffering.

More generally, the labeling of mental illness works as a system of social control. As Scarpitti and Andersen (1992) argue,

[T]hose who are labeled mentally ill are often the outgroups of society. In fact, labeling groups or individuals as mentally ill can work to contain social and political protest, if those who are disturbed are institutionalized, treated with drug therapy, or otherwise incapacitated. The historic identification of homosexuality with mental illness is a case in point. As long as gay men and women were defined as "sick," then it was less likely that other people in society would challenge the heterosexual privilege characteristic of economic, social, and political institutions. (384)

In short, this application of the medical model to individuals exhibiting certain behaviors personalizes the problem and deflects attention away from the social sources for the behaviors. Another application of the medical model is the control of violent people. The National Institute of Mental Health has considered a National Violence Initiative. Under this plan, researchers would use genetic and biochemical indicators to identify potentially violent children as young as five for biological and behavioral interventions such as drug therapy or even possibly psychosurgery (Horne, 1992–1993). This proposal specifically rejected any examination of social and economic factors such as racism, poverty, or unemployment.

Psychosurgery is another method with important implications for social control. As with drug therapy or psychotherapy, individuals who are considered abnormal are treated to correct the problem, but this time through brain surgery. With modern techniques, surgeons can operate on localized portions of the brain that govern particular behaviors (for example, sex, aggression, appetite, or fear).

Eugenics, the improvement of the human race through control of hereditary factors, is an ultimate form of social control. That is, if society decided that certain types of people should be sterilized, then those types would be eliminated in a generation. This practice was tried in Nazi Germany, where Jews, gypsies, and the so-called feebleminded were sterilized. It has also occurred in the United States. From 1907 through the mid-1970s, for instance, more than 70,000 people in thirty states were legally sterilized for perceived abnormalities such as drunkenness, criminality, sexual perversion, and feeblemindedness. The Supreme Court ruled that this practice was constitutional in 1924 (Sinderbrand, 2005).

The potential for eugenics will progress dramatically in the near future through biotechnology. Scientists are now capable of manipulating, recombining, and reorganizing living tissue into new forms and shapes. Cells have been fused from different species. Genes have been isolated and mapped—that is, the genes responsible for various physical traits have been located at specific sites on specific chromosomes. Moreover, scientists have been able to change the heredity of a cell. These breakthroughs have positive consequences. Prospective parents, for example, can have the genes of their unborn fetus checked for abnormalities. If a hereditary disorder such as hemophilia or sickle-cell anemia is found, the fetus could be aborted or the genetic makeup of the fetus could be altered before birth.

Even though this new technology has useful applications, it raises some serious questions. Will parents, doctors, and scientists correct only genetic defects, or will they intervene to make genetic improvements? Should dark skin be eliminated? Should aggression be omitted from the behavior traits of future people? If so, passive subjects could be totally controlled without fear of revolution. The social-political-economic system, whatever its composition, would go unchallenged, and society would be tranquil. The logic of genetic engineering, while positive in the sense of ridding future generations of hereditary diseases, is frightening in its basic assumption that problems arise, not from the faults of society, but from the genes of individuals in society. The Human Genome Project raises a number of fears regarding eugenics and social control.

Similar questions can be raised about the other techniques in this section. The creativity of the scientific community has presented the powerful people in society with unusually effective means to enforce conformity. Aggressive individuals in schools, prisons, mental hospitals, and society can be anesthetized. But what is aggressive behavior? What is violence?

In 1983, the Justice Department proposed a test of 2,000 boys ages nine to twelve who had already had their first contact with the police. The goal of this test was to identify the chronic offender. Proponents of the proposal argued that chronic offenders have certain characteristics that the tests could identify—such as left-handedness, dry or sweaty palms, below-normal reactions to noise and shocks, high levels of the male hormone testosterone, abnormalities in alpha waves emitted by their brains, and physical anomalies such as malformed ears, a high steepled palate, a furrowed tongue, curved fingers, and a wide gap between the first and second toes (reported in Anderson, 1983).

Such a plan, if implemented, has frightening implications. Would these tests actually separate chronic offenders from one-time offenders? Is criminal behavior actually related to the formation of one's tongue, ears, and toes? And, if the tests do identify potential problem people accurately, should such people be punished for their *potential* behaviors rather than for their actual behaviors? Most significant, what are the negative effects of being labeled a chronic offender? Such a label would doubtless have a self-fulfilling prophecy effect, as people who interact with labeled people do so on the basis of that label.

Government

The government, as the legitimate holder of power in society, is directly involved in the control of its residents. A primary objective of the government is to provide for the welfare of its citizens. This includes protection of their lives and property. It requires, further, that order be maintained within the society. There is a clear mandate, then, for the government to apprehend and punish criminals. In 2009, at year's end, the various levels of government had incarcerated about 2.3 million people in prison, jail, or juvenile facilities. Millions more were under the jurisdiction of the criminal justice system, either on probation or parole. The number of U.S. prison inmates amounts to 25 percent of the world's prisoners. The incarceration rate (number per 100,000) in the United States is six times higher than in Canada, England, and France, seven times higher than in Switzerland and Holland, and ten times higher than in Sweden and Finland (Street, 2001). For an example of a society tightly controlled by its government, see the Closer Look panel titled "Singapore: The Iron Fist in the Land of Order."

Less clear, however, is the legitimacy of a government in a democracy to stifle dissent, which is done in the interests of preserving order. The U.S. heritage, best summed up in the Declaration of Independence, provides a clear rationale for dissent:

> Governments are instituted among Men, deriving their just powers from the consent of the governed. That whenever any Form of Government becomes destructive of these ends, it is the Right of the People to alter or to abolish it, and to institute new Government, laying its foundation on such principles and organizing its powers in such form, as to them shall seem most likely to effect their Safety and Happiness.

Singapore: The Iron Fist in the Land of Order

Singapore is a small country (244 square miles) with 2,700,000 residents. The population is culturally diverse (76 percent Chinese, 15 percent Malay, and 7 percent Indian). It is a prosperous nation known for its efficiency and cleanliness. There is a very strict security system, with the largest army per capita in Asia, a relatively large police force, and the Internal Security Department. Since Singapore gained its independence from Great Britain in 1959, it has been ruled by Lee Kuan Yew and now Goh Chok Tong "in much the way a strict father might rear what he feels are errant children" (Sesser, 1992:37). The authoritarian government has many rules for its citizens and strict punishments if they are broken. Some examples:

- There is censorship, with magazines such as *Cosmopolitan* and *Playboy* banned, as well as the monitoring and censorship of newspapers, books, movies, music, and television.
- Anyone caught littering must pay a fine of up to $620 and undergo counseling.
- Eating or drinking on the subway costs the equivalent of $310.
- Smoking is illegal in public buses, elevators, restaurants, theaters, cinemas, and government offices ($300 fine).
- Videogame centers are outlawed because they allegedly harm children.
- Driving without a seatbelt costs $120.
- Jaywalkers are fined $30.
- Beginning in 1988, a law required the flushing of toilets and urinals, with violators fined.
- At the end of 1991, the government banned the import of chewing gum because it is a "perennial nuisance" in public facilities.
- Trucks and commercial vans are required to install a yellow roof light that flashes when the vehicle exceeds the speed limit.

- Cameras mounted above stop lights at intersections photograph the license plates of cars that pass through a red light, with the drivers receiving bills for the offense in the mail (fine of $150).
- Illegal immigrants, burglars, and car thieves are subject to imprisonment and lashes with a cane. As described by the Bar Association, "When the rattan hits the bared buttocks, the skin disintegrates, leaving initially a white line and then a flow of blood. The victim must lie on his front for three weeks to a month because the buttocks are so sore" (reported in Sesser, 1992:56).
- Anyone trafficking a controlled drug receives ten years in prison and five lashes with a cane. Anyone caught with more than fifteen grams of heroin or thirty grams of morphine is hanged.
- During the Vietnam War, when long hair was believed to be linked to drug use and political dissent, Singapore police would detain long-haired male youths and give them involuntary haircuts. There is still a regulation that hair must not reach below an ordinary shirt collar.
- Except for social gatherings, assemblies of more than five people in public must have police permission.
- In 1990, Parliament passed the Religious Harmony Act, which gave the government the power to arrest religious workers who it believed were engaged in politics. This act barred judicial review of these cases (that is, the courts cannot rule on the government's actions).
- Renewal of appointments and tenure in the universities are refused to academics whose work deviates from government views.
- Political dissidents, as a condition for release from detention, must make a public confession.

The U.S. government, then, is faced with a dilemma. American tradition and values affirm that dissent is appropriate. Two facts of political life work against this principle, however. First, for social order to prevail, a society needs to ensure that existing power relationships are maintained over time (otherwise, anarchy will result). Second, the well-off in society benefit from the existing power arrangements, so they use their influence (which is considerable, as noted in Chapter 14) to encourage the repression of challenges to the government. The evidence is strong that the U.S. government has opted for repression of dissent. Let us examine this evidence.

To begin, we must peruse the processes of law enactment and law enforcement. These two processes are both directly related to political authority. Some level of government determines what the law will be (that is, which behaviors are to be allowed and which ones are to be forbidden. The agents of political authorities then apprehend and punish violators. Clearly, the law is employed to control behaviors that might otherwise endanger the general welfare (for example, the crimes of murder, rape, and theft). But laws also promote certain points of view at the expense of others (for example, the majority instead of the minority, or the status quo rather than change). With this in mind, let us turn to the two schools of thought on the function of the law—the prevailing liberal view and the Marxist interpretation (Quinney, 1970:18–25; 1973).

The dominant view in U.S. society is based on liberal democratic theory and is congruent with the order model. The state exists to maintain order and stability. Law is a body of rules enacted by representatives of the people in the interests of the people. The state and law, therefore, are essentially neutral, dispensing rewards and punishments without bias. A basic assumption of this view is that the political system is pluralistic—that is, made up of the existence of a number of interest groups of more or less equal power. The laws, then, reflect compromise and consensus among these various interest groups. In this way the interests of all people are protected.

Contrary to the prevailing view of law based on consensus for the common good is the view of the radical criminologists, which is based on conflict theory. The assumptions of this model are that (1) the state exists to serve the ruling class (the owners of large corporations and financial institutions), (2) the law and the legal system reflect and serve the needs of the ruling class, and (3) the interests of the ruling class are served by the law when domestic order prevails and challenges to changing the economic and political system are successfully thwarted. In other words, the law does not serve society as a whole, but the interests of the ruling class.

Closely related to the Marxian view of the role of law in capitalist societies is the interest-group theory of Richard Quinney (1970:29–42). The essence of this theory is that a crime is behavior that conflicts with the interests of the segments of society that have the power to shape criminal policy: "Law is made by men, representing special interests, who have the power to translate their interests into public policy. Unlike the pluralist conception of politics, law does not represent a compromise of the diverse interests of society, but supports some interests at the expense of others" (Quinney, 1970:35).

Quinney's view is in the conflict-model tradition. Society is held together by some segments coercing other segments. Interest groups are unequal in power. The conflict among interest groups results in the powerful getting their way in determining public policy. Evidence for this position is seen in the successful efforts of certain interest groups to get favorable laws passed: the segregation laws of the post–Civil War South imposed by Whites on Blacks, the repression of political dissidents whose goal is to transform society, and the passage of income tax laws that benefit the rich at the expense of wage earners.

"Look, you've got to accept some curtailment of your freedom in exchange for increased security."

Quinney's model makes a good deal of sense. The model is not universally applicable, however, because certain crimes—burglary, murder, and rape—would be regarded as crimes no matter which interest group was in power. A very important part of his theory that does fit almost universally is this proposition: "The probability that criminal definitions will be applied varies according to the extent to which the behaviors of the powerless conflict with the interests of the power segments" (Quinney, 1970:18).

The Repression of Dissent Prior to September 11, 2001. All governments are interested in maintaining the existing structure of power. Thus, the resources of the government are used to control political dissent.

Government agencies have a long history of surveillance of people in the United States. The pace quickened in the 1930s and increased further with the communist threat in the 1950s. The FBI's concern with internal security, for example, dates back to 1936, when President Franklin Roosevelt directed J. Edgar Hoover to investigate domestic communist and fascist organizations in the United States. In 1939, as World War II began in Europe, President Roosevelt issued a proclamation that the FBI would be in charge of investigating subversive activities, espionage, and sabotage, and he directed that all law enforcement offices should give the FBI any relevant information on suspected activities. These directives began a pattern followed by the FBI under the administrations of Presidents Harry Truman, Dwight Eisenhower, John Kennedy, Lyndon Johnson, Richard Nixon, Gerald Ford, Jimmy Carter, Ronald Reagan, George H. W. Bush, Bill Clinton, George W. Bush, and Barack Obama.

Surveillance reached its peak during the height of antiwar and civil rights protests of the late 1960s and early 1970s. The scope of these abuses by the FBI and other government agencies such as the CIA (Central Intelligence Agency), the National Security Agency, and the Internal Revenue Service (IRS) is enormous. We focus here on what occurred under the FBI domestic surveillance program (COINTELPRO) begun in 1956. The mission of this program, according to FBI director J. Edgar Hoover, was to "neutralize the effectiveness of civil rights, New Left, anti-war and black liberation groups" (quoted in Rosen, 2000:18). Thus, in the name of national security, the FBI "used forged documents, illegal break-ins, false charges, intercepted mailings, telephone taps, and undercover provocateurs and informants" to disrupt and subvert political dissent (Michael Parenti, 2002:141). Consider a few examples of actions by the FBI against U.S. citizens:

- The FBI over the years conducted about 1,500 break-ins of foreign embassies and missions, mob hangouts, and the headquarters of such organizations as the Ku Klux Klan and the American Communist Party.
- Beginning in 1957, the FBI monitored the activities of civil rights leader Martin Luther King, Jr. The efforts included physical and photographic surveillance and the placement of electronic listening devices in his living quarters. Using the information gathered, the FBI actually made a serious effort to blackmail Dr. King into committing suicide.
- The FBI consistently monitored the activities of hundreds of U.S. writers, including Nelson Algren, Pearl S. Buck, Truman Capote, William Faulkner, Ernest Hemingway, Sinclair Lewis, Archibald MacLeish, Carl Sandburg, John Steinbeck, Thornton Wilder, Tennessee Williams, James Baldwin, and Thomas Wolfe (Robins, 1992). The question is, Why? Was it because the most acclaimed writers in the United States were part of a conspiracy or were individual lawbreakers, or was it, as has been suggested by Natalie Robins, "an unconscious effort on the FBI's part to control writers with a chilling effect that really adds up to intimidation?" (Robins, 1987:367).
- Beginning in late 1981, the FBI conducted a massive investigation of 1,330 organizations and individuals who were opposed to President Reagan's South American policy. The main target was the Committee in Solidarity with the People of El Salvador (CISPES).

For just that one organization, "although no terrorist connection was found, hundreds of people were surveilled and photographed, their meetings infiltrated, their families, friends, and employers questioned, their trash and financial and telephone records examined" (Gentry, 1991:759; Weisbrot, 2002).

- An organization of progressive lawyers, the National Lawyers Guild, was under FBI surveillance for fifty years, yet was never found to engage in illegal activity (Michael Parenti, 1995:153).
- During the 1970s, the FBI paid informants to infiltrate the Feminist Movement. Director J. Edgar Hoover told his agents that feminists "should be viewed as part of the enemy, a challenge to American values" (quoted in Rosen, 2000:20).
- During the1960s and the 1970s the FBI investigated 6,000 University of California, Berkeley, faculty members and top administrators and a number of students as Hoover wanted to squelch the student protest movement (Associated Press, 2002).

These examples are just for the FBI. Actually, the extent of the government's monitoring of the country's residents is much greater than these examples indicate. For instance, the IRS monitored the activities of ninety-nine political organizations and 11,539 individuals from 1969 to 1973; and the CIA opened and photographed nearly 250,000 first-class letters in the United States between 1953 and 1973.

Today, the techniques of surveillance by government agencies are much more sophisticated. A survey of 142 federal agencies by the Office of Technology found that one fourth of them conducted some form of electronic surveillance. The Drug Enforcement Administration, for example, uses ten separate surveillance technologies, and the FBI uses seventeen. Moreover, various federal and state agencies use computerized record systems used for law enforcement, investigative, and intelligence purposes. Government officials in Washington, DC, plan to link a thousand cameras to watch streets, public schools, the DC Metro transit system, and federal facilities. The cameras will feed a command center where surveillance images are recorded and logged by the police, Secret Service, and FBI (Christian Parenti, 2002). An early version of this surveillance network was used to monitor activists protesting NATO's fiftieth-anniversary summit in 1999 and the monitoring of crowds during mass protests against the joint World Bank and International Monetary Fund meeting in 2000. The FBI has an eavesdropping device called Carnivore that is an Internet wiretap. It is intended to sift through the Internet traffic of potential criminals, but the tool gives the FBI the ability to track not just the individual named in the court order, but also everyone who uses the same server at the Internet service provider (*USA Today*, 2000). The FBI has another computer-bugging device called a key logger system that registers every keystroke typed as it is made on a computer terminal's keyboard.

Another snooping operation, called Echelon, is conducted by the National Security Agency. Using a combination of spy satellites and listening stations, this system eavesdrops on just about every electronic communication that crosses a national border—phone calls, faxes, e-mails, radio signals—and domestic long-distance calls and local cell-phone calls. Supercomputers screen these communications for key words related to possible terrorist plots, drug smuggling, and political unrest. When target words are found, the intercept goes to humans for analysis. John E. Pike, a military analyst at the Federation of American Scientists, says, "Americans should know that every time they place an international call, the NSA is listening. Just get used to the fact—Big Brother is listening.... Surveillance technology is becoming so competent that snooping systems soon may outstrip the wildest dreams of George Orwell" (quoted in Port, 1999:110–111).

Government efforts, especially since the 1950s, have been aimed at squelching political protest, which counters the belief of Thomas Jefferson that protest is the hallmark of a democracy. The implication of government control of dissidents is that the government is beyond questioning—the dissidents are the problem. This problem became especially acute after September 11, 2001, when government officials labeled any questioning of their actions in the war on terrorism as unpatriotic.

Government Control to Combat Terrorism after September 11, 2001. Because of the excesses of the FBI and other government agencies during the 1960s and 1970s, President Ford issued an executive order placing greater controls over these agencies. The FBI, for example, was required to show evidence of a crime before engaging in domestic spying. These limited constraints were lifted following the terrorist attacks on September 11, 2001. Given the choice between security and constitutional guarantees, government officials chose increased security. President George W. Bush signed executive orders and Congress passed the USA Patriot Act of 2001, which unleashed the FBI and other agencies to spy on speech, behaviors, and ideas of citizens and noncitizens. The provisions of this Act (summarized by Eitzen, Baca Zinn, and Smith, 2011, Chapter 18):

- Expand the ability of law enforcement personnel to conduct secret searches and access a wide range of personal financial, medical, mental health, and student records, and to conduct phone and Internet surveillance. Government monitoring of communication between federal detainees and their lawyers is allowed. Judicial oversight of these investigation actions is reduced by the Act.
- Expand the legal definition of terrorism beyond previous laws in a manner that subjects ordinary political and religious organizations to surveillance, wiretapping, and criminal action. New FBI guidelines under the Act allow spying on both religious and political organizations, as well as any individual, without any evidence of wrongdoing.
- Allow FBI agents to investigate any U.S. citizen without probable cause of crime if they say it is for "intelligence purposes." As a result, some U.S. citizens, mostly of Arab and South Asian origin, have been held in secret federal custody for weeks or months, many without any charges filed against them and without access to lawyers.
- Allow noncitizens to be jailed based on suspicion, even without evidence. Suspects can be detained indefinitely without judicial review, and hundreds have been detained. Immigration hearings for post–9/11 noncitizens are conducted in secret. This provision was overturned by the Supreme Court in 2008.

Senator Russ Feingold from Wisconsin was the only senator to vote against the Patriot Act. His rationale delivered to his colleagues was:

> There is no doubt that if we lived in a police state, it would be easier to catch terrorists. If we lived in a country where the police were allowed to search your home at any time for any reason; if we lived in a country where the government was entitled to open your mail, eavesdrop on your phone conversations, or intercept your email communications; if we lived in a country where people could be held in jail indefinitely based on what they write or think, or based on mere suspicion that they were up to no good, the government would probably discover and arrest more terrorists, or would-be terrorists, just as it would find more lawbreakers generally. But that would not be a country in which we would want to live, and it would not be a country for which we could, in good conscience, ask our young people to fight and die. In short, that country would not be America. (Feingold, 2001:2)

To conduct the war on terror, domestic surveillance programs have been conducted by the FBI, the Defense Department, Homeland Security, and the National Security Agency (all of which, are justified as inherent in the "wartime" powers of the president). See the Closer Look panel titled "Homeland Security on Campus." Some examples of post–9/11 domestic spying:

Suspected terrorists are held indefinitely without judicial review.

Homeland Security on Campus

The government's war on terror has invaded the ivory tower. Concerned with preventing "violent radicalization" on university campuses, the government has engaged in the following social control tactics:

1. *Targeting potential dissident groups*, such as peace and justice organizations. In 2006, the ACLU uncovered at least 186 TALON (the Pentagon's Threat and Local Observation Notice System) reports on "anti-military protests" from student groups.

2. *Using force to quell student uprisings.* Many campus police departments are equipped with an array of weaponry. Typically, they use rubber bullets and pepper pellets and occasionally tasers to contain student demonstrations.

3. *Using electronic surveillance of students, faculty, and campus workers* to identify potential dissidents. There are surveillance cameras at more than half of college campuses.

In one case, Hussein Hussein, a professor at the University of Nevada, Reno, found a hidden camera in his office.

4. *Mining student records.* From 2001 to 2006, the Education Department teamed up with the FBI in an operation code-named Project Strike Back to examine the records of 14 million students who applied for federal financial aid to identify "people of interest" for potential terrorist activity.

5. *Tracking foreign-born students.* As of October 2007, federal agencies were actively following 713,000 internationals on campuses, and keeping more than 4.7 million names in the database.

Source: Adapted from Michael Gould-Wartofsky, "Repress U: How to Build a Homeland Security Campus in Seven Steps," *The Nation* (January 28, 2008), pp. 20–23.

- Surveillance by the FBI and local police of domestic activist organizations (e.g., American Friends Service Committee, Greenpeace, and United for Peace and Justice) (Dunn, 2006).
- The departments of Justice, State, and Homeland Security buy commercial databases that track U.S. citizens' finances, phone numbers, and biographical information (Woellert and Kopecki, 2006).
- Using a "national security letter," the FBI can demand that an Internet provider, bank, or phone company turn over records of who you call and e-mail, and where you work, fly, vacation, and the like. No judge has to approve the demand. Moreover, the individual under surveillance is unaware of what is happening because it is classified (*USA Today*, 2005).
- The Department of Homeland Security recruited utility and telephone workers, cable TV installers, poster workers, delivery drivers, and others who regularly enter private homes to become federal informants, informing on suspicious persons, activities, and items that they observed (Conason, 2007:194).

The Electronic Frontier Foundation sued the government under the Freedom of Information Act to obtain about 2,500 documents that the FBI submitted to the President's Intelligence Board. The resulting report provides a long list of FBI intelligence abuses. Among them (Electronic Frontier Foundation, 2011):

- From 2001 to 2008, there were approximately 800 violations of laws, Executive Orders, or other regulations governing intelligence investigations.
- From 2001 to 2008, the FBI investigated, at minimum, 7,000 *potential* violations of laws, Executive Orders, or other regulations governing intelligence investigations.
- Based on the proportion of violations reported to the Intelligence Oversight Board and the FBI's own statements regarding the number of violations that occurred, the *actual* number of possible violations that may have occurred in the nine years since 9/11 could approach 40,000 violations of law, Executive Orders, or other regulations governing intelligence investigations.
- The flagrant violations by the FBI included: (1) submitting false or inaccurate declarations to the courts, (2) using improper evidence to obtain federal grand jury subpoenas, and (3) accessing password protected documents without a warrant.

- The most severe restrictions on individual rights occurred under President George W. Bush in the aftermath of the 9/11 terrorist attacks. But many of them continued under President Obama. For example, the Obama administration's Justice Department asserted that the FBI can obtain telephone records of international calls made from the United States without any formal legal process or court oversight (Taylor, 2011).

Proponents of these social control activities argue that the dangers are serious, and that they are needed to make the nation secure by making it easier to identify, prevent, and punish terrorists.

Critics, on the other hand, argue that these measures go too far in expanding the government's abilities to intrude on citizens' lives, thereby weakening individual rights. Citizens have guarantees from the Constitution that protect them from the government reading their mail, listening in on phone conversations, and from general surveillance—in short, U.S. citizens have the right to privacy and freedom from unreasonable search and seizure. Moreover, there is a high probability that the invasion of privacy will not be randomly distributed, but more likely directed at noncitizens, Muslims, and any other people who look "Middle Eastern."

Issues of Privacy, Constitutional Guarantees, and the Need for Social Control. One should remember that the government must exert some control over its population. There must be a minimum of control if the fabric of society is to remain intact, and, in times of crisis, such as the very real threat of terrorist acts, the need for vigilance and social control is magnified. But in exerting control, serious problems surface. First, there is the problem of the violation of individual rights as guaranteed in the Constitution. Under what conditions can a government violate these rights—if ever? A closely related problem can be framed in the form of a question: Who monitors the monitors? The problem inherent in this question is not only the tactics of the monitors but also the criteria used to assess who should be controlled or who should not. Finally, there is the ultimate irony that the United States is waging a war to defend its free society but in doing so it restricts those very freedoms it seeks to defend. As Salim Muwakkil (2002) points out: "Soon after 9/11, Bush said the people who perpetuated the terrorist murders hate America because of 'our freedoms.' After a few more executive orders and congressional capitulations, they won't have much left to hate" (18).

Government Surveillance to Fight Crime. In 1949, George Orwell wrote a novel about life as he envisioned it to be in the year 1984. The essence of his prediction was that every word, every thought, and every facial expression of citizens would be monitored by the government using sophisticated electronic devices. With the new technology there is the very real possibility of realizing Orwell's prediction. Cities have installed cameras to monitor high crime and busy areas. Cameras are an important tool of law enforcement because they provide an accurate record of questionable behaviors and, second, in times of fiscal austerity they are cheaper than hiring more police personnel.

Cameras and other technologies intrude on the privacy of citizens in a variety of ways. For example, the faces of spectators at a Super Bowl are secretly scanned and checked against a database of potential troublemakers. When travelers pass through an EntryScan detector, air jets dislodge microscopic particles from the skin and clothing. These particles are then analyzed for traces of explosives, chemicals, or drugs. Airport security permits the searching of passengers and their luggage as well as screening their bodies. Along the one hundred miles of interstates linking Washington, DC, to its suburbs there are remote control cameras every mile or so capable of reading license plates or peering inside vehicles (there are similar systems in Chicago, Seattle, and Los Angeles).

Although the courts have ruled that people have no expectation of privacy in public settings, many question these intrusions into private lives. (Keen, 2011).

Social Control in the Private Sector: Implications for Contemporary Social Life

The private sector helps to fulfill, at least in part, Orwell's prophecy as well. Whenever we put a bank card in an ATM machine or drive through an E-ZPass lane on the highway, our whereabouts are registered. Customers in banks, 7-11s, and other stores are routinely photographed by surveillance cameras. Whenever we purchase goods over the Internet or shop by mail order, our purchasing habits are recorded. So, too, when we purchase groceries with a credit card. The books we check out of public libraries are recorded. Social networks such as Facebook remember the choices made, the statements written, and the history of relationships. Whenever we inform the postal service of a change of address, that fact is not only registered with the government but transferred to private data warehouses.

The privacy of workers is also violated routinely. Most large companies require some form of drug testing of their employees. According to *Newsweek* Scotts Miracle-Gro conducts random urine tests for nicotine and fires employees who fail. Similar, Clarian Health, an Indiana hospital system, fines employees $10 per paycheck for obesity and $5 for each failure to meet standards for cholesterol, blood pressure, and glucose levels (Dokoupil, 2011). Some employers require prospective employees to take psychological tests that ask about, among other things, sexual behavior, religious beliefs, and political attitudes. Many large corporations regularly review health information before making hiring decisions. Workers using telephones and computers may find their work watched, measured, and analyzed in detail by supervisors. Typically, corporations do one or more of the following: use video surveillance to monitor their employees, look at employees' e-mail, listen to employees' phone calls, or open employees' computer files (see the Technology and Society panel titled "The Internet's Private Eye"). Workers can be issued cell phones equipped with a GPS (global positioning system) that pinpoints their locations to computers in the main office (Levy, 2004).

This computer-stored knowledge, especially from centralized and increasingly interrelated databases (credit bureaus, banks, marketing companies, stock brokerage firms, health insurers and other insurance companies, and governments), is a threat to privacy. Added to this loss of privacy is the danger that employers, banks, and government agencies will use databases to make decisions about our lives without our knowing about it. Most especially, if the government has access to these data, it can use modern technology to monitor closely the activities of those people who threaten it. And, as we have seen in this chapter, the government is strongly inclined to do so.

But the political dissident is not the only person whose freedoms are being threatened; all of us are threatened by the power of large organizations. As Jeffrey Rothfeder (1992) says:

> Increasingly people are at the whim of ... large organizations—direct marketers, credit bureaus, the government, and the entire information economy—that view individuals as nothing but lifeless data floating like microscopic entities in vast electronic chambers, data that exist to be captured, examined, collated and sold, regardless of the individual's desire to choose what should be concealed and what should be made public. (30)

Our privacy is invaded even when we drive. About two-thirds of the new cars sold in the United States—and about 30 million cars already on the road—contain a four-inch square device called an "event data recorder." This box constantly records information about the driver such as speed, acceleration, braking, and seat belt use. In the event of an accident, the police and insurance company can access the information, even without the owner's knowledge. This raises issues of privacy such as, who owns the information—the car owner, the government, the insurance company, or the car manufacturer? Even more serious, if this device is coupled with a wireless transmitter, it could record conversations in the car (Kiser, 2005).

The Internet's Private Eye

The Internet is a digital revolution on a global scale, connecting computers, businesses, and people instantaneously around the world. This online communication is transforming society in many important ways, affecting, among other things, commerce, the knowledge explosion, and even relationships. This transformation through Internet technology is, on one hand, terrific. It is important, useful, convenient, rapid, fascinating, and almost universally available. But there is an important downside—the Internet can be and is used as a surveillance tool—and thus is a significant and new way to invade the privacy of individuals. And, as such, it is a form of social control.

In the workplace some but not all employers use software to track their employees' use of the Internet at work. The assumption is that workers may be using company time to write to contact "friends" on Facebook, track stocks, cultivate romantic relationships, check sports scores, visit sexually explicit websites, or otherwise use computers to reduce their work productivity. Consider, for example, a software tool for spying on employees. An advertisement by Spectorsoft in the June 2005 issue of PC World was titled "Record Everything Your Employees Do on the Internet." The software ("Spector CNE") on a company's network provides at the touch of a button an immediate and accurate record of every employee's:

- E-mails sent and received
- Chats/instant messages sent and received
- Keystrokes typed
- Websites visited
- Files downloaded
- Programs run

And, unlike many filtering and blocking tools, Spector CNE records everything an employee does on the Internet in exact visual detail, providing absolute proof of every activity.

Privacy is compromised when Internet sites such as Facebook and Google track users' activities and sell that information to companies so that they can target their advertising to consumers based on their online behavior. Such monitoring is big business, as online advertising accounted for $26 billion in revenue in 2010 and is projected to grow to $40 billion by 2015 (Forden, 2011).

A final caution: E-mail messages sent long ago are never lost; they can always be retrieved. Employers wishing to get rid of an employee can dredge up all his or her e-mail messages sent and received in search of a rationale for the dismissal. E-mail messages can be subpoenaed as evidence in court cases.

In effect, then, when we are alone in our cubicles at work or in our home office and using the Internet, we are being "watched."

The technology for the futuristic novel *1984* exists in drugs, human genome mapping, DNA data banks, psychosurgery, telecommunications, cyberspace, telemetry, and other high-tech devices. Currently, various arms of the government have used some of these techniques in their battle to fight crime, recidivism, political dissidence, terrorism, and other forms of nonconformity. But at what point does the government go too far in its control of nonconformity? The critical question, as stated earlier, is, Who monitors the monitors? One can easily envision a future when the government, faced with anarchy or political revolution, might justify ultimate control of its citizens—in the name of national security. If this were to take place, then, obviously, the freedoms rooted in more than 200 years of history will have been washed away.

> So, too, is there a danger from the private sector. In *1984*, George Orwell imagined a future in which a totalitarian state used spies, video surveillance, historical revisionism and control over the media to maintain its power.... Orwell thought the Communist system represented the ultimate threat to individual liberty. Over the next fifty years, we will see new kinds of threats to privacy that find their roots not in Communism but in capitalism, the free market, advanced technology and the unbridled exchange of electronic information. (Garfinkel, 2000a:11)

But are there situations when the rights of privacy ought to be curtailed for the good of society? Esteemed social scientist Amitai Etzioni argues that excessive protection of privacy in certain areas (for example, parents need to know whether one of their neighbors is a child molester, and there should be mandatory HIV testing of infants) undermines public safety and health. And, of course, the threat of terrorist acts requires government scrutiny of its citizens and noncitizens. Etzioni's communitarian philosophy holds that a good society seeks "a carefully crafted balance between individual rights and social responsibilities, between liberty and the common good" (Etzioni, 1999:5).

This raises the fundamental question: Are there situations in which society must/should place limits on individual behaviors to ensure safety, maintain clear air, preserve natural resources, and the like? But who decides what is the common good? And do we want an authoritarian government that controls us for this common good?

Social Control from the Order and Conflict Perspectives

A perennial question for many sociologists is: How is social order possible? Order theorists and conflict theorists answer this question quite differently. For order theorists, the answer to this question is that the vast majority of members of any social organization share a consensus on the norms, laws, and values. In premodern societies, social order occurs because the norms and values are shared and legitimized by deeply held religious authority. In modern complex societies, social order is maintained through a division of labor and as citizens accept the legal order and the state, which are believed to serve the common good.

Conflict theorists, on the other hand, reject the assumption of normative consensus, arguing rather that social order is the result of government force or the threat of force, economic dominants using the law, the media, or other institutions to hold power over the relatively powerless.

CHAPTER REVIEW

1. The socialization process through which the demands of the group become internalized is a fundamental mechanism of social control. This process is never complete, however; otherwise, we would be robots.

2. Ideological social control is the attempt to manipulate the consciousness of citizens so they accept the status quo and ruling ideology.

3. The agents of ideological social control are the family, education, religion, sport, and the media.

4. Direct social control refers to attempts to punish or neutralize organizations or individuals who deviate from society's norms, especially the poor, the mentally ill, criminals, and political dissidents.

5. According to Piven and Cloward, public assistance programs serve a direct social control function in times of mass unemployment by defusing social unrest.

6. Science and medicine provide the techniques for shaping and controlling the behavior of nonconformists. Drugs, psychosurgery, and genetic engineering are three such techniques.

7. The government is directly involved in the control of its citizens. It apprehends and punishes criminals. It is

also involved in the suppression of dissent, which, while important for preserving order, runs counter to the U.S. democratic heritage. Following the terrorist attacks in 2001, the government instituted a number of new rules restricting freedoms and engaged in various means of surveillance.

8. Privacy is threatened by the private sector as personal information on purchases, websites visited, and demographics is stored in huge databases. Employers can invade the personal space of employees through surveillance, intercepting e-mail messages, and psychological testing.

9. Order theorists argue that social order results from a shared consensus on the norms, laws, and values. In modern complex societies, citizens accept the legal order and the state because they are believed to serve the common good. In this view, the state and the law are neutral, dispensing rewards and punishments without bias. Conflict theorists, however, believe that the state and the law (as well as the other institutions) exist to serve the ruling class. Squelching political dissent, therefore, benefits the powerful.

Social control
Ideological social control

Direct social control
Eugenics

1. How do order and conflict theorists differ in their interpretation of the role of sport and social control?
2. What is the relationship of ideological social control to what we learned about socialization in the previous chapter?
3. What is Piven and Cloward's thesis concerning the social control function of welfare assistance programs?
4. Make the argument, as *Consumer Reports* (2002) did, that biometrics, automated identification gadgetry such as iris scans, thumbprints, hand maps, and other computer technologies may make us safer, but they also make us more vulnerable at the same time.
5. How do order theorists and conflict theorists differ in their views of the state and the law?

http://www.eugenicsarchive.org/html/eugenics/agreement.html

The Eugenics Archive website has information on the history of eugenics in America. The site contains textual information, as well as reports, charts, articles, and pedigrees made by the scientists involved with eugenics.

http://www.fbi.gov/

The Federal Bureau of Investigation has information on arrests and crime.

http://www.projectfreedom.cng1.com/part_6.html

Project Freedom explores the issue of government and how it serves as social control.

http://www.bop.gov/

The Federal Bureau of Prisons contains information on inmates and prisons. Race and gender makeup in the prison and other quick facts are available.

Deviance

The previous three chapters analyzed the ways in which human beings, as members of society, are constrained to conform. We have seen how society is not only outside us, coercing us to conform, but also inside us, making us want to behave in the culturally prescribed ways. But despite these powerful forces, people deviate from the norms. These acts and actors are the subjects of this chapter. This chapter is divided into three sections. The first section explains the characteristics of deviance. Section two examines some traditional theories for the causes of deviance, presenting theories that focus on individuals and theories that turn to society as the source of deviance. Finally, we examine deviance from the order and conflict perspectives.

The Characteristics of Deviance

Who are the deviants in U.S. society? There is considerable evidence that many of us break the law at one time or another. For example:

- A 2010 taxpayer attitude survey reveals that 12 percent of people believe that it is acceptable to cheat on income taxes (Internal Revenue Service Oversight Board, 2011). The Internal Revenue Service (IRS) estimates that waiters and waitresses underreport their cash tips by an average of 84 percent.
- Otherwise law-abiding citizens routinely copy computer software, videos, music, and other copyrighted materials, even though these activities are against the law.
- The U.S. Chamber of Commerce estimates that 75 percent of employees steal from the workplace. Time theft by employees (for example, faked illnesses, excessive breaks, and long lunches) costs U.S. business as much as $200 billion annually.
- Theft by guests costs U.S. hotels and motels more than $100 million annually. For example, Holiday Inn loses about 100,000 washcloths each year (Wilkening, 2008).
- An estimated two-thirds of all high school students admit to serious academic cheating, and 90 percent say they cheat on homework (James, 2008).
- Marijuana is the most commonly used illegal substance in the United States, and may be the country's largest cash crop, with annual harvests valued at anywhere between $10 billion and $35 billion. According to the Office of National Drug Control Policy (2010), almost 17 million Americans were current marijuana users in 2009.
- The Internet has provided a venue for sexually deviant material to be disseminated widely. Some statistics show that 72 million adults visit Internet pornographic sites each month. There are approximately 68 million pornographic search engine requests daily and 1.5 billion pornographic downloads per month. Furthermore, there are over 100,000

websites offering illegal child pornography, and one in seven youth have received sexual solicitations on the Internet (Ropelato, 2011).

These illustrations indicate that many people are guilty of cheating, stealing, and other behaviors clearly considered wrong. Are individuals who commit these illegal or immoral acts deviant?

Deviance is any behavior that does not conform to social expectations. It violates the rules of a group (custom, law, or moral code). The following discussion examines five important principles to help us understand social deviance:

1. Deviance is socially constructed.
2. Deviance is relative, not absolute.
3. The majority determines who and what is deviant.
4. Deviance is an integral part of all societies.
5. The violators of important social norms are often stigmatized.

Because deviant behavior violates the norms of a group, deviance *is socially constructed*. Social organizations create right and wrong by originating norms, the infraction of which constitutes deviance. This means that nothing inherent in a particular act makes it deviant. Whether an act is deviant depends on how other people react to it. This also means that *deviance is a relative, not an absolute, notion*. Evidence for this is found in two sources: inconsistencies between societies as to what is deviance, and inconsistencies in the labeling of behavior as deviant within a single society.

There is abundant anthropological evidence that what is right or wrong varies from society to society. Consider the following:

- The Ila of Africa encourage sexual promiscuity among their adolescents. After age ten, girls are given houses of their own during harvest time, where they can play at being a wife with boys of their choice. In contrast, the Tepoztlan Indians of Mexico do not allow girls to speak to or encourage a boy after the time of the girl's first menstruation.
- Egyptian royalty were required to marry their siblings, whereas this was prohibited as incestuous and sinful for European royalty.
- Experts estimate the average age of weaning a child from breast-feeding is around age three worldwide, and in some developing countries it is not unusual to breast-feed until age five or later. In contrast, in the United States, more than two-thirds of mothers breast-feed for six months or less, and mothers who choose to breast-feed for longer than a year or more are often stigmatized. For example, in July 2000, in Champaign, Illinois, a five-year-old boy was removed from his mother's custody when a babysitter found out that he was still being breast-fed (Corbett, 2001).

Differential treatment for similar behavior within a single society provides further proof that deviance is not a property of the act but depends on the reaction of the particular audience. Several examples illustrate that it is not the act but the situation that determines whether others interpret behavior as deviant:

- Sexual intercourse between consenting adults is not deviant except when one partner pays another for his or her services. Likewise, sex is also viewed as deviant and illegal if one person is under the age of consent (an age which varies from state to state).
- Murder is a deviant act, but the killing of an enemy during wartime is rewarded with praise and medals.
- Marriage is applauded and encouraged ... but is considered by many to be deviant when two consenting adults of the same sex desire marriage.

In a heterogeneous society, there is often widespread disagreement regarding what the rules are and therefore what constitutes deviance. For example, there are differences of opinion over sexual activities between consenting adults (regardless of sex or marital status); over smoking marijuana and drinking alcohol; over public nudism and pornography; over remaining seated during the national anthem; and over refusing to fight in a war.

This point leads to a third insight about deviance: *The majority determines who is a deviant.* If most people believe that Iraqis are the enemy, then bombing their villages is appropriate and refusing to do so is deviant. If most people believe there is a God you may talk to, then such a belief is not deviance (in fact, refusing to believe in God may be deviant). But if the majority is atheists, then those few who believe in God would be deviant and subject to ridicule, job discrimination, and treatment for mental problems.

Power is also a crucial element in deciding who or what is deviant. Certain social groups have relatively greater power and resources than others in getting their definitions of deviance to prevail. The major religious bodies in the United States, for example, have taken a strong position against homosexuality, and their opposition has influenced the laws and community norms. Or, another example that we turn to later in this chapter is the difference in sentencing for those who commit street crimes versus those who commit white-collar crimes. Both are harmful to society, but the crimes committed by the wealthy are not handled in the same way as those committed by the powerless.

A fourth characteristic of deviance is brought to us by order theorists. Classic sociological theorist Emile Durkheim has argued that *deviance is an integral part of all healthy societies* (Durkheim, 1958; 1960). Deviant behavior, according to Durkheim, actually has positive consequences for society because it gives nondeviants a sense of solidarity. By punishing the deviant, the group expresses its collective indignation and reaffirms its commitment to the rules:

> Crime brings together upright consciences and concentrates them. We have only to notice what happens, particularly in a small town, when some moral scandal has just been committed. They stop each other on the street, they visit each other, they seek to come together to talk of the event and to wax indignant in common. From all the similar expressions which are exchanged, for all the temper that gets itself expressed, there emerges a unique temper ... which is everybody's without being anybody's in particular. That is the public temper. (Durkheim, 1960:102)

For a closer look at a modern display of public temper, see the Technology and Society panel titled "Shame Sites."

TECHNOLOGY AND SOCIETY

Shame Sites

Order theorists argue that deviance has positive functions for society; most importantly, deviance serves to strengthen beliefs about society's norms and rules. Speaking about norms, Daniel Solove writes in his book *The Future of Reputation: Gossip, Rumor, and Privacy on the Internet?*

> Norms bind societies together; they regulate everyday conduct; they foster civility. They are the oil that reduces the friction of human interaction. We need to maintain norms of courtesy so that we can all get along nicely. Imagine if we didn't have norms like first-come, first-served. Fisticuffs would quickly follow. In short, norms are a central mechanism through which a society exercises social control. (2007:6)

It is no surprise, then, that people work hard to enforce social norms. The public reaction to those who break norms is what Durkheim referred to as "the public temper"

(1960:102). The public temper is what unites society in opposition to the deviant, reinforcing our social norms.

Times have changed since Durkheim's writings, and the public temper has become even more public in the form of the Internet. Websites documenting all kinds of deviant behavior (sometimes known as "shame sites") are widespread. "Web sites are increasingly naming names, or at least posting descriptions, pictures, and license plate numbers, of people supposedly caught in the act of violating social norms" (Bloom, 2008:A1).

In Solove's book about how the Internet has upped the ante regarding deviance and public shame, he says:

> From the dawn of time, people have gossiped, circulated rumors, and shamed others. These social practices are now moving over to the Internet, where they are taking on new dimensions. They transform

(continues)

from forgettable whispers within small local groups to a widespread and permanent chronicle of people's lives. An entire generation is growing up in a very different world, one where people will accumulate detailed records beginning with childhood that will stay with them for life wherever they go. In Nathaniel Hawthorne's *The Scarlet Letter*, Hester Prynne was forced by her colonial New England village to wear a scarlet letter *A* to represent her sin of adultery. The Internet is bringing back the scarlet letter in digital form—an indelible record of people's past misdeeds. (11)

Indeed, the Internet is filled with "scarlet letter" sites. Some examples include:

- Websites where you can report bad drivers, such as www.platewire.com.
- "I Saw Your Nanny" is a website where you can report on the behavior of nannies or babysitters.

- Cheaternews.com is one of many sites aimed at infidelity. Their mission is to "expose as many cheaters, liars, and abusers to the world as we can."
- Litterbutt.com has received 73,627 reports of littering in three states. Residents of Pennsylvania, Texas, and North Carolina can make a report and the litterbug will receive a letter from the state stating that they were seen and what the fine would have been if they were caught by authorities.
- Bitterwaitress.com is a website where servers can complain about the behavior of restaurant customers.

Do websites like these serve to deter people from breaking social norms? Or, as Durkheim believed, do the websites simply serve to legitimize and strengthen our belief in society's rules? One thing is certain, with the current prevalence of camera phones any behavior can end up being recorded, documented on the Internet, and judged by millions of public citizens.

Durkheim believed that the true function of punishment was not the prevention of future crimes. He asserted, rather, that the basic function of punishment is to reassert the importance of the rule being violated. It is not that a murderer is caught and put in the electric chair to keep potential murderers in line. That argument assumes people to be more rational than they really are. Instead, the extreme punishment of a murderer reminds each of us that murder is wrong. In other words, the punishment of crimes serves to strengthen our belief as individuals and as members of a collectivity in the legitimacy of society's norms. This enhances the solidarity of society as we unite in opposition to the deviant.

Crime, seen from this view, has positive functions for society. In addition to reaffirming the legitimacy of the society, defining certain acts as crimes creates the boundaries for what is acceptable behavior in the society.

A final characteristic of deviance is that the *violators of important social norms are often stigmatized*. That is, deviants are not only believed to be different from the majority, but they are also set apart by being socially disgraced. The extent of the stigmatization depends upon the type of norm violation and how the rest of society defines it. For example, as of 2010 there were over 700,000 registered sex offenders in the United States (Gramlich, 2010). Because states have made their sex offender registries public, anyone can look online and find names, addresses, and see pictures of the sex offenders in his or her state, or living in the neighborhood. Sex offenders can range from teens who were caught sending nude photos of themselves by cell phone to other teens, to rapists and pedophiles. All registered sex offenders, regardless of the type of offense, are subject to stigma and discrimination by the public.

Given the strong societal push toward conformity, what causes deviant behavior? We turn now to theories that attempt to explain why some individuals deviate from the norms of society.

Durkheim said that by punishing the deviant publicly, society expresses its collective indignation and reaffirms its commitment to society's rules.

Traditional Theories for the Causes of Deviance

The Individual as the Source of Deviance

Biological, psychological, and even some sociological theories have assumed that the fundamental reason for deviance is a fatal flaw in certain people. From this perspective, the criminal, the dropout, the addict, and the schizophrenic have something "wrong" with them. These theories are deterministic, arguing that the individual ultimately has no choice but to be different.

Biological Theories. Biological explanations for deviance have focused on physiognomy (the determination of character by facial features), phrenology (the determination of mental abilities and character traits from the configuration of the skull), somatology (the determination of character by physique), genetic anomalies (for example, XYY chromosomes in males), and brain malfunctions. Some of these theories have been discredited. Take, for example, the discredited theory of Caesare Lombroso (1835–1909) that criminals are physically different—with low foreheads, protruding ears, long arms, and hairy bodies. (These distinct characteristics suggested that criminals were throwbacks to an earlier stage of human development—closer to the ape stage than were nondeviants.) And while some other biological theories have shown a statistical link between certain physical characteristics and deviant behavior, chances are that when such a relationship is found, it also will be related to social factors. For example, the learning disability known as dyslexia is related to school failure, emotional disturbance, and juvenile delinquency. This disability is a brain malfunction in which visual signs are scrambled. Average skills in reading, spelling, and arithmetic are impossible to attain if the malady remains undiagnosed. Teachers and parents often are unaware that the child is dyslexic and assume, rather, that she or he is mentally challenged, lazy, or belligerent. The child, who actually may be very bright—Thomas Edison and Woodrow Wilson were dyslexic—finds school frustrating. Such a child is therefore more likely than those not affected to be a troublemaker, to be alienated, and to be either pushed out of school or to drop out and never reach full intellectual potential.

Similarly, XYY syndrome (where a male is born with an extra Y chromosome) is another biological trait that has been unfairly linked to crime. In the 1960s and 1970s, papers were published that indicated there was a slightly higher incarceration rate for XYY males, and the assumption was that the extra Y chromosome somehow caused aggressive behavior. However, later studies pointed to low intelligence and low socioeconomic status that placed XYY males at a higher risk of being caught committing crime (Nuffield Council on Bioethics, 2005).

Psychological Theories. Psychological theories also consider the source of deviance to reside within the individual, but they differ from the biological theories in that they assume conditions of the mind or personality to be the fault. Deviant individuals, depending on the particular psychological theory, are psychopaths (asocial, aggressive, impulsive), resulting from a lack of affection during childhood, an Oedipal conflict, a psychosexual trauma, or another traumatic early life experience. Using Freudian assumptions, the deviant is a person who has not developed an adequate ego to control deviant impulses (the id). Alternatively, deviance can result from

Psychological theories of crime are popular in movies, as seen here in the character of Jason in Friday the 13th.

a dominating superego. People with this condition are so repulsed by their own feelings (such as sexual fantasies or ambivalence toward parents and siblings) that they may commit deviant acts in order to receive the punishment they deserve. Freudians, therefore, place great stress on the relationship between children and their parents. The parents, in this view, can be too harsh, too lenient, or too inconsistent in their treatment of the child. Each situation leads to inadequately socialized children and immature, infantile behavior by adolescents and adults.

Because the fundamental assumption of the biological and psychological theories of deviance is that the fault lies within the individual, solutions are aimed at changing the individual. Screening of the population for individuals with presumed flaws is considered the best preventive approach. Doctors could routinely determine which boys have the XYY chromosome pattern. Psychological testing in the schools could find out which students are unusually aggressive, guilt-ridden, or fantasy-oriented. Although the screening for potential problem people may make some sense (to detect dyslexics, for example), there are some fundamental problems with this type of solution. First, the screening devices likely will not be perfect, thereby mislabeling some people. Second, screening is based on the assumption that there is a direct link between certain characteristics and deviance. If a person is identified as a pre-deviant by these methods, the subsequent treatment of that individual, who has a new definition of self, would likely lead to a self-fulfilling prophecy and a false validation of the screening procedures, increasing their use and acceptability.

For people identified as potential deviants or who are actually deviants, the "kinds-of-people" theorists advocate solutions aimed at changing the individuals: drug therapy, electrical brain stimulation, electronic monitoring, surgery, operant conditioning, counseling, psychotherapy, probation with guidance of a psychiatric social worker, or incarceration. The assumption is clearly that deviants are troubled and sick people who must be changed to conform to the norms of society.

The Sociological Approach. A number of sociological theories are also kinds-of-people explanations for deviance. Instead of individual characteristics distinguishing the deviant from the nondeviant, these theories focus on differing objective social and economic conditions. These theories are based on the empirical observations that crime and mental illness rates, to name two forms of deviance, vary by social location—that is, by social class, ethnicity, race, place of residence, and sex.

Let us look at some of these theories, which emphasize that certain social conditions are conducive to the internalization of values that encourage deviance.

Cultural Transmission. Edwin Sutherland's classic theory of differential association sought to explain why some people are criminals while others are not, even though both may share certain social characteristics, such as social class position (Sutherland and Cressey, 1966:81–82). Sutherland believed that through interaction, one learns to be a criminal. If our close associates are deviants, there is a strong probability that we will learn the techniques and the deviant values that make criminal acts possible. In other words, one learns to be deviant as part of the socialization process, not through any particular biological characteristics or insecure attachments to one's parents.

Societal Goals and Differential Opportunities. Robert Merton (1957) presented an explanation for why the lower classes disproportionately commit criminal acts. In Merton's view, societal values determine both appropriate goals (success through the acquisition of wealth) and the approved means for achieving these goals. The problem, however, is that some people are denied access to the legitimate means of achieving these goals. The poor (especially those from certain racial and ethnic groups) face roadblocks presented by negative stereotypes and often receive a second-class education or must drop out of school prematurely because of financial exigencies. This effectively excludes them from high-paying and prestigious occupations. Because legitimate means to success are inaccessible to them, they often resort to certain forms of deviant behavior to attain success. Viewed from this perspective, deviance is a result of social structure and not the consequence of individual pathology.

Although Merton's analysis provides many important insights, obviously it does not explain all different types of deviant behavior. Does a person use illegal drugs because he or she has not attained the goals that society deems appropriate? What about deviant behavior of the upper classes? Merton's analysis is limited in focusing only on deviance by certain social classes.

Subcultural Differences by Social Class. We explore the culture-of-poverty hypothesis in Chapter 9. (The **culture of poverty** is the view that the poor are qualitatively different in values and lifestyles from the rest of society and that these cultural differences explain their poverty.) Because it has special relevance for explaining differential crime rates, we briefly characterize it here with that emphasis. The argument is that people, because of their social class position, differ in resources, power, and prestige and hence have different experiences, lifestyles, and ways of life. The lower-class culture has its own values, many of which run counter to the values of the middle and upper classes.

Edward Banfield (1974) argues, for example, that lower-class individuals have a propensity toward criminal behavior. He asserts that a person in the lower class does not have a strong sense of morality and thus is not constrained by legal rules. These people, according to Banfield, have weak ego strength, a present-time orientation (that is, they live for the moment rather than the future), a propensity for taking risks, and a willingness to inflict injury. Many scholars accept Banfield's assertions about the "lower-class culture," but there is strong evidence that it is incorrect (see Chapter 9). Even if Banfield's characterization of the lower-class propensity to crime is correct, the critical question is whether these differences are durable. Will a change in monetary status or peer groups make a difference because the individual has a dual value system—one that is a reaction to his or her deprived situation and one that is middle class? This is a key research question because the answer determines whether to attack the problem at the individual or the societal level.

Also, this approach focuses on the presumed disproportionate deviance by those in the lower social classes. This ignores the facts about criminality. Consider the criminality of individuals within major corporations revealed in the scandals involving Enron, Bristol-Myers Squibb, and WorldCom, to name a few. In these cases, executives and their accountants "cooked the books" to make company profits seem much greater than they actually were and the value of their stocks increase. These crimes, of course, are crimes by economic elites, and thus cannot be explained by "lower-class culture." In his 2008 essay on the culture of poverty, Daniel Gross argues that we should forget about the underclass as it is the "overclass" that is hurting society. He writes: "In the under-class, unmarried fathers don't take responsibility for their children. In the overclass, twice-married, middle-aged Wall Street daddies don't own up to the consequences of their insane financial miscues." (2008:18).

The Blaming-the-Victim Critique. Although socialization theories focus on forces external to individuals that push them toward deviant behavior, they, like the biological and psychological theories, are kinds-of-people theories that find the fault within the individual. The deviant has an acquired trait—the internalization of values and beliefs favorable to deviance—that is social in origin.

There are two ways to look at deviance—blaming the victim or blaming society. The fundamental difference between these two approaches is whether the problems emanate from the pathologies of individuals or because of the situation in which deviants are immersed. The answer is doubtless somewhere between these two extremes; but because the individual blamers have held sway, let us look carefully at the critique of this approach.

We begin by considering some victims. One group of victims is composed of children in slum schools who are failures. Why do they fail? Victim blamers point to the children's **cultural deprivation**.[*] They do not do well in school because their families speak a different dialect, because their parents are uneducated, and because they have not been exposed to all the education experiences of middle-class children (for example, visits to the zoo, extensive travel, attendance at cultural events, exposure to books, exposure to correct English usage). In other words, the defect is in the children and their families. System blamers, however, look elsewhere for the sources of failure. They ask, What is it about a school that makes poor children more likely to fail? The answer for them is found in the irrelevant curriculum, the class-biased IQ tests, the tracking system, the overcrowded classrooms, the differential allocation of resources within the school district, and insensitive teachers whose low expectations for poor children comprise a prophecy that is continually fulfilled.

Another victim is the criminal. Why is the **recidivism** rate (reinvolvement in crime) of criminals so high? In a national study of prisoners released from prison in 2004, 43.3 percent were rearrested within three years (Pew Center on the States, 2011). The individual blamer would point to the faults of the individual criminals: their greed, feelings of aggression, weak impulse control, and lack of a conscience (superego). The system blamers' attention is directed to very different sources for this problem. They would look, rather, at the penal system, the employment situation for ex-criminals, and the schools. For example, some studies have shown that over 60 percent of prison inmates are functionally illiterate. This means they cannot meet minimum reading and writing demands in U.S. society, such as filling out job applications. Yet they are expected to leave prison, find a job, and stay out of trouble. Because they are illiterate and ex-criminals, they face unemployment or at best the most menial jobs (for which there are low wages, no job security, and no fringe benefits). The system blamer would argue that these people are not to blame for their illiteracy, but rather that first the schools and later the penal institutions have failed to provide the minimum requirements for productive membership in society. Moreover, the lack of employment and the unwillingness of potential employers to train functional illiterates force many to return to crime in order to survive.

African Americans (and other racial minorities) constitute another set of victims in U.S. society. What accounts for the greater probability for Blacks than Whites to be failures in school, to be unemployed, and to be incarcerated? The individualistic approach places the blame on Blacks themselves. They are culturally deprived, they have high rates of illegitimacy and a high proportion of transient males, and a relatively high proportion of Black families have a matriarchal structure. This approach neglects the pervasive effects of racism in the United States, which limits the opportunities for African Americans, provides them with a second-class education, renders them powerless to change the system through approved channels, and limits their opportunities.

Why is there a strong tendency to place the blame for deviance on individuals rather than on the social system? The answer lies in the way that people tend to define deviance. Most people define deviance as behavior that deviates from the norms and standards of society. Because people do not ordinarily question the norms or the way things are done in society, they tend to question the exceptions. The system is not only taken for granted, but it also has, for most people, an aura of sacredness because of the traditions and customs behind it. Logically, then, the people who deviate are the source of trouble. Because most people abide by society's norms, any deviation must be the result of some kind of unusual circumstance— perhaps a personality defect, character flaw, or maladjustment. The key to this approach, then, is that the flaw is within the deviant and not a function of societal arrangements.

---

[*]The term *cultural deprivation* is a loaded ethnocentric term. It implies that the culture of the group in question is not only deficient but also inferior. This label is applied by members of the majority to the culture of the minority group. The concept itself is patently false because no culture can be inferior to another, only different. The concept does remind us, however, that people can and do make invidious distinctions about cultures and subcultures. Furthermore, they act on these definitions as if they were true, resulting, often, in a self-fulfilling prophecy.

The position taken in this debate has important consequences. Let us briefly examine the effects of interpreting social problems solely within a person-blame framework. First, this interpretation of social problems frees the government, the economy, the system of stratification, the system of justice, and the educational system from any blame. The established order is protected against criticism, thereby increasing the difficulty encountered in trying to change the dominant economic, social, and political institutions. A good example is found in the strategy of social scientists studying the origins of poverty. Because the person blamer studies the poor rather than the nonpoor, the system of inequality (buttressed by the tax laws, welfare rules, and employment practices) goes unchallenged. A related consequence of the person-blame approach, then, is that the relatively advantaged segments of society retain their advantages.

Another social control function of the person-blame approach is that troublesome individuals and groups are controlled in a publicly acceptable manner. The overwhelming emphasis of government programs is on more police, courts, and prisons, rather than on changing crime-producing social conditions. This can be seen in the following facts from the Bureau of Justice Statistics (2010):

- Expenditures increased 420 percent for police departments, 660 percent for the Department of Corrections, and 502 percent for the Judicial Branch from 1982 to 2006.
- The prison population increased from 319,598 in 1980 to 1,513,559 in 2008. Currently there are 7,308,200 Americans in jail, in prison, on parole, or on probation.
- The United States incarcerates more people than any other country in the world.

In addition to social control through incarceration, a person-blame approach demands a person-change treatment program. If the cause of delinquency, for example, is defined as the result of personal pathology, then the solution lies clearly in counseling, behavior modification, psychotherapy, drugs, or some other technique aimed at changing the individual deviant. Such an interpretation of social problems provides and legitimates the right to initiate person-change rather than system-change treatment programs.

A final consequence of person-blame interpretations is that they reinforce social myths about the degree of control we have over our fate. Such interpretations provide justification for a form of **social Darwinism**—that is, a person's placement in the stratification system is a function of ability and effort. By this logic, the poor are poor because they are the dregs of society. In short, they deserve their fate, as do the successful in society. Thus, there is little sympathy for governmental programs to increase welfare to the poor.

We should recognize, however, that the contrasting position—the system-blame orientation—also has its dangers. First, it is only part of the truth. Social problems and deviance are highly complex phenomena that have both individual and systemic origins. Individuals, obviously, can be malicious and aggressive for purely psychological reasons. Perhaps only a psychologist can explain why a particular parent is a child abuser, or why a sniper shoots at cars passing on the freeway. Clearly, society needs to be protected from some

"We find that all of us, as a society, are to blame, but only the defendant is guilty."

individuals. Moreover, some people require particular forms of therapy, remedial help, or special programs on an individual basis if they are to participate in society. But much that is labeled deviant is the end product of social conditions.

A second danger in a dogmatic system-blame orientation is that it presents a rigidly deterministic explanation for social problems. Taken too far, this position views individuals as robots controlled totally by their social environment. A balanced view of people is needed, because human beings have autonomy most of the time to choose between alternative courses of action. This raises the related question as to the degree to which people are responsible for their behavior. An excessive system-blame approach absolves individuals from the responsibility for their actions. To take such a stance argues that society should never restrict deviants. This extreme view invites anarchy.

Despite the problems just noted, the system-blame approach is emphasized in this chapter. The rationale for this is, first, that the contrasting view (individual blame) is the prevailing view in U.S. society. Because average citizens, police personnel, legislators, judges, and social scientists tend to interpret social problems from an individualistic perspective, a balance is needed. Moreover, as noted earlier in this section, to hold a strict person-blame perspective has many negative consequences, and citizens must realize the effects of their ideology.

A second basis for the use of the society-blaming perspective is that the subject matter of sociology is not the individual, who is the special province of psychology, but society. If sociologists do not emphasize the social determinants of behavior, and if they do not make a critical analysis of the social structure, then who will? As noted in Chapter 1, an important ingredient of the sociological perspective is the development of a critical stance toward societal arrangements. The job of the sociologist is to look behind the facade to determine the positive and negative consequences of societal arrangements. The persistent question is, Who benefits under these arrangements and who does not? This is why there should be such a close fit between the sociological approach and the society-blaming perspective. Unfortunately, this has not always been the case.

Society as the Source of Deviance

We have seen that the traditional explanations for deviance, whether biological, psychological, or sociological, have located the source of deviance in individual deviants, their families, or their immediate social settings. The basic assumption of these theories is that because deviants do not fit in society, something is wrong with them. This section provides an antidote to the medical analogy implicit in those theories by focusing instead on two theories that place the blame for deviance on the role of society—labeling theory and conflict theory.

Labeling Theory. All the explanations for deviance described so far assume that deviants differ from nondeviants in behavior, attitude, and motivation. This assumption is buttressed by the commonly held belief that deviance is the actions of a few people who are either criminals, insane, or both. As discussed at the beginning of this chapter, in reality most people break the rules of society at one time or another. From minor infractions like stealing a towel from a hotel to major infractions like illegal drug use, deviant behavior cuts across lines of social class and race.

On the other hand, the bulk of the people processed by the criminal justice system for committing street crimes are the undereducated and the poor. Even data on mental illness demonstrate that the lower classes are more likely than the middle classes to have serious mental problems (Hudson, 2005). The difference is that most people break the rules at one time or another, even serious rules for which they could be placed in jail (for example, theft, statutory rape, vandalism, violation of drug or alcohol laws, fraud, violations of the IRS), but only some get the *label* of deviant. As one adult analyzed his ornery but normal youth:

> I recall my high school and college days, participating in vandalism, entering locked buildings at night, drinking while under age—even while I made top grades and won athletic letters. I was normal and did these things with guys who now are preachers, professors, and businessmen. A few school friends of poorer families somehow tended to get caught and we didn't. They were failing in class, and we all believed they were too dumb not to know when to have fun and when to run. Some of them did time in jail and reformatories. They were "delinquents" and we weren't. (Janzen, 1974:390)

This chapter begins with the statement that society creates deviance by creating rules, the violation of which constitutes deviance. But rule breaking itself does not make a deviant. The successful application of the label "deviant" is crucial. This is the essence of **labeling theory**, the view of deviant behavior that stresses the importance of the society in defining what is illegal and in assigning deviant status to particular individuals, which in turn dominates their identities and behaviors.

Who gets labeled as a deviant is not just a matter of luck or random selection but the result of a systematic societal bias against the powerless. Consider the typical pathway to prison: A person is caught violating a law, arrested, put on trial, found guilty, and sentenced. At every stage in this process, the lower-class person is at a disadvantage.

That there is a bias is beyond dispute (see the Diversity panel titled "The Criminal Justice System: Unreasonable Stops and Searches by Race"), because studies have compared

DIVERSITY

The Criminal Justice System: Unreasonable Stops and Searches by Race

Cornel West (1992), the highly esteemed African American philosopher and theologian at Princeton, has noted several incidents where the police stopped him because of his race:

> Years ago, while driving from New York to teach at Williams College, I was stopped on fake charges of trafficking cocaine. When I told the police officer I was a professor of religion, he replied, "Yeh, and I'm the Flying Nun. Let's go, nigger!" I was stopped three times in my first ten days in Princeton for driving too slowly on a residential street with a speed limit of twenty-five miles per hour. … Needless to say, these incidents are dwarfed by those like Rodney King's beating or the abuse of black targets of the FBI's COINTELPRO efforts in the 1960s and 1970s. Yet the memories cut like a merciless knife at my soul. (x–xi)

Similarly, an African American dentist, Elmo Randolph, has been pulled over by state troopers on the New Jersey Turnpike more than fifty times since 1991, yet has never been issued a ticket. Each time he was asked, "Do you have any drugs or weapons in your car?" (Hosenball, 1999). The harassing of Cornel West and Elmo Randolph was a consequence of "**racial profiling**," the police practice of stopping Blacks and Latino drivers for routine traffic violations and then searching them for evidence of criminal activity (for example, drugs or guns). This practice, known as stopping people for DWB (Driving While Black or Brown) is widespread. Although normally associated with Blacks

and Latinos, racial profiling also includes police stops of Asians, Native Americans, and, especially after 9/11, Arabs, Muslims, and South Asians (American Civil Liberties Union [ACLU], 2008c). Consider the following examples of racial profiling:

- An ACLU study of traffic stops in Rhode Island found that minority drivers were twice as likely to be stopped as White drivers (ACLU, 2007). Ironically, White drivers who were stopped were actually *more likely* to be found with contraband.
- According to a "stop and frisk" report released by the New York Police Department, NYPD stopped 468,932 New Yorkers in 2007. Though they make up one-quarter of New York City's population, half of those stopped were Black. Eighty seven percent of Blacks that were stopped were innocent of any wrongdoing (reported by the ACLU, 2008a).
- In April 2008, the Maryland State Police reached a settlement with individual plaintiffs ending a ten-year "Driving While Black" lawsuit. The plaintiffs were all victims of racial profiling on Maryland Interstate 95 (ACLU, 2008b).
- A study of traffic stops in Florida found that while 5 percent of the drivers on the road were Black or Latino, nearly 70 percent of those stopped and 80 percent of those searched were Black or Latino (Cole, 1999).

(continues)

defendants by socioeconomic status or race, controlling for type of crime, number of previous arrests, type of counsel, and so on. In short, research shows that the well-to-do are much more likely to avoid the label of criminal. If they are found guilty, they are much less likely to receive a punishment of imprisonment, and those who are imprisoned receive advantages over lower-class and minority inmates.

In 2011, 38.5 percent of inmates in state and federal prisons were Black, and 33.2 percent were Hispanic (Federal Bureau of Prisons, 2011). In fact, nearly one in nine Black males in the United States between the ages of twenty and twenty-nine is incarcerated. This statistic shows that the underdogs in society (the poor and the minorities) are disproportionately represented in the prison population. An important consequence of this representation is that it reinforces the negative stereotypes already present in the majority of the population. The large number of Blacks and the poor in prison "prove" that they have criminal tendencies.

The most blatant example of system bias is found by examining what type of person actually receives the death penalty and, even more particularly, those who are executed by the state. The data on capital punishment show consistently that people from disadvantaged categories (racial minorities, the poor, the illiterate) are disproportionately given the death penalty as well as disproportionately executed by the state. A good example is the difference in sentence when a White person is found guilty of killing a Black person, compared to when a Black person is the perpetrator and a White person the victim. The behavior is the same, one individual found guilty of killing another, yet juries and judges make a difference—Blacks receive the harsher sentence and punishment. To date, in cases resulting in a death row execution, 76 percent of the murder victims were White compared to 15 percent Black and 6 percent Hispanic. Nationally, only 50 percent of murder victims generally are White (Death Penalty Information Center, 2010). Furthermore, since 1976, 246 Black defendants have been executed for the murder of a White victim, compared to 15 White defendants executed for the murder of a Black victim. See Figure 7.1 for more data on death row and race.

Who gets paroled is another indicator of a bias in the system. Parole is a conditional release from prison that allows prisoners to return to their communities under the supervision of a parole officer before the completion of their maximum sentence. Typically, a parole board set up for the correctional institution or for the state grants parole. Often, the parole board members are political appointees without training. The parole board reviews a prisoner's social history, past offenses, and behavior in prison and makes its judgment. The decision is rarely subject to review and can be made arbitrarily.

The bias that disadvantages minorities and the poor throughout the system of justice continues as parole board members, corrections officers, and others make judgments that often reflect stereotypes. What type of prisoner represents the safest risk, a Latino or a White?

FIGURE 7.1

Death Penalty
Facts, 2010

*Source: Death Penalty
Information Center,
2010.* 1015 18th St. NW,
Suite 704, Washington,
DC 20036. *http://www.
deathpenaltyinfo.org.*

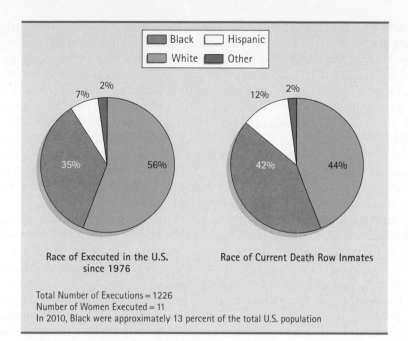

Race of Executed in the U.S. since 1976

Race of Current Death Row Inmates

Total Number of Executions = 1226
Number of Women Executed = 11
In 2010, Black were approximately 13 percent of the total U.S. population

An uneducated or an educated person? An Enron executive or a chronically unemployed, unskilled worker? The evidence is overwhelming and consistent—the parole system, like the rest of the criminal justice system, is biased against people of color and those of low socioeconomic status.

The Consequences of Labeling. We have just seen that the labeling process is a biased process, but what happens when one receives the label "deviant"? Lemert (1951) explained the difference between primary and secondary deviance. **Primary deviance** is the rule breaking that occurs before labeling. **Secondary deviance** is behavior that results from the labeling process. Informal labeling by parents, peers, and teachers, and formal labeling by the justice system results in a high probability that such a person will turn to behavior that fulfills the prophecies of others. Put another way, people labeled as deviants tend to become locked into a deviant behavior pattern (deviant career).

Criminologist Jeffrey Reiman states, "Prison produces more criminals than it cures" (2007:32). At least four factors related to the prison experience operate to fulfill the prophecy that the poor and racial minorities are likely to behave criminally. The first is that the entire criminal justice system is viewed by the underdogs as unjust. There is a growing belief among prisoners that because the system is biased against them, all prisoners are, in fact, political. This consciousness raising increases the bitterness and anger among them.

A second reason for the high rate of crime among those processed through the system of criminal justice is the accepted fact that prison is a brutal, degrading, and altogether dehumanizing experience. Mistreatment by guards, sexual assaults by fellow prisoners, overcrowding, and unsanitary conditions are commonplace in U.S. jails and prisons. Prisoners cannot escape the humiliation, anger, and frustration.

A third factor is that prisons provide learning experiences for prisoners in the art of crime. Through inmate interaction, individuals learn the techniques of crime from the experts and develop contacts that can be used later.

Finally, the ex-con faces the problems of finding a job and being accepted again in society. Long-term inmates face problems of adjusting to life without regimentation. More important, since good-paying jobs, particularly in times of economic recession, are difficult for anyone to find, the ex-con, who is automatically assumed to be untrustworthy, is faced with either unemployment or those jobs nobody else will take. Even the law works to his or her disadvantage by prohibiting certain jobs to ex-cons. A study by sociology professor Devah Pager found that 17 percent of White job applicants with criminal records received a call back from potential employers, whereas only 5 percent of Black job applicants with criminal records received a call back (Pager, 2003). Shockingly, only 14 percent of Blacks with *no* criminal record received a call back, which is less than the 17 percent of Whites *with* a criminal record!

The result of nonacceptance by society is often a return to crime. Previous offenders, on the average, are arrested for crime within six weeks after leaving prison. This, of course, justifies the beliefs by police officers, judges, parole boards, and other authorities that certain categories of people should receive punishment whereas others should not.

Ex-mental patients, like ex-convicts, also have difficulty in finding employment and establishing close relationships because of the stigma of the label. This difficulty, of course, leads to frustration, anger, low self-esteem, and other symptoms of mental illness. Moreover, the consistent messages from other people (recall Cooley's looking-glass self from Chapter 5) that one is sick are likely to lead the individual to behavior in accord with these expectations. Even while a patient is in a mental hospital, the actions of the staff may actually foster in the person a self-concept of deviant behavior consistent with that definition. Patients who show insight about their illness confirm the medical and societal diagnosis and are positively rewarded by psychiatrists and other personnel. The opposite also occurs, as illustrated so vividly by the character R. P. McMurphy in the classic novel *One Flew Over the Cuckoo's Nest* (Kesey, 1962). Although the fictitious McMurphy fought this tendency to confirm the expectations of powerful others, the pressures to conform were great. When providers saw him as mentally ill, he began to live up to their expectations.

The labeling perspective is especially helpful in understanding the bias of the criminal justice system. It shows, in summary, that when society's underdogs are disproportionately singled out for the criminal label, the subsequent problems of stigmatization and segregation they face result in a tendency toward further deviance, thereby "justifying" the society's original negative response to them.

"Solutions" for Deviance from the Labeling Perspective. The labeling theorist's approach to deviance leads to unconventional solutions. The assumption is that deviants are not basically different—except that they have been processed (and labeled) by official sources (judges and courts, psychiatrists and mental hospitals). The primary target for policy, then, should be neither the individual nor the local community setting, but the process by which some people are singled out for the negative label. From this approach, organizations produce deviants. In 1973 Edwin Schur published a book called *Radical Non-Intervention: Rethinking the Delinquency Problem*. In it he argued for **radical nonintervention**—the strategy of leaving juvenile delinquents alone as much as possible rather than giving them a negative label. Randall Shelden (2004) argues that Schur's ideas are extremely relevant in today's society, because as a society we have done exactly the opposite of what Schur proposed. Shelden argues that we only need to look at the current "zero tolerance" mentality within the school system to see how minor offenses are being processed formally within the justice system. He offers the following examples:

> Examples abound, including the following: (1) a five year prison sentence handed out to a 17-year-old Texas high school basketball player who "threw an elbow" to the head of an opposing player in a basketball game; (2) two six-year-old children were suspended for three days for playing "cops and robbers" with their fingers (pretending their fingers were guns and going "bang, bang" toward other children); (3) a girl who gave a friend a Nuprin was suspended for "dealing drugs"; (4) some high school baseball players were suspended for possessing "dangerous weapons" on school grounds—a teacher who suspected

them of having drugs found none, but instead found some baseball bats in their cars; (5) a 14-year-old boy was charged by school police with a felony for throwing a deadly missile (which turned out to be a Halloween "trick or treat" of throwing an egg). He was taken away in handcuffs and put in juvenile detention. ... (Shelden, 2004:1)

Shelden argues that the juvenile justice system is taking things too far, and that we need to reassess the ideas behind radical nonintervention. He asks:

> Why are certain acts labeled "criminal" or "delinquent" while others are not? Another pertinent question this approach asks is, how do we account for differential rates of arrest, referral to court, detention, adjudication and commitment based upon race and class? These are not merely academic questions, for the lives of real people are being impacted by recent "get tough" policies. We continue to criminalize normal adolescent behavior or behavior that should be dealt with informally, outside of the formal juvenile justice system. (Shelden, 2004:11–12)

One way to accomplish this "leave the deviants alone whenever possible" philosophy would be to treat fewer acts as criminal or deviant. For adults, this could be accomplished by decriminalizing victimless crimes, such as gambling, drug possession, and prostitution. Youth should not be treated as criminals for behavior that is legal if one is old enough. Truancy, running away from home, curfew violations, and purchasing alcohol are acts for which people below the legal age can receive the label delinquent, yet they are not crimes for adults.

Acts dangerous to society do occur, and they must be handled through legal mechanisms. But when a legal approach is required, justice must be applied evenly. Currently, the criminal label is disproportionately applied to individuals from certain social class and race backgrounds. This unfair cycle must be broken.

The strengths of labeling theory are that it (1) concentrates on the role of societal reactions in the creation of deviance, (2) realizes that the label is applied disproportionately to the powerless, and (3) explains how deviant careers are established and perpetuated. There are problems with the theory, however. First, it avoids the question of causation (primary deviance). Labeling, by definition, occurs after the fact so it does not clearly explain what caused deviant behavior in the first place.

Another problem with labeling theory involves the assumption that deviants are really normal—because we are all rule breakers. Thus, it overlooks the possibility that some people are unable to cope with the pressures of their situation and some people are dangerous. The result may be differences in quantity and quality of primary deviance.

This perspective also relieves the individual deviant from blame. The underdog is seen as victimized by the powerful labelers. Further, individuals enmeshed in the labeling process are so constrained by the forces of society that they are incapable of choice.

Perhaps its most serious deficiency, though, is that labeling theory focuses on certain types of deviance but ignores others. The attention is directed at society's underdogs, which is good. But the forms of deviance emanating from the social structure or from the powerful are not considered a very serious omission. Labeling theory focuses attention on people who have been successfully labeled as deviants, the deviant subculture, and the self-fulfilling prophecy that perpetuates their deviant patterns. Even though this is appropriate and necessary, it concentrates on the powerless. The impression is that deviance is an exclusive property of the poor in the inner cities, the minorities, and street gangs. But what about the deviance perpetuated by the powerful members of society? Another way to explain deviance—conflict theory—extends labeling theory by focusing on social structure and power.

Conflict Theory. Why is certain behavior defined as deviant? The answer, according to conflict theorists, is that powerful economic interest groups are able to get laws passed and enforced that protect their interests. They begin, then, with the law.

Of all the requirements for a just system, the most fundamental is the foundation of nondiscriminatory laws. Many criminal laws are the result of a consensus among the public as to what kinds of behaviors are a menace and should be punished (for example, murder, rape, theft). The laws devised to make these acts illegal and the extent of punishment for violators are nondiscriminatory (although, as we have seen, the administration of these laws is discriminatory), because they do not single out a particular social category as the target.

Civil Disobedience

On the first day of the 2009 United Nations climate change negotiations in Copenhagen, environmental activists engage in civil disobedience at Chevron in California.

In 1849 Henry David Thoreau wrote an essay titled "Resistance to Civil Government." His essay was a response to being jailed for refusing to pay a government poll tax, a tax that Thoreau refused to pay in protest against slavery. The phrase "civil disobedience" was thus born. **Civil disobedience** may be seen as a public, nonviolent breach of the law with the purpose of calling attention to unfair laws or practices (Brownlee, 2010). Throughout history civil disobedience has been an important tool for social change. Consider the following examples:

- The Boston Tea Party: Colonists from Massachusetts stole onto a British ship and threw its cargo (tea) into the harbor to protest the British Tea Act.
- Anti-War Protests: During the Vietnam War, students held sit-ins and rallies on college campuses to protest the war. Some men refused to enlist.
- Women's Suffrage: Women marched in the streets and engaged in hunger strikes to protest the ban on women voting.
- Rosa Parks and Civil Rights: In 1955, Rosa Parks disobeyed the law and the request of a bus driver to

give up her seat to a White passenger. She was arrested and her actions led to the Montgomery Bus Boycott, a citywide protest against racial segregation in public transit.

Today, we see numerous examples of civil disobedience in connection with special interests like the environment, animal rights, foreign policy, and globalization (Brownlee, 2010). For example, environmental activists have chained themselves to trees to protest deforestation, and animal rights activists have freed animals from cages on private company property.

In each of these historical and contemporary examples, individuals acted to convey their disapproval of certain laws or policies, to call attention to those laws and policies, and to push for social change. In addition, they were willing to face punishment for violating society's rules. While opponents may see civil disobedience as a threat to democracy, without question civil disobedience has been a key mechanism for social change.

There are laws, however, that do discriminate, because they result from special interests using their power to translate their interests into public policy. These laws may be discriminatory in that some segments of society (for example, the poor, minorities, youth) rarely have access to the lawmaking process and therefore often find the laws unfairly aimed at them. For a look at how some individuals have fought discriminatory laws, see the Human Agency panel titled "Civil Disobedience."

Not only is the formation of the law political, but so, too, is the administration of the law. This is true because at every stage in the processing of criminals, authorities make choices based on personal bias, pressures from the powerful, and the constraints of the status quo. Some examples of the political character of law administration are these: (1) The powerful attempt to coerce other people to adopt their view of morality, hence laws against pornography, drug use, and gambling; (2) the powerful may exert pressure on the authorities to crack down on certain kinds of violators, especially individuals and groups who are disruptive (protesters); (3) there may be political pressure exerted to keep certain crimes from public view (embezzlement, stock fraud, accounting tricks that make losses appear to be gains); (4) there may be pressure to protect the party in power, the elected officials, the police, the Central Intelligence Agency (CIA), and the FBI; and (5) any effort to protect and preserve the status quo is a political act.

The conflict approach is critical of the kinds-of-people explanations of order theorists and the focus of labeling theorists because both explanations center on individual deviants and their crimes. Order theorists and labeling theorists tend to emphasize street crimes and ignore the crimes of the rich and powerful, such as corporate crimes (which go largely unpoliced) and crimes by governments (which are not even considered crimes, unless they are committed by enemy governments). Conflict theorists, in contrast, emphasize corporate and political crimes, which cause many times more economic damage and harm to people than do street crimes. **Corporate crime** refers to the "illegal and/or socially harmful behaviors that result from deliberate decision making by corporate executives in accordance with the operative goals of their organizations" (Kramer, 1982:75). This definition focuses attention on corporations, rather than on individuals, as perpetrators, and it goes beyond the criminal law to include "socially harmful behaviors."

Both of these elements are critical to conflict theorists. First, deviance is not limited to troubled individuals, as is the traditional focus in sociology. Organizations, too, can be deviant.

The second part of the definition of corporate crime stresses "socially harmful behaviors," whether criminal or not. This means that conflict theorists ask such questions as these: "What about selling proven dangerous products (for example, pesticides, drugs, or food) overseas, when it is illegal to do so within the United States? What about promoting an unsafely designed automobile such as the Ford Pinto? Or, what about being excessively slow to promote a safe work environment for workers?" Analysts argue that corporate crime inflicts far more damage on society than all street crimes combined (Mokhiber, 2007). Consider the following examples of corporate crime:

- In the 1980s and 1990s, savings and loan fraud—which former Attorney General Dick Thornburgh called "the biggest white collar swindle in history" cost the United States anywhere from $300 billion to $500 billion. Note that the FBI estimates the costs to society for the street crimes of burglary and robbery to be about $3.8 billion per year (Mokhiber, 2007:1).
- In 1996, Royal Caribbean Cruise Lines was found guilty of illegally dumping oil waste in the Gulf of Mexico. They had been illegally dumping for years, and they falsified their logbooks to hide their activities (Wald, 1996).

- Fifty-six thousand Americans die every year on the job or from occupational diseases such as black lung and asbestosis. Thousands more fall victim to hazardous consumer products, contaminated foods, hospital malpractice, and pollution (Mokhiber, 2007:2).
- In 1997, Hudson foods was found guilty of lying to investigators from the U.S. Department of Agriculture about contaminated hamburger meat (Belluck, 1998).
- In August 2006, a Federal judge found Big Tobacco firms guilty of civil fraud and racketeering. For years, Big Tobacco companies claimed that they did not know that nicotine was addictive. The judge ruled that they deceived the public about the dangers of smoking in order to gain financially.
- According to the FBI, an estimated $14 billion in fraudulent loans were originated in 2009, contributing to the housing and foreclosure crisis in the United States (2009).

These are just a few of the many examples of corporate crimes that are the focus of conflict theorists.

The definition of **political crime** separates order and conflict theorists. Because order theorists assume that the law and the state are neutral, they perceive political crimes as activities against the government, such as acts of dissent and violence whose purpose is to challenge and change the existing political order. Conflict theorists, in sharp contrast, assume that the law and the state are often tools of the powerful used to keep them in power. Thus, the political order itself may be criminal because it can be unjust. Moreover, government, like a corporation, may follow policies that go against democratic principles and that do harm. Examples of political crimes from this perspective are CIA interventions in the domestic affairs of other nations, Watergate, the Iran-contra affair, war crimes, slavery, imperialism (such as forcibly taking land from Native Americans), police brutality, and using citizens experimentally without their knowledge and consent.

An extreme example of using human subjects as guinea pigs is a study begun in 1932 by the U.S. Public Health Service. The subjects were 400 African American male syphilis patients in Macon County, Alabama. The patients did not know that they had syphilis and were never informed of that fact. Because the purpose of the study was to assess the consequences of not treating the disease, the men were not treated, nor were their wives. When their children were born with congenital syphilis, they, too, were not treated. The experiment lasted forty years, until 1972 (Jones, J. H., 1981).

In sum, the focus of the conflict perspective is on the political and economic setting in society. The power of certain interests determines what gets defined as deviance (and who, then, is a deviant) and how this "problem" is to be solved. Because the powerful benefit from the status quo, they vigorously thwart efforts to reform society. The solution, from the conflict theorists, however, requires not only reform of society but also its radical transformation. The structure of society is the problem.

There are some problems with this perspective. First, there is the tendency to assume a conspiracy by the well-to-do. Because the empirical evidence is overwhelming that the poor, the uneducated, and the members of minority groups are singled out for the deviant label, some persons make the too-facile imputation of motive. Second, solutions from the conflict perspective involve the radical transformation of the power structure of society, something that is much more difficult to accomplish than solutions that focus on changing individual behavior.

The strengths of the conflict perspective on deviance are (1) its emphasis on the relationship between political order and nonconformity, (2) its understanding that the most powerful groups use the political order to protect their interests, (3) its emphasis on how the justice system is unjust and the distribution of rewards in society is skewed, and (4) its realization that the institutional framework of society is the source of so many social problems (for example, racism, sexism, pollution, unequal distribution of health care, poverty, and economic cycles).

147

CHAPTER 7
Deviance

Deviance from the Order and Conflict Perspectives

The two contrasting theoretical perspectives in sociology—the order model and the conflict model—constrain their adherents to view the causes, consequences, and remedies of deviance in opposing ways. The order perspective focuses on deviants themselves. This approach (which has been the conventional way of studying social problems) asks, Who are the deviants? What are their social and psychological backgrounds? With whom do they associate? Deviants somehow do not conform to the standards of the dominant group; they are assumed to be out of phase with conventional behavior. This is believed to occur most often as a result of inadequate socialization. In other words, deviants have not internalized the norms and values of society because they either are brought up in an environment of conflicting value systems (as are children of immigrants or the poor in a middle-class school) or are under the influence of a deviant subculture, such as a gang. Because the order theorist uses the prevailing standards to define and label deviants, the existing practices and structures of society are accepted implicitly. The remedy is to rehabilitate deviants so that they conform to the societal norms.

The conflict theorist takes a different approach to social problems. The adherents of this perspective criticize order theorists for blaming the victim. To focus on the individual deviant is to locate the symptom, not the disease. Individual deviants are a manifestation of a failure of society to meet the needs of individuals. The sources of crime, poverty, drug addiction, and racism are found in the laws; the customs; the quality of life; the distribution of wealth and power; and the accepted practices of schools, governmental units, and corporations. The established system, in this view, is not sacred. Because it is the primary source of social problems, it, not the individual deviant, must be restructured.

Because this is a text on society, we emphasize the conflict approach. The insights of this approach are clarified further in the remainder of this book as we examine the structure and consequences of social inequality in Chapters 8 through 12, followed by chapters describing the positive and negative effects of institutions.

CHAPTER REVIEW

1. Deviance is behavior that violates the laws and expectations of a group. This means that deviance is not a property inherent in a behavior but a property conferred on that behavior by other people. In short, deviance is socially created.

2. What is deviant varies from society to society, and within a society the same behavior may be interpreted differently when it is done by different categories of people.

3. The norms of the majority determine what behaviors are considered deviant.

4. Order theorists point out that deviant behavior has positive consequences for society, because it gives nondeviants a sense of solidarity and reaffirms the importance of society's rules.

5. People who violate the norms of society are often stigmatized.

6. Several traditional theories for the causes of deviance assume the source as a fatal flaw in certain people. These theories focus on physical or psychological reasons for deviant behavior.

7. Kinds-of-people explanations for deviance also apply to some theories by sociologists. One theory argues that crime results from the influences of peers. A second focuses on the propensity of the poor to be deviants because of the gap between the goal of success and the lack of the means for these people to attain it. Culture of poverty theorists argue that lower-class culture is responsible.

8. These kinds-of-people theories have been criticized for blaming the victim. Because they blame the victim, the society (government, system of justice, education) is freed from blame. Since the established order is thus protected from criticism, necessary social change is thwarted.

9. An alternative to person-blame theories is labeling theory. This approach argues that even though most people break the rules on occasion, the crucial factor in establishing a deviant career is the successful application of the label "deviant."

10. Who gets labeled as a deviant is not a matter of luck but the result of a systematic societal bias against the powerless.

11. Primary deviance is the rule breaking that occurs prior to labeling. Secondary deviance is behavior resulting from the labeling process.

12. Labeling theorists argue that because deviants are not much different from non-deviants, the problem lies in organizations that label. Thus, these organizations should (a) leave deviants alone whenever possible and (b) apply justice fairly when the legal approach is required.

13. Labeling theory has been criticized because it (a) disregards undetected deviance, (b) assumes that deviants are really normal because we are all rule breakers, (c) relieves the individual from blame, and (d) focuses on certain types of deviance but ignores deviance by the powerful.

14. Conflict theory focuses on social structure as the source of deviance. There is a historical bias in the law that favors the powerful. The administration of justice is also biased. In short, the state is a political organization controlled by the ruling class for its own advantage. The power of powerful interests in society determines what and who are deviant.

15. The conflict perspective emphasizes both corporate and political crimes that are harmful to society. From the conflict perspective, the only real and lasting solution to deviance is the radical transformation of society.

16. Order theorists focus on individual deviants. Because this perspective uses the prevailing standards to define and label deviants, the existing practices and structures of society are accepted implicitly. The remedy is to rehabilitate deviants so they conform to the societal norms.

KEY TERMS

Deviance
Culture of poverty
Cultural deprivation
Recidivism
Social Darwinism

Labeling theory
Racial profiling
Primary deviance
Secondary deviance
Radical nonintervention

Civil disobedience
Corporate crime
Political crime

STUDY QUESTIONS

1. Are there universal criteria that determine what is deviant at all times and places? Explain.
2. Most of us at one time or another behave in deviant ways. Why, then, aren't we considered deviants?
3. Explain how deviant behavior has positive social consequences for the group.
4. What is labeling theory? What are its strengths and weaknesses in understanding deviant behavior?
5. Contrast the order and conflict interpretations of deviance.

http://www.ojp.usdoj.gov/bjs/

The Bureau of Justice Statistics is a branch of the government that provides information on crime and deviance. Among the subjects on the site are criminal offenders, courts and sentencing, and key facts at a glance.

http://crimespider.com/

Crime Spider provides a list of crime and law enforcement sites arranged by topic. Topics include homicide, cybercrime, and crime studies.

http://www.asc41.com/

The American Society of Criminology is "an international organization concerned with criminology, embracing scholarly, scientific, and professional knowledge concerning the etiology, prevention, control and treatment of crime and delinquency. This includes the measurement and detection of crime, legislation and practice of criminal law, as well as the law enforcement, judicial and correctional systems."

http://www.fas.org/sgp/

Part of the Federation of American Scientists, the Project on Government Secrecy "works to challenge excessive government secrecy and to promote public oversight."

http://www.truthinjustice.org/

Truth in Justice is a nonprofit organized to "educate the public regarding the vulnerabilities in the U.S. criminal justice system that makes the criminal conviction of wholly innocent persons possible."

http://www.deathpenaltyinfo.org

The Death Penalty Information Center provides statistics and information regarding all aspects of capital punishment.

Structural Sources of Social Change: Economic and Demographic

W e are in the midst of three societal "earthquakes." For most of the twentieth century, the U.S. economy was primarily based on domestic production and consumption and its population was overwhelmingly young, White, and of European heritage. Now three massive changes are in progress: (1) the globalization and transformation of the U.S. economy, which have profound effects on jobs and security here and abroad; (2) the "new immigration," which is changing the racial composition of the United States, as Latino and Asian American populations increase dramatically; and (3) the aging of the population, which is transforming families, politics, work, and public policies. These social changes are more far-reaching and are occurring more rapidly than at any other time in human history. The purpose of this chapter is to understand these three macro social trends and the important ways that they affect individuals, families, communities, and the institutions of society.

Globalization and the Structural Transformation of the Economy

There have been two fundamental turning points in human history. The Neolithic agricultural revolution began about 8000 B.C., marking the transition from nomadic pastoral life, during which the animal and vegetable sources of food were hunted and gathered, to life in settlements based on agriculture. During this phase of human existence, tools were created and used; animals were domesticated; language, numbers, and other symbols became more sophisticated; and mining and metalworking were developed.

The second fundamental turning point, the Industrial Revolution, began in Great Britain in the 1780s. With the application of steam power and later oil and electricity as energy sources for industry, mining, manufacturing, and transportation came fundamental changes to the economy, the nature of work, family organization, and a transition from rural to urban life.

In effect, societies are transformed with each surge in invention and technological growth. Peter F. Drucker (1993) describes the historical import of such transformations:

> Every few hundred years in Western history there occurs a sharp transformation. We cross ... a "divide." Within a few short decades, society rearranges itself—its worldview; its basic values; its social and political structure; its arts; its key institutions. Fifty years later, there is a new world. And the people born then cannot even imagine the world in which their grandparents lived and into which their own parents were born. We are currently living through just such a transformation. (1)

The United States is now in the midst of a new transformation, one fueled by new technologies and applications (superfast computers, the Internet, fiber optics, biotechnology, the decoding of the human genome, artificial intelligence, and cell telephony). The amazing scientific breakthroughs have had and will continue to have immense implications for commerce, international trade, global politics, and, at the individual level, work opportunities, pay, and benefits.

Globalization

Among other changes, the new technologies have, most significantly, magnified the connections among all peoples across the globe (the following is dependent in part on Eitzen, Baca Zinn, and Smith, 2010, chapter 8; and Eitzen and Baca Zinn, 2012). The Internet makes worldwide communications instantaneous. Money moves across political boundaries with a few keystrokes. Low wages in one country affect wages elsewhere. A drought in one part of the world drives up prices for commodities everywhere, while overproduction of a product in one region brings down the prices of that product elsewhere. A collapse in the stock market of one nation has ramifications for financial markets around the world. Movies, television, and advertising from one society affect the tastes, interests, and styles in other places. Polluted air and water cross national borders. Deforestation in the developing nations has a major effect on climate change everywhere. Global warming, caused by the burning of fossil fuels, changes climates, generates megastorms, and increases the spread of tropical diseases around the world. A disease such as HIV/AIDS left Africa some fifty years ago and now infects 33 million people worldwide and 1.2 million in North America. H1N1 became a pandemic (worldwide health danger) within a few months. There has been a dramatic increase in migration flows, especially from poorer to richer nations. With sophisticated weapons systems, no nation is immune from assault from other nations or terrorist acts by revolutionary groups.

Each of these examples of **globalization** involves the processes by which everyone on Earth becomes increasingly interconnected economically, politically, culturally, and environmentally. Connections among peoples outside their tribes or political units are not new, but the linkages now are increasing geometrically, with few, if any, groups unaffected. We concentrate here on economic globalization.

Although trade between and among nations is not new, global trade entered a new phase after World War II. What have evolved are a global trade network, the integration of peoples and nations, and a global economy, with a common ideology: capitalism (see the Globalization panel titled "Sending U.S. Jobs Overseas"). Former colonies have established local industries and sell their raw materials, products, and labor on the global market. The United States emerged as the strongest economic and military power in the world, with U.S. corporations vitally interested in expanding their operations to other societies for profit. The shift to a global economy has been accelerated by the tearing down of tariff barriers. The North American Free Trade Agreement (NAFTA) and the General Agreement on Tariffs and Trade (GATT), both passed in 1994, are two examples of agreements that increased the flow of goods (and jobs) across national boundaries. In 2005 President Bush signed the Central American Free Trade Agreement (CAFTA), which institutes a Western Hemisphere-wide version of NAFTA.

The globalization of the economy is not a neutral process. Decisions are based on what will maximize profits, thus serving the owners of capital and not necessarily workers or the communities where U.S. operations are located. In this regard, private businesses, in their search for profit, make crucial investment decisions that change the dynamics in families and communities. Most significant are the corporate decisions regarding the movement of corporate money from one investment to another (called **capital flight**). This shift of capital takes several forms: investment in plants located in other nations, plant relocation within the United States, and mergers. While these investment decisions may be positive for corporations, they also take away investment (disinvestment) from others (workers and their families, communities, and suppliers).

Sending U.S. Jobs Overseas

Following the September 11, 2001, terrorist attacks, Boeing, the giant aerospace corporation, laid off nearly 30,000 workers due to many airlines canceling or delaying plane orders (the following is mostly from Stanley Holmes, 2002). A year later, Boeing announced that it would not hire back these workers but instead would shift most of its work to lower-cost suppliers in the United States, and would move the advanced design and engineering tasks to Russia and China (the Russian engineers, for example, make about $10,000 a year, compared to $72,000 that the average Boeing engineers make). Specifically, the company has already moved many of its operations outside the United States:

- Five hundred engineers and technicians from the Moscow Design Center design parts for the 777 and other commercial jetliners.
- Xian Aircraft in central China builds tail sections for the 737.
- WZK-Mielec of Poland makes aircraft doors for the 757.
- Shanghai Aircraft manufactures components for several types of Boeing planes.

- Mexmil in Mexicali, Mexico, makes fuselage-insulation blankets for all of Boeing's commercial planes.

These are examples of outsourcing by Boeing. Outsourcing is the practice of subcontracting work outside the company and its relatively well-paid (usually unionized) workers to companies inside and outside the United States where the costs are cheaper. As the head of the engineers' union affected by Boeing's moves, the Society of Professional Engineering Employees in Aerospace, puts it, "They have to stop boxing up our work and sending it to Moscow" (quoted in Holmes, 2002:75).

Boeing executives see globalization as a way to both expand sales to nations that sign on as manufacturing partners and to tap into cheaper labor markets. Philip M. Condit, the chief executive officer of Boeing, used the massive layoffs after September 11 as a window of opportunity to transform Boeing into a "global enterprise that's much less dependent on the U.S. for both brawn and brains" (quoted in Holmes, 2002:74).

Most of the manufacturing by U.S. transnational corporations is now done in low-wage economies. Manufacturers have moved offshore because profits are greater and because giant retailers (for example, Wal-Mart) have compelled manufacturers to move offshore in search of lower prices for consumers and higher profits for themselves (Meyerson, 2010: A16 A17). This migration of jobs takes two forms, both related to capital flight: offshoring and outsourcing (Friedman, 2005). **Offshoring** is when a company moves its production to another country, producing the same products in the same way, but with cheaper labor, lower taxes, and lower benefits to workers. **Outsourcing** refers to taking some specific task that a company was doing in-house—such as research, call centers, accounting, or transcribing—and transferring it to an overseas company to save money and reintegrating that work back into the overall operation.

> An explosion of new technologies—including e-mail, digitization, the Internet, broadband technology, scanners, communication satellites, undersea fiber-optic cables, and videoconferencing—has made it convenient for business to move white-collar jobs overseas. ... Now, radiologists in India are analyzing X-rays for Massachusetts General and other hospitals. Five hundred engineers in Moscow are helping Boeing design and build aircraft, as Boeing lays off engineers in the United States. The Bank of America moved 1,000 technical and back-office jobs to India while cutting 3,700 jobs in the United States. (Greenhouse, 2009:203)

This move to low-wage economies from outsourcing and offshoring has three negative effects on U.S. workers. First, U.S. jobs are exported. In 2010, for example, U.S. corporations added 1.4 million jobs—overseas (Hightower, 2011). Second, the wages of those production workers who have not lost their jobs remain relatively low because if they seek higher wages, their employers threaten to move the jobs elsewhere. And, third, workers' unions have been weakened because they, too, have lost clout. When workers had strong unions, the wages and benefits were enough for a middle-class lifestyle.

The phenomenon of outsourcing has three roots. First, there is the worldwide communications revolution spawned by the Internet. Second, there is a supply of qualified workers in

English-speaking countries, most notably India but also the Philippines, Barbados, Jamaica, Singapore, and Ireland. And, third, these workers are willing to work for one-fifth or less the salary of comparable U.S. workers. The kinds of jobs affected by outsourcing are software engineers, accountants, architects, engineers, are designers, x-ray technicians, and airplane maintenance. In this latter instance airlines such as JetBlue and U.S. Airways tune up their planes in El Salvador, where mechanics make $4,500 to $15,000 a year, compared to the average in the United States of $52,000 annually (*Business Week*, 2008). Also negatively affected are lower-level, white-collar jobs such as customer service representatives, telemarketers, record transcribers, and those who make airline and hotel reservations.

Structural Transformation of the Economy

From Manufacturing to Services. The U.S. economy was once dominated by agriculture, but in the twentieth century, while agricultural productivity increased, the number employed in agriculture declined precipitously. The economy was now dominated by manufacturing. Just as the shift from an agrarian economy to one dominated by manufacturing represented a **structural transformation of the economy**, so too is the current shift from a manufacturing economy to one characterized by service occupations and the collection, storage, manipulation, and dissemination of information. Manufacturing employment as a proportion of total U.S. private-sector jobs has declined from about 35 percent in 1950 to 8.7 percent in late 2009 (Hindery and Gerard, 2009), down from about 30 percent in 1959. Some other indicators of this shift away from manufacturing (McCormack, 2010):

- Since 2001, the United States has lost 42,000 factories.
- Total manufacturing gross domestic product (GDP) in 2008 represented 11.5 percent of U.S. economic output, down from 17 percent in 1999, and 28 percent in 1959.
- The furniture industry lost 60 percent of its production capacity in the United States from 2000 to 2008.
- The manufacture of printed circuit boards in the United States accounted for only 8 percent of global production in 2008, down from 26 percent in 2000.

Every new era poses new problems of adjustment, but this one differs from the agricultural and industrial eras. The earlier transformations were gradual enough for adaptation to take place over several decades, but conditions are significantly different now. The rate of change now is phenomenal and unprecedented.

The Changing Nature of Jobs. Joseph Schumpeter (1950) described a process inherent to capitalism that he called "creative destruction." By this he meant that as the economic structure of capitalism mutates, some sectors will lose out while others gain. For example, in 1917, the largest U.S. corporation, with three times the assets of its nearest competitor, was U.S. Steel, employing 268,000 workers. Today U.S. Steel is worth about one-fifth what it was in 1917 and employs only 26,840 workers. Replacing U.S. Steel at the apex of the nation's corporate elite are companies such as Microsoft, Intel, and Merck. Today the largest employer in the United States is Wal-Mart. These facts illustrate how manufacturing, the backbone of the U.S. economy in the twentieth century, is no longer dominant. It has been replaced by the service sector and knowledge-based companies. Whereas in the past people mostly worked at producing goods, now they tend to be doing work in offices, banking, insurance, retailing, health care, education, custodial work, restaurant work, security, and transportation.

The shift away from manufacturing to services and information/knowledge means that some sectors of the economy fade in importance or will even die out completely. These sectors are known as **sunset industries**. Over 1,500 plants in manufacturing such as steel, tires, shoes, toys, and textiles have closed permanently since 1975. And literally millions of blue-collar jobs, most of which were unionized with good pay and benefits, were lost and not replaced. See the Closer Look panel titled "Capitalism's Changing Job Market: A Process of Creative Destruction."

Capitalism's Changing Job Market: A Process of Creative Destruction

Societies experience periodic sharp economic transformations, each having dramatic effects on jobs—creating new ones and destroying others. Let's consider, briefly, two economic transformations in the United States during the twentieth century—the fall of agriculture and the rise and fall of manufacturing.

Agriculture

In 1850, 60 percent of workers were employed in agriculture. Now, less than 2.7 percent are engaged in farming (Rifkin, 1995:109–110). This dramatic shift was caused by the new technologies (for example, tractors replaced horses; trucks displaced wagons; combines deposed threshing machines; mechanized cotton, tomato, and corn pickers made field workers obsolete; and herbicides took the place of people with hoes). In effect, the combustion engine replaced oxen, mules, horses, and all but a few people. The result was that many millions of farmers changed jobs. Many occupations (harnessmakers, those who made handcrafted wood plows, farriers) became obsolete while others flourished (for example, the manufacture of farm implements, giving rise to the John Deere Company and Ford, which specialized in tractors and trucks). The science of farming also created new jobs with the need for more effective fertilizers, herbicides, and insecticides, as well as the development of new plant-breeding techniques designed to produce varieties and strains that were more uniform and easier to manipulate with machines.

Manufacturing Products

During the twentieth century, the great job growth machine was in manufacturing. Workers, many of whom formerly worked on farms or in the mines, moved to industrial centers, where work was plentiful in the steel mills, automobile plants, and other places of manufacture. With the help of unions and increased government programs (for example, Social Security), these blue-collar workers prospered.

> There is no parallel in history to the rise of the working man in the developed countries during this century.

Eighty years ago American blue-collar workers, toiling 60 hours a week, made $250 a year at most … and they had no "fringes," no seniority, no unemployment insurance, no Social Security, no paid holidays, no overtime, no pension—nothing but a cash wage of less than one dollar a day. Today's employed blue-collar worker in a unionized mass-production industry (steel, automotive, electrical machinery, paper, rubber, petroleum) working 40 hours a week earns about $50,000 a year—half in cash wages, half in benefits. … And now it is suddenly over. There is no parallel in history to the abrupt decline of the blue-collar worker during the past 15 years. As a proportion of the working population, blue-collar workers in manufacturing have decreased to [16 percent] of the American labor force from more than a third. By the year 2010 … they will constitute no larger a proportion of the labor force of every developed country than farmers do today—that is, a 20th of the total. … Yesterday's blue-collar workers in manufacturing were society's darlings; they are fast becoming stepchildren. (Drucker, 1989:81–82)

These workers are being displaced by automation and the flight of capital. In 1980, for example, U.S. Steel employed 120,000 people in steel production. Ten years later, it employed 20,000, yet maintained the same steel tonnage (Drucker, 1993:72). Even with the dramatic decline of workers in the entire manufacturing industry, U.S. companies have continued to increase output and overall production, with more and more automation, including the use of robots. "Automated technologies have been reducing the need for human labor in every manufacturing category. … Over the next quarter-century we will see the virtual elimination of the blue-collar, mass assembly-line worker from the production process" (Rifkin, 1996:11). These two transformations show that capitalism is a process of creative destruction. This is to say that with technological change, new opportunities emerge just as the old ways are destroyed. The present transformation from the industrial age to an information age presents just such a situation with winners and losers.

But while jobs have shrunk by the millions in the last two decades, many millions more have been created in **sunrise industries** (those industries characterized by increased output and employment). Such jobs are involved in the production of high-tech products (for example, computer software, medical instruments, bioengineering, and robotics). Also, lower-end service jobs such as retail clerks, janitors, and security guards have increased (and they have the advantage of being immune from offshoring and outsourcing).

Many blue-collar jobs have also been lost to automation. Robots, since the 1960s have replaced humans doing routine work such as picking fruit, welding, assembling, painting, and scanning products for defects. Now robots can see, feel, move, and work together. Similarly,

Computer Technology and Middle-Class Job Loss

Economist Paul Krugman argues that technological progress is actually reducing the demand for highly educated workers. He provides examples of legal research software, which analyzes millions of documents cheaply, tasks that once required armies of lawyers and paralegals, and software that replaces engineers in such tasks as chip design, and computer-aided medical diagnoses (2011). Similarly, fewer architects are needed as designs are created and manipulated digitally. In the medical field, the combination of computers and telecommunications has made it possible to provide services at great distances. X-rays are read and interpreted overnight in low-wage countries and returned to U.S. doctors the next day.

The Internet has eliminated many white-collar jobs. For example, the Internet allows people to make their own travel arrangements, reducing or eliminating the need for travel agents, or to buy and sell stocks, making stockbrokers unnecessary. Also, there is software that helps people do their tax returns without the need of a tax specialist. Within firms, computer programs take care of payrolls, inventory control, and delivery schedules, reducing the need for accountants. The number of letters mailed daily has declined from 207.88 billion in 2000 to 175.67 billion in 2010 (*Newsweek*, 2010), which translates into the reduction of postal service clerks, sorters, and letter carriers (Hampson, 2011). Similarly, the number of daily Google searches has increased from 100 million in 2000 to 2 billion in 2010 (*Newsweek*, 2010), drastically reducing the number of library researchers and graduate school assistants. Daily newspapers have declined from 1,480 in 2000 to 1,302 in 2010, in part because they are available free online (*Newsweek*, 2010). Thus, accompanying this decline is the reduction in jobs for journalists, columnists, investigative reporters, copyeditors, typesetters, and the like. Primarily because of voice mail, laser printers, and word processors, hundreds of thousands of secretarial and clerical jobs have been eliminated. Authors who once had secretaries type drafts find them no longer necessary because the writers compose at the computer, using spell check, grammar check, and thesaurus. The significant increase in online sales has caused a decline in the number of retail sales clerks, and related workers. Similarly, Amazon.com now sells more books online than are sold in bookstores. This trend plus the rise in e-readers has meant a decline in bookbinders, book wholesalers, and bookstore clerks.

Job scarcity, then, is not just a matter of declining manufacturing and the loss of blue-collar jobs. White-collar jobs are increasingly vulnerable, too.

many white-collar jobs are being lost because of new technologies (see the Technology and Society panel titled "Computer Technology and Middle-Class Job Loss").

The employer/employee relationship is also being reshaped. The Internet is revolutionizing how business is transacted. More than 30 million American workers work in temporary, contracted, self-employed, leased, part-time, and other "nonstandard" arrangements. These workers under **contingent employment** (that is, employees who work part-time, in temporary jobs, or as independent contractors) typically lack an explicit contract for ongoing employment and thus receive sporadic wages. They earn less than their counterparts who do the same work, and they have fewer benefits such as health insurance, family leave, and retirement, thus costing their employers up to 30 percent less than regular employees (Davidson, 2009).

One version of contingent employment is **homeshoring** or **homesourcing** in which independent contractors work from their homes. These workers make a wage but pay for their own health care and retirement plan and furnish their own equipment (telephone, computer). Typically, these folks work as reservation agents and in other call center activities. The company benefits from this arrangement by saving on employee benefits and by not having to provide workspace and equipment. The independent contractor benefits by having flexible work hours and saving on child care, transportation, and clothing.

Another type of contingent employment is that of temporary workers ("temps"). Of the 1.2 million jobs created by the private sector in 2010, for example, 26 percent were temporary positions. This trend represents a dramatic change in work. Businesses argue that they need this arrangement for flexibility in a rapidly changing competitive economy.

These growing numbers of temporary workers are not tied to an employer, which makes them free to choose from available work options. There is a downside to this trend, however: About 60 percent of these nonstandard jobs are low quality, paying less than regular full-time jobs held by similar workers. Temps earn on average 40 percent less per hour than full-time workers. In short, this trend has meant the proliferation of marginal jobs, with employers now shifting the burden of fringe benefits to individual workers and their families.

About three-fourths of those working in contingent work arrangements are women, many of whom work out of their homes. Home-based work includes word processing, editing, accounting, and telemarketing. Employers contract women to do home-based work because money is saved—the employers pay only for work delivered, they avoid unions, and they do not pay benefits such as health insurance, paid leaves, and pensions.

A generation or so ago, workers tended to work for one or two employers during their working years. Employers were loyal to their workers ("If you do your job, you'll have a job."), and workers were loyal to their employers. But the nature of work has changed dramatically. Now many workers are not allied with an employer, working, as we have seen, as contingent workers. Millions of workers are dismissed as their employers modernize the plants or move them elsewhere. Still other workers find their skills not keeping up with technological changes. Others leave jobs for other jobs. Sociologist Richard Sennett has calculated that young workers today with at least two years of college can expect to change jobs at least eleven times before retirement (reported in Schwartz, 2004).

Job Insecurity. A generation ago, workers had realistic hope of lifetime employment with the same employer. That is no longer the case. Corporate America has been downsizing for over thirty years, replacing workers with automation or with workers outside the United States. Mergers have brought more downsizing. When SBC merged with AT&T in 2005, for example, 13,000 jobs were eliminated. Those who kept their jobs found that their wages had stagnated and

Of the 1.2 million jobs created in 2010, more than one-fourth were temporary positions.

Sure, jobs are lost through downsizing, but new jobs are created to take their place.

157

that their employers often had reduced their benefits. Downsized workers, if they find work, will more than likely work for lower wages than previously.

The Bureau of Labor Statistics supplies the official unemployment statistics. The official unemployment rate in the United States since 2000 has ranged from a low of 3.9 percent in October 2000, and a high of 10.2 percent in late 2009. In November 2010, the rate was 9.8 percent (15.4 million unemployed people). The official unemployment rate is misleading, however, because it understates, dramatically, the actual magnitude of unemployment. The unemployment rate does not include those discouraged persons who have stopped looking for jobs, within the past four weeks. If these discouraged workers were added to the official unemployment rate of 9.8 percent, it would add 2.5 million people. The official rate also does not include those part-time workers who would prefer to work full-time, adding another 9 million. If both of these categories are included, the actual rate of unemployment/underemployment would be 17 percent (26,600,000 people) (*Bloomberg Business Week*, 2011:37). The official data of the government, by undercounting joblessness, diminish the perceived severity of unemployment and therefore reduce the zeal to do anything about the problem.

Benefits Insecurity. With relatively weak unions and competition from low-wage economies, U.S. corporations have been reducing their benefits to workers. Some corporations have even declared bankruptcy to renege on benefits promised to their workers (for example, United Airlines, Delta Airlines, Northwest Airlines, and Delphi Corporation, the largest U.S. auto parts maker). Others have negotiated with unions to set up a two-tiered benefits system. The first maintains benefits to those already hired. New hires, on the hand, will receive not only lower wages but a greatly reduced benefits package. Another strategy has been for employers to shift retirement plans from defined-benefit (a guaranteed retirement benefit based on years of service) to one based on the employee investments (for example, 401k). This relieves the employer from any future obligations. Most notably, many employers have reduced or eliminated health benefits to their workers.

In effect, then, corporations are shifting the risks of old age and ill health off the corporate ledger and on to the worker (Hacker, 2006).

Worker Compensation. Average wages, taking into account inflation, have not caught up with the level reached in 1973. More specifically "The income of a man in his 30s is now 12 percent below that of a man his age three decades ago" (Reich, 2008, para 6). Moreover, in this time of stagnant or declining wages, the cost for health care and college tuition have skyrocketed.

Ironically, wages declined during this prolonged period while worker productivity (that is, output per hour worked) actually rose. "The average U.S. factory worker is responsible today for more than $180,000 of annual manufacturing output, triple the $60,000 in 1972 [in constant 2005 dollars]" (Perry, 2011:A13). As a result, while the United States lost more than seven million manufacturing jobs since the late 1970s, manufacturing output has continued to grow. This increased productivity is a consequence, as shown throughout this chapter, of technology (computers, robots), efficiency of production, workers fearing that they will be laid off if they do not produce, and fewer workers working more.

Several factors depress the wages of workers. First, union membership has declined significantly, and union members make approximately 30 percent more than their nonunion peers. Second, competition from low-wage countries depresses wages in the United States. For example, Delphi Corporation in 2005, unable to compete with low-wage economies, slashed its wages for production workers from $27 an hour to $10 (decreasing a full-time worker's annual income from about $56,000 to $20,800). Third, corporations, if not moving overseas, have moved to the largely nonunion South, and the less unionized West, and to rural areas where wages are lower. Fourth, corporate management has systematically replaced workers with machines as well as contingent workers—independent contractors, temporary workers, part-time workers, and home-based workers.

159

CHAPTER 8
Structural Sources
of Social Change:
Economic and
Demographic

Consequently, many Americans are not making it financially. In 2008, some 39.8 million were living below the poverty line, and 46.3 million Americans were without health insurance. Racial and ethnic minorities were disproportionately disadvantaged. Black households had only 65 percent of the median income of Whites, and Latinos had about 72 percent of the median income of Whites in 2008. Full-time, year-round women workers made only 77 cents for every dollar earned by full-time men workers. Thus, the U.S. economy does not work for everyone. The roots of the problems found in the U.S. economy are found in the changes associated with globalization and its structural transformation.

The Working Poor. The government's official definition of the working poor is that they are individuals who were in the labor force for at least twenty-seven weeks during the year, but still had incomes below the official poverty level. About 10.7 million workers aged sixteen and older were the working poor in 2009. Having a job is not necessarily a path out of poverty. About 2.6 million in poverty were full-time year-round workers. Despite working, these people remain poor because they hold menial, dead-end jobs that have no benefits and are paid the minimum wage or below. In July 2009, the federal minimum wage increased to $7.25 an hour. This added up to $15,080 a year for full-time work, an amount $6,070 short of what a family of four needed to exceed the poverty line in 2009.

The working poor are disproportionately women, single parent families, and racial/ethnic minorities. One in three women earns poverty-level wages, compared with one out of five men. Similarly, one in three African American men, two out of five African American women and Latino men, and slightly more than half of Latina women work at jobs that pay poverty wages.

The New Poor. As we have seen, millions of workers have lost their jobs when companies closed, as companies sought cheaper labor outside the United States, and when they were replaced by robots or other forms of automation. Many of these displaced workers find other work, but usually at lower-paying jobs. They are poorer but not poor. Many others, though, especially those over forty, find gaining employment difficult because their skills are outmoded and they are considered too old to retrain.

These **new poor** are quite different from the "old poor." The old poor—that is, the poor of other generations—had hopes of breaking out of poverty; if they did not break out themselves, at least they believed their children would. This hope was based on a rapidly expanding economy with plentiful jobs. There were jobs for immigrants, farmers, and grade-school dropouts because of the needs of mass production. The new poor, however, are much more trapped in poverty. A generation ago, those who were unskilled and uneducated could usually find work and could even do quite well financially if the workplace was unionized. But now these people are displaced or misplaced. Hard physical labor is rarely needed in a high-tech society. This phenomenon undercuts the efforts of the working class, especially African Americans, Latinos, and other minorities who face the additional burden of institutional racism.

Government data reveal the contours of the new poor. Tens of millions of Americans have lost their jobs in the past two or three decades because of plant closings and layoffs. Almost half of these newly unemployed were longtime workers (workers who had held their previous jobs at least three years), and seven out of ten of them found new jobs. Of those reemployed full-time, slightly less than half make less money than before. These workers were downwardly mobile but likely not poor. About 14 percent, however, did not find employment, and they constitute the new poor. Michael Parenti (1995) summarizes the bleak picture:

> We [are] witnessing the gradual Third-Worldization of the United States, involving the abolition of high-wage jobs, a growth of low-wage and part-time employment, an increase in permanent unemployment, a shrinking middle-income population, a growing number of mortgage delinquencies, greater concentrations of wealth for the few and more poverty and privation for the many. (24)

In summary, the problems associated with the economy and work in U.S. society are structural in origin. That is, being laid off or working at low wages is not the fault of lazy and unmotivated people, but rather the result of societal forces. To understand the economy and work setting in our society, we must understand the nature of capitalism, for which profit rather than the human consequences guides managerial decisions. Transnational corporations make decisions based on global markets and where the cost of labor and doing business worldwide are the cheapest. While the transnationals prosper, U.S. labor is negatively impacted. Moreover, "the economy is shifting from a workforce of permanent employees to one in which most jobs are temporary, scarce, low-paid, without benefits and with no upward mobility" (Hightower, 2011:3). These trends are part of a profound transformation, causing many dislocations for workers, their families, communities, and society.

The New Immigration and the Changing Racial Landscape

Immigration, the movement of people across political boundaries, is one manifestation of globalization. Since the Pilgrims left Europe and arrived in what is now New England for permanent residence, this process has had important consequences for what has become the United States. The latest wave of immigration—the new immigration—is shaking up society. This **demographic** change challenges the cultural hegemony of the White European tradition; creating incredible diversity in race, ethnicity, language, religion, and culture; and leading, often, to division and hostility.

This **new immigration** represents two trends that set it apart from past immigration. First, the volume of immigration is relatively large. For example, in the ten years from 1963 to 1972, there were about 3.5 million legal immigrants; from 1973 to 1982, there were slightly fewer than 5 million; 9 million were added in the next ten years; and nearly a million have entered the United States every year since 1992. As a result, the foreign-born population has risen from 19.8 million in 1990 to 35.5 in 2009. Second, the racial landscape and rate of population growth are greatly affected, as approximately 1 million immigrants annually set up permanent residence in the United States. These new residents are primarily Latino and Asian, not European as was the case in earlier immigration eras. For example, between 1960 and 2000 the percentage of foreign-born U.S. residents of European heritage decreased from 75 percent to 16 percent. At the same time, the percentage of foreign-born U.S. residents born in Latin America increased from 6 percent to 51 percent. This demographic transition has significant implications for U.S. society, communities, families, and individuals. The facts, myths, and consequences of these two demographic changes are the subjects of this section.

Immigration Patterns

Historically, there have been four major waves of immigration, which were major sources of population growth and ethnic diversity in the United States. The first wave of immigrants arrived between 1790 and 1820 and consisted mainly of English-speaking Britons. The second wave, mostly Irish and German, came in the 1840s and 1850s and challenged the dominance of Protestantism, which led to a backlash against Catholics. The third wave, between 1880 and 1914, brought over 20 million, mostly Southern and Eastern Europeans who found factory jobs in large cities. In the 1920s, the United States placed limits on the number of immigrants it would accept, the operating principle being that the new immigrants should resemble the old ones. The "national origins" rules were designed to limit severely the immigration of Eastern Europeans and to deny the entry of Asians.

The fourth immigration wave began in 1965 and continues. The Immigration Act amendments of 1965 abandoned the quota system that had preserved the European

Popular Surnames in the United States Are No Longer Exclusively Anglo

In 2007, the Census Bureau reported that Smith remained the most common surname in the United States. One in four Americans is named Smith, Johnson, Williams, Brown, Jones, Miller, or Davis. But reflecting the surge in the Latino population, for the first time, two Latino surnames—Garcia and Rodriguez—were among the top ten most common in the United States, and Martinez nearly edged out Wilson for tenth place.

The latest surname count also revealed the growing number of Asians in the United States with the surname

Lee ranked number twenty-two. Although not all Lees are Asian, it is a very common surname in China and Korea.

Sources: Sam Roberts. (2007). "In Name Count, Garcias Are Catching Up to Joneses," *New York Times* (November 17). Online: *http://www.nytimes.com/2007/11/17/us/17surnames. html?hp?hp=&pagewanted=print*; U.S. Census Bureau. (2007). "Frequently Occurring Surnames From Census 2000" (November). Online: *www.census.gov/genealogy/www/freqnames2k.html*.

character of the United States for nearly half a century. The new law encouraged a new wave of immigrants, only this time the migrants arrived not from northern Europe but from the Third World, especially Asia and Latin America. Put another way, a hundred years ago Europeans were 90 percent of the immigrants to the United States; now, 90 percent of immigrants are from non-European countries. The result, obviously, is a dramatic alteration of the ethnic composition of the U.S. population (see the Diversity panel titled "Popular Surnames in the United States Are No Longer Exclusively Anglo"). And the size of the contemporary immigrant wave has resulted in a visible and significant number of U.S. residents who are foreign-born (slightly more than 12.5 percent in 2009, compared to 5 percent in 1970 and 8 percent in 1990).

In addition to the legal migrants (about 1 million each year), an estimated 525,000 unauthorized immigrants enter and stay (an estimated 1.5 million to 2.5 million people enter the United States illegally each year, but most return to their native countries) for a net gain of about 1.53 million U.S. immigrants annually. Although the number of immigrants who enter clandestinely is impossible to determine, the best estimate is that approximately 11.1 million unauthorized foreign nationals resided in the United States in 2009 (Department of Homeland Security, reported in Jimenez and Lopez-Sanders, 2011).

The settlement patterns of this new migration differ from previous flows into the United States. Whereas previous immigrants settled primarily in the industrial states of the Northeast and Middle Atlantic regions, or in the farming areas of the Midwest, recent immigrants have tended to locate on the two coasts and in the Southwest. Asians have tended to settle on the West Coast, Mexicans in the Southwest, with other Latinos scattered (for example, Cubans in Florida and Puerto Ricans and Dominicans in New York).[*]

California is a harbinger of the demographic future of the United States. As recently as 1970, California was 80 percent White, but since then it has been uniquely affected by immigration. The result is that Whites now are a numerical minority in California: In 2010 there were 14 million Latinos, 4.8 million Asians, and 15 million Whites. Latino children for the first time were a majority of California's under-eighteen population (Carlton, 2011). One-fourth of California's schoolchildren are studying English as a foreign language. "In another generation Latinos will be an absolute majority, and there will be 2 million fewer non-Hispanic whites than there are now" (Schrag, 2007:18). For example, Los Angeles has the largest population of Koreans outside of Korea, the biggest concentration of Iranians

---

[*]It is important to note that there is wide diversity among immigrant groups. For example, while there are over 3 million Latinos living in Florida, they come from several ethnic backgrounds: Cubans, Puerto Ricans, South Americans, Central Americans, Mexicans, and Dominicans (*USA Today*, 2008).

in the Western world, and a huge Mexican population. The diverse population of southern California speaks eighty-eight languages and dialects. The Los Angeles metropolitan area has more than fifty foreign-language newspapers, and there are television shows that broadcast in Spanish, Mandarin, Armenian, Japanese, Korean, and Vietnamese. For example, in one ZIP code—90706—lies Bellflower, where thirty-eight languages are spoken (Mohan and Simmons, 2004).

For all this diversity, though, California, especially Southern California, is becoming more and more Latino. California holds nearly half the U.S. Latino population and well over half the Mexican-origin population. Latinos are expected to surpass Whites in total California population by 2025.

Similar concentrations of Latinos are also found in Arizona and Texas. Historian David Kennedy (1996) argues that there is no precedent in U.S. history for one immigrant group to have the size and concentration that the Mexican immigrant group has in the Southwest today:

> If we seek historical guidance, the closest example we have in hand is the diagonally opposite corner of the North American continent, in Quebec. The possibility looms that in the next generation or so we will see a kind of Chicano Quebec take shape in the American Southwest, as a group emerges with strong cultural cohesiveness and sufficient economic and political strength to insist on changes in the overall society's ways of organizing itself and conducting its affairs. (68)

Immigration and Increasing Diversity

The United States is shifting from an Anglo-White society rooted in Western culture to a society with three large racial/ethnic minorities, each of them growing in size while the proportion of Whites declines. Five facts show the contours and magnitude of this demographic transformation.

- *About one-third of the people in the United States are African American, Latino, Asian, or Native American.* The non-White population is numerically significant, comprising more than one-third of the population (up from 15 percent in 1960). Four states have non-White majorities (California, Texas, New Mexico, and Hawaii). Minorities make up the majority in six of the eight U.S. cities with more than a million people—New York, Los Angeles, Chicago, Houston, Detroit, and Dallas.

- *Racial minorities are increasing faster than the majority population.* While non-Whites are now one-third of the population but they account for almost half of all births. Nationally, Whites are a minority (49.9 percent) of Americans age three and under. In eight states and the District of Columbia, minorities are the majority and pre-K and kindergarten (Meyerson, 2011). Thus, by 2023 a majority of children (under eighteen) will be from a minority background (U.S. Census estimate, reported in Yen, 2009), they will surpass Whites among working-age Americans by 2039, and by 2042 non-White minorities will exceed the White population in size (Roberts, 2008).

- *African Americans have lost their position as the most numerous racial minority.* In 1990, for the first time, African Americans were less than half of all minorities. By 2000, Latinos outnumbered African Americans 42.7 million to 39.7 million. By 2050, Latinos will comprise a projected 29 percent of the U.S. population, with African Americans at about 13 percent. This demographic transformation will make two common assumptions about race obsolete: that "race" is a "Black-and-White" issue, and that the United States is a "White" society (Chideya, 1999).

- *Immigration now accounts for a large share of the nation's population growth.* Today 12.5 percent of current U.S. residents are foreign born. The U.S. Census Bureau estimates that Latinos and Asians are growing more than ten times the pace of Whites (reported in El Nasser and Grant, 2005). Immigration accounts for over a third of the current population growth directly and adds more indirectly, as first- (those foreign-born) and second-generation (children of the foreign born) Americans have more children on average than the rest of the population.

- *New patterns of immigration are changing the racial composition of society.* Among the expanded population of first-generation immigrants, the Asian-born now outnumber the European-born, and those from Latin America, especially Mexicans, outnumber both. This contrasts sharply with what occurred as recently as the 1950s, when two-thirds of legal immigrants were from Europe and Canada.

These trends signal a transformation from a White majority to a multiracial/multicultural society:

> [Sometime after the year 2042], Whites will become a "minority." This is uncharted territory in this country, and this demographic change will affect everything. Alliances between the races are bound to shift. Political and social power will be reapportioned. Our neighborhoods, our schools and workplaces, even racial categories themselves will be altered. (Chideya, 1999:35)

The pace of these changes is quickening. During the first decade of the twenty-first century, while the White population increased by 1.2 percent, the African American population rose by 11 percent, the Native American numbers increased by 15 percent, the Asian and Latino populations each increased by 43 percent (U.S. Census Bureau, reported in the *Wall Street Journal*, 2011). One consequence of this diversity is that across the United States an estimated 84 percent of the foreign born spoke a language other than English at home. Slightly fewer than half spoke Spanish; about 18 percent spoke Chinese, Tagalog, Korean, or other Asian language; and 17 percent spoke French, German, Italian, or another European language (Martin and Midgley, 2006:25).

Consequences of the New Immigration

The new immigration raises a number of questions. We consider three: (1) Do immigrants take jobs away from U.S. citizens? (2) Are immigrants a drain on society's resources? (3) Will the increasing proportion of non-Whites, fueled by immigration, lead to a blurring of racial lines or a heightening of tensions among the racial/ethnic groups?

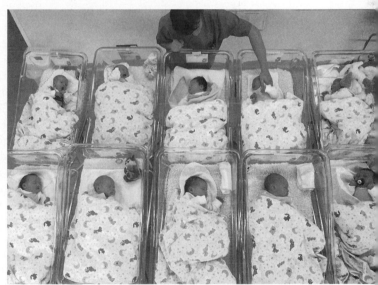

While non-Whites are about one-third of the population, they account for almost half of all births.

Do Immigrants Take Jobs from U.S. Citizens? Recent immigrants from Mexico can earn five times the wage rate in the United States that they can earn in Mexico. This is the lure. Because most do not speak English and their skills are limited, they tend to work at low-wage occupations, such as gardeners, roofers, assemblers, custodians, restaurant help, maids, and migrant farm workers. The evidence is that immigrants do not have negative effects on the wages of most Americans, but they do on the low-wage/poorly skilled/poorly educated segment of workers. Harvard economist George J. Borjas, a long-time researcher of immigration, says that "the primary losers in this country are workers who do not have high school diplomas, particularly Blacks and native-born Hispanics" (cited in Henderson, 2006). The wages of the lowest 15 percent of the workforce (typically, those with less than a high school degree) receive about 5 percent less in their paychecks because of competition from a large number of immigrants who are relatively uneducated, unskilled, and eager to work.

This problem will increase in the future as the federal and state governments no longer provide welfare benefits to legal immigrants and most nonimmigrant welfare recipients are required to leave welfare and find work, adding several million workers to compete for relatively few jobs at the low end of the occupational scale. See the Globalization panel titled "Yes, Global Free Market Mobility for Corporations; No, Global Free Market Mobility for Workers George H. Sage."

Immigration is only partly responsible for this relationship between somewhat lower wages and undereducated workers. Also pushing wages lower are the shrinking manufacturing sector, the decline in union membership, the outsourcing of jobs, and the Great Recession, which has especially brought unemployment to the construction industry where so many new immigrants have worked.

On the positive side, immigrants are more likely than the rest of the population to be self-employed and to start their own businesses, which in turn creates jobs and adds strength to local economies. For example, five years after the 1992 Los Angeles riots, there was an unexpected rebirth in some of the riot-torn areas, led largely by Asian and Latino entrepreneurs, many of whom were first-generation immigrants. These people invested locally and hired locals who spent much of their wages locally. Similar patterns of a migrant-based economy led by entrepreneurs from Jamaica, Mexico, Korea, Taiwan, and India.

To the extent that cheap, low-skilled labor helps hold down prices, there is more demand for some services, leading to more economic growth and jobs. "Lower menu prices encourage consumers to dine out more, leading to the opening of more restaurants. Lower construction costs make home-building more profitable and home remodeling more affordable" (Henderson, 2006).

Are Immigrants a Drain on Society's Resources? In the short run, immigrants consume more in public services and benefits than they pay in taxes. There are two reasons immigrants require more resources from the state than do nonimmigrant families. First, they have relatively large families, and these children go to public schools. Second, they pay less in taxes because they tend to earn low wages and have relatively little discretionary income.

Yes, Global Free Market Mobility for Corporations; No, Global Free Market Mobility for Workers George H. Sage

Throughout the United States, unauthorized immigrants—often called illegal immigrants—especially those from Mexico and Central America, have been subjected to stereotyping, scapegoating, and demonizing of the worst kind. There are several reasons for such responses, but a borderline hysteria has emerged over the accusation that these migrants are taking "American jobs" away from workers and lowering the overall wage structure. Consequently, state and federal governments are responding with legislation making it unlawful for businesses to employ unauthorized immigrants. On January 1, 2007, a new law called the employer-sanctions law went into effect in Arizona. Its purpose is to punish businesses that knowingly employ "illegal" workers, and it requires employers to use a federal online computer program known as E-Verify to check the work eligibility of all new employees hired. Although other states have passed similar laws, the Arizona law is touted as the "toughest" in the nation.

At the same time, there is another trend spreading throughout the nation that certainly has a more adverse effect on working Americans, but about which there is little public criticism, and that is the practice by corporations of closing business operations in the United States and outsourcing those "U.S. jobs" to foreign countries. Indeed, four million North American manufacturing jobs have been lost in the past decade. And where have those jobs gone? Well, a large number of them have been outsourced, as companies have closed their U.S. plants and moved productions to plants in Asia and other low-wage countries throughout the world.

In Arizona, that state has experienced a semiconductor slump. It seems that the number of jobs tied to the semiconductor chip industry is down 31 percent since 2000. It turns out that the United States now produces only about 10 percent of the world's semiconductors compared with 35 percent in 2000. So, ironically, for the state that claims to have the "toughest" anti-immigrant law, its "American" semiconductor jobs have diminished because those jobs have been outsourced to foreign countries.

Where is the outrage among politicians and "illegal immigrant" critics? Why don't we hear the same complaints against corporations that are leveled at unauthorized immigrants? Certainly closing manufacturing plants here in the United States and outsourcing those jobs to low-wage foreign countries results in laying off U.S. workers and lowering the wage structure. The answer to that is found in the old mantras: "That's the way the free market works in a global economy" and "Capitalists must be free to be mobile and invest globally to make a profit."

There is a clear contradiction here. Few politicians, businesses, and other U.S. citizens are complaining about moving capital and jobs away from the United States and into Third World countries, leaving U.S. workers to suffer the consequences. Meanwhile, these same interests voice ugly diatribes at workers who want to participate in that "free market" system by coming to the United States and competing for jobs. Why is it okay for one component of capitalism—capital—"free" to roam a virtual borderless world in the hunt for low-wage workers to maximize profits, while a second component of capitalism—workers (the producers of profit)—are restricted where they may go in search of work for their livelihood? Where is the resentment in this country for such illogical reasoning? A case can be made that what exists is a shameful case of social injustice.

Sources: "Editorial, Immigration Ground Zero; In Arizona, the Fruit of Congress's Failure," *The Washington Post* (December 26, 2007):A20. Max Jarman, "Arizona's Semiconductor Slump," *The Arizona Republic* (January 13, 2008):D1, D3. Personal communication, George H. Sage, Professor Emeritus, University of Northern Colorado. This essay was written expressly for *In Conflict and Order*, 12th edition (2010).

It is important to note that undocumented immigrants pay a variety of taxes, such as income, Social Security, Medicare, and sales taxes (West, 2010). Each year, undocumented immigrants contribute $1.5 billion to Medicare and $7 billion to Social Security, even though they will never collect benefits from them (Southern Poverty Law Center, 2010).

In the long run, however, immigrants are a good investment for society. The Academy of Sciences study (Cassidy, 1997) found that by the time a typical immigrant with a family dies, that immigrant and his or her children will have paid $80,000 more in taxes than they received in government benefits. The evidence is that immigrants are a fiscal burden for two decades or so, mainly because of educational costs. After that, the society benefits monetarily.

This conclusion fits at the national level: that is, most taxes paid by immigrants and income taxes withheld by the federal government and used in part to provide Social Security and health care benefits to the elderly. However, the state and local taxes paid by immigrants are relatively low, yet the services they consume (in particular, education) are disproportionately funded by state and local taxes. Immigration is a national problem, but one borne by the states. This unbalance is a source of growing hostility directed, unfairly, toward immigrants rather than federal policy.

Research also shows that legal and illegal immigration add $1 billion to $10 billion per year to the U.S. GDP, "largely because immigration holds down wages for some jobs, and thus prices, and increases the efficiency of the economy" (Martin and Midgley, 1999:24).

There is also a global dimension to the economic benefits derived from immigrants. Most undocumented immigrants (that is, those who entered the country illegally) are young, male, and Mexican. They leave their families in Mexico and work for months at a time as manual laborers in the United States. Typically, they send some of their earnings back to their families in Mexico—an aggregate $25 billion annually, according to the World Bank (*Economist*, 2006). As a source of foreign capital to Mexico, migrant remittances trail only oil, tourism, and illegal drugs.

Will the Increasing Proportion of Non-Whites, Fueled by Immigration, Lead to a Blurring of Racial Lines or a Heightening of Tensions among the Racial/Ethnic Groups? The latest wave of immigration has taken place in a historical context that includes the restructuring of the U.S. economy (see Chapter 14) and an increasingly conservative political climate. New immigrants have always been seen as a threat to those already in place. The typical belief is that immigrants, because they will work for lower wages, drive down wages and take jobs away from those already settled here. These fears increase during economic hard times, when businesses downsize or when they outsource jobs, pay lower wages, and replace workers with technology as they adapt to the economic transformation. The hostility toward immigrants is also the result of the common belief that the new immigrants increase taxes because they require services (education, health care, and welfare) that cost much more than the taxes they produce. Former U.S. Labor secretary Robert Reich sums up the rationale for hostility toward immigrants.

> Many Americans feel themselves overtaxed. ... They worry about schools, they are concerned about jobs, they worry about the state of social services, and they're concerned about crime. An influx of immigrants serves as a focal point of those concerns. (cited in Olinger and Florio, 2002:1A)

Previous immigration waves were White, coming mostly from Ireland, England, Germany, Italy, and Eastern Europe. Today's immigrants, in sharp contrast, are coming from Latin America and Asia. They are non-White and have distinctly non-European cultures. When these racial and ethnic differences are added to economic fears, the mix is very volatile.

The situation is worsened further by where the new immigrants locate. Typically, they move where immigrants like themselves are already established. For example, 20 percent of the 90,000 Hmong in the United States live in Minnesota, mostly around Minneapolis–St. Paul. One in twelve Asian Indians lives in Illinois, primarily in the Chicago area. Approximately 40 percent of all Asian Americans live in California. This tendency of migrants to cluster geographically by race/ethnicity provides them with a network of friends and relatives who provide them with support. This pattern of clustering in certain areas also tends to increase the fear of nonimmigrants toward them. They fear that wages will be depressed and taxes will be greater because their new neighbors are relatively poor, tend to have children with special needs in school, and likely do not have health insurance.

A second tendency is for new immigrants to locate where other poor people live for the obvious advantage of cheaper housing. A problem often arises when poor Whites live side by side with one or more racial minorities. Despite their common condition, tensions in such a situation are heightened as groups disadvantaged by society often fight each other for relative advantage. The tensions between African Americans and Asian immigrants were evidenced, for example, during the South Los Angeles riots in 1992, when roughly 2,000 Korean-owned businesses were looted or damaged by fire.

167

CHAPTER 8
Structural Sources
of Social Change:
Economic and
Demographic

The result of these factors is commonly an anti-immigrant backlash. Opinion polls taken over the past fifty years report consistently that Americans want to reduce immigration. Typically, these polls report that Americans believe that immigration in the past was a good thing for the country but that it no longer is.

The states with the most immigrants have the highest levels of anti-immigrant feeling. Several states have filed suit against the federal government, seeking reimbursement for the services provided to immigrants. Some twenty-two states have made English the official state language. The voters in California have passed two propositions that indicate anti-immigrant feelings. In 1994, they denied public welfare such as nonemergency medical care, prenatal clinics, and public schools to undocumented immigrants. In-state college tuition has been denied to noncitizens in some states. At the federal level, congress passed a bill in late 2006 that authorized fencing a third of the 2,100-mile border between the United States and Mexico.

If present immigration patterns continue, by 2042 some one-third of the U.S. population will be post-1970 immigrants and their descendants, and non-Whites will outnumber Whites. Under these circumstances of racial diversity, will the social meaning of ethnic and racial lines become increasingly blurred or more starkly defined? Will the people be pulling together or pulling apart? Will the gulf between affluent Whites and the disproportionately poor non-Whites be narrowed or widened? Will there be a de facto segregation as Whites who once lived and worked together with non-Whites move to White enclaves? Demographer William Frey has noted a "White flight" from high-immigration areas, a trend he fears may lead to the Balkanization of America (cited in Cassidy, 1997:43). Is this our future?

Anti-immigration activists are becoming more numerous and vocal. The Southern Poverty Law Center says that tension over illegal immigration is contributing to a rise in hate groups and hate crimes across the nation (Potok, 2011). White supremacy groups are growing. Vigilante groups have organized to watch the borders. What brings the anti-immigration activists together is a generalized belief "that a brown-skinned, Spanish-speaking tidal wave is about to swamp the white-skinned population of the United States" (Zeskind, 2005:A15). Former Congressman Tom Tancredo sums up this fear: "If we don't control immigration, legal and illegal, we will eventually reach the point where it won't be what kind of a nation we are, Balkanized or united; we will have to face the fact that we are no longer a nation at all" (quoted in Zeskind, 2005:A15).

Immigration and Agency

Immigration can be forced (for example, the slave trade) or freely chosen. Immigration in this latter sense is clearly an act of human agency (rather than passively accepting structural constraints, people cope with, adapt to, and change their social situations to meet their needs). Most people in developing countries do not move. Others move, breaking with their extended family and leaving neighborhood and community ties, mostly to improve their economic situations or to flee repression.

Typically, new immigrants face hostility from their hosts, who, as we have seen, fear them as competitors or hate them because they are "different" or because they fear that they may be terrorists. In this latter instance, immigrants from Muslim countries have had to confront considerable hostility and suspicion since the terrorist acts of September 11, 2001. Recent immigrants also face language barriers as they seek jobs. Often, most especially for undocumented immigrants, their initial jobs are demeaning, poorly paid, and without benefits. How do they adapt to these often very difficult circumstances? Most commonly, immigrants move to a destination area where there is already a network of friends and relatives. These networks connect new immigrants with housing (often doubling up in very crowded but inexpensive conditions), jobs, and an informal welfare system (health care, pooling resources in difficult times). These mutual-aid efforts by immigrant communities have been used by immigrant networks throughout U.S. history, whether by Swedish settlers in Minnesota, Mennonite settlers in Kansas, Irish settlers in Boston, or Mexican or Vietnamese settlers now (Martin and Midgley, 1999).

To overcome low wages, all able family members may work in the family enterprise or at different jobs and combine family resources. To overcome various manifestations of hostility by others, the immigrant community may become closer (the pejorative word is "clannish"), having as little interaction with outsiders as possible. Some may become involved in gangs for protection. Still others may move to assimilate as quickly as possible.

Effects of Immigration on Immigrants: Ethnic Identity or Assimilation? Martin and Midgley sum up the universal dilemma for immigrants:

> There is always a tension between the newcomers' desires to keep alive the culture and language of the community they left behind, and their need and wish to adapt to new surroundings and a different society. (Martin and Midgley, 1999:35–36)

Assimilation is the process by which individuals or groups adopt the culture of another group, losing their original identity. A principal indicator of assimilation is language. In 2000, slightly less than one in five Americans age five and older spoke a language other than English at home. Overall, foreign-language speakers grew by about 15 million during the 1990s (Frey, 2002:20). Assuming the experience of earlier immigrants to the United States, it is likely that the shift to English usage will take three generations—from almost exclusive use by newcomers of their traditional language, to their children being bilingual, to their children's children (third-generation immigrants) being monolingual English speakers (Martin and Midgley, 1999). According to the Pew Hispanic Center, in 2007, for example, 23 percent of adult first-generation Latinos said they could carry on a conversation very well in English, compared to 88 percent in the second generation and 94 percent in the third (reported in Gorman, 2007).

If the past is a guide, the new immigrants will assimilate. "Our society exerts tremendous pressure to conform, and cultural separatism rarely survives more than a generation" (Cole, 1994:412). But conditions now are different.

An argument countering the assumption that the new immigrants will assimilate as did previous generations of immigrants is that the new immigrants are members of racial/ethnic groups, not Whites. The early waves of immigrants (post-1965) were mostly White Europeans. Over time these groups were absorbed into the "melting pot" of society's mainstream because jobs were relatively plentiful and they did not face racial antipathy. Today's immigrants, however, face a different reality. A commonly held assumption (the reasoning of the culture of poverty—see Chapter 7) is that when new immigrants do not assimilate easily or if they continue to be poor, it is their fault. Thus, blame for many social problems and resistance to assimilation is placed on the immigrants, thereby "ignoring the impact of larger forces, such as racism and the economic order, that limit opportunities for success and present barriers to assimilation" (Pyke, 2008:212).

The current political mood is to eliminate affirmative action (as California did in 1997) and to reduce or eliminate social programs that help level the playing field so that minorities would have a fair chance to succeed. Some legislation is especially punitive toward recent immigrants, particularly the undocumented. Such public policies make it more difficult for new immigrants to assimilate than did their predecessors, should they wish to do so.

Another factor facing this generation of immigrants is that they enter the United States during a critical economic transformation and, since 2007, an economic crisis where the middle class is shrinking and the working class faces difficult economic hurdles (see Chapter 14). A possible result is that the new immigrants, different in physical characteristics, language, and culture, will become scapegoats for the difficulties that so many face (Powers, 2007). Moreover, their opportunities for advancement will be limited by the new economic realities. Sociologist Herbert Gans (1990) argues, for example, that the second generation of post-1965 immigrants likely will experience downward mobility compared to their parents because of the changing opportunity structure in the U.S. economy.

The issue of immigrant adaptation to the host society is complex, depending on a number of variables. Zhou (1997) describes a number of these critical variables, including the immigrant generation (that is, first or second), their level in the ethnic hierarchy at the point of arrival, what stratum of U.S. society absorbs them, and the degree to which they are part of a family network.

Immigrants who move to the United States permanently have four options regarding assimilation. Many try to blend into the United States as quickly as possible. Others resist the new ways by either developing an adversarial stance toward the dominant society or resisting acculturation by focusing more intensely on the social capital (that is, social networks) created through ethnic ties (Portes and Zhou, 1993). The fourth alternative is to move toward a bicultural pattern (Buriel and De Ment, 1997). That is, immigrants adopt some patterns similar to those found in the host society and retain some from their heritage. Although this concept of a bicultural pattern appears to focus on culture, the retention or abandonment of the ethnic ways depends on structural variables (Kibria, 1997:207). These variables include the socioeconomic resources of the ethnic community, the extent of continued immigration from the sending society, the linkages between the ethnic community and the sending society, and the obstacles to obtaining equal opportunity in the new society.

In sum, the new immigration, occurring at a time of economic uncertainty and reduced governmental services, is having three pronounced effects that will accelerate in the foreseeable future: (1) an increased bifurcation between the haves and the have-nots, (2) increased racial diversity, and (3) a heightened tension among the racial and ethnic groups.

The Aging Society

The population of the United States is experiencing a pronounced change in its age structure—it has become older and is on the verge of becoming much older. In 1900, about one in twenty-five residents of the United States was sixty-five years and older. By 1950, it was about one in twelve. In 2000, one in eight was sixty-five and older, and by 2030, it will likely be around one in five, with more people over sixty-five than under age eighteen. In effect, by 2030, when most of today's college students will be around fifty, there will be more grandparents than grandchildren. "The Senior Boom is coming, and it will transform our homes, our schools, our politics, our lives and our deaths. And not just for older people. For everybody" (Peyser, 1999:50).

This section is divided into two parts: (1) a demographic (demography is the study of population) description of the aged category now and in the future and (2) the implications of an aging society for social problems.

Demographic Trends

Until the twentieth century high fertility (birthrate) and high mortality (death rate) kept the United States a youthful nation. During the last century, however, the birthrate fell (except for during the post–World War II period, which was an anomaly), resulting in fewer children as a proportion of the total population. Most important, greater longevity because of advances in medical technology (everything from beta blockers for reducing hypertension to organ transplants) has increased the life expectancy of Americans. The average life expectancy in 1900 was forty-nine years, and for a baby born in 2009 it was seventy-eight and two months (up two months from 2008).

So, essentially in 130 years (from 1900 to 2030), people age sixty-five and older will have shifted from one out of twenty Americans to one in five. The surge in the number of

169

CHAPTER 8
Structural Sources
of Social Change:
Economic and
Demographic

elderly during the next few decades is the consequence of three demographic forces: a continued low fertility rate, ever-greater life expectancy rates, and the baby boom generation (the 78 million born between 1946 and 1964, representing 70 percent more people than were born during the preceding two decades) reaching old age, beginning in 2011 and ending in 2030. (See Figure 8.1 showing the population pyramids for 1950 [characteristic of a young population], 2000, and 2050. The three pyramids show the changing age structure as the baby boom group moves toward old age.)

Hidden within these statistics is another important fact about the old—they are getting older (see Figure 8.2 for the growth of the old-old, those eighty-five and older and the overall growth of those sixty-five and over). In 1900, there were just over 100,000 in the old-old category (those eighty-five and older). In 1950 the number had risen to 600,000, and by

FIGURE 8.1

Population Aging Is a Long-Term Trend

Source: U.S. Bureau of the Census. Projections for 2050 are from U.S. Census middle-series projections of U.S. population. Reprinted from "Government Spending in an Older America." *Reports on America* 3. Washington, DC: Population Reference Bureau, p. 2.

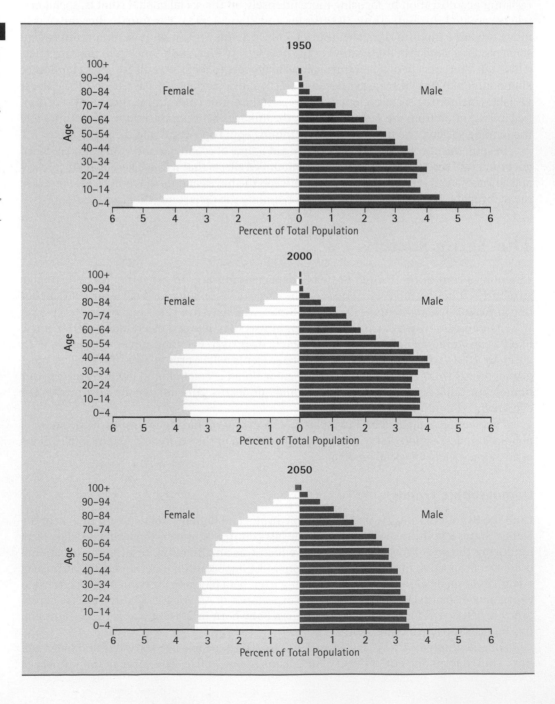

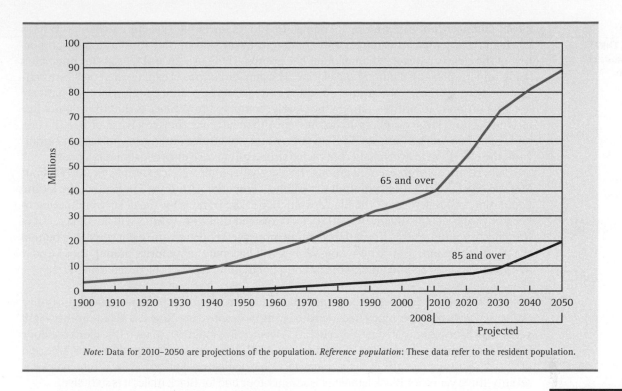

Note: Data for 2010–2050 are projections of the population. *Reference population*: These data refer to the resident population.

FIGURE 8.2

Population Age 65 and Over and Age 85 and Over, Selected Years 1900–2008 and Projected 2010–2050

Source: U.S. Census Bureau, Population Estimates and Projections, Federal Interagency Forum on Aging-Related Statistics. Older Americans 2010. Washington, D.C.; U.S. Government Printing Office, July 2010, p. 2.

2008 the number in this category had increased more than nine-fold to 5.7 million (Federal Interagency Forum on Aging-Related Statistics, 2010). In 2030, there will be 8,500,000 people age eighty-five and over, and by 2050 there will be a projected 19 million of the old-old. In 2000, some 72,000 Americans were at least one hundred years old. Because of the continued advances in medicine and nutrition, it is expected that the number of centenarians will increase to about 1 million by the middle of the twenty-first century. Children born today have a fifty-fifty chance of reaching one hundred years of age.

Demographic Portrait of the Current Elderly Population

Sex Ratio. Since life expectancy is about five years more for women than men, older women outnumber older men by a ratio of 3 to 2. As age increases, the disparity becomes greater—for those age eighty-five and older, there are about five women to every two men. By age one hundred and older, four in five are women.

A combination of biological advantages for women and social reasons explains this difference. The secondary status of women in U.S. society has provided them with extra longevity. Traditional gender roles have demanded that men be engaged in the more stressful, demanding, and dangerous occupations. It will be interesting to note whether there are any effects on female longevity as women receive a more equal share of all types of jobs. Meanwhile, though, the current situation creates problems for the majority of elderly women, who are often widows and have low incomes.

Elderly women are more likely than men to live alone usually as widows—40 percent of women and only 19 percent of men (Jacobsen, Kent, Lee, and Mather, 2011:4). This is the result of two factors: the greater longevity of women and the social norm for men to marry younger women. Thus, to the extent that isolation is a problem of the aged, it is overwhelmingly a problem for elderly women. Because of pensions through work and the traditional bias of Social Security toward women who had not worked outside the home, elderly women are much more likely than elderly men to be poor (a 13 percent poverty rate compared with 7 percent for men). African American and Latino elderly women have an even higher probability than their male counterparts of being poor.

Racial Composition. Because racial minorities have a lower life expectancy than do Whites (African Americans, for example, live about four fewer years), they form a smaller proportion of the elderly category than of other age groups. There are several reasons for minorities being underrepresented among the elderly. The gap for Latinos is explained in part by immigration, because most immigrants are young adults. But the primary reason for the relatively low proportion of minorities among the elderly, compared to Whites, is that they do not live as long because large numbers do not have health insurance, they receive poor health care, and they often work at physically demanding and sometimes dangerous jobs. Most significant, the elderly who are members of racial/ethnic groups are disproportionately poor.

Whites are overrepresented among the elderly population (for example, in 2009, about 80 percent of the elderly population was White, compared with only 7 percent of the Latino population and 8 percent of the Black population). The trend is for the elderly population to become more racially diverse (by 2050, it is expected that non-Whites will be 39 percent of the elderly population). Although becoming more racial diverse, the elderly will lag behind the rest of the population where non-Whites will become the majority among those under age eighteen in 2023 and among the nation's population in 2042 (Jacobsen et al., 2011).

Longevity. At the founding of the United States, life expectancy at birth was about thirty-five years. By 1900, life expectancy had increased to forty-seven years. Now it is about seventy-eight years. This average masks some differences: (1) women live longer than men (the life expectancy is 80.5 for women, compared to 75.5 for men) and (2) there are racial gaps that show little sign of closing. For instance, the life expectancy for White females is eighty and for White males it is seventy-three years; for Black females it is seventy-four and for Black males it is sixty-five.

Geographic Distribution. Some states and communities have disproportionately more older residents. One-fourth of all elderly Americans live in three states (California, Florida, and New York). Many rural states have a relatively high proportion of elderly, as these states experience a large out-migration of young people. Most elderly remain in their communities after retirement ("aging in place"), but those who move tend to migrate to the favorable climate found in the Sun Belt states (Florida, California, Arizona, Nevada, and Texas). The elderly who migrate are not representative of the elderly. They tend to be younger and more affluent than those who stay in their home communities. Thus, they benefit their new communities by broadening the tax base through home ownership, strong purchasing power, and not burdening the local job market. The communities they left in the Snow Belt are negatively affected. The elderly who remain are disproportionately older and poorer and require more public assistance from a lower community tax base.

Wealth, Income, and Cumulative Advantage or Disadvantage. For obvious reasons, the wealth accrued over a lifetime of work affects the quality of life during retirement. The economically challenged will continue to struggle with the exigencies of life after retirement, while those with economic advantage retain it in their later years. This changed for the relatively affluent, however, with the bursting of the economic bubble in 2007. Prior to the Great Recession, recent retirees, in general, had personal resources—education, income, and assets—unknown to previous cohorts. They benefited from a sharp rise in the stock market during the 1990s and extraordinary gains in real estate markets in the previous three decades, which ultimately they passed on to their fortunate heirs. Yet, many elderly missed out on the boom. They did not own a home or have enough assets to invest. But the boom did not last, which is discussed in greater detail in Chapter 14, presenting difficulties for many of the previously affluent.

Home equity is most significant in having a reasonable net worth. In this regard, those who are currently in the old category had an advantage because their home purchases in the 1950s and 1960s were much cheaper in interest and mortgage payments relative to wages than were homes bought in the 1970s, 1980s, and 1990s. However, in the three years after the housing bubble burst homes had lost $11 trillion in value. Moreover, the stock market lost over $7 trillion in value, with mutual funds dropping 38 percent. Investments in retirement savings [401(k)s] lost more than $1 trillion and over an eighteen-month period, the investments in public pension plans lost a combined $1.3 trillion (Byrnes and Palmeri, 2009). As a result, many who thought they had more than enough saved for retirement found that they did not. Many had to postpone retirement, remaining in the labor force indefinitely. Of course, although losing money, many of the affluent old, remained comfortable affluent.

173

CHAPTER 8
Structural Sources
of Social Change:
Economic and
Demographic

The elderly who are members of a racial or ethnic minority are disproportionately poor. This relative lack of resources for racial minorities translates into a reduced likelihood, compared to Whites, of their receiving adequate health care and, when needed, living in nursing homes with full-time skilled nursing care under a physician's supervision.

Elderly married couples tend to have greater net worth than elderly singles. Households maintained by unmarried elderly males have a greater net worth than households maintained by unmarried elderly women. Similarly, White, married-couple households with a householder age sixty-five or older will likely have higher family incomes than racial minority married couples.

Personal income is usually reduced by one-third to one-half after retirement. The important point is that those groups with advantage before becoming old maintain their economic advantage in old age—and the poor get poorer.

Typically, we assume that economic inequality narrows after age sixty-five, when benefit programs replace work as principal income sources. This is not the case as the inequalities from income and privilege tend to be magnified among elderly people. People who are initially advantaged, for example, are more likely than their less fortunate counterparts to receive good educations and obtain good jobs with better health and pension benefits, which lead to higher savings and better postretirement benefit incomes.

Most noteworthy, the government is partly responsible for these skewed advantages to the affluent. The relatively affluent are encouraged by the government, because of tax incentives, to invest in retirement income programs such as IRAs (individual retirement accounts), Keogh plans, or other tax-deferred programs. Thus, the already advantaged are given preferential tax treatment, which amounts to tax subsidization, thereby increasing their economic advantage over the disadvantaged after age sixty-five.

About 10 percent of people age sixty-five and older are poor. This proportion is lower than the overall poverty rate because Social Security benefits are indexed for inflation. This poverty rate, slightly below the poverty rate for the nation as a whole, is perceived typically as a success. However, over 3 million elderly are poor, and another 30 percent of them are in the "economically vulnerable" category—that is, they have incomes above the poverty line but below 150 percent of the official poverty rate.

The elderly spend about 20 percent of their incomes on health care, with the poor elderly spending about 35 percent of their incomes on health care. Roughly half of the incomes of the poor elderly go for food. Thus, they are especially affected by inflation at the grocery store. The only recourse for the poor in inflationary times, when their incomes do not increase with spiraling costs, is either to eat less or to eat cheaper, less nutritious food.

The elderly poor spend about 20 percent of their incomes on energy for heat and electricity, both of which increase with inflation. Those on fixed incomes are likewise negatively affected by inflationary increases in the cost of rents, taxes, and health care. The last is a special burden for the old who are poor. Health costs for the elderly are almost four times those for people under age sixty-five. The result is that the elderly poor tend to live in substandard housing, receive inadequate medical care, and have improper diets.

If the poor and the old are doubly cursed, then the elderly poor who are members of a racial or ethnic minority group experience a triple disadvantage. Individual and institutional sources of discrimination coalesce to make these people's lives especially miserable and problematic. The higher probability of older African Americans being poor is a direct consequence of their relatively low status throughout life. With average incomes only about 60 percent those of Whites, they have little chance of building a nest egg to supplement their pension incomes. African Americans are also more likely than Whites to have worked at jobs that did not provide retirement benefits and that did not qualify for Social Security (prior to 1974, for example, only 80 percent of elderly Blacks received some Social Security benefits, compared with 90 percent of older Whites). If they have worked at jobs qualifying for Social Security, minority members usually are eligible only for lower benefits because of their lower wages.

These related problems reflect the discrimination in the job market and unfair legislation. Clearly, equity in Social Security benefits will not occur until racial minorities and Whites experience similar work careers and compensation.

After a lifetime of lower earnings and receiving small or no pensions, elderly minorities must live in substandard housing. They are much more likely than elderly Whites to live in deteriorated housing with inadequate plumbing, heating, and sewage disposal. Similarly, the minority elderly suffer more health problems than do the majority elderly. For instance, among all minority elderly the prevalence of chronic disabilities is twice as high as among the White elderly.

Problems of an Aging Society

Although there are several problems brought about by an aging society, we focus on two: (1) inadequate income from pensions or Social Security and (2) the high cost of elderly health care.

Social Security. "One out of three seniors depends on Social Security for 90 percent to 100 percent of their income. Two out of three seniors depend on it for more than half their income" (Sklar, 2004). Since the introduction of Social Security in the 1930s, this program has been a significant aid to the elderly. Social Security has reduced poverty significantly among the elderly—from 35.2 percent in 1959 to 8.9 percent in 2009.

In addition to a monthly income for seniors, Social Security provides life insurance benefits to the survivors in cases of the death of a breadwinner and disability payments when a wage earner is unable to work. Most fundamental, Social Security expresses the belief that society takes responsibility for the welfare of all of its citizens. In the words of economist Robert Kuttner:

> Social Security serves, and reinforces, a kind of collective solidarity rarely articulated explicitly in the ordinary idiom of American politics. But it has precisely expressed the modern liberal view of social entitlement—the collectivity taking responsibility for unearned misfortune, not by singling out (and thus stigmatizing) the certifiably needy, but within a universal system. This approach offers a logic that is both moral and political, both redistributive and inclusive. It cultivates a politics of social empathy and, in turn, an astonishing level of political support for a surprisingly social concept in a fiercely capitalistic society. (1998:30)

Despite its considerable strengths, the Social Security program has several serious problems that place a disproportionate burden on certain categories of the elderly and on some portions of the workers paying into the program. An immediate problem is that not all workers are covered by Social Security. Some groups of workers are unable to participate because they work for states with alternative retirement programs. Also, legislation has specifically exempted certain occupations such as agricultural workers from Social Security.

For workers who are eligible for Social Security, there are wide disparities in the benefits received. The amount of benefits depends on the length of time workers have paid into the Social Security program and the amount of wages on which they paid a Social Security tax. In other words, low-paid workers receive low benefits during retirement. Thus, 30 percent of the elderly who depend almost exclusively on Social Security benefits are below the poverty line. These elderly typically are people who have been relatively poor during their working years or are widows.

On the surface, the Social Security system is gender-neutral. Benefits are based purely on employment history, earnings, and family composition. "However, gender-related differences in the American work culture mean that, in reality, Social Security provides different levels of retirement security for women and men" (American Academy of Actuaries, 2007). Some of the disadvantages for women are:

175

CHAPTER 8
Structural Sources
of Social Change:
Economic and
Demographic

- Social Security recognizes only paid work. The benefits for spouses (typically wives) who did not work in the labor force are 50 percent of the working spouse's benefits.
- Social Security benefits are based on the number of years worked and the amount earned from wages. Since women are in the workforce fewer years than men (mostly because they take time off to bear and care for children, eleven years on average), and because women generally earn less than men (a median loss of $434,000 in earnings over seventy years of unequal pay), women will receive smaller retirement benefits than men (Cawthorne and Gross, 2008).
- A divorced woman receives half of her former husband's benefit if the couple was married at least ten years. If the divorce occurs before being married ten years, then she receives nothing.
- Where wife and husband are both employed, the wife will receive Social Security benefits for her work only if her benefits exceed those earned by her husband. If she collects a benefit based on her own wages, she loses the 50 percent spouse's payment for which her husband's payroll taxes paid.
- A woman who is widowed will not receive any Social Security benefits until age sixty unless she has a child under sixteen or an older disabled child or she herself is disabled.

The Social Security system is financed through taxes on wages and salaries. From a payroll tax of 2 percent on the first $3,000 of earnings when it began in the 1930s, the rate has increased substantially over the years. The 2011 rate was 10.4 percent on the first $106,800 (the cap rises with inflation) of earnings, with the cost being split between the worker and the employer, but most economists agree that the burden of the tax is on the employee because employers finance their share by paying their employees that much less.

The method of financing Social Security is not equitable, because it disproportionately disadvantages lower-income wage earners. In other words, it is a regressive tax: It takes a larger percentage from people with the lowest incomes. The Social Security tax has the following negative features:

- It is levied at a constant rate (everyone, rich and poor, pays the same rate).
- It starts with the first dollar of earned income, offering no allowances or exemptions for the very poor.
- It applies only to wages and salaries, thus exempting income typical for the wealthy, such as interest, dividends, rents, and capital gains from the sale of property.
- It is imposed up to a ceiling ($106,800 in 2011). Thus, in effect, in 2011 a worker making $106,800 and an executive or a professional athlete making a $5 million salary paid exactly the same Social Security tax.

There is an overarching problem facing Social Security—how to finance it in the future. Three demographic factors make financing the program problematic. The first is that more people are living to age sixty-five, and the second is that people live much longer after reaching sixty-five than in earlier generations. Average life spans are fourteen years longer than they were when Social Security was created in 1935. The obvious consequence of this greater longevity is that the Social Security system pays out more and more to an ever-expanding pool of elderly who live longer and longer.

The third demographic factor working against the system is a skewed **dependency ratio** (the proportion of the population who are workers compared to the proportion not working). Social Security is financed by a tax on workers and their employers. In 1950, there were sixteen workers for each person on Social Security; in 1970 there were 3.7 workers; there were 3.4 workers in 2010; and in 2030, there will likely be 2.3 workers for each person receiving benefits (Wolf, 2010). At present, the Social Security Administration collects more in taxes than it pays out, with the surplus going into a trust fund. But as people live longer and the baby boomers reach retirement, this system will no longer support itself. Until 2010, Social Security collected more than it paid out in benefits. But that has changed with the Great Recession and because the baby boomers are starting to retire (about 10,000 each day). Estimates vary, but it appears that the Social Security Trust Fund will keep the program solvent until around 2037, and after that it will be able to pay out only about seventy cents of each dollar of promised benefits. In other words, unless major adjustments are made, Social Security funds will run short by the time today's thirty-year-olds retire.

To deal with this pending crisis in funding Social Security, Congress will have to either raise Social Security taxes, use other revenues, or cut benefits. Other options include raising the age of eligibility (this is occurring when the age will rise gradually to sixty-seven by 2022. Raising the eligibility age is unfair to certain groups: African American males, for example, live nearly eight years less than White males, meaning that relatively few would receive benefits if the retirement age were raised to seventy. Blue-collar workers also die earlier than professionals. A lifelong mine worker, for example, has only a fifty-fifty chance of reaching age sixty-five. Another plan is the reduction or elimination of the cost of living adjustment, which allows the payments to keep pace with inflation. This proposal hurts the poor most because it is regressive. Another strategy is to tax Social Security benefits as income, which would protect the poor because they pay little, if any, federal income tax. Another solution that is popular with the Republican Party is to privatize Social Security. Generally, this would allow each individual to invest part of his or her Social Security taxes in the stock market. This plan would be beneficial when the stock market goes up, but it also makes retirement savings vulnerable to stock market declines. Imagine the consequences if Social Security had been privatized prior to the Great Recession.

> Social Security is far more than a pension system, and its payouts are government guaranteed. It is also deliberately redistributive. More than three-fifths of retired Americans derive at least half their income from Social Security; without it, half would live in poverty. Dedicating some of the payroll tax to a private account system would divert that much revenue into a system that is neither redistributive nor government guaranteed. (Kuttner, 1998:34)

Paying for Health Care. Most older people are in reasonably good health. Of all age groups, however, the elderly are the most affected by ill health. Health problems escalate especially from age seventy-five onward, as the degenerative processes of aging accelerate. Consider the following facts:

- Although the elderly comprise only about 13 percent of the population presently, they consume more than one-third of all health care in the United States.
- The elderly are four times as likely as the nonelderly to be hospitalized. When hospitalized, they stay an average of about three days longer than the nonelderly.
- The medical expenses of the elderly are three times greater than those of middle-aged adults, yet their incomes are typically much less.
- The elderly account for more than one-third of all spending for prescription drugs.
- One in eight who is at least sixty-five years old has Alzheimer's disease. By 2030 the number will have doubled to one in four due to the aging of the population (Hyman, 2008). The incidence of Alzheimer's disease, the leading cause of dementia in old age, rises sharply with advancing age—from one in eight people over the age of sixty-five to a fifty-fifty chance of getting the disease after age eighty-five. Now more than 5.4 million Americans are known to have Alzheimer's; in 2050, unless effective treatment and prevention can be found, the number will triple to nearly 16 million (Bettelheim, 2011).
- Osteoarthritis, the degeneration of protective tissues around the body's joints, afflicts about half of those age sixty-five and older.
- About half of the old-old will spend some time in a nursing home before they die.
- The cost of long-term care is prohibitive. The average cost of a year in a nursing home in 2008 was $213 a day or $77,745 annually (SmartMoney.com, 2008), and in some cities it is much higher.

Fidelity Investments estimates that a sixty-five-year-old couple retiring in 2006 will need about $200,000 to cover health costs that are not covered by Medicare. That estimate does not include the cost of over-the-counter drugs, dental services, or long-term care (cited in Block, 2006). Because Medicare does not pay for most long-term care, long-term care insurance is expensive, and Medicaid will help only after the patient's resources are exhausted, resulting in many elderly spending their last years impoverished.

177

CHAPTER 8
Structural Sources
of Social Change:
Economic and
Demographic

Medicare, begun in 1965, is the federal health insurance program for those aged sixty-five and older. Everyone is automatically entitled to hospital insurance, home health care, and hospice care through this program (known as *Medicare Part A*). The supplemental medical insurance program (known as *Medicare Part B*) helps pay for doctor bills, outpatient services, diagnostic tests, physical therapy, and medical supplies. People may enroll in this program by paying a relatively modest monthly fee. Overall, Medicare is financed by payroll taxes, premiums paid by recipients, and a government subsidy.

There are three major problems with Medicare. First, it is insufficiently financed by the government. Second, from the perspective of the elderly, only about half of their health care bills are paid through the program, leaving many with substantial costs. The affluent elderly are not hurt because they can purchase supplemental health insurance. The poor are not hurt because they are also covered by Medicaid, a separate program financed by federal and state taxes that pays for the health care of indigent persons. The near poor, however, do not qualify for Medicaid, and they cannot afford additional health insurance.

A third problem with Medicare is that physicians believe the program pays them too little for their services. As a result, many physicians limit the number of Medicare patients they will serve, some even refusing to serve any Medicare patients. Thus, some elderly have difficulty in finding a physician.

A striking number of retired folks become politically active in an attempt to change some of the social conditions especially harmful to them.

Responses by the Elderly: Human Agency

People at age sixty-five today can have twenty, thirty, or even forty more years of life. Some are financially secure and many will be relatively healthy until the end. For them the choices are many involving travel, leisure activities, and social involvement. For many, life is full and meaningful.

But being old is a difficult stage in life for many. People who were once attractive, active, and powerful may no longer be so. They are no longer "tethered to society through a series of institutions—school, work, family, church, community—that structured [their] lives, defined [their] place in the world, and gave shape to [their] identity" (Rubin, 2006:93). Their lives, once organized around pursuing goals, seem empty and meaningless. Some will experience debilitating diseases that bring constant pain, that restrict their freedom, and that rob them of vitality. There is a fifty-fifty chance than anyone who survives to eighty-five "will endure years of significant mental or physical disability" (Jacoby, 2011:14).

Others are isolated in nursing homes or because they lost a spouse and their children live at a distance. Some elderly are poor and live lives of desperation and hopelessness, with inflation eating away at their meager resources.

The elderly possess a devalued status in U.S. society. Being considered old by society and by oneself is a catalyst that provokes the individual to respond in characteristic ways.

But—and this is the crucial sociological point—the elderly are reacting to socially structured inequalities and socially constructed definitions, not to age as such. In a different cultural setting in which status increases with age, observers might find different personality types and responses.

Some researchers have argued that senior citizens respond to the aging process by retreating from relationships, organizations, and society (called **disengagement**). This behavior is considered normal and even satisfying for the individual, because withdrawal brings a release from societal pressures to compete and conform. Other researchers have quarreled with the disengagement theory, arguing that many elderly people are involved in a wide range of activities.

The majority of the elderly remain active until health problems curtail their mobility and mental acuity. Some 60 percent of people over eighty continue to live independently (Rubin, 2006:90). Many older adults engage in volunteer work in churches, public libraries, charities, and the like. For example, there are three national service programs for older adults: the Retired and Senior Volunteer Program, the Foster Grandparent Program, and the Senior Companion Program annually mobilize over half a million older adults to address a variety of needs in their communities. And another nonprofit organization, Experience Corps, uses older adults as tutors and mentors in public schools to help at-risk children improve their skills (Reilly, 2006).

People age sixty-five and older consistently vote in higher proportions than other age groups. A striking number of retired people become politically active in an attempt to change some of the social conditions especially harmful for them. Senior citizens are more politically active (voting, volunteering) than any other age group in society. Faced with common problems, many join in collective efforts both locally and nationally. Several national organizations are dedicated to political action to benefit the elderly. Most significant is the American Association of Retired Persons (AARP), with more than 40 million members. Representative other groups are the National Committee to Preserve Social Security and Medicare, the National Council of Senior Citizens, the National Council on Aging, the National Caucus of Black Aged, and the Gerontological Society. These organizations work through lobbyists, mailing campaigns, advertising, and other processes to improve the lot of the elderly in the United States.

Just how effective these organizations are or will be is unknown. But as the elderly increase in numbers, their sphere of influence should increase as well. Currently, the elderly account for around 20 percent of the voting public. By 2038, they are projected to make up more than one-third of the electorate. Elderly citizens could be a significant voting bloc if they developed an age consciousness and voted alike. Politicians from states with a relatively high concentration of elderly are increasingly aware of their potential voting power, and legislation more sympathetic to the needs of the elderly may be forthcoming. It is probably only a matter of time before the elderly focus their concerns and become an effective pressure group that demands equity.

The Three Structural Transformations of Society

This chapter focuses on three major transformations in U.S. society and worldwide. These macro forces have huge consequences for societies, for communities, for families, and for individuals and the nature of work. The global economy, networked through new technologies in communications and transportation and the emergence of a relatively few large transnational corporations, moves capital and jobs around the world and within the United States to where wages are the lowest and the regulatory rules the most lenient. This phenomenon, coupled with the shift within the United States from a manufacturing to a service economy, has profoundly affected the distribution and type of jobs. Fewer and fewer workers are engaged in mass assembly-line production, jobs that paid well and had good benefits. Many assumed that new jobs in the service sector, along the information superhighway, and in cyberspace would absorb those downsized from changing industries. This occurred only to a limited extent, since the skills required are very different from those in the industrial age, and high-tech corporations also downsize their workers as they automate and use low-cost labor worldwide. As a result, the economic transformation has caused millions of workers to transfer from high-wage jobs to lower-wage jobs, to temporary or contingent work, or to no work at all. Also, unskilled and semiskilled workers have been either left out or left to work at low-wage jobs with few, if any, benefits. Thus, wages have stagnated or declined for many millions. The results, among others, are a declining middle class and an ever greater gap between the haves and the have-nots.

One aspect of the global economy is the movement of people (immigration) generally from poor societies to rich societies. The consequence for the United States is a racial/ethnic transformation as most of the recent immigrants are from Latin America and Asia. Most of these immigrants arrive without the work and language skills to fit into a knowledge society. Past immigrants have succeeded economically, but the realities of the economic transformation increase the likelihood that they will be left on the margins. Moreover, the political climate fosters the elimination of affirmative action and other compensatory programs to aid minorities, as well as the downsizing of public supports to the poor and the neglect of urban blight and inner-city schools. All of these occur as racial minorities move toward becoming the numerical majority by the mid-twenty-first century.

In addition to immigration, another demographic change—the growing proportion of the elderly—is having and will increasingly have dramatic effects on U.S. society. This increase in the dependent population places pressure on workers and families to provide for them. Their growing political power will affect public policies, the politics of elections, and the political dynamics of certain states and regions.

The consequences for U.S. society, then, of the convergence of these three powerful macro social forces are (1) a dislocation for many workers as some jobs become obsolete, their skills are no longer needed in a service/knowledge economy, their jobs have been replaced by automation, or their jobs have moved to a lower-wage environment; (2) an increasing wealth/income gap; (3) the downward economic spiral for racial minorities; (4) an increased proportion of people on the economic margins; (5) growing social unrest by the have-nots but also by workers who fear for their economic future; (6) an increase in scapegoating as animosities intensify because of economic tough times and a revival of racism; and (7) an increasing economic burden on the working population who must finance pension plans and other assistance for an ever larger elderly population.

CHAPTER REVIEW

1. Globalization refers to the processes by which the world's peoples become increasingly interconnected economically, politically, culturally, and environmentally.

2. The powerful forces affecting the U.S. economy are (a) the globalization of the economy; (b) technological change; (c) capital flight; and (d) the shift from an industrial economy to a service/information economy.

3. These forces combine to create considerable discontinuity and disequilibrium in society. In particular, low-wage labor outside the United States and the movement of business activity to low-wage areas within the United States have depressed wages and weakened unions. The result is a declining middle class,

downward social mobility for many, and the creation of the new poor.

4. The nature of work is shifting as employers downsize their workforce, replace workers with machinery, and as they hire more part-time or temporary workers. Two-thirds of these contingent workers are women.

5. The economic transformation has expanded the numbers of the working poor. This growth is a result of unemployment and underemployment (wages that do not lift a family above the poverty line).

6. The new poor are those blue-collar workers who lost manufacturing jobs with good pay and benefits because their companies closed or moved elsewhere, or

179

CHAPTER 8
Structural Sources
of Social Change:
Economic and
Demographic

who were replaced by automation. These "new poor" are much more trapped in poverty than were the "old poor" of other generations.

7. The second societal upheaval that is shaking up society and families is massive immigration. This wave of immigration differs from previous waves because the immigrants come primarily from Latin America and Asia rather than Europe.

8. Racial and ethnic diversity ("the browning of America") is increasing, with the influx of immigrants and differential fertility. The two fastest-growing minorities are Latinos and Asian Americans.

9. The reaction of Americans to the new immigrants is typically negative. This is based on two myths: (a) that immigrants take jobs away from those already here and (b) that immigrants are a drain on society's resources.

10. Immigrants face a dilemma: Do they fit into their new society, or do they retain the traditions of the society they left? Immigrants in the past, for the most part, assimilated. But conditions are different for the new immigrants: (a) They are racial/ethnics, not Whites; (b) the current political mood is to eliminate affirmative action programs and welfare programs; and (c) they have entered during difficult economic times brought about by the economic transformation.

11. The proportion of the U.S. population age sixty-five and older is growing. In this age category, women outnumber men and minorities are underrepresented. Although the elderly are not disproportionately poor, elderly women are, as are racial/ethnic minorities.

12. The Social Security program is the only source of income for about one-half of retired people and a major source of income for 80 percent of the elderly. Medicare is the universal health insurance program for the elderly. The key problem for both Social Security and Medicare is how they will be financed in the future.

13. The elderly may respond to their devalued status in several characteristic ways. They may withdraw from social relationships; they may continue to act as they have throughout their adult lives; or they may become politically active to change the laws, customs, and social structures that disadvantage them.

14. The numbers and proportion of the elderly in the U.S. population will increase. This aging population will create a difficult burden for the young, who, through taxes, are required to finance pension plans and other assistance for the elderly. Thus, there likely will be increased tensions between the generations in the future. This tension will also be racial, as the younger generation will be multiracial and multiethnic, while the elderly will be overwhelmingly White.

15. The consequences of the convergence of these three powerful forces—the structural transformation of the economy, the changing racial composition of society because of immigration, and the aging of society—are (a) an increasing wealth/income gap, (b) the downward spiral for racial minorities, (c) an increased proportion of people on the economic margins, (d) a growing social unrest, and (e) an increase in scapegoating.

KEY TERMS

Globalization
Capital flight
Offshoring
Outsourcing
Structural transformation of the
    economy

Sunset industries
Sunrise industries
Contingent employment
Homeshoring or homesourcing
New poor
Immigration

Demographic
New immigration
Assimilation
Dependency ratio
Disengagement

STUDY QUESTIONS

1. What are the consequences of globalization on individuals, communities, and the nature of work in U.S. society?
2. The U.S. economy has been transformed as it moved from one dominated by manufacturing to one based on services/knowledge. What social categories are most disadvantaged by these changes? Why?
3. A common argument is that unemployment is the consequence of individuals lacking the proper values of initiative, hard work, and a success orientation. Write an essay making the opposite case, that the fundamental reasons for unemployment are structural.

4. Compare the immigrants entering the United States in the late nineteenth century with the immigrants today. In your comparison, consider personal characteristics, where they are located, the jobs available to them, and their chances for upward mobility.
5. Are the fears toward immigrants warranted?
6. What are the sociological reasons for the contemporary rise in the numbers in such groups as "skinheads," self-appointed state militias, and other "hate" groups?
7. Why is the analysis of these two macro social forces—economic transformation and immigration— important sociologically?

http://www.ifg.org/

The International Forum on Globalization (IFG) is an alliance of sixty leading activists, scholars, economists, researchers, and writers formed to stimulate new thinking, joint activity, and public education in response to economic globalization.

http://www.guerrillanews.com/

Guerrilla News is an alternative media source that explores issues such as globalization and corporate crime. It includes information not found in mainstream news.

http://www.michaelmoore.com/

Michael Moore is an author and filmmaker from Flint, Michigan. His site contains information on his books and movies that address issues on downsizing and actions of corporations. The site also provides up-to-date information on current legislation.

http://stats.bls.gov/opub/cwc/cwcwelc.htm

Part of the Bureau of Labor Statistics, Compensation and Working Conditions Online provides articles on different labor-related topics.

http://www.usasnet.org/

United Students against Sweatshops is an international movement "that supports the struggles of working people and challenges corporate power."

http://www.helpage.org/

HelpAge International is a "global network of not-for-profit organizations with a mission to work with and for disadvantaged older people worldwide to achieve a lasting improvement in the quality of their lives."

http://www.who.int/hpr/ageing/index.htm

This site is part of the World Health Organization and deals specifically with aging and the life course. The site has news, current events, links, and publications dealing with these issues.

http://www.nia.nih.gov/

The National Institute on Aging is one center at the National Institutes of Health that seeks to "understand the nature of aging and to extend the healthy, active years of life."

http://www.ins.usdoj.gov/graphics/index.htm

The Immigration and Naturalization Services site provides various information related to immigration. The site subjects include law enforcement and border management and immigration services and benefits.

http://opr.princeton.edu/

The Office of Population Research is part of Princeton University and has a "distinguished history of contributions in formal demography and the study of fertility change."

http://cmd.princeton.edu/

The Center for Migration and Development, a center at Princeton University, is concerned with international migration and national development.

http://www.familiesusa.org/index.htm

Families USA is focused on making health care more affordable for everyone. There are sections on the site devoted to children, Medicaid, and Medicare.

http://www.umass.edu/complit/aclanet/USMigrat.html

This site describes some of the major migration and immigration laws from U.S. history.

http://www.ameristat.org/

This is the website of the Population Reference Bureau in partnership with the Social Science Data Analysis Network. It provides the latest statistics on foreign-born populations, immigration, and the elderly.

http://www.caasf.org/

Chinese for Affirmative Action has a mission "to defend and promote the civil and political rights of Chinese and Asian Americans within the context of, and in the interest of, advancing multiracial democracy in the United States."

http://www.americandemographics.com

This is the website for American Demographics magazine. It includes data and articles on various population issues.

http://globalissues.org

This site has information on "global issues that affect everyone," including trade-related, environmental, and human rights issues.

CHAPTER 9

Social Stratification

Inequality is a fact of social life. All known societies have some system of ranking individuals and groups along a superiority-inferiority scale. Consider the following examples:

In India, birth into a particular family often determines one's caste position, which in turn establishes one's social position, work, and range of marriage partners. At the bottom of this system is one group—the untouchables—that is so low that its members are not even part of the **caste system**. The untouchables do society's dirty work: sweeping floors or streets, collecting garbage, disposing of dead animals, midwifing (because of contact with the afterbirth), and washing latrines. Traditional Hindus of the upper castes believe untouchables pollute everything they touch. But there is even a hierarchy among the untouchables, with one category so sullied that they cannot be seen by others during the daylight hours. (See A Closer Look panel titled "Birth as Destiny: India's Caste System.")

In South Africa there is an unofficial caste system based on race. There are four racial castes: Whites, Blacks, Coloreds (mixed races), and Asians. The conditions for housing, work, pay, and schooling in this apartheid system are decidedly unequal by race.

In Saudi Arabia men have higher status than women. By law, custom, and religious beliefs, women are restricted from certain jobs, from driving automobiles, and from positions of authority.

Brazil was the last nation in the Western Hemisphere to abolish slavery (1888). It was made illegal in Niger in 2004. However, a form of slavery continues as workers in some situations are virtually imprisoned by their employers, working for food and shelter with no hope of paying off their debts. This is found in many societies (Bales, 1999), including the United States (Bowe, 2007).

These examples indicate a range of patterned social inequality in various societies. (See the Globalization panel titled "Inequality among Nations" for stratification across societies.) Variations on these themes are also found in the United States, where people are divided and ranked by family of origin, race, gender, and economic position.

The pattern of structured inequities is called *social stratification*, the subject of this chapter and Chapters 10 through 12. This chapter examines these ranking systems. These structured systems of inequality are crucial to the understanding of human groups because they are important determinants of human behavior and because they have significant consequences for society and its members.

Birth as Destiny: India's Caste System

The caste system in India was outlawed in 1950. Modern commerce and transportation diminished its power in urban India. It remains in force, however, in many rural villages and regions where tradition retains a powerful grip.

A caste system is a system of social stratification based on ascription. In such a system, birth into a particular family determines one's destiny—social position, type of work, and range of marriage partners—for life. In principle there is no social mobility, and each subcaste is identified with an occupation, such as priests, barbers, sweepers, or leatherworkers.

There are four major castes (varnas) in hierarchical order (and with about 3,000 subcastes—jatis—within them). About one in six Indians belongs to the lowest rung in this order. These are the untouchables (dalits). Their status is so low that it is below the caste system; "Untouchables are outcasts—people considered too impure, too polluted, to rank as worthy beings" (O'Neill, 2003:9). They are branded as impure from the moment of birth. And their "untouchability" is passed to each successive generation.

Untouchables do society's "unclean work." Even the untouchables are ranked. At the bottom of the hundreds of untouchable categories are the Bhangi, or scavengers. Their work involves physical contact with blood and the dead, such as tanning hides, cremation, cleaning up excrement and other bodily "defilements" as defined by Hindu law. They earn money by manually cleaning latrines and sewers and by removing dead animals from the streets.

Because the family transmits social position from one generation to the next, a rigid system requires that marriage occur only between social equals. Thus, a caste system mandates endogamous marriage (within one's group).

An integral part of the Indian caste system is the concern for ritual purity. Because it is believed that the higher the caste, the more pure the members, there are elaborate rules of etiquette governing social distance between the castes. Untouchables, for example, pollute their superiors by their smell, touch, or even their presence. They are required to hide whenever anyone from a higher caste is present or, if this is not possible, they must bow with their faces turned downward. Highborns must not take food or water from an untouchable because it pollutes them. Untouchables must take water only from their own well because to draw water from the same well as the other castes pollutes all others. If polluted, there are a number of practices used for ritual purification (fire, bathing, family shrine, or temple).

The caste system is supported by powerful cultural beliefs. The Hindu religion emphasizes a strong concern for duty (dharma). This involves one's duty to family, caste, age, and sex. In effect, there is a moral duty to accept one's fate. Moreover, if one does not fulfill the requirements of her or his particular caste position, there are dire consequences. Often if a dalit acts outside the caste rules (questioning a "superior," fishing in a pond used by the upper caste), a mob may attack him or her (dousing the violators with acid is a favorite punishment). Central to the Hindu religion is the belief in reincarnation—that souls are reborn after death. Thus, for people who do not observe the moral laws of their particular caste, after death their souls will be reborn into a lower caste. Conversely, faithful obedience to caste duties will result in rebirth into a higher caste. Brahmins (the highest caste), then, are being rewarded for excellence in previous lives while untouchables are being punished. This belief system provides a very strong social control mechanism for maintaining the rigid stratification system. "No one wants to be reborn as an untouchable, least of all the untouchables, who best know the miseries of this position. Furthermore, we can understand the contempt received by untouchables: they are those believed to have sinned most in a previous life" (Kerbo, 1983:20). This belief reinforces the status quo since the "haves" and the "have-nots" each believe that they are deserving of their social standing. Thus, there is no push to change the unequal system.

This chapter is divided into three sections. First, the important concepts are introduced. Second, the three major hierarchies—class, race, and gender—are described briefly. The third section describes and critiques the theories used to explain the universality of stratification systems and how hierarchies of dominant and subordinate groups are established and maintained.

Inequality among Nations

There is a huge inequality gap worldwide. Here are some representative facts:

- Nearly 10 million children die each year because their families, communities, and nations are too poor to sustain them (Sachs, 2008:38).
- The World Bank estimates that 1.1 billion people live in extreme poverty, making less than $1 a day. At the opposite extreme, are 1,210 billionaires worldwide with a combined wealth of $4.5 trillion, more than the gross domestic product of Germany (*Forbes*, 2011:41).
- The world's richest person, Carlos Slim of Mexico had a net worth of $74 billion in 2010, an increase of *$20.5 billion over the previous year* (Krantz, 2011).
- While one out of three children in wealthy countries complete some form of higher education, a smaller percent of children in sub-Saharan Africa will finish primary school (*Courier*, 2009).
- The wealthiest 20 percent consume 86 percent of the world's goods and services, while the poorest 20 percent consume but 1 percent (Williamson, 2001).
- Almost 90 percent of the world's wealth is held in North America, Europe, and high-income Asian and Pacific countries, such as Japan and Australia (Giles, 2006).
- Girls and women are disproportionately disadvantaged. Women represent two-thirds of the world's illiterate people and three-fifths of its poor.

The causes of world poverty are many. First, the poorest nations were once colonies of the richer nations, and this legacy of exploitation has left them behind (in leadership and in economies that are based on a single agricultural crop or other commodity). Second, the governments that formed following independence from colonial rule were typically corrupt and unable to control the lawlessness of criminals or warlords. Third, many poor countries are located in extreme climates where droughts or floods or earthquakes or other natural disasters are commonplace. Fourth, as their economies crumble, many of these governments have borrowed heavily from lenders such as the World Bank and the International Monetary Fund. As a condition of these loans, the poor nations are, typically, required to reduce government spending on human services. Fifth, the global economic system with free-trade policies makes it difficult for nations with a limited number of crops/commodities to cope with plunging world markets due to recessions, oversupply, and wildly fluctuating prices. The results in these countries are economic chaos, widespread unemployment, declining wages, and government instability. And, sixth, many transnational corporations continue the tradition of exploitation by using the cheap labor and cheap resources of the poor countries to their advantage.

To amplify this last point, when transnational corporations locate in poor countries, the local economies and workers should, in theory, benefit by gaining a higher standard of living and because of access to modern technology. They have not for several reasons. One reason is that the profits generated in these countries are channeled back to the home nation of the transnational corporation, not the host economy. Moreover, the assembly plants in these poor companies tend to hire young women (because they will work for lower wages than men and they are more docile in the workplace), replacing them with other young women after a few years. This pattern disrupts family arrangements, and the benefits of relatively high wages (for that economy) are short lived.

So, the global economic system results in a severe maldistribution of wealth and the accompanying life chances for people. In sum, half of the world's people live in misery while the wealthy nations and the wealthy in those nations are doing very well indeed.

Major Concepts

People differ in age, physical attributes, and what they do for a living. The process of categorizing people by age, height, occupation, or some other personal attribute is called **social differentiation**. When people are ranked in a vertical arrangement (hierarchy) that differentiates them as superior or inferior, we have **social stratification**. The key difference between differentiation and stratification is that the process of ranking or evaluation occurs only in the latter. What is ranked and how it is ranked are dependent on the values of the society.

Social stratification refers, in essence, to structured social inequality. The term *structured* refers to stratification being socially patterned. This implies that inequalities are not caused by biological differences such as sex or race. Biological traits do not become relevant in patterns of social superiority or inferiority until they are socially recognized and given importance by being incorporated into the beliefs, attitudes, and values of the people in the society. People in the United States, for example, tend to believe that gender and racial characteristics make a difference—therefore, they do.

The social patterning of stratification is also found in the distribution of rewards in any community or society, because that distribution is governed by social norms. In the United States few individuals seriously question the income differential between medical doctors and nurses or college professors and primary school teachers because the norms and values of society dictate that such inequalities are just.

Patterned behavior is also achieved through the socialization process. Each generation is taught the norms and values of the society and of its social class. The children of slaves and the children of the ruling family in a society are each taught the behavior proper for people of their station in life.

Finally, the system of stratification is always connected with other aspects of the society. The existing stratification arrangements are affected by and have effects on such matters as politics, marriage, economics, education, and religion. Harold Kerbo (1983) summarizes what is meant by social stratification:

> Social stratification means that inequality has been hardened or institutionalized, and there is a system of social relationships that determines who gets what, and why. When we say institutionalized we mean that a system of layered hierarchy has been established. People have come to expect that individuals and groups with certain positions will be able to demand more influence and respect and accumulate a greater share of goods and services. Such inequality may or may not be accepted equally by a majority in the society, but it is recognized as the way things are. (11)

The hierarchies of stratification—class, race, and gender—place groups, individuals, and families in the larger society. The crucial consequence of this so-called placement is that the rewards and resources of society such as wealth, power, and privilege are unequally distributed. And, crucially, differential access to these societal resources and rewards produces different life experiences and different life chances. **Life chances** refer to the chances throughout one's life cycle to live and to experience the good things in life. Life chances are most significant because they are those things that "(1) better-off people can purchase (good education, good medical care, comfortable homes, fine vacations, expert services of all kinds, safe and satisfying occupations) and which poor people would also purchase if they had the money; and (2) make life easier, longer, healthier, and more enjoyable" (Tumin, 1973:104). The converse, of course, is that people at the low end of the stratification hierarchies will have inadequate health care, shelter, and diets. Their lives will be more miserable and they will die sooner.

To understand U.S. society we must understand the hierarchies of class, race, and gender. Class, race, and gender are macro structures of inequality that shape our micro worlds. These structures organize society as a whole and create varied environments for individuals and families through their unequal distribution of social opportunities.

The consequence of placement in the stratification system is that the rewards and resources of society such as wealth, power, and privilege are unequally distributed.

These structures of inequality array the resources and advantages of society in patterned ways. These hierarchies are also structured systems of exploitation and discrimination in which the affluent dominate the poor, men dominate women, and Whites dominate people of color (Feagin and Feagin, 1997:26–27).

Traditionally, the family has been viewed as the principal unit in the class system because it passes on privilege (or the lack thereof) in wealth and resources from generation to generation. Even though the family is basic in maintaining stratification, life chances are affected by race and gender inequalities as well as by social class. In most families, men have greater socioeconomic resources and more power and privileges than do women, even though all family members are viewed as members of the same social class. While a family's placement in the class hierarchy does determine rewards and resources, hierarchies based on sex create different conditions for women and men even within the same family (Acker, 1973). Systems of sex stratification cut across class and racial divisions to distribute resources differently to men and women (Baca Zinn and Eitzen, 2008: Chapter 5).

Class

When a number of people occupy the same relative economic rank in the stratification system, they form a **social class**. Social class "implies having or not having the following: individual rights, privileges, power, rights over others, authority, lifestyle choices, self-determination, status, wealth, access to services, comfort, leisure, etc." (Comer, 1978:171). People are socially located in a class position on the basis of income, occupation, and education, either alone or in combination. In the past, the occupation, income, and education of the husband determined the class location of the family. But family behavior is better explained by locating families according to the more prestigious occupation, regardless of whether it is the husband's or the wife's (Yorburg, 1983:189). Occupations are part of the larger opportunity structure of society. Those that are highly valued and carry high-income rewards are unevenly distributed. The amount of income determines how well a given household can acquire the resources needed for survival and perhaps for luxury. The job or occupation that is the source of the paycheck connects families with the opportunity structure in different ways. This connection generates different kinds of class privileges for families. **Privilege** refers to the distribution of goods and services, situations, and experiences that are highly valued and beneficial (Jeffries and Ransford, 1980:68). Class privileges are those advantages, prerogatives, and options that are available to those in the middle and upper classes. They involve help from the system: banks, credit unions, medical facilities, schools, and voluntary associations. Class privileges are based on the systematic linkages between families and society. Class privilege creates many differences in family patterns.

Race and Ethnicity

Racial and ethnic stratification refers to systems of inequality in which some fixed group membership, such as race, religion, or national origin, is a major criterion for ranking social positions and their differential rewards. Like the class system, this hierarchy represents institutionalized power, privilege, and prestige. Racial and ethnic hierarchies generate domination and subordination, often referred to as majority-minority relations. Minority groups are those that are dominated by a more powerful group, stigmatized, and singled out for differential treatment.

Race is socially defined on the basis of a presumed common genetic heritage resulting in distinguishing physical characteristics. **Ethnicity** refers to the condition of being culturally rather than physically distinctive. Ethnic peoples are bound together by virtue of a common ancestry and a common cultural background.

A racial group that has a distinctive culture or subculture, shares a common heritage, and has developed a common identity is also an ethnic group. Both race and ethnicity are traditional bases for systems of inequality, although there are historical and contemporary differences in the societal placement of racial ethnics and White ethnics in this society. We examine how racial stratification deprives people of color of equal access to society's resources and thereby creates family patterns that are different from the idealized family model.

The most important feature of racial stratification is the exclusion of people of color from equal access to society's valued resources. People of color or racial ethnics have less power, wealth, and social status than do other people in the United States. African Americans, Latinos, and Asian Americans constitute the largest of the racial minorities in the United States.

Gender

Gender, like race and class, is a basic organizing principle of society. From the macro level of the societal economy, through the institutions of society, to interpersonal relations, gender shapes activities, perceptions, roles, and rewards. Gender is the patterning of difference and domination through distinctions between women and men (Acker, 1992:565).

The stratification system that assigns women's and men's roles unequally is the **sex-gender system**. It consists of two complementary yet mutually exclusive categories into which all human beings are placed. The sex-gender system combines biologically based sex roles with socially created gender roles. In everyday life, the terms *sex role* and *gender role* are used interchangeably. This use obscures important differences and underlying issues in the study of women's and men's experiences. **Sex roles** refer to behaviors determined by an individual's biological sex. **Gender roles** are social constructions; they contain self-concepts and psychological traits, as well as family, occupational, and political roles assigned dichotomously to each sex. For example, the traditional female gender role includes expectations for females to be passive, nurturant, and dependent. The standard male gender role incorporates alternative expectations—behaviors that are aggressive, competitive, and independent (Lipman-Blumen, 1984:1–2).

Patriarchy is the term for forms of social organization in which men are dominant over women. As described in Chapter 12, patriarchy is infused throughout U.S. society. Generally, men have more power than women, and, generally, they also have greater power over women. Even though there is considerable class and racial variation here, men in general gain some privilege at the expense of women. In sum, the sex-gender system distributes power, resources, prestige, and privilege unequally.

The Intersection of Class, Race, and Gender

The hierarchies of class, race, and gender do not stand alone. They are interrelated systems of stratification. Economic resources, the bases of class, are not randomly distributed but vary systematically by race and sex. For example, people of color and women have fewer occupational choices than do White males. People of color and women often experience separate and unequal education and receive less income for the work they do, resulting in different life chances.

These systems of inequality form what sociologist Patricia Hill Collins (1990) calls a **matrix of domination** in which each of us exists. The existence of these intersections has several important implications (Baca Zinn and Dill, 1996). First, people experience race, class, gender, and sexuality differently depending upon their social location in these structures of inequality. For example, people of the same race will experience race differently depending upon their location in the class structure as poor, working class, professional/ managerial class, or unemployed, their location in the gender structure as female or male, and their location in the sexuality system as heterosexual or homosexual.

Second, class, race, and gender are components of both social structure and social interaction. As a result, individuals, because of their social locations, experience different forms of privilege and subordination. In short, these intersecting forms of inequality produce both oppression and opportunity.

A third implication of the inequality matrix has to do with the relational nature of dominance and subordination. Power is embedded in each system of stratification, determining whether one is dominant or subordinate. The intersectional nature of hierarchies means that power differentials are linked in systematic ways, reinforcing power differentials across hierarchies.

Order and Conflict Theories of Stratification

Sociologists and other observers of society have pondered two fundamental questions about stratification. The first is, Why are societies stratified? The second is, Within stratified societies, why are certain categories ranked as superior while others are considered inferior? There are alternative theoretical explanations for each question, and each explanation has important implications. Let's begin with the two sociological theories for the more general and logically prior question.

All societies have some form of stratification. How is this universal phenomenon to be explained? Sociologists answer this question from either the order or the conflict perspective. The position of the order theorists is basically supportive of inequality, because the unequal distribution of rewards is assumed to be not only inevitable but also necessary. Conflict theorists, on the other hand, tend to denounce the distributive system as basically unjust, unnecessary, and the source of many social problems.

Order Theory

Adherents of the order model begin with the fact that social inequality is a ubiquitous and apparently unavoidable phenomenon. They reason that inequality must, therefore, serve a useful function for society. The argument, as presented in the classic statement by Kingsley Davis and Wilbert Moore (1945), is as follows. The smooth functioning of society requires that various tasks be accomplished through a division of labor. There is a universal problem, then, of allocation—of getting the most important tasks done by the most talented people. Some jobs are more important for societal survival than are others (typically those involved in decision making, medicine, religion, teaching, and the military). The societal problem is how to get the most talented people motivated to go through the required long periods of training and to do these important tasks well. The universally found answer, according to Davis and Moore, is differential rewards. Society must provide suitable rewards (money, prestige, and power) to induce individuals to fill these positions. The rewards must, it is argued, be distributed unevenly to various positions because the positions are not equally pleasant or equally important. Thus, a differential reward system guarantees that the important societal functions are fulfilled, thereby ensuring the maintenance of society. In this way, differential ranks actually serve to unify society through a division of labor (functional integration) and through the socialization of people to accept their positions in the system.

Although there probably is some truth to this argument, the analysts of society must also ask: Is inequality primarily integrative or divisive? Is it necessary? Must the poor always be with us? If stratification is so functional, why is it so dysfunctional for many (see Huaco, 1966; Tumin, 1953)?

Conflict Theory

Conflict theorists view stratification in a wholly different manner from the order theorists. Rather than accepting stratification as a source of societal integration, the conflict perspective assumes that stratification reflects the distribution of power in society and is therefore a major source of discord and coercion. It is a source of discord because groups compete for scarce resources and because the powerless, under certain conditions, resent their lowly position and lack of rewards. Coercion results from stratification as the powerful (who are coincidentally male, White, and wealthy) prey on the weak. From this view, then, the unequal distribution of rewards reflects the interests of the powerful and not the basic survival needs of society, as the order theorists contend.

A major contention of the conflict theorists is that the powerful people use ideology to make their value system paramount. Karl Marx argued that the dominant ideology in any society is always the ideology of the ruling class. The ruling class uses the media, schools, religion, and other institutions to legitimate systems of inequality. So powerful is this socialization process that even oppressed peoples tend to accept their low status as natural. Marx called this tendency of the oppressed to accept their oppression false consciousness (see Marx and Engels, 1959; Michael Parenti, 1978:15–18). The working class and the poor in the United States, for example, tend to accept their lack of monetary rewards, power, and prestige because they believe that the system is truly meritocratic—and that they lack the skills and brains to do the better-rewarded tasks in society. In short, they believe that they deserve their fate (see Sennett and Cobb, 1973). Consequently, they accept a differential reward system and the need to leave supervision and decision making to experts. False consciousness thus inhibits efforts by the disadvantaged to change an oppressive system. Marx argued, however, that when the oppressed become aware of their common oppression and that they have been manipulated by the powerful to serve the interests of the powerful, they will develop a class consciousness—an objective awareness of their common exploitation—thus becoming unified in a cause to advance their class interests.

Even though it is true that social stratification is an important source of societal friction, conflict theorists have not answered the important question as to its universality and necessity (neither have the order theorists, for that matter, although they address themselves directly to that question). Both theoretical perspectives have important insights that must be considered. The order theorists see stratification serving the useful function of societal maintenance by providing a mechanism (differential rewards) to ensure that all the slots in the division of labor are filled. Conflict theorists are equally valid in their contention that stratification is unjust, divisive, and a source of social instability or change.

Deficiency Theories

Some categories of people are systematically disadvantaged in the United States, most especially the poor, non-Whites, and women. Is there some flaw within these groups—perhaps biological or cultural—that explains their inferiority? Or, is it the structure of society that blocks their progress while encouraging the advancement of others? To answer these questions, we examine the various explanations for poverty. The specific explanations for inequities by race and gender are addressed in detail in Chapters 11 and 12, using the same explanatory categories used to understand poverty.

Who or what is to blame for poverty? There are two very different answers to these questions (Barrera, 1979:174–219). One is that the poor are in that condition because of some deficiency: Either they are biologically inferior or their culture fails them by promoting character traits that impede their progress in society. The other response places the blame on the structure of society: Some people are poor because society has failed to provide equality in educational opportunity, because institutions discriminate against minorities, because private industry has failed to provide enough jobs, because automation has made some jobs obsolete, and so forth. In this view, society has worked in such a way as to trap certain people and their offspring in a condition of poverty.

Biological Inferiority

In 1882, the British philosopher and sociologist Herbert Spencer came to the United States to promote a theory later known as social Darwinism. He argued that the poor were poor because they were unfit. Poverty was nature's way of "excreting ... unhealthy, imbecile, slow, vacillating, faithless members of society in order to make room for the 'fit,' who were duly entitled to the rewards of wealth. Spencer preached that the poor should not be helped through state or private charity, because such acts would interfere with nature's way of getting rid of the weak" (*Progressive*, 1980).

Social Darwinism has generally lacked support in the scientific community, although it has continued to provide a rationale for the thinking of many individuals. Recently, however, the concept has resurfaced in the work of three scientists. They suggest that the poor are in that condition because they do not measure up to the more well-to-do in intellectual endowment.

Arthur Jensen, professor emeritus of educational psychology at the University of California, has argued that there is a strong possibility that Blacks are less well endowed mentally than are Whites. From his review of the research on IQ, he claimed that approximately 80 percent of IQ is inherited, while the remaining 20 percent is attributable to environment. Because Blacks differ significantly from Whites in achievement on IQ tests and in school, Jensen claims that it is reasonable to hypothesize that the sources of these differences are genetic as well as environmental (Jensen, 1969; 1980).

The late Richard Herrnstein, a Harvard psychologist, agrees with Jensen that intelligence is largely inherited. He goes one step further, positing the formation of hereditary castes based on intelligence (Herrnstein, 1971; 1973). For Herrnstein, social stratification by inborn differences occurs because (1) mental ability is inherited and (2) success (prestige of job and earnings) depends on mental ability. Thus, a **meritocracy** (social stratification by ability) develops through the sorting process. This reasoning assumes that people close in mental ability are more likely to marry and reproduce, thereby ensuring castes by level of intelligence. According to this thesis, "in times to come, as technology advances, the tendency to be unemployed may run in the genes of a family about as certainly as bad teeth do now" (Herrnstein, 1971:63). This is another way of saying that the bright people are in the upper classes and the dregs are at the bottom. Inequality is justified, just as it was argued years ago by the social Darwinists.

Why are these children poor? Is it because their biology or culture has failed to provide them with the traits for success or is it because society has failed them through inferior schools or because their parents are denied a living wage?

Charles Murray, along with Herrnstein, wrote *The Bell Curve: Intelligence and Class Structure in American Life* (Herrnstein and Murray, 1994), a revival of social Darwinism. Their claim, an update of Herrnstein's earlier work, is that the economic and social hierarchies reflect a single dimension—cognitive ability, as measured by IQ tests.

Notwithstanding the flaws in the logic and in the evidence used by Jensen, Herrnstein, and Murray (for excellent critiques of the Herrnstein and Murray work, see Fischer et al., 1996; Gould, 1994; Hermann, 1994; Nisbett, 2007; Reed, 1994; and the symposium appearing in *Contemporary Sociology*, 1995), we must consider the implications of their biological determinism for dealing with the problem of poverty.

Jensen and Herrnstein have argued that dispassionate study is required to determine whether intelligence is inherited to the degree that they state. Objectivity is the sine qua non of scientific inquiry, and one cannot argue with its merits, although science, all science is tainted because, as the late evolutionary biologist Stephen Jay Gould has argued, all scientists are enmeshed in a web of personal and social circumstances that affect their science. Leftist geneticists, for example, are more likely to combat biological determinism just as politically conservative geneticists favor interpretations of inequality as the reflection of genetic inadequacies of people (Gould, 1982; York and Clark, 2011). We should recognize, however, the important social consequences implied by the Jensen-Herrnstein argument. First, biological determinism is a classic example of blaming the victim. The individual poor person is blamed instead of inferior schools, culturally biased IQ tests, low wages, corporate downsizing, or social barriers of race, religion, or nationality. By blaming the victim, this thesis claims a relationship between lack of success and lack of intelligence. This relationship is spurious because it ignores the advantages and disadvantages of ascribed status (statuses of individuals assigned without reference to abilities or efforts but rather on the basis of age, sex, race, ethnicity, and family background). According to William Ryan (1972), "Arthur Jensen and Richard Herrnstein confirm regretfully that Black folks and poor folks are born stupid, that little rich kids grow up rich adults, not because they inherited Daddy's stock portfolio, but rather because they inherited his brains" (54).

The Jensen-Herrnstein-Murray thesis divides people in the United States further by appealing to bigots. It provides "scientific justification" for their beliefs in the racial superiority of some groups and the inferiority of others. By implication, it legitimates the segregation and unequal treatment of so-called inferiors. The goal of integration and the fragile principle of egalitarianism are seriously threatened to the degree that members of the scientific community give this thesis credence or prominence.

Another serious implication of the biological determinism argument is the explicit validation of the IQ test as a legitimate measure of intelligence. The IQ test attempts to measure innate potential, but this is impossible, because the testing process must inevitably reflect some of the skills that develop during the individual's lifetime. For the most part, intelligence tests measure educability—that is, the prediction of conventional school achievement. Achievement in school is, of course, also associated with a cluster of other social and motivational factors, as Joanna Ryan (1972) observes:

> The test as a whole is usually validated, if at all, against the external criterion of school performance. It therefore comes as no surprise to find that IQ scores do in fact correlate highly with educational success. IQ scores are also found to correlate positively with socio-economic status, those in the upper social classes tending to have the highest IQs. Since social class, and all that this implies, is both an important determinant and also an important consequence of educational performance, this association is to be expected. (54)

Thus, the Jensen-Herrnstein-Murray thesis overlooks the important contribution of social class to achievement on IQ tests. This oversight is crucial, because most social scientists feel that these tests are biased in favor of people who have had middle- and upper-class environments and experiences. IQ tests discriminate against the poor in many ways. They discriminate obviously in the language that is used, in the instructions that are given, and in the experiences they assume the subjects have had. The discrimination can also be more subtle. For minority-group examinees, the race of the person administering the test influences the results. Another, less well-known fact about IQ tests is that in many cases they provide a self-fulfilling prophecy, as Joanna Ryan (1972) notes: "IQ scores obtained at one age often determine how an individual is subsequently treated, and, in particular, what kind of education he receives as a consequence of IQ testing will in turn contribute to his future IQ, and it is notorious that those of low and high IQ do not get equally good education" (44).

Another implication is the belief that poverty is inevitable. The "survival of the fittest" capitalist ideology is reinforced, justifying both discrimination against the poor and continued privilege for the advantaged. Inequality is rationalized so that little will be done to aid its victims. Herrnstein and Murray argue that public policies to ameliorate poverty are a waste of time and resources. "Programs designed to alter the natural dominance of the 'cognitive elite' are useless, the book argues, because the genes of the subordinate castes invariably doom them to failure" (Muwakkil, 1994:22). The acceptance of this thesis, then, has obvious consequences for what policy decisions will be made or not made in dealing with poverty. If their view prevails, then welfare programs will be abolished, as will programs such as Head Start.

This raises the serious question: Is intelligence immutable, or is there the possibility of boosting cognitive development? A number of studies have shown that Head Start–type programs raise scores among poor children by as much as nine points. These results, however, fade out entirely by the sixth grade. Yet this rise and fall of IQ scores makes the case for the role of environmental factors in cognitive development. As Beth Maschinot (1995) argues:

> [The critics of Head Start] ignore the obvious fact that once they leave Head Start, poor students typically attend substandard schools from the first grade onward. The fact that IQ scores drop again after this experience should lead one logically to conclude that intelligence as defined by IQ tests is highly responsive to environmental manipulations, not the reverse. (33)

Research on programs other than Head Start makes the same point. The Abecedarian Project conducted by the University of North Carolina studied high-risk children from 120 families. The conclusion:

> The most important policy implication of these findings is that early educational intervention for impoverished children can have long-lasting benefits, in terms of improved cognitive performance. This underscores the critical importance of good early environments and suggests that the focus of debate should now be shifted from whether government should play a role in encouraging good early environments to how these environments can be assured. (Campbell and Ramey, 1994:694–695)

Another study, by the Robert Wood Johnson Foundation, of low-birthweight infants followed their development for three years. The researchers found that the infants who had stimulating day care environments had, on average, a thirteen-point higher IQ score than the babies who did not have those experiences (reported in Richmond, 1994).

As a final example, high-risk African American children in Ypsilanti, Michigan, were randomly divided into two groups. One group received a high-quality active learning program as three- and four-year-olds. The other groups received no preschool education. The two groups were compared at age twenty-seven, with these results:

> By age 27, those who had received the preschool education had half as many arrests as the comparison group. Four times as many were earning $2,000 or more a month. Three times as many owned their own homes. One-third more had graduated from high school on schedule. One-fourth fewer of them needed welfare as adults. And they had one-third fewer children born out of wedlock. (Beck, 1995:7B)

The Jensen-Herrnstein-Murray thesis also provides justification for unequal schooling. Why should school boards allot comparable sums of money for similar programs in middle-class and lower-class schools if the natural endowments of children in each type of school are so radically different? Why should teachers expect the same performance from poor children as from children from the more well-to-do? Why spend extra money on disadvantaged children in Head Start programs if these children are doomed by genetic inferiority? The result of such beliefs is, of course, a self-fulfilling prophecy. Low expectations beget low achievement.

Finally, the Jensen-Herrnstein-Murray thesis encourages policymakers either to ignore poverty or to attack its effects rather than its causes in the structure of society itself.

Cultural Inferiority

The culture-of-poverty hypothesis contends that the poor are qualitatively different in values and lifestyles from the rest of society and that these cultural differences explain continued poverty. In other words, the poor, in adapting to their deprived condition, are found to be more permissive in raising their children, less verbal, more fatalistic, less apt to defer gratification, and less likely to be interested in formal education than are the more well-to-do. Most important is the contention that this deviant cultural pattern is transmitted from generation to generation. Thus, there is a strong implication that poverty is perpetuated by defects in the lifeways of the poor. If poverty itself were to be eliminated, the former poor would probably continue to prefer instant gratification, be immoral by middle-class standards, and so on. This reasoning blames the victim. From this view, the poor have a subculture with values that differ radically from the values of the other social classes. And this explains their poverty.

The late Edward Banfield, an eminent political scientist and advisor to Republican presidents, argued that the difference between the poor and the nonpoor is cultural—the former have a present-time orientation, while the nonpoor have a future-time orientation (Banfield, 1974). He did not see the present-time orientation of the poor as a function of the hopelessness of their situation. Yet it seems highly unlikely that the poor see little reason to complain about the slums: What about the filth, the rats, the overcrowded living conditions, the high infant mortality? What about the lack of jobs and opportunity for upward mobility? This feeling of being trapped seems to be the primary cause of hedonistic present-time orientation. If the structure were changed so that the poor could see that hard work and deferred gratification really paid off, they could adopt a future-time orientation.

Most commonly, the culture of poverty hypothesis has been dismissed by sociologists and anthropologists but recently it has received a resurgence of interest and greater acceptance (Small, Harding, and Lamont, 2010; Cohen, 2010; Battistoni, 2010). For these scholars, it is crucial to examine the structural and cultural forces.

Critics of the culture-of-poverty hypothesis argue that the poor are an integral part of U.S. society; they do not abandon the dominant values of the society, but rather, retain them while simultaneously holding an alternative set of values. This alternative set is a result of adaptation to the conditions of poverty. Elliot Liebow (1967), in his classic study of lower-class Black men, has taken this view. For him, street corner men strive to live by American values but are continually frustrated by externally imposed failure:

> From this perspective, the street corner man does not appear as a carrier of an independent cultural tradition. His behavior appears not so much as a way of realizing the distinctive goals and values of his own subculture, or of conforming to its models, but rather as his way of trying to achieve many of the goals and values of the larger society, of failing to do this and of concealing his failure from others and from himself as best he can. (222)

Stephen Steinberg is his critique of the new emphasis on culture to explain poverty (2011) states that "the question is not whether culture matters, but whether it is an independent and self-sustaining factor in the production and reproduction of poverty" (Steinberg, 2011:3). Summarizing Liebow he says:

> Liebow did not deny culture—indeed, he documented it in scrupulous detail. However, he insisted that the streetcorner man was not a carrier of an independent cultural tradition. To be sure, there were obvious similarities between parents and children, but Liebow held that these were not the product of cultural transmission, but rather reflected the fact that "the son goes out and independently experiences the same failures, in the same areas, and for much the same reasons as his father." Thus, it is not their culture that needs to be changed, but rather a political economy that fails to provide jobs that pay a living wage to millions of the nation's poor, along with a system of occupational apartheid that has excluded a who people from entire job sectors throughout American history. (Steinberg, 2011:4; emphasis added)

In short, the poor are not victims of their own vices but are victims of powerful political and economic forces.

Most people in the United States, however, believe that poverty is a combination of biological and cultural factors. Judith Chafel (1997) reviewed a number of studies on the beliefs of Americans and found that they "view economic privation as a self-inflicted condition, emanating more from personal factors (e.g., effort and ability) than the external-structural ones (e.g., an unfavorable labor market, institutional racism). Poverty is seen as inevitable, necessary, and just" (434).

Current research shows that this prevailing view is a myth. If there were a culture of poverty, then there would be a relatively large proportion of the poor that would constitute a permanent underclass. The deviant values and resulting behaviors of the poor would doom them and their children to continuous poverty. But the University of Michigan's Panel Study of Income Dynamics (Duncan, 1984) followed 5,000 representative households for ten years and found that only 2.6 percent fit the stereotype of permanent poverty. Contrary to common belief, most poor people are poor only temporarily; their financial fortunes rise and fall with widowhood, divorce, remarriage, acquiring a job with decent pay or losing one, or other changes affecting economic status. The 2.6 percent who are persistently poor are different from the temporarily poor: 62 percent are Black, compared with 19 percent of the temporarily poor; 39 percent are disabled, compared with 17 percent; one-third are elderly, compared with 14 percent; and 61 percent were female heads of households, compared with 28 percent of the temporarily poor. Examining just the two-thirds of the persistently poor who are not elderly, 65 percent live in households headed by women and almost three-quarters of these women are Black (Duncan, 1984:48–52). These facts show once again the interconnections of race and gender in understanding inequality in U.S. society and, as discussed in the next section, how inequality is structured by race and gender. The other important implication of these findings is that inequality negates the culture of poverty. Duncan and his colleagues find little evidence that poverty is a consequence of the way poor people think. Economic success is not a function of "good" values and behaviors, and failure the result of "bad" ones. Thus, the solution to poverty is not to change the attitudes of "flawed persons" but to change the opportunity structures in society (Duncan, 1984:65).

Structural Theories

In contrast to blaming the biological or cultural deficiencies of the poor, there is the view that how society is organized creates poverty and makes certain kinds of people especially vulnerable to being poor.

Institutional Discrimination

Michael Harrington (1963), whose book *The Other America: Poverty in the United States* was instrumental in sparking the federal government's war on poverty, says, "The real explanation of why the poor are where they are is that they made the mistake of being born to the wrong parents, in the wrong section of the country, in the wrong industry, or in the wrong racial or ethnic group" (21). This is another way of saying that the structural conditions of society are to blame for poverty, not the poor. When the customary ways of doing things, prevailing attitudes and expectations, and accepted structural arrangements work to the disadvantage of the poor, it is called **institutional discrimination**. Let us look at several examples of how the poor are trapped by this type of discrimination.

Most good jobs require a college degree, but the poor cannot afford to send their children to college. Scholarships go to the best-performing students. Children of the poor usually do not perform well in school, primarily because of low expectations for them among teachers and administrators. This is reflected in the system of tracking by ability as measured on class-biased examinations. Further evidence is found in the disproportionately low amounts of money given to schools in impoverished neighborhoods. All of these acts result in a self-fulfilling prophecy—the poor are not expected to do well in school, and they do not. Because they are failures as measured by so-called objective indicators (such as the disproportionately high number of dropouts and discipline problems and the very small proportion who desire to go to college), the school feels justified in its discrimination toward the children of the poor.

The poor also are trapped because they get sick more often and stay sick longer than do the more well-to-do. The reasons, of course, are that they cannot afford preventive medicine, proper diets, and proper medical attention when ill. The high incidence of sickness among the poor means either that they will be fired from their jobs or that they will not receive money for the days missed from work (unlike the more well-to-do, who usually have jobs with such fringe benefits as sick leave and paid-up medical insurance). Not receiving a paycheck for extended periods means that the poor will have even less money for proper health care—thereby ensuring an even higher incidence of sickness. Thus, there is a vicious cycle of poverty. The poor will tend to remain poor, and their children tend to perpetuate the cycle.

The traditional organization of schools and jobs in the United States has limited the opportunities of racial minorities and women. Chapters 11 and 12 describe at length how these social categories are systematically disadvantaged by the prevailing laws, customs, and expectations of society. Suffice it to say in this context that

- Racial minorities are deprived of equal opportunities for education, jobs, and income.
- Women typically work at less prestigious jobs than do men, and when working at equal-status jobs receive less pay and fewer chances for advancement.

The Political Economy of Society

The basic tenet of capitalism—that who gets what is determined by private profit rather than by collective need—explains the persistence of poverty. The primacy of maximizing profit works to promote poverty in several ways. First, employers are constrained to pay their workers the least possible in wages and benefits. Only a portion of the wealth created by the laborers is distributed to them; the rest goes to the owners for investment and profit. Therefore, employers must keep wages low. That they are successful in this is demonstrated by the more than 2.6 million people who worked full-time in 2010 but remained under the poverty level.

A second way that the primacy of profit induces poverty is by maintaining a surplus of laborers, because a surplus depresses wages. Especially important for employers is to have a supply of undereducated and desperate people who will work for very low wages. A large supply of these marginal people (such as minorities, women, and undocumented workers) aids the ownership class by depressing the wages for all workers in good times and provides the obvious category of people to be laid off from work in economic downturns.

A third impact of the primacy of profits in capitalism is that employers make investment decisions without regard for their employees (potential or actual). If costs can be reduced, employers will purchase new technologies to replace workers (such as robots to replace assembly-line workers and word processors to replace secretaries). Similarly, owners may shut down a plant and shift their operations to a foreign country where wages are significantly lower.

To reiterate, the fundamental assumption of capitalism is individual gain without regard for what the resulting behaviors may mean for other people. The capitalist system, then, should not be accepted as a neutral framework within which goods and services are produced and distributed, but rather as an economic system that perpetuates inequality.

A number of political factors complement the workings of the economy to perpetuate poverty. Political decisions to fight inflation with high interest rates, for example, hurt several industries, particularly automobiles and home construction, causing high unemployment.

The powerful in society also use their political clout to keep society unequal. Clearly, the affluent in a capitalist society will resist efforts to redistribute their wealth to the disadvantaged. Their political efforts are, rather, to increase their benefits at the expense of the poor and the powerless (see the Diversity panel titled "Who Benefits from Poverty?"). In short, they work for laws beneficial to them, sympathetic elected and appointed officials, policies based on trickle-down economics, and favorable tax laws such as low capital-gains taxes and regressive taxes.

In sum, this chapter has examined three stratification systems—the social class system, the system based on race and ethnicity, and the sex-gender system. By definition, in each stratification system certain categories of people are considered inferior and treated unfairly.

Who Benefits from Poverty?

Herbert Gans, a sociologist, has some interesting insights about the benefits of poverty. He begins with the assumption that if some social arrangement persists, it must be accomplishing something important (at least in the view of the powerful in society). What, then, does the existence of a relatively large number of people in a condition of poverty accomplish that is beneficial to the powerful?

1. Poverty provides a low-wage labor pool that is willing (or unable to be unwilling) to do society's necessary "dirty work." The middle and upper classes are subsidized by the existence of economic activities that depend on the poor (low wages to many workers in restaurants, hospitals, and truck farming).

2. The poor also subsidize a variety of economic activities for the affluent by supporting, for example, innovations in medicine (as patients in research hospitals or as guinea pigs in medical experiments) and providing servants, gardeners, and house cleaners who make life easier for the more well-to-do.

3. The existence of poverty creates jobs for a number of occupations and professions that serve the poor or protect the rest of society from them (penologists, social workers, police, pawnshop owners, numbers racketeers, and owners of liquor stores). The presence of poor people also provides incomes for doctors, lawyers, teachers, and others who are too old, poorly trained, or incompetent to attract more affluent clients.

4. Poor people subsidize merchants by purchasing products that others do not want (seconds; dilapidated cars; deteriorated housing; day-old bread, fruit, and vegetables) and that otherwise would have little or no value.

5. The poor serve as a group to be punished in order to uphold the legitimacy of conventional values (hard work, thrift, honesty, and monogamy). The poor provide living proof that moral deviance does not pay, and thus an indirect rationale for blaming the victim.

6. Poverty guarantees the status of those who are not poor. The poor, by occupying a position at the bottom of the status hierarchy, provide a reliable and relatively permanent measuring rod for status comparison, particularly by those just above them (that is, the working class, whose politics, for example, are often influenced by the need to maintain social distance between themselves and the poor).

7. The poor aid in the upward mobility of others. A number of people have entered the middle class through the profits earned from providing goods and services in the slums (pawnshops, secondhand clothing and furniture stores, gambling, prostitution, and drugs).

8. The poor, being powerless, can be made to absorb the costs of change in society. In the nineteenth century they did the backbreaking work that built the railroads and the cities. Today they are the ones pushed out of their homes by urban renewal and the building of expressways, parks, and stadiums. Many economists assume that a degree of unemployment is necessary to fight inflation. The poor, who are "first to be fired and the last to be hired," are the ones who make the sacrifice for the economy.

Gans notes:

This analysis is not intended to suggest that because it is often functional, poverty should exist, or that it must exist. For one thing, poverty has many more dysfunctions than functions; for another, it is possible to suggest functional alternatives. For example, society's dirty work could be done without poverty, either by automation or by paying "dirty workers" decent wages. Nor is it necessary for the poor to subsidize the many activities they support through their low-wage jobs. This would, however, drive up the costs of these activities, which would result in higher prices to their customers and clients.

In sum, then, many of the functions served by the poor could be replaced if poverty were eliminated, but almost always at higher costs to others, particularly more affluent others. Consequently a functional analysis equivalent to the order model must conclude that poverty persists not only because many of the functional alternatives to poverty would be quite dysfunctional for the affluent members of society. ... Poverty can be eliminated only when they become dysfunctional for the affluent or powerful, or when the powerless can obtain enough power to change society (Gans, 1971:24).

Source: From "The Uses of Power: The Poor Pay All," by Herbert J. Gans, Robert S. Lynd Professor of Sociology at Columbia University, as appeared in *Social Policy* 2 (July–August 1971):20–24. Used by permission of the author.

Various theories have provided the rationales for this alleged inferiority. A review of these explanations is found in Table 9.1, which summarizes the theories used to explain why the poor are poor as discussed in this chapter and which anticipates the discussion of racial and gender inequalities found in Chapters 11 and 12.

TABLE 9.1

Varying Explanations of Inequality by Class, Race, and Gender

Explanation for Inequality	Structures of Inequality		
	Class	Race	Gender
Biological inferiority	Social Darwinism: The poor are unfit.	Jensen-Herrnstein: Blacks are Less endowed mentally than Whites.	Women are biologically different from men: weaker, less aggressive, more nurturant, less able in mathematics and spatial relationships but better in language.
Cultural inferiority	Culture of poverty: The poor have a maladaptive value system that dooms them and their children.	Blacks have loose morals, unstable families, do not value education, and lack motivation.	Gender-role socialization leads females to accept society's devalued roles, to be passive, and to be secondary to males.
Structural discrimination	The dominant use their power to maintain advantage. The poor are trapped by segmented labor markets, tracking in schools, and other structural arrangements.	Institutional racism blocks opportunities via segmented labor markets, use of biased tests for jobs, school placement, and residential segregation.	Institutional sexism limits women's chances in the legal system, job markets, wages, etc. Patriarchy occurs where men are dominant over women through organizational norms.

CHAPTER REVIEW

1. The process of categorizing people on some dimension(s) is called social differentiation.

2. When people are ranked in a hierarchy that differentiates them as superior or inferior, this is called social stratification.

3. The three hierarchies of stratification—class, race, and gender—place groups, families, and individuals in the larger society. The rewards and resources of society are unequally distributed according to this placement. Most crucially, this social location determines for people the chances for a longer, healthier, and more enjoyable life.

4. Order model theorists accept social inequality as universal and natural. They believe that inequality serves a basic function by motivating the most talented people to perform the most important tasks.

5. Conflict theorists tend to denounce social inequality as basically unjust, unnecessary, and the source of many social problems. The irony is that the oppressed often accept their deprivation. Conflict theorists view this as the result of false consciousness—the acceptance through the socialization process of an untrue belief that works to one's disadvantage.

6. The explanations for why some categories of people are ranked at the bottom of the various hierarchies of stratification are biological, cultural, or structural.

7. The biological explanation for poverty is that the poor are innately inferior. Arthur Jensen, Richard Herrnstein, and Charles Murray, for example, have argued that certain categories of people are disadvantaged because they are less well endowed mentally (a theoretical variation of social Darwinism).

8. Another explanation that blames the poor for their poverty is the culture-of-poverty hypothesis. This theory contends that the poor are qualitatively different in values and lifestyles from the successful and that these differences explain the persistence of poverty from generation to generation.

9. Critics of innate inferiority and culture-of-poverty explanations charge that, in blaming the victim, both theories ignore how social conditions trap individuals and groups in poverty. The source of the problem lies not in the victims but in the way society is organized to advantage some and disadvantage others.

Caste system
Social differentiation
Social stratification
Life chances
Social class
Privilege

Race
Ethnicity
Gender
Sex-gender system
Sex roles
Gender roles

Patriarchy
Matrix of domination
Meritocracy
Institutional
     discrimination

STUDY QUESTIONS

1. Explain what is meant by this statement: "The structures of inequality—class, race, and gender—array the resources and advantages of society in patterned ways."
2. Within your college community, is there a system of stratification? What appear to be the criteria used in this ranking of individuals and groups on your campus? Similarly, note the voluntary seating arrangement in the cafeteria. Who sits with whom? Is this informal arrangement stratified?

3. Contrast the views of order theorists and conflict theorists on social stratification.
4. What are the sociological criticisms of the deficiency theories of social inequality? How do structural theories of inequality meet these criticisms?
5. Summarize Gans' argument in the Diversity panel titled "Who Benefits from Poverty?" on page 197. Is this analysis from the order or the conflict perspective? Elaborate.

WEB RESOURCES

http://www.census.gov/
    This is the home of the U.S. Census Bureau, which has statistics on poverty, income, and other topics.
http://www.trinity.edu/mkearl/strat.html
    This site has a comprehensive list of links related to social inequality and stratification. Topics include race, class, gender, and age stratification.
http://www.dollarsandsense.org/
    A magazine of economic justice, this site offers articles that talk about current news issues from the political left. The site also has an archive with articles starting in 1996.

http://dir.yahoo.com/Social_Science/Sociology/Social_Class_and_Stratification/
    Go to this site for links to other sites containing information on class and stratification.
http://www.hewett.norfolk.sch.uk/curric/soc/class/class.htm
    This site contains general information and definitions on social class and social stratification.
http://www.worldbank.org/poverty/data/index.htm
    The World Bank provides data on global inequality.

CHAPTER 10

Class

Ten days after the terrorist attacks on the World Trade Center and the Pentagon, Congress created the Victim Compensation Fund to compensate the families of the 3,000 who died. The total government outlay was nearly $7 billion, with the individual compensation ranging from $250,000 to $7.1 million (tax-free). The variation depended on the age, estimated lifetime earnings, and family obligations of the victim. If the victim's age was forty-five, for example, the family would receive $788,109 if the income at the time of death was $30,000; $1,023,196 if the income was $50,000; $1,536,662 if the income was $100,000; and $2,682,827 if the income level was $225,000 (U.S. Department of Justice, reported in Savage, 2001:A38; see also, Chen, 2004). Is that fair? As Frank Keating, then governor of Oklahoma, said: "The government authorizes official inequity when it compensates a dishwasher at the World Trade Center differently from the way it compensates the person whose dishes were washed" (Keating, 2002:A10). The counterargument is that the government's compensation plan was to provide for the victims' families with a safety net to ensure that they maintain their current standard of living, in short, to allow them to remain in the same economic strata in the stratification system. So, what is a life worth? Apparently, it depends on one's social class.

The democratic ideology that "all men are created equal" has been a central value throughout U.S. history. We are often reminded by politicians, editorial writers, and teachers that ours is a society in which the equality of every person is highly valued. This prevailing ideology, however, does not mesh with reality. Slavery was once legal, and discrimination against African Americans was legal until the 1960s. Women were not permitted to vote until the early 1900s. Native Americans had their land taken from them and were then forced to locate on reservations. Japanese Americans were interned against their will during World War II. Or, consider the following facts about the United States:

- At a time (2009) when the average net worth of the richest 400 people in the United States was $3.11 billion (*Forbes*, 2009), 43.6 million Americans were living below the official poverty line.
- In 2010, the highest-paid hedge fund manager made $4.9 billion, while 50.7 million Americans were without health insurance.
- The six heirs to Sam Walton's Wal-Mart fortune had a combined wealth of $89.6 billion in 2010—more than as much wealth as the bottom 120 million Americans. The chief executive officer (CEO) of Wal-Mart makes his average employee's yearly salary every hour.
- In 2009, slightly more than one in five children under age eighteen lived in poverty, the highest rate of any developed nation.

The CEO of Wal-Mart makes his average employee's yearly salary every hour.

- In the 1970s, young women and men from the top 25 percent economically were four times more likely to go to college than everyone else. Now, they are ten times more likely to attend college.

Clearly, as George Orwell wrote in his classic novel *Animal Farm*, "all ... are equal but some are more equal than others" (1946:123).

Chapter 9 considered some general principles and theories of social stratification. This chapter focuses on one hierarchy of stratification—the social class system, which is the ranking based primarily on economic resources. This chapter is divided into several parts, which describe (1) the dimensions of socioeconomic inequality, (2) the class structure in the United States, (3) the consequences of class position, (4) the degree to which people can move from one class to another—social mobility, and (5) poverty in the midst of plenty.

Dimensions of Inequality

People in the United States rank differently from one another on a number of socioeconomic dimensions: wealth, income, education, and occupation.

Wealth

One's economic circumstances are governed by wealth and income. **Wealth** is a person's net worth (assets minus liabilities). **Income** is the amount of money earned. While income is annual, wealth is generational (that is, it is cumulative and passed from generation to generation) (Collins, 2007). The distribution of both is highly unequal in U.S. society. We consider wealth first.

Wealth is unquestionably maldistributed in the United States. There exists unbelievable wealth in the hands of a few and wretched poverty for millions. At the top in 2010 were Bill Gates ($54 billion), Warren Buffett ($45 billion), Lawrence Ellison ($27 billion), Christy Walton ($24 billion), and Charles Koch and David Koch (with $21.5 billion each) (*Forbes*, 2010). At the bottom were 19 million Americans living below half of the government's poverty line.

The concentration of wealth is greatly skewed:

- The top 1 percent of wealth holders control 34 percent of total household wealth. That's more than the combined wealth of the bottom 90 percent. The top 1 percent own 50.9 percent of all stocks, bonds, and mutual fund assets.
- The richest 1 percent in 2004 had 190 times the wealth of the median household (up from 125 times in 1962) (Allegretto, 2006).
- The wealthiest 20 percent of households own over 90 percent of all the combined value of all stocks; the middle 20 percent own only about 1.7 percent, and the bottom 40 percent of households own less than 1 percent combined (Mishel, Bernstein, and Allegretto, 2007).
- The gap widens as inheritance passes from one generation to the next. Researchers at Boston College's Center for Wealth and Philanthropy estimate that by 2050, approximately $25 trillion will be passed from the elderly to their children. The upper 1 percent

'When will my suffering end?'

of U.S. households will inherit roughly one-half of that financial windfall—$12.5 trillion (reported in Marable, 2006).

- Personal wealth is badly skewed by race. Year after year the National Urban League reports in its annual "The State of Black America" that the median net worth of the average African American family is less than one-tenth the average White family's wealth.

Income

The data on wealth always show more concentration than do income statistics, but the convergence of money among the few is still very dramatic when considering income. The top 1 percent of Americans take in nearly one-fourth of all personal income. This share received by the top 1 percent is the largest since 1928 (*Nation*, 2007). Looked at another way, 5 percent of the nation's income goes to about 15,000 families.

The data in Table 10.1 show that income inequality is increasing in U.S. society. Especially noteworthy is the sharp gain in the Gini index, which measured the magnitude of income concentration from 1970 to 2009. The Gini index of 0.468 in 2009 indicates an increase of 3.3 percent from 1996 to 2006. Comparing the U.S. Gini index in 2000 of 0.460 with other rich, developed countries, the United States has the highest degree of inequality: Great Britain's was 0.346, Germany's 0.300, Canada's 0.286, and Sweden's 0.222 (Murphy, 2000).

Another measure of this increasing gap is the difference in earnings between the heads of corporations and the workers in those corporations. In 1980, the average CEO of a corporation was paid forty-two times more than the average worker. In 1990, the CEOs for the Standard & Poor's 500 companies made 96 times as much. CEOs at the top U.S. corporations had incomes in 2007 that were 344 times more than average workers. Looked at another way, the income of the CEOs of the top 500 companies averaged $9 million in 2010, a 24 percent increase from the year before. Pay for workers, however, grew 3 percent to an average wage of $40,500 (this was less than one-half of 1 percent of what the typical CEO made) (Beck, 2011).

To illustrate how income is distributed in the United States, economist Paul Samuelson described it this way: If we used children's blocks, with each portraying $500 in income, the average family's income would be 14 feet high, while at the extreme, the height of the blocks would surpass the 29,028-foot Mt. Everest (Samuelson and Nordhous, 2005).

TABLE 10.1

Start of Aggregate Income by Each Fifth of Household 1970, 1980, 1990, 2000, 2001, 2006, 2009

	Percentage Distribution of Aggregate Income					
Year	Lowest Fifth	Second Fifth	Third Fifth	Fourth Fifth	Highest Fifth	Gini* Index
2009	3.4	8.6	14.6	23.2	50.3	0.468
2006	3.4	8.6	14.5	22.9	50.5	0.470
2003	3.4	8.7	14.8	23.4	49.8	0.464
2000	3.6	8.9	14.9	23.0	49.6	0.460
1990	3.9	9.6	15.9	24.0	46.6	0.428
1980	4.3	10.3	16.9	24.9	43.7	0.403
1979	4.1	10.8	17.4	24.5	43.3	0.394

*The income inequality of a population group is commonly measured using the Gini index. The Gini index ranges from 0, indicating perfect equality (i.e., all persons having equal shares of the aggregate income), to 1, indicating perfect inequality (i.e., where all of the income is received by only one recipient or one group of recipients and the rest have none). The increase in the Gini index for household income between 1970 and 2000 indicates a significant income inequality.

Sources: U.S. Bureau of the Census, 2001, Current Population Surveys. Available online: www.census.gov/hhes/income/histinc/ ie3.html. U.S. Bureau of the Census, 2004. "Income, Poverty, and Health Insurance Coverage in the United States: 2003." Current Population Reports, P60–226 (August). Current Population Reports, P260–233 (August 2007); Current Population Reports, P60–238 (August 2010).

Clearly, wealth and income disparities in the United States are great and growing. Robert Reich (2010), former secretary of labor, warns that this widening gap may lead to trouble: "None of us can thrive in a nation divided between a small number of people receiving an ever larger share of the nation's income and wealth, and everyone else receiving a declining share. The lopsidedness not only diminishes economic growth but also tears at the fabric of our society" (146).

Education

In the United States, people also vary considerably in educational attainment. The amount of formal education an individual achieves is a major determinant of her or his occupation, income, and prestige. Despite the standard belief by people in the United States in free mass education and the almost uniform requirement that citizens complete at least eight years of formal schooling, real differences in educational attainment exist.

There is an obvious correspondence between being inadequately educated and receiving little or no income. Census data from 2008 indicate that the annual earnings of college graduates are consistently more than double that of non–high school graduates. The difference in income is compounded when race and gender are considered, as revealed in Table 10.2.

There is not only a generational correlation between education and income but an intergenerational one as well. The children of the poor and uneducated tend not to do well in school and eventually drop out (regardless of ability), while the children of the educated well-to-do tend to continue in school (regardless of ability).

- Children in the poorest families are six times as likely as children in more affluent families to drop out of school (Children's Defense Fund, 2004).
- African American, Latino, and Native American students lag behind their White peers in graduation rates and most other measures of student performance. In 2008, the graduation rate from public high schools was 81 percent for White students, 91 percent for

TABLE 10.2

Mean Earnings by Highest Degree Earned: 2008

	Mean Earnings by Level of Highest Degree (Dollars)			
Characteristic	Total Persons	Not a High School Graduate	High School Graduate Only	Bachelor's
All persons'	**42,588**	**21,023**	**31,283**	**58,613**
Age:				
25 to 34 years old	37,233	20,471	28,224	48,445
35 to 44 years old	49,605	23,793	35,233	66,332
45 to 54 years old	51,696	25,598	36,916	70,053
55 to 64 years old	50,947	27,393	35,338	64,807
65 years old and over	36,273	18,550	27,532	43,378
Sex:				
Male	51,148	24,831	36,753	72,868
Female	32,922	14,521	24,329	44,078
White[2]	43,666	21,590	32,126	59,866
Male	52,672	25,386	37,852	75,053
Female	33,115	14.370	24,610	43,848
Black[2]	32,874	18,123	27,265	46,527
Male	36,507	22,344	30,985	51,691
Female	29,734	13,976	23,195	42,858
Hispanic[3]	30,291	21,310	27,020	48,081
Male	34,240	24,340	30,618	56,980
Female	24,646	14,960	21,725	39,231

Source: U.S. Census Bureau, Current Population Survey, unpublished data, *http://www.census.gov/population/www/socderno/educ-attn.html.*

Asian students, 63.5 percent for Latino students, and 61.5 percent for African American students (National Center for Education Statistics, reported in *New York Times*, 2010).
- College students whose families are in the top income quartile earn ten times as many bachelor's degrees by age twenty-nine as students from the bottom quartile (Brown, 2011).

Thus, the cycle of inequality is maintained. To underscore how class and race interact with education the *New York Times* reported that the annual tuition at Manhattan's most elite private schools had reached $26,000 in 2004—for kindergarten as well as high school. On the same page, there was a story about a school in Mount Vernon, New York, just across the city line from the Bronx, where the student body is 97 percent African American, nine out of ten children qualify for free lunches, and one out of ten lives in a homeless shelter (reported in Moyers, 2005:1). Imagine the difference in the quality of education in these types of schools and the eventual likely outcomes for the students in each. Yet, as James Lardner says:

> America has a loud message for those who worry about being caught on the wrong side of the technological tracks: "Go to school!" Yet we design our schools to keep some people up and other people down. Half a century after *Brown v. Board of Education*, poor children across the country are routinely, and increasingly, assigned to schools filled with other poor children—a practice with a long proven record of failure. (2005:21)

TABLE 10.3

Prestige Rankings of Selected Occupation

Occupation	Prestige Ranking
Physician	86
College professor	74
Aerospace engineer	72
Dentist	72
Clergy	69
Secondary school teacher	66
Accountant	65
Elementary school teacher	64
Computer programmer	61
Sociologist	61
Police officer	60
Librarian	54
Firefighter	53
Electrician	51
Machinist	47
Mail carrier	47
Bank teller	43
Carpenter	39
Hairdresser	36
Truck driver	30
Garbage collector	28
Janitor	22

Source: National Opinion Research Center, 1994. *General Social Surveys, 1972–1994: Cumulative Codebook*. Chicago: National Opinion Research Center, pp. 881–889.

Occupation

Another demonstration that people diverge in status is that occupations vary systematically in prestige. The degree of prestige and difference accorded to occupations is variable. A justice of the Supreme Court obviously enjoys more prestige than a bartender. But society makes much more subtle prestige distinctions. There is a rather uniform tendency to rate physicians slightly higher than college professors, who in turn are somewhat higher in rank than dentists. Further down the prestige scale, mail carriers outrank carpenters, who in turn have higher prestige than do automobile mechanics (see Table 10.3).[*]

The culture provides a ready-made, well-understood, relatively uniform ranking system based on several related factors: (1) the importance of the task performed (that is, how vital the consequences of the task are for the society), (2) the degree of authority and responsibility inherent in the job, (3) the native intelligence required, (4) the knowledge and skills required, (5) the dignity of the job, and (6) the financial rewards of the occupation.

But society also presents us with warped images of occupations, which leads to the acceptance of stereotypes. The media, for example, through advertisements, television, and

[*]There is a strong correlation in these rankings over time. The National Opinion Research Centers' findings in 1994 are quite similar to those found by sociologists C. C. North and Paul K. Hatt (1947) and by Hodge, Seigel, and Rossi (1964). Also noteworthy, sociologists have found a high correlation in the rating for occupations for a number of industrialized nations (Hodge, Treiman, and Rossi, 1966).

movie portrayals, evoke positive images for middle- and upper-class occupations and negative ones for lower-prestige occupations. Professional and business leaders are White, male, cultured, and physically attractive. They are decisive, intelligent, and authoritative. At the other end of the occupational spectrum, workers are often portrayed as ethnic, bigoted, and ignorant.

Occupation, then, is a very important variable that sorts people into hierarchically arranged categories. It is highly correlated with income level, but the gender of the worker makes a tremendous difference. Regardless of the occupational category, women make considerably less, on average, than do men employed in the same category.

The Consequences of Increasing Inequality for Society

This inequality gap in the United States is the highest in the industrialized world and this divide grows between the wealthy and the nonaffluent, let alone the poor; the highly skilled and the unskilled; and the educated and the uneducated. This gap is manifested in a number of ways. The very rich live in exclusive neighborhoods, belong to exclusive clubs, play at exclusive resorts, and send their children to private schools. In each instance they interact with people like themselves. Even the less-than-rich but still affluent make major attempts to segregate themselves from those they consider below them. They, too, often send their children to private schools or home school them, and they often move from the central cities to the suburbs. Many millions of Americans live in gated communities, and millions more live in locked apartment buildings (Ehrenreich, 2008).

The ever-increasing wealth and income inequality has implications for democracy, crime, and civil unrest. The greater the wealth and income inequality in society, the greater the economic and social fragmentation. As economist Lester Thurow (1995b) asks: "How much inequality can a democracy take? The income gap in America is eroding the social contract. If the promise of a higher standard of living is limited to a few at the top, the rest of the citizenry, as history shows, is likely to grow disaffected, or worse" (78). Or, as economist James K. Galbraith (1998) puts it: "[Inequality] is now so wide it threatens, as it did in the Great Depression, the social stability of the country. It has come to undermine our sense of ourselves as a nation of equals. Economic inequality, in this way, challenges the essential unifying myth of American national life" (24). See the A Closer Look panel titled "The Widening Inequality Gap."

Evidence for this is found in our political discourse. As Galbraith (1998) says: "A high degree of inequality causes the comfortable to disavow the needy. It increases the psychological distance separating these groups, making it easier to imagine that defects of character or differences of culture, rather than an unpleasant turn in the larger schemes of economic history, lie behind the separation" (24). Since politicians represent the monied interests (see Chapter 13), the wealthy get their way, as seen in the decline in welfare programs for the poor, the demise of affirmative action, and tax breaks that benefit them disproportionately. Most telling, the inequality gap is not part of the political debate, nor is the plight of those with no effective access to health care.

The United States, compared to other advanced industrial societies, has the highest proportion of its population below the poverty line, a withering bond among those of different social classes, a growing racial divide, and an alarming move toward a two-tiered society. The consequences of an extreme bipolar society are seen in the following description by James Fallows:

> If you had a million dollars, where would you want to live, Switzerland or the Philippines? Think about all the extra costs, monetary and otherwise, if you chose a vastly unequal country like the Philippines. Maybe you'd pay less in taxes, but you'd wind up shuttling between little fenced-in enclaves. You'd have private security guards. You'd socialize only in private clubs. You'd visit only private parks and beaches. Your kids would go to private schools. They'd study in private libraries. (quoted in Carville, 1996:87)

The United States is not the Philippines, but we are seeing a dramatic rise in private schooling (about 12 percent of students), home schooling (about 2 percent), and in the number of walled and gated affluent neighborhood enclaves on the one hand, and ever greater concentration of the poor and especially poor racial minorities in segregated and

The Widening Inequality Gap

A major tear in the social fabric of society is the increasing inequality gap in U. S. This trend has worrisome consequences for all of us. The greater the gap, the more that the chances for opportunity shrinks. The greater the gap, the more political power is concentrated. The greater the gap, the more unjust the criminal justice system. The greater the gap, the more inadequate the delivery of health care to the disadvantaged. The greater the gap, the greater the deterioration of public spaces, public safety, public transportation, and public schools. In effect, money divides and the greater the gap, the greater the injustice. As examples, we have two tax systems: one for the corporations, which allows General Electric, for instance, to have global profits of $14.2 billion but pay no U.S. corporate taxes, actually getting a refund of $3.2 billion. Similarly, the affluent receive much of the income in capital gains, which is taxed at a lower rate than wages. We have two school systems one for the affluent and those who live in affluent districts and schools that are disadvantaged by the lack of wealth in their districts. And, we have two criminal justice systems, one for those with money and one for those without adequate resources.

There are many examples of the inequality gap in our society. To summarize, the fortunate few are doing extremely well but many millions of Americans are living on the edge. Here are a few examples of those at the bottom of the stratification ladder:

- 46.2 million Americans were below the poverty line in 2010 and 20.5 million were severely poor.
- More than 49.9 million Americans were without health insurance in 2010.
- On a given night one in 400 Americans is homeless and 1.6 million will be homeless at some time during the year. And, these numbers are growing.
- Currently one in 7 people and 1 in 4 children are on Food Stamps.
- One out of six Americans desiring a full-time job is not able to get one.

These and related facts yield two conclusions. First, the United States is the most unequal society in the industrialized world. And, second, the gap in the United States is widening with wealth ever more concentrated at the top.

An unequal society builds walls and barricades separating people. The rich are separated from the rest of us. In many ways they have built a self-contained world for themselves. They live in their exclusive and safe enclaves, literally and figuratively walled off from others.

They play at exclusive private clubs. They vacation at the same exclusive resorts, hobnobbing with others of similar economic and social standing. Their families intermarry. Because of their social capital, they and their children are privy to elite educations, lucrative deals, and plush jobs. Their children go to private schools, interacting with other privileged children and avoiding "others," that is, those who are not privileged. In effect, the rich are culturally, structurally, and spatially removed from the rest of us.

At the bottom of the inequality ladder, the poor are segregated as well. They live together in neighborhoods away from the more affluent. These neighborhoods are often unsafe because of criminal activity and environmental hazards. Regarding the latter, there is a relatively high likelihood that the children of the poor will be exposed to lead, industrial pollution, and other toxic chemicals that have detrimental effects on their cognitive abilities especially in the first five years of life.

Thus, there is an increasing gap between the "haves" and the "have-nots." But it is not just that the "haves" have more money, it is also that they appear to be better—that is, they succeed while the poor disproportionately fail. As a result, people are viewed as "deserving" or "undeserving." Most significant, if people are labeled as "undeserving," then we are justified in not helping them. It is assumed that they are to blame for their failures, which blames the victim.

This bias against the poor because they are thought to be "undeserving" is compounded by the physical separation of the rich from the rest of society. Because the wealthy opt out of public schools and they do not use public recreation or public transportation, they have no reason to invest in and work toward public policies for the good of the whole community. In effect, the wealthy often are numb to the plight of the needy. Their inattention and indifference to the impoverished tears at the social fabric that is supposed to hold us together.

The inequality gap is moving us toward a two-tiered society. Rather than a "rising tide lifting all boats," which is the justification for trickle down economics, the evidence from the last thirty years is that "a rising tide lifts only the yachts." In the 1950s and 1960s the income distribution was more or less a bell-shaped curve, with a strong middle class. That has changed. The middle has shrunk with many more moving downward than upward.

Source: D. Stanley Eitzen, 2011. "Tears, Snags, and Tangles in the Social Fabric of Society," speech at University of the Incarnate Word, San Antonio, TX (April 19).

deteriorating neighborhoods and inferior schools on the other. Finally, democracy is on the wane as many opt out of the electoral process. The affluent are more likely to vote, because the politicians of both parties are in tune with their wishes. The poor, near-poor, and working classes, in contrast, are not likely to vote, presumably because they are not connected to either political party and the political process works against their interests. As a result, the United States has the lowest voter turnout among the industrialized nations, further evidence of the inequality gap and the erosion of social solidarity in society.

Social Classes

Social class is a complex concept that centers on the distribution of economic resources. That is, when a number of individuals occupy the same relative economic rank in the stratification system, they form a **social class**. A significant question is, Does economic ranking place people in an identifiable class, in which they identify with and share common interests with the other members, or is the designation a fuzzy one? The dominant view is that there are no clear class boundaries, except perhaps those delineating the highest and lowest classes. A social class is not a homogeneous group, given the diversity within it, yet there is some degree of identification with other people in similar economic situations. Also, people have a sense of who is superior, equal, and inferior to them. This is evidenced in patterns of deference and feelings of comfort or uneasiness during interaction. Similarly, there tend to be commonalities in lifestyles and tastes (for example, consumption patterns, child-raising patterns, the role of women) among people in a similar economic position. But even though we can make fairly accurate generalizations about people in a social class, the heterogeneity within it precludes accurate predictions about each person included.

Sociologists agree that social classes exist and that money is a central criterion for classification, but they disagree on the meaning of social classes for people. For example, in contrast to the prevailing view that social classes are generally correlated with the society's income distribution and that their boundaries are inherently fuzzy, there is the opposing view that society is divided into conflicting classes with definite boundaries, each of which has a common interest. These two models of social class represent the views of the order model and the conflict model. Although this oversimplifies the debate, we examine these two theoretical ways to conceptualize social class. Let's examine these two positions and the resulting social class structure that results from each approach (the following discussion is dependent on Liazos, 1985:228–234; Lucal, 1994; Sanderson, 1988:191–195; Vanneman and Cannon, 1987; and Wright et al., 1982).

The Order Model's Conception of Social Class

Order theorists use the terms income, occupation, and education as the fundamental indicators of social class, with occupation as central. Occupational placement determines income, interaction patterns, opportunity, and lifestyle. Lifestyle is the key dependent variable. Each social class is viewed as having its distinct culture. There are believed to be class-specific values, attitudes, and motives that distinguish its members from other classes. These orientations stem from income level and especially from occupational experiences (Collins, 1988:29). From this perspective, "how people get the money and what they do with it is as important (perhaps even more important than) as how much they have" (Liazos, 1985:230).

The typical class system from the order perspective has these classes, distributed in an income and status hierarchy.

1. *Upper-Upper Class.* Sometimes referred to as the old rich, the members of this class are wealthy, and because they have held this wealth for several generations, they have a strong in-group solidarity. They belong to exclusive clubs and attend equally exclusive boarding schools. Their children intermarry, and the members vacation together in posh, exclusive resorts around the world (Baltzell, 1958; Domhoff, 1970; Mills, 1959).

2. *Lower-Upper Class.* The wealth of the members is of relatively recent origin (hence, the term *new rich*). The new rich differ from the old rich in prestige, but not necessarily in wealth. Great wealth alone does not ensure acceptance by the elite as a social equal. The new rich are not accepted because they differ from the old rich in behaviors and lifestyles. The new rich is composed of the self-made wealthy. These families have amassed fortunes typically through business ventures or because of special talent in music, sport, or other form of entertainment. Additionally, some professionals (doctors, lawyers) may become wealthy because of their practice and/or investments. Finally, a few people may become very wealthy by working their way to the top executive positions in corporations, where high salaries and lucrative stock options are common.

3. *Upper-Middle Class.* The key distinguishing feature of this class is high-prestige (but not necessarily high-income) jobs that require considerable formal education and have a high degree of autonomy and responsibility. This stratum is composed largely of professional people, executives, and businesspeople. They are self-made, having accomplished their relatively high status through personal education and occupational accomplishments.

4. *Lower-Middle Class.* These are white-collar workers (as opposed to manual workers) who work primarily in minor jobs in bureaucracies. They work, for example, as secretaries, clerks, salespeople, police officers, and teachers.

5. *Upper-Lower Class.* These people work at repetitive jobs with little autonomy that require no creativity. They are blue-collar workers who, typically, have no education beyond high school. They are severely blocked from upward mobility (see the Diversity panel titled "The Near Poor: The Missing Class").

6. *Lower-Lower Class.* This class is composed of unskilled laborers whose formal education is often less than high school. The chronically unemployed are in this class. When they do work, it is for low wages, no fringe benefits, and no job security. Minority-group members—African Americans, Puerto Ricans, Mexican Americans, Native Americans— are disproportionately found in this category. These people are looked down on by all others in the community. They live on the other side of the tracks. They are considered by other people to be undesirable as playmates, friends, organization members, or marriage partners. Lower-lowers are thought to have a culture of poverty—that is, their presumed traits of laziness, dependence, and immorality, which, because they are the opposite of good middle-class virtues, lock them into their inferiority.

DIVERSITY

The Near Poor: The Missing Class

Social scientists Katherine S. Newman and Victor Tan Chen have written a book portraying the "Near Poor" in the United States (2007). They assert that this category is "under the radar"—a missing class. They are "missing" because the policy-makers in Washington have abandoned them.

The missing class is comprised of families that are above the poverty line, but well below the middle class—earning between $20,000 and $40,000 for a family of four (this is at or double the poverty line). Some 57 million Americans are in this missing class—including one-fifth of the nation's children. They do not qualify for Medicaid. Most of their jobs do not include health insurance. They live on the edge just one pink slip, divorce, or health crisis from falling below the poverty line. Moreover,

> The near poor are susceptible to predatory lenders, credit-card debt, and oppressive mortgages with unfair interest rates. They struggle to find money for a child's tuition or simply to get time off work to get a checkup that they will have to pay for in cash. They need a helping hand to start to put money away to recover from the lost income of a spouse sent overseas in the National Guard or Army Reserve. Their dreams are simple—to find affordable housing near decent schools, to hold a steady job, and to give their children opportunities they didn't have. (Newman and Chen, 2007:x)

The Conflict Model's Conception of Social Class

The conception of social class presented by the order theorists has important insights. As Liazos (1985), a conflict theorist, puts it: "Only a fool would deny that occupation, education, and the various 'life-style' qualities (speech, dress, leisure activities, etc.) define a person's class. They do matter to people, and we do distinguish one person or family from another by the kind of work they do, where they went to school, and so on" (230–231).

Conflict theorists, however, argue that order theorists understate the centrality of money in determining where people fall in the class system. "Where people live, how much education they receive, what they do to earn an income (or if they do not need to earn an income), who they associate with, and so forth, depend on how much money their families earn or have" (Liazos, 1985:231). Conflict theorists, in contrast to order theorists, focus on money and power, rather than on lifestyle. Again, turning to Liazos (1985):

> In capitalist societies, the greatest class division is between the few who own and run corporations ... and the rest of the people. This is not to say that all other people belong to one class; obviously they do not. But it is to say that the one million or so people who belong to the families that own, control, and profit by the largest corporations differ fundamentally from the rest of us. It is their power and wealth that essentially distinguish them from the rest of society, not their speech, dress, education, leisure activities, and so on. (231)

Conflict theorists also differ from order theorists in how they view occupation as a criterion for social class. A social class, in this view, is not a cluster of similar occupations but, rather, a number of individuals who occupy a similar position within the social relations of economic production (Wright et al., 1982; Wright and Rogers, 2011). In other words, what is important about social classes is that they involve relationships of domination and subordination that are made possible by the systematic control of society's scarce resources. The key, then, is not the occupation itself but the control one has over one's own work, the work of others, decision making, and investments. People who own, manage, oppress, and control must be distinguished from those who are managed, oppressed, and controlled (Eshleman, 1988:216). Using these three criteria—money, relation to the means of production, and power—conflict theorists tend to distinguish five classes.

1. *Ruling Class.* The people in this class hold most of the wealth and power in society. The richest 1 percent own as much as or more than the bottom 90 percent of the population (Beeghley, 2008). But the ruling class is smaller than the richest 1 percent. These are the few who control the corporations, banks, media, and politics. They are the very rich and the very powerful. The key is that the families and individuals in the ruling class own, control, govern, and rule the society. They control capital, markets, labor, and politics. In Marxist terms, the great wealth held by the ruling class is extracted from the labor of others.

2. *Professional-Managerial Class.* Four categories of people are included in this class—managers, supervisors, professionals in business firms, and professionals outside business but whose mental work aids business.

The most powerful managers are those near the top of the organizational charts who have broad decision-making powers and responsibilities. They have considerable power over the workers below them. In the words of sociologists Vanneman and Cannon (1987):

> As firms grew, an army of managers, professionals, and white-collar employees took over some of the managerial functions previously reserved for capitalists alone. These salaried officials work for owners of productive property, just as blue-collar workers do, but earn generous incomes and enjoy substantial prestige. And—what is crucial for a class analysis—the new middle class also shares in some of the power that capital has exercised over workers. (53)

There are also lower-level managers, forepersons, and other supervisors. They have less training than do the organizational managers, have limited authority, and are extensively controlled by top and middle managers. These people hold a contradictory class position.

They have some control over others, which places them in this category, but their limited supervision of the routine work of others puts them close to the working class. The key for inclusion in this class, though, is that the role of supervisor places the individual with the interests of management in opposition to the working class (Vanneman and Cannon, 1987:55; see also Poulantzas, 1974:14). As Randall Collins (1988) argues, "The more one gives orders, the more one identifies with the organizational ideals in whose name one justifies the orders, and the more one identifies with one's formal position, the more opposed they are to the interests of the working class" (31).

Another social category within this class includes professionals employed by business enterprises. These professionals (doctors, lawyers, engineers, accountants, inspectors) have obtained their position through educational attainment, expertise, and intellect. Unlike the ruling class, these professionals do not own the major means of production, but rather they work for the ruling class. They do not have supervisory authority, but they influence how workers are organized and treated within the organization. They are dominated by the ruling class, although this is mediated somewhat by the dependence of the elite on their specialized knowledge and expertise (for an extended discussion of this growing class, see Ehrenreich, 1989).

Finally, there are professionals who have substantial control over workers' lives but who are not part of business enterprises. Their mental labor exists outside the corporation, but nonetheless their services control workers. Included in this category are social workers, who are responsible for ensuring that the unemployed and poor do not disrupt the status quo (Piven and Cloward, 1993). Educators serve as gatekeepers, sifting and sorting people for good and bad jobs, which gives them enormous power over workers and their children (Vanneman and Cannon, 1987:76). Doctors keep workers healthy, and psychologists provide help for troubled people and seek to bring deviants back into the mainstream where they can function normally. Vanneman and Cannon (1987) argue that these professionals outside business belong in the same social class as those professionals working directly for business:

> If [this class] is defined by the control it exerts over other people, then, it necessarily incorporates the social worker, teacher, and doctor as well as the first-line supervisor and plant manager. What the social worker, teacher, and doctor share with the engineer, accountant, and personnel officer is a specialization of mental labor: they all plan, design, and analyze, but their plans, designs, and analyses are largely executed by others. (76)

3. *Small-Business Owners.* The members of this class are entrepreneurs who own businesses that are not major corporations. They may employ no workers (thus, exploiting no labor power) or a relative few. The income and power over others possessed by members of this class vary considerably.

"Carpe diem."

4. *Working Class.* The members of this class are the workers in factories, restaurants, offices, and stores. They include both white-collar and blue-collar workers. White-collar workers are included because they, like blue-collar workers, do not have control over other workers or even over their own lives (Vanneman and Cannon, 1987:11). The distinguishing feature of this class is that they sell their labor power to capitalists and earn their income through wages. Their economic well-being depends on decisions made in corporate boardrooms and by managers and supervisors. They are closely supervised by other people. They take orders. This is a crucial criterion for inclusion in the working class, because "the more one takes orders, the more one is alienated from organizational ideals" (Collins, Randall, 1988:31).

Thus, they are clearly differentiated from classes whose members identify with the business firms for which they work.

5. *Poor.* These people work for minimum wages and/or are unemployed. They do society's dirty work for low wages. At the bottom in income, security, and authority, they are society's ultimate victims of oppression and domination.

Wright and his colleagues (1982) made an empirical investigation of the U.S. class structure using the conflict approach. Among their results are several interesting findings. First, it is incorrect to rank occupations, as order theorists do, because within the various occupational categories there are managers/supervisors and workers. In other words, workers in white-collar jobs can be divided into managers and workers (proletariat). So, too, can we categorize jobs for laborers, operatives, and unskilled services:

> There is a long tradition in sociology of arguing over whether or not lower white-collar jobs should be considered in the working-class or the "middle-class." Usually it is assumed in such debates that occupations as such can appropriately be grouped into classes, the issue being where a specific occupation ought to be located. ... [I]f classes are conceptualized in relational terms, this is not even the correct way to pose the problem. Instead, the empirical question is the extent of proletarianization within different occupational categories. (720)

Second, social class is closely related to gender and race. Wright and his associates found that women are more proletarianized, regardless of occupational category, than are men (54 percent occupy working-class locations, compared with only 40 percent for men). Similarly, 64 percent of all African Americans are in the working class, compared with only 44 percent of Whites. "If we examine the combined race-sex-class distributions, we see that black women are the most proletarianized of all: 65 percent of black women in the labor force are in the working class, compared to 64 percent of black men, 52 percent for white women, and only 38 percent for white men" (Wright et al., 1982:724).

Summary: Class from the Order and Conflict Perspectives

Vanneman and Cannon (1987) have summarized the fundamental differences between the order and the conflict views of social class:

> In the [conflict] vision, class divides society into two conflicting camps that contend for control: workers and bosses, labor and capital, proletariat workers and bourgeoisie [middle class]; in this dichotomous image, classes are bounded, identifiable collectivities, each one having a common interest in the struggle over control of society. In the [order] vision, class sorts out positions in society along a many-runged ladder of economic success and social prestige; in this continuous image, classes are merely relative rankings along the ladder: upper class, lower class, upper-middle class, "the Toyota set," "the BMW set," "Brahmins," and the dregs "from the other side of the tracks." People are busy climbing up (or slipping down) these social class ladders, but there is no collective conflict organized around the control of society. (39)

These radically different views on social class should not obscure the insights that both views provide for the understanding of this complex phenomenon. Occupation is critical to both, but for very different reasons. For the order theorist, occupations vary in how people evaluate them; some occupations are clearly superior to others in status. Thus, the perceptions of occupations within a population indicate clearly that there is a prestige hierarchy among them and the individuals identified with them.

The conflict theorist also focuses on occupations, but without reference to prestige. Where a person is located in the work process determines the degree of control that individual has over others and himself or herself. The key to determining class position is whether one gives orders or takes orders. Moreover, this placement determines one's fundamental interests because one is either advantaged (living off the labor of others) or disadvantaged (oppressed). Empirically, both of these views mesh with reality.

Second, order theorists focus on commonalities in lifestyles among individuals and families similar in education, income, and occupation. These varying lifestyles are real. There are differences in language use, tastes for music and art, interior decorating, dress, child-rearing practices, and the like (see Fussell, 1983). Although real, the emphasis on lifestyle misses the essential point, according to conflict theorists. For them, lifestyle is not central to social class; giving or taking orders is. This is why there is disagreement on where, for example, to place lower-level white-collar workers, such as clerks and secretaries. Order theorists place them in the middle class because the prestige of their occupations is higher than that of blue-collar workers and because their work is mental rather than manual. Conflict theorists, on the other hand, place them with workers who take orders, that is, in the worker class.

Conflict theorists also point to two important implications of the emphasis on lifestyle. First, although culture is a dependent variable (a consequence of occupation, income, and education), the culture of a social class is assumed to have a power over its members that tends to bind them to their social class (for example, the culture of poverty is believed to keep the poor, poor—see Chapters 7, 9, and 11). A second implication is the implicit assumption that these cultures are themselves ranked, with the culture of the higher classes being more valued. Conflict theorists have the opposite bias—they view the denigration of society's losers as blaming the victim. From this perspective, the higher the class, the more its members are guilty of oppressing and exploiting the labor of those below. In short, there is a strong tendency among conflict theorists to identify with the plight of underdogs and to label pejoratively the behaviors of top dogs.

Finally, each view of social class is useful for understanding social phenomena. The order model's understanding of inequality in terms of prestige and lifestyle differences has led to research that has found interesting patterns of behaviors by social location, which is one emphasis of sociology. Similarly, the focus of the order model has resulted in considerable research on mobility, mobility aspirations, and the like, which is helpful for the understanding of human motivation as well as the constraints on human behavior. The conflict model, on the other hand, examines inequality from differences in control—control over society, community, markets, labor, others, and oneself. The resulting class division is useful for understanding conflict in society—strikes, lockouts, political repression, social movements, and revolutions.

The Consequences of Social Class Positions

Regardless of the theoretical position, there is no disagreement on the proposition that one's wealth is the determining factor in a number of crucial areas, including the chance to live and the chance to obtain those things (for example, possessions or education) that are highly valued in society. As discussed in Chapter 9, life chances refer to the chances throughout one's life cycle to live and to experience the good things in life. These chances are dependent almost exclusively on the economic circumstances of the family into which one is born. Gerth and Mills (1953) contend that life chances refer to "everything from the chance to stay alive during the first year after birth to the chance to view fine art, the chance to remain healthy and grow tall, and if sick to get well again quickly, the chance to avoid becoming a juvenile delinquent—and very crucially, the chance to complete an intermediary or higher educational grade" (313).

Physical Health

Economic position has a great effect on how long one will live, or, in a crisis, who will be the last to die. For instance, the official casualty lists of the transatlantic luxury liner *Titanic*, which sank in 1912, listed 3 percent of the first-class female passengers as lost, 16 percent of the second-class female passengers, and 45 percent of the third-class female passengers (Lord, 1955:107).

TABLE 10.4	
Poverty Matters	
Outcomes	*Low-Income Children's Higher Risk*
Health	
Death in infancy	1.6 times as likely
Premature birth (under 37 weeks)	1.8 times as likely
Low birthweight	1.9 times as likely
No regular source of health care	2.7 times as likely
Inadequate prenatal care	2.8 times as likely
Family had too little food sometime in the last 4 months	8 times as likely
Education	
Math scores at ages 7 to 8	5 test points lower
Reading scores at ages 7 to 8	4 test points lower
Repeated a grade	2.0 times as likely
Expelled from school	1.4 times as likely
Being a dropout at ages 16 to 24	3.5 times as likely
Finishing a four-year college	half as likely

Source: Children's Defense Fund, 2004. *The State of America's Children*, 2004. Washington, DC. Reprinted by permission of the Children's Defense Fund.

Apparently, even in a disaster, socioeconomic position makes a real difference—the higher the economic status of the individual, the greater the probability of survival.

The greater advantage toward longer life by the well-to-do is not limited to disasters such as the *Titanic*. A consistent research finding is that health and death are influenced greatly by social class.

Economic disadvantage is closely associated with health disadvantages. Put another way: "How people live, get sick, and die depends not only on their race and gender, but primarily on the class to which they belong" (Navarro, 1991:2). The poor are more likely than the affluent to suffer from certain forms of cancer (cancers of the lung, cervix, and esophagus), hypertension, infant mortality, disabilities, and infectious diseases (especially influenza and tuberculosis). The affluent live longer, and when stricken with a disease they are more likely to survive than are the poor. For the consequences of social class on the health of children, see Table 10.4.

An obvious health advantage of the affluent is access to health-promoting and health-protecting resources and, when needed, access to medical services, paid for, at least in part, typically, with health insurance. Health insurance in the United States is typically tied to employment, with employers and employees splitting the cost. Structural changes in the U.S. economy (see Chapter 8)—the shift of employment from manufacturing to services, the rise in contingent and part-time employment, and the decline of union membership—have resulted in a decline in employment-related health insurance coverage. And the lower the prestige and the lower the wages in the job, the less likely the pay will include a health benefits package.

In 2009 about 50 million people in the United States, mostly the near-poor younger than age sixty-five, had no medical insurance, including an estimated 500,000 pregnant women, who as a result often did not receive prenatal and postnatal health care. The consequences are a high maternal death rate (typically from hemorrhage and infection) and a relatively high infant mortality rate. Of the twenty industrialized countries, eighteen have lower infant mortality rates than the United States.

The common belief is that the poor are accountable for their health deficiencies; that is, their lack of education and knowledge may lead to poor health practices. Research shows, for example, that those with lower incomes are more likely to smoke and be overweight. They are also less likely to exercise and engage in preventive health care. The essence of this argument is that the problems of ill health that beset the poor disproportionately are a consequence of their different lifestyle. This approach, however, ignores the fundamental realities of social class—that is, privilege in the social stratification system translates both directly and indirectly into better health in several major ways.

1. The privileged live in home, neighborhood, and work environments that are less stressful. The disadvantaged are more subject to stresses (and resulting ill health) from high crime rates, financial insecurity, marital instability, death of loved ones, spells of unemployment, unhealthy work conditions, and exposure to pollution and toxic materials in their neighborhoods.

2. Children of privilege have healthier environments in the crucial first five years of life.

3. The privileged have better access to and make better use of the health care system. The fewer the economic resources, the less likely a person will receive preventive care and early treatment.

4. The privileged have health insurance to pay for a major portion of their physician, hospital, diagnostic test, and pharmaceutical needs. Many people in the United States, however, cannot afford health insurance and/or their employers do not provide medical insurance, resulting in some 50 million uninsured people, about 10 million of whom are children.

The evidence is clear that the more education and income that people have, the longer they will live (Scott, 2005).

Family Instability

Research relating socioeconomic status to family discord and marital disruption has found an inverse relationship—the lower the status, the greater the proportion of divorce or desertion.

> The lack of adequate resources places a burden on intimate relationships. ... Poor two-parent families are twice as likely to break up as are two-parent families not in poverty. ... Moreover, the likelihood of marital breakup increases when a husband does not work, and it is even greater when neither spouse works. Sudden financial difficulties such as unexpected unemployment also increase the possibility of marital breakdown. (Baca Zinn, Eitzen, and Wells, 2011:3.79)

Fighting the Nation's Wars

Involuntary conscription into the U.S. Army—the draft system—works to the disadvantage of the uneducated. In 1969, during the Vietnam War, only 10 percent of the men drafted were college men. The Supreme Court has further helped the educated by ruling that a person can be a conscientious objector on a basis of either religion or philosophy. Young intellectuals can use their knowledge of history, philosophy, and even sociology to argue that they should not serve. The uneducated will not have the necessary knowledge to make such a case.

Educated young men who end up in the armed services are more likely to serve in noncombat supply and administrative jobs than are non-college-educated men. People who can type, do bookkeeping, or know computer programming will generally be selected to do jobs in which their skills can be used. Conversely, the nonskilled will generally end up in the most hazardous jobs. The chances for getting killed while in the service are greater, therefore, for the less educated than for the college educated.

When the draft is not used, as is the case at present in the war in Afghanistan, the personnel in the lower ranks of the military come disproportionately from the disadvantaged segments of society. This occurs because the military offers a job and stability for young people who find little or no opportunity in the job market. The downside, of course, is that they risk injury and even death during combat. In effect, when the United States goes to war, it is the poorer and less educated who are the most likely to die in combat (Kriner and Shen, 2010; Bacevich, 2010). Without a draft, the privileged can avoid these risks.

Prison and Poverty Line.

Justice

The administration of justice is unequal in the United States. Low-income people are more likely to be arrested, to be found guilty, and to serve longer sentences for a given violation than are people in the middle and upper classes.

Why is the system of justice unjust? The affluent can afford the services of the best lawyers for their defense, detectives to gather supporting evidence, and expert witnesses such as psychiatrists. The rich can afford to appeal the decision to a series of appellate courts. The poor, on the other hand, cannot afford bail and must await trial in jail, and they must rely on court-appointed lawyers, who are usually among the least experienced lawyers in the community and who often have heavy caseloads. All the evidence points to the regrettable truth that a defendant's wealth makes a significant difference in the administration of justice.

A class bias held by most citizens, including arresting officers, prosecuting attorneys, judges, and jury members, affects the administration of justice. This bias is revealed in a set of assumptions about people according to their socioeconomic status. The typical belief is that the affluent or the children of the affluent, if lawbreakers, are basically good people whose deviance is an aberration, a momentary act of immaturity. Thus, a warning will suffice or, if the crime is serious, a short sentence is presumed to cause enough humiliation to bring back their naturally conforming ways. Lawbreaking by the poor, on the other hand, is viewed as more troublesome and must be punished harshly, because these are essentially bad people and their deviance will persist if tolerated or mildly punished by the authorities.

Education

In general, life chances depend on wealth—they are purchased. The level of educational attainment (except for the children of the elite, where the best in life is a birthright) is the crucial determinant of one's chances of income.

Inequality of educational opportunity exists in all educational levels in many subtle and not-so-subtle forms (see Chapter 16). It occurs in the quality of education when schools are compared by district. Districts with a better tax base have superior facilities, better-motivated teachers (because those districts can pay more), and better techniques than do the poorer districts. Within each school, regardless of the type of district, children are given standardized tests that have a middle-class bias. Armed with these data, educators place children in tracks according to ability. These tracks thus become discriminatory, because the lowest track is composed disproportionately of the lower socioeconomic category. These tracks are especially harmful in that they structure the expectations of the teacher.

Consider these facts concerning college—the gateway to upward mobility (Symonds, 2003):

- Thirty-five percent of students from families with incomes of less than $25,000 enroll, compared to 80 percent of those from families with incomes of more than $75,000. Of

those who enroll, 55 percent of those in the bottom quartile of socioeconomic status graduate and 73 percent of those in the top quartile graduate.
- Seventy-eight percent of students from low-income families who rank as top achievers attend college—about the same as the 77 percent of affluent students who rank at the bottom academically.
- Although 28 percent of all eighteen-year-olds are African American or Latino, only 12 percent of the freshman classes at the top 146 colleges are African American or Latino.
- For students in the top 146 colleges only 3 percent come from families in the bottom socioeconomic quartile and just 10 percent are from families in the bottom half.

These economic disparities have serious implications for American society. Tom Mortensen of the Pell Institute for the Study of Opportunity in Higher Education says that "the trajectory we're on suggests we will become a poorer, more unequal, and less homogeneous country" (quoted in Symonds, 2003:66).

Social Mobility

This section analyzes the degree of social mobility in society. This emphasis fits with the order model. It assumes that status (as opposed to class) differences are gradations, corresponding with occupation. Moreover, there is the assumption that a high degree of social mobility exists in U.S. society, with a growing middle mass of workers enjoying a high standard of living (Knottnerus, 1987).

Societies vary in the degree to which individuals may move up in status. Probably the most rigid stratification system ever devised was the caste system of India. In brief, this system, as noted in Chapter 9, (1) determines status by heredity, (2) allows marriage to occur only within one's status group (endogamy), (3) determines occupation by heredity, and (4) restricts interaction among the status groups. Even the Indian caste system, however, is not totally rigid, for some mobility has been allowed under certain conditions.

In contrast to this closed stratification system, the United States has a relatively open system. Social mobility is not only permitted, but is also part of the U.S. value system that upward mobility is good and should be the goal of all people in the United States.

The United States, however, is not a totally open system. All U.S. children have the social rank of their parents while they are youths, which in turn has a tremendous influence on whether a child can be mobile (either upward or downward). Actually, the United States is less mobile than the other wealthy nations: "Children born into poverty in Canada, Britain, Germany or France have a statistically better chance of reaching the top than poor kids in the United States (McManus, 2011, para 3). **Social mobility** refers to an individual's movement within the class structure of society. **Vertical mobility** is movement upward or downward in social class. **Horizontal mobility** is the change from one position to another of about equal prestige. A shift in occupation from electrician to plumber is an example of horizontal mobility.

Social mobility occurs in two ways. **Intergenerational mobility** refers to vertical movement comparing a daughter with her mother or a son with his father. **Intragenerational mobility** is the vertical movement of the individual through his or her adult life.

Some societal factors increase the likelihood of people's vertical mobility regardless of their individual efforts. The availability of cheap and fertile land with abundant resources gave many thousands of Americans in the nineteenth century opportunities for advancement no longer present. Similarly, the arrival of new immigrants to the United States from 1880 to 1920 provided a status boost for the people already here. Economic booms and depressions obviously affect individuals' economic success. Technological changes also can provide increased chances for success as well as diminish the possibilities for those trained in occupations newly obsolete. Finally, the size of one's age cohort can limit or expand opportunities for success.

Sociological and economic research leads to several conclusions about social mobility in the United States (from Blau and Duncan, 1967; De Lone, 1979; Duncan et al., 1998; Mishel, Bernstein, and Allegretto, 2007; Scott and Leonhardt, 2005):

- Few children of white-collar workers become blue-collar workers.
- Most mobility moves are short in distance.
- Occupational inheritance is highest for children of professionals (physicians, lawyers, professors).
- The opportunities for the children of nonprofessionals to become professionals are very small.
- The long-term trend in social mobility has been upward, but since the 1970s (with the globalization of the economy and the shift from a manufacturing to a service/knowledge economy) this trend has reversed.
- Social mobility is the least likely at the extremes of wealth and poverty.
- While there are many individual exceptions, the overall trend by race/ethnicity is that the gap in wealth/income between African Americans and Latinos and the more privileged Whites has remained about the same.
- Women, historically, have been blocked in their occupational aspirations (being limited to low-prestige, low-paying jobs). There has been a gradual lifting of these barriers since the 1970s, but women working full-time still earn only 77 cents for each dollar as men working full-time. Moreover, while there are more and more exceptions, barriers still remain for full equality for women as they compete for the best jobs.

"Actually, Lou, I think it was more than just my being in the right place at the right time. I think it was my being the right race, the right religion, the right sex, the right socioeconomic group, having the right accent, the right clothes, going to the right schools . . ."

In sum, the commonly accepted belief of people in the United States that ours is a meritocratic society is largely a myth. Equality of opportunity does not exist because (1) employers may discriminate on the basis of age, race, sex, ethnicity, or sexuality of their employees or prospective employees; (2) educational and job training opportunities are unequal; and (3) the family has great power to enhance or retard a child's aspirations, motivation, and cognitive skills.

Education and Social Mobility

The schools play a major part in both perpetuating the meritocratic myth and legitimizing it by giving and denying educational credentials on the basis of open and objective mechanisms that sift and sort on merit. The use of IQ tests and tracking, two common devices to segregate students by cognitive abilities, are highly suspect because they label children, resulting in a positive self-fulfilling prophecy for some children and a negative one for others. Moreover, the results of the tests and the placement of children in tracks because of the tests are biased toward middle- and upper-class experiences.

Educational attainment, especially receiving a college degree, is the most important predictor of success in the United States. But a college education is becoming more difficult to attain for the less-than-affluent.

- Over the last thirty years the average cost at public and private universities has risen sixfold while the consumer price index has only increased two-and-a-half times (Archibald and Feldman, 2010).
- Federal grant programs have failed to keep up with college costs. Pell grants were instituted by the government to help students from poor families attend college. In 1986, a Pell grant covered 98 percent of tuition at a public four-year college; since 2006 funding for Pell Grants has declined.

- The majority (70 percent) of government aid to students takes the form of loans. Families of low-income students borrow about one-third of their income for their college expenses.
- Institutional scholarships have shifted their emphasis from awards based on financial need to aid based on academic achievement.
- More and more four-year schools are raising admissions standards and limiting remediation programs that help those from disadvantaged school backgrounds to attend college and overcome their academic deficiencies.
- Affirmative action programs are being challenged successfully in both the political and judicial arenas. With the loss of affirmative action, minority children, who are disproportionately poor, will be increasingly denied access to higher education. This trend is occurring at the very time that racial minorities are increasing in size.
- For students who do attend college, money stratifies. The poorest are most likely to attend community colleges, which are the least expensive; these schools emphasize technical careers and are therefore limiting in terms of later success.

To conclude, money provides access to a higher education, which in turn increases one's life chances throughout life.

Christopher Jencks and his associates provide the most methodologically sophisticated analysis of the determinants of upward mobility in their book *Who Gets Ahead?* (Jencks et al., 1979). Their findings, summarized, show the following as the most important factors leading to success.

1. Family background is the most important factor. Children coming from families in the top 20 percent in income will, as adults, have incomes of 150 to 186 percent of the national average, whereas those from the bottom 20 percent will earn 56 to 67 percent of the national average.

2. Educational attainment—especially graduating from college—is very important to later success. It is not so much what one learns in school but obtaining the credentials that counts. The probability of high educational attainment is closely tied to family background.

3. Scores from intelligence tests are by themselves poor predictors of economic success. Intelligence test scores are related to family background and educational attainment. The key remains the college degree. If people with a high IQ do not go to college, they will tend not to succeed economically.

4. Personality traits of high school students, more than grades and IQ, have an impact on economic success. No single trait emerges as the decisive determinant of economic success, but rather the combined effects of many different traits are found to be important. These are self-concept, industriousness (as rated by teachers), and the social skills or motivations that lead students to see themselves as leaders and to hold positions of leadership in high school.

Let's add another generalization to the list by Jencks. Not only are the financial, educational, and demographic assets of one's family important to success, but so, too, are the assets of one's social environment. As Fischer and his associates (1996) assert:

> The immediate neighborhood [affects] people's ways of life, whatever the family's own resources. ... It is one thing to come from a low-income family but live in a pleasant suburb with parks, low crime, and quality schools, and another thing altogether to live in an inner-city neighborhood that lacks those supports. ... The concentration of the disadvantaged in particular communities and particular schools undermines the fortunes of otherwise able youth. Schools in low-income and minority neighborhoods tend to lack resources and quality instruction. ... In the local neighborhoods, similar effects occur. Low-income areas have fewer jobs, fewer resources, and poorer-quality services than do affluent ones. (83)

The picture drawn by Jencks and other experts on social mobility in the United States is of a relatively rigid society in which being born to the right family has a profound impact, especially on the probability of graduating from college. There are opportunities for advancement in society, but they are clustered among the already advantaged. If the stratification system were open with equality of opportunity, it would make sense that people, even the disadvantaged, would support it. The irony is that although the chances of the poor being successful are small, the poor tend to support the inequality generated by capitalism—truly a case of false consciousness. This irony becomes clearer as we see the consequences of inequality for individuals.

Poverty in the United States

What separates the poor from the nonpoor? In a continuum, there is no absolute standard for wealth. The line separating the poor from the nonpoor is necessarily arbitrary. The Social Security Administration (SSA) sets the official poverty line based on what it considers the minimal amount of money required for a subsistence level of life. To determine the poverty line, the SSA computes the cost of a basic nutritionally adequate diet and multiplies that figure by three. This figure is based on a government research finding that poor people spend one-third of their income on food. Thereafter, the poverty level was readjusted annually using the consumer price index to account for inflation. If we use this official standard ($11,139 for one person under age sixty-five, $17,374 for a nonfarm family of three, and $22,314 for a nonfarm family of four) for 2010, 13.2 percent of the population (43.57 million people) were defined as living in poverty (the data on poverty in this section were taken from the DeNavas-Walt, Proctor, and Smith, U.S. Bureau of the Census, 2010). See Figure 10.1 for the poverty trend from 1959 to 2010.

The following discussion considers the poor as people below this arbitrary line, realizing that it actually minimizes the extent of poverty in the United States. Critics of the measure argue that it does not keep up with inflation, that housing now requires a much larger portion of the family budget than food, that there is a wide variation in the cost of living by locality, and that the poverty line ignores differences in medical care needs of individual families. Were a more realistic formula used, the number of poor would likely be at least 50 percent higher than the current official number (that is, around 19 percent or 64 million impoverished Americans; see the Human Agency panel titled "Coping Strategies Among the Poor").

Also, the official number of poor people is minimized because government census takers miss many poor people. Those most likely to be overlooked in a census live in high-density

FIGURE 10.1

Number in Poverty and Poverty Rate: 1959 to 2010
Source: U.S. Census Bureau, Current Population Survey, 1960 to 2010 Annual Social and Economic Supplements.

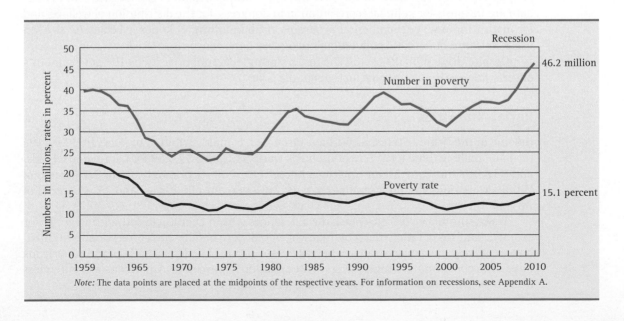

Note: The data points are placed at the midpoints of the respective years. For information on recessions, see Appendix A.

Coping Strategies Among the Poor

The lot of poor people is difficult, to say the least. If the poor receive welfare, the benefits are insufficient to meet minimal needs of food, clothing, and shelter. Suitable housing in cities is especially difficult to obtain because rents are, typically, beyond the reach of the poor. Food, clothing, banking, and other purchases/services are more expensive in the inner cities than elsewhere. How do poor people deal with the lack of money to deal with exigencies of living?

Some do not do well at all. Some are forced to live in housing that is dangerous (exposure to the cold, lead, rats, and sewage; unsafe structures that defy city building codes). Some cannot even afford those dangerous places and must live on the streets or in homeless shelters. Some are malnourished because they cannot afford enough nutritious food. Many go without visits to doctors and dentists because the cost is beyond their means or the services are unavailable.

Other poor people do better through various coping strategies. Those with family or close friendship networks may share housing costs by doubling or tripling up. They may share child care to free parents to work. Families may go together to buy food in bulk at cheaper prices. And they pool their resources in many other creative ways to manage the stresses and strains of poverty.

A few organized networks have also emerged in various inner cities (e.g., St. Louis; Miami; Chicago; New York City; Cleveland; and Norfolk, Virginia). In the case of inner-city St. Louis, several thousand people are engaged in a barter economy where people short of cash can exchange their labor/expertise for that of others without using money. Individuals earn credit ("time dollars") by cleaning, painting, providing child care, delivering goods, or repairing appliances, which can be exchanged for other services or even goods (food, clothing) that have been donated to the network. This plan has two major benefits: (1) It cushions the harshness of poverty by distributing goods and services to the people who need them; and (2) it creates a sense of community among the powerless, which may ultimately lead to power, as those in the network work together for common goals.

Sources: Peter T. Kilborn, 1996. "Build a Better Welfare System, and the World ... ," *Denver Post* (September 29):17A; Michael Hudson, 1996. *Merchants of Misery*. Monroe, ME: Common Courage Press; and Doug A. Timmer, D. Stanley Eitzen, and Kathryn D. Talley, 1994. *Paths to Homelessness: Extreme Poverty and the Urban Housing Crisis*. Boulder, CO: Westview Press.

urban areas where several families may be crowded into one apartment or in rural areas where some homes are inaccessible. Some workers and their families follow a harvest from place to place and have no permanent home, as is the case for transients and homeless people. This underestimate of the poor has important consequences, because U.S. Census data are the basis for political representation in Congress, for the distribution of welfare, and for instituting new governmental programs or abandoning old ones. Needless to say, an accurate count of the total population is necessary if the census is so used.

Despite these difficulties and the understating of actual poverty by the government's poverty line, we do know some facts about the poor.

Racial Minorities

Income in the United States, as we have discussed, is maldistributed by race. In 2010, the median family income for White households was $54,620, $37,759 for Latino households, and $32,068 and for African American households. Not surprisingly, then, 9.9 percent of Whites were officially poor, compared with 26.6 percent of Latinos, and 27.4 percent of African Americans.

These summary statistics mask the differences within each racial/ethnic category. For example, Latinos of Cuban descent, many of whom were middle-class professionals in Cuba, have relatively low poverty rates, whereas Puerto Ricans, Mexicans, and Central Americans have disproportionately high poverty rates. Similarly, Japanese Americans are much less likely to be poor than Asians from Cambodia, Laos, and Vietnam.

Nativity

In 2009, 7.16 million foreign-born individuals in the United States (19.0 percent of the foreign-born) were poor. Of these poor foreign-born, 1.7 million were naturalized citizens and 5.4 million were noncitizens, for poverty rates of 10.8 and 25.1 percent, respectively. These official statistics do not include the 11 million undocumented workers and their families who enter the United States illegally.

Gender

Women are more likely to be poor than men. For example, for female householders with no husband present the official poverty rate was 31.6 percent in 2010, compared to 15.8 percent of male householders with no wife present. This is the consequence of the prevailing institutional sexism in society that, with few exceptions, provides poor job and earnings opportunities for women. This gender disparity, combined with the high frequency of marital disruption and the number of never-married women with children, results in the high probability of women who head families being poor.

This trend, termed the **feminization of poverty**, implies that the relatively large proportion of poor women is a new phenomenon in U.S. society. Thus, the term obscures the fact that women have always been more economically vulnerable than men, especially older women and women of color. But when women's poverty was mainly limited to these groups, their economic deprivation was mostly invisible. The plight of women's poverty became a visible problem when the numbers of poor White women increased rapidly in the past decade or so with rising marital disruption. Even with the growing numbers of poor White women, the term *feminization of poverty* implies that all women are at risk, when actually the probability of economic deprivation is much greater for certain categories of women. The issue, then, is not only gender but class and race as well.

Race and gender combine to increase the probability of poverty. An African American woman is almost two and a half times more likely to be poor as a White woman and a Latino woman is almost twice as likely to be poor as a White woman.

Children

The nation's poverty rate was 15.1 percent in 2010, but the rate for children under age eighteen was 22.0 percent (16.4 million children). For the children's poverty rate by state and the percent of children living in families where no parent has a full-time, year-round job, see Table 10.5. For those under age six, the rate was 23.8 percent. Related children under age six living in families with a female head of household, no husband present, had a poverty rate of 54.3 percent, a rate more than four times that for their counterparts in married-couple families (13.4 percent).

Although there are more White children in poverty, children of color are disproportionately poor: Especially noteworthy is that the United States has the highest youth poverty rate of any Western nation.

The consequences of childhood poverty are grave. Children in poverty are more likely than their more fortunate peers to suffer from stunted growth, score lower on tests and be held back in school, suffer from lead poisoning (which may lead to mental retardation), and suffer a host of other problems.

The Elderly

Contrary to popular belief, the elderly as a category (age sixty-five and older) have a lower poverty rate (9.0 percent in 2010) than the general population (15.1 percent). Actually, there are more than four times as many children as elderly people living in poverty in the

TABLE 10.5

Children's Poverty Rate by State, 2008

Rank	State	Rate	Rank	State	Rate
1	New Hampshire	9	27	California	18
2	Hawaii	10	27	Florida	18
3	Maryland	10	27	Indiana	18
4	Alaska	11	27	Oregon	18
4	Minnesota	11	27	South Dakota	18
4	Utah	11	32	Michigan	19
7	Connecticut	12	32	Missouri	19
7	Massachusetts	12	32	New York	19
7	Wyoming	12	32	Ohio	19
10	Nebraska	13	36	Georgia	20
10	New Jersey	13	36	North Carolina	20
10	Vermont	13	38	Arizona	21
10	Wisconsin	13	38	Montana	21
14	Delaware	14	40	Alabama	22
14	Iowa	14	40	South Carolina	22
14	Virginia	14	40	Tennessee	22
14	Washington	14	43	Kentucky	23
18	Colorado	15	43	Oklahoma	23
18	Kansas	15	43	Texas	23
18	Nevada	15	43	West Virginia	23
18	North Dakota	15	47	New Mexico	24
18	Rhode Island	15	48	Arkansas	25
23	Idaho	16	48	Louisiana	25
23	Maine	16	50	Mississippi	30
25	Illinois	17	N.R.	District of Columbia	26
25	Pennsylvania	17	N.R.	Puerto Rico	56
N.R	—Not Ranked.				

Source: The Annie E. Casey Foundation, *2010 Kids Count: State Profiles of Child Well-Being* (Baltimore): 35.

United States. This seeming anomaly is the result of government programs for the elderly being indexed for inflation, whereas many welfare programs targeted for the young have been reduced or eliminated since 1980.

While the elderly are underrepresented in the poverty population, the rate increases with age. This is likely because as the age increases, the proportion of women in that category increases. Gender and race combine once again to make the economic situation especially difficult for elderly African Americans and Latino women (more than double the rate for elderly White women).

The Geography of Poverty

Poverty is not randomly distributed geographically; it tends to cluster in certain places. Regionally, the area with highest poverty is the South (19.9 percent), compared with 15.3 percent in the West, 13.9 percent in the Midwest, and 12.8 percent in the Northeast. The South and West have the highest poverty rates because they have large minority populations and relatively high concentrations of recent immigrants.

In metropolitan areas, the poverty rate in 2010 was higher in the central cities (19.7 percent) than in suburban areas (11.8 percent). For those living outside metropolitan areas, the poverty rate was 16.5 percent. With respect to central cities, two trends are significant: The proportion that is poor is increasing in the central cities; and increasingly, the poverty is more and more concentrated (that is, the poor are more and more likely to be living in already poor neighborhoods). This spatial concentration of poverty means that the poor have poor neighbors, and the area has a low tax base to finance public schools, and a shrinking number of businesses because they tend to move to areas where the local residents have more discretionary income. These factors mean a reduction in services and the elimination of local jobs. Moreover:

> Just as poverty is concentrated spatially, anything correlated with poverty is also concentrated. Therefore, as the density of poverty increases in cities ... so will the density of joblessness, crime, family dissolution, drug abuse, alcoholism, disease, and violence. Not only will the poor have to grapple with the manifold problems due to their own lack of increase; increasingly they also will have to confront the social effects of living in an environment where most of their neighbors are also poor. (Massey, 1996:407)

Although poverty is generally more concentrated in cities, the highest concentrations exist in four rural regions (Grunwald, 1999): the Mississippi Delta, which extends across seven states, where the poor are mostly African American; the Rio Grande Valley/Texas Gulf Coast/U.S.-Mexico border, a four-state region where the poor are largely Latino; the Native American reservations of the Southwest and Plains states; and Appalachia, a twelve-state region characterized by marginal farmland and a declining mining industry where the poor are predominantly White.

There are important differences between the rural and the urban poor. The rural poor have some advantages (low-cost housing, raising their own food) and many disadvantages (low-paid work, higher prices for many products, fewer social services, fewer welfare benefits) as compared with the urban poor.

Poverty is greatest among those who do not have an established residence. People in this classification are typically the homeless and migrant workers. The homeless, estimated between half a million and 3 million, are those in extreme poverty—they are the poorest of the poor (see Timmer, Eitzen, and Talley, 1994). The other category, migrant workers, is believed to be about 3 million adults and children who are seasonal farm laborers working sporadically for low wages and no benefits. It is estimated that about 50 percent of all farm workers live below the official poverty line; this percentage has not changed since the 1960s. Latinos are overrepresented in this occupation.

Finally, the United States, when compared to other major industrialized democracies, has more poverty, has more severe poverty, and supports its poor people least.

The Severely Poor

Use of the official poverty line designates all people below it as poor whether they are a few dollars short of the threshold or far below it. Most impoverished individuals and families have incomes considerably below the poverty threshold. In 2010, for example, the average deficit (the dollar amount below the poverty line) was $9,244 for all poverty households. An estimated 6.7 percent of the population (20.5 million Americans) was **severely poor** (that is, those people living at or below half the poverty line). Typically, the severely poor must use 50 percent or more of their meager income for housing.

This category of the severely poor has doubled since 1979. This upsurge in the truly destitute occurred because (1) many of them live in rural areas that have prospered less than other regions; (2) a decline in marriage (and a rise in divorce) resulted in a substantial increase in single mothers and unattached men; and (3) public assistance benefits, especially in the South, have steadily declined since 1980.

Myths about Poverty

What should be the government's role in caring for its less fortunate residents? Much of the debate on this important issue among politicians and citizens is based on erroneous assumptions and misperceptions.

Refusal to Work

Several facts belie the faulty assumption that poor people refuse to work. First, about four in five poor households contained at least one full- or part-time worker in 2009. They hold menial, dead-end jobs that have no benefits and pay the minimum wage or less. Low wages are the problem: Even with a minimum wage of $7.25 an hour, a full-time worker at that wage will have an annual income of $15,080, which is $2000 below the 2009 poverty line for a family of three. In 1968, a family of three with one minimum-wage earner had a standard of living 17 percent above the poverty line. Second, many of the poor who do not work are too young (under age eighteen), are too old (sixty-five and older), or have a work disability. Third, people of color are more likely to be poor than Whites in the same working category—that is, unemployed, having worked less than full-time, and worked full-time. Fourth, the main increase in the number of poor since 1979 has been among the working poor. This is the result of declining wages, an increase in working women who head households, and a very low minimum hourly wage that has not kept up with inflation. The lot of the working poor is similar to that of the nonworking poor on some dimensions and worse on others. They do society's dirty work for low pay and no benefits. Like the poor, they live in substandard housing and their children go to underfinanced schools. They are poor but, unlike the nonworking poor, they are not eligible for many government supports such as subsidized housing, medical care, and food stamps.

Economist Marlene Kim (1998) analyzed census data on a sample of 57,000 U.S. households and concludes:

> Most of the working poor would remain poor even if they worked 40 hours a week, 52 weeks a year. In addition, of those who could climb out of poverty if they worked such hours, two out of five are either disabled or elderly or unable to find full-time or full-year employment. Thus it appears that most of the working poor are doing all they can to support themselves. (97)

For those poor not officially in the labor force, many work (either for money or for the exchange of goods or services) in the informal economy by cleaning, painting, providing child care, repairing automobiles or appliances, or other activities. Clearly, these people are workers, they just are not in the official economy.

Welfare Dependency

In 1996, Congress passed the Personal Responsibility and Work Opportunity Reconciliation Act, which reformed the welfare system (the following is from Eitzen and Baca Zinn, 1998). This new law shifted the Aid to Families with Dependent Children (AFDC) welfare program from the federal government to the states, mandated that welfare recipients find work within two years, limited welfare assistance to five years, and cut various federal assistance programs targeted for the poor by $54.5 billion over six years. Thus, the law made assistance to poor families temporary and cut monies to supplemental programs such as food stamps and child nutrition. The assumption by policymakers was that welfare was too generous, making it easier to stay on welfare than leave for work, and welfare was believed to encourage unmarried women to have children.

We should recognize some facts about government welfare before the 1996 welfare reform (O'Hare, 1996). First, welfare accounted for about one-fourth of the income of poor adults; nearly half of the income received by poor adults came from some form of work activity. Second, about three-fourths of the poor received some type of noncash benefit (Medicaid, food stamps, or housing assistance), but only about 40 percent received cash welfare payments. Third, the poverty population changes—that is, people move in and out of poverty every year. The average welfare recipient stayed on welfare less than two years (Sklar, 1992). Only 12 percent of the poor remain poor for five or more consecutive years (O'Hare, 1996). Fourth, although the pre-reform welfare system was much more generous than now, it was inadequate to meet the needs of the poor, falling far short. The average poor family of three on welfare had an annual income much below the poverty line.

> Many poor families manage by cutting back on food, jeopardizing their health and the development of their children, or by living in substandard and sometimes dangerous housing. Some do without heat, electricity, telephone service, or plumbing for months or years. Many do without health insurance, health care, safe child care, or reliable transportation to take them to or from work. (Children's Defense Fund, cited in Sklar, 1992:10)

Fifth, contrary to the common assertion that welfare mothers keep having babies to get more welfare benefits and thereby escape working, research from a number of studies shows that most welfare recipients bring in extra money from various activities such as house cleaning, laundry, repairing clothing, child care, and selling items they have made. For example, sociologist Kathleen Harris (1996), summarizing her findings from a nationally representative sample of single mothers who received welfare, says:

> I found exclusive dependence on welfare to be rare. More than half of the single mothers whom I studied worked while they were on welfare, and two-thirds left welfare rolls when they could support themselves with jobs. However, more than half (57 percent) of the women who worked their way off public assistance later returned because their jobs ended or they still could not make ends meet. (B7)

Concerning the larger picture about government welfare programs, there is a fundamental misunderstanding by the U.S. public about where most governmental benefits are directed. We tend to assume that government monies and services go mostly to the poor (**welfare**, the receipt of financial aid and/or services from the government),when in fact the greatest government aid goes to the nonpoor ("**wealthfare**," the receipt by the nonpoor of financial aid and/or services from the government). Most (about three-fourths) of the federal outlays for human resources go to the nonpoor, such as to all children in public education programs and to most of the elderly through Social Security retirement and Medicare payments.

The upside-down welfare system, with aid mainly helping the already affluent, is accomplished by two hidden welfare systems. The first is through tax loopholes (called **tax expenditures**). Through these legal mechanisms, the government officially permits certain individuals and corporations to pay lower taxes or no taxes at all. For illustration, one of the biggest tax expenditure programs is the money that homeowners deduct from their taxes for real estate taxes and interest on their mortgages (mortgage interest is deductible on mortgages up to $1 million). In a telling irony, government provides tax breaks to homeowners ($130 billion). Ironically, while fewer than one-fourth of low-income Americans receive federal housing subsidies, more than three-quarters of Americans, many living in mansions, get housing aid from Washington.

The second hidden welfare system to the nonpoor is in the form of direct subsidies and credit to assist corporations, banks, agribusiness, defense industries, and the like. Some examples are the following:

- Tax avoidance by transnational corporations
- Lower taxes on capital gains
- Insurance loopholes
- Tax-free municipal bonds
- Agribusiness subsidies
- Aviation subsidies
- Oil and gas drillers and refiners

the Welfare Line

Totaling all of the subsidies (wealthfare) amounted to $1.053 trillion in 2010 according to the Senate Budget Committee (reported in Livingston, 2011; see also Gandhi, 2010). This amounts to nearly 25 percent of total government spending.

Finally, an assessment of the 1996 welfare reform six years after it was passed reveals premature, mixed, and uncertain results. Positively, the number of people receiving cash benefits fell from 4.6 million families in 1996 to 2.1 million families in 2002. Some 60 percent of adults formerly receiving welfare were working or engaged in activities to prepare for work. Negatively, over two-thirds still lived in poverty in 2002. Those that worked had low-wage jobs, averaging about $8.00 an hour in 2002 (Urban Institute, 2006). Research by sociologists William Julius Wilson and Andrew J. Cherlin (2001) in Boston, Chicago, and San Antonio reveals that while work has improved the sense of self-worth for former welfare recipients, three-fourths of the women who had been off welfare for two years or less had incomes below the federal poverty line. They were meeting basic expenses with government help such as food stamps. But the longer these women had been off welfare, the less likely they were to have health insurance for themselves and their children. The women facing the greatest difficulties after welfare were those with less education, poorer health, and younger children.

The first five years were extraordinary, with historically low unemployment, low inflation, and a booming economy. In 2001–2002, two powerful forces—the September 11 attacks on the World Trade Center and the Pentagon and a severe and prolonged economic downturn—combined to wreak havoc on the poor, especially those who had left welfare for work, as the 1996 Welfare Reform dictated. Then the Great Recession hit in late 2007 bringing official unemployment rates to exceed 10 percent. These rising unemployment rates hit former welfare recipients hard because, as recently hired employees, they were the most likely to be fired when the companies they worked for reduced their workforces. Moreover, the lower end of the service sector of the economy (sales clerks, janitors, restaurant workers, hotel workers), where former welfare recipients were most likely to find jobs, were especially hard hit in those difficult times. Moreover, the recessions of 2001 and 2007 were the first since the 1930s in which the "safety net" for the poor was almost nonexistent. As a result, the number of people seeking emergency food aid and the number without shelter rose significantly.

The Poor Get Special Advantages

The common belief is that the poor get a number of handouts for commodities for which other Americans have to work—food stamps, Medicaid, housing subsidies, and the like. As we have seen, these subsidies amount to much less than the more affluent receive, and recent legislation has reduced them more and more. Most significant, the poor pay more than the nonpoor for many services. This, along with low wages and paying a large proportion of their income for housing, explains why some have such difficulty getting out of poverty.

The urban poor find that their money does not go as far in the inner city. Food and commodities, for example, cost more since supermarkets, discount stores, outlet malls, and warehouse clubs have bypassed inner-city neighborhoods. Since many inner-city residents do not have transportation to get to the supermarkets and warehouse stores, they must buy from nearby stores, giving the store owners monopoly powers. As a result, the poor pay more. Consider the following:

- Hospitals routinely charge more for services to patients without health insurance, compared to those covered by a health plan.
- Check-cashing centers, largely located in poor neighborhoods, prey on customers without bank accounts, often charging 10 percent of the check's value.
- There are some WIC-only grocery stores (Women, Infants, Children). They accept just WIC vouchers as payment, not cash. Prices are 10 to 20 percent higher in these WIC-only stores.
- The "payday loan" industry offers an advance on a person's paycheck, with interest rates ranging from 500 to 2,000 percent, a devastating financial obligation for those strapped for cash.
- The insurance industry routinely charged one-third more to provide poor Blacks with burial insurance than they charged Whites. Between 2000 and 2004, sixteen major cases were settled covering 14.8 million policies sold by ninety insurance companies between 1900 and the 1980s. The settlements required the companies to pay more than $556 million in restitution to policyholders or their survivors (Donn, 2004).

The "payday loan" industry offers an advance on a person's paycheck, with interest ranging from 500 to 2,000 percent, a devastating financial obligation for those strapped for cash.

The conclusion is obvious: The poor pay more for commodities and services in absolute terms, and they pay a much larger proportion of their incomes than the nonpoor for comparable items. Similarly, when the poor pay sales taxes on the items they purchase, the tax takes more of their resources than it does from the nonpoor, making it a **regressive tax**. Thus, efforts to move federal programs to the states will cost the poor more, since state and local taxes tend to be regressive (sales taxes), while federal taxation tends to be progressive.

Welfare Is an African American and Latino Program

The myth is that most welfare monies go primarily to African Americans and Latinos. While poverty rates are higher for Blacks and Hispanics than for other racial/ethnic groups, they do not make up the majority of the poor. In 2010, non-Hispanic Whites were the most numerous racial/ethnic group in the poverty population: almost 19.6 million Whites were in poverty, compared to 10.7 million African Americans and 13.2 million Latinos in poverty.

1. People in the United States vary greatly on a number of socioeconomic dimensions. Wealth and income are maldistributed. Educational attainment varies. Occupations differ greatly in prestige and pay.

2. Order theorists place individuals into social classes according to occupation. Each social class is composed of social equals who share a similar lifestyle. Each class-specific culture is assumed to have power over its members.

3. Conflict theorists focus on money, relation to the means of production, and power as the determinants of class position. Crucial to this placement is not occupational prestige as the order theorists posit, but whether one gives orders or takes orders in the work process.

4. The consequences of one's socioeconomic status are best expressed in the concept of life chances, which refer to the chances to obtain the things highly valued in society. The data show that the higher one's economic position, the longer one's life, the healthier (physically and mentally) one will be, the more stable one's family, the less likely one will be drafted, the less likely one will be processed by the criminal justice system, and the higher one's educational attainment.

5. Societies vary in the degree to which individuals may move up in status. The most rigid societies are called caste systems. They are essentially closed hereditary groups. Class systems are more open, permitting vertical mobility.

6. Although the United States is a relatively open class system, the extent of intergenerational mobility (a son or daughter surpassing his or her parents) is limited.

7. Graduation from college is the most important predictor of upward social mobility. However, a college education is becoming more difficult to attain for the less than affluent.

8. According to the government's arbitrary line, which minimizes the actual extent of poverty, in 2003, 12.5 percent (35.9 million) of the U.S. population was officially poor. Disproportionately represented in the poor category are African Americans, Latinos, women, and children.

9. The poor are not poor because they refuse to work. Most adult poor either work at low wages, cannot find work, work part-time, are homemakers, are ill or disabled, or are in school.

10. Government assistance to the poor is not sufficient to eliminate their economic deprivation. Less than half of the poor actually receive any federal assistance. When compared with the nonpoor, their life chances are negative, with a higher incidence of health problems, malnutrition, social pathologies, and homelessness.

11. Most government assistance is targeted to the affluent rather than the poor. The nonpoor receive three-fourths of the federal monies allocated to human services. Tax expenditures and other subsidies provide enormous economic benefits to the already affluent, which further redistributes the nation's wealth upward.

12. The poor pay more than the nonpoor for services and commodities, which helps to trap them in poverty.

13. Contrary to popular belief, Whites receive more welfare than do African Americans and Latinos.

Wealth
Income
Social Class
Social mobility
Vertical mobility

Horizontal mobility
Intergenerational mobility
Intragenerational mobility
Feminization of poverty
Severely poor

Welfare
Wealthfare
Tax expenditures
Regressive tax

1. What are the key differences in the conception of social class by order-model and conflict-model theorists?
2. What are the consequences of social class position in terms of life chances?
3. What is the evidence that the gap between the haves and the have-nots is increasing in the United States?
4. To what extent is upward social mobility difficult for poor youth?

5. Which social categories are most likely to be poor? Referring to the discussion in Chapter 9, what are the fundamental reasons for the overrepresentation of these categories in the poor classification?
6. Write an essay titled "The Poor Pay More."

http://www.as.ysu.edu/~cwcs/

The Center for Working-Class Studies at Youngstown State University studies working-class life and culture. The site also has links to other class-related sites.

http://www.secondharvest.org/

Home of America's Second Harvest, a hunger relief program, this site contains facts on hunger in America and policies related to hunger. The site follows the search of Hunger in America 2001, which provides "a comprehensive profile of the incidence and nature of hunger and food insecurity in the United States."

http://www.inequality.org/

This is a site that contains extensive information on class inequality and "news, information and expertise on the divide in income, wealth, and health." Among the topics on Inequality.org are links, quotes, and the overclass.

http://www.forbes.com/people/lists/

Search the home of *Forbes* magazine to see a list of the wealthiest people in America and in the world.

http://www.ufenet.org/

United for a Fair Economy is a group that is dedicated to building a fair economy movement centered on decreasing the income gap.

http://www.pscw.uva.nl/sociosite/CLASS/bibA.html

Go to this site for a bibliography on class.

http://www.pbs.org/peoplelikeus/

This site is one that is a supplement to a PBS documentary called *People Like Us*. The site has games, resources, and information to show how class works in America and to test preconceptions people have about class.

http://www.nationalhomeless.org/

Through work in housing justice, economic justice, health care justice, and civil rights, the National Coalition for the Homeless seeks to end homelessness.

http://www.aflcio.org/paywatch/

PayWatch is part of the AFL-CIO, and it tracks earnings of CEOs. Among the features of the site is the ability of the visitor to compare her or his salary or wage to that of CEOs of various companies.

http://www.isr.umich.edu/src/psid/

The Panel Study of Income Dynamics is a "longitudinal survey of a representative sample of U.S. individuals and the families in which they reside." It emphasizes economic and demographic behaviors.

http://www.jcpr.org/

The Joint Center for Poverty Research is a research center that "seeks to advance our understanding of what it means to be poor in America."

http://www.welfareinfo.org

The Welfare Information Network provides information on government welfare programs, housing, homelessness, immigrants, food stamps, and family formation.

http://www.paffairs@ui.urban.org

The Urban Institute is a nonpartisan economic and social policy research organization. The Institute provides research information on the economy, housing, welfare, work, income, and other topics relevant to sociology.

Next, we examine explanations of racial inequality followed by a look at its effects on Blacks and Hispanics in terms of income, jobs, education, and health. Finally, the chapter turns to current trends in racial and ethnic relations.

The theme of the chapter is that racial inequalities have structural foundations. Many people think the United States is now a color-blind society where race no longer matters. For them, the election of the first African American president means that our nation has moved past race. But despite the tremendous significance of President Obama's electoral victory, and despite the changing character of racism, our society remains structured along lines of race, ethnicity, and color. In this chapter we show that racial divides persist in today's multi-racial world, and minority groups lack the same opportunities as everyone else. Keep in mind that minorities are not to blame for these racial divisions. Instead, the cause lies in our race-based system of social rights and resources. Keep in mind that our emphasis on persistent racial domination does not mean that minorities are passive victims of oppression: Their histories are filled with human agency; and for centuries, racial minorities in the United States have fought against oppression, both as individuals and in groups.

Racial and Ethnic Minorities

Racial categories are a basis of power relations and group position. Because race relations are power relations, conflict (or at least the potential for conflict) is always present. Overt conflict is most likely when minority groups try to change the distribution of power. Size is not crucial in determining whether a group is the most powerful. A numerical minority may in fact have more political representation than the majority, as is the case in South Africa. Thus, the most important characteristic of a minority group is that it is dominated by a more powerful group.

Determining who is a minority is largely a matter of history, politics, and judgment—both social and political. Population characteristics other than race and ethnicity—such as age, gender, sexual orientation, or religious preference—are sometimes used to designate minority status. However, race and ethnicity are the characteristics used most often to define the minority and majority populations in contemporary U.S. society (O'Hare, 1992:5).

Sociologists agree that race is socially constructed. This means that some groups are racially defined, even though races, per se, do not exist. What does exist is the *idea* that races are distinct biological categories. Races are thought to be physically distinguishable populations that share a common ancestry. But despite the popular belief, social scientists now reject the biological concept of race. Scientific examination of the human genome finds no genetic differences between the so-called races. Fossil and DNA evidence show that humans are all one race, evolved in the last 100,000 years from the same small number of tribes that migrated out of Africa and colonized the world (American Sociological Association, 2003; Angier, 2000; Bean et al., 2004; Mukhopadhyay and Henze, 2003). Although there is no such thing as biological race, races are real insofar as they are *socially defined*. In other words, racial categories operate as if they are real. Racial categories are a mechanism for sorting people in society. They structure and segregate "our neighborhoods, our schools, our churches, and our relationships" (Higginbotham and Andersen, 2012).

Racial classification in the United States has long been based on a Black/White dichotomy—that is, two opposing categories into which all people fit. However, social definitions of race have changed throughout the nation's history. At different points in the past, "race has taken on different meanings. Many of the people considered White and thought of as the majority group are descendants of immigrants who at one time were believed to be racially distinct from native-born White Americans, the majority of whom were Protestants" (Higginbotham and Andersen, 2009:41). Racial categories vary in different regions of the country and around the world. Someone classified as "Black" in the United States might be considered "White" in Brazil and "Coloured" (a category distinguished from both "Black" and "White") in South Africa (Bamshad and Olson, 2003:80).

In the United States, a Black/White color line has always been complicated by regional racial divides. Today, the rapidly growing presence of Latino and Asian immigrants and the resurgence of Native American identification have changed the meaning and boundaries of racial categories. Their non-White status marks them as "other and denies them many opportunities" (Lewis, Kryson, and Harris, 2004:5; Pyke, 2004:55). Skin color complicates racial differences because it is a basis of ranking that favors lighter skin over darker skin. Both within and across racial and ethnic groups, lighter-skinned people have more advantages than those with darker skin (Burton et al., 2010). Global events add still more complexity to the color lines. Since the terrorist attacks on the World Trade Center and the Pentagon, Arab Americans, Muslims, and people of Middle Eastern descent (viewed by many as a single entity) are stereotyped as different and possibly dangerous.

Racial Categories

In Chapter 8, we discussed current immigration patterns that are reshaping the U.S. racial landscape. Immigration from Asia, Latin America, and the Caribbean is also changing the character of race and ethnic relations. Sociologists Michael Omi and Howard Winant (1994:55) call this **racial formation**, meaning that society is continually creating and transforming racial categories. For example, groups once self-defined by their ethnic backgrounds (such as Mexican Americans and Japanese Americans) are now racialized as "Hispanics" and "Asian Americans." Middle Easterners coming from such countries as Syria, Lebanon, Egypt, and Iran are commonly grouped together and called "Arabs."

In the United States this continued with the 2010 census. The government has changed its racial categories over time. For the first time in Census 2000, people were allowed to record themselves in two more racial categories, and number of people identifying as mixed-race in 2010 rose in one decade from 2.4 percent in 2000 to 3 percent in 2010 (U.S. Bureau of the Census, 2010). We can expect that the use of the mixed-race or multiracial option will grow, especially among the younger population. Marrying across racial lines is on the increase, as attitudes toward interracial unions become more tolerant. Thirteen percent of U.S. marriages now involve someone of a different race (Lee and Bean, 2004:228). Already, children are much more likely to identify themselves as multiracial than adults. Four percent of the population under age eighteen was identified in more than one racial category in the 2000 Census, twice the percentage for adults (Kent et al., 2001:6; Prewitt, 2003:39).

People may now identify themselves as members of more than one racial group on the census and other federal forms.

While the Census Bureau has begun to capture the complex mix of racial groups in the United States, it uses a confusing classification for Hispanics. According to the 2000 U.S. guidelines, Hispanics were considered to be an ethnic group, not a race. People who identified their ethnicity as Hispanic could also indicate a racial background by choosing "some other race." The Census Bureau acknowledges that the distinction between race and ethnicity is flawed. The 2010 Census changed the Hispanic origin question to more clearly distinguish Hispanics as not being a race by adding the sentence "For this census, Hispanic origins are not races" (Humes et al., 2011:12). In reality, Hispanics *are racialized* in the United States. Although classified as an ethnic group, "Hispanic" encompasses a range of ethnic groups. At the same time, although Hispanics are not officially defined as a race, they are *socially defined* in racial terms. In other words, the dominant society treats them as racially inferior. When any group comes to be thought of as a race, "this means the group has become racialized" (Taylor, 2009:47).

Despite the past and present racialization of different groups, common thinking about race is flawed. We tend to see race through a Black/White lens, thereby neglecting other rapidly growing racial groups. At the same time, we think of Whites, the dominant group, as raceless, or having no race at all (McIntosh, 1992). In this view, whiteness is the natural or normal condition. It is racially unmarked and immune to investigation. This is a false picture of race. In reality, the racial order shapes the lives of all people, even Whites who are advantaged by the system. Just as social classes exist in relation to each other, "races" are labeled and judged *in relation to other races*. The categories "Black" and "Hispanic" are meaningful only insofar as they are set apart from and in distinction to "White." This point is particularly obvious when people are referred to as "non-White" (a word that ignores the differences in experiences among people of color) (Lucal, 1996:246). Race is not simply a matter of two opposite categories of people but a range of power relations among dominant and subordinate groups (Weber, 2010).

Ethnic Groups and Their Differences

How is race different from ethnicity? Whereas race is an invention used for socially marking groups based on presumed physical differences, ethnicity is a social category that allows for a broader range of affiliation. **Ethnic groups** are distinctive on the basis of national origin, language, religion, and culture.

Ethnic groups have long been present in the United States. Since colonial times, Germans, Italians, Poles, Irish and other groups arrived with their own languages, religions, and customs. Both race and ethnicity are historical bases for inequality in that they are constructed in a hierarchy from "superior" to "inferior." In the United States, some immigrants were viewed as belonging to an inferior race. For example, Jews were once racialized and later reconstructed as White (Brodkin, 2009). Nevertheless, race and ethnicity have differed in how they incorporated groups into society. Race was the social construction setting people of color apart from European immigrant groups (Takaki, 1993:10). Groups identified as races came into contact with the dominant society through force and state-sanctioned discrimination in work that was unfree and offered little opportunity for upward mobility. In contrast, European ethnics migrated to the United States voluntarily to enhance their status or to market their skills in a land of opportunity. They came with hope and sometimes with resources to provide a foundation for their upward mobility. Unlike racial groups, most had the option of returning if they found the conditions here unsatisfactory. The voluntary immigrants came to the United States and suffered discrimination in employment, housing, and other areas (Pollard and O'Hare, 1995).

Over time, White ethnic groups were incorporated into society while keeping their cultures alive in their families or for cultural celebrations. Sociologists call this "optional ethnicity" (Waters, 1996), that is the ability to choose whether or not to identify with their group of origin and which cultural traits to keep. This option is possible for some White groups, but generally not for people of color who remain different from the dominant society because racial discrimination sets them apart from others.

Today, globalization and transnational migration (See Chapter 8.) are changing the landscape of countries throughout the world. In the United States some groups have given up their ethnic customs, while others remain distinctive. As European countries struggle with political and economic integration, people may no longer identify as Italian, but as Lombardians or Sicilians (Wali, 1992). Expanding communications networks and the increased social interaction that have resulted from immigration have not suppressed ethnic conflicts. During the last decade of the twentieth century, ethnic and religious differences have led to massacres of ethnic Tutsis by Hutus in Rwanda; full-scale war involving Serb, Bosnian, Albanian, and other ethnic groups in the Balkans; and violence against ethnic Chinese in Indonesia (Pollard and O'Hare, 1999:5). Across Europe today, anti-immigrant racism is on the rise. Growing fears of a mounting foreign influx are fueling political movements to stop immigration.

Racial-Ethnic Groups in the United States

In the United States, race and ethnicity both serve to mark groups as different. Groups *labeled as races* by the wider society are bound together by their common social and economic conditions. As a result, they develop distinctive cultural or ethnic characteristics. Today, we often refer to them as **racial-ethnic groups** (or racially defined ethnic groups). The term *racial-ethnic group* refers to groups that are socially subordinated and remain culturally distinct within U.S. society. It includes (1) the systematic discrimination of socially constructed racial groups and (2) their distinctive cultural arrangements. The categories of African American, Latino, Asian American, and Native American have been constructed as both racially and culturally distinct. Each group has a distinctive culture, shares a common heritage, and has a common identity within a larger society that subordinates it. The racial characteristics of these groups have become meaningful in a society that continues to change (Baca Zinn and Dill, 1994).

Terms of reference are also changing, and the changes are contested within groups and between them. For example, *Blacks* continue to debate the merits of the term *African American*, while *Latinos* disagree on the label *Hispanic*. In this chapter, we use such interchangeable terms because they are currently used in both popular and scholarly discourse.

African Americans. In 2010, African Americans were 13 percent of the population (U.S. Bureau of the Census, 2010). Before 1990, virtually all descended from people who were brought involuntarily to the United States before the slave trade ended in the nineteenth century. They entered the southern states to provide free labor to plantations, and as late as 1890, 90 percent of all Blacks lived in the South, 80 percent as rural dwellers. In the South, they endured harsh, violent, and arbitrary conditions under slavery, an institution that would have consequences for centuries to come. During the nineteenth century, the political storm over slavery almost destroyed the nation. Although Blacks left the South in large numbers after 1890, within northern cities they also encountered discrimination and an extreme level of segregation that exposed them to unusually high concentrations of poverty and other social problems (Massey, 1993:7; Takaki, 1993:7). African Americans have a distinctive history of slavery and oppression.

In the past two decades, the Black population has changed due to immigration from Africa and the Caribbean. In fact, more Blacks are coming from Africa than during the slave trade. About 50,000 legal immigrants arrive annually, and overall more have migrated here than in nearly the entire preceding centuries (Roberts, 2005:A1). The increase in Black immigration from Africa and the Caribbean is making the population more diverse and posing challenges to today's Black immigrants (Shaw-Taylor, 2009). The increase in Black immigration is also changing what it means to be Black. It has sparked a new debate about the "African American" label. It ignores the enormous linguistic, physical, and cultural diversity of the peoples of Africa. The term "Black" is also problematic in that it risks conflating people of African descent who were brought here as slaves with recent immigrants from Africa and the Caribbean (Mukhopadhyay and Henze, 2003:675). In fact, the experiences of today's immigrants are markedly different from those who have descended as slaves.

Latinos. As we saw in Chapter 5, the size of the U.S. Latino population has now surpassed the African American population to become the nation's largest minority. In many respects, the Latino population is the driving force of this society's racial and ethnic transformation (Saenz, 2004:29). In 2010, Hispanics or Latinos made up 16 percent of the total U.S. population (U.S. Bureau of the Census, 2010). Although Latinos are the largest minority, they are a varied collection of ethnic groups. They include diverse people who originate from Spanish-speaking countries in Latin America, the Caribbean, and Spain. Two-thirds (66 percent) of all Latinos are Chicanos or Mexican Americans, 9 percent are Puerto Ricans, 3.5 percent are Cubans, and 23 percent are "other Hispanic" (U.S. Bureau of the Census, 2010).

The *Hispanic* category was created by the federal government to provide data on people of Mexican, Cuban, Puerto Rican, and other Hispanic origins in the United States. The term was chosen as a label that could be applied to all people from the Spanish-speaking countries of Latin America and from Spain. Because the population is so diverse, there is no precise definition of group membership. Even the term *Latino*, which many prefer, is a new invention. While Latinos as often viewed as immigrants, the majority (63 percent) of the population was born in the United States Nonetheless, a significant proportion of the population immigrated to the United States only recently (Saenz, 2010).

The national origins of Latinos are diverse, and so is the timing of their arrival in the United States. As a result, Mexicans, Puerto Ricans, Cubans, and other Latino groups have varied histories that set them apart from each other. Cubans arrived largely in the period between 1960 and 1980; Mexicans originally became part of the United States in 1848, with the forcible annexation of much of what is the southwest and because of the Treaty of Guadalupe Hidalgo. Other Mexicans have been migrating continuously since around 1890. Puerto Ricans came under U.S. control in 1898 and obtained citizenship in 1917; Salvadorans and Guatemalans have been migrating to the United States in substantial numbers during the past two decades.

As a result of these different histories, Hispanics are found in many legal and social statuses—from fifth-generation to new immigrants, from affluent and well educated to poor and unschooled. Such diversity means that there is no "Hispanic" population in the sense that there is a Black population. Hispanics do not have a common history. They do not compose a single community. Rather, they are a collection of groups with different national origins, languages, racial identifications, and socioeconomic statuses. Saying that someone is "Hispanic" or "Latino" reveals little about attitudes, behaviors, beliefs, race, religion, class, or legal situation in the United States (Massey, 1993; Saenz, 2010).

Despite these differences, Latinos in the United States have endured a long history of discrimination. Mexican Americans in the Southwest lost property and political rights as Anglos moved into the region in the 1800s. As late as the 1940s, local ordinances in some Texas cities blocked Mexican Americans from owning real estate or voting. Also, Mexican Americans were required to attend segregated public schools in many jurisdictions before 1950 (Pollard and O'Hare, 1999:6).

Asian Americans. Asian Americans are another rapidly growing minority group in the country. In 2010, Asian Americans made up 5 percent of the U.S. population (U.S. Bureau of the Census, 2010). Foreign-born Asians now make up 23.9 percent of the nation's immigrants.

Like the Latino population, the Asian population in the United States is extremely diverse, giving rise to the term *Pan-Asian*, which encompasses immigrants from Asian and Pacific Island countries and native-born citizens descended from those ethnic groups (Lott and Felt, 1991:6). Until recently, immigrants who arrived in the United States from Asian countries did not think of themselves as "Asians," or even as Chinese, Japanese, Korean, and so forth, but rather people from Toisan, Hoeping, or some other district in Guangdong Province in China, or from Hiroshima, Yamaguchi, or some other place. It was not until the late 1960s, with the advent of the Asian American movement, that a Pan-Asian consciousness was formed (Espiritu, 1996:51).

The largest Asian American groups are Chinese (22 percent), Filipinos (18 percent), Japanese (5.6 percent), Vietnamese (10 percent), Koreans (10 percent), and Asian Indians (18 percent) (U.S. Bureau of the Census, 2009). There also are Laotians, Kampucheans, Thais, Pakistanis, Indonesians, Hmongs, and Samoans (Lee, 1998:15).

The characteristics of Asians vary widely according to their national origins and time of entry into the United States. Most come from recent immigrant families, but many Asian Americans can trace their families' history in the United States more than 150 years. Much of this period was marked by anti-Asian laws and discrimination. The 1879 California constitution barred the hiring of Chinese workers, and the federal Chinese Exclusion Act of 1882 halted the entry of most Chinese immigrants until 1943. Americans of Japanese ancestry were interned in camps during World War II by an executive order signed by President Franklin D. Roosevelt. Not until 1952 were Japanese immigrants granted the right to become naturalized U.S. citizens (Pollard and O'Hare, 1999:6–7).

Whereas most of the pre–World War II Asian immigrants were peasants, the recent immigrants vary considerably by education and social class. On one hand, many arrived as educated middle-class professionals with highly valued skills and some knowledge of English. Others, such as the Indo-Chinese, arrived as uneducated, impoverished refugees. These differences are reflected in the differences in income and poverty level by ethnic category. Asian Americans taken together have higher average incomes than do other groups in the United States. Although a large segment of this population is financially well off, many are poor. Asian Americans are seen as "the model minority," a well-educated and upwardly mobile group. But this stereotype is misleading. Not only is it used to blame other racial minorities for their own inequality, but it also ignores both the history of discrimination against Asians and their wide differences. Even the term *Asian American* masks great diversity.

Native Americans. Once thought to be destined for extinction, the Native American or American Indian population today is larger than it has been for centuries. Now at 2 percent of the total U.S. population (U.S. Bureau of the Census, 2010), Native Americans have more autonomy and are more self-sufficient than at any time since the last century (Snipp, 1996:390). Nevertheless, the population remains barred from full participation in U.S. society.

The tribes located in North America were and are extremely heterogeneous, with major differences in physical characteristics, language, and social organization. As many as 7 million indigenous people lived in North America when the Europeans arrived. The conquest made them "Indians." By 1890, they were reduced to fewer than 250,000 by disease, warfare, and in some cases genocide. In the first half of the nineteenth century, the U.S. government forced Indians from their homelands. Those forced migrations accelerated after President Andrew Jackson signed the Indian Removal Act of 1830. Many tribes were then forced to live on marginal land that was reserved solely for them.

The current political and economic status of American Indians stems from the process that forced them into U.S. society. Many factors led to the disparities we now observe between Native Americans and others, including the appropriation of Indian land for the gain of White settlers, the mismanagement by the Bureau of Indian Affairs of resources found on native lands, and the underinvestment of land by the Federal government in Native American education and health care (Adamson, 2009).

Important changes have occurred in the social and economic well-being of the Native American population from 1960 to the present. At the time of the 1970 Census, American Indians were the poorest group in the United States, with incomes well below those of the Black population. By 1980, despite poverty rates as high as 60 percent on many Indian reservations, poverty among American Indians had declined. At the end of the twentieth century, Native Americans were better off than they were in the 1900s. Over the past few decades, Native Americans have made important gains in cutting poverty rates and increasing their educational levels. Yet even with these gains, Native Americans are nowhere near poverty with White Americans. Today, Native Americans have a poverty rate of 27 percent, twice the White poverty rate. Native peoples rank at the bottom of most U.S. socioeconomic indicators, with low levels of life expectancy, per capita income, employment, and education (Harjo, 1996; Pollard and O'Hare, 1999; Thornton, 1996; Muhammad, 2009; U.S. Bureau of the Census, 2009 American Community Survey).

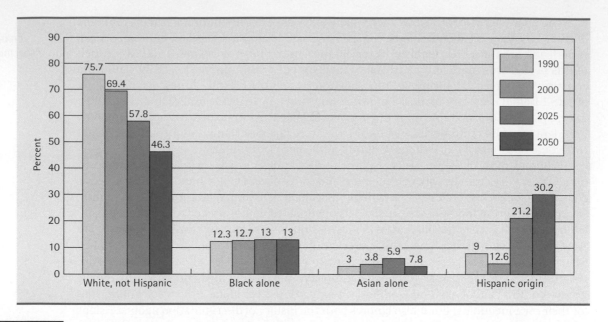

FIGURE 11.1

Percent of the
Population by
Race and Hispanic
Origin: 1990,
2000, 2025 and
2050

Sources: U.S. Census
Bureau, 1997. "Popula-
tion of the United States:
1997" Current Popula-
tion reports. Series
P23-194. Washington,
DC: U.S. Government
Printing Office, p.9. U.S.
Census Bureau, 2004.
"U.S. interim projections
by Age, Sex, race, and
Hispanic Origin," http://
www.census.gov/ipc/
www/usinterimproj/. U.S.
Census Bureau, 2008.
Population Division."
Table 4: Projections of
the Population by Sex,
race, and Hispanic Origin
for the United States:
2010 to 2050.

Although Third World conditions prevail on many reservations, a renaissance has occurred in American Indian communities. In cities, modern pan-Indian organizations have been successful in making the presence of American Indians known to the larger community and have mobilized to meet the needs of their people (Snipp, 1996:390). A college-educated Indian middle class has emerged, American Indian business ownership has increased, and some tribes are creating good jobs for their members (Fost, 1991:26).

To summarize this section, the combined population of the four racial minority groups accounts for 30 percent of the total U.S. population. New waves of immigration from non-European countries, high birth rates among these groups, and a relatively young age structure account for the rapid increase in minorities. By the middle of the twenty-first century, today's minorities will comprise nearly one-half of the U.S. population. (See Figure 11.1 for population projections through the year 2050.) African Americans, Latinos, Asian Americans, and Native Americans are different in many respects. Each group encounters different forms of exclusion. Nevertheless, as racial minorities they remain at the lowest rungs of society.

Explanations of Racial and Ethnic Inequality

Why are some racial and ethnic groups consistently disadvantaged? Some ethnic groups, such as the Irish and the Jews, have experienced discrimination but managed to overcome their initial disadvantages. But, African Americans, Latinos, Asian Americans, and Native Americans have not been able to cast off their secondary status. Three types of theories have been used to explain why some groups are treated differently: deficiency theories, bias theories, and structural discrimination theories.

Deficiency Theories

A number of analysts have argued that some groups are disadvantaged because they *are* inferior. That is, when compared with the majority, they are deficient in some important way. There are two variations of **deficiency theories**.

Biological Deficiency. This classical explanation for racial inferiority maintains that group inferiority is the result of flawed genetic—and, therefore, hereditary—traits. This is the position of Arthur Jensen, Richard Herrnstein, and Charles Murray (as discussed in Chapter 7). Their book, *The Bell Curve* (Herrnstein and Murray, 1994), claims that Blacks are genetically inferior to Whites, and this explains differences in the successes of racial groups. Despite the media attention given the work of these and other theorists, there is no definitive evidence for the thesis that racial groups differ in intelligence. Biological deficiency theories are generally not accepted in the scientific community (see *Contemporary Sociology*, 1995).

Cultural Deficiency. Many explanations of racial subordination rest on group-specific cultural traits handed down from generation to generation. According to this explanation, the cultural beliefs and practices of minority groups are dysfunctional when compared to the dominant group. In addition, these groups remain at the bottom because they fail to take advantage of the opportunities in society (Brown and Wellman, 2005:188). From this perspective, minorities are disadvantaged because of their own heritage and customs. Cultural deficiency was the basis for Daniel Patrick Moynihan's famous 1967 report, which charged that the "tangle of pathology" within Black ghettos was rooted in the deterioration of the Negro family (U.S. Department of Labor, 1965). High rates of marital dissolution, female-headed households, out-of-wedlock births, and welfare dependency were said to be the residues of slavery and discrimination, a complex web of pathological patterns passed down through the generations. The Moynihan report was widely criticized for being a classic case of "blaming the victim." It finds the problem within Black culture, not in the structure of society.

For over four decades, many social scientists strongly opposed cultural explanations. However, the culture of poverty is now back on the sociological agenda, this time using new definitions of culture and arguing that culture and social structural conditions work together to produce poverty and racial inequality (Small et al., 2010; Wilson, 2010). (See A Closer Look panel titled "Culture and Structure in Today's Poverty Debates.") Still, the old cultural approach dominates in popular thought. Today, much of the public discussion about race and poverty rests on false assumptions about minorities (Bonilla-Silva, 2003; di Leonardo, 1992; Reed, 1990). "Family breakdown" is still used to explain African Americans, while a backward culture is said to produce Latino problems. Today's immigrant debates use culture to generate fear. For example, in his book, *Who Are We? The Challenges to American Identity* (2005), Samuel P. Huntington argues that a culture alien to Anglo-Saxon ways makes unchecked Latino immigration a threat to U.S. society.

Bias Theories

The deficiency theories blame minorities for their plight. **Bias theories**, on the other hand, blame the members of the dominant group. They blame individuals who hold *prejudiced attitudes* toward minorities. Gunnar Myrdal (1944), for example, argues in his classic book *An American Dilemma* that prejudiced attitudes toward an entire group of people are the problem. This argument reduces racism to the "prejudiced" acts of individual White Americans (Brown and Wellman, 2005:189).

Many sociologists have argued that prejudiced attitudes are not the essence of racism. For example, David Wellman (1977) has challenged the notion that the hostile attitudes of White Americans, especially lower-class Whites, are the major cause of racism. Instead, he shows that many unprejudiced White people defend the traditional arrangements that negatively affect minorities. Research by Lawrence Bobo (2009:81) shows that although prejudice has declined, most White Americans are still unwilling to support social practices and policies to address racial inequalities. Unbiased people fight to preserve the status quo by favoring, for example, the seniority system in occupations, or they oppose affirmative action, quota systems, busing to achieve racial balance, and open enrollment in higher education.

Culture and Structure in Today's Poverty Debates

Why are people poor? Is this a result of their family history? Choices they have made? Or the values they hold? And why is it some people are able to "overcome" poverty and some are not? These questions have long held the interest of social scientists and the public alike. In the 1960s, Oscar Lewis and Daniel Patrick Moynihan were two of the social scientists examining this relationship. They argued that individual and group behavior, norms, and values, or culture, were key in determining who stayed poor and why. In this way, they believed that poverty is caused by unmarried mothers, welfare dependence, and outmoded cultural lifestyles.

This perspective became known as the *culture of poverty*, which many social scientists applied to people of color. These explanations situated poverty at the group level, blaming those in poverty for their own condition, without looking at the larger structural factors and daily informal barriers that produce unequal opportunities based on race and class. The use of these cultural arguments to explain poverty was highly problematic and generated huge debates about whether culture was a useful tool to explain why people are unable to escape poverty. Many scholars shied away from using cultural explanations to explain poverty in the decades that followed.

Recently, there has been a resurgence of interest in the field of cultural studies which evidence the fact that culture is back on the poverty agenda (Cohen, 2010). This resurgence explains how culture may explain poverty, without falling into some of the old pitfalls. Current scholarship defines culture in a more complex way than the literature of the 1960s and typically recognizes the ways numerous social factors, such as culture, race, gender, sexuality and local space work together to determine an individual's socioeconomic status. In addition, this scholarship often questions the existence of clear-cut boundaries between structure and culture. Using these definitions, this set of scholars argues that cultural forces and structural forces work together to shape the lives of those living in poverty. William Julius Wilson is one of the scholars leading the new cultural debates. He

argues, "structural conditions provide the context within which cultural responses to chronic economic and racial subordination are developed" (Wilson, 2010:61).

Many social scientists strongly disagree that culture is a useful concept for understanding poverty in the twenty-first century. Stephen Steinberg is one of these critics who says that the new wave of arguments about the relationship between culture and poverty are just regurgitations of the old arguments in a more clever and catchy disguise. He contends that the current revision still places too much emphasis on culture and not enough on macro structural forces. The scholars he reviews give a nod to the importance of structure in shaping individual and group responses to poverty, but ultimately view culture as an "independent and self-sustaining factor in the production and reproduction of poverty" (Steinberg, 2011) and in this way still blame the culture of the individual or the group for their own poverty.

How, then, should we explain poverty? Is it culture? Is it structure? Is it both? This is no ordinary sociological debate. The stakes are high because poverty explanations shape social policy with real consequences for poor people everywhere. No doubt, sociologists and policy makers will continue debating culture, structure, and poverty for years to come.

Source: Paula Miller, Department of Sociology, Michigan State University, 2011. This essay was written expressly for *In Conflict and Order*, 13th Edition.

References

Cohen, Patricia. 2010. "Culture of Poverty Makes a Comeback". *New York Times*. October 17. Accessible from: http://www.nytimes.com/2010/10/18/us/18poverty.html.

Steinberg, Stephen. 2011. "Poor Reason: Culture Still Doesn't Explain Poverty." *Boston Review*. January 13. Accessible from: http://www.bostonreview.net/BR36.1/steinberg.php.

Wilson, William Julius. 2010. *More than Just Race: Being Black and Poor in the Inner City.* New York, New York: W.W. Norton and Company.

Today, we live in an era when laws to protect citizens from racial discrimination are firmly in place. The new conventional wisdom views racism as a remnant of the past, the result of individual White bigotry, which is diminishing (Brown and Wellman, 2005). The focus strictly on prejudice is inaccurate because it concentrates on the bigots and ignores the structural foundation of racism. The determining feature of majority-minority relations is not prejudice, but differential systems of privilege and disadvantage. "The subordination of people of color is functional to the operation of American society as we know it and the color of one's skin is a primary determinant of people's position in the social structure" (Wellman, 1977:35). Even if active dislike of minorities ceases, "persistent social patterns can endure over time, affecting whom we marry, where we live, what we believe and do, and so forth" (Elliot and Pais, 2006:300).

Thus, institutional and individual racism generate privilege for Whites. Discrimination provides the privileged with disproportionate advantages in the social, economic, and political spheres. Racist acts, in this view, are based not only on stereotypes, hatred, or prejudgment, but are also rational responses to the struggle over scarce resources by individuals acting to preserve their own advantage.

Structural Discrimination Theories

Deficiency and bias theories focus, incorrectly, on individuals: the first on minority flaws, and the second on the flawed attitudes of the majority. Both kinds of theory ignore the social organization that oppresses minorities. Michael Parenti criticizes those who ignore the system as victim blamers. "Focusing on the poor and ignoring the system of power, privilege, and profit which makes them poor, is a little like blaming the corpse for the murder" (1978:24). The alternative view is that racial inequality is not fundamentally a matter of what is in people's heads, not a matter of their private individual intentions, but rather a matter of public institutions and practices that create racism or keep it alive. **Structural discrimination theories** move away from thinking about "racism in the head" toward understanding "racism in the world" (Lichtenberg, 1992:5).

Many sociologists have examined race as a structural force that permeates every aspect of life. Those who use this framework make a distinction between individual racism and institutionalized racism (Carmichael and Hamilton, 1967). **Individual racism** is related to prejudice. It consists of individual behavior that harms other individuals or their property. **Institutional racism** is structural. It comprises more than attitudes or behavior. It is structural, that is, *a complex pattern of racial advantage built into the structure of society—* a system of power and privilege that advantages some groups over others (Higginbotham and Andersen, 2009:78). Because institutional racism views inequality as part of society's structure, individuals and groups discriminate whether they are bigots or not. These individuals and groups operate within a social milieu that ensures racial dominance. The social milieu includes laws, customs, religious beliefs, and the stable arrangements and practices through which things get done in society.

Institutional or structural racism is not about beliefs. It is not only about actions directed at those considered racially different (meaning those not considered White). According to Howard Winant:

> ... structural racism is about ... the ways things work, regardless of the reasons of why, it's about outcomes, not intentions or beliefs. So, if vast inequalities in wealth persist across racial lines, for example, they may persist not because White people presently intend to impoverish Black or Brown people; they may persist because of years and years of some people doing better than others do. Inequality accumulates; injustice becomes normal ... taken for granted. (Winant, 2009:58)

While there are different structural theories of racial inequality, they all agree on the following points. First, history is important in determining present conditions and resistance to change. Historically, institutions defined and enforced norms and role relationships that were racially distinct. The United States was founded and its institutions established when Blacks were slaves, uneducated, and different culturally from the dominant Whites (Patterson, 2007:58). From the beginning, Blacks were considered inferior (the original Constitution, for example, counted a slave as three-fifths of a person). Religious beliefs buttressed this notion of the inferiority of Blacks and justified the differential allocation of privileges and sanctions in society.

Second, discrimination can occur without conscious bigotry. Everyday practices reinforce racial discrimination and deprivation. Although actions by the Ku Klux Klan have an unmistakable racial tone, many other actions (choosing to live in a suburban neighborhood, sending one's children to a private school, or opposing government intervention in hiring policies) also maintain racial dominance (Bonilla-Silva, 1996:475). With or without malicious intent, racial discrimination is the "normal" outcome of the system. Even if "racism in the head" disappeared, "racism in the world" would not, because it is the *system* that disadvantages (Lichtenberg, 1992).

Finally, institutional discrimination is reinforced because institutions are interrelated. The exclusion of minorities from the upper levels of education, for example, is likely to affect their opportunities in other institutions (type of job, level of remuneration). Similarly, poor children will probably receive an inferior education, be propertyless, suffer from bad health, and be treated unjustly by the criminal justice system. These inequities are cumulative.

Institutional derogation occurs when minority groups and their members are made to seem inferior or to possess negative stereotypes through legitimate means by the powerful in society. The portrayal of minority-group members in the media (movies, television, newspapers, and magazines) is often derogatory. For example, many studies depict Black men disproportionately as drug users, criminals, lower class, and "pathological." (Muwakkil, 1998b:18). Such stereotypes are "controlling images" that define perceptions of minorities (Collins, 1990). If we based our perceptions of certain minority populations on media images, we would have considerably skewed views. The media also provide us with explanations and interpretations intended to help us make sense of our society, including its multiracial composition. The ideas that pervade today's mass media obscure pervasive racial inequality. Instead, we are bombarded by depictions of race relations that suggest discriminatory racial barriers have been dismantled and that the United States has become a truly color-blind nation (Gallagher, 2010; Weber, 2010). Color-blind racism is the belief that ignoring race and racial differences will produce equality (Gallagher, 2010; Bonilla-Silva, 2009).

Why is the United States structured along racist lines? Structural theorists have a long-standing debate over the relative importance of race and class in shaping racial stratification. Those emphasizing class contend that the economy and the class system are what produce racial inequality. (See the discussion of the underclass later in the chapter.) Some scholars argue that modern race relations are produced by world capitalism. Using the labor of non-White peoples began as a means for White owners to accumulate profits. This perspective contends that capitalism as a system of class exploitation has shaped race and racism in the United States and the world (Bonacich, 1992a).

Other structural theories point to race itself as a primary shaper of inequality. For example, racial-formation theory proposes that the United States is organized along racial lines from top to bottom—a racial state, composed of institutions and policies to support and justify racial stratification (Omi and Winant, 1986; 1994). Another theory, called *systematic racism*, also argues that race is paramount in explaining inequality. Systematic racism includes a diverse assortment of structural practices; the unjustly gained economic and political power of Whites; the continuing resource inequalities; and the White-racist ideologies, attitudes, and institutions created to preserve White advantages and power. Systematic racism is both structural and interpersonal. "At the macro level, large-scale institutions ... routinely perpetuate racial subordination and inequalities. These institutions are created and recreated by routine actions at the micro level by individuals" (Feagin, 2000:16). Systemic racism is far more than a matter of individual bigotry, for it has been from the beginning, a material, social, and ideological reality (Feagin, 2006: xiii).

Why does the United States have this tremendous degree of racial inequality even though most White people are not "racist"? According to sociologist Bonilla-Silva (2009:176), racial inequality exists because it benefits members of the dominant race.

Racial Stratification from the Order and Conflict Perspectives

Order perspectives of race and ethnic relations have assumed that the United States is a land of opportunity and that all groups—ethnic and racial—would eventually assimilate or blend into the country's social melting pot. This was the experience of the European immigrants who came to the United States in the nineteenth and early twentieth centuries and who were absorbed into the broader society a few generations after they arrived (Pollard and O'Hare, 1999:44). Order theories accent patterns of inclusion, orderly integration, and the assimilation of racial and ethnic groups. The word *assimilate* comes from the Latin word *assimulare*, meaning "to make similar" (Feagin and Feagin, 1993:27). Order theories are concerned with how minorities adapt to the core society. These theories see the situations of Blacks and non-Whites as similar to those of earlier White immigrants. Just as White ethnics made a place for themselves in the land of opportunity, so should racial minorities. With the right motivation and behaviors, minorities can lift themselves up and succeed in the U.S. mainstream.

Conflict (or power-conflict) theories are critical of assimilation theories for ignoring social conditions that exclude racial minorities from full participation in U.S. society. Most conflict theories emphasize the deep-lying roots of racial and ethnic inequalities in the U.S. economy. Social institutions, not group culture, keep minorities stuck on the bottom rungs of society. Conflict theories argue that racial-ethnics were never meant to assimilate. Racial stratification exists because certain segments of society benefit from it. Racial-ethnics are located in the larger society in ways that prevent their assimilation. The melting pot does not apply to people of color. Differences between Whites and people of color produce conflict, not consensus, across race lines.

Neither the conflict nor the order model captures the complexity of today's multiracial society. While some minorities remain at the bottom, racially defined immigrants are entering a U.S. society that is unlike the country that absorbed the European immigrants. New theories are needed to illuminate the experiences of different racial groups and their connections to global transformations.

Discrimination against Blacks and Hispanics: Continuity and Change

The treatment of Blacks and Hispanics has been disgraceful throughout American history. Through public policies and everyday practices, they have been denied the opportunities that should be open to all people. Since World War II, however, under pressure from civil rights advocates, the government has led the way in breaking down these discriminatory practices.

"...and the winner of this week's "Race to the Bottom" is..."

Community organizing, civil rights legislation, landmark court decisions, and rising education have advanced the cause of racial equality. By the close of the twentieth century, many well-educated people of color had climbed into the middle class.

In 2008, 35 percent of African Americans and 41 percent of Latino families had incomes of $50,000 or more compared with 54 percent of White families (U.S. Bureau of the Census, 2009). They have taken advantage of fair-housing legislation and moved to the suburbs looking for better schools, safer streets, and better services. Yet having "made it" in the United States does not shield African Americans from discrimination. Studies of public accommodation have found that in stores, bars, restaurants, and theaters, middle-class Blacks are ignored or treated with hostility (Feagin and Sikes, 1994). No matter how affluent or influential, Black people are vulnerable to "micro-insults" such as being followed around in stores (Bonilla-Silva, 2003; Feagin, 2006; Muwakkil, 1998a:11).

Substantial growth of the minority middle class has not erased the problem of segregation. A class divide now characterizes minority communities across the country. As some successful people of color have become richer, many more unsuccessful ones have been marginalized. To be sure, much progress is evident in some areas. But in others, racial injustice remains deeply entrenched and is worsening (Lewis et al., 2004:104; Warren, 2011).

Racism was clearly present in the aftermath of Hurricane Katrina, the costliest natural disaster ever to hit the United States. For days, the world watched as federal officials moved slowly to assist those stranded and dying in flooded houses and overcrowded shelters in New Orleans and the Gulf Coast areas. What was exposed was not just a broken levee but race and class divides both familiar and yet new. Even media commentators raised the reasonable question of whether the fact that a majority of those hardest hit in New Orleans—low-income Black residents—had affected the slowness of the federal government response (De Parle, 2007:163; Feagin, 2006:xv).

The present segregation of African Americans cannot be dismissed as wrongs committed in the past. Today, U.S. neighborhoods remain segregated. Although residential segregation is declining it is not disappearing. Despite some progress toward integration in the last decades of the twentieth century, neighborhood segregation is a key feature of the U.S. social landscape. African Americans, in particular, continue to live in segregated neighborhoods in exceptionally high numbers (Farley and Squires, 2012:315). Levels of Hispanic segregation have been rising, with dark-skinned Hispanics having high levels of segregation than their lighter-skinned counterparts (Rugh and Massey, 2010). Residential segregation deprives minorities of economic and educational opportunities.

Income

The average income for White families and households is greater than the average income for those of Blacks and Hispanics. Racial income disparities have remained unchanged over time. In 2009, the median income of Black households was about $33,000, the median income of White households was about $53,400, and the median income of Hispanic households was about $39,000 (U.S. Bureau of the Census, 2009). Even though the median household income for Blacks is still below that of Hispanics, per-person income for Hispanics is actually lower because Hispanics tend to have larger households. (See Figure 11.2.)

Although the racial income gap is wide, the *racial wealth gap* is even wider. White families are generally wealthier than Black or Latino families (Collins et al., 1999). *Wealth* is the sum of important assets a family owns. It includes home ownership, pension funds, savings accounts, and investments. Many of these resources are inherited across the generations. White families generally have greater resources for their children and bequeath them as

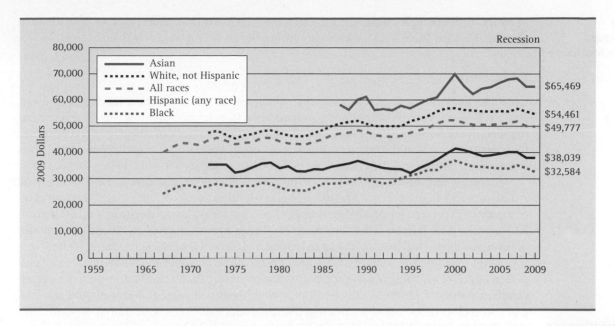

FIGURE 11.2

Real Median
Household Income
by Race and
Hispanic Origin:
1967 to 2009

Source: Carmen De
Navas-Walt, Bernadette
Proctor, and Jessica
C. Smith, 2010. U.S.
Census Bureau, Current
Population Reports,
P60-238, *Income,
Poverty, and Health
Insurance Coverage in
the United States: 2009.*
Washington, DC: U.S.
Government Printing
Office, p.6.

assets at death. Sociologists call this "the cost of being Black" (Oliver and Shapiro, 1995). According to this line of thought the African American disadvantage will persist until the wealth divide is closed (Shapiro, 2004).

One important indicator of a family's wealth is home ownership. Paying off a home mortgage is the way most people build net worth over their lifetimes. But because racial minorities encounter discrimination in their efforts to buy, finance, or insure a home, a great race gap remains (Farley and Squires, 2010:315). Fewer than half of Blacks and Latinos and fewer than 60 percent of Asians and American Indians own their own homes, compared to three-quarters of Whites. Rampant racial discrimination prevails in the housing market, even after forty years of federal fair housing laws (Briggs, 2005; Crowley, 2002:25; Leondar-Wright et al., 2005:11).

Poverty rates for all minority groups are higher than those of Whites. The percentage of Blacks, Hispanics, and Native Americans in poverty is about three times that of Whites. Even Asian Americans, who have a higher average income than Whites, are more likely to live in families with incomes below the poverty line (O'Hare, 1992:37). Although most poor people are White, Blacks remain disproportionately poor, followed by Hispanics and then Whites. In 2009, 11 percent of Whites were poor, compared with 11 percent of Asian Americans, 23 percent of Hispanics, and 25 percent of Blacks (U.S. Bureau of the Census, 2009). Although this is an advance for African Americans in recent decades brought about by the growth of the Black middle class, it is still a shamefully high number. By contrast, immigration has increased poverty rates among Hispanics (Alter, 2007:37).

Many factors explain the difference in White and minority earnings. Racial-ethnics are concentrated in the South and Southwest, where incomes are lower for everyone. Another part of the explanation is the differing age structure of minorities. They are younger, on average, than is the White population. A group with a higher proportion of young people of working age will have a lower average earning level, higher rates of unemployment, and lower rates of labor-force participation.

Looking at racial inequalities by age reveals another disturbing pattern. The degree of inequality increases after the teenage years. Racial disparities become greater in peak earning years. This fact suggests that another part of the explanation for racial inequalities in earnings lies in the lack of education and skill levels required to move out of poor-paying jobs. All these explanations leave a substantial amount of inequality unexplained. Minorities at all levels of unemployment and education still earn less than do Whites, as we will see in Chapter 13. (See Table 11.1 for average earnings by race, Hispanic origin, and sex.)

Education

In 1954, the Supreme Court outlawed segregation in the schools. Yet the landmark *Brown v. Board of Education* ruling did not end segregation. In fact, schools are now rapidly resegregating. Following Supreme Court decisions in the early 1990s, school resegregation continues to grow in all parts of the country. Black and Latino segregation is usually race and class segregation, both from Whites and from middle-class students (Orfield and Lee, 2010:331).

Among young adults, Hispanics have the lowest educational attainment, while Whites and Asians have the highest. The 2009 high school graduation rate for Whites was 87 percent compared with 85 percent for Asian Americans, 81 percent for African Americans, and 60 percent for Hispanics (U.S. Bureau of the Census, 2009). This is a growing problem, since most new jobs in the new century will require education beyond high school (Pollard and O'Hare, 1999:30).

What explains the minority education gap? Although some educators point to a "culture of oppression" that causes underperformance among Black and Latino students, recent research points to larger social conditions. Neighborhood segregation, unequal schools, and social class differences all work together to produce different educational opportunities (Lewis et al., 2004; Orfield and Lee, 2012; Rothstein, 2007:120).

Minority participation in higher education has risen since the 1960s. College campuses are far more diverse than they were a century ago (Rothstein, 2007). Nevertheless, there are large racial gaps in college enrollment. Although many colleges actively recruit students of color, many factors contribute to low retention rates. Even when they reach college, students of color often confront a range of discriminatory barriers. Studies have consistently found that they are more alienated than White students and drop out more often than White students. Discrimination by Whites on and off campus is a recurring problem (Feagin, 2000:170).

All these disparities translate into economic inequalities. Yet education alone is not the answer. Even with a college degree, African Americans and Latinos had far higher

---

TABLE 11.1

Mean Personal Income by Race-Ethnicity, Sex, and Education (2008)

			Educational Attainment			
		All	*No High School Diploma*	*High School or College*	*Some College*	*Bachelor's Degree or Higher*
White	Male	55,900	23,961	39,996	47,175	93,765
	Female	35,748	13,676	26,978	30,759	53,816
Black or African American	Male	38,185	20,517	31,909	36,277	64,717
	Female	31,591	15,059	24,752	29,456	51,450
Asian	Male	61,369	22,777	33,699	38,597	83,084
	Female	43,393	18,597	25,416	30,344	58,446
Hispanic	Male	35,032	24,056	31,818	39,772	70,416
	Female	25,805	15,358	22,902	26,936	45,716
Totals	Male	54,063	23,398	38,670	45,561	90,795
	Female	35,429	14,118	26,527	30,484	53,873

Source: U.S. Census Bureau (2009). "Current Population Survey, Annual Social and Economic Supplement," Table generated at url: *http://www.census.gov/hhes/www/cpstc/cps_table_creator.html.*

unemployment rates than their White counterparts. This is compounded by the fact that education does not pay equally. Minority membership, regardless of level of education, is underpaid compared with Whites of similar education. A highly educated White man still makes more money than anyone else. (See Table 11.1.)

Unemployment

African Americans and Latinos are more likely than Whites to be unemployed. For the last three decades, unemployment rates among Black workers have been twice that of White workers, with Latinos in between. In 2011, the unemployment rate for Latinos was 11 percent, compared with 15 percent for African Americans and 8 percent for Whites (Bureau of Labor Statistics, 2011; U.S. Department of Labor, 2007). Minority teenagers had an even harder time. The unemployment rate among Black teens was 37 percent, for Latinos it was 30 percent, and for Whites it was 21 percent (Bureau of Labor Statistics, 2011).

These government rates are misleading because they count as employed the almost 6 million people who work part-time because they cannot find full-time jobs, and they do not count as unemployed the discouraged former workers, numbering more than 1 million, who have given up their search for work.

Type of Employment

African Americans and Latinos have always been an important component of the U.S. labor force. However, their job prospects and the jobs they hold are different from those of other people in the United States. Minorities are twice as likely as Whites to be unemployed; they are more likely to work in low-skilled occupations and less likely to work in managerial or professional occupations. (See Table 11.2.) Black and Latino workers are more likely to be in jobs with pay too low to lift a family of four above the poverty line (Leondar-Wright et al., 2005:9). Sociological research shows racial inequalities in workplace recruitment, hiring, firing, job levels, pay scales, promotion, and degree of autonomy on the job. Seemingly neutral practices can advantage some groups and adversely affect others (American Sociological Association, 2003).

TABLE 11.2

Selected Labor Force characteristics by Race and Ethnicity

		Total %	Black %	Hispanic %	Asian %	White %
In civilian labor force	Men	71.2	65	77.8	73.2	72
	Women	58.6	59.9	56.5	57	58.7
Unemployed	Men	10.5	18.4	12.7	7.8	9.6
	Women	8.6	13.8	12.3	7.1	7.7
Occupations						
Management and professional	Men	34.2	23.5	15.3	47.7	34.8
	Women	40.6	33.8	24.1	46.1	41.5
Sales and service	Men	31.4	39.5	35.9	32.7	30.3
	Women	53.3	59	64.9	46.5	52.7
Skilled and unskilled manual	Men	34.4	37	48.9	19.6	34.9
	Women	6.1	7.2	7.9	7.3	5.9

Source: Bureau of Labor Statistics, 2010. "Current Population Survey, Household Data Annual Averages," Tables 4, 5, and 10. Can be accessed from *http://www.bls.gov/cps/tables.htm*

Immigrants generally work in the lowest rungs of the low-wage workforce. They are more likely than natives to be food-preparation workers, sewing machine operators, parking lot attendants, housekeepers, waiters, private household cleaners, food processing workers, agricultural workers, elevator operators, janitors, operators, fabricators, and laborers (Schulman, 2007:101). Although Hispanic and Native American minorities are in the least-rewarding jobs, and many face discrimination in hiring and promotion, the occupational status of minorities improved slowly during the last decade. Between 1990 and 2010, the percentage of Blacks in management and professional occupations increased from 17 to 29 percent, while the percentage increased from 13 to 18 percent for Hispanics (Pollard and O'Hare, 1999:33; Bureau of Labor Statistics, 2011). Despite these gains, however, a huge gap remains. As more minorities enter high-status work, they are confronting new forms of job discrimination in the form of "job ceilings" that keep them out of executive suites and boardrooms (Higginbotham, 1994).

Globalization and shifts in the U.S. economy have diminished work opportunities across the land and have produced a job crisis in minority communities. (See Chapter 8.) The Great Recession has affected minority communities much like a depression and has threatened the viability of many Black communities. In 2009, joblessness for 16–24-year-old Black men reached Great Depression proportions with a rate of 34 percent—more than three times the rate for the general U.S. population (Ehrenreich and Muhammad, 2009; Haynes, 2009).

Because African Americans and Latinos established successful niches in civil service, they are also being replaced by government downsizing (American Sociological Association, 2003). The new economy will be increasingly made up of people of color. If they continue to be denied equal access to higher-paying jobs, the entire society will be at risk for poverty and other problems associated with economic inequality.

Health

The health of the U.S. population is distributed unevenly across race. Hispanics are the most likely to be without health coverage. 31 percent of Hispanics, 18 percent of African Americans, 14 percent of Asian Americans, and 13 percent of Whites were not covered by private or government medical insurance in 2009 (U.S. Bureau of the Census, 2009). Hispanics born outside the United States were almost twice as likely to lack health insurance as their U.S.-born counterparts. Many are unfamiliar with the U.S. health care system, and a few are illegal immigrants who are afraid to seek medical assistance (del Pinal and Singer, 1997:37; Folbre, Heintz, and the Center for Popular Economics, 2000).

In the United States we emphasize the role of personal responsibility in determining health. But research finds that health disparities are affected by social conditions. For example, racial minorities are more likely than other groups to live near hazardous waste facilities. **Environmental racism** is the disproportionate exposure of some racial groups to environmental toxic substances. Race is the strongest predictor of hazardous waste facilities in the country, even after adjustment for social class. Even before Hurricane Katrina struck in 2005, New Orleans was already struggling with environmental assaults that ranged from floodwaters to toxic debris. People of color were the most vulnerable to these assaults. Although public

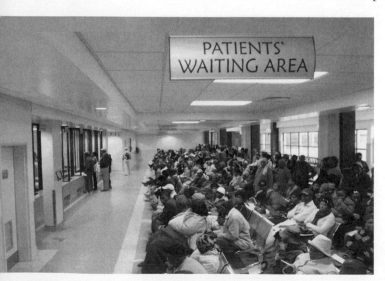

Lower income and minorities rely on hospital emergency rooms for general health care.

attention has focused on rebuilding the Gulf coast, a lesser-known crisis of lethal debris lingers, left over from hurricane damage (Bullard and Wright, 2009). Nationally, three out of five people of color live in communities with abandoned toxic waste sites because of land use, housing patterns, and infrastructure development (Bullard, 2007:87).

The health disadvantages of living in impoverished neighborhoods cannot be overstated. Those living in "high opportunity" neighborhoods, which are typically White, can expect to live up to twenty years longer than residents of a "low opportunity" neighborhood in the same city. Researchers at the Health Policy Institute of the Joint Center for Political and Economic Studies in Washington, D.C., claim that zip code is more important than genetic code in determining a person's health! (Coffey, 2011:A12).

Racial disparities are found in access to health care and treatment of serious disease. Minorities receive lower-quality health care than Whites, even when their insurance and income are the same, because of racial prejudice and difference in the quality of health care plans (Stolberg, 2002; Brown and Wellman, 2005:191).On virtually every measure of health, African Americans and Latinos are disadvantaged, as revealed in the following selected facts:

- Compared to the general population, Blacks and Hispanics are less likely to have a consistent source of medical care and more likely to use emergency rooms as a primary source of care (Forrest and Whelan, 2000).
- Pharmacies in segregated neighborhoods are less likely to have adequate medical supplies, and hospitals in these neighborhoods are more likely to close (Williams and Jackson, 2005).
- Hispanic/Latino children are more likely than non-Hispanic White children to live in poverty and experience a disproportionate burden of infant mortality, low-birth weight asthma, endocrine, neurological, and behavioral disorders which may be associated with exposure to toxic substances (Office of Minority Health and Health Disparities, 2011).
- HIV/AIDS has had a devastating impact on minorities across the United States. Racial and ethnic minorities accounted for 68 percent of the newly diagnosed cases of HIV and AIDS in 2007 (U.S. Department of Health and Human Services, 2009).

Contemporary Trends and Issues in U.S. Racial and Ethnic Relations

Racial diversity presents new social conditions that reflect differences in group power and access to social resources. Three major trends reveal old and new forms of racial inequality: growing racial strife, the economic polarization of minorities, and a national shift in U.S. racial policies. These trends are occurring in a global context, closely associated with macro social forces at work around the world.

Growing Racial Strife

Although the social dynamics of race are changing, the United States is still plagued by racial divisions. The growing immigrant and minority presence together with the economic crisis gripping the nation are adding *new* tensions in society. Here, as in other countries racial and ethnic diversity is marked by growing conflict. Some cities are divided societies where minorities seldom meet Whites as neighbors, as classmates in public schools, in church or in the new ethnic shopping centers now springing up across the country (Harris and Bennett, 1995:158).

Anti-Hispanic incidents increased steadily during the last two decades. Crimes against Hispanics are on the rise. Anti-immigration movements often translate into hate-related activities. One effect of the increasing anti-immigrant sentiment in the nation is the surge in incidents of vigilantism—unauthorized attempts to enforce immigration laws by ordinary citizens. Some private citizens are increasingly taking the law into their own hands to stem the perceived "flood" of illegal immigrants in the country (National Council of La Raza, 1999; Southern Poverty Law Center, 2006; 2007).

Current debates about foreigners have produced anti-immigration laws and policies such as Arizona's 2010 legislation requiring immigrants to carry proof of their legal status and to show IDs to police officers who suspect they may be illegally in the United States (Martin and Midgely, 2010; Navarro, 2011). We also see new expressions of anti-Muslim/anti-Arab racism. Like old-fashioned forms of Bigotry and hate crimes, this racism is also fueled by misbeliefs about minorities (Blauner, 2001:191).

Racial conflict is often associated with uncertain economic conditions. Lack of jobs, housing, and other resources can add to fear and minority scapegoating on the part of Whites. In Florida and many parts of the West and Southwest, perceptions that Cubans, Mexicans, and other Hispanics are taking jobs from Anglos have touched off racial tensions. Racial tensions often erupt in violence between Whites and minorities and among minorities themselves as individuals compete for a shrinking number of jobs and other opportunities.

Instead of moving society "past race," the historic election of the first African American president has thrust some incidents of racial conflict onto center stage. Prominent Democrats such as former President Carter have publically speculated that race—and by implication racism—is behind some of the partisan attacks of President Obama at venues ranging from town hall meetings to the floor of congress, and the "birther" movement's rumors about the president's birthplace.

More Racially Based Groups and Activities

The Southern Poverty Law Center documented 1,000 hate groups in forty-eight states and the District of Columbia in 2010, a number that has swelled by 66 percent since 2000 (Potok, 2011). Hate groups include White supremacist groups with such diverse elements as the Ku Klux Klan, Neo-Confederate groups (those describing Southern culture as fundamentally White), Nazi-identified parties, and skinheads. Many groups use the Internet to spread their literature to young people. As a result, more than half of all hate crimes are now committed by young people, ages fifteen to twenty-four. In addition to racist websites, cyber extremism flourishes on e-mail and in discussion groups and chat rooms (Intelligence Report, 2001). (See the panel Technology and Society titled "Race and Computer Technology.") Racism is also fueled by the proliferation of cable TV hosts, who spread and legitimize extremist propaganda. The rise in racial extremism is driven by changing racial composition of the country and the nation's economic difficulties.

Profiling and Maltreatment. Racial discrimination in the criminal justice system has drawn scrutiny in recent years. The past three decades have seen "numerous cases of race-related police brutality and misconduct, and official acknowledgements of systematic racial profiling (Lewis et al., 2004:95). Blacks and dark-skinned Latinos are disproportionately targeted by police officers. Lower-class communities where minorities reside are subjected to a higher level of policy suspicion, stops, interrogations, and searches (Bonilla-Silva, 2003; Warren et al., 2006). Racial profiling is the use of race and ethnicity as clues to criminality and potential terrorism. According to the Federal Bureau of Justice Statistics, in 2005, Black drivers were twice as likely to be arrested during traffic stops, while Hispanic drivers were more likely than Black or White drivers to receive a ticket (Robinson, 2007). Racial profiling on the highways has become so prevalent that a term has emerged to explain it: "driving while Black" (Bonilla-Silva, 2003). Since September 11, Arab Americans, Muslims, and other Middle Easterners have been the targets of threats, gunshots, firebombs, and other forms of

Race and Computer Technology

Computer and internet access affords great advantages in all areas of life including jobs, health, family, social networking, and entertainment. People without these skills are seriously handicapped. The disparity impedes social mobility and reinforces racial inequality. Racial differences in computer access and use reflect larger social divisions.

- Lower income racial minorities have less internet access to health and employment information because they lack home computers (Kaiser Family Foundation, 2010).
- Without home computers the less advantaged must use the internet more for entertainment than for empowering themselves (The Associated Press, 2011).
- Social networking sites that reproduce racial categories in the wider society are gaining friends and expanding swiftly (The Associated Press, 2011).

Studies have found that as technology evolves new forms of online racism emerge and overt racism is more pervasive.

- White supremacist web pages cloak their messages to mirror objective discussion about race. Less critical users do not see their overt racism and imbedded distortions of fact (Statzel, 2010).
- An interactive video gaming discussion panel noted that the addition of less anonymous voice chat features introduced racial bias. The way gamers "sounded" to each other became a factor where texting did not. The panel also noted that increased contact among various groups might ease racism (Young, 2011).
- A genocidal pattern emerged from a popular Chinese fantasy role-playing game. Characters with certain physical attributes were shunned (Young, 2011).

vigilante violence (Fahim, 2003). Fear of terrorism has provoked a rash of hate crimes and a national debate about the official use of profiling—that is, the use of race and ethnicity as clues to criminality and potential terrorism.

Campus Racial Tensions. Recent headlines about racism on college campuses have surprised many people because educational institutions are formally integrated. Yet campus racism is widespread. Over the past few years, students of color have reported dramatic increases in acts of racial discrimination, intolerance, hate crimes and insensitivity among cultures at institutions of higher education. In 2010, Arizona abolished ethnic studies programs throughout the state.

According to the U.S. Department of Education and watchdog and advocacy groups, every year, more than a half million college students are targets of bias-driven slurs or physical assaults. Every day, at least one hate crime occurs on a college campus and every minute, a college student somewhere sees or hears racist, sexist, homophobic, or otherwise biased words or images. These problems are not isolated or unusual events. Instead, they reflect racial trends in the wider society.

Social and Economic Isolation in U.S. Cities

The notion of a troubled "underclass," locked in U.S. inner cities by a deficient culture, is commonly used to explain racial poverty. According to this reasoning, broken families and bad lifestyles prevent minorities from taking advantage of the opportunities created by anti-discrimination laws. However, like the older cultural-deficiency models we discussed earlier, this explanation is wrong on many counts. It relies heavily on behavioral traits to explain poverty. It blames the victims for conditions that are actually rooted in social structure. Social and economic changes have removed jobs and resources from inner-city residents. This reality is a better explanation of poverty among African Americans.

Hurricane Katrina exposed relationship between racial disparities and emergency preparedness in the northern Gulf Coast. But disparities between Blacks and Whites are not unique to New Orleans. In large cities across the nation, African Americans are much more likely than Whites to live in communities that are geographically and economically isolated from the economic opportunities, services, and institutions that people need to succeed. Of the fifteen U.S. metropolitan areas with the most African Americans in absolute numbers in 2000, New Orleans had the highest Black poverty rate at 33 percent. But racial differences in poverty were stark in each of these metropolitan areas except New York. In Chicago, Newark, Memphis, and St. Louis, African Americans were about five times more likely than Whites to be impoverished. High poverty rates for African Americans are linked to lower levels of education and employment. In 2000, Blacks in these large cities were also far less likely to own a car or phone (Saenz, 2005:1).

Not having a home computer impedes social and job mobility for low-income minorities.

Without jobs, cars, or phones, inner-city residents are utterly vulnerable to urban disasters. This social entrapment can be explained *structurally*. In his classic studies of African American poverty at the end of the twentieth century, sociologist William J. Wilson found that the social problems of the inner city are due to transformations of the larger economy and to the class structure of ghetto neighborhoods (1987; 1996). The movement of middle-class Black professionals from the inner city has left behind a concentration of the most disadvantaged segments of the Black urban population. Wilson's research reveals how family dissolution and welfare are connected to the structural removal of work from the inner city. The Black inner city is not destroying itself by its own culture; rather, it is being destroyed by economic forces.

Rising poverty rates among Latinos have led many policy makers and media analysts to conclude that Latinos have joined inner-city African Americans to form a hopeless "underclass." Although changes in the U.S. economy have also hit Latinos hard because of their low educational attainment and their labor market position, structural unemployment has a different effect on the many diverse Latino barrios across the nation (Moore and Pinderhughes, 1994). The loss of jobs in Rust Belt cities has left many Puerto Ricans living in a bleak ghetto economy. Mexicans living in the Southwest, where low-paying jobs remain, have not suffered the same degree of economic dislocation. Despite high levels of poverty, Latino communities do not conform to the conventional portrait of the underclass.

A structural analysis of concentrated poverty does not deny that inner cities are beset with a disproportionate share of social problems. As poverty is more concentrated in inner cities, crime and violence proliferate. The poor may adopt violence as survival strategies. This escalates violence even further (Massey, 1996). As Wilson explains, "... structural conditions provide the context within which cultural responses to chronic economic and racial subordination are developed" (Wilson, 2010:61). A structural analysis focuses on social conditions, not immoral people. Vanishing jobs and many forms of unemployment are related to changes in the organization of work that accompany corporate globalization. (See Chapter 8.)

Racial Policies in the New Century

The 1960s civil rights movement legalized race-specific remedies to end racial bias. Government policies based on race overturned segregation laws, opened voting booths, created new job opportunities, and brought hopes of racial justice for people of color. As long as it appeared that conditions were improving, government policies to end racial justice remained in place.

But by the end of the 1980s, the United States had become a very different society from the one in which civil rights legislation was enacted. Economic restructuring brought new dislocations to both Whites and minorities. As racial minorities became an ever larger share of the U.S. population, racial matters grew more politicized. Many Whites began to feel uncomfortable with race-conscious policies in schools and the workplace. The social climate fostered an imaginary White disadvantage, said to be caused by affirmative action multiculturalism. Although there is no research evidence for White disadvantage, a powerful conservative movement is producing new debates about the fairness of racial policies. A new form of racism has emerged. **Color-blind racism** is the belief that race no longer matters in people's experiences (Gallagher, 2012).

Color-blindness is the basis for the current downsizing of policies related to affirmative action, school desegregation, and voting rights. Growing racial populations are controlled through many different forms of discrimination, including employment practices, neighborhood and school segregation, and other inequalities discussed in this chapter. In addition, the demise of the welfare state and the retreat from health care and other forms of social responsibility have caused minorities to lose ground. Finally, international systems of dominance (global capitalism and geopolitical relations are producing still more racial inequalities in the United States) (Allen and Chung, 2000:802; Barlow, 2003).

Despite claims about color-blindness, race does matter. As Higginbotham and Andersen put it, "race and ethnicity are present throughout day-to-day life; they are embedded in social institutions and in social relationships. And they have real and recurring social and historical consequences. Neither race nor ethnicity just go away by denying that they are there (Higginbotham and Andersen, 2012:x).

While racism is a tool for exclusion, it is also the basis for political mobilization. Since the country was founded, people of color have struggled for social change. All racially defined groups have rich histories of resistance, community building, and social protest. Racial projects, according to Omi and Winant (1994), are organized efforts to distribute social and economic resources along racial lines. Through social movements, groups organize and act to bring about social change. Despite the new racial climate, the struggle against racism continues. Multiracial organizations, composed of racial-ethnic and White antiracist activists, continue to work at national and local levels to fight and eradicate racist prejudices and institutional racism.

CHAPTER REVIEW

1. Racial and ethnic stratification are basic features of U.S. society. They are also found throughout the world and are important features of globalization. Patterns of inequality are built into everyday social practices. They exclude people from full and equal participation in social institutions. Racial and ethnic stratification exist because they benefit certain segments of society.

2. The concept of race is a social invention. It is not biologically significant. Racial groups are set apart and singled out for unequal treatment.

3. An ethnic group is culturally distinct in race, religion, or national origin. The group has a distinctive culture. Some ethnic groups such as Jews, Poles, and Italians have distinguishing cultural characteristics that stem from religion and national origin. Because racial groups also have distinctive cultural characteristics, they are referred to as *racial-ethnic groups*.

4. Minority racial and ethnic groups are systematically disadvantaged by society's institutions. Both race and ethnicity are traditional bases for systems of inequality, although there are historical and contemporary differences in the societal placement of racial-ethnics and White ethnics in this society.

5. Racial-ethnic groups are socially subordinated and remain culturally distinct within U.S. society. African Americans, Latinos, Asian Americans, and Native Americans are constructed as both racially and culturally distinct. Each group has a distinctive culture, shares a common history, and has developed a common identity within a larger society that subordinates it.

6. Deficiency theories view minority-group members as unequal because they lack some important feature common among the majority. These deficiencies may be biological (such as low intelligence) or cultural (such as the culture of poverty).

7. Bias theories place the blame for inequality on the prejudiced attitudes of the dominant group. These theories, however, do not explain the discriminatory acts of the unprejudiced, which are aimed at preserving privilege.

8. Structural theories argue that inequality is the result of external constraints in society rather than internal cultural factors. There are four main features of institutional discrimination: (a) forces of history shape present conditions; (b) discrimination can occur without conscious bigotry; (c) institutional discrimination is less visible than are individual acts of discrimination; and (d) discrimination is reinforced by the interrelationships among the institutions of society.

9. Civil rights legislation improved the status of some racial-ethnics, yet the overall position of Blacks and Latinos relative to Whites has not improved. Large gaps remain in work, earnings, and education. Global and economic transformations have contributed to the persistent poverty in U.S. urban centers.

10. The racial demography of the United States is changing dramatically. Immigration and high birth rates among minorities are making this a multiracial, multicultural society. These trends are also creating racial anxiety and racial conflict.

11. Public policy has shifted from race-conscious remedies to a color-blind climate that is dismantling historic civil rights reforms.

KEY TERMS

Dominant group	Racial-ethnic groups	Individual racism
Minority group	Deficiency theories	Institutional racism
Racial formation	Bias theories	Environmental racism
Ethnic group	Structural discrimination theories	Color-blind racism

STUDY QUESTIONS

1. What constitutes a minority group?
2. What is the key difference between deficiency theories and bias theories as they explain the existence of minorities?
3. Order theories argue that minorities should eventually assimilate. What does this mean, and why does the conflict perspective disagree with this assumption?
4. How do everyday social arrangements work to keep minorities subordinate?
5. What is meant by the changing demography of race? What are the anticipated consequences of this trend for schools, employment, incidents of violence, and life chances?
6. Is the persistent poverty of minorities a consequence of culture or structure?

WEB RESOURCES

http://www.census.gov/pubinfo/www/hotlinks.html
This is the U.S. Census Bureau site that contains the most recent census data collected on racial-ethnic groups in the United States.

http://www.usanetwork.com/functions/nohate/erasehate.html
Erase the Hate is affiliated with USA Network and is "dedicated to combating hate and racism while promoting respect and understanding."

http://www.abacon.com/sociology/soclinks/race.html
This site, by Allyn and Bacon, offers sociology links to race, ethnicity, and inequality.

http://www.webcom.com/~intvoice/
Interracial Voice is "an independent, information-oriented, networking newsjournal, serving the mixed-race/interracial community in cyberspace."

http://www.nativeweb.org/
The Native Web offers information about and resources for indigenous cultures around the world.

http://www.hispaniconline.com/
Hispanic Online has a mission "to offer more news, resources, and entertainment options that are relevant to Latinos than any other site."

http://www.asianamerican.net/index.html

Asia American Net "is the first and the only web site whose mission is to serve all Asian American communities and to promote and strengthen cultural, educational, and commercial ties between Asia and North America." This site is for people looking to learn more about Asia and also for "Asian American communities to remind them of their national and cultural origins they can be proud of."

http://www.omhrc.gov/

The Office of Minority Health looks to improve the health of racial and ethnic minorities and to eliminate the racial disparities in health.

http://afroamhistory.about.com/

This site contains information on African American history. Information on influential African Americans and details of important historical events related to African Americans can be found here.

http://usinfo.state.gov/usa/race/hate/homepage.htm

This site has links to and information about hate crimes.

http://www.ctwo.org/

Center for Third World Organizing is "a racial justice organization dedicated to building a social justice movement led by people of color."

http://www.arc.org/

Applied Research Center is "a public policy, educational and research institute whose work emphasizes issues of race and social change."

CHAPTER 12

Gender Inequality

Every society treats women and men differently. Today, there is no nation where women and men are equals. Worldwide, women perform an estimated 60 percent of the work, yet they earn only 10 percent of the income and own only 10 percent of the land. Two-thirds of the world's illiterate are women. Despite massive political changes and economic progress in countries throughout the world, women continue to be the victims of abuse and discrimination. Even where women have made important strides in politics and the professions, women's overall progress remains uneven.

This chapter examines the social basis of gender inequality. We show how gender disparity is built into the larger social world we inhabit. From the macro level of the global economy, through the institutions of society, to interpersonal relations, gender is the basis for dividing labor, assigning roles, and allocating social rewards. Until recently, these differences seemed natural. However, new research shows that gender is not natural at all. Instead, "women" and "men" are social creations. To emphasize this point, sociologists distinguish between *sex* and *gender*. **Sex** refers to the biological differences between females and males. **Gender** refers to the social and cultural patterns attached to women and men. Both sex and gender organize social life throughout the world.

Gender is not only about women. Men often think of themselves as "genderless," as if gender did not matter in the daily experience of their lives. Yet, from birth through old age, men are also **gendered**. This gendering process, the transformation of biological males into socially interacting men, is a central experience for men (Kimmel and Messner, 2007:xvi). In the big picture, gender divisions make women and men unequal. But we cannot understand gender, or women's and men's experiences, by looking at gender alone; gender operates together with other power systems such as race, class, and sexual orientation. These overlapping categories produce different gender experiences for women and men of different races and classes. Nevertheless, the gender system denies both women and men the full range of human and social possibilities. This chapter examines gender stratification in U.S. society at both structural and interpersonal levels of organization. We take a **feminist approach** (one in support of women's equality) to show that social factors make women unequal to men.

Women and Men Are Differentiated and Ranked

Gender stratification refers to the hierarchical placement of the sexes that gives women unequal opportunities, resources, and power. Although there is worldwide variation in women's and men's roles, gender inequality exists in most parts of the world. Every society has certain ideas about what women and men should be like as well as ways of producing people who are much like these expectations.

Scientists have competing explanations for gender differences. Biological models argue that innate biological differences between men and women produce different social behaviors. Anthropological models look at masculinity and femininity cross-culturally, stressing the variations in women's and men's roles. Sociologists treat gender as social creation deeply embedded in society.

Is Gender Biological or Social?

We know that there *are* biological differences between the two sexes. Debates about gender differences often fall back on "nature vs. nurture" arguments. The nurture camp argues that most differences are socially constructed. The opposing camp claims that differences between women and men are rooted in evolution. In 2005, Larry Summers, then president of Harvard University, caused a storm by suggesting that innate ability could be a reason there were so few women in the top positions in mathematics, engineering, and the physical sciences. Biological explanations have also become a favorite theme in the media (Barnett and Rivers, 2004; The Economist, 2006:70). Is the popular biological explanation correct? Are men hardwired to dominate women? To answer this question, let us first review the evidence for each position.

Biological Bases for Gender Roles. Males and females are different from the moment of conception. Chromosomal and hormonal differences make females and males physically different. Hormonal differences in the sexes are also significant. The male hormones (androgens) and female hormones (estrogens) direct the process of sex differentiation from about six weeks after conception throughout life. They make males taller, heavier, and more muscular. At puberty, they trigger the production of secondary sexual characteristics. In males, these include body and facial hair, a deeper voice, broader shoulders, and a muscular body. In females, puberty brings pubic hair, menstruation, the ability to lactate, prominent breasts, and relatively broad hips. Actually, males and females have both sets of hormones. The relative proportion of androgens and estrogens gives a person masculine or feminine physical traits.

These hormonal differences may explain in part why males tend to be more active, aggressive, and dominant than females. However, there are only slight differences in the level of hormones between girls and boys in childhood. Yet, researchers find differences in aggression between young girls and boys (Fausto-Sterling, 1992).

Biological differences between women and men are only averages. They are often influenced by other factors. For example, although men are on the average larger than women, body size is influenced by diet and physical activity, which in turn may be influenced by culture, class, and race. The all-or-none categorizing of gender traits is misleading because there is considerable overlap in the distribution of traits possessed by women and men. Although most men are stronger than most women, some men are weaker than some women, and vice versa. And although males are on the average more aggressive than females, greater difference may be found among males than among males and females (Barnett and Rivers, 2004; Basow, 1996:81). Furthermore, gender is constantly changing. Femininity and masculinity are not uniformly shaped from genetic makeup. Instead, they are modeled differently (1) from one culture to another, (2) within any one culture over time, (3) over the course of all men's and women's lives, and (4) between and among different groups of women and men, depending on class, race, ethnicity, and sexuality (Kimmel, 1992:166).

The Social Bases for Gender Roles. Cross-cultural evidence shows a wide variation of behaviors for the sexes. Table 12.1 provides some interesting cross-cultural data from 224 societies on the division of labor by sex. This table shows that for the majority of activities, societies are not uniform in their gendered division of labor. Even activities requiring strength, presumably a male trait, are not strictly apportioned to men. In fact, activities such as burden bearing and water carrying are done by females more than by males. Even an activity such as house building is not exclusively male. Although there is a wide variety in the social roles assigned to women and men, their roles seldom vary "randomly" (O'Kelly, 1980:41). Despite the widespread cultural variation in women's and men's activities, every known society makes gender a major category for organizing social life. This is the social construction of gender. It is a sociological perspective that calls on social rather than biological differences to show how all societies transform biological females and males into social, interacting women and men (Andersen, 2011).

TABLE 12.1

Gender Allocation in Selected Technological Activities in 224 Societies

	Number of Societies in Which the Activity Is Performed by:					
Activity	Males Exclusively	Males Usually	Both Sexes Equally	Females Usually	Females Exclusively	Percent Male
Smelting of ores	37	0	0	0	0	100.0
Hunting	139	5	0	0	0	99.3
Boat building	84	3	3	0	1	96.6
Mining and quarrying	31	1	2	0	1	93.7
Land clearing	95	34	6	3	1	90.5
Fishing	83	45	8	5	2	86.7
Herding	54	24	14	3	3	82.4
House building	105	30	14	9	20	77.4
Generation of fire	40	6	16	4	20	62.3
Preparation of skins	39	4	2	5	31	54.6
Crop planting	27	35	33	26	20	54.4
Manufacture of leather products	35	3	2	5	29	53.2
Crop tending	22	23	24	30	32	44.6
Milking	15	2	8	2	21	43.8
Carrying	18	12	46	34	36	39.3
Loom weaving	24	0	6	8	50	32.5
Fuel gathering	25	12	12	23	94	27.2
Manufacture of clothing	16	4	11	13	78	22.4
Pottery making	14	5	6	6	74	21.1
Dairy production	4	0	0	0	24	14.3
Cooking	0	2	2	63	117	8.3
Preparation of vegetables	3	1	4	21	145	5.7

Source: Adapted from George P. Murdock and Caterina Provost, 1973. "Factors in the Division of Labor by Sex. A Cross-Cultural Analysis." *Ethnology* 12 (April):207. Reprinted by permission.

Gender and Power

Gender differences are social creations that are embedded in society. The term **gendered institutions** means that entire institutions are patterned by gender (Acker, 1992; Lorber, 2005). Everywhere we look—the global economy, politics, religion, education, and family life—men are in power. But men are not uniformly dominant. Some men have great power over other men. In fact, most men do not feel powerful; most feel powerless, trapped in stifling old roles and unable to implement the changes in their lives that they want (Kimmel, 1992:171). Nevertheless, socially defined differences between women and men legitimate **male dominance**, which refers to the beliefs and placement that value men over women and that institutionalize male control of socially valued resources. **Patriarchy** is the term used for forms of social organization in which men are dominant over women.

Like race and class, "gender is a multilevel system of differences and disadvantages that includes socioeconomic arrangements and widely held cultural beliefs at the macro level, ways of behaving in relation to others, at the interactional level, and acquired traits and identities at the individual level" (Ridgeway, 1997:219). Gender inequality is tied to other inequalities such as race, class, and sexuality to sort women and men differently. These inequalities also work together to produce differences *among women* and differences *among men*. Some women derive benefits from their race and their class while they are simultaneously restricted by gender. Such women are subordinated by patriarchy, yet race and class intersect to create for them privileged opportunities and ways of living (Baca Zinn, Hondagneu-Sotelo, and Messner, 2010). For example, men are encouraged to behave in a "masculine" fashion to prove that they are not gay (Connell, 1992). In defining masculinity as the negation of homosexuality, **compulsory heterosexuality** is an important component of the gender system. Compulsory heterosexuality imposes negative sanctions on those who are homosexual or bisexual. This system of sexuality shapes the gender order by discouraging attachment with members of the same sex. This enforces the dichotomy of "opposite" sexes. **Sexuality** is also a form of inequality in its own right because it systematically grants privileges to those in heterosexual relationships. Like race, class, and gender, sexual identities are socially constructed categories. Sexuality is a way of organizing the social world based on sexual identity and a key linking process in the matrix of domination structured along the lines of race, class, and gender (Messner, 1996:223).

Gender scholars have debated the question of universal male dominance, asking whether it is universal, found in all societies across time and space. Many scholars once claimed that all societies exhibit some forms of patriarchy in marriage and family forms, in division of labor, and in society at large (Ortner, 1974; Rosaldo, 1974). Other scholars have challenged universal patriarchy with cases that serve as counterexamples (Shapiro, 1981). Current thought follows the latter course. Sexual differentiation, it seems, is found in all societies, but it does not always indicate low female status (Rogers, 1978). Male dominance is not homogeneous. Instead, it varies from society to society.

We should keep in mind that although gender stratification makes women subordinate to men, they are not simply the passive victims of patriarchy. Like other oppressed groups, women find ways to resist domination. Through personal and political struggles, they act on their own behalf, often changing the conditions that subordinate them.

Gender Stratification from the Order and Conflict Perspectives

The Order Perspective

From the order perspective, biology, history, and society's needs combine to separate men and women into distinct gender roles. Biologically, men are stronger, while women bear and nurse children. As a result, men fill the "instrumental" roles in society, while women fill the "expressive" roles. According to this view, role division is "functional" or beneficial for society.

The need for women to nurse their infants and stay near home meant that for most of human history, they have done the domestic work, while men were free to hunt and leave the village for extended periods. Thus, a whole set of customs supporting men as the providers and women as the nurturers established the norms for future generations.

Although modern technology has freed women from the need to stay at home and has allowed them to work at jobs formerly requiring great strength, order theorists believe that distinct and separate roles are good for society. Clear-cut gender roles promote stable institutions and an efficient system in which girls and boys are socialized to take their places in society.

Talcott Parsons, a major order theorist, argued in the 1950s that with industrialization, the family and the role of women as nurturers and caretakers was more important than ever. The husband in the competitive world outside the home needs a place of affection. As women take on the roles of providing affection and emotional support within the family, men perform instrumental roles outside the family that provide economic support. Parsons argued that not only is this division of labor practical, but it is also necessary because it assures that the important societal tasks are accomplished (Parsons and Bales, 1955:3–9).

The Conflict Perspective

A different view of gender emerges from the conflict perspective. Conflict theorists are critical of the order model because it neglects what is most important about gender roles—that they are unequal in resources, power, and opportunities. According to the conflict view, gender roles are not neutral ways of meeting societies' needs but are part of the larger system of power and domination.

There are several conflict explanations for gender inequality. Most of them focus on the divisions of labor and power between women and men, and the different values placed on their work. This idea originated in the work of Friedrich Engels and Karl Marx. They wrote that industrialism and the shift to a capitalist economy widened the gap between the power and value of men and women. As production moved out of the home, the gendered division of labor left men with the greater share of economic and other forms of power (Chafetz, 1997; Sapiro, 1999:67).

Most conflict theories explain gender inequality as an outcome of how women and men are tied to the economic structure of society (Nielson, 1990:215). These theories say that women's economic role in society is a primary determinant of their overall status (Dunn, 1996:60). The division between domestic and public spheres of activity gives men and women different positions of advantage and disadvantage. Their roles in the labor force and in the family are interdependent. Whether or not they work outside of the home, women do the vast majority of child care and household labor. Men are freed from these responsibilities. Women's reproductive roles and their responsibilities for domestic labor limit their association with the resources that are highly valued (Ridgeway, 1997; Rosaldo, 1980). Men's economic obligations in the public sphere assure them control of highly valued resources and give rise to male privilege.

In capitalist societies the domestic-public split is even more significant, because highly valued goods and services are exchanged in the public, not the domestic, sphere. Women's domestic labor, although important for survival, ranks low in prestige and power because it does not produce exchangeable commodities (Sacks, 1974). Because of the connections between the class relations of production (capitalism) and the hierarchical gender relations of its society (patriarchy) (Eisenstein, 1979), the United States is a **capitalist patriarchy** where male supremacy keeps women in subordinate roles at work and in the home.

The Implications of the Order and Conflict Perspectives

A point should be made about the implications of the conflict and order perspectives. Each position, with its emphasis on different factors, calls for a different approach to the study of gender. One consequence of the focus on gender roles by the order model has been to treat gender inequality as a problem of roles. Outmoded masculine and feminine roles are thought to be responsible for keeping women from achieving their full potential. This interpretation ignores the ways in which gender roles are rooted in power relations.

The difference between the order and conflict models lies in whether the individual or the society is the primary unit of analysis. The **gender roles** approach emphasizes traits that individuals acquire during the course of socialization, such as independent or dependent behaviors and ways of relating. The **gender structure** approach emphasizes factors that are external to individuals, such as the social structures and social interactions that reward women and men differently. These approaches differ in how they view the sexes, in how they explain the causes and effects of sexism, and in the solutions they suggest for ending inequality. Understanding sexism requires both the individual and the structural approaches. Though gender roles are learned by individuals and produce differences in the personalities, behaviors, and motivations of women and men, gender stratification essentially is maintained by societal forces. This chapter places primary emphasis on social *structure as the cause of inequality*.

Learning Gender

The most complex role that a member of society must learn to play is that of female or male. "Casting" for one's gender role takes place at birth, after a quick biological inspection; and the role of "female" or "male" is assigned. It is an assignment that will last one's entire lifetime and affect virtually everything one ever does. A large part of the next twenty years or so will be spent gradually learning and perfecting one's assigned role (David and Brannon, 1980:117).

Sociologists use the term *gender socialization* to describe how we learn gender. Gender socialization takes place throughout life. Understanding socialization is important not only to explain gender, but to explain gender inequality (Martin, 2005:457). From infancy through early childhood and beyond, children learn what is expected of boys and girls, and they learn to behave according to those expectations.

The traits associated with traditional gender roles are those valued by the dominant society. Keep in mind that the gender is not the same in all classes and races. However, most research on gender socialization reflects the experience of White, middle-class people—those who are most often the research subjects of these studies. How gender is learned depends on a variety of social conditions affecting the socialization practices of girls and boys. Still, society molds boys and girls along different lines.

Children at Home

Girls and boys are perceived and treated differently from the moment of birth. Their access to clothes, toys, books, playmates, and expressions of emotion are severely limited by gender (Martin, 2005:457). Parents and "congratulations" greeting cards describe newborn daughters as "sweet" and "soft," whereas boys are immediately described as "strong" and "hardy." Cards sent to parents depict ribbons, hearts, and flowers for girls, but mobiles, sports equipment, and vehicles for boys. Newborn greeting cards thus project a gender scheme that introduces two "classes" of babies: one decorative, the other physically active (Valian, 1998:19–20).

Children learn at an early age what it means to be a boy or a girl in our society. One of the strongest influences on gender role development in children occurs within the family setting, with parents passing on, both overtly and covertly, their own beliefs about gender (Witt, 1997:254). From the time their children are babies, parents treat sons and daughters differently, dressing infants in gender-specific colors, giving them gender-differentiated toys, and expecting different behavior from boys and girls (Thorne, 1993; Witt, 1997). While both mothers and fathers contribute to the gender stereotyping of their children, fathers have been found to reinforce gender stereotyping more often than mothers (Campenni, 1999; Idle, Wood, and Desmarias, 1993; Valian, 1998; Witt, 1997).

In addition to the parents' active role in reinforcing society's gender demands, a subtler message is emitted from picture books for preschool children. A classic sociological study of eighteen award-winning children's books conducted forty years ago found the following characteristics (Weitzman et al., 1972):

- Females were virtually invisible. The ratio of male pictures to female pictures was 11:1. The ratio of male to female animals was 95:1.
- The activities of boys and girls varied greatly. Boys were active in outdoor activities, while girls were passive and most often found indoors. The activity of the girls typically was that of some service for boys.
- Adult men and women (role models) were very different. Men led, women followed. Females were passive and males active. Not one woman in these books had a job or profession; they were always mothers and wives.

We have seen improvements in how girls and women are portrayed. Females are no longer invisible; they are as likely as males to be included in the books, and they have roles beyond their family roles. In many respects, however, gendered messages in children's books still exist (Crabb and Bielawski, 1994; Mc Cabe et al., 2011). An update of the classic Weitzman study found that while the proportion of female characters were portrayed as dependent and submissive, male characters were commonly portrayed as being independent and creative (Oskamp, Kaufman, and Wolterbeek, 1996). Subsequent studies have found that despite some improvement, women and girls are still underrepresented in book titles and as central characters (Nilges and Spencer, 2002; Mc Cabe et al., 2011).

Gendered socialization is found even where gender roles are becoming more flexible or androgynous. **Androgyny** refers to the integration of traditional feminine and masculine characteristics in the same individual. Are girls more androgynous than boys? If so, what explains the difference? And what difference does androgyny make in an individual's overall well-being? Research has found that fathers who display the most traditional attitudes about gender transmit their ideas onto their sons more so than onto their daughters, whereas mothers who tend to have more liberal attitudes do not transmit their attitudes onto their daughters more than their sons. Consequently, "when the sons establish their own families, they will be more likely than the daughters to transmit traditional attitudes to their own sons" (Kulik, 2002:450). Other researchers have found that while adolescent girls tend to be more supportive of egalitarian gender roles than their parents (especially their fathers), adolescent boys follow their fathers' resistance to changes in traditional male roles. Therefore, it is predictable that males would be less likely than females to develop androgynous characteristics (Burt and Scott, 2002). In a study of child care books and parenting websites, sociologist Karen Martin found some evidence of gender-neutral child rearing. But she also found that children's nonconformity to gender roles is still viewed as problematic because it is linked with homosexuality (Martin, 2005).

Gender identities affect individuals' well-being in various ways. Witt (1997) found that parents who foster androgynous attitudes and behaviors in their children ultimately cause their girls and boys to have high self-esteem and self-worth. Androgynous individuals appear to be able to more effectively manage stress and practice good health (Edwards and Hamilton, 2004), and androgynous college students report having better relationships with their parents (Guastello and Guastello, 2003:664).

Studies have shown that children construct gender in their everyday lives.

Children at Play

Children teach each other to behave according to cultural expectations. Same-sex peers exert a strong influence on how gender is learned. In a classic study of children's play groups, Janet Lever (1976) discovered how children's play groups stress particular social skills and capabilities for boys and others for girls. Her research among fifth graders, most of whom were White and middle class, found that boys, more than girls: (1) played outdoors, (2) played in larger groups, (3) played in age-heterogeneous groups, (4) were less likely to play in games dominated by the opposite sex, (5) played more competitive games, and (6) played in games that lasted longer.

Barrie Thorne's (1993) study of gender play in multiracial school settings found that boys control more space, more often violate girls' activities, and treat girls as contaminating. According to Thorne, these common ritualized interactions reflect larger structures of male dominance. In reality, the fun and games of everyday schoolchildren are *power play*, a complex social process involving both gender separation and togetherness. Children's power play changes with age, ethnicity, race, class, and social context. In her analysis of how children themselves construct gender in their daily play, Thorne shifts the focus from individuals to *social relations*:

> The social construction of gender is an active and ongoing process. ... Gender categories, gender identities, gender divisions, gender-based groups, gender meanings—all are produced actively and collaboratively, in everyday life. When kids maneuver to form same-gender groups on the playground or organize a kickball game as "boys-against-the-girls," they produce a sense of gender as dichotomy and opposition. And when girls and boys work cooperatively on a classroom project, they actively undermine a sense of gender as opposition. This emphasis on action and activity, and on everyday social interactions that are sometimes contradictory, provides an antidote to the view of children as passively socialized. Gender is not something one passively "is" or "has." (Thorne, 1993:4–5)

Subsequent research on fourth-grade children in schoolyards supports Thorne's conclusions about gendered interaction in schoolyards. Boyle and her colleagues (Boyle, Marshall, and Robeson, 2003), found a great deal of intragender variation in the schoolyard with girls engaging in many different activities. They also found that boys were more easily accepted into play with girls than was the case when girls tried to play with a group of boys, and that boys tend to use more space in the schoolyard and are more likely to violate girls' space and games than the reverse.

Toys play a major part in gender socialization. Toys entertain children; they also encourage different skills in girls and boys. For example, they afford opportunities for girls to develop communication skills, nurturance, and attractiveness and for boys to develop technical knowledge competition, and aggression (Renzetti and Curan, 2003; Frances, 2010). Today, most toys for sale are gender-linked, some say more gender-specific than in the past (Delamont, 2001; Frances, 2010).

Girls are often involved in cross-gender or neutral toy behavior. While girls are often encouraged by both parents to branch out and play with neutral toys some of the time, boys tend not to be given this same encouragement (Campenni, 1999; England, 2010). While we may be seeing some breakdown of traditional play patterns and socialization of girls, the same does not appear true for boys. Studies have also found that messages transmitted to children from advertisements affect their toy use and that the effects are different for boys and girls. Research finds that the messages in commercials have stronger effects on boys than girls (Pike and Jennings, 2005).

Although girls are now encouraged to engage in activities such as playing video games, traditional gender stereotypes still underlie this pastime. Feminine toys are certainly not out—in fact, these pink-and-purple-gendered games are doing quite well with little girls all over the world. Research finds that girls tend to become less stereotypical in their play as they age—choosing more neutral toys, sports, and computer games (while boys remain masculine in their play) (Orenstein, 2008).

Dichotomous gender experiences may be more characteristic among White, middle-class children than among children of other races. An important study on African American adolescent girls by Joyce Ladner (1971) has shown that these girls develop in a more independent fashion. Other research has also found that among African Americans, both girls and boys are expected to be nurturant and expressive emotionally as well as independent, confident, and assertive (McAdoo, 1988; Stack, 1990). Recent studies examining whether or not the socialization of African American children is more gender-neutral than that in other groups are inconsistent. Most scholars now say there is too much variation in any group to make generalizations (Hill and Sprague, 1999; Smith, 2001).

Formal Education

In 1972, Congress outlawed sex discrimination in public schools through Title IX of the Educational Amendments Act. More than four decades later, schools continue to be powerful agents of socialization. Studies by the American Association of University Women (AAUW, 1992; 1999) have offered compelling evidence that two decades after the passage of Title IX, girls and boys are not receiving the same education.

Recent media discussions of "the boy crisis," in U.S. schools portray young men as marginalized, while girls are taking over the schools. But numerous studies find that "over the past three decades, boys' tests scores are mostly up, more boys are going to college, and more are getting bachelor's degrees" (Matthews, 2006:A01; Von Drehle, 2007). Although males do drop out of school more often than females, the trend is most pronounced among minorities and boys from low-income homes (Barnett and Rivers, 2004; Gibbs, 2008; Matthews, 2006; Mead, 2006). The "boy crisis" is an issue of race and class disadvantage, not one of gender difference.

Schools shortchange girls in every dimension of education. Let us examine the following areas: curriculum, teacher–student interactions, sports, and female role models.

Curriculum. Schools are charged with the responsibility of equipping students to study subjects (for example, reading, writing, mathematics, and history) known collectively as the formal curriculum. But schools also teach students particular social, political, and economic values that constitute the so-called hidden curriculum operating alongside the more formal one. Both formal and informal curricula are powerful shapers of gender (Renzetti and Curran, 2003:109; Booher-Jennings, 2008).

Numerous studies find gender differences in the curriculum students are exposed to. For example, girls are more likely to participate in biological sciences and boys in the physical sciences (Adamuti-Trache and Andres, 2007; Sadker, 2002:238). In math, although girls and boys tend to take the same number of math courses, there are differences in what courses they take. Girls are more likely to end their math courses after a second algebra course; in fact, girls now outnumber boys in taking algebra and geometry. But boys are more likely to take trigonometry and calculus, which give them an advantage in higher level math skills (AAUW, 1999; Andersen, 2011).

Although girls on the average receive higher grades in high school than boys, they tend to score lower on some standardized tests, which are particularly important because such test scores are used to make decisions on the awarding of scholarships and admissions. Schools ignore topics that matter in students' lives. The "evaded curriculum" is a term coined in the AAUW Report to refer to matters central to students' lives that are touched on only briefly, if at all, in most schools. Students receive inadequate education on sexuality, teen pregnancy, the AIDS crisis, and the increase of sexually transmitted diseases among adolescents. According to the AAUW Report, gender bias also affects males. Three out of four boys currently report that they were the targets of sexual harassment in schools—usually of taunts challenging their masculinity. In addition, while girls receive lower test grades, boys often receive lower overall course grades.

Teacher–Student Interactions. Even when girls and boys are in the same classrooms, boys are given preferential treatment. Girls receive less attention and different types of attention from classroom teachers.

Since the 1980s, educational reforms have been in place to foster gender equity in schools. Teachers are advised to encourage cooperative cross-sex learning, to monitor their own (teacher) behavior, to be sure that they reward male and female students equally, and actively familiarize students with gender-atypical roles by assigning them specific duties as leaders, recording secretary, and so on (Lockheed, 1985, cited in Giele, 1988).

Despite the fact that many teachers are trying to interact with their students in nongendered ways, studies show that they nonetheless continue to do so. In her study of third-grade classes, Garrahy (2001) found that while the teachers were claiming to be gender-neutral, they voiced beliefs about gendered differences among students and interacted with their students in gendered ways. Spencer and Tolman (2003), found that teachers spent more time with the male students when they were working independently and in small groups; perhaps most troubling, the students normalized and naturalized these gendered differences. Unfortunately, despite the increasing awareness of gender inequality within schools, new teachers are not adequately being taught about gender-equity issues.

Sports. Sports in U.S. high schools and colleges have historically been almost exclusively a male preserve (this section is based on Eitzen and Sage, 2010). The truth of this observation is evident if one compares by sex the number of participants, facilities, the support of school administrations, and financial support.

Such disparities have been based on the traditional assumptions that competitive sport is basically a masculine activity and that the proper roles of girls and women are as spectators and cheerleaders. What is the impact on a society that encourages its boys and young men to participate in sports while expecting its girls and young women to be spectators and cheerleaders? Sports reinforce societal expectations for males and females. Males are to be dominant and aggressive—the doers—while females are expected to be passive supporters of men, attaining status through the efforts of their men folk.

An important consequence of this traditional view is that approximately one-half of the population was denied access to all that sport has to offer (physical conditioning, enjoyment, teamwork, goal attainment, ego enhancement, social status, and competitiveness). School administrators, school boards, and citizens of local communities have long assumed that sports participation has general educational value. If so, then girls and women should also be allowed to receive the benefits.

In 1972, passage of Title IX of the Educational Amendments Act required that schools receiving federal funds must provide equal opportunities for males and females. Despite considerable opposition by school administrators, athletic directors, and school boards, major changes have occurred over time because of this federal legislation. More monies were spent on women's sports; better facilities and equipment were provided; and women were gradually accepted as athletes. The most significant result was an increase in female participation. The number of high school girls participating in interscholastic sports increased from 300,000 in 1971 to 3.11 million in 2008. By the 2008 school year, 41 percent of all high school participants were female, and the number of sports available to them was more than twice the number available in 1970. Similar growth patterns have occurred in colleges and universities.

At the intercollegiate level, on the positive side, budgets for women's sports have improved dramatically, from less than 1 percent of the men's budgets and no athletic scholarships in 1970 at the college level to approximately 38 percent of the men's budgets and 33 percent of the scholarships in 2008. Despite this marked improvement, women athletics remain underfunded. Although women account for 57 percent of the college student population, female athletes receive only 43 percent of participation opportunities. And male athletes receive $179 million more in athletic scholarships than their female counterparts (Lopiano, 2008). This inequality is reinforced by unequal media attention, the scheduling of games (men's games are always the featured games), and the increasing lack of women in positions of power. One ironic consequence of Title IX has been that as opportunities for female athletes increased and programs expanded, the majority of coaching and administration diminished. In the early 1970s, most coaches of women's intercollegiate teams were women. By 2008, women coached 46 percent of women's teams (Lopiano, 2008). Females who aspire to coaching and athletic administration have fewer opportunities than males; girls see fewer women as role models in such positions. Thus, even with federal legislation mandating gender equality, male dominance is maintained.

Female Role Models. The work that women and men do in the schools supports gender inequality. The pattern is the familiar one found in hospitals, in business offices, and throughout the occupational world: Women occupy the bottom rungs while men are in the more powerful positions. Women make up a large percentage of the nation's classroom teachers but a much smaller percentage of school district superintendents. In 2010, women comprised 81 percent of all elementary school teachers, more than half of all secondary school teachers (54 percent), and 62 percent of all school administrators (Bureau of Labor Statistics, 2010).

As the level of education increases, the proportion of female teachers declines. Even after four decades of attention to gender equity in higher education, women have not achieved the same status as men. Women are less likely than men to be employed as full-time tenure track faculty members, less likely to hold tenured or full professor positions, and comprise less than a quarter of all college and university presidents (Curtis, 2011).

In 2009 (more than two decades after the Office of Civil Rights issued guidelines spelling out the obligations of colleges and universities in the development of affirmative action programs), women represented only 42 percent of full-time faculty. Furthermore, they remained overwhelmingly in the lower faculty ranks, where faculty is much less likely to hold tenure. In 2009, women comprised 30 percent of full professors, 41 percent of associate professors, 48 percent of assistant professors, and 54 percent of instructors/lecturers, and 23 percent of college presidents were women (National Center for Education Statistics, 2010).

Socialization as Blaming the Victim

The discussion so far demonstrates that gender differences are learned. This does not mean that socialization alone explains women's place in society. In fact, a socialization approach alone can be misused in such a way that it blames women themselves for sex inequality. This is the critique offered by Linda Peterson and Elaine Enarson (1974). Many years ago, they developed the argument that socialization diverts attention from structured inequality: "Misuse of the concept of socialization plays directly into the Blaming the Victim ideology; by focusing on the victim, responsibility for 'the woman problem' rests not in the social system with its sex-structured distribution of inequality, but in socialized sex differences and sex roles" (8).

Not only is the cause of the problem displaced, but so are the solutions: "Rather than directing efforts toward radical social change, the solution seems to be to change women themselves, perhaps through exhortation ('If we want to be liberated, we'll have to act more aggressive ...') or, for example, changing children's literature and mothers' child rearing practice" (8).

This issue raises a critical question: If the socialization perspective is limited and perhaps biased, what is a better way of analyzing gender inequality? To answer this question, let us look at how male dominance affects our society.

Reinforcing Male Dominance

Male dominance is both a force that socializes and a force that structures the social world. It exists at all levels of society, from interpersonal relations to outside institutions. This section describes the interpersonal and institutional reinforcement of gender inequality.

Language

Language perpetuates male dominance by ignoring, trivializing, and sexualizing women. Use of the pronoun *he* when the sex of the person is unspecified and of the generic term *mankind* to refer to humanity in general are obvious examples of how the English language ignores women. Common sayings such as "that's women's work" (as opposed to "that's men's work!"), jokes about female drivers, and phrases such as *women and children first*, or *wine, women, and song* are trivializing. Women, more than men, are commonly referred to in terms that have sexual connotations. Terms referring to men (*studs, jocks*) that do have sexual meanings imply power and success, whereas terms applied to women (*broads, bimbos, hos*) imply promiscuity or being dominated. In fact, the term *promiscuous* is usually applied only to women, although its literal meaning applies to either sex (Richmond-Abbott, 1992:93). Research shows that there are many derogatory or at least disrespectful generic terms for women, but few for men (Sapiro, 1999:329). Not only are there fewer derogatory terms that refer to men, but of those that exist, such terms are considered derogatory because they invoke the images of women. "Some of the more common derogatory terms applied to men such as *bastard, motherfucker*, and *son of a bitch* actually degrade women in their role as mothers" (Romaine, 1999:999).

Interpersonal Behavior

Gender inequality is different than other forms of inequality because individuals on both sides of the power divide (the divide being between women and men) interact very frequently (in the home, in the workplace, and in other role relations). Consequently, gender inequalities can be reproduced and resisted in everyday interactions (Ridgeway and Smith-Lovin, 1999:191). New research even finds gender differences in Internet social networking. (See the Technology and Society panel titled "Gender and Social Networking.")

Sociologists have done extensive research on the ways in which women and men interact, with particular attention being paid to communication styles. This research finds that in mixed-sex groups men talk more, show more visual dominance, and interrupt more, whereas women display more tentative and polite speech patterns (Ridgeway and Smith-Lovin, 1999).

Various forms of nonverbal communication also sustain male dominance. Men take up more space than do women and also touch women without permission more than women touch men. Women, on the other hand, engage in more eye contact, smile more, and generally exhibit behavior associated with low status. These behaviors show how gender is continually being created in various kinds of social interaction that occur between women and men. Candace West and Don Zimmerman (1987) call this "doing gender." It involves following the rules and behaviors expected of us as males or females. We "do gender," because if we don't, we are judged incompetent as men and women. Gender is something we create in interaction, not something we are (Risman, 1998:6).

Producing gender through interaction is becoming a lively sociological topic. Instead of treating gender only as identity, or socialization, or stratification, this perspective emphasizes gender as dynamic *practices*—what people say and do as they engage in social interaction (Martin, 2003; Ridgeway, 1997). In this view, gender is a system of action in which gendered practices are learned and enacted in all social settings throughout an individual's life. Gender is enacted in school, families, workplaces, houses of worship, and social movements. "In time, like riding a bicycle, gendering practices become almost automatic" (Martin, 2003:325).

Mass Media

Much of the information we receive about the world around us comes from the mass media—radio, television, newspapers, magazines, and the Internet. Although media are often blamed for the problems of modern society, they are not monolithic and do not present

Gender and Social Networking

We can examine data provided by Internet media rating services such as comScore to advertisers and marketing researchers to analyze gender differences among users. The data show that women use Internet networking more than men. Studies of social networking, principally Facebook, show that women use social network sites (SNS) not only more but differently.

- Women use SNS more than men. Data collected by Google Ad Planner from nineteen different sites show that 53 percent of total users are women.
- Women are the majority of users on the top sites such as Facebook. Both sexes use more content-based sites such as LinkedIn and YouTube equally. Men dominate social news sites, where they represent 64 percent of total users. The world's largest and most popular social networking site Facebook has a majority of female users (57 percent). They are also more active on the site having, on average, 8 percent more "friends" than men and sharing 62 percent of information and photos (Solis, 2010).
- Data collected in a 2010 comScore report show that, across the world, a higher percentage of women use social networking sites than men. 75.8 percent of all women with Internet access logged on to a social networking site compared to 69.7 percent of men. Women also spent more time on these sites logging an average of 5.5 hours a month compared to 4 hours for men (Solis, 2010).
- Research done in England by Ohio State University shows women spend their leisure time doing social networking differently than men. Their increased amount of housework and childcare compared to men shapes their SNS activity. Women socialize, make connections, and share their personal life. Men are more interested in obtaining information and increasing their status (Sayer and Mattingly, 2006).
- Data shows that women are more likely to disclose information about themselves, publicize photos and have low privacy settings. (wikigender.org contributors, 2011).
- Smartphone usage also reflects a SNS gender difference with women making up 55 percent of mobile activity (wikigender.org contributors, 2011).
- Research done at University of Buffalo suggested to researchers that females who base their self worth on their appearance tend to share more photos online and maintain larger networks on SNSs (Stefanone, 2011).

us with a simple message. The media have tremendous power. They can distort women's images, and they can bring about change as well (Sapiro, 1999:224). Women are still underrepresented on the op-ed pages, on Sunday chat shows, and as experts in news stories (Pollit, 2010; Media Report to Women, 2011). Studies show that women journalists' role in newsrooms is shrinking even though women predominate in undergraduate and graduate journalism programs and have for decades (Lauer, 2002). In magazines, women's portrayal has become less monolithic since the 1980s. With the rise of feminism, many magazines devoted attention to women's achievements. Alongside these new magazines for the new woman, many "ladies" magazines continue to define the lives of women in terms of men— husbands or lovers.

One network news program is now anchored by a woman (Diane Sawyer) while "Rachel Maddow rules on cable" (Pollit, 2010). Still, women are underrepresented in television newsrooms. In 2010, women made up 40 percent of the television news workforce, whereas the percentage of women news directors in television was at 28 (Papper, 2010).

Studies have continually demonstrated that highly stereotyped behavior characterizes child and adult programming as well as commercials. Male role models are provided in greater numbers than are female, with the exception of daytime soap operas, in which men and women are equally represented. Prime-time television is distorted. Although men represent 49 percent of the U.S. population, they represented 60 percent of prime-time television characters in 2007 (Media Report to Women, 2007).

Images of women on entertainment television have changed greatly in recent decades. A report by the National Commission on Working Women has found increasing diversity of characters portraying working women as television's most significant improvement. In many serials, women do play strong and intelligent roles, but in just as many shows, men are still the major characters and women are cast as glamorous sidekicks or scheming villains (Andersen, 2009:62). In response to the imbalances in prime-time television, the National Organization for Women states, "If you are a middle-aged woman, a lesbian, a Latina, a woman with a disability, a women of size, a low-income mom struggling to get by ... good luck finding programming that even pretends to reflect your life" (National Organization for Women, 2002).

Television commercials have long presented the sexes in stereotyped ways. Women appear less frequently in ads than men, are much more likely to appear in ads for food, home, and beauty/clothing products. Men are less likely to be shown cooking, cleaning, shopping, or washing dishes. When men are shown in the context of family life, they are usually engaged in activities stereotypically associated with men—in cars or mowing the lawn. Moreover, they are usually seen with boys not girls, and rarely with infants (Andersen, 2011:62). In the past decades, however, the potential buying power of working women has caused the advertising industry to modify women's image. Working women have become targets of advertising campaigns. But most advertising aimed at women with jobs sends the message that they should be superwomen, managing multiple roles of wife, mother, and career woman, and be glamorous as well. Such multifarious expectations are not imposed on men.

The advertising aimed at the "new woman" places additional stresses on women and at the same time upholds male privilege. Television commercials that show women breezing in from their jobs to sort the laundry or pop dinner in the oven reinforce the notion that it is all right for a woman to pursue a career as long as she can still handle the housework.

Religion

Most U.S. religions follow a typical pattern. The clergy is male, while the vast majority of worshippers are women (Paulson, 2000). Despite important differences in religious doctrines, there are common views about gender. Among these are the beliefs that (1) women and men have different missions and different standards of behavior, and (2) although men and women are equal in the eyes of the deity, women are subordinate to men (Sapiro, 1999:219; Thomas, 2007). Limiting discussion to the Judeo–Christian heritage, let us examine some teachings about women's place from the Old and New Testaments. The Old Testament established male supremacy in a number of ways. Images of God are male. Females were second to men because Eve was created from Adam's rib. According to the Scriptures, only a man could divorce a spouse. A woman who was not a virgin at marriage could be stoned to death. Girls could be purchased for marriage. Employers were enjoined to pay women only three-fifths the wages of men: "If a male from 20 to 60 years of age, the equivalent is 50 shekels of silver by the sanctuary weight; if it is a female, the equivalent is 30 shekels" (Leviticus 27:4). As Gilman (1971) notes:

> The Old Testament devotes inordinate space to the listing of long lines of male descent to the point where it would seem that for centuries women "begat" nothing but male offspring. Although there are heroines in the Old Testament—Judith, Esther and the like—it's clear that they functioned like the heroines of Greek drama and later of French: as counterweights in the imaginations of certain sensitive men to the degraded position of women in actual life. The true spirit of the tradition was unabashedly revealed in the prayer men recited every day in the synagogue: "Blessed art Thou, O Lord ... for not making me a woman." (51)

The New Testament retained the tradition of male dominance. Jesus was the son of a male god, not of Mary, who remained a virgin. All the disciples were male. The great leader of the early church, the apostle Paul, was especially adamant in arguing for the primacy of males over females. According to Paul, "the husband is supreme over his wife," "woman was created for man's sake," and "women should not teach nor usurp authority over the man, but to be silent." Contemporary religious thought reflects this heritage. In 1998, the Southern Baptist Convention, the nation's biggest Protestant denomination, amended its statement of beliefs to include a declaration that "a woman shall submit herself graciously to her husband's leadership and a husband should provide for, protect and lead his family." Some denominations limit or even forbid women from any decision making. Others allow women to vote but limit their participation in leadership roles.

There are, however, many indications of change. Throughout the West, women are more involved in churches and religious life (Paulson, 2000; Thomas, 2007; Van Biema, 2004). The National Council of Churches seeks to end sexist language and to use "inclusive language" in the Revised Standard Version of the Bible. Terms such as man, mankind, brothers, sons, churchmen, and laymen would be replaced by neutral terms that include reference to female gender. But these terms, while helpful, do not address a fundamental theological cause: "When God is perceived as a male, then expecting a male voice interpreting the word of God naturally follows" (Zelizer, 2004:1A).

The percentage of female seminary students has exploded in the past few decades. Women now make up only 17 percent of the nation's clergy (Bureau of Labor Statistics, 2010). Across the United States, female clergy are struggling for equal rights, bumping up against what many call a "stained-glass ceiling." Today, half of all religious denominations in the United States ordain women. At the same time, the formal rules and practices discriminate against women. In denominations that ordain women and those that do not, women often fill the same jobs: leading small churches, directing special church programs, preaching and evangelizing (Van Biema, 2004). Despite the opposition of organized religion, many women are making advances within established churches and leaving their mark on the ministerial profession.

The Law

That the law has been discriminatory against women is beyond dispute. We need only recall that women were specifically denied the right to vote prior to the passage of the Nineteenth Amendment.

During the past three decades, legal reforms and public policy changes have attempted to place women and men on more equal footing. Some laws that focus on employment include the 1963 Equal Pay Act, Title VII of the 1964 Civil Rights Act, and the 1978 Pregnancy Discrimination Act. The 1972 Educational Amendments Act calls for gender equality in education. Other reforms have provided the framework for important institutional changes. For example, sexist discrimination in the granting of credit has been ruled illegal, and discrimination against pregnant women in the workforce is now prohibited by the law. Affirmative action (which is now under assault) remedied some kinds of gender discrimination in employment. Sexist discrimination in housing is prohibited, and the differential requirements by gender as traditionally practiced by the airline industry have been eliminated. Such laws now provide a basis for the equal treatment of women and men. But the force of the laws depends on how well they are enforced and how they are interpreted in the courts when they are disputed.

Legal discrimination remains in a number of areas. There are still hundreds of sections of the U.S. legal code and of state laws that are riddled with sex bias or sex-based terminology, in conflict with the ideal of equal rights for women (Benokraitis and Feagin, 1995:24). State laws vary considerably concerning property ownership by spouses, welfare benefits, and the legal status of homemakers.

Today, many legal reforms are threatened by recent Supreme Court decisions. For example, the right to abortion became the law of the land in the *Roe v. Wade* decision of 1973. *Roe v. Wade* was a major breakthrough for women, giving them the choice to control their own bodies. But in 1989 and 1992, the Supreme Court narrowed women's rights by allowing states to impose restrictions on abortion.

Roe v. Wade is still on the books, but the Supreme Court has returned the nation to a pre-*Roe* patchwork of state regulations. Forty-nine states now have restrictions that make it more difficult for women to obtain abortions.

Politics

Women's political participation has always been different from that of men. Women received the right to vote in 1920, when the Nineteenth Amendment was ratified. Although women make up a very small percentage of officeholders, 1992 was a turning point for women in politics. Controversies such as Anita Hill's harassment allegations, the abortion rights battle, and the lack of representation at all levels of politics propelled women into the political arena. In 1992, Congress experienced the biggest influx of women (and minorities) in history. Subsequent elections have increased the number of women in our national legislature. But ninety years after the first woman was elected to congress, women still hold less than a fifth of all national seats. They do only slightly better at the state level (Dokoupil, 2011). As of 2011, seventeen U.S. senators are women, and seventy-one women are in the House of Representatives (Center for American Women and Politics, 2011) (see Table 12.2 for the percentages of women in elective offices). If Congress were representative of the nation, the Senate would have 51 women and the House 222 (Sklar, 2004).

The gender gap in our nation's capital is scandalous at all levels. In Washington, DC's, less visible workforce of professional staff employees, women hold 60 percent of the jobs, but they are nowhere equal to men. Congress has two classes of personal staff employees: highly paid men who hold most of the power and lower-paid women who tend to be relegated to clerical and support staff. Many answer the phones and write letters to constituents—invisible labor that is crucial to their bosses' reelection.

Hillary Clinton's 2008 presidential candidacy sparked a national debate about women's access to political power. But globally, women are making substantial gains in politics. Although some facets of the gender gap appear to be narrowing with Nancy Pelosi as the first female speaker of the House of Representatives, sixty-five countries do better than the

TABLE 12.2

Percentages of Women in Elective Offices

Year	U.S. Congress (%)	Statewide Elective (%)	State Legislatures (%)	Year	U.S. Congress (%)	Statewide Elective (%)	State Legislatures (%)
1979	3	11	10	2001	13.6	27.6	22.4
1981	4	11	12	2003	13.6	26.0	22.4
1983	4	11	13	2004	13.8	26.0	22.5
1985	6	14	15	2005	15.0	25.7	22.7
1987	5	14	16	2006	15.0	25.1	22.8
1989	5	14	17	2007	16.1	24.1	23.5
1991	6	18	18	2008	16.5	23.2	23.7
1993	10.1	22.2	20.5	2009	16.8	22.6	24.3
1996	10.3	25.9	20.6	2010	16.8	22.5	24.5
1997	11.0	25.4	21.6	2011	16.6	21.9	23.5
1999	12.1	27.6	22.4				

Source: Center for Women in Politics. 2011. "Facts on Women in Congress 2011." http://www.cawp.rutgers.edu/fast_facts/levels_of_office/Congress-CurrentFacts.php.

United States when it comes to women serving in national legislatures. For example, in Norway, 37 percent of lawmakers are women. In Sweden, it is 45 percent (Wheatcroft, 2007). Furthermore women have served as heads of state in nations such as Canada, France, Germany, the United Kingdom, Turkey, Pakistan, Chile, South Korea, and Liberia (Falk, 2008). In the 200-year history of the United States, there has never been a female president of the United States or vice president (just two vice-presidential candidates). Today, there are only three female justices on the U.S. Supreme Court.

The gender gap refers to differences in political attitudes and voting patterns of women and men. Voting studies of national elections since 1980 demonstrate that women often vote differently from men, especially on issues of economics, social welfare, and war and peace (Renzetti and Curran, 2003:299).

Just fifteen percent of women work in jobs traditionally held by men.

Structured Gender Inequality in the Workplace

In this section of the chapter, we focus on the contemporary U.S. workplace, which has one of the highest levels of workplace gender inequality in the industrial world (Kimmel, 2004:186). The workplace distributes women and men in different settings, assigns them different duties, and rewards them unequally.

Occupational Distribution

The new economy discussed in Chapter 8 has changed both women's and men's employment rates. Increasingly, it is viewed as "normal" for adult women and men, regardless of parental status, to be employed (Bianchi, 1995:110). Women's labor force participation rates have grown at a faster pace than men's in recent decades. Between 1070 and 1990, women's numbers in the labor force increased twice as fast as those of men (see the labor force participation rates for men and women, 1950 through 2009, in Figure 12.1). At present, women's rate of labor force participation is holding steadily, while men's is declining. In 2010, 58 percent of women over sixteen were in the labor force, compared with 71 percent of men. Today, as in the past, the proportions of employed women vary by race. African American women have had a long history of high workforce participation rates. In 2004, they edged ahead of other women. By 2010, they participated in the labor force at a rate of 59 percent; 58 percent of White women were in the labor force in 2010, compared with 56 percent of Hispanic women (Bureau of Labor Statistics, 2010). (See the projected labor force participation rates for women by race in Table 12.3.)

The increase in women's participation in the U.S. labor force is among the most important social, economic, and cultural trends of the past century. Today's working woman may be any age. She may be any race. She may be a nurse or a secretary or a factory worker or a department store clerk or a public schoolteacher. Or she may be—though it is much less likely—a physician or the president of a corporation or the head of a school system. Hers may be the familiar face seen daily behind the counter at the neighborhood coffee shop, or she may work virtually unseen, mopping floors at midnight in an empty office building.

Although the increase in women's labor force participation is among the most important social and cultural trends of the past century, women have not achieved equality in the workforce. Some occupations have changed more than others and there has been little

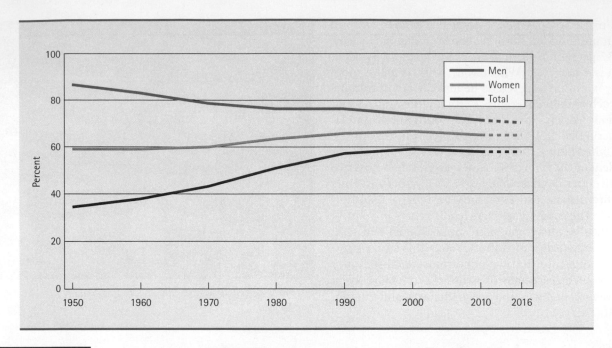

FIGURE 12.1

Labor Force
Participation Rate
by Sex, 1950–2009,
and Projected,
2009–2016

*Sources: Occupational
Outlook Quarterly, Winter
2001–2002.* Washington
DC: U.S. Department of
Labor, Bureau of Labor
Statistics, p. 39; "Employment Projections." U.S.
Department of Labor,
2007. Online: http://
www.bls.gov/emp/
emplab05.htm

change in how traditionally female jobs are viewed and rewarded (England, 2010). The typical female worker is a wage earner in clerical, service, manufacturing, or some technical job
that pays poorly and gives her little possibility for advancement and little control over her
work. More women work as sales workers, secretaries, and cashiers than in any line of work.
The largest share of women (54 percent) works in "service" and "sales and office" jobs (Bureau of Labor Statistics, 2010). (See Table 12.4 for a listing of the twenty leading occupations of employed women.)

Economic restructuring has altered the gender distribution of the labor force. Since 1980,
women have taken 80 percent of the new jobs created in the economy. This gender shift in the
U.S. workforce has accelerated in the current economic downturn, which has affected women
and men differently. The Great Recession has disproportionately laid off men, who are more
likely to work in industries such as manufacturing and construction. Women, on the other
hand, are overrepresented in economic sectors such as education and health care.

Gender segregation refers to the pattern whereby women and men are situated in different jobs throughout the labor force (Andersen, 2011:128). The overall degree of gender
segregation has not changed much since 1900. Women and men are still concentrated in
different occupations (Dubeck and Dunn, 2002; England, 2010).

TABLE 12.3

Labor Force Participation Rates for Women, by Race, Selected Years and Projected 2016

Year	Black	White	Hispanic	Asian
1975	48.8	45.9	n.a.	n.a.
1986	56.9	55.4	50.1	57.0
1996	60.4	59.8	53.4	58.8
2006	61.5	59.3	56.1	57.6
2016	63.1	58.8	57.8	58.7

Source: "Employment Projections," U.S. Department of Labor, 2007. Table 3. Online http://www.bls.gov/emp/
emplab05.htm

TABLE 12.4

Twenty Leading Occupations of Employed Women

Occupation	2009 Annual Averages (employment in thousands)			
	Total Employed Women	Total Employed (Men and Women)	Percent Women (%)	Women's Median Weekly Earnings ($)
Total, 16 years and older (all employed women)	66,208	139,877	47.4	657
Secretaries and administrative assistants	3,074	3,176	96.8	619
Registered nurses	2,612	2,839	92.0	1,035
Elementary and middle school teachers	2,343	2,862	81.9	891
Cashiers	2,273	3,056	74.4	361
Nursing, psychiatric, and home health aides	1,770	2,002	88.5	430
Retail salespersons	1,650	3,182	51.9	443
First-line supervisors/managers of retail sales workers	1,459	3,311	44.1	597
Waiters and waitresses	1,434	2,005	71.6	363
Maids and housekeeping cleaners	1,282	1,428	89.8	371
Customer service representatives	1,263	1,862	67.9	587
Childcare workers	1,228	1,292	95.1	364
Bookkeeping, accounting, and auditing clerks	1,205	1,306	92.3	627
Receptionists and information clerks	1,168	1,277	91.5	516
First-line supervisors/managers of office and administrative support	1,163	1,632	71.3	705
Managers, all others	1,106	3,249	34.1	1,037
Accountants and auditors	1,084	1,754	61.8	902
Teacher assistants	921	1,006	91.6	474
Cooks	831	2,004	41.5	371
Office clerks, general	821	1,002	82.0	594
Personal and home care aides	789	926	85.2	406

Source: U.S. Department of Labor, Bureau of Labor Statistics, Annual Averages 2009. "20 Leading Occupations of Employed Women 2009 Annual Averages." http://www.dol.gov/wb/factsheets/201ead2009.htmSource.

Media reports of women's gains in traditionally male jobs are often misleading. In blue-collar work, for example, gains appear dramatic at first glance, with the number of women in blue-collar jobs rising by 80 percent in the 1970s. But the increase was so high because women had been virtually excluded from these occupations until then. Women's entry into skilled blue-collar work such as construction and automating was limited by the very slow growth in those jobs (Amott, 1993:76). In 2010, only 1.8 percent of automotive service technicians and mechanics, 2.7 percent of construction workers, and 0.8 percent of tool and die makers were women (Bureau of Labor Statistics, 2010). The years from 1970 to 1990 found more women in the fields of law, medicine, journalism, and higher education. Today, women fill 42 percent of all management positions (up from 19 percent in 1972). Still, there are fewer women in prestige jobs. Only 30 percent of lawyers, 32 percent of doctors, and 42 percent of full-time university or college teachers were women (Bureau of Labor Statistics, 2010).

Although women have made inroads in high-paying and high-prestige professions, not all have fared equally. White women were the major beneficiaries of the new opportunities. There has been an occupational trickle-down effect, as White women improved their occupational status by moving into the male-dominated professions such as law and medicine, while African American women moved into the female-dominated jobs, such as social work and teaching, which had been vacated by White women. This upscale movement for White women was related to federal civil rights legislation, particularly the requirement that firms receiving federal contracts comply with affirmative action guidelines (Amott, 1993:76).

The Earnings Gap

Although women's labor-force participation rates have risen, the gap between women's and men's earnings has remained relatively constant for three decades. Women do not approach earnings parity with men, even when they work in similar occupations and have the same levels of education.

The pay gap between women and men has narrowed. It hovered between 70 and 74 percent throughout the 1990s. Today, women who work year-round and full-time earn 80 cents for every dollar men earn. Closing the wage gap has been slow, amounting to less than half a cent per year! At this rate, 87 more years could go by before women and men reach parity (Sklar, 2004).

For women of color, earnings discrimination is even greater. Women's incomes are lower than men's in every racial group. Among women and men working year-round and full-time in 2009, White women earned 79 percent of White men's earnings; Black women earned 93 percent of Black men's earnings; Hispanic women earned 89 percent of Hispanic men's earnings (Bureau of Labor Statistics, 2010). The earnings gap affects the well-being of women and their families. If women earned the same as men, their annual family incomes would rise by $4,000 and poverty rates would be cut in half. Their lost earnings could have bought a home, educated their children, and been set aside for retirement (Greim, 1998; Love, 1998; The Wage Gap, 2003).

The earnings gap persists for several reasons:

- Women are concentrated in lower-paying occupations.
- Women enter the labor force at different and lower-paying levels than do men.
- Women as a group have less education and experience than do men; therefore, they are paid less than men.
- Women tend to work less overtime than men.

These conditions explain only part of the earnings gap between women and men. They do not explain why female workers earn substantially less than do male workers with the same number of years of education and with the same work histories, skills, and work experience. Men with professional degrees may expect to earn almost $2 million more than their female counterparts (Sklar, 2004). Study after study finds that if women were men with the same credentials, they would earn substantially more. Research on the income gap has found that women's and men's credentials explained some differences, but that experience accounted for only about one-third of the wage gap. The largest part of the wage gap is caused by sex discrimination in the labor market that blocks women's access to better-paying jobs through hiring or promotion or simply paying women less than men in any job (Dubeck and Dunn, 2002; ISR Newsletter, 1982; Leinwand, 1999). (See the Human Agency panel titled "Take Control: How to Negotiate Your Salary.")

Take Control: How to Negotiate Your Salary

Research by the University Association of University Women (UAUW) found that just one year out of college women working full time already earn less than their male colleagues, even when they work in the same field. Ten years after graduating, the pay gap widens (the UAUW report can be viewed in its entirety on the UAUW website www.UAUW.org).

The wage gap persists for many reasons including overt discrimination. A wage gap may be traced in part to the negotiation process, which is something we can often control. Men negotiate more often than women (Johnson, 2007).

Tory Johnson offers the following tips for women to make the most of the negotiation process:

- **Commit to negotiating.** Smart women talk about money even though it may be uncomfortable. Do all the homework needed to get comfortable with negotiating.
- **Research salary data.** Use online tools (salary.com and payscale.com are two resources), as well as salary data compiled by industry-specific associations, career services, and alumni relations to know what positions should pay based on industry, geography, company size, level of experience, and education.
- **Remove the emotion.** Women often fail to negotiate because we don't want to be disliked. Negotiating salary is not about being well-liked or disliked, it is about speaking up for fair compensation based on position and performance.
- **Anticipate the opposition.** What are some of the reasons the decision makers might say no? If the objection is "this is all we budgeted for," you might ask for a signing bonus, guaranteed salary review, or year-end bonus.
- **Negotiate as if the salary is for someone else.** Women are great at speaking up for charity, or for friends, but not for ourselves. Pretend you are speaking up for your mother, your daughter, or your best friend.

Johnson offers a final thought: Keep in mind that since the company has made you a job offer, they clearly want you and they value your skills and experience. That should bolster your confidence in negotiating your salary (Johnson, 2007).

Intersection of Race and Gender in the Workplace

There are important racial differences in the occupational concentration of women and men. Women of color make up over 14 percent of the U.S. workforce (Bureau of Labor Statistics, 2010). They are concentrated in the least paid, lowest status jobs in the labor market, with few fringe benefits, poor working conditions, high turnover, and little chance of advancement. Mexican American women, for example, are concentrated in secretarial, cashier, and janitorial jobs; Central American women in jobs such as household cleaners, janitors, and textile machine operators; Filipinas as nurses, nurses' aides, and cashiers; and African American women as nursing aides, cashiers, and secretaries (Andersen, 2011; Reskin, 1999). White women are a privileged group in the workplace compared with women of color. A much larger share of White women (41 percent) than African American women (33 percent) of Latinas (24 percent) hold managerial and professional specialty jobs (Bureau of Labor Statistics, 2010).

Workplace inequality, then, is patterned by both gender and race—and also by social class and other group characteristics. One's placement in a job hierarchy as well as the rewards one receives depend on how these characteristics "combine" (Dubeck and Dunn, 2002:48). Earnings for all workers are lowest in those areas of the labor market where women of color predominate.

How Workplace Inequality Operates

Why are women unequal in the workplace? Several theories are used to explain job segregation and wage inequality. Some focus on individuals, some focus on structural conditions, and others call on interactional processes to explain women's disadvantages in the workplace.

Popular explanations for gender differentials point to women themselves. They claim that women's socialization, their education, and the "choices" they make to take time out of the workforce to have children produce different work experiences for women and men. *Human capital theory*, for example, rests on the individual characteristics that workers bring to their jobs. Of course, time in the workplace, education, and experience all play a part. But the reality is far more complex. Research finds that women's individual characteristics, or their human capital, explain only a small part of employment inequality (Ridgeway, 1997:224). Research shows that ideas and practices about gender are embedded in workplace structures. This means that the workplace itself produces gender disparities (Acker, 1990; Williams, 1995; Martin, 2003). The structure of work itself is responsible for gender differences in the workplace. Let us examine the organization of the labor force that disadvantage women and advantage men.

Dual labor market theory centers on the labor market itself. The labor market is divided into two separate segments, with different characteristics, different roles, and different rewards. The primary segment is characterized by stability, high wages, promotion ladders, opportunities for advancement, good working conditions, and provisions for job security. The secondary market is characterized by low wages, fewer or no promotion ladders, poor working conditions, and little provision for job security. Women's work tends to fall in the secondary segment. For example, clerical work, the largest single occupation for women, has many of the characteristics associated with the secondary segment.

To understand women's disadvantages, we must look at the structural arrangements that women confront in the workplace. A classic study by Rosabeth Moss Kanter (1977), *Men and Women of the Corporation*, found that organizational location is more important than gender in shaping workers' behavior. Although women and men behave differently at work, Kanter demonstrated that the differences were created by organizational locations. Workers in low-mobility situations (regardless of their sex) tend to limit their aspirations, seek satisfactions in activities outside work, dream of escape, and create peer groups in which interpersonal relationships take over other aspects of work. Kanter argued that "when women seem to be less motivated or committed, it is probably because their jobs carry less opportunity" (Kanter, 1977:159).

Many features of work itself block women's advancement. For example, some structural conditions call on gender segregation, per se, in which women are concentrated in occupational categories based on gender. Much research in this tradition has explained why job segregation and wage inequality persist even as women have flooded the workforce and moved into "male jobs." Sociologists Barbara Reskin and Patricia Roos (1990) studied eleven once-male-dominated fields that had become integrated between 1979 and 1988: book editing, pharmacy, public relations, bank management, systems analysis, insurance sales, real estate sales, insurance adjusting and examining, bartending, baking, and typesetting and composition. Reskin and Roos found that women gained entry into these fields only *after* earnings and upward mobility in each of these fields declined; that is, salaries had gone down, prestige had diminished, or the work had become more like "women's work" (Kroeger, 1994:50). Furthermore, in each of these occupations, women specialized in lower-status specialties, in different and less desirable work settings, and in lower-paid industries. Reskin and Roos call this process *ghettoization*. Some occupations changed their sex-typing completely, while some became resegregated by race as well as gender (Amott, 1993:80; Reskin and Roos, 1990).

Many fields that have opened up to women no longer have the economic or social status they once possessed. Their structures now have two tiers: (1) higher-paying, higher-ranking jobs with more authority, and (2) lower-paying, more routinized jobs with less authority. Women are concentrated in the new, more routinized sectors of professional employment, but the upper tier of relatively autonomous work continues to be male-dominated, with only token increases in female employment (Carter and Carter, 1981). For example, women's entry into three prestige professions—medicine, college teaching, and law—has been accompanied by organizational changes. In medicine, hospital-based practice has grown as more women have entered the profession. Women doctors are more likely than men to be found in hospital-based practice, which provides less autonomy than the more traditional office practice. In college teaching, many women are employed in two-year colleges, where heavy teaching responsibilities leave little time or energy for writing and publishing—the keys to academic career advancement. And in law, women's advancement to prestigious positions is being eroded by the growth of the legal clinic, where much legal work is routinized.

Many organizational features block women's advancement. In the white-collar workforce, the well-documented phenomenon of women going just so far—and no further—in their occupations and professions is called the **glass ceiling**. This refers to the invisible barriers that limit women's mobility despite their motivation and capacity for positions of power and prestige (Lorber, 1994:227). In contrast, men who enter female-dominated professions generally encounter *structural advantages*, a "glass escalator," which tend to enhance their careers (Williams, 1992).

Many of the old discriminatory patterns are difficult to change. In the professions, for example, sponsor-protégé systems and informal interactions among colleagues limit women's mobility. Sponsorship is important in training personnel and ensuring leadership continuity. Women are less likely to be acceptable as protégés. Furthermore, their sex status limits or excludes their involvement in the buddy system or the old-boy network (Epstein, 1970). Such informal interactions continually re-create gender inequality. *Interactional theories* also explain why gender is such a major force in the labor process. Taken-for-granted interactions block women's progress:

> Interactional processes contribute to the sex-labeling of jobs, to the devaluation of women's jobs, to forms of sex discrimination ... to differences between men's and women's reward expectations, and to the processes by which women's entrance into male occupations sometimes leads to feminization or resegregation by specialty. (Ridgeway, 1997: 231)

Individual, structural, and interactional explanations of women's workplace inequality rest on *social processes* rather than outright discrimination. But it is important to recognize that outright discrimination can be found in the workplace. For example, sexual harassment affects women in all types of jobs. Sexual harassment can include unwanted leers, comments, suggestions, or physical contact of a sexual nature as well as unwelcome requests for sexual favors. Some research finds that sexual harassment is prevalent in male-dominated jobs in which women are new hires, because it is a way for male workers to dominate and control women who should be their equals.

Gender in the Global Economy

Gender relations in the United States and the world are linked to the global economy. Private businesses make investment decisions that affect the lives of women and men all around the world. In their search for profit, transnational corporations turn to developing nations where women and children provide a cheap work force. The demand for cheap labor has produced a global system of production with a strong gendered component. The international division of labor affects both men and women. As manufacturing jobs switch to low-wage economies, men are often displaced. The *global assembly line* uses the labor of women, many of them young, single, and from poor rural areas. Women workers of particular classes/castes and races from low-income countries provide a cheap supply of labor for the manufacture of commodities distributed in the wealthier industrial nations.

The global economy is altering gender relations around the world by bringing women into the public sphere (Walby, 2000). While this presents new opportunities for women, the disruption of male dominance can also result in the reaffirmation of local gender hierarchies through right-wing militia movements, religious revivalism, and other forms of masculine fundamentalism (Connell, 1998). In addition, old forms of women's exploitation and abuse are being replaced by new forms of control. For example, women's work in the sex industry is now an important part of the global economy. The worldwide expansion of the sex club industry is closely linked to organized crime and the trafficking of women and girls across national boundaries (Jeffries, 2008). (See the Globalization panel titled "Trafficking Sex for a Globalized Market.")

Trafficking Sex for a Globalized Market

What do oil, "Big Macs," and women all have in common? Although the link may seem elusive, it is a very important one. Each of these is largely connected to the global market. They are each commodities that are bought and sold in countries across the world. Many things and many people are affected in different ways by globalization, but women especially are negatively affected. Some even find themselves in what has come to be known as the global sex industry. The global sex industry can be understood as all of the activities, legal and illegal, performed by individuals and institutions around the world that service the system by which sex is bought and sold. Those who work in the sex industry are mostly women, but children are also involved. The process by which the sex industry has taken hold is complex, involving different actions by corporations. The requirement of companies to make a profit to stay in business and the desire to increase consumption by consumers in order to gain these profits have led to increased "needs" in various places across the world. Employing diverse tactics, companies make whatever their product is seem attractive and necessary, thus increasing the need for and consumption of the product. All of this is done in the name of profit. This has pervaded all sectors of society, including the sex industry (Doezema and Kempadoo, 1998:16–17). By relocating and creating new "needs" for people, as well as by creating fractured local economies, globalization has set the stage for the development of the sex industry.

The industrialization of sex work can be best illustrated by a common practice referred to as "trafficking." Trafficking is the profit-seeking system whereby women (and children) are moved from one place to another in order to perform sexual work for money. Involved in the trafficking are groups who want these workers to be brought to a certain area to perform sex acts as a draw to increase tourist interest in the area. This heightened interest brings consumers (mostly men) to the region, thus stimulating the economy. Also involved are those who are paid to ensure that women and children are available to be bought and sold, and those who are in control of the women and children when they arrive at their new location. Trafficking, then, requires an agreement between different groups whose common goal is money. While some of those involved may enter voluntarily, the majority is coerced into their situation. This coercion can occur because of the lack of other monetary options, which is often created either by large corporations leaving a city, causing joblessness, or by large corporations entering a city, creating competition that cannot be handled by local businesses. Thus, women may migrate to find better jobs and in this migration become involved in sex work (Doezema and Kempadoo, 1998:16–17). Also, promises of a better life or a better job, which are rarely, if ever, realized, are often used to lure women. "In this sense, sex tourism is like any other multinational industry, extracting enormous profits from grotesquely underpaid local labor and ... in the context of the global economy" (Hennessy and Ingraham, 1997:256).

Corporations and globalization, then, put women workers in a precarious position by making them work in horrible conditions for low pay, forcing them to migrate to find better jobs. These jobs, which may include being involved in sex trafficking, whether entered voluntarily or involuntarily, are exploitative and work to undermine the autonomy and livelihood of women across the world.

Sources: Jo Doezema and Kamala Kempadoo (eds.), 1998. Global Sex Workers: Rights, Resistance, and Redefinition. New York: Routledge, pp. 16–17. Rosemary Hennessy and Chrys Ingraham (eds.), 1997. Materialist Feminism: A Reader in Class, Difference, and Women's Lives. New York: Routledge, p. 256.

This essay was written expressly for *In Conflict and Order,* by Katie Thurman, Department of Sociology, Michigan State University (2003).

The Costs and Consequences of Sexism

Who Benefits?

Clearly, gender inequality enters all aspects of social life both in the United States and globally. This inequality is profitable to certain segments of the economy, and it also gives privileges to individual men.

Transnational corporations derive extra profits from paying women less than men. Worldwide, the workplace is segregated by gender. Women's segregation in low-paying jobs produces higher profits for certain economic sectors—namely, those where most of the workers are women. Women who are sole breadwinners and those who are in the workforce on a temporary basis have always been a source of easily exploitable labor. These women provide a significant proportion of the marginal labor force capitalists need to draw on during upswings in the business cycle and to release during downswings (Edwards, Reich, and Weisskopf, 1978:333).

Gender inequality is suited to the needs of the economy in other ways as well. The U.S. economy must accumulate capital and maintain labor power. This requires that all workers be physically and emotionally maintained. Who provides the daily maintenance that enables workers to be a part of the labor force? Women! They maintain the workers through the unpaid work they do caring for home, children, and elders. This keeps the economy going, and it also provides privileges for individual men at women's expense.

The Social and Individual Costs

Gender inequality benefits certain segments of society. Nevertheless, society at large and individual women and men pay a high price for inequality. Sexism diminishes the quality of life for all people. Our society is deprived of half of its resources when women are denied full and equal participation in its institutions. If women are systematically kept from jobs requiring leadership, creativity, and productivity, the economy suffers. The pool of talent consisting of half the population will continue to be underutilized.

Women's inequality also produces suffering for millions. We have seen that individual women pay for economic discrimination. Their children pay as well. The poverty caused by gender inequality is a pressing problem in the new century. Adult women's chances of living in poverty are still higher than men's at every age. This is called *the feminization of poverty* (Pearce, 1978). Economist Nancy Folbre points out that the highest risk of poverty comes from being female and having children—which helps explain the high rates of both female and child poverty in the United States. Folbre calls this trend the "pauperization of motherhood" (Folbre, 1985, cited in Albelda and Tilly, 1997:24). Of course, sexism produces suffering around the world. Some women are persecuted simply because they are women.

Sexism also denies *men* the potential for full human development, because gender segregation denies employment opportunities to men who wish to enter such fields as nursing, grade school teaching, or secretarial work. Eradicating sexism would benefit such males. It would benefit all males who have been forced into stereotypic male behaviors. In learning to be men, boys express their masculinity through toughness, competitiveness, and aggression. Expressions typically associated with femininity, such as gentleness and expressiveness, are seen as undesirable for males. Rigid gender norms make men pay a price for their masculinity.

Male inexpressiveness can hinder communication between husbands and wives and between fathers and children; it has been called "a tragedy of American society" (Balswick and Peck, 1971). Certainly, it is a tragedy for the man himself, crippled by an inability to show the best part of being human—exhibiting warm and tender feelings for other people (Balswick and Collier, 1976:59).

Fighting the System

Feminist Movements in the United States

Gender inequality in this society has led to feminist social movements. Three stages of feminism have been aimed at overcoming sex discrimination. The first stage grew out of the abolition movement of the 1830s. Working to abolish slavery, women found that they were not equal with their male abolitionist friends. They became convinced that women's freedom was as important as freedom from slavery. In July 1848, the first convention in history devoted to women's rights was held at Seneca Falls, New York. Participants in the Seneca Falls convention approved a declaration of independence, asserting that men and women are created equal and that they are endowed with certain inalienable rights.

During the Civil War, feminists turned their attention to the emancipation of Blacks. After the war and the ratification of the Thirteenth Amendment abolishing slavery, feminists were divided between those seeking broad social reforms and those seeking voting rights for women. The second stage of feminism gave priority to voting. The women's suffrage amendment, introduced into every session of Congress from 1878 on, was ratified on August 26, 1920, nearly three-quarters of a century after the demand for women's suffrage had been made at the Seneca Falls convention. From 1920 until the 1960s, feminism was dormant: "So much energy had been expended in achieving the right to vote that the woman's movement virtually collapsed from exhaustion" (Hole and Levine, 1979:554).

Feminism was reawakened in the 1960s. Social movements of that era gave rise to an important branch of contemporary feminism. The civil rights movement and other protest movements of the 1960s spread the ideology of equality. But like the early feminists, women involved in political protest movements found male dominance even in social movements seeking equality. Finding injustice in freedom movements, they broadened their protest to concerns such as health care, family life, and relationships between the sexes. Another strand of contemporary feminism emerged among professional women who discovered sex discrimination in earnings and advancement. Formal organizations such as the National Organization for Women evolved, seeking legislation to overcome sex discrimination (Freeman, 1979).

These two branches of contemporary feminism gave rise to a feminist consciousness among millions of U.S. women. During the 1960s and early 1970s, this produced many changes in the roles of women and men. However, periods of recession, high unemployment, and inflation in the late 1970s fed a backlash against feminism. Today's women's movement may be the first in U.S. history to face an antifeminist social movement. From the mid-1970s, a coalition of groups calling themselves profamily and prolife emerged. These groups, drawn from right-wing political organizations and religious organizations, oppose feminist gains in reproductive, family, and antidiscrimination policies. Many gains have been set back by opposition to affirmative action programs and other equal rights policies. Political, legal, and media opposition to feminism continues to undermine women's equality (Faludi, 1991).

Women's Struggles in the Twenty-First Century

The women's movement is not over. Quite the contrary, the women's movement remains one of the most influential sources of social change, even though there is not a unified organization that represents feminism (Andersen, 2011:354). Not only do mainstream feminist organizations persist, but the struggles for women's rights continue. Today, many feminist activities occur at the grassroots level, where issues of race, class, and sexuality are important. In communities across the country, women and men fight

> against the abuse of women, against corporate poisoning of their neighborhoods, against homophobia, and racism, and for people-oriented economic development, immigrants' rights, educational equity, and adequate wages. Many have been engaged in such struggles for most of their lives and continue despite the decline in the wider society's support for a progressive social agenda. (Naples, 1998:1)

Whether or not they call themselves feminists, activists across the country and around the world are using their community-based organizing to fight for social justice (Ferree, 2006). Instead of responding passively to the outside world, women are forging new agendas and strategies to benefit women.

CHAPTER REVIEW

1. U.S. society, like other societies, ranks and rewards women and men unequally.

2. Gender differences are not natural. They are social inventions. Although gender divisions make women unequal to men, different groups of men exhibit varying degrees of power, and different groups of women exhibit varying levels of inequality.

3. Men as well as women are gendered beings.

4. Gender works with the inequalities of race, class, and sexuality to produce different experiences for all women and men.

5. The conflict and order perspectives provide different explanations of women's inequality. Order theorists emphasize division of labor and social integration. Conflict theorists emphasize the economic structure of society in producing women's inequality.

6. Many sociologists have viewed gender inequality as the consequence of learned behavior. More recently,

sociologists have moved from studying gender as the individual traits of women and men to studying gender as social structure and social interaction.

7. Gender inequality is reinforced through language, interpersonal behavior, mass media, religion, the law, and politics.

8. The segregation of women in a few gendered occupations contrasts with that of men, who are distributed throughout the occupational hierarchy; and women, even with the same amount of education and when doing the same work, earn less than men in all occupations.

9. Gender segregation is the basic source of gender inequality in the labor force. Work opportunities for women tend to concentrate in a secondary market that has few advancement opportunities, fewer job benefits, and lower pay.

10. The combined effects of gender and racial segregation in the labor force keep women of color at the bottom of the work hierarchy, where working conditions are harsh and earnings are low.

11. The global economy is strongly gendered. The global assembly line is dependent on women's labor.

12. Gender inequality deprives society of the potential contributions of half its members, creates poverty among families headed by women, and limits the capacities of all women and men.

13. Feminist movements aimed at eliminating inequality have created significant changes at all levels of society. Despite a backlash against feminism, women across the country continue to struggle for equal rights.

KEY TERMS

Sex	Male dominance	Gender structure
Gender	Patriarchy	Androgyny
Gendered	Compulsory heterosexuality	Gender segregation
Feminist approach	Sexuality	Glass ceiling
Gender stratification	Capitalist patriarchy	
Gendered institutions	Gender roles	

STUDY QUESTIONS

1. In explaining gender inequality, order theorists emphasize the gender-roles approach, whereas conflict theorists focus on structural factors. Compare and assess these two approaches.
2. What are the individual and institutional mechanisms that reinforce gender inequality in society?
3. The incomes of men and women differ significantly. Why?
4. How do female officeholders make a difference?
5. Who benefits from gender inequality?

WEB RESOURCES

http://www.dol.gov/wb/
The U.S. Department of Labor Women's Bureau site has important publications put out by the bureau, as well as statistics that are pertinent to women.

http://www.chicanas.com/huh.html
Making Face, Making Soul is a Chicana feminist site. The site offers news relevant to Chicana women, information on academics, including a list of Chicana professors, and other useful information.

http://www.feminist.com/fairpay/
The National Committee on Pay Equity is a coalition to eliminate discrimination in pay based on both race and sex.

http://www.cluw.org/
The Coalition of Labor Union Women looks to empower women workers in their lives, at work, and in their unions. Links and current events information are available.

http://www.catwinternational.org/about/
The Coalition against Trafficking in Women "promotes women's rights. It works internationally to combat sexual exploitation in all its forms, especially prostitution and trafficking in women and children, in particular girls."

http://www.femina.com/
Femina is a site that offers links, from A to Y, to "sites for, by, and about women."

http://www.rslevinson.com/gaylesissues/
All Things Queer is a gay and lesbian site devoted to issues surrounding the community, including coming-out stories, news, and other resources with relevant information.

http://www.feminist.org
The Feminist Majority is a private organization dedicated to women's equality. The website provides information on a wide array of subjects, including global issues, reproductive rights, health and safety, and other subjects.

NO JOBS

↓

NO TAXES

↓

NO BUDGET!!!

KICKIN ASS
FOR THE
MIDDLECLA

EGY
18
WE
BE

FIGHT THE
ATTACK ON THE
AMERICAN
DREAM

LEGISLATORS
STOP
THE ATTACK

LEGISLATORS
STOP
THE ATTACK
ON
THE MIDDLE
CLASS

CHAPTER 13

The Economy

In the past decade or so Wal-Mart has been ranked at or near the top of Fortune's list of the 500 biggest U.S. companies. Wal-Mart's premier status underscores the economic transformation of the economy, since Wal-Mart, unlike previous Number Ones (such as General Motors or ExxonMobil) does not make or produce anything. Thus, it symbolizes the "New Economy." But just what does the ascendancy of Wal-Mart signify? It signifies the dark side of the "New Economy": low-skilled, non-union jobs; big stores driving small stores out of business, which means fewer options for consumers; reliance on low-wage economies to supply goods; and endless sprawl with huge stores and parking lots (Callahan, 2002).

The next five chapters of this book describe the fundamental institutions of society. As noted in Chapter 2, institutions are social arrangements that channel behavior in prescribed ways in the important areas of social life. They are interrelated sets of normative elements— norms, values, and role expectations—that the people making up the society have devised and passed on to succeeding generations in order to provide solutions to society's perpetually unfinished business. The institutions of society—family, education, religion, polity, and economy—are interrelated. But even though there are reciprocal effects among the institutions, the economy and the polity are the core institutions. The way society is organized to produce and distribute goods and services and the way power is organized are the crucial determinants of the way the other institutions are organized. We begin, then, with a chapter on the economy, followed by a chapter on the polity. The remaining three chapters focus on the supporting institutions of family, education, and religion. Each of these institutions is strongly affected by the form of the economy and power arrangements in the contemporary United States.

This chapter describes the economy of the United States. Four areas are emphasized: the domination of huge corporations, the maldistribution of wealth, the social organization of work, and the current economic crises. We start, though, with a brief description of the two fundamental ways societies can organize their economic activities.

Capitalism and Socialism

Industrialized societies organize their economic activities according to one of two fundamental forms: capitalism or socialism. Although no society has a purely capitalist or socialist economy, the ideal types provide opposite extremes on a scale that helps us measure the U.S. economy more accurately.

Capitalism

Three conditions must be present for pure **capitalism** to exist—private ownership of the means of production, personal profit, and competition. These necessary conditions constitute the underlying principles of a pure capitalist system. The first is private ownership of the means of production. Individuals own not only private possessions but also, most important, the capital necessary to produce and distribute goods and services. In a purely capitalist society, there would be no public ownership of any potentially profitable activity.

The pursuit of maximum profit, the second essential principle, implies that individuals are free to maximize their personal gains. This means the proponents of capitalism argue that profit seeking by individuals has positive consequences for society (that is, job creation, economic growth). Thus, seeking individual gain through personal profit is considered morally acceptable and socially desirable.

Competition, the third ingredient, is the mechanism for determining what is produced and at what price. The market forces of supply and demand ensure that capitalists will produce the goods and services wanted by the public, that the goods will be high in quality, and that they will be sold at the lowest possible price. Moreover, competition is the mechanism that keeps individual profit-seeking in check. Potential abuses such as fraud, faulty products, and exorbitant prices are negated by the existence of competitors, who will soon take business away from those who violate good business judgment. So, too, economic inefficiency is minimized as market forces cause the inept to fail and the efficient to succeed.

These three principles—private property, personal profit, and competition—require a fourth condition if true capitalism is to work: a government policy of **laissez-faire**, allowing the marketplace to operate unhindered. Any government intervention in the marketplace will, argue capitalists, distort the economy by negatively affecting incentives and freedom of individual choice. If left unhindered by government, the profit motive, private ownership, and competition will achieve the greatest good for the greatest number in the form of individual self-fulfillment and the general material progress of society.

Critics argue that capitalism promotes inequality and a host of social problems because the object is profit, not enhancing the human condition. Consider this critique by the Reverend Jesse Jackson (1998):

> The operation of free markets is a wondrous and mighty thing. To allocate goods and services, to adjust supply with demand, the market has no equal. But the market sets the price—not the value—of things. It counts consumers, not citizens. ... The market has no opinion on the distribution of income, wealth and opportunity in society. ... The market does not care if kids in Appalachia or Brooklyn go to school in buildings that are dangerous to their health. The market has no opinion on whether opportunity is open to the many, or limited to the few. The market does not care that [50] million Americans go to bed every night without health insurance. ... The market does not care if the economy is swimming in speculative capital, but large segments of the country are effectively redlined [a banking practice of not loaning money within certain boundaries, most typically where the poor and racial minorities are located] as banks merge. The market does not care if the shows our children watch on television are filled with sex, violence, and racial stereotyping. The market measures TV shows by the price of their advertising. On the values they impart, the market has no opinion. (19)

As the late political observer Molly Ivins (2000) observed: "Capitalism ... is a dandy system for creating wealth, but it doesn't do squat for social justice. No reason to expect it to—that's not its job" (22).

The economy of the United States is not purely capitalistic. Taxes are levied on people and business operations to raise monies for the common good such as a federal interstate highway system; the air traffic control system and the subsidizing of airports; flood control projects; the defense establishment; the postal system; and disaster relief. In many ways the government interferes with the market by monitoring the safety of food and drugs, prohibiting the sale of certain products, issuing licenses, protecting the civil rights of women and minorities, taxing income, subsidizing business activities, overseeing the banking and insurance industries, and by raising or lowering interest rates.

Moreover, while U.S. social programs are less generous than found in the social welfare states, there is nonetheless minimal help for victims of natural disasters, for preschool training for low-income children, for victims of predatory low-interest student loans, and for aid to the unemployed.

Socialism

Socialism is an economic system in which the means of production are owned by the people for their collective benefit. The five principles of socialism are democratization, egalitarianism, community, public ownership of the means of production, and planning for common purposes. True socialism must be democratic. Representatives of a socialist state must be answerable and responsive to the wishes of the public they serve. Nations that claim to be socialist but are totalitarian violate this fundamental aspect of socialism. The key to differentiating between authentic and spurious socialism is to determine who is making the decisions and whose interests are being served. Thus, it is a fallacy to equate true socialism with the politicoeconomic systems of the former Soviet Union, the People's Republic of China, or Cuba. These societies are socialistic in some respects; that is, their material benefits are more evenly distributed than those in the United States. But their economies and governments are controlled by a single political party in an inflexible and authoritarian manner. Although these countries claim to have democratic elections, in fact, the citizens have no electoral choice but to rubber-stamp the candidates of the ruling party. The people are denied civil liberties and freedoms that should be the hallmark of a socialist society. In a pure socialist society, democratic relations must operate throughout the social structure: in government, at work, at school, and in the community.

The second principle of socialism is egalitarianism: equality of opportunity for the self-fulfillment of all, equality rather than hierarchy in decision making, and equality in sharing the benefits of society. For some socialists, the goal is absolute equality. For most, though, equality means a limit to inequality, with some acceptable disparities in living standards. This more realistic goal of socialism requires a fundamental commitment to achieving a rough parity by evening out gross inequities in income, property, and opportunities. The key is a leveling of advantages so that all citizens receive the necessities (food, clothing, shelter, medical care, living wages, sick pay, and retirement benefits).

The third feature of socialism is community, which is the "idea that social relations should be characterized by cooperation and a sense of collective belonging rather than by conflict and competition" (Miller, 1991:406). This sense of the collective is evidenced by a relatively high taxation rate to provide for the common good—such as universal health care, paid maternity leave, subsidized child care, universal preschool programs, and a generous retirement program.

The fourth characteristic of socialism is the public ownership of the means of production. The people own the basic industries, financial institutions, utilities, transportation, and communication companies. The goal is serving the public, not making a profit.

"See? No socialists."

Mike Twohy/The New Yorker Collection/www.cartoonbank.com

The fifth principle of socialism is planning. The society must direct social activities to meet common goals. This means that socialists oppose the heart of capitalism, which is to let individuals and corporations acting in their own interests in the marketplace determine overall outcomes. For socialists, these uncoordinated activities invite chaos and, while possibly helping some in the society, will do damage to others. Thus, a purely socialist economy requires societal planning to provide, at the least possible individual and collective cost, the best conditions to meet the material needs of its citizens. Planning also aims to achieve societal goals such as protecting the environment, combating pollution, saving natural resources, and developing new technologies. Public policy is decided through the rational assessment of the needs of society and of how the economy might best be organized to achieve them. In this situation the economy must be regulated by the government, which acts as the agent of the people. The government sets prices and wages; important industries are run at a loss if necessary. Dislocations such as surpluses or shortages or unemployment are minimized by central planning. The goal is to run the economy for the good of the society.

Critics of democratic socialism argue that it minimizes individual freedom and choice. Government monopoly is inefficient because of a centralized bureaucracy making "one size fits all" decisions. Taxes are high to pay for the expensive social programs. And, the argument goes, the "cradle to grave" social programs for individuals and families reduce their motivation to succeed, an attitude that when held by many limits creativity, economic productivity, growth, and the striving for excellence.

The Corporation-Dominated Economy

The U.S. economy has always been based on the principles of capitalism; however, the present economy is far removed from a free enterprise system. The major discrepancy between the ideal system and the real one is that the U.S. economy is no longer based on competition among more or less equal private capitalists. It is now dominated by huge corporations that, contrary to classical economic theory, control demand rather than respond to the demands of the market. However well the economic system might once have worked, the increasing size and power of corporations disrupt it. This development calls into question the appropriate economic form for a modern postindustrial society.

Monopolistic Capitalism

Karl Marx, more than 130 years ago, when bigness was the exception, predicted that capitalism was doomed by several inherent contradictions that would produce a class of people bent on destroying it. The most significant of these contradictions for our purposes is the inevitability of monopolies.* Marx hypothesized that free enterprise would result in some firms becoming bigger and bigger as they eliminate their opposition or absorb smaller competing firms. The ultimate result of this process is the existence of a monopoly in each of the various sectors of the economy. Monopolies, of course, are antithetical to the free enterprise system because they, not supply and demand, determine the price and the quality of the product.

For the most part, the evidence in U.S. society upholds Marx's prediction. Less than 1 percent of all corporations produce over 80 percent of the private-sector output. Most sectors of the economy are dominated by few corporations. Instead of one corporation controlling an industry, the typical situation is domination by a small number of firms. When four or fewer firms supply 50 percent or more of a particular market, a **shared monopoly** results, which performs much as a monopoly or cartel would. Most economists agree that above this level of concentration—a four-firm ratio of 50 percent or more—the economic costs of a shared monopoly are manifest (for example, higher prices by 25 percent). Government data show that a number of industries are highly concentrated (for example, each of the following industries has four or fewer firms controlling at least 60 percent): light bulbs, breakfast cereals, turbines/generators, aluminum, tobacco, beer, chocolate/cocoa, photography equipment, trucks, cosmetics, film distribution, soft drinks, snack foods, guided missiles, and roasted coffee.

This trend toward ever greater concentration among the largest U.S. business concerns has accelerated because of two activities—mergers and **interlocking directorates**.

Megamergers.   There are thousands of mergers each year, as giant corporations become even larger. Some of the ten largest mergers in U.S. history have occurred in recent years (for example, Time, Inc., and AOL joining with Warner Communications; Disney merging with Capital Cities/ABC; NBC merging with Comcast; United Airlines taking over Continental Airlines; the merger of NationsBank and BankAmerica; Bank of America taking over Merrill Lynch; J.P. Morgan buying out Bear Sterns; Philip Morris taking over Miller Brewing; Citicorp merging with Travelers Group; Texaco buying out Getty Oil; and Exxon merging with Mobil Oil). There have also been megamergers combining U.S. and foreign firms (for example, Daimler and Chrysler, British Petroleum and Amoco, and Deutsche Bank and Bankers Trust). The federal government encouraged these mergers by relaxing antitrust law enforcement on the grounds that efficient firms should not be hobbled.

This trend toward megamergers has at least six negative consequences: (1) It increases the centralization of capital, which reduces competition and raises prices for consumers; (2) it increases the power of huge corporations over workers, unions, and governments;

---

*Marx prophesied that capitalism carried the seeds of its own destruction. In addition to resulting in monopolies, capitalism (1) encourages crises—inflation, slumps, gluts, depressions—because the lack of central planning means the overproduction of some goods and the underproduction of others; (2) encourages mass production for expansion and profits, but in so doing, a social class, the proletariat (working class), is created that has the goal of equalizing the distribution of profits; (3) demands the introduction of labor-saving machinery, which forces unemployment and a more hostile proletariat; and (4) will control the state, the effect of which is that the state will pass laws favoring the wealthy, thereby incurring the further wrath of the proletariat. All of these contradictions of capitalism increase the probability of the proletariat building class consciousness, which is the condition necessary before class conflict and the ushering in of a new economic system (Marx, 1967).

(3) the benefits to local communities are diminished ("Superlarge companies with interests and commitments stretching from Boston to Brisbane are unlikely to focus as intensely as smaller ones do on support for the local neighborhoods—the schools, the arts, the development of research activities, the training of potential workers" [Garten, 1999:28].); (4) it reduces the number of jobs (for example, when Citicorp and Travelers combined to make Citigroup, 10,400 jobs were cut); (5) it increases corporate debt (currently, U.S. corporations spend about half their earnings on interest payments); and (6) it is nonproductive. Elaborating on this last point, mergers and takeovers do not create new plants, products, or jobs. Rather, they create profits for lawyers, accountants, brokers, bankers, and big investors.

Interlocking Directorates. Another mechanism for the ever greater concentration of the size and power of the largest corporations is interlocking directorates, the linkage between corporations that results when an individual serves on the board of directors of two companies (a **direct interlock**) or when two companies each have a director on the board of a third company (an **indirect interlock**). Such arrangements have great potential to benefit the interlocked companies by reducing competition through the sharing of information and the coordination of policies.

In 1914, passage of the Clayton Act made it illegal for a person to serve simultaneously on the corporate boards of two companies that were in direct competition with each other. Financial institutions and indirect interlocks, however, were exempt. Moreover, the government has had difficulty in determining what constitutes "direct competition." The result is that despite the prohibition, over 90 percent of large U.S. corporations have some interlocking directors with other corporations.

Interlocking directorates proliferate throughout U.S. industry. When directors are linked directly or indirectly, there is the potential for cohesiveness, common action, and unified power. Clearly, the principles of capitalism are compromised when this phenomenon occurs.

Transnational Corporations

The thesis of the previous section is that there is a trend for corporations to increase in size, eventually resulting in huge enterprises that join with other large companies to form effective monopolies. This process of economic concentration provides the largest companies with enormous economic and political power. If, for example, we compare government budgets with gross corporate revenues, in 2009 the total sales of Wal-Mart, Royal Dutch Shell, and ExxonMobil each exceeded the gross domestic product of Indonesia (the fourth most populous nation in the world). Combining these three transnational corporations, their sales revenues were more than the combined economies of the world's poorest 118 countries with a total population of over 800 million (Teller-Elsberg, Folbre, and Heintz, 2006:15).

Another trend—the globalization of the largest U.S. corporations—makes their power all the greater. This fact of international economic life has very important implications for social problems, both domestically and abroad.

A number of U.S. corporations have substantial assets overseas. In 2009, six of the top fifteen multinationals in sales were U.S.-based corporations (*Forbes*, 2010a). U.S. corporations are shifting more and more of their total assets outside the United States to increase profits. Resources necessary for manufacture and production tend to be cheaper in many other nations. Most significant, U.S. corporations increase their profits by moving their production facilities from high-wage situations to low-wage nonunion countries. Moreover, foreign production costs are lower because labor safety laws and environmental protection laws are much more lax than in the United States.

The consequences of this shift in production from the United States to outside this country are significant. Most important is the reduction of, even drying up of, many semiskilled and unskilled jobs in the United States. The effects of increased unemployment are twofold: increased welfare costs and increased discontent among those in the working class.

Another result of the twin processes of concentration and internationalization of corporations is the enormous power wielded by the gigantic multinational corporations. In essence, the largest corporations control the world economy. Their decisions to build or not to build, where to relocate a plant, and to start a new product or to scrap an old one have tremendous impacts on the lives of ordinary citizens in the countries they operate from and invest in and in their disinvestment in U.S.-based operations.

Finally, multinational corporations tend to meddle in the internal affairs of other nations in order to protect their investments and maximize profits. These activities include attempts to overthrow governments considered unfriendly to corporate interests and payment of millions of dollars in bribes and political contributions to reactionary governments and conservative leaders in various countries.

Capitalism and Inequality

Inequality is endemic to capitalism. In the competition for profits there are winners and losers. But, as economist Lester Thurow puts it:

> In the theology of capitalism the distributions of wealth, income and earnings are of no consequence. There is no concept of fairness other than that those who produce in the market are fairly compensated by the market. Those who do not produce are shoved aside by the market. They do not get to consume—they do not deserve to consume. (quoted in Collins, Leondar-Wright, and Sklar, 1999:1)

We have seen how corporate wealth is concentrated through shared monopolies and interlocking directorates. Let's begin by reviewing the degree to which corporate wealth is concentrated.

Concentration of Corporate Wealth

Wealth in the business community is centralized in a relatively few corporations, and this concentration is increasing. In 2009, for example, the corporation with the most assets ($2.22 trillion) was Bank of America and the top corporation in sales—Wal-Mart—had $408.2 billion in revenues, and the greatest producer of profits was ExxonMobil at $19.28 billion (*Forbes*, 2010a). The following examples reveal just how concentrated wealth is among the major U.S. corporations:

Less than 1 percent of all corporations account for over 80 percent of the total output of the private sector.

- Of the 15,000 commercial U.S. banks, the largest fifty hold more than one-third of all assets.
- One percent of all food corporations control 80 percent of all the industry's assets and about 90 percent of the profits.
- Six U.S.-based transnational corporations ship 90 percent of the grain in the world market.
- Five massive conglomerates (Viacom/CBS, Disney/ABC, News Corp./Fox, NBC/Comcast, and AOL/Time Warner) now command 75 percent of prime-time television. Similarly, two conglomerates (Clear Channel and Viacom) together own radio stations with 42 percent of the nation's listeners.

Concentration of Private Wealth and Income

Capitalism generates inequality. Wealth is concentrated not only in the largest corporations but also among individuals and families. As noted in Chapter 10, Bill Gates of Microsoft was the wealthiest person in 2010 at about $54 billion, followed by Warren Buffett of Berkshire Hathaway at $45 billion.

A few families are fabulously wealthy and colossal in corporate magnitude. The six heirs to Sam Walton's fortune were worth a combined $89.6 billion in 2010. Dividends from their Wal-Mart stock add a cumulative total of $1 billion annually. The 400 richest Americans own about as much wealth as the bottom half of the population. Michael Parenti (2002) describes the holdings of few "old-rich" families:

> A handful of giant business conglomerates, controlled by the Mellons, Morgans, DuPonts, Rockefellers, and a few others, dominate the U.S. economy. The DuPonts control ten corporations, each worth billions of dollars, including General Motors, Coca-Cola, and United Brands, along with many smaller firms. The DuPonts serve as trustees of dozens of colleges. They own about forty manorial estates and private museums in Delaware alone and have set up thirty-one tax-exempt foundations. ...
>
> Another powerful financial empire, that of the Rockefellers, extends into just about every industry in every state of the Union and every nation of the world. The Rockefellers control five of the world's twelve largest oil companies and four of the biggest banks. (12)

Concentration of Want and Misery

The inequality generated by a capitalist economy has a dark side. Summarizing the 2010 data on poverty in the United States (found in Chapter 10), 15.1 percent of the population (46.2 million people) were below the poverty line. According to the National Council on Economic Opportunity, another 30 million were on the edge of poverty. The data indicate that the poor are concentrated among certain social categories, especially people of color and families headed by women.

Again, summarizing from earlier chapters, research strongly substantiates how the life chances of the poor are jeopardized by their lack of resources. The fewer resources available, the greater the possibilities for any of the following to occur:

- Premature births and babies born mentally retarded because of prenatal malnourishment
- Below-average life expectancy
- Disproportionate death from tuberculosis, influenza, pneumonia; from cancer of the stomach, lung, bronchus, and trachea; and from accidents
- Impaired health because of differences in diet, sanitary facilities, shelter, and medical care
- More frequent and longer periods of illness
- An arrest, conviction, and serving of a longer sentence for a given violation
- A lower-than-average level of educational attainment
- Spouse and child abuse, divorce, and desertion

Thus, the economic position of a family has very telling consequences on the probability of good health, educational attainment, justice, and a stable marriage.

Work in U.S. Society

Work is central to the human experience. Societies are organized to allocate work in order to produce the goods and services needed by the society and its members for sustenance, clothing, shelter, defense, and even luxury. Work provides individuals with their social identity, economic resources, and social location. Work dominates their time and is a primary source of life's meaning because it constitutes their contributions to other people.

The world of work also has a dark side, however. The structure of work is a major source of social problems. Work is alienating for many people. The organization of work sometimes exploits, does harm to workers, and often dehumanizes them. The distribution of work and how it is rewarded are major sources of inequality in society. This section focuses on the social problems generated by the social organization of work.

The Problems of Work

Work is a universal human activity. People everywhere engage in physical and mental activities that enhance the physical and social survival of themselves and others. Although people universally must work to meet their material needs, the way work is structured varies by society. Let's examine problems that emanate from the way work is structured in U.S. society.

The Control of Workers. With the advent of the Industrial Revolution, more and more families left agrarian life, moved to cities, and worked in factories. Work in these factories was sometimes difficult, often tedious, and usually boring. There was always the threat of lowered productivity and worker unrest under these adverse conditions. The factory owners and their managers used several tactics to counteract these potential problems and especially to maintain high productivity—scientific management, hierarchical control, technical control, and extortion.

Scientific management (called Taylorization, after its founder, Frederick Taylor) came to the fore in U.S. industry around 1900. The emphasis was on breaking down work into very specialized tasks, standardization of tools and procedures, and speeding up repetitive work. These efforts to increase worker efficiency and therefore to increase profits meant that workers developed a very limited range of skills. Instead of a wide knowledge of building cars or furniture, their knowledge was severely curtailed. This specialization had the effect of making workers highly susceptible to automation and to being easily replaced by cheaper workers. But the scientific-management approach also had a contradictory effect. In its attempt to increase efficiency by having workers do ever more compartmentalized tasks, it increased the repetition, boredom, and meaninglessness of work—hence, the strong tendency for workers to become alienated and restless. Because a worker does specific production task, it is clear to supervisors and co-workers when the worker fails to perform (Ritzer, 2000:31).

Closely related to scientific management is the use of bureaucracy to control workers. Work settings, whether in factories, offices, or corporations, are organized into bureaucratized hierarchies. In this hierarchy of authority (chain of command), each position in the chain gives orders to those below, taking responsibility for their actions and following orders from above. The hierarchical arrangement controls workers by holding out the possibility of advancement, with more prestigious job titles, higher wages, and greater benefits as one moves up the ladder. Those who hope to be upwardly mobile in the organization must become obedient rule followers who do not question authority.

Similarly, work organized along an assembly line permits maximum control over workers. "Workers must do certain tasks at specific points during the production process. It is immediately obvious when a worker fails to perform the required tasks" (Ritzer, 2000:31).

Workers are also controlled by management's use of technology to monitor and supervise them (see Chapter 6). Some businesses use lie detectors to assess worker loyalty. Psychological tests and drug tests are used to screen applicants for work. Telephone taps have been used to determine whether workers use company time for personal use. Closed-circuit television, two-way mirrors, and other devices have been used by management to determine whether workers are using their time most productively. The most common contemporary technology for worker control is the computer. The computer can count keystrokes, time phone calls, monitor frequency of errors, assess overall employee performance, and even issue warnings when the employee falls short of the ideal.

A final management tool to control workers is extortion. If workers become too militant in their demands for higher wages, safe working conditions, or benefits, management can threaten them with reprisals. In the past, owners threatened to hire cheaper labor (new immigrants, for example) or to use force to end a strike. Today, the most common and successful management tool is the threat to move the plant to a nonunion state or outside the United States if the union does not reduce its demands or to replace the workers with robots or other forms of automation.

Alienation. **Alienation** refers to the separation of human beings from each other, from themselves, and from the products they create. In capitalism, according to Karl Marx, worker alienation occurs because the workers do not have any control over their labor; because they are manipulated by managers; because they tend to work in large, impersonal settings; and because they work at specialized tasks. Martin Nicolaus in his foreword to Karl Marx's *Grundrisse* summarizes Marx on alienation:

> With the advance of the division of labor and the growing scale of capitalist production, the role of the worker in the industrial process has a tendency to be transformed from active to passive, from master to cog, and even from participant to observer, as the system of machinery becomes more automatic. (1973:51)

Under these circumstances, workers use only a fraction of their talents and have no pride in their own creativity and in the final product. Thus, we see that worker alienation is linked with unfulfilled personal satisfaction. As Blauner (1964) describes it,

> [a]lienation exists when workers are unable to control their immediate work processes, to develop a sense of purpose and function which connects their jobs to the overall organization of production, to belong to integrated industrial communities, and when they fail to become involved in the activity of work as a mode of personal self-expression. (5)

Put another way, this time by philosopher Albert Camus, "Without work all life goes rotten. But when work is soulless, life stifles and dies" (quoted in Levitan and Johnson, 1982:63).

In the absence of satisfaction and personal fulfillment, work becomes meaningless. When this meaninglessness is coupled with management's efforts to control workers, the repetitive nature of the work, and the requirement of punching a time clock, many workers feel a profound resentment. This resentment may lead workers to join together in a union or other collective group to improve their working conditions. For many workers, though, the alienation remains at a personal level and is manifested by higher worker dissatisfaction, absenteeism, disruption in the workplace, and alcohol or other drug abuse on the job.

Alienation is not limited to manual workers. The work of white-collar workers such as salesclerks, administrative assistants, and bank tellers is mostly routine, repetitive, boring, and unchallenging. These workers, like assembly line workers, follow orders, do limited tasks, and have little sense of accomplishment.

Studs Terkel (1975), in introducing his book *Working*, summarizes the personal impact of alienating work:

> This book, being about work, is, by its very nature, about violence—to the spirit as well as to the body. It is about ulcers as well as accidents, about shouting matches as well as fistfights, about nervous breakdowns as well as kicking the dog around. It is, above all (or beneath all), about daily humiliations. To survive the day is triumph enough for the walking wounded among the great many of us.
>
> It is about a search, too, for daily meaning as well as daily bread, for recognition as well as for cash, for astonishment rather than torpor; in short, for a sort of life rather than a Monday through Friday sort of dying. Perhaps immortality, too, is part of the quest. To be remembered was the wish, spoken and unspoken, of the heroes and heroines of this book.
>
> For the many, there is a hardly concealed discontent. The blue-collar blues is no more bitterly sung than the white-collar moan. "I'm a machine," says the spotwelder. "I'm caged," says the steelworker. "A monkey can do what I do," says the receptionist. "I'm less than a farm implement," says the migrant worker. "I'm an object," says the high-fashion model. Blue collar and white call upon the identical phrase: "I'm a robot." (xiii–xiv)

Many forms of work are alienating because the work is routine, repetitive, boring, and unchallenging.

Dangerous Working Conditions. In a capitalist economy, workers represent a cost to profit-seeking corporations. The lower the management can keep labor costs, the greater will be their profits. Historically, low labor costs meant that workers received low wages, had inferior or nonexistent fringe benefits such as health care, and worked in unhealthy conditions. Mines and factories were often extremely unsafe. The labor movement early in this century gathered momentum because of the abuse experienced by workers.

After a long and sometimes violent struggle, the unions succeeded in raising wages for workers, adding fringe benefits, and making work conditions safer. But the owners were slow to change; and worker safety was, and continues to be, one of the most difficult areas. Many owners of mills, mines, and factories continue to consider the safety of their workers a low-priority item, presumably because of the high cost.

About thirty-five years ago, the federal government instituted the Occupational Safety and Health Administration (OSHA) to make the workplace safer. The result has been a 75 percent drop in workplace fatalities, despite resistance by the business community and weak enforcement by the government. Even with this dramatic drop in worker deaths, the problem of worker safety remains.

> There is currently one OSHA inspector for every 66,258 workers, according to [a report by the AFL-CIO]. At these staffing and inspection levels it would take federal OSHA 137 years to inspect each workplace under its jurisdiction just once. ... (Wedekind, 2009:7)
>
> Around 6,000 workers are killed every year on the job, and 4.5 million are injured. Another 10,000 die later on from job injuries and 50,000 from occupational diseases caused by things as chemicals, asbestos, pesticides, and solvents. Some 50,000 to 60,000 sustain permanent disability, and millions more suffer from work-related illnesses. (Parenti, 2008:99)

Minorities, especially Latinos, have the highest work-related death rates. From 1992 to 2007, the number of Latino worker deaths increased by 76 percent (Jervis, 2009). The reason for the higher Latino rate is the influx of Latino immigrants who took the dangerous and hard-to-fill jobs in construction, meat packing plants, and as farm laborers. Undocumented workers often are exploited because if they complain they will be deported. They usually do not join unions, which help protect workers, and they do not protest when conditions are dangerous.

Significant occupational dangers continue to plague workers, especially in certain jobs such as loggers, fishers, structural iron and steel workers, refuse collectors, roofers, electrical power line installers and repairers, miners, and farmers. In addition to falls, fires, explosions, cave-ins, violent weather, and equipment malfunctions, there are also dangers from invisible contaminants such as nuclear radiation, chemical compounds, coal tars, dust, and asbestos fibers in the air. These dangers from invisible contaminants are increasing because the production of synthetic chemicals has increased so dramatically. The following examples describe the specific risks of continued exposure to dangerous chemicals in certain industries:

Workers in the dyestuffs industry (working with aromatic hydrocarbons) have about thirty times the risk of the general population of dying from bladder cancer.

- About 10 percent of coal miners suffer from black lung, caused by years of breathing coal dust in areas with inadequate ventilation.
- Migrant farm workers have a life expectancy thirty years below the national average. This low rate is a consequence of living in poverty or near-poverty and, most significant, of the exposure to herbicides and pesticides sprayed on the fields where they work.
- Workers in the semiconductor industry face special dangers from exposure to acids, gases, and solvents used in chip manufacturing. "About 75,000 workers in semiconductor plants breath or come in contact with dozens of known or suspected carcinogens, including toluene, cadmium, arsenic, benzene, and trichloroethylene" (Stranahan, 2002:45).
- Pregnant operators of video display terminals have disproportionate numbers of miscarriages or babies with birth defects, apparently from exposure to nonionizing radiation.

The record of industry has often been one of ignoring the scientific data, or of stalling through court actions, or of claims that jobs will be lost because of the cost to clean up the factories or mills, resulting in higher prices to consumers. Most important, some companies have not informed workers of the dangers.

This discussion raises some critical questions: Should profits supersede human life? Are owners guilty of murder if their decisions to minimize plant safety result in industrial deaths? Who is a greater threat, the thugs in the streets or the executives in the suites? Jeffrey Reiman (2004) answers these questions:

> Is a person who kills another in a bar brawl a greater threat to society than a business executive who refuses to cut into his profits to make his plant a safe place to work? By any measure of death and suffering the latter is by far a greater danger than the former. Because he wishes his workers no harm, because he is only indirectly responsible for death and disability while pursuing legitimate economic goals, his acts are not labelled "crimes." Once we free our imagination from the blinders of the one-on-one model of crime, can there be any doubt that the criminal justice system does not protect us from the gravest threats to life and limb? It seeks to protect us when danger comes from a young-lower-class male in the inner city. When a threat comes from an upper-class business executive in an office, the criminal justice system looks the other way. (87)

Sweatshops. A sweatshop is a substandard work environment where workers are paid less than the minimum wage, workers are not paid overtime premiums, and other labor laws are violated. Although sweatshops occur in various types of manufacturing, they occur most frequently in the garment industry. Garment sweatshops are common in New York City, San Francisco, Los Angeles, El Paso, and Seattle. The workers in these places make clothes for such brands as Levi Strauss, Esprit, Casual Corner, the Limited, the Gap, and for such merchandisers as JC Penny, Sears, and Wal-Mart. The workers, mostly Latina and Asian immigrant women, are paid much below the minimum wage, receive no benefits, and work in crowded, unsafe, and stifling conditions.

Modern-day slavery exists in the United States. The Central Intelligence Agency estimates that "50,000 people are trafficked into or transited through the United States annual as sex slaves, domestic servants, garment slaves, and agricultural laborers" (quoted in Kralis, 2006, para 2; see also Bales, 1999 and Cockburn, 2009).

U.S. corporations also sell products produced by workers in sweatshop conditions in other countries. Soccer balls are sewn together by child laborers in Pakistan. Mattel makes tens of millions of Barbies a year in China. Many of Disney's products are made in Sri Lanka and Haiti—countries notorious for their lack of labor and human rights. Nike, Reebok, and other shoe manufacturers have exploited workers in many Asian countries. See the Globalization panel titled "Modern Day Slavery in the United States."

Unions and Their Decline. Historically, labor unions have been extremely important in changing management-labor relations. Joining together, workers challenged owners to increase wages, add benefits, provide worker security, and promote safety in the workplace. Through the use of strikes, work slowdowns, public relations, and political lobbying, working conditions improved and union members, for the most part, prospered. In wages and benefits, union workers earn about 34 percent more than nonunion workers. Consider the following differences between union workers and unorganized workers in comparable jobs:

The median earnings of full-time wage and salary workers in 2009 were $908 per week for union workers, compared with $710 for employees not represented by unions (Bureau of Labor Statistics, reported in Hananel, 2010).

- Union members are 59 percent more likely to have employer-provided health insurance than their non-union counterparts (Reich, 2009).
- Union women earn 33 percent more than nonunion women.
- African American union members earn 35 percent more than comparable nonunion members; and Latino unionists earn 51 percent more.

Modern Day Slavery in the United States

The United States outlawed slavery in 1865. According to history and political science textbooks, the United States is a free country. Yet the U.S. Central Intelligence Agency estimates that 50,000 people are trafficked into or transited through the United States annually as prostitutes, domestics, garment, and agricultural slaves (reported in U.S. State Department, 2007). These people are immigrants from East Asia, Eastern Europe, Mexico, and Central America. Some are in the United States involuntarily. Some migrated willingly, legally and illegally, but are subjected to conditions of involuntary servitude. In the latter case, these immigrants came to the States to work, only to find themselves owing money to those who helped them get here, for housing and food, and even for the tools of their employment.

> In cases like these, the workers' employers are often in league with those who helped them immigrate, or perhaps they rent out the squalid quarters where the workers stay or charge exorbitant prices for minor services like check-cashing. Finding themselves in such debt, the workers are forced to stay on—at risk of violent retribution if they leave—and surrender their wages until their obligation is paid. (Colin, 2007:2)

These workers are trapped in bonded labor—a modern day version of slavery. This type of slavery differs from slavery of the past since legal ownership has been replaced by domination and power. The perpetrators do not rely on chains, or guns. "All they require is some method of coercion: threats of beating, deportation, death, or, perhaps most effective, harm to the victim's family back home should he or she ever speak up" (Bowe, 2007:xvii).

Concerning what to do about this problem, researchers from the University of California, Berkeley's Human Rights Center and the Washington D.C.-based anti-slavery group, Free the Slaves, state that:

> New federal laws have been passed to combat these crimes . . . but much more needs to be done— especially at the local level. Police officers, rather than federal agents, are most likely to encounter forced labor but often mistake it for illegal immigration and treat victims as part of a criminal enterprise. [They] recommend launching a broad-based awareness campaign; improving monitoring of industries vulnerable to forced labor; increasing training and coordination among law enforcement officials in the United States; and strengthening protections for survivors of forced labor. (Gilmore, 2004)

But unions have lost their strength since about 1980, as membership declined from a high of about 35 percent of wage and salary workers in the mid-1950s to 11.9 percent in 2010. With such small and dwindling numbers, labor unions are in danger of becoming irrelevant. Most significant, they have already become enfeebled politically. This decline in power by unions is linked to the decline in progressive politics. Once, unions were a major force behind such progressive programs as Social Security, Medicare, unemployment insurance, and the minimum wage. When unions were a political force, even Republicans had to occasionally give in to their demands.

The reasons for the decline in union membership (and clout) are several. First, there was a direct assault against unions by Republican Presidents Ronald Reagan, George H. W. Bush, and George W. Bush. Each of these administrations was unsympathetic with strikes and sometimes used federal leverage to weaken them. Similarly, their appointees to the post of Secretary of Labor and the National Labor Relations Board (NLRB) were probusiness rather than prolabor. For instance, the Republican-dominated NLRB voted in 2006 in three cases, known collectively as the Kentucky River cases, to slash long-time federal labor laws protecting workers' freedom to form unions, by allowing employers to classify millions of workers as supervisors. Under federal labor law, supervisors are prohibited from forming unions.

Second, public opinion has turned against unions because some of them are undemocratic, scandal-ridden, and too zealous in their demands. Public opinion has also turned against organized labor because of a probusiness, procapitalist bias that increased during the era of supply-side economics that dominated the Reagan and first Bush administrations and much of Congress during that time. That bias, although muted a bit, continued during the Clinton administration but was resurrected during George W. Bush's administration.

Third, businesses do all they can to block unions. Typically, companies are required to have a union vote if 30 percent of workers sign a petition. When such an election does occur, companies have won more than half the time, versus 28 percent in the early 1950s. The antiunion vote by workers is the result usually of an all-out assault by the company, including information arguing that unionization may lead to downsizing or even the closing of plants, "worker appreciation" days with free barbeque or pizza, and selective firing of workers who are union activists (an illegal activity, but it happens in about one-fourth of union drives, according to a commission study established by President Clinton), and other forms of intimidation.

A major reason for the decline of union strength is the transformation of the economy brought about by globalization (discussed in Chapter 8). Manufacturing jobs, which are in decline, have historically been prounion, while service jobs, which are increasing, have been typically nonunionized. Many businesses, faced with stiff competition from low-wage economies, have insisted on reducing wages and/or worker benefits or have said they would go bankrupt or move overseas themselves. The increased use of microchip technology threatens jobs with increased automation in the factory (robots to replace assembly-line workers) and in the office (computers to displace typists and file clerks). Similarly, the advent of computers, modems, and fax machines has increased the number of workers who work at home, as temporaries, and part-time. These workers are the least likely to join unions.

These forces have given the strong advantage to management, a trend that has several negative consequences. First, faced with the threat of plants closing or moving to nonunion localities or to low-wage nations, unions have chosen, typically, to give back many of the gains they made during the 1960s and 1970s. Thus, workers have lost real wages and benefits.

A second consequence of union decline is that the workplace may be less safe. "Some of the most injury-prone industries, like food processing and textiles, have clustered in right-to-work (nonunion) states across the South" (Lacayo, 1991:29).

A major consequence of union decline is the further dwindling of the middle class. In the words of Albert Shanker (1992), the late president of the American Federation of Teachers,

> The union movement took a lot of workers who were relatively unskilled and turned them into middle class people who educated their children and supported the United States economy. Now, we've got businesses turning their employees into third-world workers. (E9)

Implied in this statement is a related consequence: If businesses turn their employees into Third World workers, then these workers will not be able to purchase enough goods and services to encourage economic growth and society-wide prosperity. As Norman Birnbaum (1992) has said, "Nations with strong unions and social contracts have the highest living standards" (319).

Another consequence is a weakened voice and political power for working people. Instead of a unified voice that argues for conditions favorable to workers and their families, nonunion workers go in a number of political directions, sometimes against their economic interests.

A final consequence points to a possible contradiction—the precipitous decline in unions may actually lead to labor's regeneration. As the unions decline, with workers poorly compensated and ever fearful of losing their jobs, with management becoming more arrogant and demanding, the situation may get bad enough that there will be a turnaround—a surge in union membership and worker militancy. Or, as occurred in Wisconsin, Ohio, and other states following the Republican landslide in 2010, Republican governors sought to weaken or even ban public employee unions. These attacks on unions elicited outrage among union *and* non-union workers. Is this the precipitating event that could lead not only to a stronger collective voice in the work arena but also in the nation's politics. Those nations with strong unionized labor (for example, Canada, Germany, France, and Sweden) have a social democratic conception of society, which means universal health care, progressive income taxes, and more equitable government programs.

Of course, this scenario may not occur. Unions may continue to decline in size and influence; pay and benefits to workers may continue to erode; and workers may be fragmented rather than united.

Discrimination in the Workplace: The Perpetuation of Inequality

Women and minorities have long been the objects of discrimination in U.S. industry. Currently (and we have progressed mightily), approximately 50,000 charges of discrimination by organizations are filed annually with the U.S. Equal Opportunity Commission. The charges now and in the past have centered on hiring policies, seniority rights, restricted job placement, limited opportunities for advancement, and lower pay for equal work. A number of court suits (and those settled out of court) illustrate that discriminatory policies have been common among such major corporations as AT&T, General Motors, and Northwest Airlines and in such industries as banking and steel.

Two mechanisms operating in the U.S. economy perpetuate inequalities in the job market by social class, race, and gender—the segmented labor market and male dominance in the workplace.

Segmented Labor Market. The capitalist economy is divided into two separate sectors that have different characteristics, different roles, and different rewards for laborers within each. This organization of the economy is called the segmented labor market, or the dual labor market. The primary sector is composed of large, bureaucratic organizations with relatively stable production and sales. Jobs within this sector require developed skills, are relatively well paid, occur in good working conditions, and are stable. Within this sector there are two types of jobs. The first type, those in the upper tier, is high-status professional and managerial jobs. The pay is very good for the highly educated people in these jobs. They have a high degree of personal autonomy, and the jobs offer variety, creativity, and initiative. Upward mobility is likely for those who are successful. The second type, the lower-tier jobs within the primary sector, is held by working-class people. The jobs are either white-collar clerical or blue-collar skilled and semiskilled. The jobs are repetitive, and mobility is limited. The jobs are relatively secure because of unionization, although they are much more vulnerable than those in the upper tier. When times are difficult, these workers tend to be laid off rather than terminated.

The secondary economic sector is composed of marginal firms in which product demand is unstable. Jobs within this sector are characterized by poor working conditions, low wages, few opportunities for advancement, and weak job security. Little education or skill is required to perform these tasks. Workers beginning in the secondary sector tend to get locked in because they lack the skills required in the primary sector and they usually have unstable work histories. A common interpretation of this problem is that secondary-sector workers are in these dead-end jobs because of their pathology—poor work history, lack of skills, and lack of motivation. Such an explanation, however, blames the victim. Poor work histories tend to be the result of unemployment caused by the production of marginal products and the lack of job security. Similarly, these workers have few, if any, incentives to learn new skills or to stay for long periods with an employer because of the structural impediments to upward mobility. And unlike workers in the primary sector, workers in the secondary sector are more likely to experience harsh and capricious work discipline from supervisors, primarily because there are no unions.

"How could we discriminate against minority employees... we don't even have any."

The significance of this dual labor market is threefold. First, placement in one of these segments corresponds with social class, which tends to be perpetuated from generation to generation. Second, employment in the secondary sector is often so inadequately paid that many full-time workers live in poverty, as noted in Chapter 2. And third, the existence of a dual labor market reinforces racial, ethnic, and gender divisions in the labor force. White males, while found in both segments, tend to predominate in the upper tier of the primary sector. White females tend to be clerks in the lower tier of the primary sector, and White ethnics tend to be clerks in the lower tier of the primary sector. Males and females of color are found disproportionately in the secondary sector. These findings explain why unemployment rates for African Americans and Latinos are consistently much higher than (usually at least double) the rate for Whites. They also explain the persistent wage differences found by race and gender.

Male Dominance at Work. Closely tied to segmented labor markets is the dominance of men in work-related roles (also known as capitalist patriarchy). This dominance is reflected in two ways—men tend to make the rules and enforce them, and men receive unequal (that is, greater) rewards (see Figure 13.1).

Current gender inequality results from a long history of patriarchal social relations in which men have consciously kept women in subordinate roles at work and in the home. Men as workers consistently have acted in their own interests to retain power and to keep women either out of their occupations or in subordinate and poorly paid work roles. Historically, through their unions, males insisted that the higher-status and better-paying jobs be exclusively male. They lobbied legislatures to pass legislation supportive of male exclusiveness in occupations and in opposition to such equalization measures as minimum wages for women. Also, the male unions prevented women from gaining the skills that would lead them to equal-paying jobs. The National Typographical Union in 1854, for example, insisted not only that women be refused jobs as compositors but also that they not be taught the skills necessary to be a compositor (Hartmann, 1976).

Throughout U.S. history, capitalists have used gender inequality in the workplace to their advantage. Women were hired because they would work for less money than men, which made men all the more fearful of women in the workplace. Capitalists even used the threat of hiring lower-paid women to take the place of higher-paid men to keep the wages of both sexes down and to lessen labor militancy.

In contemporary U.S. society, men and women, with some exceptions, are accorded different and unequal positions in religious, government, school, work, and family activities.

FIGURE 13.1

Female-to-Male Earnings Ratio and Median Earnings of Full-Time, Year-Round Workers fifteen Years Old and Over by Sex: 1960–2009

Source: U.S. Census Bureau, Current Population Survey, 1961 to 2009 Annual Social and Economic Supplements.

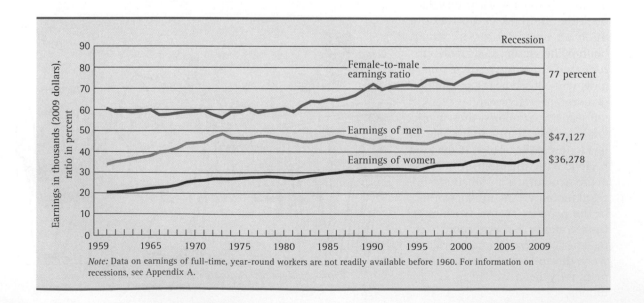

Note: Data on earnings of full-time, year-round workers are not readily available before 1960. For information on recessions, see Appendix A.

"If we pay them starvation wages—
why do they need a lunch break?"

Looking only at work, women and men perform different tasks in the labor force. This division of labor between the sexes preserves the differential power, privilege, and prestige of men (see Chapter 12). Men are overrepresented in administrative and supervisory roles. Women are found disproportionately in jobs in which they follow orders. Women are found, as noted earlier, more often than men in the secondary job market where jobs are menial, poorly paid, and with little or no benefits.

Unemployment

The Bureau of Labor Statistics supplies the official unemployment statistics. In 2009, during the Great Recession, the official unemployment rate reached 10 percent. The rate is misleading, however, because it understates, dramatically, the actual amount of unemployment. Not included in the data are the 60 million or so people who are not in the labor force because they are in school, are disabled or retired, are homemakers, or are not seeking work.

The data are distorted by undercounting the unemployed in two ways. First, people who have not actively sought work in the four weeks prior to being interviewed are not counted in the unemployed category. Women and minorities are overrepresented among these **discouraged workers**. The rationale of the Bureau of Labor Statistics for excluding dispirited workers is that the function of the statistic is to chart fluctuations in the conditions of the active labor force, not to provide a complete portrait of the jobless. Regardless of the reasoning, the official data of the government, by undercounting joblessness, diminish the perceived severity of unemployment and therefore reduce the zeal to do anything about the problem. The extent to which the public perceives unemployment as a problem is further lessened by counting as employed anyone who had worked for as little as an hour for pay in the week before being interviewed. There are almost 5 million part-time workers who want to work full-time. Thus, people who subsist on odd jobs, temporary work, or minimal part-time work are counted as fully employed by the government. If the discouraged workers were counted as unemployed, along with those who work part-time but want to work full-time, then the rate would be 16.7 percent, or one in six Americans of working age, instead of the official rate of 10 percent.

Unemployment is commonly believed to be functional (that is, have positive consequences) for society by reducing inflationary pressures. Capitalists like high unemployment because it tends to deflate wages and therefore increases profits. When there are unemployed people willing to work, workers will not make inordinate demands for higher wages for fear that they will be replaced by cheaper labor. Thus, even unionized labor becomes relatively docile when unemployment is high. Fred and Harry Magdoff (2004) have summarized the capitalist argument:

> One of the central features of capitalism is the oversupply of labor, a large mass of people that enter and leave the labor force according to the needs of capital. During an upswing in the business cycle, additional labor is necessary to utilize a business's full capacity. As sales slacken during a recession, workers no longer needed are then dismissed. The reserve army of labor—with brief and very unusual exceptions—is always present. ...
>
> When considering the surplus of workers in the reserve army of labor, it is important constantly to keep in mind two points. First, there is not an absolute surplus population, but rather a surplus in the context of a society ruled by the profit motive and the golden rule of accumulation for the sake of accumulation. Second, there would be no surplus of labor if everyone had enough to eat, a decent place to live, health care, and education, and workers had shorter work hours and longer vacations so they could have more leisure and creative time. (20–21)

FIGURE 13.2

Black and White Unemployment for the Last Two Recessions and Recoveries

Source: U.S. Census Bureau, "Current Population Survey" (census. gov/cps). Data are three month moving averages.

Unemployment affects some groups more than others. This **reserve army of the unemployed** is disproportionately composed of people of color (Latinos, African Americans, Native Americans), immigrants, teenagers, and residents in declining cities and regions. Typically, the official unemployment rates for African Americans and Latinos are around twice as high as the rate for Whites. For example, at the beginning of 2010, the official unemployment rate for Whites was 8.7 percent and 17.2 percent for Blacks (Haynes, 2010). These proportions by race tend to be relatively constant, whether the overall unemployment rate is high or low or whether the economy is in a boom or a slump (see Figure 13.2). Thus, the labor market assigns people of color disproportionately not only to the low-paying jobs but also to the jobs that are most unstable, precisely the situation of the secondary sector in the segmented labor market.

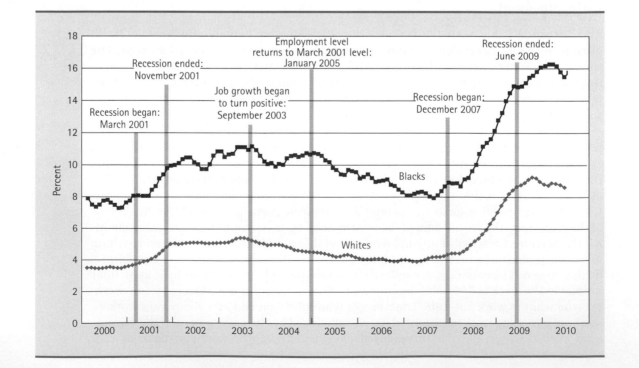

An important consequence of the reserve army of the unemployed being composed primarily of racial minorities is that it inflames racial antipathies against them by people who hold unstable jobs. These job holders perceive their enemy as the people below them who will work for lower wages, rather than the capitalists who oppose full employment and adequate wages for all people.

In summary, the problems associated with work in U.S. society are structural in origin. The source is not in unmotivated or unwilling workers. To understand the work setting in our society, we must understand the nature of capitalism, for which profit rather than human consequences guides managerial decisions. And in looking at unemployment, we must recognize that the economy fails to produce enough jobs with living wages and adequate benefits for the workers to maintain a middle-class lifestyle. Finally, in examining this labor market, we must understand that the economy is undergoing a profound transformation (Chapter 8). The next few generations will be caught in the nexus between one stage and another, and many will suffer because of the dislocations. So, too, will a society that refuses to plan, but rather lets the marketplace dictate the choices of economic firms.

Capitalism in Crisis

The Great Recession (2007–2010)

The transformation and the economy and the effects of globalization have created considerable economic havoc in the past few decades, as noted in Chapter 2. Adding to the dislocations brought about by these epochal changes of change is the Great Recession, which began in 2007 and ended in 2010, although its effects continue.

Prelude to the Economic Crisis. As the economy shifted away from manufacturing to services and information/knowledge some sectors (sunset industries) of the economy faded in importance or even died. Tens of millions of jobs lost permanently, mostly unionized jobs with good pay and benefits. Moreover, weak unions plus the competition from low-wage economies, led many U.S. corporations to reduce or eliminate their benefits (health insurance, retirement) to workers. Wages were also negatively affected.

Thus, the transformation of the economy, at least in the short run, marginalized millions, increased unemployment, drove social mobility downward, and made many millions insecure about their jobs, health care, and retirement. To cope with these problems, employees worked more hours a week, putting in 350 more hours a year than the average European, more women worked in the labor force (70 percent, almost double the percentage in 1970), and families went deeper into debt with credit cards, car loans, college loans, and home equity loans.

Families were also buying homes because home values had risen for half a century, most steeply from 1997 to 2006 when they rose by an inflation-adjusted 85 percent. This price appreciation tempted many to speculate, "flipping" recently purchased houses for a quick profit. Others took advantage of easy credit to refinance by taking out second mortgages in order to remodel their homes or to purchase "big ticket" items such as automobiles and boats.

> Homeowners, armed with easy credit, snapped up properties as if they were playing Monopoly. As prices soared, buyers were able to afford ever-larger properties only by taking out risky mortgages that lenders were happily approving with little documentation or money down. (Gandel and Lim, 2008:90)

Mortgage market lenders encouraged this housing "bubble." About 20 percent of home loans in 2005 were subprime—that is, loans sold to low-income people who had little chance of paying their mortgages. These subprime loans were "often given out under predatory terms that were especially unfavourable to the unsuspecting borrowers" (Foster and Magdoff, 2010:52). They were offered no-money down loans, with what appeared to be low interest rates. The "low" rates were for the first two years but then the loans increased

The Subprime Crisis for African Americans and Latinos

In 2008 and 2009, the housing industry was in a deep crisis as many homeowners could no longer make their payments, banks foreclosed, and some debtors just walked away from their debts leaving the lending companies holding the devalued properties. Under these conditions the value of housing depreciated rapidly (making many properties worth less than the mortgage), many neighborhoods declined as people moved out and houses were boarded up, and the crisis deepened. All of this eroded the tax base, which limited governmental services.

Subprime loans played a large role in this crisis. Subprime lending refers to high interest loans to people who would otherwise be considered too risky for a conventional loan. Historically, racial minorities have been excluded from home ownership. This has changed in the last couple of decades, but because African Americans and Latinos tend to have low-income jobs and lack good credit, they were charged higher-than-conventional interest rates or they were given "adjustable rate" loans, which offer initial low interest rates that increase sharply some years later. As a result, according to the United for a Fair Economy, African Americans and Latinos will lose between $163 billion and $278 billion from subprime loans taken out between 1999 and 2007. African Americans will lose $71 billion to $122 billion, while Latino borrowers will lose between $76 billion and $129 billion for the same period (Rivera, Cotto-Escalera, and Desai, 2008).

Adding to the problem is a practice known as predatory lending, in which borrowers are steered to subprime loans even when they are qualified for a conventional loan rate. Unscrupulous mortgage brokers may either ignore a homeowner's ability to repay the loan or not divulge the important details of a loan, such as the pros and cons of an adjustable rate mortgage. Low-income people of color were the prime targets of the subprime mortgage industry. The result, for example, is that 56 percent of subprime loans were made to African Americans. Since homeownership is an important component of wealth, the long-term consequence of the subprime fiasco is an increase in the wealth gap between Whites and people of color.

Add to this mix the reckless and irresponsible dealmaking on Wall Street, which involved an intricate, intertwined system of loan brokers, mortgage lenders, Wall Street trusts, hedge funds, offshore tax havens, and other predators (Moyers and Winship, 2009). For example, subprime loans were bundled and sold to third parties "around the world [thus serving] to spread significant risk far and wide" (Foster and Magdoff, 2010:52). These "derivatives" were financial contracts between a buyer and a seller that derive value from an underlying asset, such as a mortgage or a stock. This allowed banks and insurance firms to leverage their assets by as much as 40 times the value of the underlying asset. In the case of subprime mortgages, this was "financial alchemy that turned low-quality mortgages into trillions of dollars of high-priced derivatives" (Karabell, 2009:35). The government stood by without interfering with the market when it indulged in these reckless ventures. There were five financial agencies at the federal level that could have regulated these practices but did not because they assumed in accordance with a basic premise of capitalism that the financial players would police themselves (Hightower, 2007).

---

substantially when the "variable rate" clause (found in the fine print of the loan contract) was enforced. See A Closer Look panel titled "The Subprime Crisis for African Americans and Latinos."

The Ensuing Economic Crisis. These forces converged in 2007 creating a "perfect storm" of economic devastation. It began when subprime borrowers began defaulting on their mortgages. That sent housing prices tumbling, unleashing a domino effect on mortgage-backed securities (Gandel and Lim, 2008). Banks and brokerages that had borrowed money to increase their leverage had to raise capital quickly. Some, like Merrill Lynch and Bear Sterns, were forced to sell their assets to other banks at bargain rates (Bear Sterns was sold to J.P.Morgan for $236 million, down from its value of $20 billion a year earlier.). Others, like Lehman Brothers, failed. The stock market dropped precipitously. Credit dried up. Business slowed causing companies to lay off workers by the hundreds of thousands. What was happening in the United States affected markets elsewhere causing a worldwide recession and a further slowing of business activity here and abroad. The result was the worst economic downturn in the United States since the Great Depression of the 1930s. Let's consider the contours of the crisis, beginning with unemployment.

Christopher Weyant/The New Yorker Collection/www.cartoonbank.com

"At this point, I'm just happy to still have a job."

Unemployment. Since the 1970s, retaining a job has become more precarious (Kalleberg, 2009). This trend accelerated in the recent recession as some 7.5 million American workers lost their jobs from late 2007 to December 2009. The official government's unemployment rate jumped from 4.6 percent in mid-2007 to 10 percent through January 1, 2010. The rate of 10 percent represents 14 million people but this underreports the actual number of unemployed, as noted earlier.

A major shift in unemployment is evident—fewer adult men are working. In 1954 about 96 percent of American men between the ages of 25 and 54 worked. Now it is 80 percent. And the men most likely to be unemployed are those without a high school diploma. The reason, in part, has to do with structural changes in the economy. The growth areas are in government, health care, and leisure generating jobs for college graduates. Sectors like manufacturing and agriculture, while productive, are not generating jobs, using, rather, machines or foreign workers (Brooks, 2011).

Housing Woes. The value of homes grew rapidly in the new millennium, reaching a peak in 2006. By this time many homeowners were on the financial edge as they purchased overvalued houses, assuming their value would increase even more. But the housing bubble burst causing values to decline precipitously, losing $4 trillion in value from 2005 to the end of 2008 (*Economist*, 2009:47). The newly unemployed found they could not meet their monthly payments. Those who purchased subprime mortgages were especially vulnerable. By 2009 some 1.5 million homes owned mostly by African Americans were lost through subprime foreclosures. In 2010 banks repossessed 1 million homes, and about 5 million borrowers were at least two months behind on their mortgage payments (Herron, 2011). In the fourth quarter of 2010 some 27 percent of homeowners owed more money on their homes than they were worth (Konczal, 2011). All of this created a downward spiral, decreasing home values further.

Renters were not immune from the nation's housing crisis. This occurs in several ways. First, when owners of apartments are foreclosed on, their renters are evicted even though they have been paying their rents. According to the National Low Income Housing Coalition, renters were an estimated 40 percent of families facing eviction because of foreclosure

(Fireside, 2009). Those who were evicted usually lost their security deposits and any prepaid rent. Second, homeowners forced into foreclosure often became tenants, increasing the demand for rentals. This coupled with the lack of apartment construction drives up rents (Schmit, 2011). As a consequence, more than half (51.5 percent) of renters are spending more than 30 percent of their household income for housing—the threshold set by the government to determine if housing is unaffordable (Davidson and Hansen, 2010). Similarly, 37 percent of homeowners with mortgages are spending 30 percent or more of the before-tax income on housing.

Financial Decline. Consider just the financial losses that occurred in 2008 (Marquardt and Shinkle, 2009):

- Stock market value declined by $7.3 trillion.
- The Standard & Poor's 500 lost 38.5 percent, its worst fall since 1937.
- Average loss by mutual funds: 38 percent.
- Household wealth dropped $11.1 trillion (18 percent).
- Americans lost over $1 trillion in their 401(k)s (retirement savings). Individuals who had contributed to 401(k)s for twenty years or more, lost an average of 20 percent of value, even after counting the money they had added through the years.
- Over an eighteen-month period, the investments of public pension plans—the retirement security for 22 million police officers, firefighters, teachers, and their survivors—lost a combined $1.3 trillion.
- From the start of the Great Recession to May 2009, 2.4 million workers lost health insurance they were getting through their jobs.

In sum, according to the Federal Reserve, the net worth of more than two-thirds of Americans declined, suffering a median drop of 18 percent (reported in Block, 2011). Put another way, surveys revealed that more than 24 million Americans shifted in 2008 from lives that were "thriving" to ones that were "struggling" (Page, 2009).

Personal Bankruptcies. The current economic crisis with rising unemployment, plummeting home values, staggering stock market losses, and increased indebtedness have added to these usual reasons for bankruptcy (medical catastrophe, financial missteps, and divorce). In 2009 there were 1,402,816 bankruptcies. In 2009 a record number of consumers (4.2 percent) were falling delinquent or into default on their loans, meaning that they were only a step or two away from bankruptcy.

A major source of bankruptcy is the inability to pay for catastrophic health care needs. Employers have increasingly cut back on their contribution to health insurance, either dropping coverage altogether, or by decreasing their obligation to provide health insurance, including introducing high-deductible health insurance. Of course, those who lose jobs also lose their health insurance. Since the cost of health care is so expensive (for example, a heart bypass costs $200,000; a premature baby close to $1 million), the uninsured are just a catastrophic illness or accident away from economic ruin. The Public Broadcasting System (PBS) reported that 700,000 go bankrupt each year because of medical bills (PBS, 2009).

Hunger. The poorest among us are suffering the harshest effects of the economic decline. Already on the economic margins, they have been pushed down even further. The welfare "safety net," which has eroded since 1980, was further cut by the welfare reform of 1996, which ended the idea of welfare as an entitlement.

> Despite soaring unemployment and the worst economic crisis in decades, 18 states cut their welfare rolls last year, and nationally the number of people receiving cash assistance remained at or near the lowest in more than 40 years. (DeParle, 2009: para 1)

Some facts about hunger amid the economic crisis:

- According to the U.S. Department of Agriculture, the number of people receiving food stamps from July 2008 to July 2009 increased from 29.2 million to 35.9 million.
- One in eight Americans (37.0 million, including 14 million children) received emergency food assistance in 2009. This was an increase of 46 percent over 2006.
- The demand at food banks across the country increased by 30 percent in 2008 from the previous year.
- By early 2009 some 16.5 million children received free school lunches, up 6.5 percent from the previous year. Another 3.2 million students received reduced-price lunches.

This surge in the hungry in the United States indicates the struggle by the new poor to cope with their desperate situations.

> The message is simple. Ever more Americans need food they can't afford. As tough economic times take their toll, increasing numbers of Americans are on tightened budgets and, in some cases, facing outright hunger. As a result, they may be learning a lot more about food banks and soup kitchens than most of them ever wanted to know. ... Families who just months ago didn't even know what a food bank was and would never have considered visiting a food pantry now have far more intimate knowledge of both. ... Other formerly middle class Americans who have never dealt with, or even thought about, food insecurity before simply don't know whom to call or where to turn. (Turse, 2009: para 1, 4)

The New Homeless. The extent of homelessness is difficult to know since those without a permanent home may be doubling up with relatives, sleeping in vehicles, and the like, not just in shelters. Thus the numbers of the homeless understate the actual count. Given that caveat, the official number of homeless prior to the Great Recession was about 1 in 400 Americans (750,000) on any given night; and about 1.6 million experienced homelessness at some point in a given year. Around 40 percent of the homeless population were families, typically a single mother and her children.

During the Great Recession millions more Americans were at greater risk of becoming homeless. Some 9.6 million families were spending more than half of their income on housing. Foreclosures brought evictions, even for renters when their apartment buildings were foreclosed. The newly unemployed could not make their mortgage payments or their rents. Costly medical care put some in bankruptcy. As a result, according to the National Alliance to End Homelessness, as many as 3.4 million Americans were assumed to be homeless at some point in 2009—a 35 percent increase since the recession started in December 2007 (Vestal, 2009). Unlike the traditional homeless composed mostly of the long time poor and near poor, the new homeless included the "working poor, who were among the hardest hit by the collapse in subprime mortgages. But others are middle-class families who scarcely expected to find themselves unable to afford homes" (Armour, 2008:2B). For example, the Chicago Coalition for the Homeless found that in 2008, 22 percent of families seeking emergency shelter were homeless for the first time (Keen, 2010).

Legacy of the Great Recession. The Great Recession, while technically over in 2010, will have lasting social consequences.

First, federal, state, and local governments lost significant tax revenues, causing them to face serious budget shortfalls. Politicians had two possible remedies: increase taxes or decrease spending. In the current political climate, the emphasis is on decreasing spending. At the federal level, there have been cuts to programs such as Head Start, Women Infants and Children, Pell grants for college students, and support for public education. In 2011 nine states, for example, cut spending for preschool programs by at least 10 percent (*Economist*, 2011). The main targets, however, will be programs for seniors—Medicare and Social Security. State governments experiencing financial difficulties have made significant cuts in public education

(K-12 and college), unemployment benefits, and various types of welfare. In short, the Great Recession gave politicians cover to repeal the progressive legislation passed since the 1930s.

Second, the economic crunch gave employers reason to reduce or eliminate worker benefits. In this time of economic uncertainty, corporations also did little hiring or even decreased their workforce, relying more heavily on temporary workers or independent contractors. Throughout the economy "good, secure, well-paid positions—tenured appointments in the academy, union jobs on the factory floor—are being replaced by temporary, low-wage employment" (Deresiewicz, 2011:28).

Third, the "American dream," has become a dream rather than a reality for more and more Americans. The "American Dream" is the belief that in this land of opportunity anyone can succeed with hard work (McNamee and Miller, 2009). Through the 1950s and 1960s, this dream was realized by increasingly more Americans as average real wages (that is, wages adjusted for inflation) and family incomes expanded and the economy created new jobs and opportunities. The result was that many Americans after World War II were able to move up into a growing and vibrant middle class. This trend peaked in 1973, and since then families have tended to either stagnate or decline in their level of affluence. The transformation of the economy away from manufacturing and toward service, fueled by globalization, had the effect of shrinking the middle class as the gap between the "haves" and the "have-nots" increased. This trend downward accelerated with "the Great Recession," with unemployment rates climbing dramatically, personal debt rising, and the housing bubble bursting. All of this occurred while the costs for health care, college, consumer goods, and transportation continued to rise. The result: many middle-class families plunged in income and resources, thus moving down in social class. Some declared bankruptcy. Some were forced from their homes and had to relocate. Some families became poor, hungry, and even homeless.

Various polling organizations have asked a question regarding the American Dream: "In America, each generation has tried to have a better life than their parents, with a better living standard, better homes, a better education, and so on. How likely do you think it is that today's youth will have a better life than their parents? In December 2001, the measure peaked at 71 percent. In April 2011, only 44 percent expressed that view, reflecting an increasingly dim optimism for young Americans" (Rampell, 2011). See A Closer Look panel titled "The Effects of the Great Recession on Recent College Graduates."

A CLOSER LOOK

The Effects of the Great Recession on Recent College Graduates

A major *Demos* study entitled "The Economic State of Young America," begins with this: "Today's 20-somethings are likely to be the first generation to not be better off than their parents" (Draut, 2008:1). Today's young adults have the unfortunate luck to come of age and start careers while facing strong headwinds of the Great Recession. Let's focus here on the sober outlook for today's college graduates.

The official unemployment rate for those aged 16 to 24 in 2010 was the highest in 60 years—18.4 percent. For college graduates, the rate was 9.7 percent, up from just over 5 percent in 2007, the beginning of the Great Recession. The job market for racial minorities is especially daunting, with the total Black unemployment rate at 19 percent, and for Latinos 13.8 percent, compared to 8.3 percent for Whites (Huffington, 2011 paras 6, 7).

The average salary for 2011 college graduates was $36,866. In 2009 it was $46,500. Moreover, research shows that workers who begin their careers during economic downturns earn lower wages (5 to 15 percent lower each year) than similar workers who begin careers at other times, lasting from five to ten years after starting work (Wozniak, 2011).

Not only are job prospects grim but two-thirds of today's graduates leave college with a large debt, averaging $22,900, the most indebted students ever. This amount of indebtedness is 8 percent higher than the previous year and 47 percent greater than a decade earlier (Whitehouse, 2011).

How will these newly minted graduates react to an economy that has stacked the deck against them? Some will be risk-averse, playing it safe. Others will see that their plight is not their fault, but the consequence of a faulty U.S. economy. Armed with that awareness, they might join with others to seek meaningful change.

Fourth, the Great Recession has affected families and personal behavior. Personal economic difficulties have resulted in many families and individuals changing their patterns of consumption such as buying cheaper merchandise and second-hand goods. There is a greater likelihood of renting rather than buying a home. Two reasons: the housing market is unstable and when one rents, he or she is more able to move for a better situation. If homes are purchased or built, there is a trend toward downsizing. In 2007 the median home size was 2,300 square feet, in 2010 it was 2,100 with more than one-third saying that their ideal home size was less than 2,000 square feet (Perman, 2010).

Families have also adjusted, usually downward, to the conditions of the Great Recession. Couples were marrying later and having fewer children. The number of cohabiting couples increased. Divorce actually decreased, not because couples were more compatible but rather that the divorce process was expensive and homes were difficult to sell. Household size increased, reversing a half-century slide, as high unemployment and the housing bust forced some people to double up. Most notable is the rise in young adults ages nineteen to twenty-nine living with their parents (34 percent compared to 25 percent in 1980) (El Nasser, 2011).

Many families experienced the unemployment of one of its members. In 2010, for example, more than 1 million two-earner couples became one-earner (Uchitelle, 2011). The obvious consequence is that these families lost significant income, as well as self-esteem. Since there was a greater likelihood of men losing jobs than women, many families experienced role reversal, with the wife as breadwinner and the husband now in the role of "house husband."

A final consequence of the Great Recession is a diminished trust in the U.S. economic system. Clearly, the institution of the economy did not work to keep markets stable. Rather, rampant speculation by banks and lending organizations made the situation worse, as did the lack of government oversight, a condition sought by corporations and their lobbyists. Lenders sometimes engaged in fraud, taking advantage of the disadvantaged with their subprime schemes. Clearly, the self-regulating market did not work, requiring the federal government to bail out failing banks and insurance companies. After the bubble burst in 2008 the government stepped in to avoid a deepening crisis. It seized control of Fannie Mae and Freddie Mac, the nation's largest housing finance entities, guaranteeing up to $100 billion for each company to ensure they would not fall into bankruptcy. The government also bailed out American International Group with $85 billion; set aside $700 billion to ease the credit crunch among banks; the government purchased $250 billion in stock in the nine major banks and financial institutions; and it loaned significant amounts to General Motors and Chrysler. These actions were a recognition that the self-cleansing nature of markets had failed. Now the government was involved in overseeing the business world and having a financial stake in these troubled enterprises. This marks an ideological sea change from the laissez-faire philosophy that has prevailed since the Reagan presidency.

The Negative Consequences of Private Profitability over Social Need

We have written elsewhere (Eitzen, Baca Zinn, and Smith, 2011) that the major social problems in the United States are in large measure the result of the form of the economy. This is illustrated by the role of capitalists as they seek profit in the climate engendered by the economic transformation discussed in Chapter 8. Entrepreneurs, as they seek to maximize profit, shut down plants, reduce workforces, replace workers with machines, or threaten to move operations overseas to force workers to accept lower wages and benefits. They also continue to pollute the environment and fight government attempts to enforce worker and consumer safety. These entrepreneurs, corporate boards of directors, and corporate executives have no allegiance to consumers, workers, or the communities in which their operations are located. Their ultimate loyalty is to the bottom line. Michael Parenti (1986) describes this fundamental logic of capitalism and capitalists:

> Capitalism's purpose is not to create jobs; in fact, capitalists are constantly devising ways of eliminating jobs in order to cut labor costs. Nor is its purpose to build communities, for capitalists will build or destroy communities as investment opportunities dictate.

Nor is capitalism dedicated to protecting the family or traditional life, for no system in human history has been more relentless in battering down ancient practices and destroying both rural and urban homegrown cultures. Nor is capitalism intent upon protecting the environment on behalf of generations yet to come; for corporations will treat the environment like a septic tank in order to cut production costs and maximize profits without regard for future generations or for the generation enduring it all today. Nor can we say that capitalists are committed to economic efficiency as such, since they regularly pass on their hidden dis-economies to the public in the form of overproduction, overpricing, pollution, unemployment, population dislocation, harmful products, and personal injury. And as the military budget shows, they actively court waste and duplication if it brings fatter contracts and bigger profits.

Capitalism has no loyalty to anything but its own process of capital accumulation, no loyalty to anything but itself. Nor could it be otherwise if one wished to survive as a capitalist; for the first law of the market is to make a profit off other people's labor or go out of business. Private profitability rather than social need is the determining condition of capital investment. (1–2)

Can society continue to allow capitalists the freedom to make investment decisions unfettered by the concerns of society? Can corporations pollute the environment and produce waste with impunity? Should businesses be allowed to shut down a plant without sufficient warning and compensation to the affected workers and communities? Should taxes be levied on robots, with the monies spent on job retraining of workers displaced by them? As Chapter 14 shows, the close relationship between economic power and political power appears to preclude government curbs on the abuses created by capitalists. And the rationale provided by many people for the lack of governmental control of business will likely be that capitalism is not the problem but really the solution to society's problems—if allowed to operate without restraints.

Declining Wages, Jobs, Consumerism, and Profits

According to Karl Marx, one of the contradictions of capitalism that will bring its downfall is the "**falling rate of profit**." This refers to the propensity of employers to maximize profits by reducing labor expenses. This is accomplished by using labor-saving machines and by paying the minimum in wages and benefits. The result of this capitalist rationale, argued Marx, would actually be to reduce profits because the workers would be less and less able to purchase products. Some industrialists, such as Henry Ford, recognized this problem. "Mass production," Ford said, "requires mass consumption, which means higher wages" (cited in Harrington, 1986:13). The logic, more commonly held by capitalists, though, is to increase profits by keeping wages low. This, as seen in Chapter 8, is evidenced by the purchase of new microelectronic technology to replace workers, the movement of production sites from relative high-wage areas to low-wage ones such as in the southern United States or to foreign countries, and the hiring of part-time or temporary workers in order to escape paying benefits.

There are a number of indicators of personal and family economic decline as noted throughout this chapter. The middle class is smaller. More and more workers receive substandard wages, substandard pensions, and substandard fringe benefits. The result is a reduction in lifestyle. For families on the economic margin, purchases will be limited to necessities. As more and more people in the United States are adversely affected, the sale of consumer goods and services will decline. This means that corporate profits will suffer, causing further efforts by management to reduce expenses. Thus, one possible future scenario is that of an economic downward spiral. The way out, to repeat Henry Ford's admonition, is to encourage mass consumption through higher wages. The prospect for higher-wage jobs, however, is bleak as corporations downsize and U.S. corporations and U.S. workers compete with even lower-wage economies elsewhere.

The Lack of Economic Planning

The capitalist philosophy dating back to Adam Smith argues that the government should stay out of economic affairs. According to this view, the marketplace will force businesses to make the decisions that will best benefit them and, indirectly, the citizenry. Yet, when the government does receive valuable information with which it could make decisions to avert future crises, the strong tendency in the United States is to remain aloof.

Ironically, the government is involved in central planning in the areas of space exploration, military goals, and homeland security from terrorists.

The issue of central planning revolves around whether the society is able and willing to respond to present and future social problems. Is a capitalist society capable of meeting the problems of poverty, unemployment, social injustice, population growth, energy shortages, global warming and climate change, environmental damage, and monopoly? Robert Heilbroner (1974), a distinguished economist, argues that we will not prepare for the problems of the future: "The outlook is for what we may call 'convulsive change'—change forced upon us by external events rather than by conscious choice, by catastrophe rather than by calculation" (132).

The lack of central planning points to the undemocratic nature of U.S. society. It is commonly believed that the people, through their economic choices, actually govern business decisions. While this is partially true, it ignores the manipulation of the public by business interests through advertising and other hypes. Neither the public nor its elected representatives are involved in the economic decisions of the giant corporations—and these decisions often have dire consequences domestically and internationally. As Andrew Hacker (1970) argues:

> The power to make investment decisions is concentrated in a few hands, and it is this power which will decide what kind of a nation America will be. Instead of government planning there is boardroom planning that is accountable to no outside agency; and these plans set the order of priorities on national growth, technological innovation, and ultimately, the values and behavior of human beings. Investment decisions are sweeping in their ramifications—no one is unaffected by their consequences. Yet this is an area where neither the public nor its government is able to participate. (52)

The lack of central planning is also a result of the resistance of powerful interest groups in society. Short-term goals such as employment for labor groups or profit for corporations lead special interests to block government efforts to meet future needs. Thus, the power of the economic dominants in society has the effect of superseding the interests of the nation, as shown in Chapter 14.

CHAPTER REVIEW

1. Economic activity involves the production and distribution of goods and services.

2. There are two fundamental ways society can organize its economic activities: capitalism and socialism.

3. Capitalism in its pure form involves (a) the private ownership of the means of production, (b) the pursuit of personal profit, (c) competition, and (d) a government policy of allowing the marketplace to function unhindered.

4. Socialism in its pure form involves (a) democracy throughout the social structure; (b) equality—equality of opportunity, equality rather than hierarchy in making decisions, and equality in sharing the benefits of society; and (c) efficiency in providing the best conditions to meet the material needs of the citizens.

5. Marx's prediction that capitalism will result in an economy dominated by monopolies has been fulfilled in the United States. But rather than a single corporation dominating a sector of the economy, the United States is characterized by the existence of shared monopolies—in which four or fewer corporations supply 50 percent or more of a particular market.

6. Economic power is concentrated in a few major corporations and banks. This concentration has been

accomplished primarily through mergers and interlocking directorates.

7. The power of the largest corporations in the United States is increased by their international activities. Multinational corporations have important consequences: (a) a decline in domestic jobs, (b) a crippling of union's power, (c) a crippling of the government through lost revenues in taxes and a negative balance of payments, (d) an increase in corporate power over the world economy and world events, and (e) an exploitation of workers and natural resources in Third World countries.

8. Inequality is endemic to capitalism. Corporate wealth and private wealth are highly concentrated. Poverty, too, is concentrated disproportionately among people of color and in households headed by women.

9. Societies are organized to allocate work in order to produce the goods and services required for survival. The way work is organized generates important social problems.

10. Owners and managers of firms and factories control workers in several ways: (a) through scientific management, (b) through bureaucracy, (c) through extortion, and (d) by monitoring worker behavior.

11. Blue- and white-collar workers in bureaucracies and factories are susceptible to alienation, which is the separation of human beings from each other, from themselves, and from the products they create. Specialized work in impersonal settings leads to dissatisfaction and meaninglessness.

12. A primary goal of business firms in a capitalist society is to reduce costs and thus increase profits. One way to reduce costs is not to provide adequately for worker safety.

13. Labor unions have declined in numbers and power. This has resulted in lower real wages and benefits, less-safe work conditions, and a declining middle class.

14. Another work-related problem is discrimination, in which women and minorities have long received unfair treatment in jobs, pay, and opportunities for advancement. Two features of the U.S. economy promote these inequities: (a) the segmented labor market and (b) the capitalist patriarchy.

15. The official government data on unemployment hide the actual amount by undercounting the unemployed in two ways: (a) People not actively seeking work (discouraged workers) are not counted; and (b) people who work at part-time jobs are counted as fully employed.

16. Unemployment has positive consequences for some people. Having a certain portion unemployed tends to keep inflation in check, according to some economists. Also, unemployment benefits capitalists by keeping wages down.

17. U.S. capitalism is facing four crises: (a) the Great Recession; (b) the primacy of profit over human considerations; (c) the propensity of corporate managers to increase profitability by reducing the workforce and lowering wages, which means that ultimately profits will fall because workers will be forced to reduce their purchases; and (d) the lack of central planning to solve current problems and anticipate future ones.

18. Two facts about institutions of society are especially important: (a) Although they are interrelated, the economy is the most dominant and shapes each of the other institutions; and (b) the particular way that an institution is organized is at once a source of stability and a source of problems.

KEY TERMS

Capitalism
Laissez-faire
Socialism
Shared monopoly

Interlocking directorates
Direct interlock
Indirect interlock
Scientific management

Alienation
Discouraged workers
Reserve army of the unemployed
Falling rate of profit

STUDY QUESTIONS

1. What are the mechanisms within the U.S. economy that work against the capitalist ideal of free enterprise?
2. Why is inequality endemic to capitalism? Is this good?
3. A major assumption of conflict theorists is that capitalism is a primary source for many social problems. Michael Parenti's critique of capitalism (in the section titled "The Negative Consequences of Private Profitability over Social Need") is an example

of this approach. Do you agree or disagree? Why?
4. Given the conditions of the "structural transformation of the economy" (Chapter 8) and the "Great Recession," should the government become more involved in the economy (violating laissez-faire) with policies to alleviate current problems and central planning to lessen or eliminate future problems?

http://www.dol.gov/

The U.S. Department of Labor provides facts and statistics on labor, including unemployment.

http://www.bls.gov/

"The Bureau of Labor Statistics is the principal fact-finding agency for the Federal Government in the broad field of labor economics and statistics."

http://www.labornet.org/

Labornet offers information on the current labor movement, including news, archives, links, and protests.

http://www.northlandposter.com/cgi-bin/Web_store/web_store.cgi

This is the home of the Northland Poster Collective, which sells posters, buttons, bumper stickers, and more with slogans related to social justice, particularly labor.

http://www.umwa.org/homepage.shtml

This is the homepage of the United Mine Workers of America, a union fighting for the rights of workers since 1890.

http://unions.org/default2.asp

The Union Resource Network is a searchable index of unions on the Internet. It also contains union labor news.

http://www.sweatshops.org

Sweatshops.org provides general information on sweatshops, why they form, ideas on how to eliminate them, and links to other relevant sites. There is also the option of searching the green pages for socially and environmentally responsible products.

http://www.tao.ca/~resist/womeninglobalcapitalism.html

This site discusses the position of women in global capitalism. It includes information on sweatshops and trafficking in women, as well as links to similar sites.

http://www.cartoonweb.com/lobby.asp

Cartoons related to the economy and other issues can be found at this site.

http://www.dsausa.org/dsa.html

Democratic Socialists of America is an organization that advocates for a more humane social order with an "equitable distribution of resources, meaningful work, gender and racial equality, a healthy environment, sustainable growth, and non-oppressive relationships."

http://www.globalexchange.org/

Global Exchange is a human rights organization that looks to create environmental, political, and social justice around the world. The site explores global campaigns, provides information on issues in different countries, and offers opportunities to get involved.

http://www.corpwatch.org/

Corpwatch is a site looking to hold corporations responsible for their actions. It contains information on issues dealing with sweatshops and politics.

http://epinet.org

The Economic Policy Institute website provides information on jobs, living wages, Social Security, and more.

Washington's favors? Clearly, from this perspective, power in Washington is centralized and represents the powerful few.

The compelling questions of this chapter are, Who are the real power wielders in U.S. society? Are they an elite, or are the people sovereign? The location and exercise of power are difficult to determine, especially in a large and complex society such as the United States. Decisions are necessarily made by a few people, but in a democracy these few are to be representatives of the masses and therefore subject to their influence. But what of nonrepresentatives who aid in shaping policy? What about the pressure on the decision makers by powerful groups? What about those pressures on the decision makers that are so diffuse that the leaders may not even know who is applying the pressure? And, perhaps most significant of all, what is the power of money?

Models of the National Power Structure

There are two basic views of the power structure—the **elitist model of power** and the **pluralist model of power**. The elitist view of power is that there is a pyramid of power. The people at the apex control the rest of the pyramid. Pluralists, on the other hand, see power as dispersed rather than concentrated. Power is broadly distributed among a number of organizations, special interests, and the voters. This chapter examines different elitist and pluralist conceptions of power in the United States. As each is surveyed, the fundamental questions are How does a particular model mesh with the facts of our contemporary society? Does the model portray things as they are or as they should be?

Pluralist Models

Pluralism I: Representative Democracy. Many people in the United States accept the notion promoted in high school civics books that the country is a "government of the people, by the people, for the people." **Democracy** is the form of government in which the people have the ultimate power, where the will of the majority prevails, where there is equality before the law, and decisions are made to maximize the common good. In a complex society of more than 310 million people, the people cannot make all decisions; they must elect representatives to make most decisions. So, decision making is concentrated at the top, but it is to be controlled by the people who elect the decision makers. This model is shown in Figure 14.1. (See A Closer Look panel titled "Structural Barriers to Democracy.")

The most important component of a democratic model is that the representatives, because they are elected by the people, are responsive to the wishes of the people. This model, however, does not conform to reality. The United States is undemocratic in many important ways. The people, although they do vote for their representatives every few years, are really quite powerless. For example, who makes the really important decisions about war and peace, economic policies, and foreign policy? The people certainly do not. The record shows that many times the people have been deceived when the object was to conceal clandestine illegal operations, mistakes, undemocratic practices, and the like. These illicit and deceptive activities have been carried out by Democratic and Republican presidents alike.

FIGURE 14.1

Representative
Democracy

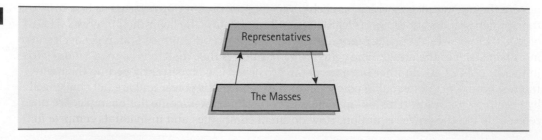

Structural Barriers to Democracy

In the 2004 presidential election the actual vote by the adult U.S. population was as follows (Zinn, 2005):

- Only 60 percent of the eligible voters actually voted. Stated another way, 40 percent of those eligible chose not to vote.
- Bush won the approval of 31 percent of the eligible voters. Kerry won 28 percent of the eligible voters.

In short, George W. Bush became president of the United States receiving slightly more than three out of ten of the possible votes.

Those who voted were disproportionately White, relatively affluent, educated, and suburban. What about low-income and borderline low-income citizens, racial minorities, blue-collar laborers, and city dwellers who chose not to vote? Why did they not vote? What is the source of their alienation? Is the problem with the apathetic voting population or is it with the system? Let's look at the systemic sources that thwart democracy in the United States.

The two-party system that has emerged (political parties are not mentioned in the Constitution) is a major impediment to democracy. Corporations, special interests, and wealthy individuals sponsor both parties. Since candidates from minor parties rarely win, they do not receive monetary support, which fulfills the prophecy. They also remain minor parties because the government subsidizes the two major parties in two ways: First, the Republican and Democratic Parties receive millions from the federal government to fund their nominating conventions and receive federal matching campaign funds based on their presumed viability. On the surface, this "matching funds" approach seems fair, but in practice it keeps the strong parties strong and the weak parties weak.

The bias toward the two-party system was revealed again when a "bipartisan" commission ruled that Ross Perot could not participate in the 1996 presidential debates and Ralph Nader could not be part of the 2000, 2004, and 2008 presidential debates. They could not take part, it was argued, because they had no chance of winning. Of course, not being part of the debates makes that prophecy a certainty. The commission, by the way, was composed of members selected from the Republican and Democratic Parties!

Another obstacle to third parties is that they cannot break the two-party control at every level of government. Even if the candidate of a third party were successful in winning the presidency, he or she would have difficulty in governing because both houses of Congress would be controlled by one or the other of the major parties. Moreover, since the two major parties control both houses of Congress (chairing committees, majorities on committees and in Congress), independents (in 2010 there were two,

both senators, Bernie Sanders of Vermont who is part of the Democratic Caucus and Joe Lieberman, who is nominally part of the Democratic Caucus) have no power.

The framers of the Constitution set up the Electoral College, which is a device that gave the ultimate power of electing the president to the elite in each state and gave extraordinary power to the least populous states. Now most of these undemocratic principles have been overturned by amendments to the Constitution. But the Electoral College remains, allowing for the possibility of a president being elected with fewer votes than his or her opponent (for example, in 2000 George W. Bush was elected president with 539,893 *fewer* votes than Al Gore).

The Electoral College gives all electoral votes from a state to the winner in that state (for example, in 2000 with nearly 3 million votes cast in Florida, George W. Bush won by a disputed margin of 437 votes and received *all* of Florida's electoral votes, giving Bush a majority in the Electoral College. And, to top it all, an electoral vote in Wyoming corresponded to 167,081 persons, while an electoral vote in California represented 645,172 persons because the number of electors is determined by the number of senators and representatives in that state, giving states with small populations disproportionate votes.

A major problem lies with the winner-take-all system. A state with a 30 percent Latino population may not have any Latino representation in Congress because a White majority in each congressional district voted for the White candidate. Similarly, a city may have a seven-member city council elected at large by majority vote. The usual result is that not one council member represents a poor section of the city. One critic said: "[The] Winner Take All is downright dangerous. It distorts national policy, robs voters of representation, and pits partisan voters as well as racial, ethnic, and religious minorities against each other for a scarce commodity —political representation" (Hill, Stevens, 2002:xi).

Consider what happened in Alabama in the 1992 election. George H. W. Bush won the state handily with 47.9 percent of the vote, claiming all nine of its electoral votes. But exit polls indicated that 91 percent of African American voters in Alabama—who make up roughly two-ninths of the state's electorate—voted for Bill Clinton. Despite this overwhelming level of support, Clinton, with only 30 percent of the White vote, did not secure a single electoral vote in Alabama. African American voters might just as well have stayed home (Hoffman, 1996:15).

Just as many voters are disenfranchised by the winner-take-all system, many are also shut out by the process in which state legislatures under partisan control deliberately shape congressional districts (called gerrymandering) to be overwhelmingly Republican or Democrat. This rigging of

(continues)

Structural Barriers to Democracy *(continued)*

the system means, in effect, that the public is denied a choice. As *USA Today* (2002d) editorialized: "Little wonder turnout at the polls has been declining for years. By trying to fix the outcomes of House races before Election Day, professional partisans are effectively disenfranchising voters" (13A).

Both parties seek the largest number of voters by appealing to those who are most likely to vote (upper-middle-class, White fiscal conservatives from the suburbs). Both parties push for middle-class tax cuts, "family values," and a tougher stance on crime. Both parties are beholden to business. As Ralph Nader put it: The difference between his major party foes was merely the "velocity with which their knees hit the floor when Big Business enters the room" (quoted in Willing, 2000:9A). All of these similarities leave out many who find each of the two major parties irrelevant to their interests. Neither party, for example, has a plan to revitalize the cities, desegregate housing, and provide affordable housing for the working poor. Neither

the Republicans nor the Democrats have been willing "or professed to see the necessity to mount an attack on the economic trends that had created the inner-city ghetto and that also were keeping many Whites and non-ghetto Blacks in poverty and hopelessness" (Wicker, 1996:12). Neither party has pressed hard for further racial gains or for the enforcement of what has been accomplished. In short, many if not most of the nation's eligible voters are electorally homeless (Hightower, 1996).

The U.S. system is in sharp contrast to the multinational party systems found in the European democracies, where religious minorities, racial groups, the working class, and other special interests form viable political parties. The result is that citizens can find a political party with an agenda compatible to their interests. As a consequence, voter turnout in Canada and Europe ranges between 80 percent and 90 percent, compared to the 50 percent in U.S. presidential elections.

Not only have the people in the United States been misinformed at times, but the basic democratic tenet that the public be informed has also been defied on occasion. On one hand, Congress has shown its contempt for the electorate by the use of secret meetings. The executive branch, too, has acted in secret. Recent presidents have gone months without holding a press conference, have used executive privilege to keep presidential advisors from testifying before congressional committees, and have refused to debate opponents in election campaigns. Many people who are appointed rather than elected wield tremendous power. Technical experts, for example, evaluate extremely complicated issues; they can virtually dictate to the president and Congress what is needed for defense, shoring up the economy, or winning friends abroad because they are the experts. The coterie of advisors may convince the president to act in particular ways. Members appointed to the regulatory agencies have tremendous power to shape various aspects of the economy.

Perhaps one of the most undemocratic features (at least in its consequences) of the U.S. political system is a result of how campaigns are financed. Political campaigns are becoming more and more expensive, with money needed to pay for staff, direct-mail operations, phone banks, polling, computers, consultants, and media advertising. The campaigns for Congress and president in 2008 cost $5.3 billion overall (up from $3.5 billion in 2000), including monies from the federal government, individuals, political parties, and organizations. Candidate Barack Obama raised $750 million for his presidential campaign in 2008 and is expected to raise $1 billion for the 2012 campaign. Compare these amounts with the $650 million that President George W. Bush and Senator John Kerry collected together for their campaigns in 2004.

In 2002, Congress passed the Bipartisan Campaign Reform Act (also known as the McCain-Feingold law). This law limited the use of "soft money" in federal elections. The use of "soft money" had allowed individuals, corporations, unions, and other organizations to give unlimited amounts of money to political parties or to private organizations that are technically independent of the candidates. Since this tactic was not covered by the election laws, the amounts raised were unlimited. This loophole was used by wealthy persons to contribute to the Republican and Democratic national parties (and indirectly to the presidential candidates).

McCain-Feingold did eliminate "soft money" in federal elections (buttressed by a favorable Supreme Court ruling in 2003) but it did not limit the giving of large sums to affect election outcomes. A number of ways were employed to navigate the system and give large donations to build support among Democrat or Republican voters. The loophole used is called 527s, which are advocacy groups, tax exempt under Section 527 of the Internal Revenue Code, that finance political advertisements while not directly calling for the election of defeat of specific candidates.

McCain-Feingold also limited maximum contributions to $2,300. While technically adhering to this limitation, corporate executives, lobbyists, and other insiders could maximize their political influence through a sophisticated system of bundling—the pooling of a large number of contributions, a tactic used by both political parties.

Another method to raise money is through contributions to a "foundation" or charity of a candidate. Through this loophole, donors could give unlimited contributions to a candidate with their identities hidden from the public record. A fourth source of money is the contributions to the political conventions or to inauguration expenses. While technically not a political contribution, it is clear that a corporation or interest group is helping to underwrite the expenses of a political party.

As noted, there were ways around the McCain-Feingold attempted to control spending. With a Supreme Court decision in 2010 (*Citizens United v. Federal Election Commission*), however, these efforts to get around McCain-Feingold were no longer necessary. By a landmark 5-4 decision the Supreme Court struck down the laws of twenty-two states and the federal government. It invalidated part of the McCain-Feingold campaign finance reform law that sought to limit corporate influence by ruling that the constitutional guarantee of free speech means that corporations, labor unions, and other organizations can spend unlimited sums to help elect or defeat political candidates.[*] These organizations are still barred from making direct contributions to politicians but they can now legally give unlimited amounts for ads to sway voters, as long as the ads are produced independently and not coordinated with a candidate's campaign. As the *New York Times* editorialized: "The court's conservative majority has paved the way for corporations to use their vast treasuries to overwhelm elections and intimidate elected officials into doing their bidding" (*New York Times*, 2010, para 1).

What do the contributors of large sums receive for their donations? Obviously, they have access to the politician, perhaps even influence. It is difficult to prove conclusively that receiving campaign contributions from a special interest buys a vote, but there is some indirect evidence that such contributors do gain advantage:

- Interest groups often give to candidates who run unopposed.
- Some interest groups give money to both sides in an election. Others contribute after the election to the candidate they opposed but who won anyway.
- Interest groups overwhelmingly support incumbents. By giving to the incumbent, the giver is almost assured of giving to the winner.
- The most money disproportionately goes to the most powerful members of the House and Senate (those in leadership roles).

See A Closer Look panel titled "The Best Democracy Money Can Buy."

---

[*]It is important to point out that although labor unions have the same right as corporations to spend freely in elections, they are no match to the corporations. The Center for Responsive Politics provides the data from the 2007–2008 election cycle: (1) corporations gave $1.964 billion in federal campaign contributions, compared to labor, which spent $74.8 million—a 15-1 disadvantage for labor (cited in Bybee, 2010); and (2) business and corporate interests accounted for 70.8 percent of the total political contributions, while only 2.7 percent came from labor (Chapin, 2010). Furthermore, these disparities occurred before the 2010 Supreme Court decision, freeing up the entities to spend in unlimited amounts.

The Best Democracy Money Can Buy

Billions are spent in election campaigns. The consequence of this flood of money in elections is that it sabotages democracy. This occurs in several ways. First, it makes it harder for government to solve social problems.

> How can we produce smart defense, environmental, and health policies if arms contractors, oil firms, and HMOs have a hammerlock over the committees charged with considering reforms? How can we adequately fund education and child care if special interests win tax breaks that deplete public resources? (Green, 2002:4)

Second, and related to the first, the "have-nots" of society are not represented among the decision makers. Moreover, since the successful candidate must either be wealthy or be beholden to them, they are a different class of people, from a different social world than most Americans. Thus, the money-politics connection is undemocratic because "democracy requires diversity in its legislatures in order to reflect the popular will" (Green, 2002:18).

Third, the money chase creates part-time elected officials and full-time fundraisers. For example, "senators from the ten largest states have to raise an average of over $34,000 a week, every week, for six years to stay in office" (Green, 2002:2).

Fourth, money diminishes the gap between the two major political parties because the candidates and parties seek and receive funds from the same corporate sources and wealthy individuals. Democrats in need of funds, even though they are more inclined than Republicans to support social programs and raising taxes to pay for them, must temper these tendencies or lose their monetary support from wealthy interests. As Robert Reich has observed, "it is difficult to represent the little fellow when the big fellow pays the tab" (Reich, 1989:A29).

Fifth, the money chase in politics discourages voting and civic participation (of the twenty-four Western democracies, the United States ranks twenty-third in voting turnout).

Sixth, big money in politics means that special interests get special access to the decision makers and receive special treatment from them.

> The pay-to-play mentality has so seeped into our system that there now exist two classes of citizens. There are those for whom tax breaks, bailouts, and subsidies are granted; for whom running for and winning office is plausible; and with who elected officials take time to meet. And then there are the rest of us—the nondonors for whom taxes go up, consumer prices rise, and influence evaporates. (Green, 2002:148)

What the hell, Senator—let's cut to the chase

© Lee Lorenz/The New Yorker Collection/www.cartoonbank.com

Money presents a fundamental obstacle to democracy because only the interests of the wealthy tend to be served. It takes money—and lots of it—to be a successful politician. The candidate must either be rich or be willing to accept contributions from other people. In either case, the political leaders will be part of or beholden to the wealthy.

Closely related to campaign financing is the process by which political candidates are nominated. Being wealthy or having access to wealth is essential for victory because of the enormous cost. This means that the candidates tend to represent a limited constituency—the wealthy.

The two-party system also works to limit choices among candidates to a rather narrow range. Each party is financed by the special interests—especially business:

> Campaign donations from members of the corporate community and upper class are a central element in determining who enters politics with any hope of winning a nomination. It is the need for a large amount of start-up money—to travel around the district or the country,

Is the United States a Plutocracy? Some Warnings

A **plutocracy** is a government by or in the interest of the rich. Many observers are concerned that the political system in the United States has become a plutocracy. Consider the following statements:

> The U.S. system of campaign finance is "an elaborate influence-peddling scheme in which both parties conspire to stay in office by selling the country to the highest bidder."
>
> SENATOR JOHN MCCAIN

Big money and big business, corporations and commerce are again the undisputed overlords of politics and government. The White House, the Congress and, increasingly, the judiciary, reflect their interests. We appear to have a government run by remote control from the U.S. Chamber of Commerce, the National Association of Manufacturers and the American Petroleum Institute. To hell with everyone else....

We are creeping toward an oligarchic society where a relative handful of the rich and privileged decide with their money, who will run, who will win, and how they will govern.

BILL MOYERS

Money not only determines who is elected, it determines who runs for office. Ultimately, it determines what government accomplishes—or fails to accomplish. Congress, except in unusual moments, will listen to the 900,000 Americans who give $200 or more to their campaigns ahead of the 259,600,000 who don't. Real reform of democracy, reform as radical as those of the Progressive era and deep enough to get government moving again, must begin by completely breaking the connection between money and politics.

SENATOR BILL BRADLEY

[Instead of a government of, by, and for the people, we have a government] of the 1%, by the 1%, and for the 1%.

NOBEL LAUREATE ECONOMIST JOSEPH STIGLITZ

to send out large mailings, to schedule radio and television time in advance—that gives members of the power elite a very direct role in the process right from the beginning and thereby provides them with personal access to politicians of both parties. (Domhoff, 1998:225)

Affluent individuals and the largest corporations influence candidate selection by giving financial aid to those sympathetic with their views and withholding support from those who differ. The parties, then, are constrained to choose candidates with views congruent with the monied interests. See A Closer Look panel titled "Is the United States a Plutocracy? Some Warnings," which discusses this linkage between money and power.

Pluralism II: Veto Groups. Although some groups and some individuals have more power than others, the power structure in the United States is viewed according to the veto groups' model as a plurality of interest groups (Riesman, 1950:213–217). Each interest group (for example, the military, labor, business, farmers, education, medicine, law, veterans, the aged, African Americans, and consumers) is primarily concerned with protecting its own interests. The group that primarily exercises power varies with the issue at stake. There is a balance of power, since each veto group mobilizes to prevent the others from actions threatening its interests. Thus, these groups tend to neutralize each other.

The masses are sought as an ally (rather than dominated, as is the case in the various elitist models) by the interest groups in their attempts to exert power over issues in their jurisdiction. Figure 14.2 shows the relationship between the various levels in this model. This pluralist model assumes that there are a number of sectors of power. The most powerful people in each sector are usually wealthy—probably upper class. But the pluralist view is that the upper class is not a unified group—there is considerable disagreement within the upper-class category because of differing interests. Power is not concentrated but is viewed as a shifting coalition depending on the issue. The basic difference between pluralists and elitists depends on the question of whether there is a basic unity or disagreement among the powerful from different sectors (basically, those who are wealthy enough to be upper class).

FIGURE 14.2

Veto-Groups
Model

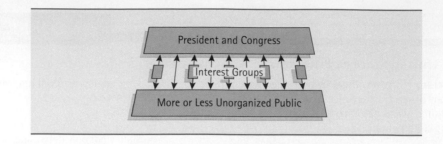

Several criticisms of this pluralistic model stem from the knowledge that it, like the other pluralistic model (for representative democracy), is an idealized conception of the distribution of power—and as such, it does not conform with reality and is subject to question on several grounds. First, is the power structure so amorphous that power shifts constantly from one power source to another? Second, are the interest groups so equal in power that they neutralize each other? The special bias of this view is that it does not give attention to the power differentials among the various interest groups. It is absurd to claim that the power of big business is neutralized by the countervailing power of farmers. The business sector spends much more than does organized labor to get its way. Moreover, only 13 percent of workers now belong to unions and while union members tend to vote Democratic, a significant minority now vote Republican. Similarly, the business community has many more resources to affect the political process than do environmental groups. Then, there are the powerless, such as migrant workers, the homeless, welfare recipients, immigrants, the poor, and the near-poor, who present no countervailing power against the rich and powerful. Thus, the conclusion that there is a hierarchy of power among these so-called "veto groups."

A final criticism is that the leaders in each sector come disproportionately from the upper-economic stratum. If this assertion is correct, the possibility of a power elite that transcends narrow interest groups is present, since they may know each other, tend to intermarry, and have similar economic interests (as discussed later in this chapter).

The pluralist models are not altogether faulty. A number of possible power centers often compete for advantage. Shifting coalitions are possible. There are instances when elected officials are responsive to public opinion (for example, the banning of soft money contributions to political parties in 2002). However, it seems to us that most of the evidence supports an elitist view, although each of the three types described next also has its faults.

Elitist Models

The elitist views of societal power are usually structured quite similarly to the views of Karl Marx. For Marx, economics was the basis for the stratification system (that is, unequal distribution of rewards, including power). The economic elite, because of its ownership and control of the economy, exerts tremendous influence on government policies and actions and is, therefore, a ruling class. The elite manipulate the masses through religion, nationalism, control of the media, and control of the visible governmental leaders (Marx and Engels, 1947:39). Marxists agree that the state serves the interests of the capitalist class. They disagree on how this is accomplished. One position is called the **instrumentalist view** (the following is from Marger, 1987:42–44). Here, the ruling class rules by controlling political officials and institutions through money and influence. Research shows, for example, the connections (social backgrounds) between top corporate and political decision makers. The state is seen as functioning "in terms of the instrumental exercise of power by people in strategic positions, either directly through the manipulation of state policies or indirectly through the exercise of pressure on the state" (Gold, Lo, and Wright, 1975:34). In effect, then, the government is an active instrument of the ruling class, used to accomplish its goals.

The second way Marxists see the ruling class is the **structuralist view**. From this perspective, the linkage between the economic elite and the political elite is not important. Rather, the ruling class gets its way because "the structure of political and economic institutions in capitalist society makes it imperative that the state serve those interests regardless of whether big businessmen directly or indirectly take part in state affairs" (Marger, 1987:43). From this perspective, then, the system is viewed as biased in favor of the elite without their active manipulation.

Power Elite I: The Thesis of C. Wright Mills. C. Wright Mills' (1956) view of the U.S. structure of power posits that the key people in three sectors—the corporate rich, the executive branch of the government, and the military—combine to form a power elite that makes all-important decisions.

The elite are a small group of people who routinely interact together. They also, as Mills assumed, have similar interests and goals. The elite are the power elite because the members have key institutional positions—that is, they command great authority and resources in specific and important sectors, and each sector depends on the other sectors.

There are three levels in Mills' pyramid of power. The uppermost is the power elite—composed of the leaders of three sectors. Mills implied that of the three, the corporate rich are perhaps the most powerful (first among equals). The middle level of power is composed of local opinion leaders, the legislative branch of government, and the plurality of interest groups. These bodies, according to Mills, do the bidding of the power elite. The third level is the powerless mass of unorganized people who are controlled from above. They are exploited economically and politically. The three levels of power are depicted in Figure 14.3.

Mills (who was writing in the 1950s) believed that the power elite was a relatively new phenomenon resulting from a number of historical and social forces that have enlarged and centralized the facilities of power, making the decisions of small groups much more consequential than in any other age (Mills, 1968).

The two important and related factors giving rise to the recent emergence of the power elite are that the means of power and violence (1) are now infinitely greater than they were in the past, and (2) are also increasingly centralized. The decisions of a few people become ultimately crucial when they have the power to activate a system that has the capability of destroying hundreds of cities within minutes. Transportation, communication, the economy, and the instruments of warfare are examples of several areas that have become centralized—making a power elite possible. The federal government taxes, regulates, and passes laws so that the lives of almost all people in the United States are affected.

This same bureaucratic process is evident in the military, in which decisions are more and more centralized. The Pentagon, which oversees the largest and most expensive feature of the government, is a relatively new phenomenon. The economy in the United States was once composed of many, many small productive units that were more or less autonomous. But over time the number of semiautonomous economic units has dwindled through

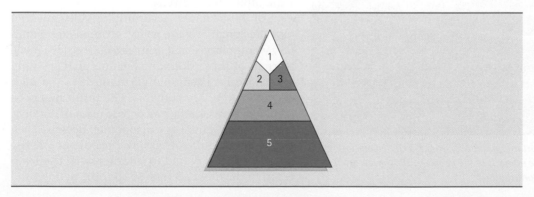

FIGURE 14.3

Mills' Pyramid of Power

1 = corporate rich;
2 = executive branch;
3 = military leaders;
4 = leaders of interest groups, legislative branch, local opinion leaders;
5 = unorganized masses

mergers, interlocking directorates, and chain stores, putting the financial squeeze on the small businessperson. The result is that the economy has become dominated by less than 200 giant corporations.

The tremendous advances in transportation and communication have made it much more likely that the people holding key positions in the political, economic, and military hierarchies can be in contact with each other if they wish to do so. If, as Mills assumed, they have similar interests, then they must be in contact so that their activities can be coordinated to the best mutual advantage.

The key decision makers also have instruments to influence the masses, such as television, public relations firms, and techniques of propaganda that are unsurpassed in the history of humankind. Hence, if there is a power elite and they want to manipulate the masses to accept their decisions, they have the instruments of mass persuasion at their disposal. Mills also contended that the importance of institutions has shifted. Whereas the family and religion were once the most important U.S. institutions, they (along with education) have become subordinate to the three power institutions of the economy, polity, and military—thus making the leaders of these three domains the power elite. Mills (1968) said, "Families and churches and schools adapt to modern life; governments and armies and corporations shape it; and, as they do so, they turn these lesser institutions into means for their ends" (267). For example, religious institutions supply chaplains to the armed forces, where they increase the effectiveness of the combat units by raising morale. Schools train people for their places in the giant corporations. Fathers and sons, mothers and daughters are sometimes taken from their homes to fight and die for their country. And, Mills said, the symbols of these lesser institutions are used to legitimate the decisions of the power elite who dominate the powerful institutions.

A most important impetus for the formation of the power elite was World War II. United States participation in a worldwide war, where the possibility of defeat was very real, meant, among other things, that a reorganization of various sectors had to be accomplished. The national government, particularly the executive department, had to be granted dictatorial powers so that the war could be conducted. Decisions had to be made quickly and in secret, two qualities not compatible with a democracy. The nation's corporations had to be mobilized for war. They made huge profits. Finally, the military became very prominent in decision making. Their expertise was essential to the making of wartime strategy.

The important question is: Do these elected officials represent the interests of the people or the narrow interests of their contributors?

Following World War II, the United States was faced with another threat—the spread of communism. This meant, in effect, that the executive department, the corporations, and the military did not shift back to their peacetime ways. The military remained in the decision-making process, the corporations remained dependent on lucrative defense contracts, and the executive branch continued to exercise its autonomous or at least semiautonomous powers.

All these factors, according to Mills, ensured that the domains of the polity, economy, and military were enlarged and centralized. Decisions made in each of these domains became increasingly crucial to all citizens, but particularly to the leaders of the other key domains. The result had to be a linkage between the key people in each domain. It was in their interests to cooperate. Because each sector affected the others, the people at the top of each hierarchy had to interact with the leaders from the other sectors, so that the actions and decisions would benefit all. Thus, they have come to form a triangle of power, an interlocking directorate of people in the three key domains making coordinated decisions—a **power elite**.

The important question is: Do these elected officials represent the interests of the people or the narrow interests of their contributors?

An important ingredient in Mills' view is that the elite are a self-conscious cohesive unit. This unity is based on three factors: psychological similarity, social interaction, and coinciding interests.

1. *Psychological similarity.* The institutional positions men and women occupy throughout their lifetimes determine the values they will hold. For example, career military men hold certain values by virtue of being socialized into the military subculture. The famous quote "What's good for General Motors is good for the country" by Secretary of Defense (under President Eisenhower) Charles Wilson is also indicative of this probability. Thus, for Mills, the psychology of these leaders is largely shaped by the values they develop in their institutional roles. Additionally, the psychological similarity among the members of the elite is derived from their similar social origins and lifestyles.
2. *Social interaction.* Mills (1956) argued that the members of the ruling elite interact socially, their children go to the same schools, and they do business with each other. Hence, these people who are the inner circle of the "upper social classes" tend to see the world alike.
3. *Coinciding interests.* A third unifying condition hypothesized by Mills is the existence of similar interests among the elite. The interest of the elite is, among other things, maintenance of the capitalist system with themselves at the top. Additionally, the government needs adequate defense systems, to which the military agree and that the corporations gladly sell for a profit. The huge corporations have large holdings in foreign countries. They therefore expect the government to make policy decisions that will be beneficial (profitable) for these U.S. interests. These similar interests result in unity and a need for planning and coordination of their efforts. Because each sector affects the other, the people at the top of each hierarchy must interact with leaders of the other sectors so that their actions will benefit all. Top decisions, Mills argued, thus become coordinated decisions.

Much of Mills' argument seems to fit with the realities of U.S. politics. Certainly those at the top of the key sectors wield enormous power. Some elements in Mills' thesis, however, have not held completely during the intervening fifty years (see Wolfe, 1999). First, Mills believed that the three sub-elites that compose the power elite are more or less equal, with the corporate rich probably having the most power. The equality of these groups is not proved. With the dismantling of the Soviet Empire, the power of the military elite diminished only to rise again after the terrorist attacks on the World Trade Center and the Pentagon in 2001. Military leaders are influential only in their advisory capacities and their ability to convince the executive branch and Congress. What looks like military power is often actually the power of the corporations and/or the executive branch carried out in military terms. In the view of many observers (especially Domhoff, as we see in the next section), business leaders compose the real power elite. Even though this is debatable, the fact is that they surpass the military in power, and because the executive branch is composed of people with close ties to the leading corporations, the logical conclusion is that business interests prevail in that sector as well.

Conflict occurs among the three sectors. There is often bitter disagreement between corporations and the government, between the military and the executive branch, and between the military and some elements in the business community. How is this conflict to be explained if, as Mills contended, the power elite is a group that acts in concert, with joint efforts planned and coordinated to accomplish the agreed-on goals? A good deal of empirical evidence shows that the heads of the three major sectors do not compose a group.

Mills relegates a number of powerful (or potentially powerful) forces to the middle ranges of power. What about the power of pressure groups that represent interests other than business or the military? Certainly, organized labor, farmers, professional organizations such as the American Medical Association, and consumers exert power over particular issues. Sometimes business interests even lose. How is this to be explained?

Finally, is Congress only in the middle level of the power structure? In Mills' view, Congress is a rubber stamp for the interests of business, the executive branch, and the military. Congress is apparently not composed of puppets for these interests, although the laws most often seem to favor these interests. But Congress does have its mavericks, and some of these people, by virtue of seniority, exert tremendous power (for either the blockage or passage of legislation). Should not the key congressional leaders be included in the power elite? The problem is that they often have interests that do not coincide with those of the presumed elite.

Power Elite II: Domhoff's "Governing Class" Theory. In Mills' view, power is concentrated in a relatively small, cohesive elite; G. William Domhoff's model of power is more broadly based in a "dominant class." Domhoff (1998) defined this dominant class as the uppermost social group (approximately 1 percent of the population), which owns a disproportionate amount of the country's wealth and contributes a disproportionate number of its members to the controlling institutions and key decision-making groups of the country:

> The owners and top-level managers in large income-producing properties are far and away the dominant power figures in the United States. Their corporations, banks, and agribusinesses come together as a corporate community that dominates the federal government in Washington. Their real estate, construction, and land development companies form growth coalitions that dominate most local governments. Granted, there is competition within both the corporate community and the local growth coalitions for profits and investment opportunities, and there are sometimes tensions between national corporations and local growth coalitions, but both are cohesive on policy issues affecting their general welfare, and in the face of demands by organized workers, liberals, environmentalists, and neighborhoods. (Domhoff, 1998:1)

This status group is composed mainly of rich businesspeople and their families, many of whom are, according to Domhoff's convincing evidence, closely knit through stock ownership, trust funds, intermarriages, private schools, social clubs, exclusive summer resorts, and corporation boards.

The dominant class in Domhoff's analysis controls the executive branch of the federal government, the major corporations, the mass media, foundations, universities, and the important councils for domestic and foreign affairs (for example, the Council on Foreign Relations, the Committee for Economic Development, the National Security Council, the National Industrial Conference Board, and the Twentieth Century Fund). Since they can control the executive branch, Domhoff argues, this dominant class controls the very important regulatory agencies, the federal judiciary, the military, the Central Intelligence Agency, and the Federal Bureau of Investigation.

The dominant class has greater influence on (but not control of) Congress and state and local governments than any other group. These parts of the formal power structure are not directly controlled by the governing class in Domhoff's analysis, but because he claims that such a class controls the executive and judicial branches, Congress is effectively blocked by two of the three divisions of government. Thus, U.S. foreign and domestic policies are initiated, planned, and carried out by members and organizations of a power elite that serve the interests of an upper class of rich businesspeople. Decisions are made that are considered appropriate for the interests of the United States—a strong economy, an adequate defense, and social stability. While perhaps beneficial to all people in the country, policies designed to accomplish these goals especially favor the rich. Consequently, U.S. corporations overseas are protected, foreign trade agreements are made that benefit U.S. corporations, and the tax structure benefits corporations or the very wealthy (by means of allowances for oil depletion, for capital gains and capital losses, for depreciation of equipment, and for other business expenses).

Domhoff demonstrates in detail the manner in which the governing class interacts (which we examined in Chapter 10). Once he established the interlocking ties brought about by common interests and through interaction, he cites circumstances that show the impact of individuals and subgroups within the elite on the decision-making structure of the United States:

- *Control of presidential nominations through the financing of political campaigns:* The evidence is clear that unless candidates have large financial reserves or the backing of wealthy people, they cannot hope to develop a national following or compete in party primaries.
- *Control of both major political parties:* Even though the Democratic Party is usually considered the party of the common person, Domhoff shows that it, like the Republican Party, is controlled by aristocrats (Parenti, 1995; this is documented well in Greider, 1992).
- *Almost total staffing of important appointive governmental positions (cabinet members, members of regulatory agencies, judges, diplomats, and presidential advisors):* These appointees are either members of the upper class or people who have held positions in the major corporations, and are thereby people who accord with the wishes of the upper class.

As a result of these circumstances (and others), all important foreign and domestic decisions are seen as made by the governing class. Domhoff's view of the power structure is reconstructed graphically in Figure 14.4.

In many ways, Domhoff's model of the U.S. power structure was a refinement of the one posited earlier by Mills. Domhoff's assessment of the power structure was similar to Mills' in that they both (1) view the power structure as a single pyramid, (2) see the corporate rich as the most powerful interest group, (3) relegate Congress to a relatively minor role and place the executive branch in an important role in the decision-making process, and (4) view the masses as being dominated by powerful forces rather than having much grassroots power.

The major difference between the views of Mills and Domhoff is that Domhoff has asserted the complete ascendancy of the upper class to the apex of power. The executive branch is controlled by upper-class businesspeople, industrialists, and financiers, rather than the two groups being more or less equal partners in the power elite, as Mills saw it. Moreover, the placement of

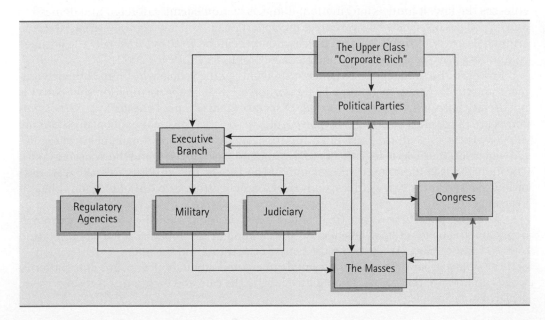

FIGURE 14.4

Domhoff's View of the Structure of Power

Black line = control; Blue line = influence. This model is based on our interpretation of Domhoff and is therefore subject to minor errors in emphasis.

Golden rule

Reprinted by permission of Johnny Hart and Creators Syndicate, Inc.

the military in the pyramid of power is quite different. Mills saw the military as part of the alliance of the troika, whereas Domhoff saw the military as having much less power and being dominated by the corporate rich through the executive branch.

Domhoff's view of power is quite persuasive, but there are also several criticisms. First, much of Domhoff's proof is in the form of listing the upper-class pedigrees of presidential advisors, cabinet members, ambassadors, regulatory agency members, and so on. Even though people in these positions are disproportionately from upper-class backgrounds (as evidenced by their attendance at prestige schools, their membership in exclusive social clubs, and their placement in the various social registries), we are given no proof that these people actually promote the interests of the corporate rich. This is an assumption by Domhoff that appears reasonable, but it is an oversimplification. There are many examples of wealthy people who make decisions on bases other than economics, such as religious or moral altruism, or civil or human rights. Thus, Domhoff's assumption is one of Marxian economic determinism, and as such is subject to the criticism of oversimplification of a complex process. Even though an economic motive of some kind explains a great deal of social behavior, its operation with other prestige factors is very complex and does not explain all of human behavior.

Power Elite III: Parenti's "Bias of the System" Theory. We commonly think of the machinery of government as a beneficial force promoting the common good. The government can be organized for the benefit of the majority, but it is not always neutral. The state regulates; it stifles opposition; it makes and enforces the law; it funnels information; it makes war on enemies (foreign and domestic); and its policies determine how resources are apportioned. And in all of these areas, the government is generally biased toward policies that benefit the wealthy, especially the business community (this section is taken from Michael Parenti, 1978; 1995; 2002).

Power in the United States is concentrated among the people who control the government and the largest corporations. This assertion is based on the assumption that power is not an attribute of individuals but rather of social organizations. The elite in U.S. society is composed of people who occupy the power roles in society. The great political decisions are made by the president, the president's advisors, cabinet members, the members of regulatory agencies, the Federal Reserve Board, key members of Congress, and the Supreme Court. The individuals in these government command posts have the authority to make war, raise or lower interest rates, levy taxes, dam rivers, and institute or withhold national health insurance.

Economic activity was once the result of many decisions made by individual entrepreneurs and the heads of small businesses. Now, a handful of companies have virtual control over the marketplace. Decisions by the boards of directors and the management personnel of these huge corporations determine employment and production, consumption patterns, wages and prices, the extent of foreign trade, and the rate at which natural resources are depleted, for example.

The Dark Side of Lobbying

Special interests in 2010 spent $3.5 billion lobbying elected officials and candidates to influence them to legislate or administer in their favor. Lobbying is a constitutionally protected activity (that is, the First Amendment guarantees the right of free speech). There are several problems with this common practice. First, there is a great imbalance between those organizations with huge resources such as corporations (ExxonMobil, General Electric), Realtors (National Association of Realtors), physicians (American Medical Association), business (U.S. Chamber of Commerce), labor unions (United Automobile Workers), the elderly (American Association of Retired People), and those groups without power, resources, and organizational clout such as migrant workers, single parents, the homeless, and the chronically unemployed. Moreover, lobbyists do not advance "the interrelated causes of peace, justice, social health, ecological sustainability, and democracy at home and abroad" (Street, 2007:31) but rather the advantages in power and profits.

A second problem with lobbying is the close link between elected officials and lobbyists. This occurs in several ways. For instance, lobbyists pay exorbitant prices to attend fundraisers for their legislative friends. Also, key legislators, when defeated for office or after retiring, are often hired by lobbying firms to influence their former colleagues.

Third, lobbyists often sway legislative decisions away from what would benefit the common good. Some examples:

- Congress passed a Medicare bill that specifically prohibited negotiations over prices. Medicare could have used its bargaining power to extract lower drug prices but the pharmaceutical industry opposed that because it would hurt its profits.
- It is in lobbyists' best interest to present information, sometimes biased, that will support their interests. ExxonMobil, for example, has used disinformation to raise doubts about climate change in an effort to preempt the public's demand for action on the issue (Mooney, 2006).
- Since 2001 through 2007, Philip Morris, the leader in the tobacco industry, spent over $75 million on lobbying expenses to keep tobacco regulations and increased cigarette taxes at a minimum (Beall, 2008; *New York Times*, 2007), even though tobacco use is a leading health hazard.

A final problem with lobbying is that its excesses can lead to corruption scandals. A recent example is the once-powerful lobbyist Jack Abramoff, who pleaded guilty to fraud, tax evasion, and conspiracy to bribe public officials. Abramoff admitted to providing lavish luxury trips, skybox fundraisers, entertainment, support for political campaigns, and employment for relatives of officials. Among the political casualties were former House Majority Leader Tom DeLay who resigned from Congress, Congressmen Robert Ney who decided to not run for reelection in 2006, and Senator Conrad Burns who was defeated in his 2006 reelection attempt. Burns, by the way, following his defeat, was hired by a Washington lobbying firm.

The few thousand people who compose this power elite tend to come from backgrounds of privilege and wealth. It would be a mistake, however, to equate personal wealth with power. Great power is manifested only through decision making in the very large corporations or in government. We have seen that this elite exercises great power. Decisions are made by the powerful, and these decisions tend to benefit the wealthy disproportionately. But the power elite is not organized and conspiratorial.

The interests of the powerful (and the wealthy) are served, nevertheless, because of the way society is organized. This bias occurs in three ways—by their influence over elected and appointed governmental officials at all levels, through systemic imperatives, and through the ideological control of the masses.

As discussed in an earlier section, the wealthy receive favorable treatment by actually occupying positions of power or by having direct influence over those who do. Moreover, the financially advantaged spend huge sums to influence Congress and the executive branch through lobbying—spending $3.47 billion in 2009 to influence legislation and executive actions (Eaton and Bell, 2010). The laws, court decisions, and administrative decisions give advantage to those individuals, corporations, and interest groups with financial clout. (See the A Closer Look panel titled "The Dark Side of Lobbying" for more on the arguments for and against the practice.)

More subtly, the power elite can get its way without actually being mobilized at all. The choices of decision makers are often limited by various systemic imperatives; that is, the institutions of society are patterned to produce prearranged results regardless of the personalities of the decision makers. In other words, there is a bias that pressures the government to do certain things and not to do other things. Inevitably, this bias favors the status quo, allowing people with power to continue to exercise it. No change is easier than change. The current political and economic systems have worked and generally are not subject to question, let alone change. In this way, the laws, customs, and institutions of society resist change. Thus, the propertied and the wealthy benefit, while the propertyless and the poor remain disadvantaged. As Parenti (1978) argues: "The law does not exist as an abstraction. It gathers shape and substance from a context of power, within a real-life social structure. Like other institutions, the legal system is class-bound. The question is not whether the law should or should not be neutral, for as a product of its society, it cannot be neutral in purpose or effect" (188).

In addition to the inertia of institutions, other systemic imperatives benefit the power elite and the wealthy. One such imperative is for the government to strive to provide an adequate defense against our enemies, which stifles any external threat to the status quo. Thus, Congress, the president, and the general public tend to support large appropriations for defense, which, in turn, provide extraordinary profit to many corporations. In addition, the government protects U.S. transnational corporations in their overseas operations, so that they enjoy a healthy and profitable business climate. Domestic government policy also is shaped by the systemic imperative for stability. The government promotes domestic tranquility by squelching dissidence.

Power is the ability to get what one wants from someone else. This can be achieved by force or by getting that someone to think and believe in accordance with your interests. "The ability to control the definition of interests is the ability to define the agenda of issues, a capacity tantamount to winning battles without having to fight them" (Parenti, 1978:41). U.S. schools, churches, and families possess this power. The schools, for instance, consciously teach youth that capitalism is the only correct economic system.

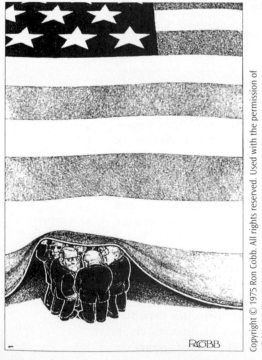

This indoctrination to conservative values achieves a consensus among the citizenry concerning the status quo. In other words, each of us comes to accept the present arrangements in society because they seem to be the only options that make sense. Thus, there is a general agreement on what is right and wrong. In sum, the dominance of the wealthy is legitimized. "The interests of an economically dominant class never stand naked. They are enshrouded in the flag, fortified by the law, protected by the police, nurtured by the media, taught by the schools, and blessed by the church" (Parenti, 1978:84). Finally, the belief in democracy works to the advantage of the power elite, as Parenti (1978) notes in the following passage:

As now constituted, elections serve as a great asset in consolidating the existing social order by propagating the appearances of popular rule. History demonstrates that the people might be moved to overthrow a tyrant who shows himself provocatively indifferent to their woes, but they are far less inclined to make war upon a state, even one dominated by the propertied class, if it preserves what Madison called "the spirit and form of popular government." Elections legitimate the rule of the propertied class by investing it with the moral authority of popular consent. By the magic of the ballot, class dominance becomes "democratic" governance. (201)

The Consequences of Concentrated Power

Who benefits from how power is concentrated in the United States? At times, most everyone does; but for the most part, the decisions made tend to benefit the wealthy. Whenever the interests of the wealthy clash with those of other groups or even of the majority, the interests of the wealthy are served. Consider how the president and Congress deal with the problems of increasing government debt, energy shortages, inflation, or deflation. Who is asked to make the sacrifices? Where is the budget cut—are military expenditures reduced or are funds for food stamps slashed? When the Congress considers tax reform, after the roar of rhetoric recedes, which groups benefit by the new legislation or by the laws that are left unchanged? When a corporation is found guilty of fraud, violation of antitrust laws, or bribery, what are the penalties? How do they compare with the penalties for crimes committed by poor individuals? When there is an oil spill or other ecological disaster caused by huge enterprise, what are the penalties? Who pays for the cleanup and the restoration of the environment? The answers to these questions are obvious—the wealthy benefit at the expense of the less well-to-do. In short, the government is an institution made up of people—the rich and powerful or their agents—who seek to maintain their advantageous positions in society.

Two journalists, Barlett and Steele (2000), argue that there are two ways to get favorable treatment by Congress and the White House: contribute generously to the right people and spend lavishly on lobbying (Barlett and Steele, 2004:40–42). (See the Technology and Society panel titled "Facebook Lobbies Washington.") If you do you will get, for example, favorable tax rates, immunity from certain laws, government subsidies, and even a government bailout if needed. If you do not make generous political contributions and have lobbyists to make your case, then you will, according to Barlett and Steele, pay a disproportionate share of taxes, pay higher prices for a range of products, be compelled to pay all of your debts, and you will see legislation for the social good weakened or killed. In essence, we have a political system where spending money for political purposes makes a huge difference, dividing Americans into the fortunate few and second-class citizens.

The bias of the system today is nothing new. Since the nation's founding, the government's policy has primarily favored the needs of the wealthy. The founding fathers were upper-class holders of wealth. The Constitution they wrote gave the power to people like themselves—White male property owners.

This bias continued throughout the nineteenth century as bankers, railroad entrepreneurs, and manufacturers joined the landed gentry to make the power elite. The shift from local business to large-scale manufacturing during the last half of the nineteenth century saw a concomitant increase in governmental activity in the economy. Business was protected from competition by protective tariffs, public subsidies, price regulation, patents, and trademarks. Throughout that century, when there was unrest by troubled miners, farmers, and laborers, the government inevitably sided with the strong against the weak. The militia and federal troops were used to crush the railroad strikes. Antitrust laws, which were not used to stop the monopolistic practices of business, were invoked against labor unions.

During this time, approximately 1 billion acres of land in the public domain (almost half the present size of the United States) were given to private individuals and corporations. The railroads in particular were given huge tracts of land as a subsidy. These lands were and continue to be very rich in timber and natural resources. This active intervention of the government in the nation's economy during the nineteenth century was almost solely on the behalf of business. Michael Parenti notes, "The government remained laissez-faire in regard to the needs of the common people, giving little attention to poverty, unemployment, unsafe working conditions, child labor, and the spoliation of natural resources" (Parenti, 2008:56).

The early twentieth century was a time of great governmental activity in the economy, which gave the appearance of restraining big business. However, the actual result of federal regulation of business was to increase the power of the largest corporations. The Interstate

Facebook Lobbies Washington

Tech companies have steadily increased their lobbying activities. Microsoft spent $6.9 million in 2010 and has a staff of sixteen. Google, with a staff of twenty-five has increased its spending on lobbying Washington DC insiders from $260,000 in 2005 to $5.16 million in 2010.

Facebook, the world's largest social networking site, is a relative newcomer in the tech world, founded in 2004. It is also new to lobbying, having spent only $351,390 in 2010, but up 30 percent from the previous year. Facebook in 2011 had four registered lobbyists, two Republicans and two Democrats, both part of a twelve-member staff. Facebook has turned to lobbying lawmakers, congressional staff, and privacy experts as they consider sweeping challenges to their activities. The points of contention between Facebook and Washington include (Williamson, Schatz, and Fowler, 2011):

- Issues of privacy, particularly government concerns for greater protections of online users' identities

and personal information, their consumption habits, and sharing user information with third parties and websites. Facebook fears regulatory actions that might hinder its revenue from ads targeted at users (Swartz, 2011).

- Internet freedoms. Facebook seeks to expand its operations worldwide, especially in China. This raises questions concerning the use of Facebook by dissidents in a country with little tolerance for dissent. Should Facebook be allowed by Congress to play by China's rules?

Although Facebook has a small lobbying presence, it has a unique advantage in cultivating influence in Washington: "basically every single politician in Washington (or at least their staff) uses Facebook every day to reach out to constituents and campaign" (Gobry, 2011: para 4).

Commerce Commission, for instance, helped the railroads by establishing common rates to replace ruinous competition. Federal regulations in meat packing, drugs, banking, and mining weeded out the weaker cost-cutting competitors, leaving a few to control the markets at higher prices and higher profits. Even the actions of that great trustbuster, Teddy Roosevelt, were largely ceremonial. His major legislative proposals reflected the desires of corporate interests. Like other presidents before and since, he enjoyed close relations with big businessmen and invited them into his administration (Parenti, 2008:57).

World War I intensified the governmental bias on behalf of business. Industry was converted to war production. Corporate interests became more actively involved in the councils of government. Governmental actions clearly favored business in labor disputes. The police and military were used against rebellious workers, because strikes were treated as efforts to weaken the war effort and therefore as treasonous.

The New Deal is typically assumed to be a time when the needs of those impoverished by the Great Depression were paramount in government policies. But, as Parenti has argued, "the central dedication of the Franklin Roosevelt administration was to business recovery rather than to social reform" (Parenti, 1980:74). Business was subsidized by credits, price supports, bank guarantees, stimulation of the housing industry, and the like. Welfare programs were instituted to prevent widespread starvation, but even these humanitarian programs also advantaged the big-business community. The government provision of jobs, minimum wages, unemployment compensation, and retirement benefits obviously was aimed at people in dire economic straits. But these programs were actually promoted by the business community because of benefits to them. The government and business favored social programs at this time not because millions of people were in misery but because violent political and social unrest posed a real threat, as noted in Chapter 6 (see Piven and Cloward, 1993).

The historical trend for government to favor business over less powerful interests continues in current public policy.

Subsidies to Big Business

There is a general principle that applies to the government's relationship to big business—business can conduct its affairs either undisturbed by or encouraged by government, whichever is of greater benefit to the business community. The government benefits the business community with hundreds of billions in subsidies annually. Corporations receive a wide range of favors and tax breaks, direct government subsidies pay for advertising, research, and training costs and incentives to pursue overseas production and sales. The following are examples of government decisions that were beneficial to business:

- State and local governments woo corporations with various subsidies including tax breaks, low-interest loans, infrastructure improvements, and relatively cheap land. In 2006, for example, Mississippi offered Kia, the Korean automaker, $1 billion in incentives to build a plant (Georgia offered Kia $400 million). Citizens for Tax Justice argues that when these subsidies occur corporations manage to shield as much as two-thirds of their profits from state corporate income taxes. "The result: Money that could be spent on real economic development opportunities flows instead into the pockets of executives and the bill gets passed along to small taxpayers—local businesses and workers" (Singer, 2006:6).
- In 1996, Congress gave broadcasters spectrum rights to broadcast one channel of super-high-resolution digital programs or several channels that could be used for digital interactive services or TV programs of high, but not super-high, resolution. To which the *New York Times* (2000a) editorialized: "By giving the new spectrum away instead of auctioning it off to the highest bidders, Congress deprived the treasury, and thus taxpayers, of tens of billions of dollars" (1).
- Eleven days after the terrorist attacks of September 11, 2001, Congress appropriated $15 billion for the airline industry. The bailout went to the airline companies, not the workers laid off by the companies and allied industries (travel and tourism).
- The government installs price supports on certain commodities, increasing the profits of those engaged in those industries and simultaneously costing consumers. For example, subsidies to agriculture were $15.4 billion in 2010.
- Taxpayers give farming business up to 45 cents per gallon in subsidies for ethanol, the fuel made from corn. In addition to taking farmland out of food production and raising supermarket prices for meat and grains, the annual subsidy amounts in $5.7 billion.
- The federal government directly subsidizes the shipping industry, railroads, airlines, and exporters of iron, steel, textiles, paper, and other products.
- The government often funds research and develops new technologies at public expense and then turns them over to private corporations for their profit. This transfer occurs routinely with nuclear energy, synthetics, space communications, mineral exploration, and pharmaceuticals. Although the pharmaceutical industry, for example, argues that it must charge high prices on drugs to recoup its costly research, the Joint Economic Committee of Congress found that public research led to fifteen of the twenty-one drugs considered to have the highest therapeutic value introduced between 1965 and 1992 (reported in Goozner, 2000). Three of these drugs—Capoten, Prozac, and Zovirax—have sales of more than $1 billion each. Not incidentally, the drug makers are the most powerful lobby in Washington, with nearly 15,000 registered federal lobbyists spent almost $200 million to influence legislators in 2009.
- Transnational corporations are permitted to set up tax havens overseas to make various intracompany transactions from a unit in one foreign country to another, thus legally sheltering them from U.S. taxes. Apple Computer, for example, allocates a portion of the profits on iPads and MacBooks sold in the United States to the offshore subsidiary that owns the patent (Collins, 2011).
- In 2003, Congress passed the Medicare Prescription Bill. The pharmaceutical industry, using 675 lobbyists from 138 firms, nearly seven lobbyists for each senator, was successful in achieving favorable treatment in the legislation, including: (1) a prohibition on the Medicare program from using its bargaining clout to directly negotiate deep drug price

G.E. reported $3.1 billion in domestic profits in 2010, but paid no federal taxes because of loopholes in the tax code.

discounts (one estimate is that this will increase profits by $139 billion over eight years); and (2) a ban on the reimportation of prescription drugs from Canada, which cost about 50 percent less than in the United States (*Public Citizen*, 2003).

- The more than $1 trillion in government bailouts to the banks and financial firms in 2008 actually rewarded them for their reckless behavior. Bank of America, for example, one of four banks that controlled 95 percent of commercial bank derivatives activity, which inflated the housing bubble, received $45 billion in a government bailout.

Perhaps the best illustration of how business benefits from government policies is the system of legal loopholes provided by the tax code. Using these tax breaks, eleven corporations including General Electric, Boeing, Wells Fargo, ExxonMobil, IBM, and Verizon, reported $62 billion in domestic profits in 2010, but paid a negative 3.6 percent federal tax rate (in other words they received money back). To illustrate: General Electric, the nation's largest corporation reported worldwide profits of $14.2 billion in 2010, $5.1 billion of which came from its U.S. operations. Although the top corporate tax rate is 35 percent, G.E. paid no U.S. taxes, actually receiving a tax refund of $3.2 billion. G.E.'s success is "based on an aggressive strategy that mixes fierce lobbying for tax breaks and innovative accounting that enables it to concentrate its profits offshore" (Kocieniewski, 2011: para 5). Closing corporate loopholes would add nearly $200 billion to federal government revenues (Miller, 2011).

Trickle-Down Solutions

Periodically, the government is faced with the problem of finding a way to stimulate the economy during an economic downturn. One solution is to spend federal monies through unemployment insurance, government jobs, and housing subsidies. In this way, the funds go directly to the people most hurt by shortages, unemployment, inadequate housing, and the like. Opponents of such plans advocate that the subsidies should go directly to business, which would help the economy by encouraging companies to hire more workers, add to their inventories, and build new plants. Subsidizing business in this way, the advocates argue, benefits everyone. In effect, proponents argue, because the government provides direct benefits to businesses and investors, the economic benefits indirectly trickle down to all.

Opponents of "trickle-down" economics argue that this is an inefficient way to help the less-than-affluent.

> One way to understand "trickle-down" economics is to use a more graphic metaphor: horse-and-sparrow economics—that is, if you feed the horse well, some will pass on through and be there on the ground for the sparrow. There is no doubt that sparrows can be nourished in this manner; and the more the horses get fed, the more there will be on the ground for the sparrows to pick through. It is, however, probably not a very pleasant way for sparrows to get their sustenance, and if one's primary goal is to feed the sparrows, it is a pretty silly—and inefficient—way to do the job…. Why waste the money on the horses when it might go directly to the sparrows? (MacEwan, 2001:40)

There are at least two reasons government officials tend to opt for these trickle-down solutions. First, because they tend to come from the business class, government officials believe in the conservative ideology that says what is good for business is good for the United States. The second reason for the probusiness choice is that government officials are more likely to hear arguments from the powerful. Because the weak, by definition, are not organized, their voice is not heard or, if heard, not taken seriously in decision-making circles.

Although the government most often opts for trickle-down solutions, such plans are not very effective in fulfilling the promise that benefits will trickle down to the poor. The higher corporate profits generated by tax credits and other tax incentives do not necessarily mean that companies will increase wages or hire more workers. What is more likely is that corporations will increase dividends to the stockholders, which further increases the inequality gap. Job creation is also not guaranteed because companies may use their newly acquired wealth to purchase labor-saving devices. If so, then the government programs will actually have widened the gulf between the haves and the have-nots.

The Powerless Bear the Burden

Robert Hutchins in his critique of U.S. governmental policy, characterized the basic principle guiding internal affairs in this way: "Domestic policy is conducted according to one infallible rule: the costs and burdens of whatever is done must be borne by those least able to bear them" (Hutchins, 1976:4). Let us review several examples that support this statement.

After the Great Recession hit in late 2007 federal and state governments had to reduce or eliminate programs. Where were the cuts made? Typically, social programs for the disadvantaged were targeted, not subsidies for business or tax breaks to homeowners. In the 2008–2009 school year, twenty-four states reduced their funding for early childhood education (most needed by children from low-income families). Low-income children's access to health care has also declined because of state budget cuts. So, too, have programs providing low-income families with temporary cash-assistance support and child care subsidies been reduced (Austin, 2010). Public school education has taken the biggest hit with thirty-four states reducing school budgets in 2010 and at least twenty-one states proposing spending cuts in 2011–2012. The result is the laying off of large numbers of teachers, raising class sizes, cutting electives such as music, art, and sports, eliminating summer school programs, and shortening the academic year.

When threatened by war, the government institutes a military draft. A careful analysis of the draft reveals that it is really a tax on the poor. During the height of the Vietnam War, for instance, only 10 percent of men in college were drafted, although 40 percent of draft-age men were in college. Even for educated young men who ended up in the armed services, there was a greater likelihood of their serving in noncombat jobs than for the non-college-educated. Thus, the chances for getting killed while in the service were about three times greater for the less-educated than for the college-educated (Baskir and Strauss, 1978; Zeitlin, Lutterman, and Russell, 1977). Even more blatant was the practice that occurred legally during the Civil War. The law at that time allowed the affluent who were drafted to hire someone to take their place in the service.

In the Iraq and Afghanistan wars beginning in 2003, the government decided not to have a draft, relying rather on volunteers. While patriotism was undoubtedly a factor in the decision to enlist, economic incentives (for example, enlistment bonus) to those from disadvantaged backgrounds was also a powerful motive. In effect, the battles were fought overwhelmingly by young men and women from the working and lower classes. As one critic put it: "If this war is truly worth fighting, then the burdens of doing so should fall on all Americans.... If it's not worth your family fighting it, then it's not worth it, period" (Broyles, 2004:A25). See A Closer Look panel titled "Guns or Butter? Who's Paying for the War?."

Guns or Butter? Who's Paying for the War?

In addition to the $600 billion or so to fund the military annually, another $300 billion directly funds the Iraq and Afghanistan wars (and does not count the indirect costs of providing medical care and disability compensation for veterans, the interest on the federal debt incurred by the war, higher oil prices, and other costs) (Bilmes, 2008). Ultimately, these wars could cost as much as $3 trillion, according to Nobel Prize Laureate in Economics Joseph Stiglitz (Stiglitz and Bilmes, 2008).

This war is fully funded. But sacrifices must be made, so federal expenditures are cut from domestic programs. Badly needed infrastructure projects go unfunded. Universal health care does not happen. Federal spending on efforts aimed as ensuring safety and health such as the Consumer Product Safety Commission, the National Transportation Safety Board, the Occupational Safety and Health Administration, and the Food and Drug Administration are underfunded (*Chicago Tribune*, 2007). In late 2007, President George W. Bush signed a spending bill that benefited the Pentagon but vetoed an appropriations bill that provided funding for low-income programs such as Head Start, rural health, job training, and programs providing block grants to the states for low-income people and people with disabilities and for energy assistance to help low-income families pay for rising home heating costs (Wolf, 2007).

The poor, being powerless, can be made to absorb the costs of societal changes. In the nineteenth century the poor did the back-breaking work that built the railroads and the cities. Today, they are the ones pushed out of their homes by gentrification, urban renewal, and the building of expressways, parks, and stadiums.

Following the devastation from Hurricane Katrina in Louisiana and Mississippi in 2005, priorities were set by decision makers as to where rebuilding should be initiated and where it should be delayed or even ignored. In New Orleans, the bulk of the money spent first went to the business community and for repairing the Super Dome (home field for the New Orleans Saints). Left behind were low-income families. Although Congress required that half of federal grant money help low-income people, some 90 percent of $1.7 billion in federal money spent in Mississippi went to affluent homeowners and to rebuild casinos and hotels, and expand the Port of Gulfport (Eaton, 2007).

The government's attempts to solve economic problems generally obey the principle that the poor must bear the burden. A common solution for runaway inflation, for example, is to increase the amount of unemployment. Of course the poor, especially minorities (whose rate of unemployment is consistently twice the rate for Whites), are the ones who make the sacrifice for the economy. This solution, aside from being socially cruel, is economically ineffective because it ignores the real sources of inflation—excessive military spending, excessive profits by energy companies (foreign and domestic), and administered prices set by shared monopolies, which, contrary to classical economic theory, do not decline during economic downturns (Harrington, 1979).

More fundamentally, a certain level of unemployment is maintained continuously, not just during economic downturns. Genuine full employment for all job seekers is a myth. But why is it a myth, since all political candidates extol the work ethic and it is declared national policy to have full employment? Economist Robert Lekachman (1979) has argued that it is no accident that we tolerate millions of unemployed people. The reason is that a moderate unemployment rate is beneficial to the affluent. These benefits include the following: (1) People are willing to work at humble tasks for low wages, (2) the children of the middle and upper classes avoid the draft as the unemployed join the volunteer army, (3) the unions are less demanding, (4) workers are less likely to demand costly safety equipment, (5) corporations do not have to pay their share of taxes because local and state governments give them concessions to lure them to their area, and (6) the existing wide differentials between White males and the various powerless categories such as females, Latinos, and African Americans are retained.

The operant principle here is that "foreign policy seems to be carried on in the light of the needs of the munitions makers, the Pentagon, the CIA, and the multinational corporations" (Hutchins, 1976:4). For example, military goods are sold overseas for the profit of the arms merchants. Sometimes arms are sold to both sides in a potential conflict, the argument being that if we did not sell them the arms, then other nations would, so we might as well make the profits.

The government has supported foreign governments that are supportive of U.S. transnational companies regardless of how tyrannical these governments might be. The U.S. government has directly intervened in the domestic affairs of foreign governments to protect U.S. corporate interests and to prevent the rise of any government based on an alternative to the capitalist model (Parenti, 2008:85). In Latin America, for example, since 1950 the United States has intervened militarily in Guatemala, the Dominican Republic, Chile, Uruguay, Nicaragua, Grenada, and Panama. As Parenti (1988) characterizes it:

> Sometimes the sword has rushed in to protect the dollar, and sometimes the dollar has rushed in to enjoy the advantages won by the sword. To make the world safe for capitalism, the United States government has embarked on a global counterrevolutionary strategy, suppressing insurgent peasant and worker movements throughout Asia, Africa, and Latin America. But the interests of the corporate elites never stand naked; rather they are wrapped in the flag and coated with patriotic appearances. (94)

In summary, this view of power argues that the power of wealthy individuals and the largest corporations is translated into public policy that disproportionately benefits the power elite. Throughout U.S. history, there has been a bias that pervades government and its policies. This bias is perhaps best seen in the aphorism once enunciated by President Calvin Coolidge and repeated by contemporary presidents: "The business of America is business."

The Order and Conflict Perspectives on the Distribution of Power

Power is unequally distributed in all social organizations. In our examination of the structure of power at the societal level, two basic views were presented—the pluralist and the elitist. The former is consistent with the world view of order theorists, while the latter is congruent with the way conflict theorists perceive reality (see Table 14.1).

TABLE 14.1

Assumptions of the Order and Conflict Models about Politics

Order Model	*Conflict Model*
1. People in positions of power occupy bureaucratic roles necessary for the rational accomplishment of society's objectives.	1. People in positions of power are motivated largely by their own selfish interests.
2. The state works for the benefit of all. Laws reflect the customs of society and ensure order, stability, and justice—in short; the common good.	2. The state exists for the benefit of the ruling class (law, police, and courts protect the interests of the wealthy).
3. Pluralism: (1) competing interest groups: (2) majority rule; (3) power is diffused.	3. Power is concentrated (power elite).

One glaring weakness of many pluralists and elitists is that they are not objective. Their writings tend often to be polemics because so much effort is spent attempting to prove what they believe is the nature of the power structure. The evidence is presented to ensure the absolute negation of the opposite stance. This points to a fundamental research problem. Are the data reliable? Are our observations distorted by bias? Sociologists or political scientists are forced in the study of power to rely on either the perceptions of other people (who are presumed to be knowledgeable) or on their own observations, which are distorted by their not being present during all aspects of the decision-making process. Unfortunately, one's perceptions are also affected by one's model (conflict or order). Ideological concerns often cause either faulty perceptions or a rigidity of thought that automatically rejects conflicting evidence.

The task for sociologists is to determine the real distribution of power with our ideological distortion. Given these problems with objectivity, we must ask: (1) What is the power structure really like? (2) What facts are consonant with the pluralist model and what facts fit the elitist model?

CHAPTER REVIEW

1. In answering the question of who the real power wielders are in U.S. society, there are two contrasting answers from pluralists and elitists.

2. The representative-democracy version of pluralism emphasizes that the people have the ultimate power. The people elect representatives who are responsive to the people's wishes. This version ignores the many instances in which the people have been deliberately misled by their leaders, secrecy, and the undemocratic manner in which election campaigns are funded.

3. The veto-groups version of pluralism recognizes the existence of a number of organizations and special-interest groups that vie for power. There is a balance of power, however, with no one sector getting its way. The groups tend to neutralize each other, resulting in compromise. Critics of this view of power argue that it is an idealized version that ignores reality. The interest groups are not equal in power. Power does not shift from issue to issue. Also, at the apex of each of the competing groups are members of the upper class, suggesting the possibility of a power elite.

4. Marxists assert that there is a ruling class. There are two variations on this theme. The instrumentalist view is that the ruling class (capitalists) does not govern (that is, hold office) but that it rules by controlling political officials and institutions. The structuralist view is that the state serves the interests of the capitalist class because whoever holds government office will make decisions that promote stability and a healthy business climate—both of which enhance the interests of the capitalist class.

5. In C. Wright Mills' view of power, there is a power elite composed of the top people in the executive branch of the federal government, the military, and the corporate sector. Although these people represent different interests, they tend to perceive the world in a like manner because

of their similar social class backgrounds and similar role expectations, because they interact socially, because their children go to the same schools and intermarry, and because they share similar interests. There is considerable evidence for the linkages among these three sectors. There are some problems with this view, however. The equality of these three groups is not a fact. There is conflict among the three sectors. Other sectors of power are ignored.

6. In G. William Domhoff's view of power, there is a dominant class—the uppermost social class. The very rich control the nation's assets, control the corporations, are overrepresented in the key decision-making groups in society, and through contributions and activities control both major political parties. The major criticism of this view is that while the people in key positions tend to have upper-class pedigrees, there is no evidence that these people actually promote the interests of the corporate rich.

7. Michael Parenti's bias-of-the-system view is another elitist theory. The powerful in society (those who control the government and the largest corporations) tend to come from backgrounds of privilege and wealth. Their decisions tend to benefit the wealthy disproportionately, but the power elite is not organized and conspiratorial. The interests of the wealthy are served, nevertheless, by the way society is organized. This bias occurs by their influence over elected and appointed officials, systemic imperatives, and through the ideological control of the masses.

8. The pluralist model of power is congruent with the order model: (a) People in powerful positions work for the accomplishment of society's objectives; (b) the state works for the benefit of all; and (c) power is diffused through competing interest groups.

9. The elitist model of power fits with the conflict model: (a) People in powerful positions are motivated largely by selfish interests; (b) the state exists for the benefit of the ruling class; and (c) power is concentrated in a power elite model of power.

10. The consequences of concentrated power are one-sided. The benefits accrue to the already advantaged in tax breaks, protections for business at home and abroad, and having the powerless bear the burden of change, war, and economic uncertainty.

KEY TERMS

Elitist model of power
Pluralist model of power
Democracy

Plutocracy
Instrumentalist view
Structuralist view

Power elite
Power

STUDY QUESTIONS

1. How does the way political campaigns are financed have undemocratic consequences?
2. What is your reaction to the A Closer Look panel titled "Structural Barriers to Democracy"? Is the United States a democracy? (Consider also your response to Study Question 1 here.) Elaborate.
3. Classify Mills, Domhoff, and Parenti as either instrumentalists or structuralists. Justify your placement of each.
4. Summarize the three variations of the conflict view of politics by Mills, Domhoff, and Parenti. Which variation most closely approximates politics in the contemporary United States? Why? Or, alternatively, is each variation incorrect? If so, why?
5. How have government decisions tended to increase the gap between the haves and the have-nots?

WEB RESOURCES

http://www.lib.umich.edu/govdocs/govweb.html
For government resources on the Web, go to this University of Michigan site. It has information on each branch of the U.S. government, as well as links to sites about governments in other countries.

http://www.udel.edu/htr/Psc105/Texts/whogovern.html
This site offers a discussion of the pluralist and elitist models of power and other ideas pertaining to theories of power and who governs the United States.

http://www.thirdworldtraveler.com/Book_Excerpts/PowerElite.html
This site contains excerpts from C. Wright Mills' *The Power Elite*.

http://opensecrets.org/
The Center for Responsive Politics is a group that "tracks money in politics, and its effect on elections and public policy. The Center's work is aimed at creating a more educated voter, an involved citizenry, and a more responsive government."

http://www.brook.edu/dybdocroot
The Brookings Institution "functions as an independent analyst and critic, committed to publishing its findings for the information of the public. In its conferences and activities, it serves as a bridge between scholarship and public policy, bringing new knowledge to the attention of decision makers and affording scholars a better insight into public policy issues."

http://www.ncl.org/
The National Civic League is a "non-profit, non-partisan organization dedicated to strengthening citizen democracy by transforming democratic institutions."

http://www.commoncause.org/
Common Cause is a nonpartisan citizen's lobbying organization promoting open, honest, and accountable government.

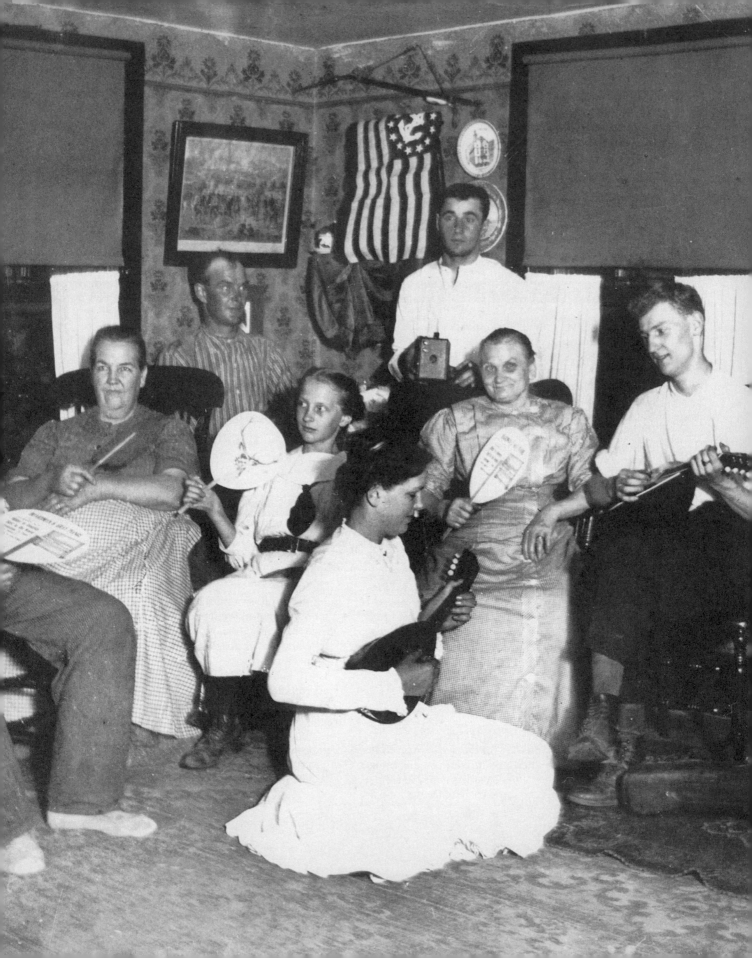

CHAPTER 15

Families

amilies are far different from what they used to be. They are more diverse; they include more diverse household arrangements; they are more easily fractured; family members spend less time together; and parents have less influence over their children, to name a few differences from earlier times. Many find these changes threatening. They yearn for a time when families were more stable, when fathers were providers and mothers stayed home to raise the children.

Family changes occurring in the last few decades have led some social analysts to conclude that the family is in serious trouble, that we have lost our family values, and that the "breakdown of the family" causes social problems. This view of the world is flawed in two fundamental respects. First, it reverses the relationship between family and society by treating families as the building blocks of society rather than as a product of *social conditions*. Second, it ignores the structural reasons for recent family changes and the profound transformations occurring throughout the world. Even in different societies, families and households are undergoing similar shifts as a result of global economic changes.

This chapter examines the family as a social institution. It relates families to the larger society. Families in the United States are diverse, with regional, social class, religious, racial, and ethnic differences; nonetheless, distinct patterns can be found in family life. The theme of the chapter is that families are not isolated units free from outside constraints, but that social forces outside the family affect life inside families.

The Mythical Family in the United States

There are many myths about families. These beliefs are bound up with nostalgia and cultural values concerning what is typical and true about families. The following myths, based on folk wisdom and common beliefs, are rarely challenged except by social scientists and family scholars.

1. *The myth of a stable and harmonious family of the past.* Most people think that families of the past were better than families of the present. They are believed to have been more stable, better adjusted, and happier. However, family historians have found that there is no golden age of the family. Many children were raised by single parents or stepparents, just as now. Divorce rates were lower because of strong religious prohibitions and community norms against divorce, but this does not mean that love was stronger in the past. Many "empty" marriages continued without love and happiness to bind them.

Historian Stephanie Coontz has reexamined our deepest assumptions about the history of the family. Her book *The Way We Never Were* (Coontz, 1992) explodes the myth that family life has recently "gone bad." In her more recent book, *Marriage, A History*

(Coontz, 2005), she shows how marriage changed from an economic and political institution to a voluntary love relationship. This change, not the loss of family values, is what makes marriage more fragile today. Family life of the past was quite different from the stereotype. Desertion by spouses, illegitimate children, and other conditions that are considered modern problems existed in the past. Part of the family nostalgia holds that there were three generations living under one roof or in close proximity. This image of the three-generational family is also false. Few examples of this "classical family of western nostalgia" (Goode, 1984:43) have been found by family historians.

2. *The myth of separate worlds.* This is the positive image of the family as a place of love and trust, where individuals escape from the outside world. It makes a distinction between "public" and "private" realms with the family as a "haven in a heartless world." Here, social relations are thought to be different from those in the world at large. Of course, love and trust are the glue for many families, but this glorification of private life tends to mask the dark side of some families, where emotional and physical aggression are commonplace, and where competition between spouses and among children sometimes destroys relationships. This myth ignores the harsh effects of economic conditions (for example, poverty or near-poverty, unemployment, and **downward mobility** or the threat of downward mobility). It ignores the social inequalities (racism, sexism, ageism, homophobia) that prevent many people from experiencing the good things in life. And the idealized family view masks the inevitable problems that arise in intimate settings (tensions, anger, and even violence in some instances).

3. *The myth of the monolithic family form.* We all know what a family is *supposed* to look like. It should resemble the Ozzie and Harriet form. We get this image from our ministers and priests, from children's literature, and from television. This image is of a White, middle-class, heterosexual, father-as-breadwinner, mother-as-homemaker, and children-at-home living in a one-family house. This model, however, represents a small proportion of U.S. households. Less than 10 percent of all households consist of married couples with children in which only the husband works. Today, it makes more sense to talk about "types of families" (Mabry et al., 2004). Contemporary family types represent a multitude of family forms, including single-parent households (resulting either from unmarried parenthood or divorce), stepparent families, extended multigenerational households, gay and straight cohabiting couples, child-free couples, lone householders with ties to various types of families, and many other kinds of families.

4. *The myth of a unified family experience.* We assume that all family members experience family life in the same way. This image hides the diversity *within* families. The family is a gendered institution. Women and men experience marriage differently. There are gender differences in decision making, in household division of labor, and in forms of intimacy and sexuality. Similarly, divorce affects men and women differently. Remarriage patterns differ by gender, as well. Girls and boys experience their childhoods differently, as there are different expectations, different rules, and different punishments according to gender.

5. *The myth of family decline as the cause of social problems.* Partly because of the myths about the past, and partly because the family has changed so much in the past few decades, many conclude that the breakdown of the family is responsible for today's social ills. Fatherless families, or women working outside the home, are said to be the reasons for poverty, violence, and crime. Divorced and unwed mothers, in this view, are damaging children, destroying families, and tearing apart the fabric of society.

U. S. Families in Historical Perspective

The Family in Capitalism

Family forms in the United States are closely related to economic development. Industrialization moved the center of production from the domestic family unit to the workplace. Families became private domestic retreats set off from the rest of society. Men went off to earn a wage in factories and offices, while women remained in the home to nurture their children. From the rise of the industrial economy until World War II, capitalism operated within a simple framework. Employers assumed that most families included one main breadwinner—a male—and one adult working at home directing domestic work—a female; in short, jobs with wives. As a result, many men received the income intended to support a family.

The private family with a breadwinner father and a homemaker mother pattern was an important historical development, but economic conditions precluded this pattern for many families. With industrialization, wave after wave of immigrants filled the industrial labor force. Through their labor, entire families became a part of society. Immigrant families did not separate themselves into privatized units. Instead, they used kinship connections to adjust in the new society. Families were crucial in assisting their newly arrived kin to adapt to the new society.

Many immigrants came to the United States in family groupings, or they sent for families once they were established in cities. Kin helped in locating jobs and housing, and they provided other forms of support. Contrary to the typical portrayal of immigrants, their transplanted kinship and ethnic bonds did not disintegrate, but rather were rebuilt in the new society (Early, 1983; Vecoli, 1964).

The developing capitalist economy did not provide equal opportunities for all people. Racial-ethnic people did not have the opportunity to become part of the industrial labor force. Instead, they labored in nonindustrial sectors of the economy. This often required family arrangements that were different from those in the dominant society. The breadwinner–homemaker pattern never applied to immigrants and racial minorities because they were denied the opportunities to earn a family wage. So, many married women took jobs to make ends meet. Some women took in boarders or did piecework; some worked as maids in middle-class and upper-class homes; and some became wage workers in sweatshops, department stores, and offices. For these families, the support of the community and extended family members was crucial (Albelda, 1992:7).

Families have always varied with the social conditions surrounding them. From the original settlement of the American colonies through the mid-twentieth century, families of European descent often received economic and social supports to maintain families. Following World War II, the G.I. Bill, the National Defense Education Act, the expansion of the Federal Housing Authority and Veterans Administration loan subsidy programs, and government funding of new highways provided the means through which middle-class Whites were able to achieve the stable suburban family lives that became the ideal against which other families were judged (Coontz, 1992). These kinds of supports have rarely been available for people of color and, until quite recently, were actively denied them through various forms of housing and job discrimination. Family history makes it clear that social forces have always created many different family types.

What we think of as "the family" is an ideal. It implies a private retreat set apart from society. This image masks the real relationship between families and the larger society. A better way of understanding how families are related to social institutions is to distinguish between families and households: **Family** refers to a set of social relationships, whereas **household** refers to residence or living arrangements (Rapp, 1982; Jarrett and Burton, 1999). To put it another way, a household is a residence group that carries out domestic functions, whereas a family is a kinship group (Holstein and Gubrium, 1999:31). A good example of the importance of distinguishing between family and household is the restructuring of family obligations and household composition after divorce (Ferree, 1991:107).

Stratification and Family Life: Unequal Life Chances

In previous chapters, we examined growing inequalities in the distribution of social opportunities. These stratification hierarchies—class, race, and gender—are changing and reshuffling families and individuals. In this section, we examine the effects of social class on

TABLE 15.1

People and Families in Poverty by Selected Characteristics, 2009

Characteristics	Below Poverty Percent	Characteristics	Below Poverty Percent
People		**Nativity**	
Total	14.3	Native	13.7
Family Status		Foreign born	19
In families	12.5	Naturalized citizen	10.8
Householder	11.1	Not a citizen	25.1
Related children under 18	20.1	**Region**	
In unrelated subfamilies	51.1	Northeast	12.2
Reference person	48.7	Midwest	13.3
Children under 18	56.6	South	15.7
Unrelated individual	22	West	14.8
Male	20	**Residence**	
Female	24	Inside metropolitan areas	13.9
Race		Inside central cities	18.7
White	12.3	Outside central cities	11
Black	25.8	**Type of Family**	
Asian	12.5	Married-couple	5.8
Hispanic origin	25.3	Female householder (no	
Age		husband present)	29.9
Under 18	20.7	Male householder (no	
18-64 years	12.9	wife present)	16.9
65 years and older	8.9		

Source: DeNavas-Walt, Carmen, Bernadette D. Proctor, and Jessica C. Smith, U.S. Census Bureau, Current Population Reports, P60–238, *Income, Poverty, and Health Insurance Coverage in the United States: 2009*, U.S. Government Printing Office, Washington, DC, 2010.

families in the United States. Of course, the social patterning of inequality occurs along many other dimensions including age, family characteristics, and place of residence (see Table 15.1).

Families are embedded in a class hierarchy that is "pulling apart" to shrink the middle class while more families join the ranks of the rich or the poor (Usdansky, 1992). This movement creates great differences in family living and no longer guarantees that children's placement in the class system will follow that of their parents. Still, a family's location in the class system is the single most important determinant of family life.

Social and economic forces produce different family configurations. In a stratified society, family structures differ because households vary in their ability to hook into, accumulate, and transmit wealth, wages, or welfare (Rapp, 1982). Households in different parts of the class structure have different ways of acquiring the necessities of life. Inheritance, salaries, wages, welfare, or various involvements with the hidden economy, the illegal economy, or the irregular economy provide different connections with society's opportunity structures. The social networks and relationships outside the family—at work, school, church, and voluntary associations—are the social forces that shape class and racial differences in family life.

The middle-class family form is idealized in our society. This form, a self-reliant unit composed of a breadwinning father, homemaker mother, and their children, has long been most characteristic of middle-class and upper-middle-class families. Middle-class families of the twenty-first century are quite different from television's stereotyped family of the 1950s. Today, many families can sustain their class status only through the economic contributions of employed wives. Such families must find ways to provide care for their children. How families in different class locations provide child care is the subject of a recent study by sociologist Karen Hansen. Her research challenges the myth that middle-class families are self-sufficient and disconnected from kin. Even if they are middle class, families with two breadwinners must build social networks to help them care for children. In today's world they have increased their reliance on kin. Hansen concludes that structural changes have given rise to middle-class families that are "not-so-nuclear" (Hansen, 2005).

Although many families *appear* to be autonomous, they are supported by conditions in the larger society. When exceptional economic resources are called for, nonfamilial institutions usually are available in the form of better medical coverage, expense accounts, and credit at banks (Rapp, 1982:181).

These links with nonfamily institutions are precisely the ones that distinguish life in middle-class families from families in other economic groups. The strongest links are with the occupations of middle-class family members, especially those of the husband-father. Occupational roles greatly affect family roles and the quality of family life (Schneider and Smith, 1973). Occupations are part of the larger opportunity structure of society: Occupations that are highly valued and carry high-income rewards are unevenly distributed. The amount of the paycheck determines how well a given household can acquire needed resources.

In the working class, material resources depend on wages acquired in exchange for labor. When hourly wages are insufficient or unstable, individuals in households must pool their resources with other people in the larger family network. The pooling of resources may involve exchanging babysitting, sharing meals, or lending money. Pooling is a way of coping with the tenuous connections between households and opportunity structures of society. It requires that the boundaries of "the family" be expanded. This is one reason that the idealized nuclear family is impossible for many people to sustain. At the lower levels of the class hierarchy, people lack the material resources to form autonomous households.

The fluid boundaries of these families do not make them unstable. Instead, this family flexibility is a way of sustaining the limited resources that result from their place in the class hierarchy. Minority single-parent families, which are criticized as being disorganized, are often embedded in a network of sharing and support. Variation in family organization is often a way of adapting to society.

Middle-class families with husbands (and perhaps wives) in careers have both economic resources and built-in ties with supportive institutions such as banks, credit unions, medical facilities, and voluntary associations. These ties are intrinsic to some occupations and to middle-class neighborhoods. They are structurally determined. Such connections strengthen the autonomy of middle-class families. But the middle class is shrinking, and many middle-class families are without middle-class incomes because of changes in the larger economy. Changes in family structure have also contributed to the lowering of family income. High divorce rates, for example, create many more family units with lower incomes.

Turning to the upper class, we find that family boundaries are more open than are those of the middle class, even though class boundaries are quite closed. Among the elite, family constitutes not only a nuclear family but also the extended family. The elite have multiple households (Rapp, 1982:182). Their day-to-day life exists within the larger context of a network of relatives (Dyer, 1979:209).

Wealthy families are nationally connected by a web of institutions they control. In this social class, families throughout the country are connected by such institutions as boarding schools, exclusive colleges, exclusive clubs, and fashionable vacation resorts. In this way, the elite remain intact, and the marriage market is restricted to a small (but national) market (Blumberg and Paul, 1975:69). Marriage legally clarifies the lines of inheritance in a way that is less important to those without property (Hansen, 2005:69). Family life of the elite is privileged in every sense, as Stein, Richman, and Hannon (1977) report: "Wealthy families can afford an elaborate support structure to take care of the details of everyday life. Persons can be hired to cook and prepare meals and do laundry and to care for the children" (9). The vast economic holdings of these families allow them a high degree of control over the rewards and resources of society. They enjoy freedoms and choices not available to other families in society. These families maintain privileged access to **life chances** and lifestyles.

Kinship ties, obligations, and interests are more extended in classes at the two extremes than they are in the middle (McKinley, 1964:22). In the upper extreme and toward the lower end of the class structure, kinship networks serve decisively different functions. At both extremes they are institutions of resource management. The kin-based family form of the elite serves to preserve inherited wealth. It is intricately tied to other national institutions that control the wealth of society. The kin-based family form of the working and lower classes is a primary institution through which individuals participate in social life as they pool and exchange their limited resources to ensure survival. It is influenced by society's institutions, but it remains separate from them.

Economic Transformation and Family Life

Family life is intertwined with other institutions. (The following is adapted from Baca Zinn, Eitzen, and Wells, 2010:92–132.) In Chapter 8, we discussed the powerful forces that are transforming the U.S. economy: (1) globalization, (2) technological change, (3) capital flight, and (4) the shift from an industrial economy to a service economy. These forces combine to affect families both directly and indirectly. They have reduced the number of jobs providing a middle-class standard of living and have expanded the number of lower-standard-of-living jobs. This results in increased job and benefit insecurity, a shrinking middle class, and downward social mobility for many.

The Great Recession (also detailed in Chapter 8) has magnified these difficulties and created considerable discontinuity for family life. For example, wages for the employed have stagnated, and their benefits have been reduced or eliminated. Unemployment has risen sharply. Investments in stocks and home buying have declined precipitously, causing high rates of foreclosures and bankruptcies. The economic decline has increased the numbers of individuals and families who are "food insecure" and homeless. Tough economic conditions have caused couples to delay marriage and if married to delay childbearing. Financial woes are a major source of family discord. The economic transformation and the Great Recession have had dire consequences for many in the middle class. Katherine Newman (1988) describes the experience of the downwardly mobile middle class:

> They once "had it made" in American society, filling slots from affluent blue-collar jobs to professional and managerial occupations. They have job skills, education, and decades of steady work experience. Many are, or were, homeowners. Their marriages were (at least initially) intact. As a group they savored the American dream. They found a place higher up the ladder in this society and then, inexplicably, found their grip loosening and their status sliding. Some downwardly mobile middle-class families end up in poverty, but many do not. Usually they come to rest at a standard of living above the poverty level but far below the affluence they enjoyed in the past. They must, therefore, contend not only with financial hardship but with the psychological, social, and practical consequences of "falling from grace, of losing their proper place" in the world. (8)

Thus, individual self-esteem and family honor are bruised. Moreover, this ordeal impairs the chances of the children, as children and later as adults, to enjoy economic security and a comfortable lifestyle.

Downward mobility also occurs within the stable working class, whose links with resource-granting opportunity structures have always been tenuous. Many downwardly mobile families find successful coping strategies to deal with their adverse situations. Some families develop a tighter bond to meet their common problems. Others find support from families in similar situations or from their personal kin networks. But for many families, downward mobility adds tensions that make family life especially difficult. Family members experience stress, marital tension, and depression. Newman suggests that these conditions are normal, given the persistent tensions generated by downward mobility. Many families experience some degree of these pathologies and yet somehow endure. But some families disintegrate under these pressures, with serious problems of physical brutality, incapacitating alcoholism, desertion, and even suicide (Newman, 1988:134–140).

Although families throughout society are changing as a result of macroeconomic forces, the changes are most profound among the working class. Blue-collar workers have been hardest hit by the economic transformation. Their jobs have been eliminated by the millions because of new technologies and competition from other lower-wage (much lower) economies. They have disproportionately been fired or periodically laid off. Sometimes their places of work have shut down entirely and moved to other societies. Their unions have lost strength (in numbers and clout). And their wages have declined.

Because family life is intertwined with social forces, we should not be surprised that economic transformations are producing changes that make family life difficult for many. In 1950, some 60 percent of U.S. households fit this pattern: an intact nuclear household composed of a male breadwinner, his full-time homemaker wife, and their dependent children. Sociologist Judith Stacey (1990; 1991) calls this type of family the **modern family**. Although this family form was dominant in society, its prevalence varied by social class. The pattern clearly prevailed in working-class families, for example, but was much less likely among low-income families, where women have always had to work outside the home to supplement family income.

This model for the family was disrupted by the destabilizing effects of globalization on jobs in the United States and by the challenges women face in maintaining traditional ways. Stacey found that working-class families, especially the women in them, created innovative ways to cope with economic uncertainty and domestic upheavals. In effect, these women were and are the pioneers of emergent family forms. Stacey calls these new family forms **postmodern families** because they do not fit the criteria for a "modern" family. Now there are divorce-extended families that include ex-spouses and their lovers, children, and friends. Households now expand and contract as adult children leave and then return home only to leave again. The vast majority of these postmodern families have dual earners. Many now involve husbands in greater child care and domestic work than in earlier times. Kin networks have expanded to meet economic pressures. Parents now deal with their children's cohabitation, single and unwed parenthood, and divorce. The result is that fewer than 10 percent of households now conform to the "modern" family form. According to Stacey (1991):

> No longer is there a single culturally dominant family pattern, like the modern one, to which the majority of Americans conform and most of the rest aspire. Instead, Americans today have crafted a multiplicity of family and household arrangements that we inhabit uneasily and reconstitute frequently in response to changing personal and occupational circumstances. (19)

These postmodern family forms are new to working-class and middle-class families as they adjust to the structural transformation, *but they are not new to those in poverty*. The economic deprivation faced by the poor has always forced them to adapt in similar ways: by running single-parent households, by relying on kin networks, by sharing household costs, and by encouraging multiple wage-earners among a family unit.

Today's Diverse Family Forms

Families are constantly changing through their interactions with other social institutions. Among the most prominent changes are those in family form and composition. To understand current trends in family life, we must return to the distinction between households and families discussed earlier in this chapter. (The following is based on Ahlburg and De Vita

FIGURE 15.1

Households by Size: 1970–2009

Source: U.S. Census Bureau, 2009. American Community Survey. "Table B1: Household Type by Household Size." Online: http://factfinder.census.gov.

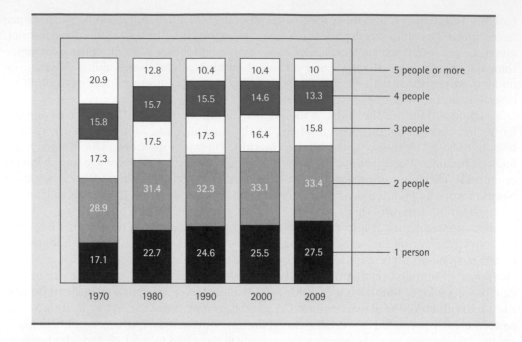

[1992], Bianchi and Casper [2000:8], and Lichter and Qian [2004]). The U.S. Census Bureau defines a household as all persons living in a household unit. A household may consist of one person who lives alone or of several people who share a dwelling. A family, on the other hand, is two or more persons related by birth, marriage, or adoption who reside together. All families comprise households but not all households are families under the Census Bureau's definition. Over the years, households have changed in several important ways. Households have become smaller, with the greatest differences occurring in the largest and smallest households (see Figure 15.1). Family households include families in which a family member is the householder—the person who owns or rents the residence. These households can include nonfamily members such as a boarder or friend. A **nonfamily household** includes the householders who live alone or share a residence with individuals unrelated to the householder, such as college friends sharing an apartment. Some nonfamily households substitute for families and serve many of the same functions. Same-sex couples are one example (Lichter and Qian, 2004:2). The growth of the nonfamily household (that is, persons who live alone or with unrelated individuals) is one of the most dramatic changes to occur during the past four decades. In 1970, 81 percent of household were family households, but the proportion dropped to 66 percent by 2009. At the same time, nonfamily households, which consist primarily of people who live alone or who share a residence with roommates or with a partner, have been on the rise. The fastest growth has been among persons living alone. Nonfamily households are a diverse group. They may consist of elderly individuals who live alone, college-age youths who share an apartment, cohabiting couples, individuals who delay or forego marriage, or those who are "between marriages" (Ahlberg and De Vita, 1992:5; Rawlings, 1995:22).

Figure 15.2 divides family and nonfamily households into various categories: married couples with and without children, other family households, men and women living alone, and other nonfamily households. The most dramatic shift in household composition has been the decline in the percentage of households with children. Two-parent households with children dropped from 40 percent to 22 percent for households between 1970 and 2009 (Fields, 2004; U.S. Bureau of the Census, 2010). This downward trend reflects the postponement of children and the shift toward smaller families. However, household composition varies considerably among different segments of the population. Minorities are more likely than Whites to live in households that include children. This difference arises primarily because

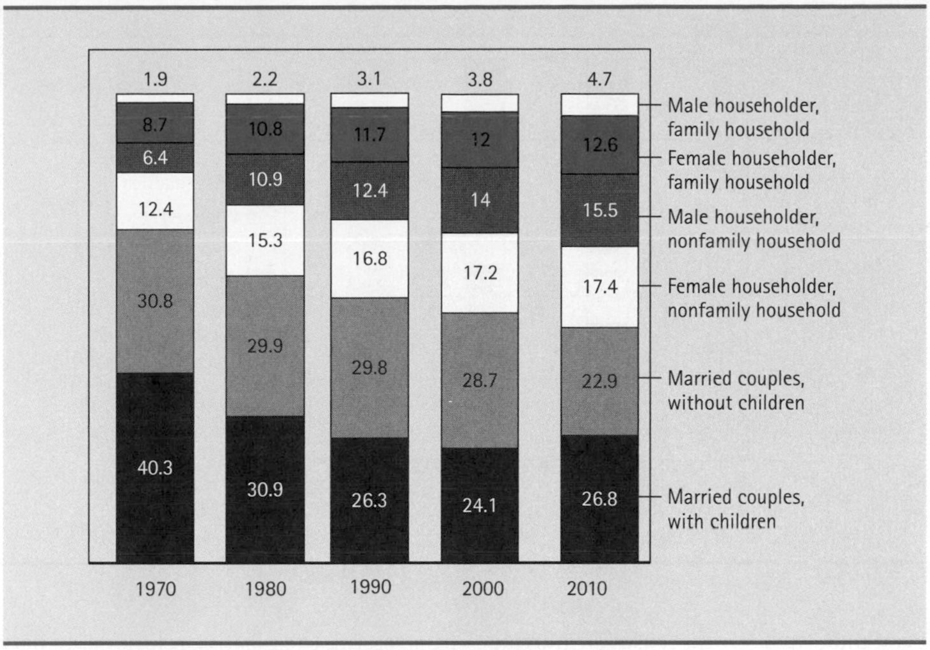
1.9
2.2
3.1
3.8
4.7
8.7
6.4
12.4
30.8
40.3
10.8
10.9
15.3
29.9
30.9
11.7
12.4
16.8
29.8
26.3
12
14
17.2
28.7
24.1
12.6
15.5
17.4
22.9
26.8
Male householder, family household
Female householder, family household
Male householder, nonfamily household
Female householder, nonfamily household
Married couples, without children
Married couples, with children
1970
1980
1990
2000
2010

FIGURE 15.2

Households by Type: 1970–2010 (percent distribution)

Source: Fields, Jason. 2004. "America's Families and Living Arrangements: 2003" Current Population Reports, P20-553. Washington, DC: U.S. Bureau of the Census, p.4. U.S. Census Bureau, 2010. Families and Living Arrangements: Historical Time Series. Table HH-1: Households, by Type: 1940 to Present. Can be accessed at: http://www.census.gov/population/www/socdemo/hh-fam.html#ht.

minority populations tend to have a younger age structure than the White population (that is, a greater share of minorities are in the prime childbearing ages), and minorities tend to have higher fertility rates than Whites (De Vita, 1996:34). In the next decade, the overall composition of households is projected to continue to shift, with a decreasing proportion of family households and continued growth of nonfamily households.

Macrolevel changes produce a wide range of family structures, including one-parent families, cohabiting couples (both gay and straight) with children, dual worker families, and many varieties of extended families such as divorce-extended families and multigenerational families. Still, married couples with children continue to be a prominent family pattern. Parents and children now live increasingly in diverse settings, including intact biological families, stepfamilies, and blended families, and single-parent families. Structural changes have made families more diverse and altered family experiences.

Changes in Marriage and Family Roles

Ongoing social changes are transforming all features of family life. Marriage, in particular, has changed in such a way that it no longer occupies a central place in families as it did in the past. Marriage behaviors are shifting—the young delay it, older people get out of it, and some skip it altogether. Married people now represent a smaller proportion of adults. In 2009, 54 percent of all adults were married compared with 72 percent in 1970. The decline in marriage has many causes, including increased rates of cohabitation, later age at first marriage, and a high divorce rate. (See Figure 15.3.) According to sociologist Kathleen Gerson, changes in intimate relationships, work trajectories, and gender arrangements have combined to produce a revolution in living, working, and family building (Gerson, 2011).

How do we as a society respond to the trends that have reshaped family life over the past several decades? (Much of the following is based on Baca Zinn, Eitzen, and Wells, 2011: 265–271.) One of the responses to the declining significance of marriage is a "marriage movement" that seeks to raise public awareness of the benefits of marriage to both individuals and society. The marriage movement is made up of family scholars and therapists, educators, policymakers and religious leaders who have proposed a number of strategies for improving marriage and reducing divorce (Amato et al., 2007:244). Some family scholars

FIGURE 15.3

Diversity in U.S. Families

Source: U.S. Census Bureau. American Community Survey. 2009. "Table B1: Sex by Marital Status for the Population 15 Years and Over (by Race/Ethnicity)." Can be accessed at factfinder.census.gov.

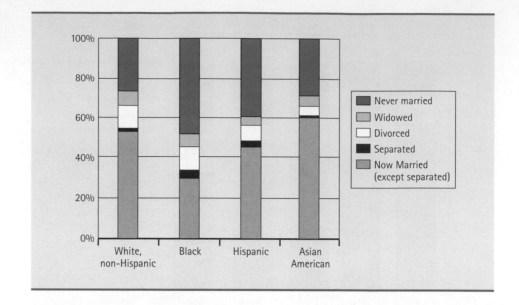

are even making a strong "case for marriage" by stressing the positive relationship between marriage and individual well-being. For example, sociologist Linda Waite (2000) contends that married individuals are healthier, happier, and better off financially than those who never married, are divorced, or widowed. Her arguments represent one side in a national debate between those who wish to promote traditional marriage (organizations such as the Institute for American Values) and those who argue that family forms are shaped by social and economic forces (organizations such as the Council on Contemporary Families).

The Social and Individual Benefits of Marriage

Individuals marry for a variety of reasons. These include the obvious ones, such as the desire for companionship and intimacy. But there are other benefits to being married. To begin with, the marriage relationship promotes healthy behaviors. Research shows that the unmarried are far more likely than the married to die from all causes, including heart disease, stroke, pneumonia, many kinds of cancer, automobile accidents, cirrhosis of the liver, murder, and suicide. There are many reasons why marriage promotes better health. When the married are compared with the unmarried of the same age and the divorced, the married (especially husbands) are less likely to engage in risky behaviors such as excessive drinking, dangerous driving, substance abuse, and multiple sexual partners. Waite and Gallagher (2000) posit that marriage affects health by providing individuals, again especially men, with someone who monitors their health and who encourages self-regulation. Marriage also provides individuals with a sense of meaning in their lives and a sense of obligation and responsibility to others.

The married also have better mental health than the unmarried. Summarizing the research, Waite and Gallagher say, "Married men and women report less depression, less anxiety, and lower levels of other types of psychological distress than those who are single, divorced, or widowed" (2000:67).

Marriage also enhances the sex lives of the partners. Waite and Gallagher, after surveying the research, conclude that "married people have both more and better sex than singles do. They not only have sex more often, but they enjoy it more, both physically and emotionally, than do their unmarried counterparts. ... Marriage, it turns out, is not only good for you, it is good for your libido too" (Waite and Gallagher, 2000:70).

The married have more economic resources (income, pension and Social Security benefits, financial assets, and the value of their primary residence) than the unmarried.

This economic activity stems from the increase in productivity by husbands (compared to unmarried men) and the fact that both spouses in so many marriages are now in the labor force. The greater economic advantage of married couples explains many of the benefits that Waite and others associate with the marriage bond itself. With greater affluence comes better nutrition, better access to physicians and hospitals, a greater likelihood of living in a safe neighborhood, more travel and quality leisure, and the opportunity to experience the good things in life. So it may not be true that the marriage bond itself generates better emotional and physical health for the partners, but greater resources are generated.

The Benefits of Marriage Reconsidered

Marriage matters. Married people have more resources, are better networked, and are healthier, leaving little doubt that marriage is beneficial. But we must evaluate this generalization cautiously. Obviously, not all marriages are advantageous to their partners. Some marriages are abusive. Some marriages are empty of love and caring. The relatively high divorce rate is ample evidence that marriages are not blissful for millions of couples. But let's go beyond these negatives. Consider, first, the generalization that marriage is beneficial economically. Recent research finds the economic benefits of marriage to be uneven; that is, they differ by social class and race. The likelihood that cohabiting couples anticipate they will eventually marry depends on men's socioeconomic circumstances (Manning and Smock, 2002). Women are generally reluctant to marry men who are jobless or have unstable employment.

The economic transformations of the past three decades are closely associated with what has been called the "retreat from marriage" (Lichter et al., 2002). A society that produces an increasing proportion of low-wage, unstable jobs is a society that is likely to have lower marriage rates because economic insecurity discourages marriage and makes existing marriages less stable.

The obstacles to achieving economic stability through marriage are especially difficult for people of color. As we saw in Chapter 8, poverty rates for minorities continue to be much higher than for the White population. Lower wages, also more common to racial minorities than to Whites, require working longer hours, which means less companionship and more pressure on the marital bond.

The evidence documenting the economic benefits of marriage is strong; nonetheless, marriage turns out to be more economically beneficial to some groups in society than others. Gender is a crucial factor in evaluating the benefits of marriage. Each marriage is the creation of a new social unit. The two members of this unit—in which the interaction is intense and the feelings intimate—do not, strange as it may seem, always share the same interpretations and reap the same rewards from their shared life. The fundamental reason for this is that the two members in a marriage differ by gender. By dissecting the family, we see that the sex-gender system structures women's and men's family lives differently. One of the most useful ways of understanding this is Jessie Bernard's concept of "his" and "her" marriages. Bernard's classic work (1972) revealed that every marital union actually contains two marriages, which do not always coincide.

The generalization that marriage is beneficial to the spouses is too facile. We can only answer the question "Who benefits from marriage?" by examining the social location of the partners in a marriage. This means including the social class and race/ethnicity of the spouses. And we must learn the lesson of Bernard that every marriage is actually two marriages. In effect then, marriage matters, but the degree to which it matters is affected by social class, race, and gender.

Same-Sex Marriage

Another issue dominating today's marriage debate is the definition (and legality) of marriage. At issue is whether marriage is limited to a woman and a man or whether it can be between members of the same sex.

Supporters of same-sex marriage argue that homosexual couples should have the same rights as heterosexuals. Legalizing same-sex marriage would provide gays the privileges of marriage such as Social Security benefits, health care, and pension benefits. If marriage is denied to lesbians and gays, then they are being discriminated against on the basis of sexuality.

Opponents argue that making same-sex unions legal denigrates marriage and abandons the basic building block of the family. This view dominated politics in the U. S. until 2012 when President Obama announced his support for same-sex marriage. Most states have passed legislation banning same-sex marriage. In 2003, Massachusetts became the first state to offer civil marriage to same-sex couples on the same basis that it did to heterosexual brides and grooms. Today, the following states issue marriage licenses to same-sex couples: Massachusetts, Connecticut, California, Iowa, Vermont, New Hampshire, New York, and the District of Colombia. In 2008, the California Supreme Court overturned the state's ban on gay marriage.

Most states exclude same-sex couples from the benefits and protections that married heterosexual couples enjoy under state law. The following states, however, now recognize gay civil unions: Delaware, Hawaii, Illinois, and New Jersey. Other states, including Nevada, Oregon, and Washington offer a range of rights and benefits to same-sex couples (NCSL, 2011).

The United States trails some other countries on gay rights: Gay and lesbian couples have full marriage rights in Canada, Spain, the Netherlands, Belgium, South Africa, Norway, Sweden, Portugal, Iceland, and Argentina.

Divorce and Remarriage

Most people in the United States marry, but not all marriages last forever; some eventually are dissolved. Recent divorce rates show that between 40 percent and 50 percent of all first marriages end in divorce (Visher et al., 2003). Divorce and marital separation are not evenly distributed through the population, but vary according to social and economic characteristics. Various government documents reveal the following patterns for first marriages (summarized in Coontz, 2007).The following patterns are some generalizations about divorce in the United States:

- One in five marriages ends in divorce or separation within five years.
- Couples who separate do so, on average, after seven years and divorce after eight years.
- One in three marriages dissolves within ten years.
- Divorce patterns for African Americans and Latinos differ from those of Whites. Latinos have divorce rates that are about the same as Whites, but African Americans are more likely to experience economic hardships that lead to marital disruption and divorce rates that are twice as high as Whites.

Some of the many reasons for the increased divorce rate include the increased independence (social and financial) of women; the economic restructuring that eliminates many jobs for men and makes women's employment necessary; the greater tolerance of divorce by religious groups; and the reform of divorce laws, especially the adoption of no-fault divorce in many states (that is, no longer does one spouse have to prove that the other was at fault in order to obtain a divorce). An important reason is the striking change in public attitudes toward divorce. Divorce is a difficult step and one

"So where do we spend this Thanksgiving? Your father's place, your mother's place, my mother's place or my father's place?"

Whitney Darrow, Jr./The New Yorker Collection/www.cartoonbank.com

that commands sympathy for the partners and children. But it is no longer considered a moral violation. Instead, divorce is generally accepted today as a possible solution for marital difficulties.

Divorce does not mean a permanent withdrawal from the marriage arena. Now, close to 90 percent of those remarrying have been divorced. This increase in remarriage by the divorced is the result of two demographic facts. The first is that people are living longer, reducing the time of widowhood. Second, this trend is also simply the consequence of the ever-greater proportion of divorced people in the population. The probability of remarriage is affected by four important variables: age, socioeconomic status, race, and religion. The age of women is crucial, with older women much less likely to remarry than younger women. The marriage prospect of younger women with children is less than it is for younger women without children. Socioeconomic status is also important. Income, for example, is significant, but the relationship differs by gender. The more money a divorced man has, the more likely he is to remarry. The reverse is true for women (Coleman and Ganong, 1991:193). Race is also significant. African Americans and Latinos remarry at lower rates than Whites (Amato et al., 2007). Religion also affects remarriage rates. In the past, most Christian religious groups disapproved strongly of divorce, with varying severity in sanctions for those who defied the doctrines of the church on this matter. The ultimate church sanction was to consider as adulterers the divorced who remarried. Most denominations have shifted considerably on this issue and show ever greater tolerance, even bestowing the church's blessing on remarriages. The exception has been the Catholic Church, which officially does not recognize remarriage.

Remarriage may solve the economic problems of single-parent families by adding a male income. It may also relieve the many burdens of running a household alone. Partners in a remarriage should, when compared to first marrieds, be more tolerant, more willing to compromise, more aware of the need to integrate their different styles of living, and better able to anticipate problems and work them out before they snowball. Moreover, the pooling of economic resources and the greater probability of better-paying jobs (because of being older) should ease or eliminate the economic problems that plague many first marriages.

Work and Family Roles

In today's world, it is impossible for work and family to be separate worlds. Work shapes family life and family overlaps with work. The economy provides goods and services for consumption by families. Families use their earned income to buy these goods and services. The economy provides jobs to family members, while the family supplies skilled workers to the economy. (The following is based on Baca Zinn, Eitzen, and Wells, 2011:187–193.)

Among the most important changes affecting U.S. families is the increase in married-couple families in which both spouses are in the labor force, or dual-worker marriages. Since 1960, the rise of women's participation in the labor force has been dramatic (see Chapter 12).

Work–family relationships generate difficulties for workers. Jobs impose different constraints on families, such as the amount of time spent working and the scheduling of work, which determine the amount of time workers can spend with their families. In addition work has psychological costs and benefits that influence family interaction. Extensive research on work and family in recent years has given us new information on how these "greedy institutions" operate.

The term **work–family interference** refers to the way in which the connections between jobs and family life may be a source of tension for workers and family members (Hughes et al., 1992:32). One of the ways that the work-family relationship is expressed is through **spillover**—that is, the transfer of moods, feelings, and behavior between work and family settings. Spillover can be positive or negative. Researchers are finding that work-to-family spillover is more negative than family-to-work spillover (Roehling et al., 2003). Spillover appears to be a gendered phenomenon, with men's work stress more likely to affect their family life and women's family stress more likely to affect their work life (Zvonkovic et al., 2006;149).

This gendered and uneven relationship of work and family, or the "work-family role system" (Pleck, 1977), reinforces traditional division of labor in both work and family. The system also ensures that wives' employment does not affect their core responsibilities for housework and childcare. Employed wives generally have two jobs—work and family—while employed husbands have only one. For wives, this produces a second work shift. In her study of working families, sociologist Arlie Hochschild (Hochschild and Machung, 1989) found enormous conflicts between work and family. (See the Research Methods panel titled "Researching Families.") Women were much more deeply torn between the demands of work and family than were their husbands. The additional hours that working women put in on the second shift of housework, she calculated, add up to an extra month of work each year. Even though social class is important in determining how the household labor gets done (more affluent families can afford to purchase more labor-saving services), Hochschild has found that social class, race/ethnicity, and personality give limited clues about who does and does not share the second shift. Gender is paramount. This finding is repeated in study after study. Child care, one of the most fundamental problems of employed parents, remains unsolved. In general,

RESEARCH METHODS

Researching Families: How Sociologist Arlie Hochschild Interviewed Couples about the Demands of Work and Family

With my research associates Anne Machung and Elaine Kaplan, I interviewed fifty couples very intensively, and I observed in a dozen homes. We first began interviewing artisans, students, and professionals in Berkeley, California, in the late 1970s. This was at the height of the women's movement, and many of these couples were earnestly and self-consciously struggling to modernize the ground rules of their marriages. Enjoying flexible job schedules and intense cultural support to do so, many succeeded. Since their circumstances were unusual they became our "comparison group" as we sought other couples more typical of mainstream America. In 1980 we located more typical couples by sending a questionnaire on work and family life to every thirteenth name—from top to bottom—of the personnel roster of a large, urban manufacturing company. At the end of the questionnaire, we asked members of working couples raising children under six and working full time jobs if they would be willing to talk to us in greater depth. Interviewed from 1980 through 1988, these couples, their neighbors and friends, their children's teachers, daycare workers and baby-sitters, form the heart of this book. . . .

We also talked with other men and women who were not part of two-job couples: divorced parents who were war-weary veterans of two-job marriages, and traditional couples, to see how much of the strain we were seeing was unique to two-job couples.

I also watched daily life in a dozen homes during a weekday evening, during the week-end, and during the months that followed, when I was invited on outings, to dinner, or just to talk. I found myself waiting on the front doorstep as weary parents and hungry children tumbled out of the family car. I shopped with them, visited friends, watched television, ate with them, walked through parks, and came along when they dropped their children at

daycare, often staying on at the baby-sitter's house after parents waved good-bye. In their homes, I sat on the living-room floor and drew pictures and played house with the children. I watched as parents gave them baths, read bedtime stories, and said good night. Most couples tried to bring me into the family scene, inviting me to eat with them and talk. I responded if they spoke to me, from time to time asked questions, but I rarely initiated conversations. I tried to become as unobtrusive as a family dog. Often I would base myself in the living room, quietly taking notes. Sometimes I would follow a wife upstairs or down, accompany a child on her way out to "help Dad" fix the car, or watch television with the other watchers. Sometimes I would break out of my peculiar role to join in the jokes they often made about acting like the "model" two-job couple. Or perhaps the joking was a subtle part of my role, to put them at ease so they could act more naturally. For a period of two to five years, I phoned or visited these couples to keep in touch even as I moved on to study the daily lives of other working couples—black, Chicano, white, from every social class and walk of life.

I asked who did how much of a wide variety of household tasks. I asked who cooks? Vacuums? Makes the beds? Sews? Cares for plants? Sends Christmas or Hanukkah cards? I also asked: Who washes the car? Repairs household appliances? Does the taxes? Tends the yard? I asked who did most household planning, who noticed such things as when a child's fingernails need clipping, cared more how the house looked or about the change in a child's mood.

U.S. society is unresponsive to the needs of working parents. The traditional organization of work—an inflexible eight-hour workday—makes it difficult for parents to cope with family problems or with the conflicting schedules of family members. The policies of federal and state governments lag behind the child support policies of other Western nations.

Despite these different orientations to work and family, pressures are increasingly an issue for men as well as women. Rather, involvement in family life is taking place across race and class. Research on men's family lives offers a hopeful perspective in gender equality. Although true "role sharing" couples remain a minority, men are taking on more of the family workload, a step in the transformation of both the male role and the patriarchal family (Coltrane, 1996).

Obstacles remain to achieving a society in which men and women share equally the responsibilities for balancing work and family. For men, fatherhood continues to include assumptions about breadwinning. Nicholas Townsend's *The Package Deal: Marriage, Work, and Fatherhood in Men's Lives* (2002) finds that men today view their lives in terms of a "package deal" in which marriage, fatherhood, employment, and home ownership are interconnected. In this package, supporting a family is "crucial to successful fatherhood." Men who do not adequately support their families have failed to be good fathers. The continued linkage between successful fatherhood and the good provider role encourage men to invest their energies in labor market success and make the goal of involved fatherhood difficult to achieve.

Children and Adolescents

Family changes have profoundly affected children. Over the past few decades, the living arrangements of children changed substantially. In 1980, 85 percent of children lived with two parents, but by 2009, this proportion had dropped to 66 percent (Kids Count, 2009). Living arrangements of children have become more varied. For example, in the early 1990s, researchers and policymakers began to notice an increase in the number of children living in a home maintained by a grandparent. By 2009, 7 percent of children were living in such homes (U.S. Bureau of the Census, 2006).

Research comparing the last decade of the twentieth century with the first decade of the twenty-first century finds that children's well-being across the nation is improving. Many indicators of child well-being including infant mortality, child and teen death rates, and teen birth rates show improvement (Annie E. Casey Foundation, 2002). The poverty rate of children has dropped substantially in recent years. Now at 20 percent, it is still well above the lows of the late 1960s and 1970s of around 14 percent. (See Figure 15.4 on poverty

FIGURE 15.4

Poverty Rates by Age: 1959 to 2009

Source: Carmen De Navas-Walt, Bernadette Proctor, and Jessica C. Smith, U. S. Census Bureau, Current Population Reports, P60-238, *Income, Poverty, and Health Insurance Coverage in the United States: 2009*, U. S. Government Printing Office, Washington, DC, 2010.

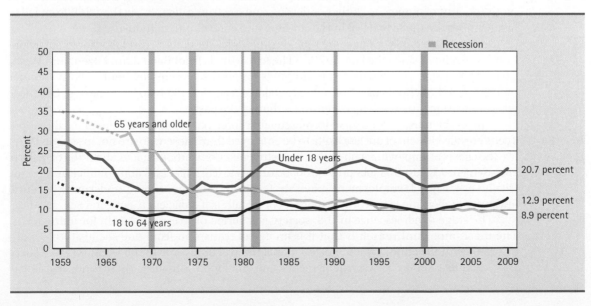

rates by age.) Furthermore, the lowered child poverty rate masks disparities by race. Child poverty stands at 35 percent for African Americans, 30 percent for Latinos, and 15 percent for Whites (U.S. Bureau of the Census, 2009).

Child poverty is related to the changes in family structure discussed in this chapter. A child's likelihood of experiencing poverty during the formative years is partially determined by the type of family he or she lives in. U.S. child poverty rates are often linked to the surge in families headed by single women. The share of children living in single-parent families has stabilized and inched downward over the past five years. Today, about one-fourth of all U.S. children live in single-parent families. However, changes in the proportion of mother-only families are but one factor contributing to changes in child poverty rates. There are vast numbers of low-income two-parent families with children. Young parents, whether living alone or as married couples, are especially vulnerable to poverty because they are likely to have less job experience than older workers and to lose their jobs during economic downturns. Because they have less job experience than older workers, they are often the first to lose their jobs during economic downturns (O'Hare, 1996:19–20).

Children and adolescents are strongly influenced by the amount of economic resources available to their families and the degree of esteem the family members receive from others outside the family. Basically, social class position provides for their life chances. The greater the family's economic resources, the better the chance they have to live past infancy, to be in good health, to receive a good education, to have a satisfying job, to avoid being labeled a criminal, to avoid death in war, and to live the good life. Negatively, this means that millions of the nation's children are denied these advantages because they were born to parents who were unemployed, stuck in the lower tier of the segmented labor market, or victims of institutional racism or sexism.

Material resources produce different social resources and different ways in which families interact with society. Annette Lareau's study of middle-class and working-class families shows class differences in parenting styles, which transmit different advantages to their children. Her book *Unequal Childhoods* (2003) reveals how middle-class families engage in practices of "concerted cultivation," centering on verbal skills and organized activities. In contrast, working-class families allow their children to develop more naturally. While both forms of child rearing have benefits, middle-class practices are those more highly valued by society. They transmit greater social advantages to children.

About 13 percent of the total population is between the ages of thirteen and nineteen (U.S. Bureau of the Census, 2009). This is a very significant category in U.S. society, for several reasons. First, teenagers are a strong economic force. Collectively, they spend an enormous amount of money on clothes, toiletries, and electronic devices. As they shift from fad to fad, fortunes are made and lost in the clothing and entertainment industries.

Many U.S. teens work at some time during high school, but teen labor force participation has declined since the late 1970s. (The following is from Baca Zinn, Eitzen, and Wells, 2011:188–189). The downward trend holds for adolescent employment in both summer months and the school year. Not only are today's teens less likely to be employed, but those who are working are working fewer hours than in the past.

One of the reasons for teens' decreased labor force participation is related to education. Teens enrolled in school are less likely to be employed than those who are not in school. What are the effects of employment on high school students? Conventional ideas about the benefits of employment suggest that jobs provide opportunities to learn life skills and enhance autonomy. On the other hand, employment may interfere with schoolwork and undermine parental authority as working teens become more economically self-sufficient (Gecas and Seff, 1991).

The stage of adolescence in U.S. society is a period of stress and strain for many teens. The most important reason is that it is an age of transition from one social status to another. (See the Technology and Society Panel titled "Family Life in the Digital Age.") There is no clear distinction between adolescence and childhood. Similarly, there is no clear line of

Bruce Eric Kaplan/The New Yorker Collection/www.cartoonbank.com

"I thought driving around all day picking kids up and dropping them off, then waiting for them, would be more fulfilling."

demarcation between adolescence and adulthood. Are people considered adult when they can get a full-time job, when they are physically capable of producing children? Conversely, are they still adolescents when they continue to live at home with their parents? Unlike premodern societies, which have rites of passage serving to identify the individual as a child or an adult, adulthood in U.S. society is unclear. Surely much of the acting out by adolescents in the United States can be at least partially explained by these status ambiguities.

Recent changes in family life have altered childhood and adolescence. Along with changes in family structure, parents spend more time working and less time at home. Busy schedules create a time crunch for all family members. Kids are leading much more hectic lives, their time carefully parceled out among school, after-school care, soccer, ballet, karate, piano, horseback riding, and "play dates," with less time not only for pure play but also for family meals. While time is a scare commodity in family life, many studies show that today's parents manage to maximize time with their children. Bianchi, Robinson, and Milkie (2006) compared mothers' and fathers' time in 1975 and 2000 and found that contemporary parents spend more time playing with and reading or talking with their children than was the case twenty-five years earlier. Parents increasingly include children in their leisure-time activities. This suggests either that leisure-time is becoming more family-oriented or that parents are more likely to include their children in their own leisure activities. Parents have managed to create more time for their children despite women's increased labor force participation by spending more hours in multi-tasking, that is, engaging in multiple activities simultaneously.

Along with the changing pace of life, technology is decreasing family interactions. Although living in the same house, parents or children may tune each other out. Watching television, often in separate parts of the house, along with using video games, smartphones, and headsets have all worked to loosen the bond between parents and children. The results for some people are attenuated family relationships and adverse outcomes for infants, children, and adolescents (Hamburg, 1993). Other parents and children manage well even with these deficits in interaction time.

Family Life in the Digital Age

Technological innovations have dramatic effects on today's families. Parents and children live in a screen-saturated society dominated by electronic devices that transmit information. The average American now spends more than eight hours in front of screens perched side by side. According to the Pew Research Center's Internet and American Life project, 88 percent of adults now own a cell phone and nearly half of these are smart phones. 57 percent own a laptop computer, 55 percent a desk-top model, 44 percent a game console, 19 percent an e-book reader, and 19 percent a tablet computer. Among young people aged 12 to 17, nearly 80 percent own a cell phone, and 30 percent have a smart phone (Kahn, 2012).

Does expanding screen use reduce the time family members spend interacting face to face? Research conducted in 2010 by the Annenberg Center for the Digital Future found that "over the last decade, the amount of time family members in Internet-connected households spend in shared interaction dropped from an average of 26 hours per week to less than 18 hours" (Kahn, 2012:A6). In staying connected and constantly monitoring work messages, social media sites, and texts, family members are becoming disconnected from one another. In her latest book, *Alone Together* (2011), social scientist Sherry Turkle argues that technology is a substitute for human relationships.

Computers, TVs, cellphones and other screen technologies have other complex effects on family relationships. For example, technology makes it possible for parents to be closely connected to their adolescent children—a text or call away. Turkle reveals how technologies introduce new complications that *restrain* adolescent independence when teens need to become separate. Several boys in her study refer to the mistake of having taught their parents how to text and send instant messages (IMs). As one put it: "I taught my parents to IM. They didn't know how. It was the stupidest thing I could do. Now my parents IM me all the time. It is really annoying. My parents are upsetting me. I feel trapped and less independent" (Turkle, 2011:174).

The Aged

During the twentieth century, the population of the United States experienced a profound change—it became older and is on the verge of becoming much older. (See Figure 15.5.) The "senior boom" discussed in Chapter 8 affects family life in many ways. First, aging has produced personal and family relationships that never existed before. Although we think of grandparenthood as a universal stage of family life, this is a post–World War II phenomenon. For the first time in history, most adults live long enough to know their grandchildren, and grandparents are a regular part of children's experiences growing up (Cherlin and Furstenberg, 1994a).

A second way in which increased longevity transforms family life involves the emergence of new family and household forms. For example, households with grandparents present are more common today than in previous decades. Multigenerational family households, that is, family households that contain at least two adult generations or a grandparent and at least one other adult are on the rise. As of 2008, 16 percent of the total U.S. population lived in a multigenerational family household (Pew Research Center, 2010).

Violence in Families

The family has two faces. It can be a haven from an uncaring, impersonal world, a place where love and security prevail. The family members love each other, care for each other, and are accepting of each other. But there is also a dark side to the family. The family is a common context for violence in society. "People are more likely to be killed, physically assaulted, sexually victimized, hit, beat up, slapped, or spanked in their own homes by other family members than anywhere else in our society" (Gelles, 1995:450). The intensity that characterizes

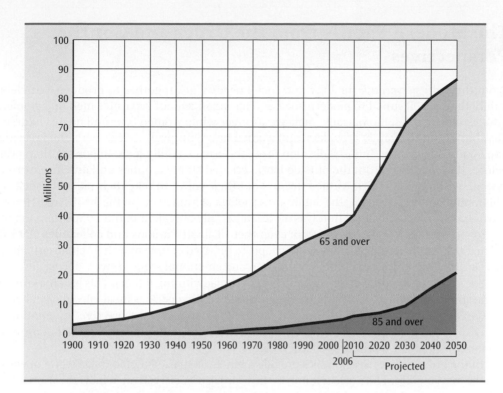

FIGURE 15.5

Number of People Age 65 and Over, by Age Group, Selected Years 1900–2006 and Projected 2010–2050

Source: Agingstats. gov. 2009. "Number of people age 65 and over, by age group, selected years 1900–2006 and projected 2010–2050." Can be accessed at: http://www.aoa.gov/ agingstatsdotnet/ Main_Site/Data/2008_ Documents/Population. aspx

intimate relationships can give way to conflict. Some families resolve the inevitable tensions that arise in the course of daily living, but in other families conflict gives way to violence.

Although the family is based on love among its members, the way it is organized encourages conflict. The family, like all other social organizations, is a power system; that is, power is unequally distributed between parents and children and between spouses, with the male typically dominant. Parents have authority over their children. They feel they have the right to punish children in order to shape them in the ways they consider important. As we saw in Chapter 12, male dominance has been perpetuated by the legal system and religious teaching. Threats to male dominance are often resisted through violence.

Unlike most organizations in which activities and interests are relatively narrow, the family encompasses almost everything. Thus, there are more "events" over which a dispute can develop. Closely related to this phenomenon is a vast amount of time during each day when family members can interact. This lengthy interaction increases the probability of disagreements, irritations, violations of privacy, and the like, which increase the risk of violence.

The rule in our society that the home is private has two negative consequences. First, it insulates the family members from the protection that society could provide if a family member gets too abusive. Second, the rule of privacy often prevents victims of abuse from seeking outside help.

Violence in the family presents the ultimate paradox—the physical abuse of loved ones in the most intimate of social relationships. The bonds between wife and husband, parent and child, and adult child and parent are based on love, yet for many people these bonds represent a trap in which they are victims of unspeakable abuses.

Although it is impossible to know the extent of battering that takes place in families, the problem these forms of violence represent is not trivial. The threat of violence in intimate relationships exists for all couples and for parents and children. Violence in the family is not only a problem at the micro level of family units, it also represents an indictment of the macro level of society, its institutions, and the cultural norms that support violence.

The Modern Family from the Order and Conflict Perspectives

From the *order perspective*, biology and social needs work together to produce a nuclear family that is well suited to modern society. This arrangement separates men and women into distinctive roles. Biologically, men are stronger while women bear and nurse children. Men have been the family providers, and women have "naturally" dealt with child rearing and family nurturance. Industrialization made the private family more important than ever before. Its separation from the outside world created stable families and an efficient role system, with boys and girls trained throughout their youth to take their places in society. This family prototype became the dominant sociological framework in the 1950s and 1960s. It was based on a family form that was more statistically prevalent in the 1950s than today, but by no means the only family form even then. Talcott Parsons and colleagues (1955) defined the family as a particular set of people (a married couple and their children) filling two central functions (socialization of children and emotional support) with a fixed division of labor (a stay-at-home, nurturing mother and a breadwinning father). This became known as the standard family. According to this view, the family operates most effectively when a division of labor is present in the nuclear family. Women fill the "expressive" or emotional roles of providing affection and support, while men fill the "instrumental" roles that provide economic support by working outside the family.

In the order perspective, families provide a haven from the harsh outside world of work and the marketplace. The nuclear family is the bedrock of society in an achievement-oriented world. The family fits with other social institutions and contributes to social order. The order perspective gives rise to the argument that changes in the family are destroying the country's social fabric. "Family values" is code for reinstating the two-parent family.

The *conflict perspective* is different. Here, families are closely connected to material inequalities in the larger society. Conflict theorists are especially interested in how families are affected by class, race, and gender. This perspective sees different family arrangements emerging out of different social and economic contexts.

The family is a vital part of capitalism in that it produces both workers and consumers to keep the economy going. The family is important in producing social inequality because it is the vehicle through which property and social status are acquired. Wealth is locked up in elite families and then passed down through intergenerational inheritance. This limits the resources and opportunities of those who are lower in the socioeconomic hierarchy. As we have seen, families pass on their advantages and disadvantages to their offspring. While this transmission of social class position promotes stability in society—which the order theorists cherish—it also promotes inequality based on ascribed status.

The family serves the requirements of capitalism in another way—by glorifying the realm of the personal. This serves the economy through heightened consumerism. It also supports the interests of the dominant class by promoting false consciousness. The family is one of the primary socialization agents of youth, and as such it promotes the status quo by transmitting the culture of society. Children are taught to accept the inequalities of society as natural, and they are taught to accept the political and economic systems without question.

From the conflict perspective, the family is not the haven posited by the order theorists. Broader social systems enter into the family and reproduce the conflicts and tensions found in the rest of society. Family relations are not simply matters of love and agreement, but political arrangements as well. What is thought to be a private relationship of love is really a social relationship of power. At the micro level, conflict is generated by (1) women's resistance to men's dominance, and (2) employment and economic hardships, which work against family companionship. Thus, the modern family is not a tranquil institution, but one fraught with potential and actual conflict.

Conflict theorists argue that the nuclear family has positive consequences for capitalism, but can be negative for individuals (Zaretsky, 1976). The economic system benefits when employers can move individuals from place to place. The economy is served when employers do not have to worry about satisfying the emotional needs of workers. Finally, the system benefits when the family is isolated and therefore cannot affect society.

Conflict theorists maintain that because the family has sole responsibility for maintaining a private refuge from an impersonal society and for providing personal fulfillment, it is structured to fail. The demands are too great. The family alone cannot provide for all the emotional needs of its members, although its members try to fulfill these needs through consumerism, leisure, and family fun. Conflict theorists argue that society should be restructured so that personal fulfillment is met not only in the family but also in the community, at work, and in the other institutions of society.

Families of the Future

We have examined a number of trends that characterize contemporary families. Several key societal trends are dramatically altering the future prospects for families in the United States and around the world. (Much of the following is taken from Joseph F. Coates, 2002.)

Multi-generational households will continue to increase in the United States.

- *Stresses on family functions will continue to reshape families.* Schools, businesses, and government institutions will be under more demand for meeting human services once provided in families.
- *Economics will continue to drive family changes.* The rise of the two-income family will make family life more complicated, but will provide women broader opportunities and will result in men's greater involvement in family life.
- *Divorce will continue.* Society will focus on creating more effective families as "profamily" movements emerge.
- *Nontraditional family forms shaped by social and economic changes will proliferate.* Emerging patterns include cohabitation relationships, blended families resulting from divorced parents who remarry, "boomerang families" resulting from young people returning home to live with parents, single-parent families, and gay and lesbian families. Other emerging family forms include those formed through technology (surrogate parents and eventually children from cloned embryos) and transnational families in which family members live in different countries with a pattern of moving back and forth across national boundaries.
- *An aging society will redefine families.* Parents will "boomerang" back to their adult children. Elders will enter into cohabitation and other shared living arrangements including retirement communities with dorm-style living.

These trends lead to the conclusion that family variation is typical. Most significant, at the personal level most of us have been and will be participants in a variety of family forms as we move through the life cycle. This is not only the case for individuals but also for individual families, for they, too, will change forms as members enter and leave and work situations change. As the new century moves forward, many different family arrangements will emerge. They will exist alongside traditional families. This will contribute to the diversity and flexibility of the family.

1. The family is idealized and mythologized. New sociological research has given us a better understanding of the U.S. family in the past and present.

2. Families are a product of social structure. They have different connections with institutions that provide resources for family support. Class and race are important determinants of family life.

3. Changes in the U.S. economy have created discontinuity in family life. Globalization and other transformations have reduced the number of jobs. As the need for skilled labor has diminished, many blue-collar families have experienced underemployment or unemployment. Jobs providing a middle-class standard of living have also disappeared and produced downward mobility for families across the country. These difficulties have been magnified by the Great Recession, which has produced high rates of unemployment and changed the shape of families in many ways.

4. As blue-collar workers in this century have experienced a rapid rise and fall in their fortunes, they moved from the modern family (an intact nuclear household of male breadwinner, his full-time homemaker wife, and their children) to the postmodern family (emergent family forms that vary considerably).

5. A major demographic trend since World War II has been the sharp rise in mothers who work outside the home. This takes a toll on the well-being of women workers, even though men in all classes and racial groups are taking on more of the family workload.

6. More than one-fourth of all households with children are single-parent families; more than one-half of all Black families, one-third of Hispanic families, and one-fifth of White families are in this category. In 80 percent of these cases, these families are headed by women. Single-parent families have a number of unique problems, the most prominent one being a lack of economic resources.

7. Twenty percent of all children in the United States live in poverty.

8. Although work and family are interdependent, husbands give priority to jobs over families, and employed wives give priority to families over jobs. Gender inequality in the larger society reinforces the gendered family. Women and men experience the family in different ways, and men benefit more than women from family arrangements.

9. Although women and men both benefit from marriage, men gain more. Marriage matters for most couples. However, the benefits are decreased, even reversed, for some poor couples, especially minority poor who face greater threats of unemployment, underemployment, and lower wages than Whites.

10. The family is not a tranquil institution, but one fraught with potential and actual conflict. Families are a major setting for violence in this society.

11. The divorce rate in U.S. society is the highest in the world. The probability of divorce is correlated with a number of variables, including socioeconomic status, age at first marriage, education, race, and religion.

12. Adolescence is a difficult time in U.S. society for many young people and their parents. A fundamental reason for this is that adolescents are in a transitional stage between childhood and adulthood, with no clear distinction to indicate when adulthood is reached. Rapidly changing social conditions are exacerbating this tension.

13. The aging of U.S. society has produced new family relationships and new household forms, including multigenerational households.

14. Order theorists view the family as a source of stability for individuals and society. According to this view, the traditional division of labor by sex contributes to social order.

15. Conflict theorists argue that the traditional family supports the economy but individuals and families pay a high price. The family is a major source of false consciousness and a primary agent of social stratification.

16. A number of trends indicate that families in the United States will continue to change—for example, economic changes, stress on families, the high divorce rate, and demographic changes, including the aging of society and immigration.

KEY TERMS

Downward mobility
Family
Household

Life chances
Modern family
Postmodern families

Nonfamily household
Work–family interference
Spillover

1. What are the myths about U.S. families?
2. What is the relationship between the economy and family patterns?
3. Explain the following statement: Families are embedded in class and race hierarchies. What are the consequences of this fact for family life?
4. Explain how family and work are interconnected.
5. What are the benefits of marriage by class, race, and gender?

6. What social factors are related to variation in divorce rates in the United States?
7. What are the consequences for families of an aging population?
8. Contrast the differing views of families by order and conflict theorists.

http://www.familiesandwork.org/index.html

The Families and Work Institute is a "non-profit center for research that provides data to inform decision-making on the changing workplace, changing family, and changing community."

http://www.contemporaryfamilies.org/

The Council on Contemporary Families, founded in 1996, is a nonprofit organization dedicated to enhancing the national conversation about what contemporary families need and how these needs can be met. Divorce, gay and lesbian families, and welfare reform are just a few of the many topics discussed.

http://laborproject.berkeley.edu/

In order to advocate for family-friendly policies in the workplace, the Labor Project for Working Families works with unions on collective bargaining, legislation, and public policy related to balancing work and family. Issues dealt with include child care, elder care, family leave, and flexible work schedules.

http://www.nationalpartnership.org/

The National Partnership for Women and Families promotes "fairness in the workplace, access to quality affordable healthcare, and policies that help women and men meet the dual demands of work and family."

http://www.trinity.edu/~mkearl/family.html

This site contains various information about families, including myths, violence, divorce, and marriage roles.

http://www.pscw.uva.nl/sociosite/TOPICS/familychild.html

Go to this site for links on family and children.

http://www.nccep.org/

The National Center for Children in Poverty promotes "strategies that prevent child poverty in the United States and that improve the lives of low-income children and families."

http://www.atask.org/

The Asian Task Force against Domestic Violence has a mission to eliminate family violence and to strengthen Asian families and communities. It addresses the need for multicultural and multilingual resources for Asian American families.

http://www.ncadv.org/

This is the home of the National Coalition against Domestic Violence, which has information on domestic violence, how to get help, and legislation dealing with domestic violence.

http://www.hrc.org/

The Human Rights Campaign works for lesbian, gay, bisexual, and transgender rights. Included in the website is information on LGBT adoption, partner benefits, and recent news related to the community.

http://www.ngltf.org/

The National Gay and Lesbian Task Force fights for the civil rights of those in the gay, lesbian, bisexual, and transgender community.

http://www.childrensdefense.org

This website for the Children's Defense Fund provides information on children's issues such as health, education, safety, and poverty.

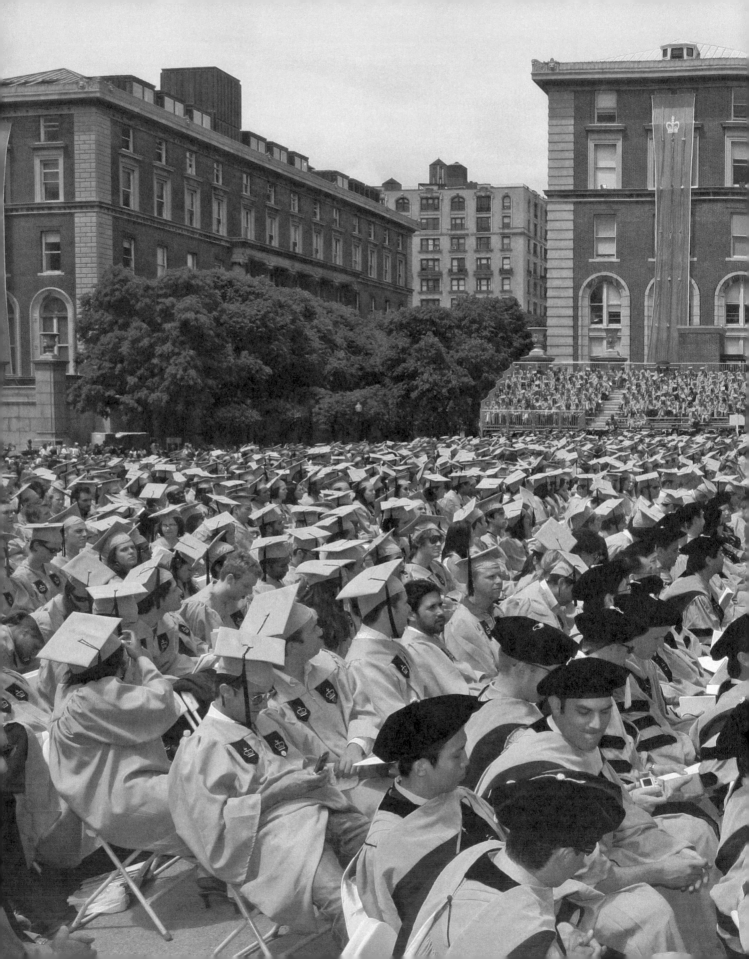

CHAPTER 16

Education

The United States is falling behind other countries in the resource that matters most in the new global economy: human capital. American 15-year-olds ranked 25th in math and 21st in science achievement on the most recent international assessment conducted in 2006. At the same time, the U.S. ranked high in inequity, with the third largest gap in science scores between students from different socioeconomic groups. (National Governors Association et al., 2008:5)

This chapter examines one of society's basic institutions—education. The organization of education in society is both a source and a potential solution to some of our most vexing social problems. The chapter is divided into three sections. The first describes the characteristics of U.S. education. The second section describes the current role of education in perpetuating inequality in society. The concluding section summarizes the chapter by looking at education from the order and conflict perspectives.

The Characteristics of U.S. Education

Education as a Conserving Force

The formal system of education in U.S. society (and in all societies) is conservative, since the avowed function of the schools is to teach newcomers the attitudes, values, roles, specialties, and training necessary for the maintenance of society. In other words, the special task of the schools is to preserve the culture, not to transform it. Thus, the schools indoctrinate their pupils in the culturally prescribed ways. Children are taught to be patriotic. As Terry Everton (2004) notes:

> Compulsory schooling defines good citizens as those who play by the rules, stay in line, and do as they're told. Learning is defined by how well we memorize and regurgitate what someone else has deemed we need to know. Creativity is permitted within the parameters of the guidance of licensed professionals whose duty it is to make sure we don't get too wacky with our ideas or stray very far from the boundaries of normalcy. (55)

There is always an explicit or implicit assumption in U.S. schools that the American way is the only really right way. When this assumption is violated on the primary and secondary school levels by the rare teacher who asks students to consider the viability of world government, or who proposes a class on the life and teachings of Karl Marx or about world religions, then strong enough pressures usually occur from within the school (administrators, school board) or from without (parents, the American Legion, the Christian right) to quell the disturbance. As a consequence, creativity and a questioning attitude are curtailed in school.

Mass Education

People in the United States have a basic faith in education. This faith is based on the assumption that a democratic society requires an educated citizenry so that individuals can participate in the decisions of public policy. It is for this reason that the government not only provides education for all citizens but also compels children to go at least to the eighth grade or until age sixteen (although this varies somewhat from state to state).

Who can quarrel with the belief that all children should be compelled to attend school, since it is for their own good? After all, the greater the educational attainment, the greater the likelihood of larger economic rewards and upward social mobility. However, to compel a child to attend school for six hours a day, five days a week, forty weeks a year, for at least ten years, is quite a demand. The result is that many students are in school for the wrong reason. The motivation is compulsion, not interest in acquiring skills or curiosity about their world. This involuntary feature of U.S. schools is unfortunate because so many school problems are related to the lack of student interest. It is no surprise that in spite of two decades of intense educational reform, approximately 30 percent of public high school students will drop out before graduation (Thornburgh, 2006).

On the positive side, as a result of the goal and commitment to mass education, an increasing proportion of the population has received a formal education. In 1940, for example, 38 percent of the people in the United States age twenty-five to twenty-nine had completed high school. Between 2006 and 2008, 84.5 percent of Americans over the age of twenty-five were high school graduates, and another 27.4 percent had a bachelor's degree or higher (U.S. Bureau of the Census, 2009).

The Preoccupation with Order and Control

Most administrators and teachers share a fundamental assumption that school is a collective experience requiring subordination of individual needs to those of the school. U.S. schools are characterized, then, by constraints on individual freedom. The school day is regimented by the dictates of the clock. Activities begin and cease on a timetable, not in accordance with the degree of interest shown or whether students have mastered the subject. Another indicator of order is the preoccupation with discipline (that is, absence of unwarranted noise and movement, and concern with the following of orders).

In their quest for order, some schools also demand conformity in clothing and hairstyles. Dress codes are infamous for their constraints on the freedom to dress as one pleases. School athletic teams also restrict freedom, and the school authorities condone these restrictions. Conformity is also demanded in what to read and how to give the answers the teacher wants.

The many rules and regulations found in schools meet a number of expressed and implicit goals, but many of those goals may be outdated. Zuckerman writes:

U.S. schools are characterized by a preoccupation with order and discipline.

> We are on the threshold of the most radical change in American education in over a century as schools leave the industrial age to join the information age. For most of the past century, our schools were designed to prepare children for jobs on factory lines. Kids lived by the bell, moved through schools as if on conveyor belts, and learned to follow instructions. But today many of these factories are overseas, leaving behind a factory-based school system for an information age. (2005:68)

There are certain trends that indicate the educational system in the United States is moving toward more fragmentation rather than less. According to the National Center for Education Statistics (2010), more and more parents are opting to send their children to private schools (about 11 percent or 6 million children) or to school them at home (about 2.9 percent or 1.5 million children). Taxpayer-funded charter schools are also growing rapidly. These schools are based on a hybrid "free market" system in which educators, students, and parents choose a curriculum and educational philosophy free from the dictates of school boards and educational bureaucracies but financed publicly. In 2007, there were almost 4,000 charter schools with more than 1 million students, half of which were low income or minority students.

Vouchers are another plan that splinters the educational system. This plan gives parents a stipulated amount of money per child that can be used to finance that child's education in any school, public or private. This plan sets up an educational "free market" in which schools have to compete for students. This competition will, theoretically, improve schools because they must provide what parents want for their children, whether that be better discipline, emphasis on learning the fundamentals, religious instruction, focus on the arts, vocational training, or college preparation. While some parents will use vouchers to send their children to other public schools outside their district, there is the constitutional question as to whether it is appropriate to use public funds to pay tuition in religious-based schools. The Supreme Court ruled (five to four) in 2002 that spending public money to pay tuition costs at religious schools was constitutional and did not violate the separation of church and state.

Each of these educational reforms has strengths and weaknesses. Most important, they represent a trend that is rapidly dividing and subdividing the educational system. For many, this is viewed as a positive, representing the core American values of individualism and competition. Others see this trend as fragmenting further an already disaggregated educational system. Moreover, they see private schools, charter schools, and voucher systems as working against inclusiveness through segregation. For example, 70 percent of Black charter students attend schools where at least 90 percent of the students are minorities (Blume, 2010). This segregation serves to increase the gap between racial-ethnic groups and social classes in U.S. society.

Local Control of Education

Although the state and federal governments finance and control education in part, the bulk of the money and control for education comes from local communities. There is a general fear of centralization of education—into a statewide educational system or, even worse, federal control. Local school boards (and the communities themselves) jealously guard their autonomy. Because, as it is commonly argued, local people know best the special needs of their children, local boards control allocation of monies, curricular content, and the rules for running the schools, as well as the hiring and firing of personnel.

There are several problems with this emphasis on local control. First, tax money from the local area traditionally finances the schools. Whether the tax base is strong or weak has a pronounced effect on the quality of education received (a point we return to later in this chapter).

Second, local taxes are almost the only outlet for a taxpayers' revolt. Dissatisfaction with high taxes (federal, state, and local) on income, property, and purchases is often expressed at the local level in defeated school bonds and school tax levies. The growing proportion of people age sixty-five and older increases the likelihood of the defeat of school issues.

The separation of church and state is a contentious issue in the United States.

Third, because the democratic ideal requires that schools be locally controlled, the ruling body (school board) should represent all segments of that community. Typically, however, the composition of school boards has overrepresented the business and professional sectors and overwhelmingly underrepresented blue-collar workers, the poor, and various minority groups. The result is a governing body that is typically conservative in outlook and unresponsive to the wishes of people unlike themselves.

Fourth, local control of education may mean that the religious views of the majority (or at least, the majority of the school board) may intrude in public education. An explicit goal of the Christian Coalition, a conservative religious organization founded by Pat Robertson (see Chapter 17), is to win control of local school boards. Their agenda opposes globalism, restricts sex education to abstinence from sexual intercourse, promotes the teaching of biblical creationism in science classes, encourages school prayer, and censors books that denigrate Christian values (favorite targets are, for example, J. D. Salinger's *Catcher in the Rye* and John Steinbeck's *The Grapes of Wrath*).

The following are some examples of attempts by states and cities to install religious values in schools:

- In 2002, the Cobb County Board of Education in Georgia voted to insert a sticker in school biology textbooks that reads: "This textbook contains material on evolution. Evolution is a theory, not a fact, regarding the origin of living things. The material should be approached with an open mind, studied carefully, and critically considered" (Slevin, 2005). Eleven parents filed suit against the school board, challenging the constitutionality of the textbook warning sticker. On December 19, 2006, a settlement was announced in which the school board agreed not to restore the warning sticker or take any actions that would prevent or hinder the teaching of evolution (National Center for Science Education, 2006).
- In 2005, the Kansas State Board of Education adopted standards of teaching science where evolution was to be represented as scientifically controversial. In February 2007, the board overturned that decision, ruling that evolution should be treated in a scientifically appropriate and responsible way (National Center for Science Education, 2007).
- Although the U.S. Supreme Court outlawed the posting of the Ten Commandments in public schools, numerous local school boards believe they can survive legal challenges if the commandments are posted in a display with other historical documents, such as the Magna Carta and the Declaration of Independence (Johnson, 2000).
- In 2002, the Texas Board of Education objected to a sixth-grade social studies book that read, "Glaciers formed the Great Lakes millions of years ago," because this was counter to the creation time line of religious conservatives. The book was changed to read, "Glaciers formed the Great Lakes in the distant past" (Russell, 2003).
- In March 2010, the Texas Board of Education voted to approve a social studies curriculum that portrays conservative ideas in a more positive light, emphasizes the role of Christianity in the nation's founding, and stresses the superiority of American capitalism (McKinley, 2010). Furthermore, the board adopted a resolution that seeks to curtail references to Islam in Texas textbooks, "as social conservative board members warned of what they describe as a creeping Middle Eastern influence in the nation's publishing industry" (Castro, 2010:1).

As illustrated by these and a number of other lawsuits in recent years, the separation of church and state remains a volatile subject in the United States.

A Lack of Curriculum Standardization

Another potential problem with local control is the lack of curriculum standardization across more than 14,000 school districts and fifty states. The late Albert Shanker, former president of the American Federation of Teachers, compared the United States with other countries that have a common curriculum: "In the U.S., we have no such agreement about curriculum—and there is little connection between what students are supposed to learn, the knowledge on which they are assessed, and what we expect our teachers to know" (1991:E7).

Since Shanker wrote this in 1991, there has been a national push for education based on common standards while at the same time preserving local control. This idea is embodied in the 2001 **No Child Left Behind Act**. Signed by George W. Bush in 2002, the goal of this legislation was to close the gaps that plague education in the United States and make schools accountable for success or failure. For example, according to the National Assessment of Educational Progress (2009) only 32 percent of the nation's eighth-graders are proficient in mathematics and just 30 percent are proficient in reading (the percentages of students performing *below* basic levels are 29 percent in math and 26 percent in reading). Compared with other industrialized nations, which have prescribed national curricula or highly specified national standards, U.S. students rank near the bottom in achievement. To improve performance, the No Child Left Behind legislation requires states to develop academic standards in reading, math, and science. States, districts, and schools would then be responsible to ensure that all children achieve these state standards by 2013–2014. Adequate yearly progress is measured by a single statewide assessment system given annually to all students from third to eighth grade. On the basis of these tests, schools are given a grade of "passing" or "failing." In the 2009–2010 school year, 38 percent of schools were labeled as "failing to make adequate yearly progress" (Education News, 2011). This percentage varies by state, with a low of 5 percent of schools in Texas failing to make progress, to a high of 91 percent of schools in the District of Columbia. In 2007, more than 1,000 of California's 9,500 schools were branded as "chronic failures," and state officials predict that all 6,063 public schools serving poor students will be declared in need of restructuring by 2014 (Schemo, 2007).

Under the No Child Left Behind Act, schools receive a rating each year based on standardized testing.

While this legislation has been heralded as the most ambitious federal overhaul of public schools since the 1960s, a number of problems have become apparent. First and foremost, instead of one system, we have fifty. Each state was permitted to set its own proficiency benchmarks, with some setting a high and others setting a low standard. Because the federal government rewards those who meet the standards, the states with high standards are punished, while the states with low standards are unfairly rewarded. In their 2007 report "The Proficiency Illusion" (Cronin et al., 2007), researchers from the Thomas B. Fordham Institute examine No Child Left Behind in detail. In their comprehensive review, they find:

- State tests vary greatly in their difficulty, with Colorado, Wisconsin, and Michigan having the lowest proficiency standards in reading and math.
- Improvements in the passing rates on state tests can largely be explained by declines in the difficulty on those tests, rather than true growth in student learning.
- The tests in eighth grade are consistently and dramatically more difficult than those in earlier grades. Many states set the bar much lower in elementary school, giving false impressions to parents and teachers that students are doing well.

Critics of No Child Left Behind argue that there is no attempt to address the funding inequities among rich and poor districts within a state that perpetuate the achievement gaps, the chronic underfunding of poorer schools, or child poverty itself (Metcalf, 2002). To rectify this, in March 2010 President Obama announced that an allocation of $900 million in grants would be awarded to help turn around the nation's lowest-performing schools. Unfortunately, the 2007–2009 economic recession has left states in fiscal crisis, and budget cuts to education are rampant, resulting in teacher layoffs and the reduction in school programs and supplies. It remains to be seen what effect this will have on state standards and educational outcomes.

In sum, the lack of a common national curriculum has several negative consequences. First, there is a wide variation in the preparation of students, as states have the ability to raise or lower their standards. Second, because families move on the average of once every five years, there are large numbers of children each year who find the requirements of their new schools different from their previous schools. Finally, not only are many American students graduating without the skills necessary to compete in an information economy, but they also appear to be ill poised to compete in a global economy.

In a push for a common national curriculum, the National Governors Association Center for Best Practices has joined with others to form the Common Core State Standards Initiative, an initiative to develop international benchmarks for all states so that all students are prepared to be competitive in a globalized market. The federal government was not involved in the development of the standards; this is purely a state-driven initiative. Parents, teachers, school administrators, and experts across the country have developed the set of common standards, and as of April 2012 forty-eight states have voluntarily adopted them.

As for No Child Left Behind, in October 2011 the Senate Education Committee voted in favor of a bipartisan bill to dismantle the part of the law that labels thousands of schools as failing on the basis of standardized test scores. The bill gives states more leeway for holding schools accountable, and some critics argue that it will set the country back to pre-NCLB legislation. The chances that the bill will become law are slim due to divisions in Congress, and the future of No Child Left Behind remains in doubt.

The Competitive Nature of U.S. Education

Not surprisingly, schools in a highly competitive society are competitive. Competition extends to virtually all school activities. The compositions of athletic teams, cheerleading squads, debate teams, choruses, drill teams, bands, and dramatic play casts are almost always determined by competition among classmates. Grading in courses, too, is often based on the comparison of individuals (grading on a curve) rather than on measurement against a standard. In all these cases, the individual learns at least two lessons: (1) Your classmates are enemies, for if they succeed, they do so at your expense; and (2) fear of failure is the great motivator, not intellectual curiosity or love of knowledge.

The Sifting and Sorting Function of Schools

Schools play a considerable part in choosing the youth who come to occupy the higher-status positions in society. Conversely, school performance also sorts out those who will occupy the lower rungs in the occupational prestige ladder. Education is, therefore, a selection process. The sorting is done with respect to two different criteria: a child's ability and his or her social class background. Although the goal of education is to select on ability alone, ascribed social status (the status of one's family, race, sex, and religion) has a pronounced effect on the degree of success in the educational system (for a closer look at gender and education, see A Closer Look panel titled "Leaving Boys Behind?"). The school is analogous to a conveyor belt, with people of all social classes getting on at the same time but leaving the belt in accordance with social class—the lower the class, the shorter the ride.

Leaving Boys Behind?

In the 1990s, researchers and popular writers started writing about the "girl crisis" in America. According to books like *Reviving Ophelia: Saving the Selves of Adolescent Girls* (Pipher, 1994) and *Failing at Fairness: How Our Schools Cheat Girls* (Sadker and Sadker, 1994), girls were believed to be suffering when they hit adolescence. In 1992, the American Association of University Women (AAUW) published "How Schools Shortchange Girls," a study conducted by the Wellesley College Center for Research on Women. The report claimed that girls across the country were victims of a pervasive bias in schools. Teachers paid more attention to male students, gave them more time and feedback on their work, and did not encourage girls, especially in the areas of math and science. As a result, millions of dollars in grants were awarded to study the plight of girls in education (Sommers, 2000).

More recently, writers have been focusing on a different crisis in education. Christina Hoff Sommers (2000) writes that the research used to justify the girl crisis is full of errors and some of the data are even missing. She argues that it is actually boys, not girls, that are shortchanged in schools.

According to writer Gerry Garibaldi, boys are increasingly disengaged in the "feminized" classroom (2006). Through movies, television, and rap music, pop culture teaches young boys it is not "cool" to like or do well in school and that to be masculine is to be disengaged and anti-authority (Wenzl, 2007). Those who propose that it is boys who are in crisis offer the following arguments:

- Boys are less likely to graduate from high school (65 percent versus 72 percent of girls) (Greene and Winters, 2006).
- Boys are, on average, a year and a half behind girls in reading and writing (Sommers, 2000).
- Each year women receive more bachelor's and master's degrees than men (Mead, 2006).
- Boys are more likely to be held back a grade, drop out, and be suspended from school (Sommers, 2000).

- Girls continue to score higher on the Scholastic Aptitude Test (SAT) in the area of writing. On the newly revamped SAT in 2006, girls scored an average of 11 points higher in writing (College Board, 2006).

So what is the truth concerning the gender gap in education? In a 2006 report by the Education Sector, Mead argues that "the real story is not bad news about boys doing worse; it's good news about girls doing better" (2006:1). In the report, using data from the National Assessment of Education Progress, Mead argues that American boys are scoring higher and achieving more than they have in the past, but girls have improved their performance on some measures even faster, which makes it appear as though boys are doing "worse." The data seem to indicate that younger boys are doing quite well, but older boys are starting to slip when they reach twelfth grade. Mead argues that twelfth-grade girls are sliding as well, which indicates the problem is not necessarily gender-related.

In the battle over who is in crisis and more disadvantaged, two very important ideas seem to get left out. First of all, regardless of the statistics that more boys are dropping out of school and are less likely to go to college, women still, on average, earn less than men at every level of education. Furthermore, women continue to attain a small percentage of high-level jobs in corporations, politics, and other occupations, and they continue to be responsible for the majority of domestic work.

Second, for every statistic that indicates a gender gap, there is an even larger gap by social class and race. Mead argues that test scores show that poor, Black, and Hispanic boys have an achievement gap that is anywhere from two to five times larger than the gap between genders. Educational reform that is focused solely on gender will miss the mark by ignoring these racial and economic achievement gaps.

Education and Inequality

Education is presumed by many people to be the great equalizer in U.S. society—the process by which the disadvantaged get their chance to be upwardly mobile. The data in Figure 16.1 show, for example, that the higher the educational attainment, the higher the income. But these data do not in any way demonstrate equality of opportunity through education. They show clearly that African American and Hispanic men with the same educational attainment as White men receive lower economic rewards. Note that this figure is for males only. As indicated in Chapter 12 women earn less than men at every level of education. These differences by race and sex reflect discrimination in society, not just in schools. This section focuses on how the schools help perpetuate class and race inequities.

FIGURE 16.1

Median Annual Earnings of Male Full-time Workers age 25 Years and Older by Race and Education, 2007

Sources: National Center for Education Statistics, 2010, U.S. Department of Education. http://nces.ed.gov/pubs2010/2010015.pdf

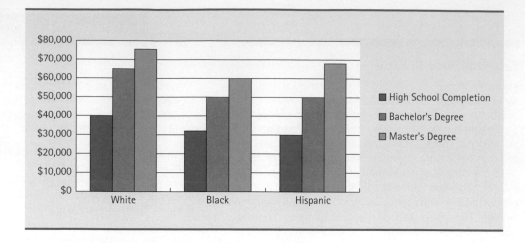

The evidence that educational performance is linked to socioeconomic background is clear and irrefutable. (We include race/ethnicity along with economic status since they are highly correlated.)

- The 2009 Nation's Report Card shows that at grade eight, only 33 percent of Black students and 43 percent of Hispanic students demonstrated a basic proficiency in science. At grade twelve, only 29 percent of Black students achieved basic proficiency or better in science, compared to 72 percent of White students (Nagel, 2011).
- In 2009 among eighth graders, only 41 percent of students who qualified for free lunches achieved basic proficiency or better in science (Nagel, 2011).
- Assessment tests given to fourth and eighth graders show that for every year from 2000 to 2009, average reading scores and average math scores are lower for students in high poverty schools compared to students in low poverty schools (National Assessment of Educational Progress, 2009).
- Achievement gaps in reading, writing, and mathematics persist between minority and White students. Table 16.1 shows the difference in the math achievement levels of eighth-graders in 2009. With the exception of Asian/Pacific Islander students, minority students are much more likely to be below the basic levels of math upon entering high school. In Table 16.1, notice that eighth-grade Asian students are more likely to be at advanced levels in math. For a closer look, see the Diversity panel titled "The Tiger Mom Controversy."
- African American, Latino, and Native American students lag behind their White peers in graduation rates and most other measures of student performance. The National

TABLE 16.1

Eighth-Grade Math Proficiency by Race/Ethnicity

	At or Above Basic (%)	At or Above Proficient (%)	At Advanced (%)
White	83	44	11
Black	50	12	1
Hispanic	57	17	2
Asian/Pacific Islander	85	54	20
American Indian	56	18	3

Source: National Center for Education Statistics, U.S. Department of Education. "The Condition of Education: 2010." *http://nces.ed.gov/pubs2010/2010028.pdf.*

The Tiger Mom Controversy

On January 11, 2011, Yale Professor Amy Chua published her book *Battle Hymn of the Tiger Mother*, a comic memoir about how she tried to raise her two daughters the same way her strict Chinese immigrant parents raised her, but was forced to pull back when her younger daughter rebelled. Her book set off a firestorm of controversy and she found herself on various talk shows defending her strict parenting. The following is an excerpt from the book's first chapter, before she "was humbled by (her) thirteen-year-old":

A lot of people wonder how Chinese parents raise such stereotypically successful kids. They wonder what these parents do to produce so many math whizzes and music prodigies, what it's like inside the family and whether they could do it too. Well, I can tell them, because I've done it. Here are some things my daughters, Sophia and Louisa, were never allowed to do:

- Attend a sleepover
- Have a playdate
- Be in a school play
- Complain about not being in a school play
- Choose their own extracurricular activities
- Get any grade less than an A
- Not be the No. 1 student in every subject except gym and drama
- Play any instrument other than the piano or violin
- Not play the piano or violin.

I'm using the term "Chinese Mother" loosely. I know some Korean, Indian, Jamaican, Irish and Ghanaian parents who qualify too. Conversely, I know some mothers of Chinese heritage, almost always born in the West, who are not Chinese mothers, by choice or otherwise. I'm also using the term "Western parents" loosely. Western parents come in all varieties.

All the same, even when Western parents think they're being strict, they usually don't come close to being Chinese mothers. For example, my Western friends who consider themselves strict make their children practice their instruments 30 minutes every day. An hour at most. For a Chinese mother, the first hour is the easy part. It's hours two and three that get tough.

Despite our squeamishness about cultural stereotypes, there are tons of studies out there showing marked and quantifiable differences between Chinese and Westerners when it comes to parenting. In one study of 50 Western American mothers and 48 Chinese immigrant mothers, almost 70% of the Western mothers said either that "stressing academic success is not good for children" or that "parents need to foster the idea that learning is fun." By contrast, roughly 0% of the Chinese mothers felt the same way. Instead, the vast majority of the Chinese mothers said that they believe their children can be "the best" students, that "academic achievement reflects successful parenting," and that if children did not excel at school then there was "a problem" and parents "were not doing their job." Other studies indicate that compared to Western parents, Chinese parents spend approximately 10 times as long every day drilling academic activities with their children. By contrast, Western kids are more likely to participate in sports teams.

Source: Chua, Amy. 2011. "Why Chinese Mothers Are Superior," The *Wall Street Journal* (January 8). Available online: *http://online.wsj. com/article/sb10001424052748704111504576059713528698754. html?keywords=chinese+mothers*

Assessment of Educational Progress (NAEP) defines the **status dropout rate** as the percentage of sixteen to twenty-four-year-olds that are not enrolled in school and have not earned a high school diploma or equivalency. In 2009, the NAEP found that the status dropout rate was 6 percent for Whites, 11 percent for Blacks and Hispanics, and 3 percent for Asian Americans. Note that all of these are native-born students.

- The status dropout rate for foreign-born Hispanic students is a shocking 35 percent. According to Nathan Thornburgh (2006), "Dropping out of high school today is to your societal health what smoking is to your physical health, an indicator of a host of poor outcomes to follow, from low lifetime earnings to high incarceration rates to a high likelihood that your children will drop out of high school and start the cycle anew" (32).

These social class and racial gaps in academic achievement are found in almost every school and district in the United States. On the surface these patterns reinforce the social Darwinist assumptions that the affluent are successful because they are intelligent, and, conversely, the poor and minorities are at society's bottom because they do not have the requisite abilities to be successful. Similarly, dysfunctional families, unmotivated students, and the culture of poverty are commonly believed by some to explain the academic achievement gap. We argue, to the contrary, that structural factors explain why the poor and minorities are disadvantaged in our supposedly meritocratic education system. In effect, the educational system is stacked in favor of middle- and upper-class children and against children from poor backgrounds. Many interrelated factors explain why the education system tends to reinforce the socioeconomic status differentials in the United States. We examine a few of these in the following sections.

Financing Public Education

Schools in the United States reflect the economic divide that exists in society: "In America, the type of education provided, the way it is funded, and the content of the curriculum are local matters directed by local authorities. The result is easy to see. Across America one sees the extremes: from schools that resemble shining mansions on a hill to ramshackle, dilapidated structures" (Kamau, 2001:81).

Approximately 50 million U.S. children attend public schools. These schools receive funds from three governmental sources—about 9 percent from the federal government, about 47 percent from the state (depending on the allocation within each state), and 44 percent from local taxes in each district within the state (Villano, 2009). The result of this distribution is that schools are funded unequally in the United States, with public schools being more successful in educating children in middle-class communities but often failing children in poor neighborhoods.

Equal opportunity in education (at least as measured by equal finances) has not been accomplished nationwide because wealthier states are able to pay much more per pupil than are poor states. The top-spending states, for example, invest more than double the amount per pupil than those states spending the least. Because the federal government provides only about 9 percent of the money for public schools, equalization from state to state is impossible as long as primarily state and local governments fund education because both entities vary in wealth and commitment to public education. See Figure 16.2 for a closer look at per pupil spending by state.

The disparities in per-pupil expenditures within a given state are also great, largely because of the tradition of funding public schools primarily through local property taxes. This procedure is discriminatory because rich school districts can spend more than poor ones on each student—and at a lower tax rate. Thus, suburban students are more advantaged than are students from the inner city; districts with business enterprises are favored over

FIGURE 16.2

States with the Highest and Lowest Spending Per Public School Student, 2008

Sources: U.S. Census Bureau, Public Education Finances, 2008. http://www2.census.gov/govs/school/08f33pub.pdf

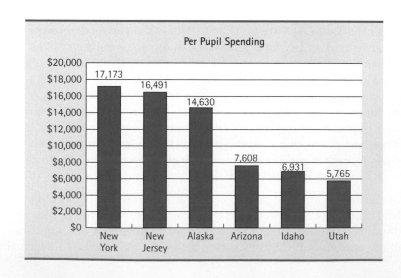

agricultural districts; and districts with natural resources are better able to provide for their children than are districts with few resources. Following are some examples:

- In Illinois, in 2007–08 the New Trier Township High School District spent $21,137 per student, while the Farmington Central Community Unit School District spent only $6,728 per student, reflecting the large disparity in their local tax bases (New America Foundation, 2009).
- In New York City, per-pupil spending of $11,700 is just about half the $22,000 per student in the Long Island suburb of Manhasset (Kozol, 2005).
- Including all the costs of operating a public school, a third-grade class of twenty-five children in the schools of Great Neck, New York, receives at least $200,000 more per year than does a class of the same size in Mott Haven, New York, where 99.8 percent of the children are African American or Latino (Kozol, 2002).
- In the Los Angeles area, the students of McKittrick School in the Central Valley receive $17,000 each, more than twice as much as students in Laguna Beach schools (*Los Angeles Times*, 2003).

According to Carey and Rosa, "At every level of government—federal, state, and local—policymakers give more resources to students who have more resources, and less to those who have less. These funding disparities accumulate as they cascade through layers of government, with the end result being massive disparities between otherwise similar schools" (2008:1).

There have been a number of court challenges to unequal funding within states with systems in several states judged unconstitutional. Various schemes have been proposed to meet the objections of the courts, but inequities remain even in the more progressive states. Progressive plans to address financial inequities are fought by the affluent districts and their constituents because, they argue, their taxes should be spent on their children, not others.

Research shows that low-income students and the schools serving them have fewer computers and other supplies; have teachers who are underpaid and have less teaching experience; are more likely to attend schools in need of repairs and modernization; and have higher student-teacher ratios.

In sum, the financing of public education is upside down. The schools and students who need the most help receive the least, while those with advantages are advantaged all the more. In a study of school construction spending across the nation between 1995 and 2004, Filardo et al. find that out of the billions of dollars spent on school facilities, the least affluent school districts (also those with predominantly minority student enrollment) made the lowest investment per student while the most affluent districts made the highest investment (2006). Further, the money spent on schools serving low-income students was more likely used to fund basic repairs, while schools in more affluent districts were more likely to add science labs, technology, or other new programs. As stated by President Barack Obama "For low income students, the schools are made less decrepit; for wealthier students, they are made more enriching. ... For all students to achieve, all must be provided adequate resources: effective teachers, inspiring school leaders, and enriching classroom environments" (2006:1).

Family Economic Resources

The average SAT scores for youth from families whose income was $200,000 or more was 381 points higher than youth from families whose income was $20,000 or less. By race, Whites scored about 300 points higher than African Americans on average (Marklein, 2009). How are we to explain these differences on the SATs by income and race? Among the reasons are the benefits that come from economic privilege. Low-income parents (disproportionately people of color), most without health insurance, are unable to afford prenatal care, which increases the risk of babies being born at low birth weight, a condition that may lead to learning disabilities. As these children age, they are less likely than more affluent children to receive adequate nutrition, decent medical care, and a safe and secure environment. These deficiencies increase the probability of their being less alert, less curious, and less able to interact effectively with their environment than are healthy children.

Low-income children are more likely than the children of the affluent to attend schools with poor resources, which, as we have seen, means that they are less likely to receive an enriched educational experience. In their analysis of a nationally representative sample of kindergarten children, Lee and Burkam argue:

> Low-SES [socioeconomic status] children begin school in kindergarten in systematically lower-quality elementary schools than their more advantaged counterparts. However school quality is defined—in terms of higher student achievement, more school resources, more qualified teachers, more positive teacher attitudes, better neighborhood or school conditions, private vs. public schools—the least advantaged U.S. children begin their formal schooling in consistently lower-quality schools. This reinforces the inequalities that develop even before children reach school age. (2002:3)

Similarly, most low-income youths live in communities that have few opportunities to apply academic skills and build new ones because they are either not available or not accessible (libraries, planetariums, summer camps, zoos, nature preserves, museums). The lack of community resources is especially destructive during the summer months, the time when children doing least well in school (a group that is disproportionately poor) slide backward the furthest.

"You're moving into a place where all the parents live well and all the kids test well."

Edward Koren/The New Yorker Collection/www.cartoonbank.com

Children from low-income families cannot afford private early development programs, which prepare children for school. They can be in Head Start, but these government programs have the funding for only about 60 percent of those eligible.

The level of affluence also affects how long children will stay in school, because schools, even public schools, are costly. There are school fees (many school districts charge fees for participation in music, athletics, and drama), supplies, meals, transportation, and other costs of education. These financial demands pressure youth from low-income families to drop out of school prematurely to go to work. The children from the middle and upper classes, not constrained by financial difficulties, tend to stay in school longer, which means better jobs and pay in the long run.

The affluent also give their children educational advantages such as home computers, travel experiences abroad and throughout the United States, visits to zoos, libraries, and various cultural activities, and summer camps to hone their skills and enrich their experiences in such activities as sports, music, writing, and computers. Another advantage available to the affluent is the hiring of tutors to help children having difficulty in school or to transform good students into outstanding ones.

Affluent parents may also use their privilege to get other advantages for their children. For example, in addition to spending money for their children to enroll in SAT-preparation classes, they may get a psychologist's or medical doctor's recommendation for their child to be identified as having a learning disability so that he or she would be given extra time to complete tests such as the SAT. The College Board reports that while only a tiny fraction—1.9 percent—of students nationwide are given special accommodations for taking the SAT, the percentage jumps fivefold for students from New England prep schools (exclusive private schools that send their students to elite colleges and universities). In contrast, at ten Los Angeles inner-city high schools, no students sought the time accommodation. This is ironic given the fact that learning disabilities are more frequently found in economically disadvantaged populations (Weiss, 2000).

The well-to-do often send their children to private schools (about 11 percent of U.S. children attend these schools). Parents offer several rationales for sending their children to private schools. Some do so for religious reasons. Some choose them because private schools, unlike public schools, are selective in whom they accept. Thus, parents can ensure that their children will interact with children similar to theirs in race (some private schools were expressly created so that White children could avoid attending integrated public schools) and social class. Similarly, private schools are much more likely than are public schools to get rid of troublesome students (those with behavioral problems and low achievers), thereby providing an educational environment more conducive to achievement. A final reason for attending private schools is that the most elite of them provide a demanding education and entry to the most elite universities, which, in turn, may lead to placement in top positions in the professional and corporate occupational worlds.

The preceding arguments show that a family's economic resources are correlated to their child's educational success. From test scores to dropout rates, some students are more advantaged than others.

Higher Education and Stratification

Obtaining a college degree is the most important avenue to later success. Because the payoff in jobs and pay is directly related to the prestige of the college or university attended, colleges play an important role in maintaining the stratified structure of society. From those who receive no college education to those who attend private, elite universities, each tier in the hierarchy results in different life chances.

On the lowest tier of the hierarchy are those who cannot afford to attend college. While economic success is possible without a college degree, for most individuals no college education translates into a lifetime of lower earnings and low-mobility jobs. The cost of college is high and getting higher. In 2009–2010, on average, the total annual expenses to attend a four-year private school as a resident were $26,273 compared to $7,020 for a four-year public school for in-state students and $11,528 for out-of-state students (College Board, 2010). The cost of room, board, fees, and tuition at the nation's most exclusive schools is $40,000 or more for a single school year. The high costs, coupled with declining scholarship monies, prohibit college attendance not only for the able poor but also increasingly for children of the working and lower middle classes. A comparison of students from different income groups shows that 14 percent of those from the lowest income group will enroll in college, compared to 64 percent of those from the highest income group (Symonds, 2006).

The ability to pay for college reinforces the class system in two ways: The lack of money shuts out the possibility of college for some students, and for those who do attend college, money stratifies. The poorest, even those who are talented, are most likely to attend community colleges, which are the least expensive; they emphasize technical careers and are therefore limiting in terms of later success (about 44 percent of the nation's college students attended community colleges). Students with greater resources are likely to attend public universities. Finally, those with the greatest financial backing are most likely to attend elite and prestigious private schools. It is important to note that, although ability is an important variable, it is money—not ability—that places college students in this stratified system. Children of the affluent are also advantaged in admittance to elite universities because of admission criteria that favor the children of alumni and the children of big contributors to the university's fund-raising campaigns.

The annual cost to attend Harvard University is over $50,000 per year.

Minorities and Higher Education

Because racial minorities are much more likely than Whites to be low income or just above, they are underrepresented in college educati on. The following facts make this point.

First, even though more minorities are attending college than ever, they continue to be underrepresented in higher education. In 2008, 63 percent of college students were White, 14 percent were Black, and 12 percent were Hispanic (National Center for Education Statistics, 2010).

Racial minorities also receive a disproportionately low number of college degrees. This is reflected in the relatively low number of minority students who attend and graduate from graduate school. For example, in 2009, 4 percent of African Americans and 2 percent of Hispanics earned a Master's degree.

Curriculum

U.S. schools are essentially middle or upper class. The written and spoken language in the schools is expected to be middle class. This is always a problem to some extent because some children, especially some children from economically disadvantaged backgrounds, do not speak English (at least middle-class English) and, for many, English may be a second language. The language gap is increasing with the recent wave of immigrants from Latin America and Asia. In 2005, enrollment of students with limited proficiency in English reached 5.1 million, a 57 percent increase over the previous ten years (Zehr, 2009). This presents problems for the schools not only in urban areas such as Los Angeles but also in many rural areas. The schools, in general, have failed to recognize the special needs of these and other bilingual students, which results in their overall poor student performance.

Segregation

U.S. schools tend to be segregated by social class and race, both by neighborhood and, within schools, by ability grouping. Schools are based in neighborhoods that tend to be relatively homogeneous by socioeconomic status. Racial and economic segregation is especially prevalent at the elementary school level, carrying over to a lesser degree in the secondary schools. Colleges and universities, as we have seen, are peopled by a middle- and upper-class clientele. Thus, at every level, children tend to attend a school with others like themselves in socioeconomic status and race. A study by Harvard University found that public schools are highly segregated and becoming more so: "Although minority enrollment now approaches 40 percent nationwide, the average White student attends a public school that is 80 percent White. At the same time, one-sixth of Black students—the figure is one-quarter in the Northeast and Midwest—attend schools that are nearly 100 percent non-White" (reported in the *New York Times*, 2003:1). According to Fuentes (2007), Latinos living in New York attend schools that are 80 percent non-White. These figures are the same in the West, which has seen a swell in the Latino population overall. In short, the progress toward desegregation peaked in the late 1980s and has retreated over the past fifteen years due to racially segregated neighborhoods and school districts across the country challenging integration policies.

Two recent cases illustrate this challenge to integration: Louisville and Seattle. In both cases,

Some argue that charter schools contribute to segregation in education. Approximately 70 percent of black charter students attend schools where 90 percent of the students are minorities.

officials have worked to ensure that the student bodies of their public schools reflect their city's ethnic composition. Based on the belief that students learn best in a diverse environment, students are assigned by race to some kindergarten through twelfth-grade public schools. White parents have challenged these policies in court, and the George W. Bush administration came forward in siding with these opponents, saying that race-conscious admissions policies violate the Constitution (Lane, 2006).

At the college level, some universities have also addressed the issue of segregation through the use of race-conscious admissions. At the University of Michigan, for example, the admissions committee uses a point scale where students need 100 points to be accepted to the university. Prior to 2003, underrepresented ethnic minorities received an automatic twenty point bonus toward admission. A 2003 Supreme Court decision (*Gratz v. Bollinger*) found this system to be unconstitutional and too close to a quota system. At the same time, however, another Supreme Court decision (*Grutter v. Bollinger*) upheld that race could still be considered in the admission process, but minorities could not be awarded a fixed quantity of extra points. This decision has come under fire from the public. In 2006, Michigan residents voted overwhelmingly in favor of barring the state from granting preferences based on skin color or gender in public contracting, employment, and education (Brown, 2006).

Tracking and Teachers' Expectations

In 1954, the Supreme Court declared segregated schools unconstitutional. As we have seen, many schools remain at least partially segregated by social class and race because schools draw students from residential areas that are more or less homogeneous by class and race. Segregation is reinforced further by the tracking system within the schools. **Tracking** (also known as ability grouping) sorts students into different groups or classes according to their perceived intellectual ability. The decision is based on grades and teachers' judgments but primarily through standardized tests. The result is that children from low-income families and from ethnic minorities are overrepresented in the slow track, while children from advantaged backgrounds are disproportionately in the middle and upper tracks.

The rationale for tracking is that it provides a better fit between the needs and capabilities of the student and the demands and opportunities of the curriculum. Slower students do not retard the progress of brighter ones, and teachers can adapt their teaching more efficiently to the level of the class if the students are relatively homogeneous in ability. The special problems of the different ability groups, from gifted to challenged, can be dealt with more easily when groups of students share the same or similar problems. The arguments are persuasive.

Although these benefits may be real, tracking is open to serious criticisms. First, students in lower tracks are discouraged from producing up to their potential. They tend to be given repetitive and low-level tasks that reinforce the gap between them and students in the higher tracks. Kozol (2005) found evidence of tracking in his discussions with poor high school students. For example, he found that minority students were funneled into vocational classes geared toward low-level employment (like sewing classes) rather than classes with academic substance which would prepare them for college.

Another criticism of the tracking system is that students in the upper track develop feelings of superiority, whereas those in the lower track tend to define themselves as inferior. As early as the second grade, students know where they stand on the smart-or-dumb continuum, and this knowledge profoundly affects their self-esteem. These psychological wounds can have devastating effects.

A third criticism is that the low-track students are tracked to fail. The negative labels, low teacher expectations, poor education resources (the highest track is much more likely to have access to computers and to have the most talented teachers), and because teachers typically do not want to teach these classes (there is a subtle labeling among teachers regarding who gets to teach what level) all lead to a high probability of failure among students assigned to the lowest track. Given all of these negatives, it is not surprising that students who have discipline problems or who eventually drop out come disproportionately from the low track. To summarize, Datnow and Cooper (2002) argue:

> Because of tracking practices, educational institutions, like the communities in which they are embedded, sort individuals by race, social class, language, and ability. Tracking serves as the major vehicle to sort and institutionalize the division between the "haves" and "have-nots," resulting in racially identifiable groups of students, with African-American, Latino, and low-income students receiving an unequal distribution of educational access and opportunity. (690)

The tracking system is powerful in its negative effects. There are four principal reasons this system stunts the success of students who are negatively labeled: stigma, self-fulfilling prophesies, beliefs about future payoffs to education, and the creation of negative student subcultures.

Stigma. Assignment to a lower track carries a strong **stigma** (a label of social disgrace). Such students are labeled as intellectual inferiors. Their self-esteem wanes as they see how other people perceive them and behave toward them. Thus, individuals assigned to a track other than college prep perceive themselves as second class, unworthy, stupid, and in the way. Clearly, assignment to a low track is destructive to a student's self-concept.

The Self-Fulfilling Prophecy. A **self-fulfilling prophecy** (see Chapter 7) is an event that occurs because it is predicted and people alter their behavior to conform to the prediction. This effect is closely related to stigma. If placed in the college-prep track, students are likely to receive better instruction, have access to better facilities, and be pushed more nearly to their capacity than are those assigned to other tracks. The reason is clear: The teachers and administration expect great things from the one group and lesser things from the other. Moreover, these expectations are fulfilled. Those in the higher track do better, and those in the lower track do not. These behaviors justify the greater expenditures of time, faculties, and experimental curricula for those in the higher track.

An example comes from a classic controversial study by Rosenthal and Jacobson (1968). Although this study has been criticized for a number of methodological shortcomings, the findings are consistent with theories of interpersonal influence and with the labeling view of deviant behavior. In the spring of 1964, all students in an elementary school in San Francisco were given an IQ test. The following fall the teachers were given the names of children identified by the test as potential academic "spurters," and five of these were assigned to each classroom. The spurters were chosen by means of a table of random numbers. The only difference between the experimental group (those labeled as spurters) and the control group (the rest of the class) was in the imaginations of the teachers. At the end of the year all the children were again tested, and the children from whom the teachers expected greater intellectual gains showed such gains (in IQ and grades). Moreover, they were rated by their teachers as being more curious, interesting, and happy, and more likely to succeed than the children in the control group.

The implications of this example are clear and profound. Teachers' expectations have a profound effect on students' performance. When students are overrated, they tend to overproduce; when they are underrated, they underachieve. The tracking system is a labeling process that affects the expectations of teachers (and fellow students and parents). The limits of these expectations are crucial in the educational process. Yet the self-fulfilling prophecy can work in a positive direction if teachers have an unshakable conviction that their students can learn. Concomitant with this belief, teachers should hold *themselves*, not the students, accountable if the latter should fail. Used in this manner, the self-fulfilling prophecy can work to the benefit of all students.

Future Payoff. School is perceived as relevant for students going to college. Grades are a means of qualifying for college. For the non-college-bound student, however, school and grades are much less important for entry into a job. At most, they need a high school diploma, and grades really do not matter as long as one does not flunk out. Thus, non-college-bound students often develop negative attitudes toward school, grades, and teachers. This is reflected in the statistic that students from the lowest income quarter are more than six times as likely to drop out of high school as students from the highest income quarter (U.S. Department of Education, National Center for Educational Statistics, 2006).

As we have seen, being on the lower track has negative consequences. These students are more rebellious both in school and out and do not participate as much in school activities. Finally, what is being taught is often not relevant to their world. Thus, we are led to conclude that many of these students tend to feel that they are not only second-class citizens but perhaps even pariahs (outcasts). What other interpretation is plausible in a system that disadvantages them, shuns them, and makes demands of them that are irrelevant?

The Student Subculture. The reasons given previously suggest that a natural reaction of students in the lower track would be to band together in a **student subculture** that is antagonistic toward school. This subculture would quite naturally develop its own system of rewards, since those of the school are inaccessible.

These factors (stigma, negative self-fulfilling prophecy, low future payoff, and a contrary student subculture) show how the tracking system is at least partly responsible for the tendency of students in the lower tracks to be low achievers, unmotivated, uninvolved in school activities, and more prone to break school rules and drop out of school. To segregate students either by ability or by future plans is detrimental to the students labeled as inferior. It is an elitist system that for the most part takes the children of the elite and educates them to take the elite positions in society. Conversely, children of the non-elite are trained to repeat the experiences of their parents.

The conclusion is inescapable: Inequality in the educational system causes many people to fail in U.S. schools. This phenomenon is the fault of the schools, not of the children who fail and to focus on these victims is to divert attention from the inadequacies of the schools and of the broader societal system of stratification.

Education from the Order and Conflict Perspectives

From the order perspective, schools are crucially important for the maintenance of social integration. They are a vital link between the individual and society, deliberately indoctrinating youth with the values of society and teaching the skills necessary to fit into society. Most important, the schools sift and sort children so that they will find and accept their appropriate niche in the societal division of labor.

The conflict perspective emphasizes that the educational system reinforces the existing inequalities in society by giving the advantaged the much greater probability of success (in grades, in achievement tests, in IQ tests, in getting an advanced education; all of which translate into economic and social success outside school). Conflict adherents also object to the **hidden curriculum** in schools—that is, learning to follow orders, to be quiet, to please people in authority regardless of the situation. In short, students learn to fit in, to conform. This may be functional for society and for students who will act out their lives in large bureaucracies, but it is not conducive to personal integrity and to acting out against situations that ought to be changed. Furthermore, does an educational system built on order, a rigid time schedule, and the lecture method adequately prepare youngsters for life as it is and will be? Critics argue that the hidden curriculum and current school format leaves students unprepared to meet the demands of the twenty-first century global economy.

CHAPTER REVIEW

1. The U.S. system of education is characterized by (a) conservatism—the preservation of culture, roles, values, and training necessary for the maintenance of society; (b) belief in mass education; (c) preoccupation with order and control; (d) fragmentation; (e) local control; (f) a lack of curriculum standardization; (g) competition; and (h) reinforcement of the stratification system.

2. No Child Left Behind was meant to ensure that all children meet their state's academic standards and make schools accountable for failure. The problem lies in the fact that states set different proficiency standards.

3. Education, instead of being the great equalizer, reinforces social inequality.

4. The system of education reinforces social inequality: (a) by being financed principally through local property taxes, thus richer districts have advantages; (b) by family resources (or lack of resources) determining the kind of education one receives; (c) by making higher education only affordable to certain groups of people; (d) by schools failing to recognize the needs of bilingual students; (e) through class and race segregation; and (f) by tracking students according to presumed level of ability.

5. The tracking system is closely correlated with social class; students from low-income families are disproportionately placed in the lowest track. Tracking thwarts the equality of educational opportunity for the poor by generating four effects: (a) stigma, which lowers self-esteem; (b) self-fulfilling prophecy; (c) a perception of school as having no future payoff; and (d) a negative student subculture.

6. The order perspective views the system of schooling as vital in preparing children to accept their place in society and their place in the societal division of labor. The conflict perspective views the system of schooling as a system of exploitation, where some end up on top and many end up on the bottom of the stratification system.

KEY TERMS

No Child Left Behind Act
Status dropout rate
Tracking

Stigma
Self-fulfilling prophecy
Student subculture

Hidden curriculum

STUDY QUESTIONS

1. Formal education reinforces the status quo. Should it? Must it? Should there be some point in the educational process when schools promote a critical assessment of society?
2. Explain the No Child Left Behind Act. Is it working? How could it be improved?
3. How does the formal system of education reinforce the social stratification system in society?
4. Contrast the order and conflict perspectives on formal education.

WEB RESOURCES

http://www.uscharterschools.org/
U.S. Charter Schools.Org is an online learning community designed to serve and support the United States' charter schools and to educate others about them.

http://www.rethinkingschools.org/
Fifteen years ago, a group of Milwaukee-area teachers had a vision. They wanted not only to improve education in their own classrooms and schools, but to help shape reform throughout the public school system in the United States. Today that vision is embodied in Rethinking Schools. Rethinking Schools began as a local effort to address problems such as basal readers, standardized testing, and textbook-dominated curriculum. Since its founding in 1986, it has grown into a nationally prominent publisher of educational materials, with subscribers in all fifty states, all ten Canadian provinces, and many other countries.

http://www.americatakingaction.com/
America Taking Action is a national network of school websites linking kids and communities across America. The network has been created entirely by involved parents, teachers, and community leaders as a public service, with no financial backing or influence. The goals of the network are to connect schools nationwide by providing a network of free school websites; providing numerous resources for teachers, students, and parents; fostering communication between teachers, students, and parents; and providing funding for education.

http://www.aihec.org/

The mission of American Indian Higher Education Consortium (AIHEC) is to maintain commonly held standards of quality in American Indian education; to support the development of new tribally controlled colleges; to promote and assist in the development of legislation to support American Indian higher education; and to encourage greater participation by American Indians in the development of higher education policy.

http://www.hacu.net/hacu/Default_EN.asp

The mission of Hispanic Association of Colleges and Universities (HACU) is to promote the development of member colleges and universities; to improve access to and the quality of postsecondary educational opportunities for Hispanic students; and to meet the needs of business, industry, and government through the development and sharing of resources, information, and expertise.

http://www.nafeo.org

National Association for Equal Opportunity in Higher Education (NAFEO) is the national umbrella and public policy advocacy organization for 118 of the nation's historically and predominantly Black colleges and universities. Its mission is to champion the interests of Historically Black Colleges and Universities (HBCUs) through the executive, legislative, regulatory, and judicial branches of federal and state government.

http://www.nhsa.org/

The National Head Start Association (NHSA) is a private not-for-profit membership organization representing more than one million children, upward of 200,000 staff, and 2,700 Head Start programs in America. NHSA provides a national forum for the continued enhancement of Head Start services for low-income children ages zero through five, and their families. It is the only national organization dedicated exclusively to the concerns of the Head Start community.

http://www.nea.org/

The National Education Association is America's oldest and largest organization committed to advancing the cause of public education. Founded in 1857 in Philadelphia and now headquartered in Washington, DC, NEA proudly claims 3.2 million members who work at every level of education, from preschool to university graduate programs. NEA has affiliates in every state, as well as in over 14,000 local communities across the United States.

http://www.ed.gov/

U.S. Department of Education's "award-winning site is designed to help pursue the President's initiatives, including *No Child Left Behind,* and advance our mission as a Department—to ensure equal access to education and to promote educational excellence for all Americans."

http://nces.ed.gov/

The National Center for Education Statistics collects, analyzes, and makes available data related to education in the United States and other nations.

http://www.natcenscied.org/

The National Center for Science Education is a nationally recognized clearinghouse for information and advice to keep evolution in the science classroom.

CHAPTER 17

Religion

Robert D. Putnam and David E. Campbell in their tour de force on religion—*American Grace* (2010)—argue that in the past fifty years the religious landscape in the United States has been reshaped. Following World War II, the mainline churches dominated and moderated. Church attendance and other forms of religious observance were common. But then, American religion experienced three seismic shocks. The first, the rebellious 1960s with libertine views on sex and drugs, was accompanied by a decline in religious observance. The tumultuous 1960s was followed by a second shockwave—the conservative reaction in the 1970s and 1980s characterized by the rise of evangelicalism and the Religious Right. Most notably, there was a blending of the theological with the political, with "religion" increasingly associated with the Republican Party and with conservative stances on divisive social issues such as abortion, gay marriage, and prayer in schools. The third shockwave was characterized by a negative reaction to the blending of religiosity with conservative politics since the 1990s especially by young people, leading to a number of them abandoning organized religion.

Despite all of this religious upheaval, Putnam and Campbell state:

> Any discussion of religion in America must begin with the incontrovertible fact that Americans are a highly religious people. One can quibble over just how religion and religiosity, should be gauged, but any standard, the United States (as a whole) is a religious nation. In general, Americans have high rates of religious belonging, behaving, and believing—what social scientists call the three Bs of religiosity. (Putnam and Campbell, 2010:7)

Sociologists study religion for two fundamental reasons. First, religion is a ubiquitous phenomenon that has a tremendous impact on human behavior. In the words of sociologist Meredith McGuire (1992): "Religion is one of the most powerful, deeply felt, and influential forces in human society. It has shaped people's relationships with each other, influencing family, community, economic, and political life. ... Religious values influence their actions, and religious meanings help them interpret their experiences" (3).

Second, sociologists study religion because of its influence on society and society's impact on religion. Religion is part of a larger social system, affected by and affecting the other institutions of the society—that is, patterns of the family, the economy, education, and the polity. Because religious trends may be responses to fundamental changes in society, and some religious ideas may constrain social behaviors in a narrowly prescribed manner, the understanding of any society is incomplete unless one comprehends the religion of that society.

But what is religion? The variety of activities and belief systems that have fallen under this rubric is almost infinite. There are some elements essential to religion, however, that allow us to distinguish it from other phenomena (taken from Nottingham, 1954:1–11). A starting point is that religion is a social construction—that is, it is created by people and is a part of culture. In the words of Harvard theologian Gordon Kaufman:

> The image or concept of God that we have in our books and our minds is a humanly constructed one by means of which we (in our religious and cultural traditions) attempt to focus our attention on the ultimate resource [of life]. ... [But it is our image, the creation of our human minds]. (Kaufman, 1997:6)

Religion is an integrated set of ideas by which a group attempts to explain the meaning of life and death. Religion is also a normative system, defining immorality and sin as well as morality and righteousness. The following amplify some of these statements further:

- Religion deals with the ultimate of human concerns—the meaning of life and death. It provides answers as to the individual's place in society and in the universe.
- There is an emphasis on human conduct. There are prescriptions for what one ought to do as well as the consequences for one's misconduct. This setting of limits on behavior is an important social control mechanism.
- There is a distinction between the sacred and the secular. Some objects and entities are believed to have supernatural powers and are therefore treated with respect, reverence, and awe. What is sacred and what is not are matters of belief. The range of items believed to be sacred is limitless. They may be objects (idols, altars, or amulets), animals or animal totems, parts of the natural world (sun, moon, mountains, volcanos, or rivers), transcendental beings (gods, angels, devils), or people (living or dead, such as prophets, messiahs, or saints).
- Because the sacred is held in awe, there are beliefs (theologies, cosmologies) to express and reinforce proper attitudes among believers about the sacred. The set of beliefs attempts to explain the meaning of life. McGuire (1992) says: "Religion shapes what the adherent knows about the world. This cosmic knowledge organizes the individual's perceptions of the world and serves as a basis for action" (16).
- **Ritual** consists of symbolic actions (for example, processions, sacraments, candles, chanting, singing) that reinforce the collective remembering of the group's shared meanings. Ritual, then, evokes shared understandings among the believers (awe, reverence, ecstasy, fear), which lead to group unity.
- An essential ingredient of religion is the existence of a community of believers. There must be a social group that shares a set of beliefs and practices, moral values, and a sense of community (a unique identity). Again, turning to McGuire (1992), "Coming together with fellow believers reminds members of what they collectively believe and value. It can also impart a sense of empowerment to accomplish their religious and everyday goals" (20).

One important consequence of a group of people having the same religious heritage and beliefs is unity. All believers, whether of high or low status, young or old, are united through the sharing of religious beliefs. Thus, religion, through the holding of common values to be cherished, sins to be avoided, rules to be followed, and symbols to be revered, integrates. Group unity is also accomplished through the universal feeling that God or the gods look on this particular group with special favor (the ethnocentric notion that "God is on our side"). An example of this is found in a verse of the national anthem of Great Britain:

> O lord our God, arise
> Scatter our enemies
> And make them fall.
> Confound their politics,

Frustrate their knavish tricks,
On thee our hopes, we fix,
God save us all.

Another consequence of religion is that it constrains the behavior of the community of believers, thus providing a social control function. This is accomplished in two ways. First, there are explicit rules to obey that, if violated, are punished. Second, in the process of socialization, children internalize the religious beliefs and rules. In other words, they each develop a conscience, which keeps them in line through guilt and fear.

A final consequence of religion is the legitimation of social structures that have profane (secular) origins (Berger, 1967a:343–344). There is a strong tendency for religious beliefs to become intertwined with secular beliefs, thereby providing religious blessings to the values and institutions of society: For example, during the period of extreme racial separation "clergy in the Dutch Reformed Church of South Africa ... used the Bible (Genesis 9:18–27; Joshua 9:21–27) to defend apartheid, arguing that Blacks were considered the children of Ham and therefore destined to be the 'hewers of wood and the drawers of water'" (Parenti, 1994:121).

Similarly, in U.S. society, the church has endorsed a number of secular activities. The Puritan Church of the early settlers condoned witch hunts. The defeat of the Native Americans was justified by most Christian groups on the grounds that the Indians were heathens and in need of Christianity. Finally, most religious denominations sought biblical rationalizations for slavery (van den Berghe, 1967:82).

The same religious bases that promote group integration also divide. Religious groups tend to emphasize separateness and superiority, thereby defining others as inferior (infidels, heathens, heretics, or nonbelievers). There are some 10,000 extant religious sects— each with its own cosmology, each with its own answer for the meaning of life and death. Most assert that the other 9,999 not only have it completely wrong but are instruments of evil, besides (Krakauer, 2003:338). This occurs because each religious group tends to feel it has the way (and often the only way) to achieve salvation or reach nirvana or whatever the goal.

Religious differences accentuate the differences among societies, denominations, and even within local churches. Because religious groups have feelings of superiority, there may be conflict brought about by discrimination, competition for converts, or feelings of hatred. Also, because religious ideas tend to be strongly held, groups may split rather than compromise. Liberals and fundamentalists, even within the same religion, denomination, or local church, will, doubtless, disagree on numerous issues. A common result, of course, is division.

A major divisive characteristic of religion is its tendency, through established churches, to accept the acts of the state. Within the church, there have always been people who spoke out against the church's cohabitation with the secular. This ability of the church to rationalize the activities of the state, no matter how onerous, has split many churches and denominations. The slavery issue, for example, split Baptists into American Baptists and Southern Baptists. In 1995, after 150 years of being hostile to Black progress, the Southern Baptist Convention, an association of about 40,000 congregations, issued a public apology for their history of bigotry (Salmon, 2008).

Conflict itself can occur between religious groups (with the sanction of each religion). Recent events in Iraq, Lebanon, Palestine, Ireland, Nigeria, the Philippines, Indonesia, and Bosnia provide bloody evidence of this occurrence (see the Globalization panel titled "The Global Reach of the World's Major Religions"). Religious conflict has also occurred within the United States at various times. Confrontations between Catholics and Protestants, Christians and Muslims, between warring sects of Muslims, Muslims and Jews, as well as between Protestants and Jews, have been fairly commonplace. Clearly, religious values are reason enough for individuals and groups to clash.

The Global Reach of the World's Major Religions

Some 70 percent of the world's inhabitants identify with one of five major world religions. The largest is Christianity, with some 2 billion followers (one-third of the world's population). This religion originated with a cult of the followers of Jesus of Nazareth. Its source of truth is the Bible.

Islam is the world's second largest religion (1.3 billion—about 20 percent of the world's population). It is also growing the fastest as eight of the ten countries in the world with the most rapid growth have Islamic majorities. Islam is the word of God (Allah) as revealed to Muhammad, God's messenger (born A.D. 570), who wrote the Koran (Qur'an). Its roots go back to Abraham (as do the roots of Christianity and Judaism). While Islam is found everywhere (there are 7 million Islamics in the United States), it is concentrated in the Arab countries of the Middle East, northern Africa, and Indonesia.

Judaism began with God's covenant with Abraham some 4,000 years ago, granting Abraham and his descendents exclusive rights to what is now Palestine and the designation as "God's chosen people." Following numerous battles and enslavement in Old Testament times, the Jews scattered during the first century, experiencing prejudice and persecution wherever they settled. There are only 15 million Jews worldwide, with 6 million residing in the United States.

Hinduism is the oldest of the world's major religions, dating back about 4,500 years. It is the third largest with over 800 million followers (14 percent of the world's population). Hinduism differs from Christianity, Islam, and Judaism in that it is polytheistic (several gods and goddesses with no one supreme being), and it has no single sacred text, but many. Also, unlike Christianity and Islam, Hindus do not proselytize or use force to add to their numbers. Hinduism grows primarily through high birth rates in India, its primary location. Hinduism is also found in Pakistan, southern Africa, and Indonesia (there are 1.4 million Hindus in the United States).

Buddhism has 350 million followers (6 percent of the world's population), primarily in Asia, with majorities in Thailand, Cambodia, Japan, and Myanmar (Burma). Siddhartha Gautama, born in 563 B.C., became the "Buddha." His message was that by living a rigidly prescribed life of meditation and proper conduct, one could achieve enlightenment, the highest level of human consciousness. Buddhism does not recognize a god or gods, since each human being has the potential of godliness.

These brief descriptions of the world's major religions mask the diversity of religious expression found within each (for example, Christianity split into the Eastern Orthodox Church and the Roman Catholic Church in the eleventh century and then split again with the Protestant Reformation in the sixteenth century). Each religion is a powerful source of unity among its followers as well as division within the religion (fundamentalists and liberals, radicals and moderates, as well as denominations). For our purposes here, however, we focus on the global dimensions of these religions.

- Through missionary activity, the followers of a religion travel to various countries trying to convert nonbelievers to their religious beliefs (called proselytizing). For example, in 1900, about 9 percent of Africa's population was Christian. By 2000, that number had risen to 46 percent, with much of the increase the result of missionary activity (Jenkins, 2002:55). Or take the global reach of The Church of Jesus Christ of Latter-day Saints (Mormons). This religion began in the United States and had (in 2000) some 5.1 million members in the United States. Because of a strong missionary zeal (young Mormon men give two years to missionary activity), there are now some 2.5 million Mormons in South America; 711,000 in Asia; 228,000 in Europe; as well as hundreds of thousands each in Mexico, Central America, the South Pacific, United Kingdom, Canada, Africa, and the Caribbean (Sheler, 2000:61).

- Historically, some religions have used military actions to convert nonbelievers (for example, the Crusades were attempts by European Christians to drive Muslims out of the Holy Land; part of the zeal behind the colonial expansion of the sixteenth and seventeenth centuries was a missionary zeal to convert the indigenous peoples of these non-Christian lands to Christianity).

- Religious ideology is the source of tensions, political instability, terrorism, and wars. In contemporary times, there are many examples, such as Muslims versus Hindus in India and Pakistan; Muslims versus Jews in the Middle East; Catholics versus Protestants in Northern Ireland; Catholics and Christian Serbs fighting Bosnian and Kosovar Muslims in the Balkans; Muslim guerrillas versus Catholics in the Philippines; clashes between Christians and Muslims in Indonesia and Nigeria; Hindus fighting Buddhists in Sri Lanka; and Muslim extremists using terrorist attacks against Christian targets worldwide.

- While there are nations in which one religion prevails (for example, Saudi Arabia is 99 percent Muslim), immigration brings religious diversity to other nations. Both Europe and the United States, for example, are experiencing an influx of non-Christian immigrants. These immigrants practice the religions of their country of origin, build churches, mosques, or temples, and often send their children to religious-based schools.

- Policy decisions by governments are sometimes affected by religious ideology. For example, the voting in the United Nations often divides Muslim and Christian nations. U.S. policy toward Israel is consistently pro-Jewish, regardless of whether Republicans or Democrats are in power. Abortion politics in the United States, which divide liberals and conservatives and have a strong religious component for some (for example, the Christian Right), have implications for policy. For instance, in 2002, President George W. Bush canceled the financial contribution of the United States to the United Nations Population Fund, a fund providing poor women worldwide with access to prenatal care, family planning, and other reproductive health services. Similarly, some religious traditions are a primary force of backlash against modernization (for example, the Taliban in Afghanistan, the Muslim clerics in Iran).

Classical Sociology's Differing Interpretations of Religion

The great classical sociologists—Emile Durkheim (1858–1917), Karl Marx (1818–1883), and Max Weber (1864–1920)—wrote perceptively about religion. From different perspectives and asking different questions, each theorist adds to our sociological understanding of the differing consequences of religion on society and its members.

Religion from the Order Perspective of Emile Durkheim

Durkheim, the French sociologist, wrote *The Elementary Forms of Religious Life* in 1912 (1965). This classic work explored the question of why religion is universal in human societies. He reasoned that religion must help maintain society. Durkheim studied the religion of the Australian aborigines to understand the possible role of religion in societal survival.

Durkheim found that each aborigine clan had its own totem, an object it considered sacred. The totem—a kangaroo, lizard, tree, river, or rock formation—was sacred because the clan believed that it symbolized the unique qualities of the clan. Two of Durkheim's interpretations are important in this regard. First, people bestow the notion of the sacred onto something, rather than that object being intrinsically sacred. Second, what the group worships is really society itself. Thus, people create religion.[*] Because the members of a society share religious beliefs, they are a moral community and as such the solidarity of the society is enhanced.

The society is held together by religious rituals and festivals in which the group's values and beliefs are reaffirmed. Each new generation is socialized to accept these beliefs, ensuring consensus on what is right and wrong. Religion, then, whether it be among the preindustrial Australian aborigines, the Muslims of the Middle East, the Buddhists of Asia, or the Christians of North America, serves the same functions of promoting order and unity. In short, as people meet to affirm common beliefs and values, they are bound together in a moral community.

Religion from the Conflict Perspective of Karl Marx

Whereas Durkheim interpreted the unity achieved through religion as positive, Marx viewed it as negative. Religion inhibits societal change by making existing social arrangements seem right and inevitable. The dominant form of economics in society, the type of government, the

---

[*]This raises an important question: Do we create God or is there a supernatural force somewhere that human beings grope to find? Durkheim is correct in stating that religion is a social product. This universal response, however, does not prove or disprove the existence of God (or gods). Sociologists as individuals may have strong religious beliefs, but as sociologists they focus on the complex relationship between religion and society.

law, and other social creations are given religious sanction. Thus, the system remains stable, which the order theorists see as good, when it perhaps should be transformed to meet the needs of all of the people.

Religion promotes the status quo in other ways. The powerless are taught to accept religious beliefs that are against their own interests. The Hindus, for example, believe that it is each person's duty to accept his or her caste. Failure to do so will result in being reincarnated to a lower caste or even as an animal.

> A good example of [the legitimation of inequality through religion] occurs in Hinduism in which the concepts of karma, dharma, and samsara combine to explain and justify the continuous inequality generation after generation. Karma indicates the belief that a person's present situation is the result of his or her actions in a previous life, and dharma refers to the duties and norms attached to each caste. Finally, samsara refers to the continual birth and rebirth of life. In other words, central beliefs in Hinduism absolve society or others from responsibility for social inequality. It is the result of individual actions. (Hurst, 2001:309–310)

Christianity proclaims that the poor should accept their lot in this life, for they will be rewarded. As the Bible says, "The meek shall inherit the earth." This says, in effect, do not assert yourself, accept oppression, and good things will happen ultimately. From this perspective, oppression and poverty are reinterpreted by religion to be a special form of righteousness. Thus, religion is the ultimate tool to promote false consciousness.

Max Weber's View of Religion and Social Change

Max Weber disagreed fundamentally with Marx's notions that (1) religion impedes social change by being an **opiate of the masses** and by encouraging the oppressed to accept their lot, and that (2) economic considerations supersede ideology. Weber's 1904 classic *The Protestant Ethic and the Spirit of Capitalism* (1958) refuted Marx on both grounds. Weber demonstrated that the religious beliefs of John Calvin (1509–1564) were instrumental to the rise of capitalism in Europe. The Calvinist doctrine of predestination was the key. Because God, by definition, knows everything, God knows who will go to heaven (the elect) and who will be condemned to hell even before they are born. This view was disconcerting to believers because it meant that one's future was locked in (predestined). Calvinists dealt with their anxiety by emphasizing economic success as the indicator to themselves and others of being one of God's elect. The rationale for this emphasis was that surely God would reward the chosen in this life as well as in the afterlife. This belief led Calvinists to work very hard, to live frugally, to accumulate savings, and to invest those savings in more land, equipment, and labor. Thus, the particular religious beliefs of the Calvinists were conducive to the development of capitalism in Europe and later among the colonies in America. Religious ideology, in this case, led to economic change.

Religious ideology has led to social changes in other settings as well. Martin Luther King, Jr., and the Southern Christian Leadership Council used religion to inspire followers to break down racial segregation in the United States. Liberation theology practiced by many priests and nuns and their followers in Central and South America fueled protest against Latin American dictatorships. Similarly, Catholicism was a force for change in communist Eastern Europe (Hurst, 2001:311).

Some Distinctive Features of U.S. Religion

Civil Religion

One feature of U.S. religion, traditionally, has been the separation of church and state (established by the First Amendment to the Constitution). This is both a consequence and the cause of the religious diversity found in the United States. There is a relationship between religion and the state in the United States, but it differs from the usual conception of one dominant church that is inseparable from the state. In many respects, "God and country" are conceived by most people as one. This notion that the United States and its institutions are sanctified by God has been labeled the civil religion of the United States (Bellah, 1967).

Civil religion in the United States is seemingly antithetical to the constitutional demand for separation of church and state. The paradox is that the government sanctions God as "religious imagery, language, and concepts [that] pervade public discourse, appear on the currency, and are present in the pledge to the flag" (Wilcox, 2000:16). Every presidential inaugural address except Washington's second has mentioned God; and present-day presidents have regularly scheduled prayer breakfasts, while at the same time declaring it illegal to have prayer and/or religious instruction in the public schools. The basis for the paradox is that the civil religion is not a specific creed. It is a set of beliefs, symbols, and rituals that are broad enough for all citizens to accept. The God of the civil religion is all things to all people. One thing is certain—politicians, if they want to be successful, must show some semblance of piety by occasionally invoking the blessings of this nondenominational, nonsectarian God.

Several central themes of the civil religion are important for understanding U.S. society. First, there is the belief that God has a special destiny for the United States, that it has been chosen by God to fulfill His will (Wilcox, 2000:16). This implies that God is actively involved in history and, most important, that the country has a holy mission to carry out God's will on earth. John F. Kennedy phrased this message well in the conclusion to his inaugural address: "With a good conscience our only sure reward, with history the final judge of our deeds, let us go forth to lead the land we love, asking His blessing and His help, but knowing that here on earth God's work must truly be our own" (quoted in Bellah, 1967:1–2). This belief has been the source of self-righteousness in foreign relations. It has allowed people to subdue the pagan Natives, to win the frontier, following a policy of manifest destiny, and later to defeat fascism and communism. President Reagan, for example, exhorted people in the United States to understand that communism was evil and that God wanted us to be strong. Thus, he invoked Scripture to justify a strong defense:

> I found myself wanting to remind you of what Jesus said in Luke 14:31: "Oh, what king, when he sets out to make [war]—or meet another king in battle will not first sit down and take counsel whether he is strong enough with 10,000 men to encounter the one coming against him with 20,000. Or else, while the other is still far away, sends a delegation and asks the terms of peace." I don't think the Lord that blessed this country, as no other country has ever been blessed, intends for us to have to someday negotiate because of our weakness. (quoted in Pierard and Linder, 1988:280)

Similarly, President George H. W. Bush argued that God was on our side in the Persian Gulf War: "During the 1992 presidential campaign, Bush cited Jesus Christ as the moral force behind his military interventionism, claiming that during the Persian Gulf War 'America, as Christ ordained' was 'a light unto the world'" (Parenti, 1992:43).

President George W. Bush—in an address to the nation on the first anniversary of the September 11, 2001, terrorist acts—said this:

> We cannot know all that lies ahead. Yet we do know that God has placed us together in this moment, to grieve together, to stand together, to serve each other and our country. And the duty we have been given—defending America and our freedom—is also a privilege we share. We are prepared for this journey. And our prayer tonight is that God will see us through, and keep us worthy.

As a final example of the presidential invoking of God, recent presidents, including George W. Bush and Barack Obama, have ended their speeches with the prayer "God bless America."

We're thinking maybe it's time you started getting some religious instruction. There's Catholic, Protestant, and Jewish—any of those sound good to you.

A second aspect of the civil religion is maintenance of the status quo. The God of civil religion is more closely allied to law and order than to changing the system. Thus, civil religion tends strongly toward uncritical endorsement of U.S. values and the system of stratification. Order and unity are the traditional ways of God, not change and dissent. Thus, public policy tends to receive religious legitimation.

At the same time, however, the civil religion enjoins people in the United States to stand up for certain principles—freedom, individualism, equal opportunity. Consequently, there are occasions when current governmental policy or the policy of some group is criticized because it does not measure up to certain ideals. The civil religion of the United States, then, accomplishes both the priestly role of religion (acceptance of what is) and the prophetic role of religion (challenging the existing system), with emphasis, however, on the former.

The Variety of Religious Beliefs in the United States

Some societies are unified by religion. All people in those societies believe the same religious ideas, worship the same deities, obey the same moral commandments, and identify strongly with each other. Superficially, through its civil religion, the United States appears to be homogeneous along religious lines. In 2010, some 92 percent of Americans professed to believe in God or a universal spirit. About 76 percent of Americans identify themselves as Christians. And 54 percent of Americans say that religion is "very important" to them in daily life (Gallup Poll, 2010). While Christians are the clear majority in the United States, there are also about 7 million Jews, 4 million Muslims (the estimates vary from 2.5 million to 7 million), more than 1 million Hindus, and millions of other non-Christians, including Buddhists as well as atheists (see the Diversity panel titled "Islam in the United States").

The proportions by religious affiliation are (Gallup, 2010):

- Protestant, 45 percent
- Christian (non-specific), 8 percent
- Catholic, 21 percent
- Mormon, 2 percent
- Jewish, 2 percent
- Muslim, 2 percent
- Other, 4 percent
- No affiliation, 17 percent in 2010 (up from 7 percent in 1990) (this category includes atheists, but it consists mostly of people who believe in Christian basics) (Putnam and Campbell, 2010).

The range of attitudes and beliefs among U.S. Christians is fantastically wide. Among Roman Catholics, for example, there are radical priests, nuns, and parishioners who disobey the instructions of bishops, cardinals, and even the pope. At the same time, however, there are Catholics who rigidly adhere to all the rules set down by the church authorities. Some even insist on Latin spoken in Masses. The range within Protestantism is even greater. Many

Islam in the United States

Islam has about 1.6 billion followers worldwide, second only to Christianity. Muslims believe in one god, Allah, as their creator and the sustainer of the universe. They accept the Hebrew Bible, and venerate Jesus as a prophet. The founder of Islam was Muhammad, an Arab born in Mecca about A.D. 570, who is believed to be Allah's messenger. Islamic scripture, the Koran, is a recording of divine revelation as revealed by the prophet Muhammad. Observant Muslims perform five key duties (the Five Pillars of Islam): accepting no god but Allah and Muhammad as his prophet, prayer five times a day, fasting during the ninth month in the Islamic lunar year, giving to charity, and making a pilgrimage to Mecca at least once in a lifetime.

Islam is the nation's fastest-growing faith, with about 4 million to 7 million adherents in the United States, nearly double the number a decade ago, and are expected to double again by 2030 (Grossman, 2011). Muslims outnumber Jews, Episcopalians, and Presbyterians in the United States. Their growth in the United States is evidenced by the huge growth in the number of Islamic houses of worship (mosques) since 1960—from 104 to about 2,000 in 2011. More than half of American Muslims reside in ten states—California, New York, Illinois, New Jersey, Indiana, Michigan, Virginia, Texas, Ohio, and Maryland. Most notably, in 2006 Keith Ellison, an African American from Minneapolis, became the first Muslim elected to the House of Representatives. He was reelected in 2008 and 2010.

American Muslims are not a monolithic group. Some 65 percent were born in 80 different countries; 35 percent were born in the United States. The ethnic makeup in Muslims is 33 percent South Asian, including people from such countries as India, Pakistan, Bangladesh, and Sri Lanka (the top countries of origin for Muslim immigrants to the United States in 2009 were Pakistan and Bangladesh), 30 percent African American, and 25 percent from the Arab world (Pew Research Center, 2011). About 20,000 people convert to Islam each year in the United States (IslamaConcepts.com, 2009). Of the U.S.-born converts to Islam, 42 percent are African Americans. Although most Muslims are conservative on social issues (opposing abortion, premarital sex, homosexuality, divorce, alcohol use, and dancing), there are differences in beliefs and levels of activism. For example, although Muslim women are encouraged to dress modestly, their clothing varies from head scarfs and floor-length dresses to fashions not unlike that of other U.S. women. Only 10 percent of U.S. Muslims practice Islam's Five Pillars. Like any other religious group, Muslims have different sects within; there are Sunnis and Shiites (they differ on who are the descendents of Muhammad); there are about 20,000 who belong to Louis Farrakhan's Nation of Islam.

Islam differs from Christianity; Islamists are typically people of color, and they are stereotyped as religious and political zealots, perhaps even terrorists. Therefore, Muslims in the United States are often objects of discrimination, hostility, and hate crimes. Many object to the building of Mosques in their city or neighborhood. Hate crimes (arsons, bombings, physical assaults) against Arab Americans were especially prevalent after the terrorist attacks on September 11, 2001, but remain an ongoing problem for Muslims. While Muslims comprise less than 2 percent of the U.S. population, they were the objects of approximately one quarter of the religious discrimination claims filed with the Equal Employment Opportunity Commission during 2009 (*Right Truth*, 2010).

The estimated number of Muslims in the United States ranges from 2.5 million to 7 million. The largest concentration is in Dearborn, Michigan.

Outsourcing Prayer

Outsourcing is the practice of shifting work done domestically to an entity in another society. An unusual version of outsourcing is where Catholic clergy, in short supply in the United States, Canada, and Europe, pay priests in India to say Mass for special intentions (Rai, 2004:13).

In the Catholic tradition, the intention is a prayer, typically, for the repose of the soul of a deceased person, for a sick person, or a prayer for a newborn. In Kerala, India, the Indian state with the largest concentration of Catholics, priests are sometimes asked to say Mass for Catholics in other countries where there are too few priests. Priests receive a donation of 40 rupees (90 cents) to say a Mass for special intentions for one of their parishioners. They receive $5 for fulfilling a prayer request from the United States.

Protestants believe that the Bible is to be taken literally, word for word; for others, the Bible is purely allegorical. Some religious groups have so much faith in the healing power of religion that their members refuse to see physicians under any circumstances. Within Protestantism are Amish, Hutterites, Quakers, high-church Episcopalians, Pentecostal Holiness groups, Congregationalists, and even snake handlers (see the Globalization panel titled "Outsourcing Prayer" for an unusual, but accepted, practice).

Religious Organization

Very broadly, U.S. religious organizations can be divided according to their secular commitments into two categories—churches and sects (Troeltsch, 1931). Religious groups have a choice—to reject and withdraw from the secular society, or to accommodate to it. The basis for a decision to reject the social environment is maintenance of spiritual and ethical purity. Such a choice, by definition, entails withdrawal from the world, thereby consciously avoiding any chance to change it. The opposite choice—accommodation—requires compromise and the loss of distinctive ideals, but it also means that the groups can influence the larger society. The accommodation or resistance to the secular world is the fundamental difference between a church and a sect.

A **church**, as an ideal type (that is, in its purest form), has the following attributes:

- The tendency to compromise with the larger society and its values and institutions.
- The tendency to be inclusive in that their standards for membership are relatively loose.
- Membership that tends to occur by being born to parents who belong to the church.
- Membership, moreover, takes place through infant baptism, which implies that all members are saved.
- A hierarchy of authority, with those at the top being trained for their vocation.
- Acceptance of a diversity of beliefs, because the membership is large; for many, the scriptures are interpreted metaphorically rather than literally.
- Tolerance of the popular vices.

A **sect** in its perfect form is exactly opposite a church in every way:

- There is a fundamental withdrawal from and rejection of the world. A sect is a moral community separate from and in many ways hostile toward the secular world.
- Membership is only through a conversion experience. Membership is therefore exclusive, voluntary, and limited to adults. Hence, adult baptism is the only accepted form of baptism.
- Organization is informal and unstructured. Ministers are untrained. They became ministers by being called from the group.

- The belief system is rigid with an emphasis on the purity of doctrine. The Bible is the source, and it is interpreted literally.
- There are rigid ethical requirements restraining the members from the popular vices of drinking, smoking, card playing, dancing, and cursing.

The church–sect dichotomy does not exhaust all the possibilities. Some religious groups fit somewhere in between—as institutionalized sects. These groups (for example, Mormons, Disciples of Christ, and Southern Baptists) incorporate features of both a church (trained leadership, some accommodation to the larger society) with the sectlike attributes of adult baptism and an unwillingness to compromise on some theological questions.

For our purposes, however, the church–sect dichotomy, while oversimplifying the situation, is useful in two ways: to depict a form of social change, and to show why certain categories of people are attracted to one type and not the other.

The church–sect dichotomy illustrates an important sociological phenomenon—the process of organization deflects away from the original goal of the group. A group may form to pursue a goal such as religious purity, but in so doing it creates a new organization, which means that some of the group's energies will be spent in organizational maintenance. Consequently, a sect may form with the explicit intention of eliminating a hierarchy and a codification of beliefs. Patterns of behavior emerge, however, as certain practices are found to be more effective. In particular, the selection of ministers tends to become routinized, and a system of religious instruction for children is developed so that they will learn the catechism in the proper sequence.

Sects, then, tend to become churches. This is illustrated by the type of leader found in each. Often a sect is formed by a charismatic person and his or her followers. This person is followed because he or she is believed to possess extraordinary qualities of leadership, saintliness, gifts of prophecy, or ability to heal.

What happens to such an organization when this leadership is gone? The organization is faced with a crisis of succession. Groups typically find ways to pass on the **charisma** (the extraordinary attributes) of the original leader. This process is called the **routinization of charisma** (whereby an organization attempts to transmit the charisma of the former leader to a new one). This is done by (1) selection of the successor by the original charismatic leader, (2) designation of a successor by the group closest to the original leader ("disciples"), (3) hereditary transmission, or (4) transmission of charisma by ritual ("laying on of hands") (Weber, 1947:358–366). In this last instance there is the recognition of a **charisma of office**—that is, whoever holds the position possesses charisma. When this occurs, the organizational machinery is advanced enough to move the group away from its sectlike qualities toward a church. The important sociological point here is that organizations seldom remain the same. The simple tends to become complex. But the process does not stop at complexity; as the original goal of the sect (religious purity with the necessity of separation from the world) is superseded when the organization gets larger and more bureaucratic, some persons will become dissatisfied enough to break away and form a new sect. Thus, the process tends to be cyclical.

Increased bureaucratization (and subsequent splintering) is characteristic of modern urban society. This leads us to a final consideration relative to the church–sect dichotomy—the motivation to join sects. At the risk of oversimplification, two important features of sects help explain why some categories of people are especially drawn to sects rather than churches. The first is that a sect (more so than a church) may provide a total world of meaning and social identity and a close circle of people to whom members can turn when troubled. The sect provides precisely those things missing in the lives of many who live in large metropolitan areas and work in huge bureaucracies, and whose world is rapidly changing. The sect provides meaning in a meaningless world. The members find friends in a sea of strangers. They find stability in a setting that is rapidly undergoing change. Thus, the alienated are especially attracted to sects. So, too, are new migrants to the city. In the city, they are confronted with a variety of new and difficult problems—industrialized work, work insecurity, loss of kinship ties, and disruption of other primary-group ties. The sects, unlike the established city churches, appeal to such people through their form of worship, emphasis on individual attention, and lack of formal organization (Yinger, 1961:21–25).

A second variable affecting attraction to a sect or church is social class. Generally, low-status people tend to be attracted to sects rather than to churches because religious status is substituted for social status (or as the Bible puts it, "and the last shall be first"). It makes sense for people of low social or economic status to reject this world and the religious bodies that accommodate to it. Such people would be especially attracted to a religious group that rejects this world and assures its followers that in the next world true believers—those who are religiously pure—will have the highest status. The sect represents to its followers a reaction against or escape from the dominant religious and economic systems in society. It is a protest against the failure of established churches to meet the needs of marginal groups (Pope, 1942:140). The sect, moreover, rejects the social classes as irrelevant and, in fact, as a system of rewards that is in exact reverse order from God's will.*

Churches, on the other hand, attract the middle and upper classes. Since these people are successful, they obviously would not turn to a religious organization that rejects their world. As Max Weber (1963) has said: "Other things being equal, classes with high social and economic privilege will scarcely be prone to evolve the ideas of salvation. Rather, they assign to religion the primary function of legitimizing their own life pattern and situation in this world" (107).

Both the sect and the church, consequently, have well-developed theodicies (Berger, 1967b). A **theodicy** is a religious legitimation for a situation that otherwise might cause guilt or anger (such as defeat in a war or the existence of poverty among affluence). Sects tend to have a theodicy of suffering—that is, a religious explanation for their lack of power and privilege. Churches must explain the inequalities of society, too, but their emphasis is on legitimation of possessing power and privilege. This tendency to develop theodicies has the important social function of preserving the status quo. Churches convince their adherents that all is well, that one should accept one's fate as God-given. This makes people's situations less intolerable and the possibility of revolution remote—the suffering know they will be rewarded, while the guilt of the well-off is assuaged. Consequently, there is no reason to change the system.

Cults. A **cult** is a new religion with practices and teachings at odds with the dominant culture and religion. In other words, a cult rejects society and established religions. Typically, the members of a cult give extreme devotion to a charismatic leader who requires much of them (their material resources, their work, a demanding lifestyle, and a total, intense commitment). Although not true for all cults, some are totalistic, self-enriching, and guru-worshiping. "As the master is elevated, the followers are infantilized and diminished" (Parenti, 2010:114). A cult differs from a sect in one fundamental way. A sect is a religious group that leaves an established church to recapture what it considers the essence of its religious tradition. A cult, on the other hand, represents religious innovation, a new religious expression. Consider, for example, the Church of Scientology, founded in 1953 by science fiction author L. Ron Hubbard. Among its teachings is the belief in reincarnation and that souls have lived on other planets before living on Earth.

We tend to think of cults and their followers as bizarre (for example, the mass suicides by the followers of Jim Jones' People's Temple and Heaven's Gate). They are, by definition, different from the rest of us; they reject society and claim to have religious experiences that are alien to most of us. Many of these groups ultimately fail. The message fades; the predictions misfire; the charismatic leader dies and his or her replacement disappoints. But while we tend to think of these groups as weird and transitory, we should remember that many of the major religious groups of today, including Christianity, Mormonism, Islam, and Judaism, began as cults.

---

*It is incorrect to say, however, that all lower-class people who are alienated will join religious sects in order to attack the establishment. Their estrangement may lead them to join other kinds of social movements (for example, labor or political) or toward social isolation.

Class, Race, Gender, Sexuality, and Religion

The Relationship between Social Class and Religion

The dominant religion in the United States, Christianity, stresses the equality of all people in the sight of God. All people, regardless of socioeconomic status, are welcomed in Christianity. We might expect, therefore, that the distribution of members by socioeconomic status within any denomination would be randomly distributed. We might also assume that the organization of any local congregation would ignore status distinctions. Although these two assumptions seem to have surface validity, the empirical situation refutes them.

We have seen that sects and churches tend to have a social-class bias—the lower the socioeconomic status, the greater the probability of belonging to a sect. There also seems to be a ranking of denominations in terms of the socioeconomic status of their members. Although there is always a range of social classes within any one denomination, there is a modal status that characterizes each. The reasons for this are varied: the proportion of members living in rural or urban areas, which immigrant groups brought the religion to the colonies or United States and during what historical period, and the appeal of the religious experience (ritual, evangelism, close personal ties, salvation, legitimation of the social system, or attacks on the establishment). This last point is especially important because "life conditions affect men's religious propensities, and life conditions are significantly correlated with the facts of stratification in all societies" (O'Dea, 1966:60).

There is a relationship between economic status, educational attainment, and denominational affiliation. The most affluent of the major religions is Reform Judaism with 67 percent of households making more than $75,000 a year in 2010. At the other end are Pentecostals, Jehovah's Witnesses, and Baptists, with 20 percent or fewer in each case making at least $75,000 (Leonhardt, 2011). Judaism has the highest proportion of high-education and high-income members, followed by Episcopalians and Presbyterians. At the low-education and low-income end of the social class system are the Assembly of God, Southern Baptists, and Jehovah's Witnesses. This is an oversimplification, however, since each denomination includes people of high, middle, and low economic and educational status.

Local churches, even more so than denominations, tend to be homogeneous in socioeconomic status. This is partly the result of residential patterns—that is, neighborhoods are relatively homogeneous by socioeconomic status, and the local churches are attended mostly by people living nearby. Another reason, and perhaps just as important, is the tendency for people to seek organizations composed of people like themselves. They do not want to feel out of place, so they are attracted to churches where the members have the same lifestyle (for example, speech patterns, clothing tastes, and educational backgrounds). The result, then, is that people belonging to a particular denomination often look for the local congregation where they feel most comfortable.

There is some range, however, in every local church. Probably no one congregation is composed totally of people from exactly the same status niche. Although the status differentials may be minimal within a local congregation, they are evidently important to the parishioners. The rule is that the higher the socioeconomic status of the member, the greater his or her influence in the running of the local church. There is greater likelihood that such people will be elected or appointed to office (elder, deacon, trustee, Sunday school superintendent) and that their opinions will carry greater weight than those of people of lower social status. This may be partly a function of the disproportionately large financial contributions by the more well-to-do, but the important point here is that the secular world intrudes in the organization of each local congregation. The common indicators of religious involvement—church membership, attendance at church services, and participation in the church's activities—demonstrate a relationship to socioeconomic status. On each of these measures, people of high status are more involved than those of low status. Unfortunately, these are not very good measures of religiosity, although they are often assumed to be. The problem is that upper-class people are much more likely to join and actively participate in all sorts of organizations. The joining of churches and attending services are the manifestations of a more general phenomenon—the tendency for middle- and upper-class people to be joiners, while lower-class individuals tend to isolate themselves from all types of organizations. The spuriousness of the relationship between socioeconomic status and religiosity is more clearly seen when we analyze the importance of religion to people of varying socioeconomic circumstances, as well as differences in religious beliefs and the degree to which church activities are secular by social class.

William J. Goode (1966), after comparing white-collar church members with working-class church members, found that while the former were more likely to belong to and participate in formal activities of the church, the latter were actually more religious:

> They participate less in formal church activities, but their religious activity does not appear to be nearly so secularized. It is more specifically religious in character. This is indicated by the fact that on a number of other religious dimensions, dimensions not dependent on extraneous nonreligious variables, individuals of manual-status levels appear to display a considerably higher level of religious response. This is true particularly of psychological variables, such as religious "salience," the greater feeling that the church and religion are great forces in the lives of respondents. It is also true for "religiosity" as measured by a higher level of religious concern, and for religious "involvement," the extent to which the individual is psychologically dependent on some sort of specifically religious association in his life. (111)

There is evidence for the "secularization of religion" by social class. Polling data reveal that the more education and income one has, the less likely one is to find religion important and to hold traditional religious beliefs.

In summary, there is a rather complex relationship between socioeconomic status and religion. Although the relatively poor and uneducated are more likely to be indifferent to religion than are the better educated and financially well off, those who are religious tend to make religion a more integral part of their lives than do better-off people. They go to church more for religious than secular reasons. They believe much more strongly than do the well-to-do in the fundamental beliefs as expressed in the Bible. They are more likely to accept the literal interpretation of the Bible. Thus, we have the paradox that on many objective measures of religious involvement—church attendance and participation in formal church activities—middle- and upper-status people exceed those of less status, whereas if importance of religion in the life of the individual is considered, the poor who go to church outstrip their more economically favored brethren.

Religion and Race: The Case of African Americans

As with other social phenomena, race and religion separate people. As noted earlier, historically most White churches in the United States chose to ignore or to actively support racial segregation. The issue of the legitimacy of slavery divided some White congregations and denominations. For example, the Southern Baptist Convention was a denomination conceived out of support for slavery. In 1995, 150 years after taking that proslavery stand, the Southern Baptist Convention passed a resolution confessing to a sin of historic proportion: "We lament and repudiate historic acts of evil such as slavery from which we continue to reap a bitter harvest" (quoted in Sheler, 1995:10). Similarly, Pope John Paul II apologized for the church's complicity in the African slave trade. Also, of historic importance to Blacks everywhere, the Dutch Reformed Church in 1991 formally apologized to Black South Africans for having provided religious justification for apartheid. While these sweeping apologies are important symbolically, we should note that they were slow in coming. It took the Southern Baptists, for example, 150 years—and a full thirty years after the height of the civil rights struggle—to finally admit to their support of racism.

Local churches are among the most segregated organizations. They tend to be exclusively of one race or predominantly White or African American. Some observers have suggested, for example, that the most segregated hour left in the United States is eleven o'clock on Sunday morning.

This segregation by race is the consequence of a number of factors: a reflection of residential segregation patterns, past and present discrimination, and denominational loyalty (Jaynes and Williams, 1989:92). Most significant for African Americans is that their local churches are one of the few organizations over which they have control. Moreover, these historic Black churches have been not only the focus of their religion but also a key component of the Black community's social life, sources for helping those in need, and centers for Black political activities. Segregated churches gave African Americans, who were denied equal opportunity in the larger society, opportunities for the talented to express and hone their abilities. Significantly, the leaders of the civil rights movement in the 1960s were almost exclusively African American clergy.

Religion and Ethnicity: The Case of Recent Immigrants

Recent immigrants arrive with religious beliefs from their country of origin, adding to the diversity of religious expression in U.S. society. Recent East Indian immigrants tend to be Hindu; Chinese are Confucians; Southeast Asians are Buddhists; those from Middle East countries tend to be Muslim; and Latinos are overwhelmingly Catholic. But these generalizations mislead, since there are wide variations within each ethnic group. For example, there are differences among Muslims between Sunni and Shia. There are political moderates and there are extremists. There are the devout and the secular (Barrett, 2007).

The rapid growth of Latinos has a considerable effect on the Catholic Church. From 1990 to 2008 the Catholic Church added 11 million adults, of which 9 million were Latinos (Jayson, 2010). Thus, Latinos were 32 percent of all U.S. Catholics in 2008, compared to 20 percent in 1990. However, the proportion of Latino adults identifying with Catholics has declined from 66 percent in 1990 to 60 percent in 2008. Those Latinos leaving the Catholic Church have taken one of two paths: (1) There has been a rise in the number of Latinos who do not identify with any religion (in 1990 this was 6 percent, compared to 12 percent in 2008); and (2) Latinos abandoning Catholicism for another denomination have tended toward an exuberant form of Protestantism known as Pentecostalism (15 percent of all U.S. Latinos).

Religion and Gender

The three dominant religions in the United States—Christianity, Judaism, and Islam—have been and remain patriarchal. Each worships a male God (as feminist theologian Mary Daly has put it: "As long as God is male, the male is God," quoted in Stange, 2010:7A). Each of these traditions recognizes only males as prophets, and has historically given men the highest religious leadership roles. Significantly, their belief systems have been used to legitimize female subordination to males (see the Diversity panel titled "Religion and Patriarchy").

These religions began in historical times and places where women were clearly subservient to men in all aspects of society. However, this patriarchal tradition continues. Women are formally denied the role of pastor, minister, priest, or rabbi in the Missouri Synod Lutheran Church, the Greek Orthodox Church, the Church of Jesus Christ of Latter-day Saints (Mormon), the Catholic Church, the Southern Baptist Church, the Mennonite Brethren Church, and Orthodox Judaism. Pope John Paul II, for example, stated in 1995 that the Roman Catholic Church's ban on women priests is "founded on the written Word of God and that it is to be held always, everywhere and by all" (quoted in Religion News Service, 1995). In other denominations there have been bitter disputes over this matter, with some dissidents breaking away to form separate organizations when women were allowed to become pastors. The majority of Protestant denominations now have women in the ministry, as do Reform and Conservative Judaism. These breakthroughs are relatively recent in origin. The United Methodist Church and the Presbyterians began ordaining women in 1956, Evangelical Lutherans

Religion and Patriarchy

The great religions and their leaders have consistently taught that women were secondary to men. Consider the following examples of this thought, which supported men as God's chosen leaders:

- One hundred women are not worth a single testicle.—Confucius (551–479 B.C.)
- In childhood a woman must be subject to her father; in youth to her husband; when her husband is dead, to her sons. A woman must never be free of subjugation.—The Hindu Code of Manu (circa A.D. 100)
- If ... the tokens of virginity are not found in the young woman, then they shall bring out the young woman to the door of her father's house, and the men of the city shall stone her to death with stones because she has wrought folly ... so you shall purge the evil from the midst of you.—Deuteronomy 22: 20–21 (Old Testament)
- Blessed art thou, O Lord our God and King of the Universe, that thou didst not create me a woman.—Daily prayer (ancient and contemporary) of the Orthodox Jewish male
- Let a woman learn in silence with all submissiveness. I permit no woman to teach or to have authority over men; she is to keep silent.—I Timothy 2:11–15 (New Testament)

- Men are superior to women.—The Koran (circa A.D. 650)
- Women should remain at home, sit still, keep house, and bear and bring up children.—Martin Luther (1438–1546)
- Woman in her greatest perfection was made to serve and obey man, not rule and command him.—John Knox (1505–1572)

Given these pronouncements, we should not be surprised that women traditionally have not held positions of spiritual leadership within organized religion. But these statements were made long ago at historical times when women were clearly subservient to men in all aspects of society.

Serious questions remain: Will congregations accept female clergy in the same way they do men? Will female clergy be called to lead the largest and most prestigious congregations? Will the hierarchy in the various denominations promote women to the highest offices? And will some religious groups continue to deny women the clergy role?

Source: The quotations were taken from a list compiled by Meg Bowman, 1983. "Why We Burn: Sexism Exorcised." *The Humanist* 43 (November/December): 28–29.

in 1960, and Episcopalians in 1979. But even in the more liberal denominations such as the Episcopal Church, some congregations have refused to accept women ministers. The irony is that while women are denied leadership roles in religious organizations, they are, on average, more religious than men. Putnam and Campbell conclude from their research:

> In the average Sabbath service women outnumber men by three to two. Women believe more fervently in God, they aver that religion is more important to their daily lives, they pray more often, they read scripture more often and interpret it more literally, they talk about religion more often—in short, by virtually every measure they are more religious. To be sure, not all women are religiously inclined, but the correlation between gender and religiosity is robust. (Putnam and Campbell, 2010:233)

Clearly, female clergy are not only underrepresented but have not kept up with the gains by women in other professions—women now account for 25 percent of lawyers and 21 percent of physicians, but only 10 percent of the mainline Protestant clergy. Moreover, female clergy are paid less than male clergy, even though women in the pulpit are generally more highly educated than their male counterparts (Burke, 2009).

Religion and Sexuality

The Judeo-Christian tradition considers homosexual behavior a heinous sin. A few passages of the Old Testament condemn homosexuality. The New Testament continued this tradition.[*] The apostle Paul, for example, wrote in Corinthians that homosexuals would never inherit

---

[*]For a critique of the Biblical condemnation of homosexuality by Episcopal Bishop John Shelby Spong, see The Sins of Scripture, 2005, chapters 12–15.

the kingdom of God. Contemporary Christian churches and denominations have varied in their response to homosexuality. For fundamentalists the twin pillars of their fight in the culture wars are to outlaw abortions and same-sex marriages. Regarding the latter, there is no issue for fundamentalists—homosexuality is a sin. The late Rev. Jerry Falwell, fundamentalist preacher and founder of the Moral Majority, for example, called the outbreak of AIDS among homosexuals a "form of judgment of God upon a society" (quoted in Crooks and Baur, 1987:312). Similarly, Rev. John Hagee, pastor of a megachurch in San Antonio, proclaimed that Hurricane Katrina was God's punishment for America's liberal attitudes toward homosexuality. The fundamentalists also try to affect public and corporate policy regarding their values. The Southern Baptist Convention in 1996, for instance, voted to boycott the Walt Disney Corporation because Disney provides the same health care benefits for the live-in partners of gay employees as it does for the spouses of straight workers (while still denouncing homosexuality, the Southern Baptists did rescind its boycott of Disney in 2005). Even some mainline churches have taken a stand against homosexuals, especially their ordination into the clergy and same-sex marriages. The United Methodist Church added these words to its Book of Discipline in 1996: "Ceremonies that celebrate homosexual unions shall not be conducted by our ministers and shall not be conducted in our churches" (Kerr, 1999:37A). On the other hand, the United Church of Christ in 2005 declared that it would sanction same-sex marriages.

THE DECLINE OF MORALITY IN AMERICA

As an example of an inclusive church, consider this statement in its weekly church service bulletin:

> Bethel College Mennonite Church [North Newton, Kansas] welcomes into fellowship and membership all persons who confess faith in Jesus Christ, without regard to their race, ethnic background, gender, age, sexual orientation, education, ability, and other factors which give rise to discrimination and marginalization.

Even in the more liberal denominations and churches, the issue has often been divisive, with some resisting doctrinal change while others seek the acceptance of homosexuals, the recognition of loving unions outside of marriage, and even the ordination of gay and lesbian clergy. For example, in defiance of the Methodist ban on same-sex marriages, ninety United Methodist ministers married two women before more than 1,000 clergy, lay leaders, gay men, lesbians, and other supporters in the Sacramento Convention Center in early 1999. So, too, for Episcopalians as the Episcopal Church USA formally accepted gay bishops and same-sex unions but this has led to several parishes' and a few dioceses' opting out of the church. Moreover, there is the threat of a split over this issue between the Episcopal Church and the Anglican Communion, the third largest Christian organization representing 77 million members worldwide.

One Christian denomination, the Universal Fellowship of Metropolitan Community Churches, was founded in 1968 as a fellowship of Christian Churches with a special outreach to the world's gay, lesbian, bisexual, and transgender communities. It has grown from twelve worshipers to a denomination claiming 42,000 members in the United States and 352 churches in nineteen countries. More than twenty of their churches in the United States have been bombed or set on fire by arsonists.

Religious Trends

Religion in U.S. society is a paradox. On the one hand, religion seems to be losing its vitality. The data show, for example, that in the past forty years or so there has been a slight downward trend in church attendance (see Table 17.1). There are differences across social categories. For example, people age 65 and older are more than twice as likely as eighteen-to thirty-year-olds to attend religious services at least once a week; women are much more likely to attend than men; southerners are substantially greater church attenders than those from other regions; and Protestants are more likely to attend than Catholics. Among the denominations Church of Christ had the highest weekly attendance (68 percent), followed by Mormons (67 percent), Pentecostal (65 percent), and Southern Baptist (60 percent). Attendance at the mainline churches continues to decline. Episcopalians, for instance, had but a 32 percent weekly attendance rate (*Christian Chronicle*, 2006).

Another indicator of slippage in the religiosity of Americans is that the number saying that they have no religion has jumped from 7 percent in 1990 to 17 percent now. Moreover these "nones" are concentrated among young adults, where 27 percent say that they have no religious affiliation. As noted at the beginning of this chapter, Robert Putnam and David Campbell (2010) suggest in that this youthful disaffection from organized religion is the result of the public face of American religion shifting sharply to the right during the 1980s. Their analysis showed that rejection of religion by youth was due especially to religion's intolerance of homosexuality.

There are other indications that people in the United States are just as religious as ever, and in some areas there is even dramatic growth. Bill Moyers (1996) argues that there is a current surge in the search for an understanding of core principles of belief. "We shouldn't be surprised by all this stirring. It's a confusing time, marked by social and moral ambivalence and, for many, economic insecurity. People yearn for spiritual certainty and collective self-confidence" (4). This theme is amplified by sociologist Rodney Stark: "Besides providing a sense

TABLE 17.1

Percentage Attending Church during Average Week (1954–2005)[*]

Year	Percentage	Year	Percentage	Year	Percentage	Year	Percentage
1954	46	1969	42	1984	40	1999	41
1955	49	1970	42	1985	42	2000	42
1956	46	1971	40	1986	40	2001	42
1957	47	1972	40	1987	40	2002	46
1958	49	1973	40	1988	42	2003	46
1959	47	1974	40	1989	43	2004	42
1960	47	1975	40	1990	43	2005	40
1961	47	1976	41	1991	43	2006	40
1962	46	1977	41	1992	43	2007	41
1963	46	1978	41	1993	41	2008	38
1964	45	1979	40	1994	38	2009	42
1965	44	1980	40	1995	44	2010	39
1966	44	1981	41	1996	39		
1967	43	1982	41	1997	35		
1968	43	1983	40	1998	40		

[*]The number saying that they attend church on any given Sunday actually overstates the case. The number represents, rather, the proportion of the population that represent themselves as regular churchgoers (Smietana, 2006).

Source: The Gallup Poll Monthly, various issues, and www.pollingreport.com/religion.html.

of orientation and insecurity in an insecure world, one of the functions of religion is to satisfy the need to know where we come from and where we're going" (quoted in Morin, 1998:37).

Americans have consistently and overwhelmingly believed in God, with survey findings showing that more than nine out of ten adults in the United States believe in God or a universal spirit (Gallup Poll, 2010). Surveys show uniformly that Americans are far more likely than their counterparts in Europe and Scandinavia to attend church regularly and to respond that religion is important in their lives.

Some religious groups are growing rapidly in members and interest. The fastest growing in percentage gain are the Pentecostals and the Church of Jesus Christ of Latter-day Saints (Mormons). More significant because of their growing numbers nationwide and their political leverage are the evangelical denominations and sects.

In this section we highlight three major trends of U.S. religion: (1) the decline of the mainline churches, (2) the rise of the evangelicals, and (3) the new political activism of the evangelicals and the decline of religious pluralism. Because social conditions have led to these shifts, the focus is on the societal conditions that have given impetus to these trends.

The Decline of the Mainline Denominations

The pattern of denominational growth and decline is stable. Together, the mainline denominations of the United Church of Christ (which includes most Congregationalists), the Presbyterian Church, the Episcopal Church, the American Baptist Churches, the United Methodist Church, the Evangelical Lutheran Church, and the Lutheran Church (Missouri Synod), have lost millions of members since the 1970s and continue to do so. The Church of Jesus Christ of Latter-day Saints (also known as the Mormon Church), African American Protestant groups, and Assemblies of God, Jehovah's Witnesses, and other conservative evangelical and Pentecostal groups continue to gain members (Lindner, 2011). Reflecting the trend away from mainline churches, not one of the Republican candidates for president in 2012 is a member of the Protestant denominations that have dominated American politics: Episcopalian, Presbyterian, or Methodist. Rather two of the candidates are Mormons, one is a member of an interdenominational evangelical church, one belongs to an evangelical Lutheran church, and two are Catholics (McManus, 2011).

The reasons for the decline in the mainline denominations are not altogether clear, but the following appear plausible. These denominations have lost their vitality as they have become more and more churchlike (that is, they have moved away from the qualities characterizing sects) and do not require enough commitment, theologically or evangelistically, from congregants (Van Biema, 2004). The beliefs within these churches have become so pluralistic that to many people the faith seems watered down. Many churchgoers want authority, but they too often receive only more ambiguity. The mainline churches also have lost members because of a preoccupation with social issues at the expense of an emphasis on an old-fashioned faith and biblical teachings for personal growth (Reeves, 1996).

Because other parts of society emphasize rationality, efficiency, and bureaucracy, many people seek a religion that will emphasize feelings and fellowship. However, the mainline churches, for the most part, are just as impersonal and ossified as the other bureaucracies in society.

The growth of the Catholic Church is mixed. Overall, it has gained membership because of the large numbers of immigrants from Mexico and other Catholic countries and a relatively high fertility rate. At the same time it is vulnerable to losses in attendance. In this case, the rigidity of the Catholic hierarchy is partly responsible. The Church has taken strong stances against contraception, abortion, gender equality, homosexuality, and divorce. Many Catholics feel that church authorities are out of step with contemporary life. The continuing revelations of the pedophilia scandals (priests sexually abusing children) engulfing a number of Catholic parishes and the subsequent cover-ups by church officials have turned many away from Catholicism. The prohibition on marriage of priests is, in large part, the cause of a drastic reduction in the number of priests (an average of one for every 1,400 Catholics with an average age of nearly 60) (Kristof, 2005). The Catholic and some other traditional churches have also lost credence with some people for their refusal to accept women in leadership roles. This patriarchal emphasis by some churches, however, is a positive attraction for some individuals.

An interesting recent development has been the defection of many Latino Catholics to Evangelical Protestant denominations, as noted earlier. There are several reasons for this shift away from traditional membership patterns. First, the emotional power of the evangelicals appeals to many Whites and Latinos alike. Second, evangelical churches often provide a sense of community and social services sometimes lacking in Catholic churches. Third, Latino Catholics often find linguistic and cultural barriers in the church. Only 2 percent of Catholic priests (fewer than 2,000), for example, are Latino. Meanwhile, the Southern Baptists, to name just one evangelical denomination, have 2,300 Latino pastors and 500 more in seminary training. Finally, critics charge that Latino Americans suffer various forms of discrimination within the U.S. Catholic Church. These charges include the failure of the church hierarchy to encourage religious vocations among Latino Americans, a hesitancy to elevate Latino priests to higher posts, and a reluctance to accept rituals meaningful to Latinos, such as devotions to the Virgin of Guadalupe.

The Rise of Christian Fundamentalism

Beginning in the late 1960s, there has been a rise in Christian fundamentalism. Although there are variations among fundamentalists, they share four central features. First, there is a personal relationship with Jesus brought about by being born again and a repentance of sins. This personal experience is reflected in a believer's daily life. Second, there is an emphasis on evangelism, a responsibility to convert others to their faith. Not only is this an effort to change individuals, it also includes an intense wish to bring the wider culture back to its religious roots, to restore the Christian character of American society. A third feature of fundamentalism is the belief that every word of the Bible is literally true. Scripture, thus, provides an exact description of history and absolute moral truths. Moreover, it provides prophecy of future world events. Fourth, fundamentalists are true believers separate from those who do not take the Bible literally. As holders of certain truth, they reject religious pluralism.

There are two categories of fundamentalists—evangelicals and pentecostals. Evangelicals emphasize a personal relationship with Jesus, public declaration of their faith, and spreading the faith to nonbelievers. Pentecostals share these beliefs with fundamentalists and also emphasize the active presence of the Holy Spirit in their lives and church services. Their church services are very emotional (crying, laughing, shouting, applauding, waving arms, moving about) with special emotional experiences involving faith healing and "speaking in tongues."

Both of these strands of religious fundamentalism are growing rapidly in the United States and worldwide. This growth caught many religious observers and sociologists by surprise, because they assumed that modernizing societies undergo processes that tend to make religion increasingly irrelevant to the affairs of society (Lechner, 1989). What, then, are the reasons for this unforeseen rise?

The most obvious reason that fundamentalists are increasing in number is their great emphasis on converting other people to their faith. They stress this activity because Christ commanded, "Go ye into all the world and preach the gospel to every creature."

Second, fundamentalist congregations emphasize community. The people are friendly, accepting, and caring in a world that for many people is unfriendly, rejecting, and uncaring. Thus, fundamentalists tend to provide for many people the ingredients they find missing in the mainline churches and in the other impersonal bureaucracies of which they are a part.

Third, fundamentalists offer the truth. They believe intensely that they are right and other people are wrong. In a society characterized by rapid change and a plurality of ideas and too many choices, many people seek authority, a foundation to provide consistency and constancy in their lives. Fundamentalists provide a rigid set of beliefs based on the infallibility of the Bible as the word of God.

A fourth appeal of fundamentalists is their insistence that society has made wrong choices and that we must go back to laws and customs based on biblical truths. For example, in keeping with their reading of the Bible, the Southern Baptists declared at their 1998 convention that a woman should "submit herself graciously" to her husband's leadership and a husband should "provide for, protect and lead his family" (Niebuhr, 1998). Thus, fundamentalism offers not only a critique of modern society but also an action program based on its set of absolute beliefs.

Fifth, evangelicals appeal directly to youth and young adults. The approach to people is warm rather than aloof (parishioners and clergy are more apt to hug). The buildings, lighting, staging, and music are contemporary. Compare evangelical music, for example, with that found in mainline churches. Instead of hymns and organ music, there is music of praise, music with a beat with guitars and drums.

Sixth, some of these churches have become huge (the Lakewood megachurch in Houston has 47,000 regular attendees).[*] There are about 2,000 of these **megachurches** (with at least 2,000 in attendance each week). Typically, they are found in the Sun Belt, in the suburbs around sprawling cities such as Atlanta, Dallas, Houston, Phoenix, and Los Angeles. They are theologically conservative and evangelical but the message is a more generalized "feel-good" theology.

> The megachurches are studiously nondenominational, run by CEOs and businesspeople who avoid pentecostal riffs and sulfuric eschatology. Instead they market a feel-good Jesus. They preach to people's "felt needs" and personal problems, trying to be relevant to their lives, as might any self-help organization. They establish small affinity groups to boost self-esteem and foster a sense of belonging. They hold seminars on "God's Plan to Make You a Winner." (Parenti, 2010:107)

Their growth is fueled by entertaining church services (fast-paced, scripted productions, with high-energy music, dramatic skits, and sermons with real-life applications), a number of services during the week, cafes, bookstores, sports facilities, child care, youth programs, and movies, and specialized ministries for targeted groups (elderly, newly divorced, parents of teenagers, Vietnamese immigrants, compulsive eaters) (Fitzgerald, 2007; Keilholtz, 2008).

Finally, fundamentalists have increased their popularity through an emphasis on modern marketing techniques (for example, direct-mail advertising, radio, television, and social media). This type of ministry, which is particularly effective in reaching the disabled and the elderly, began with the advent of radio in the 1920s and expanded greatly with the growth of television in the 1950s and 1960s, cable television in the late 1970s, and satellite transmission in the 1980s.

The Spread of the Evangelical Message via Savvy Marketing

Many religious leaders have become entrepreneurs using contemporary marketing techniques and various forms of the media to reach millions and to make millions. Let's look at a few examples.

- Pastor Joel Osteen of Houston's Lakewood's megachurch is the largest church in the United States with 47,000 attending a Sunday service in 2010, a staff of 350, and a multimillion-dollar budget. Each week seven million watch his sermon on national cable and network channels, bringing in about $70 million a year. His book *Your Best Life Now* sold 2.5 million in its first year and was on *USA Today*'s Best-Selling Books list for 125 weeks. In 2005, the congregation moved into the newly renovated 18,000-seat complex at Houston's Compaq Center. The $90 million remodel features two waterfalls, three large television screens, and a state-of-the-art lighting system.
- Willow Creek Community Church in suburban Chicago has a $48 million budget and $143 million in assets and 427 employees. Its bookstore brings in $3.2 million; its

---

[*]As large as this church is it pales in comparison with the world's largest megachurch, Yoido Full Gospel Church in Seoul, South Korea. This church has 830,000 members, rising by 3,000 a month (*Economist*, 2007).

Rick Warren, pastor of a megachurch in Southern California is the author of the fastest-selling nonfiction book of all time—The Purpose-Driven Life.

restaurants another $2.5 million; and its auto repair has revenue of $1 million. An arm of the church, the Willow Creek Association, provides consulting services for other churches, running workshops and conferences on Willow Creek's methods for creating effective services. The pastor of Willow Creek, Bill Hybels, started with a congregation of 125 in 1975; today he attracts about 23,400 people to its weekly services.

- Rick Warren, pastor of Saddleback Church, a Southern California megachurch, launched a book, *The Purpose-Driven Life*, which has sold about 35 million copies worldwide to become the fastest-selling nonfiction book of all time. This book has been taught in 20,000 churches in 162 countries, and translated into twenty-five languages. The marketing tool identified evangelical pastors who would take their church members on a forty-day period of spiritual reflection that the book recommends. Weekly attendance, which was 250 in 1980 is now about 22,000, with over 100,000 on the Saddleback Church's membership roles.

- Creflo A. Dollar (his actual family name) presides over the World Changers Church with its annual budget of $80 million. He is a leading proponent of the "Prosperity Gospel," along with many others including Kenneth Copeland, Benny Hinn, Joyce Meyer, and Joel Osteen. This is the belief that "Poverty is just a matter of bad faith and negative thinking. God wants us to be wealthy, but only our prayers and offerings can unleash his power" (Bilger, 2004:70). Or, as Pastor Mac Hammond of the Living Word Christian megachurch in Minneapolis preached "you can never have too much money. ... God's highest and best is that your whole life becomes a reflection of His abundant provision" (quoted in Putnam and Campbell, 2010: 326).

Contemporary Christianity and Politics

Religious organizations are sometimes organized for political action. The National Council of Churches, for example, tends to take liberal political positions on social issues, while the Christian Coalition supports far-right causes and candidates. Political concerns tend to unite fundamentalist churches, while the membership of many mainline churches is split on political issues.

The Religious Right

Fundamentalists and evangelicals believe that they live in a society that is suffering from a moral breakdown. The family is no longer stable with both spouses working outside the home and a high divorce rate. Crime is rampant. The public schools give away condoms but will not allow Bible study. The media promote sexual promiscuity, violence, and drug use. Abortion is legal. Gays and lesbians openly espouse what the Religious Right considers a sinful lifestyle. Thus, they fight for practices consistent with their biblical view of the Christian family and the Christian society. The political beliefs that emanate from this view are described by sociologist Sara Diamond:

> [The political beliefs of the Christian Right have a] consistent yet contradictory pattern. That is that the right, typically, [these are generalizations] supports state institutions or government institutions or government action when the role that's being played is what I call an "enforcer" role. So the right, for example, has historically supported U.S. military

intervention all over the world, until fairly recently; supports, under the rubric of "law and order," very tough law enforcement, draconian measures, even, draconian police power, even violations of people's civil liberties. Also, the right typically supports what they call a "traditional morality," a religiously-derived code of behavior and therefore supports a very strong role for the state in regulating, if not outlawing abortion, access to contraception, sex education; and wants the government to maintain sodomy laws.

At the same time the right is anti-government, rhetorically, at least, when it comes to the state's role as distributor of wealth and power. The right does not want the government to be active in terms of anti-poverty programs, spreading the wealth more equitably throughout society via the tax structure, or through funding various welfare programs. (quoted in Barsamian, 1996:36–37)

The Religious Right has become especially politically energized recently by what they feel is a move away from the Christian roots of the United States. The courts, composed of judges with lifetime appointments, have been responsible, in their view, for this shift. Since the 1960s, court decisions have ruled against prayer in schools, against religious displays in public spaces, and have made abortion legal. With two Supreme Court vacancies in 2005, conservative religious leaders aggressively pressured President George W. Bush to appoint replacements compatible with their views, which he did.

The Religious Right is a social movement with a network of leaders and organizations. There is Pat Robertson's Christian Coalition, James Dobson's Focus on the Family Action (the political arm of Focus on the Family), Beverly LaHaye's Concerned Women of America (which promotes traditional roles for women), Donald Wildmon's American Family Association (which opposes pornography), Robert Simond's Citizens for Excellence in Education, Phyllis Schlafly's The Eagle Forum, and Gary Bauer's Family Research Council. But the Christian Right is as much a political force as a religious movement. Its organizations use their bloc voting and substantial financial resources to support politicians (almost always Republicans) who share their religion-based agenda and to influence the positions of the Republican Party (nationally and in each of the states). They also organize cadres of church-based workers as volunteers to disseminate political information to people most likely to be compatible with their religious and political views. Also, the Christian Coalition actively works to defeat candidates who they feel hold what they believe to be antibiblical positions.

The Religious Right has had a powerful influence in U.S. politics since the early 1980s. It became a powerful wing of the Republican Party and evangelicals remain the largest single voting bloc. Kevin Phillips argues that during this period "The Republican Party [became] the first religious party in U.S. history" (Phillips, 2006:21). But by 2008, the influence of the Religious Right was beginning to wane and its favored policies to shift. Jerry Falwell, founder of the Moral Majority, was dead. Other leaders of the movement such as Pat Robertson, James Dobson, and Phyllis Schlafly were in their seventy's and being replaced by younger pastors with more nuanced politics. While still focused on anti-abortion and antigay marriage, the New Religious Right is, while not liberal, somewhat more progressive (Kuo, 2008). A poll of 1,000 evangelicals by Beliefnet. com found that 60 percent identified themselves as part of a political

movement interested in protecting the environment, tackling HIV/AIDS, helping the poor, and promoting human rights; they were less interested in identifying with those opposed to abortion and homosexuality (reported in Kuo, 2008). Another poll by *Relevant*, a magazine targeting evangelicals under twenty-five, asked respondents prior to the 2008 election who they believed "Jesus would vote for," and a plurality said Democrat Barack Obama. Cameron Stang, *Relevant*'s founder and publisher, says that "young Christians simply don't seem to feel a connection to the traditional religious right. Many differ strongly on domestic policy issues—namely issues that affect the poor—and are dissatisfied with America's foreign policy and the war" (cited in Kuo, 2008:26). In other words, there appears to be a generational shift among the Religious Right toward a kinder, gentler, conservatism (Moser, 2008; Pinsky, 2006).

The Role of Mainline Churches: Comfort or Challenge?

The political activism among fundamentalists is different from that found in mainline churches. The difference is that while fundamentalist congregations are relatively homogeneous in religious and political ideologies, mainline congregations are much more pluralistic. This pluralism places the clergy in a precarious position, a dilemma brought about by the two contradictory roles (analogous to the order and conflict approaches to the social order) of the church—to comfort the afflicted and to afflict the comforted (or to comfort and to challenge). The comforting role is one of aiding individuals in surmounting trials and tribulations of sickness, the death of loved ones, financial woes, and social interaction with family, neighbors, colleagues, or enemies. The church helps by such means as pastoral counseling and collecting and distributing food and clothing to the needy. Another way the church comforts the afflicted is through providing a rationale for suffering (theodicy), the consequence of which is sanctification of the status quo.

Three related criticisms of the comforting function are immediately apparent. First, some would say that the church (and the clergy) has allowed this function to supersede the other role of challenger. Second, if the church would do more challenging and less comforting, human suffering would be reduced. By helping people to accept an imperfect society, the church preserves the status quo—that is, the injustice and inequality that caused the problems in the first place. In this way, religion is an "opiate of the masses" because it persuades them to accept an unjust situation rather than working to change it from below. Third, the comfortable will not feel guilty, thereby preventing them from working to change the system from above.

The other function of the church—to challenge—is the injunction to be an agent of social protest and social reform. The church, through its pronouncements and leadership, seeks to lead in the fight for social justice. A fundamental problem is in winning the support of the members. Change is almost by definition controversial, because some people benefit under the existing social arrangements. When the church takes a stand for or against patriarchy, abortion, same-sex marriage, war, or the abuses of business or labor, some members will become alienated. They may withdraw their financial support or even leave the church. The church, of course, has a commitment to its members. Because it cannot afford to lose its membership, the church may compromise its principles. Such an action, however, may make other members angry at the church because of its hypocrisy. Consequently, the church is in the unenviable position of trying to maintain a precarious balance between compromise and purity.

Of course, the clergy vary in their interpretation of the role of the church. They are truly people in conflict. There are conflicting expectations of the clergy from all sides (resulting in **role conflict**). The church hierarchy expects the clergy to behave in a particular way (consider the rules issued by the Catholic hierarchy, such as celibacy and absolute obedience to authority). Most parishioners favor the comforting role. They want counsel in times of personal crisis. If poor, they want to be assured that they will be rewarded later, and if rich, they want their holding of wealth and power legitimized.

Although they are a minority in most congregations, some parishioners wish the clergy to take stands on controversial issues and work for social change. This wish puts their clergy in a bind because to take a public stand on controversial issues is divisive.

A final source of the clergy's role conflict arises from their own definition of the role. These various expectations, and the resulting role conflict of the clergy, amount to one reason they may drop out. Another is that if they take a stand (or do not), they may automatically alienate a segment of the parish and perhaps the church hierarchy. They may, consequently, be forced to resign.

Clergy who do not resign may solve their dilemma by being noncontroversial. This non-boat-rocking stance is all too familiar and results in another problem—irrelevancy. By ignoring social issues, one in fact legitimates the status quo. Hence, the inequities of the society continue, because the moral force of the churches is mainly quiet.

Not all clergy are content with the emphasis on comfort. As noted in the previous section, increasing numbers of clergy have become politically active on the moral issues of abortion, homosexuality, and pornography. Typically, though, this view of morality ignores the social problems of inequalities and injustices. Other clergy are not content to let the church continue to perpetuate injustice by not speaking and acting out. They are committed to a socially relevant church, one that seeks social solutions to social problems.

A recent trend appears to be a resurgence in religious activism on social issues, not only by religious fundamentalist groups opposed to such things as sex education in the schools, gay rights, and abortion, but also by the leadership in the mainline churches. The leaders in almost every mainline religious organization have gone on record as opposing the government's budget cuts to the disadvantaged, U.S. military aid to dictatorships, and the arms race. For example, the bishops of the Roman Catholic Church in the United States have formally challenged the fundamental assumptions and strategies of the U.S. defense system.

But political stands from the general leadership of a denomination are viewed quite differently than political activism by local ministers or priests. When local ministers or priests speak out, participate in marches, work for integrated housing, and demonstrate against the War in Afghanistan, many of their parishioners become upset. As a result, the socially active clergy often become objects of discrimination by their parishioners. Another consequence is that the laity trust their clergy less and less. As behavior in one area is questioned (for example, social activism), church members are likely to withdraw confidence in others as well. Finally, churches have divided on this issue. Some want social action instead of just pious talk. Others want to preserve the status quo. The hypocrisy found in many churches forces splits, the formation of underground churches, or total rejection of Christianity as the source of social action. Other members may leave because they feel that the church has wandered too far from the beliefs on which the faith was founded. This dilemma accelerates the current dropout problem among mainline churches—by parishioners and clergy alike. The problem seems to be that for the most part those who drop out are the social activists who leave the church with a residue of comforters. If this is the case, the future of the church is bleak unless there is a reversal, and prophets of social action ascend—an unlikely possibility, given the propensity of most parishioners for the message of comfort over the message of challenge. Meanwhile, the political message and action from the religious right unite and energize its clergy and followers.

Religion from the Order and Conflict Perspectives

As usual, order and conflict theorists view this social phenomenon—religion—very differently. Also, as is common, the unity and diversity found within this institution suggest that both models of society are partially correct.

Proponents of the order model emphasize the solidarity functions of religion. Religion helps individuals through times of stress, and it benefits society by binding people together through a common set of beliefs, reaffirmed through regularly scheduled ceremonial rituals.

Conflict theorists acknowledge that religion may unify in small societies, but in diverse societies religious differences divide. Religious conflict occurs commonly at all levels, however, from intersocietal religious warfare to schisms in local congregations. From the conflict perspective, religious unity within a society, if it does occur, has negative consequences. Such unity is used to legitimate the interests of the powerful (for example, slavery, racial segregation, conquest of pagans, and war; see Spong, 2005). Similarly, the interests of the powerful are served if the poor believe that they will be rewarded in the next life. Such a theodicy prevents revolutions by the oppressed and serves, as Marx suggested, as "an opiate of the masses."

CHAPTER REVIEW

1. Religion is socially created and has a tremendous impact on society. It is an integrated set of beliefs by which a group attempts to explain the meaning of life and death. Religion defines immorality and sin as well as morality and righteousness.

2. The consequences of religion are unity among the believers, conformity in behavior, and the legitimation of social structures. Religion also divides. It separates believers from nonbelievers, denominations, religions, and even the members of local religious groups.

3. Emile Durkheim, an order theorist, explored the question of why religion is universal. He reasoned that what any group worships is really society itself. The society is held together by religious rituals and festivals in which the group's values and beliefs are reaffirmed.

4. Karl Marx, a conflict theorist, saw religion as inhibiting social change by making existing social arrangements seem right and inevitable. Religion further promotes the status quo by teaching the faithful to accept their condition—thus, religion is the ultimate tool to promote false consciousness.

5. Max Weber, contrary to Marx, saw religious ideology as the catalyst for economic change. He demonstrated this with his analysis of the relationship between Calvinist ideology (predestination) and the rise of capitalism.

6. Civil religion is the belief that "God and country" are one. God is believed to have a special destiny for the United States. Order and unity are thus given religious sanction.

7. Although most people in the United States identify with Christianity, there is a wide of religious belief in U.S. society.

8. U.S. religious organizations can be divided according to their secular commitment into two categories. A church tends to compromise with the larger society, tolerates popular vices, and accepts a diversity of beliefs. A sect, in sharp contrast, rejects the world. It is a moral community with rigid ethical requirements and a narrow belief system.

9. A theodicy is a religious legitimation for a situation that otherwise might cause guilt or anger. Sects tend to have a theodicy of suffering, explaining their lack of power and privilege. Churches have theodicies that legitimate the possession of power and privilege.

10. A cult is a religious group that rejects the society and religions of the mainstream. It provides a new religious expression that some are willing to follow completely. A cult differs from a sect in one fundamental way. A sect results from a breakoff from an existing religious organization. The members do not seek a new religion but rather seek to recapture the true faith. Cults, on the other hand, represent a new religion. Most cults fail, but a few have become major religions.

11. There is a relationship between social class and religion: (a) The lower the social class, the greater the probability of belonging to a sect; (b) there is a relationship between social class and denominational affiliation (for example, the lower the social class, the more likely to be Baptist, and the higher the social class, the more likely to be Episcopalian); (c) the higher the social class of the member, the greater his or her involvement and influence in the local church.

12. Religious groups hold beliefs or behave in ways that support the racial, gender, and sexuality norms of society.

13. One trend is the decline in the mainline denominations. These churches are often bureaucratic and impersonal. Their beliefs are pluralistic. The Catholic Church is losing members because its stands against contraception and divorce are out of tune with contemporary life.

14. Another trend is the rise of Christian fundamentalism. The two categories of fundamentalists are evangelicals and pentecostals. They are alike except that pentecostal congregations are more emotional—personally experiencing the Holy Spirit. Fundamentalists are growing (while the mainline churches are declining) because they (a) emphasize evangelism; (b) tend to be friendly, accepting, and caring communities; (c) offer the truth based on the infallibility of the Bible; (d) offer a critique of modern society and a prescription for its change back to a God-centered society; and (e) use modern marketing techniques and radio and television.

15. The contemporary mainline Christian churches are faced with a basic dilemma brought about by their two contradictory roles—to comfort the afflicted and to afflict the comforted. The comforting function is criticized because it focuses on helping the individual but ignores the problems of society. The challenging function—the

injunction to be an agent of social protest and social reform—is criticized because it is divisive, alienating some members who disagree with the position taken. The evidence is clear that the majority of clergy is opting for the comforting function over the challenging function.

16. The order model emphasizes the solidarity functions of religion, which order theorists interpret as good.

17. From the conflict perspective, religious beliefs have negative consequences because they sanctify the status quo; that is, religion legitimates the interests of the powerful while also justifying the existence of inequality. Thus, revolutionary activity by the oppressed is suppressed by religion because it serves, as Marx suggested, as "an opiate of the masses."

KEY TERMS

Religion
Ritual
Opiate of the masses
Civil religion
Church

Sect
Charisma
Routinization of charisma
Charisma of office
Theodicy

Cult
Megachurches
Role conflict

STUDY QUESTIONS

1. What are the social consequences for a community of believers?
2. Explain the contradiction that religion is both a source of stability and a source of conflict.
3. Contrast the views of religion by Durkheim, Marx, and Weber.

4. Is religion generally supportive of existing class and gender hierarchies? Give evidence to support your position.
5. Explain the contrast in growth patterns by the mainline denominations and the more fundamentalist denominations.

WEB RESOURCES

http://durkheim.itgo.com/main.html
This page is the home of the Emile Durkheim Archive. It offers excerpts from Durkheim's work and some explanation on his theories, including those that he held on religion.

http://www.angelfire.com/or/sociologyshop/msor.html
This page offers a look at Karl Marx's theories on religion and how they pertain to the study of religion in sociology.

http://www.ne.jp/asahi/moriyuki/abukuma/
The Weberian Sociology of Religion page contains texts about religion written by Max Weber and links to other pertinent sites.

http://www.infidels.org/index.shtml
The Secular Web is "an online community of nonbelievers dedicated to the pursuit of knowledge, understanding, and tolerance."

http://www.religioustolerance.org/welcome.htm#new
For information on current and historical events in the news related to religion, as well as descriptions of different religions and links to other religion sites, visit ReligiousTolerance.org.

http://www.earlham.edu/~libr/acrlwss/wsstheo.html
Part of WSSLINKS, created by the Women's Studies Section of the Association of College and Research Libraries, this site has links to websites that are generally related to women and religion, as well as those that pertain to specific religions, including Christianity, Judaism, and Buddhism.

http://www.calltorenewal.com/about_us.html
Call to Renewal is a faith-based group attempting to overcome racism and poverty.

http://www.barna.org
This is the website for the Barna Research Group. This group specializes in research on religious issues.

http://www.parishioners.org/
This site provides information on various religious issues.

http://www.princeton.edu/~nadelman/csar/csar.html
This is the site for the Center for the Study of American religion. It has links to many other sites for the study of American religion.

http://www.igc.apc.org/culturewatch
Culture Watch provides information about the Religious Right in the United States.

Human Agency: Individuals and Groups in Society Changing Social Structures

The Sociological Paradox: Social Structure and Agency

Sociology is the study of all things social. This book, focusing on the societal level, emphasizes the social context and the social forces that so strongly affect human behavior. As sociologist Peter Berger (1963) says (as quoted in Chapter 1): "Society not only controls our movements, but shapes our identity, our thoughts and our emotions. The structures of society become the structures of our own consciousness. Society does not stop at the surface of our skins. Society penetrates us as much as it envelops us" (121).

This **deterministic** view is too strong, however. While society constrains what we do, it does not determine what we do (Giddens, 1991:863). While society and its structures are powerful, the members of society are not totally controlled. We are not passive actors. We can take control of the conditions of our own lives. Human beings cope with, adapt to, and change social structures to meet their needs. Individuals, acting alone or with others, can shape, resist, challenge, and sometimes change the social institutions that impinge on them. These actions constitute human agency. This chapter focuses on the macro dimensions of agency—that is, those collective actions that change and overcome societal constraints.

The paradox of sociology—the power of society over its members versus the power of social actors to change society—has several important meanings and implications (see Chapters 1 and 2). Foremost, society is not a rigid, static entity composed of robots. People in interaction are the architects of society in an ongoing project; that is, society is created, sustained, and changed by people.

Second, the social forms that people create often take on a sacred quality—the sanctity of tradition—that constrains behavior in socially prescribed ways. The sociological insight is, to restate the previous point, that what many consider sacred and therefore unchangeable is a social construction and can, therefore, be reconstructed.

A third implication is that since social structures are created and sustained by people, they are imperfect. There are positive and negative consequences of the way people have organized. Many are content with the status quo because they benefit from it. Others accept it even though they are disadvantaged by it. But there are also those who seek change to improve it or, perhaps, to change it completely. They are the agents of change.

In sum, the essence of agency is that individuals through collective action are capable of changing the structure of society and even the course of history. But, while agency is important, we should not minimize the power of the structures that subordinate people, making change difficult or, at times, impossible.

This chapter is divided into two major parts. The first is conceptual, considering social movements, the collective and organized efforts of human actors to change society. This section describes the types of social movements and the conditions under which they succeed or fail. The second part is illustrative, providing two case studies of agency—the civil rights movement and the movement to bring gender equity to sport—and a third case of the potential for a massive social movement now.

Social Movements

Individuals seeking to change social life in some way are limited in what they can accomplish by themselves. We need to join with others who share our goals, if we are to have any hope of success. Sociologists Kenneth Kammeyer, George Ritzer, and Norman Yetman (1997) show the importance of social movements if we are to be effective agents of change:

> As individuals, we are limited in our ability to make the societal changes we would like. There are massive social forces that make change difficult; these forces include the government, large and powerful organizations, and the prevailing values, norms, and attitudes. As individuals going to a voting booth, we have minimal power. As individuals protesting to officials, we have minimal power. As individuals standing against the tide of public opinion, we have little hope of exerting influence. As individuals confronting a corporate structure, we are doomed to frustration and failure. But if we combine with others who share our convictions, organize ourselves, and map out a course of action, we may be able to bring about numerous and significant changes in the social order. Through participation in a social movement, we can break through the social constraints that overwhelm us as individuals. (632–633)

Individual actors seeking change typically join with others for greater power to become part of a social movement. A **social movement** is a collective attempt to promote or resist change. These movements arise when people are sufficiently discontented that they will work for a better system. Hence, social movements are inherently political because they seek to affect public policy. A social movement is a goal-directed effort by a substantial number of people. It is an enduring organization with leaders, a division of labor, an ideology, a blueprint for collective action, and a set of roles and norms for the members (see Blumer, 1951; Smelser, 1962). Although money and organizational skills are important, ideology is the key to a movement's success. The ideology provides the goal and the rationale for action, binds diverse members together in a common cause, and submerges individuals to the movement. An **ideology** is a set of ideas that explains reality, provides guidelines for behavior, and expresses the interests of a group. An ideology may be elaborate, such as Christianity, Marxism, or capitalism. Such an ideology provides a consistent framework from which to act and believe on a number of issues. Or the ideology may be narrowly aimed at one side or the other on issues such as animal rights, abortion, protection of the environment, capital punishment, gun control, gay rights, U.S. involvement in preemptive war, nuclear energy, universal health insurance, pay equity, living wage, and welfare. For each of these issues, groups on either side have an ideology that explains their position, provides the goal, brings members together, and offers a compelling argument used to recruit new members.

Types of Social Movements

Three types of social movements are political in nature: resistance movements, which are organized to prevent changes; reform movements, which seek to alter a specific part of society; and revolutionary movements, which seek radical changes.

One type of social movement—**resistance movements**—is explicitly organized either to resist change or it is reactionary in that it seeks to reverse changes that have already occurred and restore "traditional values."

Because periods of rapid change foster resistance movements, there are numerous contemporary examples of this phenomenon. There are current efforts to stop the trend toward the use of nuclear power for energy. People have organized to stop the damming of rivers or the logging of forests because they want to protect the environment. The move by feminists to make the Equal Rights Amendment part of the Constitution was met with considerable organized resistance, even from women. Antiabortion groups have formed to reverse legislation and judicial acts that make abortion legal or easy to obtain. Evangelicals in a number of communities have organized to pressure school boards to reverse school policies that they consider opposite to Christian principles. As examples, they oppose the teaching of evolution and seek to have the schools also teach creationism or intelligent design. They want prayer in the schools. They want Christian symbols in public spaces. They oppose the teaching of sex education (unless it teaches abstinence exclusively). They oppose same-sex marriage.

Gallows with handicapped ramp

Reform movements seek to alter a specific part of society. These movements commonly focus on a single issue, such as women's rights, gay rights, or global warming. Typically, there is an aggrieved group such as women, African Americans, Native Americans, gays, people with disabilities, farmers, or workers that focuses its strategy on changing the laws and customs to improve its situation (see the Human Agency panel titled "The Political Muscle of Americans with Disabilities"). At various times in U.S. history, oppressed groups have organized successful drives to change the system to provide more equity. The civil rights movement of the 1950s and 1960s provides an example. Another example is the student movement in the late 1990s to eliminate foreign sweatshops that produce goods that bring profits to U.S. colleges and universities (see the Globalization panel titled "Students against Sweatshops").

The third type of social movement—the **revolutionary movement**—seeks radical changes. Such movements go beyond reform by seeking to replace the existing social institutions with new ones that conform to a radically different vision of society. The bottom-up uprisings in various Middle East countries are clear examples of revolutionary social movements. Similarly, throughout Eastern Europe, new nations have been created out of the former Soviet Union and its satellites. These nations, newly independent, have adopted new forms of government and new economies that are drastically different from what they had in the previous fifty years. These changes have dramatically changed all areas of social life.

The Life Course of Social Movements

Social movements move through predictable stages. For a movement to begin, it must attract members. Usually there is some societal condition—institutional racism, institutional sexism, economic depression, war, an immigration wave, the passage of a controversial law or court decision, technological change—that threatens or harms some segment of society. As William Sloan Coffin wrote, "You cannot have a revolt without revolting conditions" (Coffin, 2004:62). This causes social unrest, but it is unfocused.

The second stage of a movement is when grievances become focused. A leader or leaders emerge who use ideology and charisma (extraordinary personal attributes) to define the central problem(s) they face, and to challenge and inspire followers to join in a common quest to change society for the better. Sometimes there are individuals whose acts of personal courage, such as provoking the powerful, or getting jailed, injured, or killed, serve to coalesce the previously unfocused. This is especially important in an age of instant communication, in which public attention is centered on the charismatic leader's message and personal valor, the heroism of martyrs, the repressive acts by authorities, the terrorism of those opposing

The Political Muscle of Americans with Disabilities

The disability rights movement began in the late 1960s. In 1972, Disable in Action with 1,500 members, organized protests targeted at inaccessible public buildings, the Jerry Lewis telethon (which they believed perpetuated demeaning stereotypes of people with disabilities), and media organizations that either neglected or provided prejudicial coverage of disability issues). They also blocked traffic in front of Richard Nixon's 1972 New York campaign headquarters to protest his veto of the Rehabilitation Act. Congress did pass the Rehabilitation Act of 1973, which prohibited government agencies and contractors from discrimination against people with disabilities. Other favorable legislation also passed during the 1970s, in keeping with the politics of the times.

Following the election of Ronald Reagan in 1980, the political climate changed for disability rights activists. The 1980s were characterized, in general, by weakened federal requirements, reduced budgets, deregulation, and unfavorable judicial decisions.

In 1989, Congress passed historic legislation to protect the civil rights of people with disabilities. This bill, the Americans with Disabilities Act, extends to people with disabilities the same protections against discrimination that were given to African Americans and women in the 1960s and 1970s.

Some 20 percent of people in the United States have some form of impairment (more than 55 million). About 5 percent of people with a disability were born with it, 85 percent will experience a disabling condition in the course of their lives, usually from accidents, disease, environmental hazards, or criminal victimization (Russell, 2000). This category of disability includes a wide range of people, such as people with mental retardation, paraplegics, the blind, those with cerebral palsy, and those with AIDS, and those with Alzheimer's disease.

Before the Americans with Disabilities Act became law with President George H. W. Bush's signature in 1990, people with disabilities faced discrimination in jobs, social situations, and transportation. The new law prohibited stores, hotels, restaurants, and theaters from denying access to people with disabilities. Employers could no longer reject qualified workers just because they are disabled. Moreover, employers had to modify the workplace to make it accessible to their workers with disabilities. Public buildings under construction or undergoing remodeling now must be made accessible to wheelchair users under the new legislation. So, too, must public transportation vehicles be equipped with lifts to accommodate wheelchair users. Finally, telephone companies must now have operators who can take messages typed by deaf people on a Telecommunications Device for the Deaf and then relay it orally to a hearing person on another phone.

The sweeping 1989 victory for people with disabilities was won despite the contrary efforts of many in the business community who argued that the provisions were too costly to businesses. Success was achieved over this considerable opposition through a number of means. Foremost, people with disabilities have developed a common identity (class consciousness) through a shared outrage at the discrimination they experience. Now, instead of feelings of isolation, feelings of a common bond and empowerment have emerged among the disabled. Many became active in what became known as the disabilities movement. Some of these people joined advocacy groups; others joined together to use tactics of civil disobedience, such as disrupting public transportation or blocking access to city hall, in order to make their plight more visible. In one celebrated case, the students at Gallaudet University, a college for the deaf, protested the selection of a hearing president in 1988. They refused to go to classes and occupied the administration building, eventually forcing the newly appointed president to resign and the governing board to appoint the university's first deaf president.

The 1989 Americans with Disabilities Act victory was also fueled by increased numbers of people with disabilities, including people with AIDS and the aged, and people who had become disabled with Alzheimer's, blindness, deafness, arthritis, and other ailments. With the realization that about one-fifth of Americans have disabilities, politicians have found it difficult to vote against them. As a cohesive group, people with disabilities have considerable potential political clout. Their growing sense of a shared condition and common identity has made their voting as a bloc on certain issues more likely than ever. The result has been, finally, legislation guaranteeing their civil rights.

Sources: The content of this essay has been taken from a number of sources, especially De Parle, 1989; Eitzen, Baca Zinn, and Smith, 2011; Johnson, 1991; Russell, 1998; 2000; and Shapiro, Joseph, 1989:chapter 11.

the movement, and the continuing inequities in society on which the movement is centered. This is a critical stage when those in similar situations realize that others share their feelings of discontent, anger, or injustice and that together they can make a difference. They begin to acquire a collective identity and a sense of common purpose. It is a time of excitement over the possibilities for collectively bringing about needed social change.

The third phase involves moving toward organization. Resources (money, equipment, and members) are mobilized. A formal organizational structure is developed with rules, policies,

Students against Sweatshops

The collegiate apparel industry generates $4.0 billion annually, with each university receiving a share of the sales using its logo on sweatshirts, caps, and other items. Each university sells its right to use the logo to the Collegiate Licensing Corporation, a trademark company that acts as an agent for Nike, Champion, and Reebok and more than 200 universities involved. Major universities earn several million dollars annually from these sales.

Students on a number of campuses have taken this opportunity to indicate to the world that they do not want their universities engaged in enterprises that manufacture clothing made in foreign sweatshops. Investigations of the production of Nike footwear in Asia found, for example, that:

75 to 80 percent of Nike workers were women, mostly under the age of twenty-four, who regularly put in ten- to thirteen-hour days, worked six days a week, and were forced to work overtime two to three times per week; worker abuse by supervisors was widespread. The typical worker earned around 50 percent of the wage that governments considered as meeting "minimum physical needs"—meaning subsistence for a single adult worker in a given country. (Sage, 2010:119)

Looked at another way, a baseball cap with a university logo selling retail for $19.95, for example, earns the university $1.50, while the worker in the Dominican Republic who made it earns eight cents (Capellaro, 1999).

To right the injustices accompanying sweatshops and the complicity of U.S. corporations and universities in these injustices, students on a number of campuses have battled to ensure that collegiate apparel is made under humane conditions. The students used various tactics: Students at the University of Michigan occupied a dean's office for a three-day "sweat-in"; students at the University of Arizona blocked an administration building for an afternoon; students at the University of Wisconsin, Madison, defied the use of pepper spray and night sticks by campus police to sit-in at the chancellor's office; students at Purdue held an eleven-day hunger strike; at Yale, forty students engaged in a "knit-in," doing needlework in the center of

campus; at Holy Cross and the University of California at Santa Barbara, students held mock fashion shows, lecturing on sweatshops while parading down the catwalk; at Harvard, 350 students held a rally, as did 250 at Princeton, to demand that their schools not use sweatshops to create merchandise; and students at the University of North Carolina held a nude-optional party titled "I'd Rather Go Naked Than Wear Sweatshop Clothes." Students at other colleges and universities circulated petitions, picketed college bookstores, and launched websites calling for "sweat-free" clothing. These protests were coordinated through United Students against Sweatshops, which was founded in 1997 and in 2009 had chapters on more than 250 college and university campuses in the United States and another 200 campus organizations worldwide (Sage, 2010:123). As a result of these protests, individual universities have changed their policies. Duke University, for example, notified Nike and other licensees of Duke products that they must disclose to the school the locations of their factories or Duke would not renew their contracts (similar demands were made by the University of Wisconsin, Madison; the University of Michigan; and Georgetown University). The presidents of various universities agreed to the demands of student activists and, in turn, demanded the monitoring of factories independent of industry influence (through the Worker Rights Consortium) that make college-name apparel, full disclosure, living wages, and women's rights guarantees.

The social movement initiated by students against sweatshops in the garment industry eventually enlarged its goals to include worker struggles in other industries and to struggle against racism, sexism, homophobia, classism, and other forms of oppression. The thrust was to bring justice to workers who were being exploited in the global economy.

Clearly, students acting collectively on their campuses have been and continue to be change agents from the bottom up, changing the policies of their universities and those of corporations to create more humane working conditions for those who labored to make profits for those universities.

and procedures to be followed. Power is centralized and levels of organization are delineated. Strategies are formed to confront the authorities, attract new members, and keep older members energized. Alliances may be formed with other groups with similar goals (allowing them to share computerized mailing lists of likely contributors or new members, and the like). In short, this is a bureaucratization (or formalization) stage when a once unfocused number of people now have become an organization. Where once leadership was charismatic, it is now composed of administrators and managers (this is called the routinization of charisma).

The final stage occurs if the movement is successful. If so, the movement becomes integrated into society. The goals of the movement have been accomplished. This is the stage of **institutionalization**. While this is the goal of the social movement, this stage has its dangers. A common danger is **goal displacement**. This occurs when the goal of maintaining the formal structure of the movement's organization supersedes the original goals of the social movement. Another threat involves power struggles within the movement, which divert effort from the common goal. Finally, and related to the last point, success can lead to the leadership elite using its power to keep power and the extraordinary status and rewards that come with that power. In effect, then, "organizational success and its consequences can corrupt the original goals of the movement" (Hess, Markson, and Stein, 1993:596).

Agency: Social Change from the Bottom Up

Often the people lead and the leaders of government and business follow. Harlan Cleveland (1992) states:

> The tidal waves of social change of our lifetimes—environmental sensitivity, civil rights for all races, the enhanced status of women, recognition of the rights of consumers and small investors—were not generated by the established leaders in government, business, labor, religion, or higher education. They boiled up from people (and new leaders) who had not previously been heard from. (16)

This section provides two case studies in which the efforts of seemingly powerless individuals and groups changed powerful social structures. The first case involves the centuries-long struggle by African Americans to obtain the civil rights due all citizens. The second case study is of the specific situation in which recent actions by individuals and groups have brought significant changes moving toward gender equity within athletics.

The Civil Rights Movement

Many believe that the civil rights movement began when Rosa Parks was arrested for not giving up her seat to a White man on a bus in Montgomery, Alabama, in 1955, and a successful bus boycott followed. The civil rights movement is not the result of one event but the "inevitable outcome of centuries of mistreatment of black people by white people and their governments" (Powledge, 1991:xi). Or, as Vincent Harding (1981) puts it, the movement is long and continuous,

> flowing like a river, sometimes powerful, tumultuous, and roiling with life; at other times meandering and turgid. ... The river of black struggle is people, but it is also the hope, the movement, the transformative power that humans create and that create them, us, and makes them, us, new persons. So we black people are the river; the river is us. The river is in us, created by us, flowing out of us, surrounding us, re-creating us and this entire nation. (xix)

Africans were brought to this country as slaves and as slaves they were exploited, demeaned, and kept powerless (this section is taken in part from Berry, 1994; Harding, 1981; Powledge, 1991; Zinn, 1980). The laws and the customs permitted the oppression of the slaves:

> Beginning in Virginia at the end of the 1630s, laws establishing lifelong African slavery were instituted. They were followed by laws prohibiting black-white intermarriage, laws against the ownership of property by Africans, laws denying blacks all basic political rights. ... In addition, there were laws against the education of Africans, laws against the assembling of Africans, laws against the ownership of weapons by Africans, laws perpetuating the slavery of their parents to African children, laws forbidding Africans to raise their hands against whites even in self-defense. ... [The laws] outlawed many rituals connected with African religious practices, including dancing and the use of drums. In many places they also banned African languages. Thus they attempted to shut black people out from both cultures, to make them wholly dependent neuters. (Harding, 1981:27)

Despite the oppressive control of Blacks and the severe punishments for their violations of the laws and customs, many African men and women struggled against the domination of

White power. Some engaged in individual acts of rebellion. Some ran away, heading north. At times, Black fugitives formed small guerrilla bands, creating bases from which to harass neighboring plantations and places to which others might flee. These fugitives (known as *outlyers*) were very significant to the oppressed. Their existence meant that the apparently total institution of slavery was actually not all-encompassing. Most important, "the outlyers represented a hidden, submerged black power that the masters could not break. They were a radical presence, challenging blacks and whites alike" (Harding, 1981:40). For those who remained in bondage, some chose to resist, using such tactics as refusing to learn how to use a tool without breaking it, work slowdowns, persistent noncooperation, arson, and even poisoning.

Around 1800, Blacks constituted about 20 percent of the U.S. population. Of the 1 million, 900,000 were held in legal slavery. In that year, Gabriel Prosser and forty other slaves were executed for daring to revolt against their masters. This insurrection and the punishment ushered in a period of some thirty-five years of intensified slave rebellions. Efforts to escape also escalated, as the chances for success increased with the Underground Railroad, a network of Blacks and Whites who smuggled thousands of slaves to the North. Among the slaves who stayed behind, agency took many forms such as keeping African traditions, fighting to keep family ties, maintaining community solidarity, and creating their own rituals that recognized marriage and parenthood. Summarizing the pre–Civil War situation for Blacks, historian Vincent Harding (1981) states:

> [The slave community] was not a community caught in the flatness of despair. It was not a
> community without hope. It lived with brutality, but did not become brutish. Often it was
> treated inhumanely, but it clung to its humanity. There was too much in the river [Harding's metaphor of the cumulative effects of the Black struggle, see p. 531] which suggested
> other possibilities, announced new comings, and hurled restless movements against the
> dam of white oppression. Always, under the surface of slavery, the river of black struggle
> flowed with, and was created by, a black community that moved actively in search of
> freedom, integrity, and home—a community that could not be dehumanized. (74)

After the Civil War, the Emancipation Proclamation, and the passage of the Thirteenth, Fourteenth, and Fifteenth Amendments to the Constitution, Blacks were freed from slavery and given certain rights. But while they were technically free, they remained oppressed. One form of oppression—slavery—was lifted, only to be replaced by other modes of oppression—economic slavery through low-wage jobs and sharecropping arrangements with landowners, and being treated as inferiors by Whites. In the 1880s, the average wage of Black farmworkers in the South was about fifty cents a day. They were usually paid in "orders," not money, which could only be used at a store controlled by the landowner. The sharecropper had to borrow from the store to get the seed to plant the crop. "When everything was added up at the end of the year he was in debt, so his crop was constantly owed to someone, and he was tied to the land, with the records kept by the planter and storekeeper so that the Negroes are swindled and kept forever in debt" (Zinn, 1980:204).

Despite these roadblocks, there was more freedom than before, and many Blacks found ways to reinforce their liberty such as hunting with guns, driving carriages, meeting with other Blacks in public places, forming political unions, changing their names, asserting their rights to Whites, and omitting the long-standing and deeply understood signs of inferior status:

> One of the most significant movements toward the definition of freedom came as black
> families all over the South made a momentous decision to withdraw their women from the
> full-time agricultural labor force. In many cases children moved out of the role of full-time
> field hands as well. Everywhere in slavery's former domain, black families were openly
> declaring the autonomy they had fought so hard to develop and maintain under the old
> regime; they were establishing their right to decide who should work and how. Now mothers
> and wives were often free to give more attention to their own families and work; children
> could attend the schools now being created at great cost by blacks and their white allies.
> (Harding, 1981:282)

421

CHAPTER 18
Human Agency:
Individuals and
Groups in Society
Changing Social
Structures

White violence toward Blacks escalated in response to the behavioral changes of the former slaves. The Ku Klux Klan and local vigilante groups used raids, lynchings, beatings, and burnings to intimidate Blacks. The courts were much more likely to send Blacks to prison than Whites. And in the penitentiary system of the South, there were beatings, chain gangs, and forced labor as contractors purchased their labor cheaply (Blackman, 2008).

The Black Codes were laws passed by Southern states and local governments to keep Blacks "in their place." These codes were intended to keep Blacks from achieving equality, to control Blacks, and to keep Blacks bound to jobs and land controlled by Whites. Although the laws varied from state to state and city to city, the patterns were essentially the same. There were restrictions against land ownership or rental by Blacks. There were vagrancy laws insisting that Blacks have lawful employment. In South Carolina, for example, a vagrant could be sentenced to a year of hard labor and be hired out to an individual. The laws created harsh penalties against Black workers who broke contracts with landowners or other employers. Other laws placed severe restrictions on the kinds of work that Blacks could do. In effect these laws meant that Blacks were subjected to many special punishments that did not apply to Whites. "The patterns were clear: in almost every situation having to do with black-white relationships, freedom of movement, freedom of choice in jobs, a personal sense of independence, and control over their own families, the Black Codes were the slave codes revived" (Harding, 1981:314).

Moving to the early twentieth century, a rigid system of segregation emerged in the South, where interaction between the races as equals was denied. These "Jim Crow" laws (supported by an 1896 U.S. Supreme Court decision *Plessy v. Ferguson*, which justified the principle of "separate but equal") meant that all public facilities in the South such as restaurants, restrooms, schools, and public transportation could be segregated. Nevertheless, African Americans often banded together to fight injustice, share resources, and maintain control over their lives. The National Association for the Advancement of Colored People (NAACP) was founded in 1909, and the National Urban League began a year later. Both fought for civil rights in public opinion and in the courts, but with little success until after World War II.

The military was segregated during World War II, although defense industries were prohibited from discrimination based on racial differences (by executive order of President Roosevelt). Toward the conclusion of the war, the Black press and a few Whites in the media pushed for integration, arguing that since Blacks had fought in the war for the principles of equality, freedom, and democracy, they should have the same rights.

Shortly after World War II, the NAACP challenged the concept of separate but equal schooling in the courts. This effort was rewarded in 1954 when the Supreme Court ruled in *Brown v. Board of Education of Topeka, Kansas*, that "separate educational facilities are inherently unequal." This ruling was resisted in the South by the Ku Klux Klan, White citizens councils, mayors, school boards, and governors.

In addition to this momentous court decision, two events in the next year galvanized Blacks into a mass movement that ultimately changed race relations in the United States. The first incident was the lynching of Emmitt Till in Mississippi. Till, a fourteen-year-old African American from Chicago, was visiting relatives. To show off to his cousins, he violated the unwritten code of conduct for Blacks in the rural South by making a "smart" remark to a White woman. The woman's husband and brother-in-law kidnapped Till from his uncle's house. Later, young Till's mutilated and lifeless body was found in a river. In court, Till's uncle identified the two men who took his nephew from his house (the first time in Southern history that a Black man accused Whites of a felony crime in court). Despite this heroic act, the all-White jury found Till's murderers not guilty (who later admitted, with pride, that they had killed him).

The second case involved the jailing of a Black woman, Rosa Parks, in Montgomery, Alabama, for not giving her seat on a bus to a White man as was the custom fortified by the law (the following is adapted from Eitzen and Stewart, 2007:1–3). This simple act of civil disobedience by one courageous person set off a chain of events that changed the South. Following Parks' arrest, more than 5,000 people packed a church and passed a resolution backing a bus boycott. A leader emerged, a young local minister, Martin Luther King, Jr., who inspired African Americans to use nonviolent resistance to overthrow their oppressors and their unfair laws and practices.

The immediate target was the segregated public bus system. Over 40,000 Blacks boycotted the transportation system for 381 days, walking to work or using a carpooling network. The city eventually abolished segregation in public transportation—a clear case of agency, as the powerless successfully changed an unfair system.

Under King's leadership, Blacks along with White sympathizers mobilized to desegregate other public facilities. There were sit-ins in restaurants, waiting rooms, and churches, and wade-ins at public beaches. Economic boycotts were organized. Court cases were initiated. Brave students became the first African Americans to integrate schools. And there were protest marches to publicize grievances. These efforts were violently resisted by Whites. King and others were jailed. Demonstrators were abused verbally and physically. Lynchings took place, the most infamous being the murder by Klansmen of three civil rights workers in Mississippi. Birmingham police got involved when the commissioner, "Bull" Conner, ordered the police to disperse protesters with fire hoses, clubs, and police dogs, an event watched by millions on television. Drive-by shootings and other forms of intimidation were attempted to keep Blacks from registering to vote.

However, King's reform movement was bent on tearing down the segregationist norms and values and substituting new ones. To a limited, but nonetheless significant extent, the movement succeeded. Schools were desegregated with the help of federal troops. The 1964 Civil Rights Bill banned discrimination in public facilities, education, employment, and in any agency receiving government funds. The 1965 Voting Rights Act prohibited the use of literacy and similar tests to screen voting applicants and allowed federal examiners to monitor elections.

But the civil rights movement has not completely achieved equality. As noted in various parts of this text, considerable residential segregation occurs in the North and the South, many schools remain racially segregated, African Americans have less spent on their education than Whites, Black unemployment is twice that of Whites, wages are considerably less for Blacks, the poverty rate for Blacks is triple that of Whites, racial discrimination continues in the loans business, and the economic position of Black women is far worse than that of White women.

In short, while civil rights battles have been won, the war for equality is still being fought in legislatures, in the courts, in school districts, and in neighborhoods. As before, individuals and groups are taking agency seriously, working to change institutional racism in all its forms.

Civil rights leaders lead an estimated 10,000 followers in their Selma to Montgomery march. This and other peaceful tactics by those in the Civil Rights Movement led to the downfall of the Jim Crow South.

Gender Equity in Sports

In the last century or so, women have made several significant advances. The courts have ruled that women are not the property of their husbands. Women now own property. Women vote. Women serve on juries. Women are now elected to public office. In each case, women fought against a patriarchal social order where it just seemed "natural" for men to have the power (Kuttner, 1996). The battles for gender equity are ongoing, especially regarding equal employment and promotion opportunities and the acceptance of women in leadership roles (religion, government, education, corporations). One of the most recent, interesting, and successful battles for gender equity has occurred in sports—the case study described here.

Historically, sport has been a male preserve (this section is dependent on a number of sources: Coakley, 2007:chapter 8; Eitzen, 2012; Sage and Eitzen, 2013:chapter 14; Malec, 1997). When women did participate, they were ignored by fans and the media, trivialized (given team nicknames such as the "Wildkittens" or the "Teddy Bears")

(Eitzen and Baca Zinn, 1989a), or demeaned for being "masculine" or lesbians. Thus, sport was (and is) an institution that contributes to and perpetuates male dominance in society (Hall, 1985).

With a few exceptions, U.S. sport in the early 1970s was for men and boys. At that time, *Sports Illustrated* writers Bil Gilbert and Nancy Williamson (1973) said: "There may be worse (more socially serious) forms of prejudice in the United States, but there is no sharper example of discrimination today than that which operates against girls and women who take part in competitive sports, wish to take part, or might wish to if society did not scorn such endeavors" (90).

Compare this statement with the situation now. U.S. women have been celebrated for their successes in recent Olympic Games. Female professionals in tennis and golf are on television and highly rewarded for victories. Now professional leagues for women are found in basketball, soccer, and other sports. At the collegiate level, schools with successful teams, especially in basketball, are given strong fan and media support (in a few cases more than for the men's teams). In 1972, women athletes received a total of $100,000 in athletic scholarships. Now, more than 150,000 women play college sports and share more than $400 million a year in scholarships, yet men receive more than $227 million in athletic financial aid than women. About 15,000 women are employed in intercollegiate athletics as athletic directors, coaches, trainers, or sports information directors (Acosta and Carpenter, 2009). At the high school level, just one girl in twenty-seven (less than 300,000) participated in interscholastic competition in 1971. Now, more than 3.17 million girls participate (still 1.3 million fewer girls than boys). Youth sports now have girls' teams, and some have boys and girls playing on the same teams, in sharp contrast to a generation ago when many youth sports programs had formal policies excluding girls from any participation.

These important changes were not initiated by the powerful—by the federal government, state governments, the National Collegiate Athletic Association, the various state high school associations, local school boards, Little League Baseball, or other youth sports organizations. The changes came about because of a wider social movement for women's rights and the acts of individual parents, athletes, and groups who challenged patriarchal tradition, laws, and the policies of various athletic and school organizations. As a result of their acts of agency, sport has been changed so that "the next generation of sportswomen will likely find equality in athletics so ordinary and natural that they could forget where it came from" (Kuttner, 1996:5).

The 1960s and early 1970s were a time of societal upheaval. Rebellion was ubiquitous. The powerless (for example, racial minorities, people with disabilities, gays, and lesbians) challenged discriminatory laws and practices. Students confronted school administrations about their archaic and paternalistic practices. Young people contested the government's war in Southeast Asia. Rather than be drafted to serve in a war they did not believe in, some young men fled to Canada and others chose jail. Youth defied traditions and the materialistic ways of their parents and the older generation. In this time of insurgence, insubordination, defiance, and reforms, the women's movement took root. Actually, women had fought for equality for a hundred years or more, but in the 1960s the movement gained many followers and significant momentum. There were intellectual strands such as Betty Friedan's *The Feminine Mystique* (1963), which argued for an all-out effort to remove the obstructions that had restricted women's access to equal opportunities in society. Feminist intellectuals argued also that girls and women are enhanced as human beings when they are given the opportunities to become competent intellectually and physically. The women's movement also redefined occupational and family roles for women, providing them with increased time and resources for other pursuits.

Organizations emerged, such as the National Organization for Women (NOW), with branches throughout the United States. This organization was instrumental in promoting progress in women's sports in two major ways. First, it asked local organizations to gather information about the differences for boys and girls and men and women in local schools and community programs (number of teams, participants, budgets, equipment, and facilities). This provided a national database for proposed legislation and court cases, as well as information for each participating community so that strong arguments for equity could be made before school boards or the courts. Indirectly, this survey was important because local women learned about the inequities of their communities firsthand and thus were likely candidates for more activist responses later.

425

CHAPTER 18
Human Agency:
Individuals and
Groups in Society
Changing Social
Structures

The second contribution of NOW was its lobbying effort for national legislation to correct gender inequities. Armed with national data, women as individuals and as members of women's groups applied pressure on political representatives. After two years of intense lobbying, Congress passed Title IX of the Educational Amendments of 1972, which declared, "No person in the United States shall, on the basis of sex, be excluded from participation in, be denied the benefits of, or be subjected to discrimination under any educational program or activity receiving federal financial assistance."

Title IX was resisted vigorously by the male establishment in athletic organizations and schools as being too radical, impractical, and burdensome. As a result, enforcement in the early years was sporadic at best. There was a setback in 1984 when the Supreme Court in *Grove City v. Bell* ruled that Title IX did not apply to school athletic programs because they did not receive federal monies directly (even though the schools did). Congress made Title IX stronger in 1988 with the passage of the Civil Rights Restoration Act (over President Reagan's veto), which mandated equal opportunity to all programs in any organization receiving federal money. Most significant, the U.S. Supreme Court ruled that schools could be sued for financial damages if the schools had intentionally violated Title IX.

Court cases have been used throughout the struggle for gender equity in sports. Regarding youth sports, in 1973 Little League Baseball's ban against participation by girls was challenged and overturned in several lawsuits by individual parents. As a result, the various youth sports have permitted female participation.

At the high school level, lawsuits have been brought by girls and their parents against school districts or state high school regulatory bodies. Typically, these cases involve one of three situations: (1) a girl wishing to participate on a boys' team because her school did not provide a girls' team (the courts generally ruled in favor of the girl in these cases); (2) a girl wanting to be on a boys' team even though her school provided a girls' team (the courts generally ruled against her in this type of case because equal opportunity had not been denied to her); and (3) girls wanting equality with a boys' team in a particular sport (Sage and Eitzen, 2013). As an example of this last situation, Nebraska settled four class-action lawsuits in 1996, agreeing that high schools must provide girls' softball with facilities and equipment equal to boys' baseball (Pera, 1996).

Gender inequity in intercollegiate athletics has been challenged officially in two ways (Sage and Eitzen, 2012). Since the passage of Title IX, thousands of complaints have been filed on behalf of women with the Department of Education's Office of Civil Rights. In addition, dozens of lawsuits have been filed against colleges and universities because of gender inequity. For example, in 1992 Colorado State University (CSU) dropped several sports, including the women's softball team, because of budgetary constraints. Nine members of the softball team filed suit against CSU, claiming the university violated Title IX. The Colorado Supreme Court ruled that CSU had to reinstate women's softball. In another case, the California chapter of NOW filed a sex-discrimination lawsuit against the California State University system in 1993, claiming that only 30 percent of its participants in sports are women and that women's sports receive less than 25 percent of the athletics budget. Within a year, the California State University system agreed to increase significantly its athletics opportunities and finances for women. In 1994 after five years of litigation, a U.S. district court, reacting to a suit brought by female athletes at Brown University, ordered that the school reinstate women's gymnastics and volleyball teams and provide "equal treatment" to women's athletics. In 1998 a federal court approved a settlement that Brown had reached, agreeing to maintain women's athletics participation within 3.5 percent of women's enrollment at the university and to increase spending on four women's sports.

Aside from the courts, there are other challenges by women to the male-dominated system of athletics. Some female athletes compete with men in the traditional male sports of football and wrestling. There are a few female coaches of men's teams. There are also female athletic directors (even a few at NCAA Division I schools), female sportswriters, and a few women umpires and referees. In each instance, these women invaded a male domain, and, as a result, they have often encountered hostility, disrespect, and various uncooperative actions from men. But by crossing traditional gender boundaries, these pioneers are extremely important players in this struggle for gender equity.

The past forty years have seen dramatic changes in sports opportunities for women and girls. Participation is way up. Public interest in women's sports is growing rapidly. The number of sports for girls and women offered by schools has risen dramatically. Budgets, resources, and facilities are enormously better. Gender equality in sport, however, is still a goal, not a reality. For example, women in Division I colleges, while representing 53 percent of college student bodies, receive only 45 percent of the participation opportunities, 34 percent of the total money spent on athletics, 45 percent of the total scholarship dollars, and 32 percent of the recruiting dollars (National Women's Law Center, 2011). Men's football is the culprit, since it has been allowed to be exempt from the accounting. It is not uncommon for a school with a big-time football program to spend twice as much on its men's football team as it spends on all women's sports. A second area of concern is the decrease, since Title IX, in the proportion of women's teams with women in leadership positions (the number of men exceed the number of women as head coaches and top administrator of women's athletics) at both the high school and college levels. Third, media attention is not equal. The argument by television networks and newspapers is that they give the public what they want, and the public wants male sports. This, of course, is a self-fulfilling prophecy. Fourth, opportunities in sports careers (professional sports, sports journalism, athletic trainers, referees) for women still lag behind the opportunities and rewards for men. Fifth, female athletes, especially those involved in sports requiring strength and aggression, continue to battle stereotypes, because they do not conform to the dominant cultural definitions of femininity.

So, despite dramatic and positive changes, sport is still contested terrain for those wishing to achieve gender equity. Continued acts of agency, collectively and individually, are required if the positive trend is to stay on track.

Is There Hope for a People's Social Movement Now?

U.S. society is fragmented and in danger of pulling apart (Eitzen, 2011). There is a declining trust in societal institutions, especially in an economy that does not supply enough jobs at a living wage and a polity that is increasingly undemocratic; increasing walls between the affluent and the poor; a polarization in politics and in the media that makes compromise nearly impossible; and an ever widening inequality gap. These problems have been highlighted throughout this book. The question is: Is there any ray of hope that somehow we can achieve a society that is fair and democratic, and where all citizens have a sense that everyone is pulling together for the common good?

There are reasons for cautious optimism. An examination of U.S. history reveals examples of when the federal government acted boldly and with public support to overcome serious social problems. In effect progressive change occurred from the top down.

Over 100 years ago, the Progressive movement began as a reaction to unchecked capitalism, the robber barons, economic exploitation, and political corruption. Out of the Progressive Era emerged an activist government led by a Republican, President Teddy Roosevelt, that addressed problems of the workplace—safety regulations, prohibition against child labor, mandating the eight-hour workday, and providing disability compensation. The government broke up business monopolies, established a national parks system, and allowed women the vote.

The government responded to the near collapse of the market economy in the Great Depression eighty years ago by regulating banks and stock markets, initiating federal welfare programs (Aid to Families with Dependent Children and Social Security), and by funding massive public works to provide jobs and infrastructure.

As a final example, after World War II, about seventy years ago, the government instituted large-scale federal investment with strong public support such as the interstate highway system, the space program, the GI Bill (education and low cost mortgages for veterans), and Medicare.

Each of these examples of federal activism for the public good had strong public support. Are we ready to support progressive legislation now, against the wishes of current political leaders and the money from special interests?

427

CHAPTER 18
Human Agency:
Individuals and
Groups in Society
Changing Social
Structures

The problem with top-down solutions is that they rely on the powerful to give up some of their power, and they allow people to be relatively passive, waiting for a leader to inspire and lead. The more positive solution lies with an active citizenry pushing for change from the bottom up. The late historian Howard Zinn's book *A People's History of the United States* (1980), shows over and over how oppressed and aroused Americans organized at various times to change the system with success, most notably the women's suffrage movement, various labor struggles and strikes that resulted in major advances for workers in safety, wages, and benefits, and the civil rights movement that brought positive changes for racial/ethnic minorities, women, and gays. See A Closer Look panel titled "The Paradox of Social Progress and Economic Reaction."

A populist movement, known as the Tea Party, emerged during the Great Recession and the election of President Obama. It was antigovernment, reacting to the government's response to the economic collapse with bailouts to the powerful. Its philosophy is libertarian, holding individual rights and freedom as its supreme values and that the government is the prime obstacle to personal liberty (Wallis, 2010). Their "bible" is Ayn Rand's *Atlas Shrugged*, first published in 1957, which held as primary: individual rights, low taxes, and very limited government. Thus, they oppose, for example, universal health care, the redistribution of wealth, and the government regulation of businesses.

The Tea Party movement is a loose confederation of national and local groups with no central leadership, with protests occurring at both levels, focusing on taxes and government intrusion into the lives of citizens. The 2010 elections reflected the power of the movement with 140 candidates running (as Republicans) with Tea Party support (130 running for the House and 10 for the Senate). About one-third of these candidates won—forty new House members and five Senators with Tea Party support. The Tea Partiers in the House changed that body with increased resistance to compromise. Significant also, was that in several Republican primaries, incumbent moderates were defeated by doctrinaire Tea Partiers, thus further eroding cooperation in Congress.

What are the chances of change from the people based on progressive changes and an active role of government in solving social problems?

Is there any chance of change from the bottom up now? There are a number of forces converging that have the potential for heightened massive unrest—the potential spark for a people's social movement. First, the gap between the wealthy and the rest of is greater than ever. In the past thirty years workers' wages have stagnated while the wealthy have experienced huge gains. Second, the Congress continues to benefit the already rich with tax shelters, loopholes, and other subsidies in return for contributions. In effect, we have the best Congress money can buy. Those with little or no money have no political power. Third, when the Great Recession occurred in late 2007 the banks were bailed out while the little people were not. The perpetrators of fraud went free while the victims experienced bankruptcy and foreclosures. Now businesses want more subsidies and even less government oversight. Fourth, the 2010 election resulted in a Republican landslide and efforts by the winners to impose their ideological agenda. The solution offered by the winners was to weaken unions, slash benefits for the poor and the old, and provide more subsidies for business and the affluent. In particular, new Republican governors in Wisconsin, Ohio, Maine, Florida, and Michigan waged an all-out battle against unions, but also against women (reproductive rights), gays (opposition to gay marriage), and immigrants. Fifth, the union busting efforts caused many to coalesce against them. There have been massive demonstrations, recall efforts against anti-worker politicians, and a significant loss of public support for these newly elected officials. Many working class White males have switched sides. Thirty years ago they left the Democratic Party for the Republicans and thus, were called "Reagan Democrats." But now many are seeing that the Republican Party works against the interests of working people and they are moving back to the Democrats. Sixth, the Republicans are trying to squash efforts to increase voting by the poor and ethnics (groups that tend to vote Democrat). They oppose automatic registration along with driver's licenses. They want voters to show photo IDs. They especially fear the Latino vote, which likely will be reduced by the redistricting (gerrymandering) that will be controlled by mostly Republican governors and Republican-dominated legislatures. Seventh,

The Paradox of Social Progress and Economic Reaction

Robert Kuttner

New York state became the sixth state to legalize same-sex marriage. In 2012 President Obama affirmed his support of gay and lesbian unions. This issue is becoming more of a decisive headache for Republicans than a theme to rally their base. Time is not on the right's side, either, because sexual orientation is just less and less of a big deal for younger voters.

Sunday's *New York Times* gave three whole pages to a Father's Day story about an extended family made up of a mom, her toddler, the lad's donor dad and his gay partner. In a few more years, this story would be no more newsworthy than a piece about how divorced and remarried straight couples and their children manage complex relationships that go well beyond traditional nuclear families.

It's worth reflecting on two questions. First, how did we make such stunning progress in three decades on issues involving tolerance and inclusiveness? And how is it that, during the same period, we have gone steadily backwards on a whole set of economic issues? The society has become more inclusive in according rights to women, African-Americans, the Lesbian, Gay, Bisexual, and Transgender community, people with disabilities—and far more unequal and precarious economically.

This is not to say, of course, that the struggles for tolerance and inclusion are over. Bigotry still persists; it is especially vicious when it comes to immigrants. And immigrant rights issues connect to economic issues. At a time of dwindling opportunity and security, immigrants, who can easily be exploited and compelled to work for less than their economic worth, are sometimes seen as an economic threat to the locals.

Still, to invoke Dr. King, there is little doubt that the arc is bending toward justice. The momentum is in the direction of more acceptance, less bigotry.

So, what happened? It's not as if homophobia and racism were exactly pushovers.

The entire social order based on white privilege was very handy if you happened to be caucasian. Blacks did all the scut work and they did it for cheap wages, reserving the good jobs for white folks. Likewise, male privilege: very convenient for men. And gays and lesbians were the last group who could be openly ridiculed even in polite liberal company.

What happened, simply, was political struggle—and from the bottom up. To review the various documentaries commemorating the 50th anniversary of the sit-ins and freedom rides is to appreciate the sheer impossibility of the odds, and the extraordinary personal bravery. To challenge the racist order, especially in the south was to risk economic ruin and death. Feminists and gays were the object of scorn. Disability rights were not even on the radar screen. Individual acts of gays coming out slowly engendered compassion. The HIV epidemic moved from an object of disgust to one of empathy.

But these individual acts of heroism only gained traction because they combined with a social movement. They changed norms, then laws, which reinforced the shift in norms.

Slowly, we have become a kinder, more inclusive society.

Why, then, are we going backwards when it comes to economic justice? It comes down to power. Owners of financial wealth have become more and more politically powerful, while the countervailing movements have become steadily weaker.

I recently wrote about the bravery of the housekeeper at the Times Square Sofitel who reported the assault by Dominique Strauss-Kahn. But she could take this step without fear because she was not alone. The Times Square Sofitel, like nearly every one of New York's large hotels, is unionized. And the union, Local 6 of the hotel and restaurant workers, backed by a powerful hotel and motel trades council, is one of the strongest local unions anywhere in America—not strong because of union bosses, but because the union is intrinsic to the daily life of the workplace.

When the manager of the Sofitel balked at letting some housekeepers join a vigil in support of their colleague on the morning that Strauss-Kahn was to be arraigned, workers at the hotel told him they would suspend their jobs and sit down in his lobby. He quickly relented.

A housekeeper in a non-union hotel would think twice about complaining about an assault from a rich and powerful guest. She could get fired. In the "hospitality" industry, by definition, the guests come first. But members of Local 6 are protected by a contract that requires due process, and a whole system of shop stewards called union delegates who assure that rights are enforced.

A housekeeper at a non-union hotel in much of America makes eight or nine dollars an hour. In Manhattan, a union housekeeper makes almost $25 an hour, or $50,000 a year, enough to live a middle class life, even in New York. The difference between a living wage and a starvation wage affects the client's hotel bill by a few bucks.

There is no good reason why all people in service occupations, from Wal-Mart clerks to nurse aides and pre-k teachers, can't be paid a living wage. But this will take political struggle and social movements—just as progress in the battles for inclusion did.

As bankers call the tune in both parties, and as the economy becomes more precarious for the working middle class, the political base of a just society needs to be rebuilt from the ground up. For all the hopes we've placed in the Obama administration, it won't be built from the top down.

Source: Robert Kuttner. 2011. "The Paradox of Social Progress and Economic Reaction," *Huffington Post* (June 19).

around 25 million Americans are unemployed or working part-time but want to work full-time. With just one job available for every five people looking for work, many of these people have been unemployed for a long time. Eighth, over 21 percent of sixteen—twenty-four year-olds are unemployed. Their outlook is bleak. The odds are that they will be downwardly mobile from their parents. It's not their fault; society as it is currently structured has let them down. Finally, events in the Egypt, Libya, Syria, and elsewhere in the Middle East reveal how the powerless gain power through social movements. These countries had been ruled by despots for generations without a revolution. But now, extreme social inequality, high unemployment especially among the young, and continuing poverty provided the conditions for social unrest, leadership emerged, and the powerless came together in part because of social media and the young.

These forces combine for a world class recipe for social unrest. Together they constitute the structural conduciveness (necessary preconditions) for a social movement. Two additional ingredients are required: First, there must be a massive public outrage over the unjust system. That seems to be building. Second, there needs to be a precipitating event that brings people together in a social movement. This spark may have come from the newly elected extreme conservatives who have overreached when they attacked public workers (teachers, firefighters, police, and social workers). Perhaps it is the budget plan to reduce the federal debt by Representative Paul Ryan that would ultimately eliminate Medicare, while simultaneously lowering taxes for the wealthy. Or, it may be the retention of the massive George W. Bush tax cuts for the wealthy while cutting programs for Women, Infants, and Children, Food Stamps, and other programs for the needy. Have these actions tipped the scales, generating outrage?

In 2010 newly elected Republicans governors and Republican-dominated legislatures passed legislation that was anti-union, opposed women's reproductive rights, and was punitive toward recent immigrants. These efforts spawned organized protests.

So, is there hope? Consider the humble beginnings of the civil rights movement. A young preacher in Birmingham, Martin Luther King, Jr., organized a protest that began when Rosa Parks refused to give her seat on a bus to a White man and ended in a Supreme Court decision ending the segregation of public transportation. A few courageous Blacks sat in a segregated Woolworth's restaurant in Greensboro, North Carolina, and two weeks later sit-ins spread to fifteen cities. These and other efforts such as the Freedom Riders, brought down the Jim Crow laws of the South, and ended in the 1965 Voting Rights legislation. It can be done. And, it was done from the bottom up.

Not all social movements are successful. But some are. Working together with other like-minded folks in a massive social movement, the people can challenge the unequal arrangements and thereby stitch our torn societal quilt back together. History shows that such movements can succeed.

Conclusion

This book is an introduction to sociology. The primary purpose was to make you more perceptive and more analytical regarding things social. Our hope is that you will build on this knowledge in a lifelong quest to understand society and your place in it.

The theme of this last chapter is the importance of human beings in constructing and reconstructing society. This has two important implications for each of us. First, we do not have to be passive actors who accept society's institutional imperatives as inevitable. To the contrary, we can be actively engaged in social life, working for the improvement or even radical change of faulty social structures. Second, the personal is political. While there are broad political struggles within society that involve us, politics also occurs at the micro level. Issues of social justice may be present in our work situations, at church and other organizations to which we belong, in our neighborhoods, in our families, and in our personal relationships. We can promote social justice in these situations or thwart it. In each instance, our actions have political implications.

At the macro level, the most important struggles involve overturning existing structures of exploitation and domination. These include collective efforts to bring about universal programs for greater equality such as universal health care, pensions, equal opportunity education, and expanding and upgrading the societal infrastructure (highways, bridges, water supply, airports, mass transit). New family forms require programs such as paid parental leave and a national system of dependent care. The changing economy requires management-labor cooperation to increase productivity while providing fair wages and protecting job security, job safety, job training, and collective bargaining rights. Issues of social justice involve progressive taxation (the more money made, the higher proportion paid in taxes), pay equity, and programs to guard against race, gender, and sexuality biases in employment, housing, and lending practices.

In sum, society's structural arrangements are not inevitable. Individuals converging across lines of race, ethnicity, gender, and sexual orientation can work at the grassroots level organizing opposition, educating the public, demonstrating to promote a cause, electing allied candidates, using the courts, or employing other tactics to transform society. Human beings are agents of change if they choose to be. The choice is ours.

Frances Fox Piven (1996), the eminent social scientist, in writing about the need for social change to solve social problems, says: "No one has ever successfully predicted the movements when ordinary people find their footing, discover new capacities for solidarity and power and new visions of the possible. Still, the development of American democracy depended on the perennial emergence of popular revolt in the past, and it does once again" (67).

CHAPTER REVIEW

1. The sociological paradox is that while society has power over its members, social actors have the power to change society. This means that (a) society is not a rigid entity, composed of robots; (b) what people consider sacred, and therefore unchangeable, is a social construction that can be reconstructed; and (c) since social structures are created by people, they are imperfect, always in need of reform or transformation.

2. A social movement is a collective attempt to promote or resist change.

3. There are three types of social movements: (a) resistance movements, which are organized to resist change or to reverse changes that have occurred; (b) reform movements, which seek to alter a specific part of society; and (c) revolutionary movements, which go beyond reform by seeking the transformation of the entire society.

4. Social movements move through predictable stages. Initially, a number of people share feelings of discontent or anger over some societal condition. The second stage is when the grievances of these people become more focused. A leader emerges who defines the goals, identifies the enemies, and challenges and inspires followers to work together for positive change. The followers are further galvanized as their target is provoked

and the powerful attack them. Stage three involves organization, with formal rules, policies, procedures, and tactics. Alliances are formed with similar groups for mutual advantage. When the goals of the movement are accepted by society, the movement has arrived at the final stage, institutionalization.

5. The point of social movements and individual acts of agency is that institutional changes tend not to come from the leaders of government and business, but rather boil up from the people.

6. The civil rights movement did not begin in the 1960s, but rather from the time Blacks arrived here as slaves. Moreover, the civil rights movement is not the result of a single event. It carries the cumulative effects of centuries of mistreatment of Blacks by Whites and White governments.

7. Despite the oppressive control of Blacks, many of them exhibited agency by individual acts of rebellion, work slowdowns, and running away to join with others in bands that harassed Whites. Others fought the slave codes by promoting community solidarity, fighting to keep family ties, and creating their own rituals that recognized marriage and parenthood. After the Civil War, Blacks remained oppressed by low wages and sharecropping arrangements. Black Codes, laws that were biased against

Blacks, were passed to keep Blacks from achieving equality. Similarly, in the early twentieth century, Jim Crow laws enforced rigid segregation. Again, in the face of these indignities, Blacks engaged in various forms of agency.

8. The civil rights movement came together in the 1950s, with the passage of the Supreme Court decision desegregating the schools, the outrage of the lynching of Emmitt Till, and the Montgomery bus boycott. Sit-ins were organized. Economic boycotts against White businesses were initiated. Grievances were taken to court. The movement was partially successful, as segregationist laws and practices were soon abolished. Racial equality has not yet been achieved, however, as measured by wages, employment opportunities, unemployment rates, poverty rates, desegregated neighborhoods, and differences in money spent on education.

9. Before 1970, U.S. sport was almost exclusively for men and boys. However, as a consequence of court cases, individual acts of courage by women pioneers in sport as athletes, coaches, administrators, and referees; and the efforts of women's organizations, dramatic moves toward gender equity in sports have been accomplished. Archaic rules by athletic organizations prohibiting girls from competition have been overturned. Legislation, most prominently Title IX, was passed, giving impetus to greater participation by girls and women in school sports. Later rulings by the courts have given women greater equity in this previously male preserve. Full gender equity, however, has not yet been reached.

10. Society's structural arrangements are not inevitable. Individuals acting alone or with others in grassroots organizations can be agents of change.

KEY TERMS

Determinism	Resistance movements	Institutionalization
Social movement	Reform movements	Goal displacement
Ideology	Revolutionary movement	

STUDY QUESTIONS

1. What is the fundamental sociological paradox?
2. Provide contemporary examples (in the United States and worldwide) of the three types of social movements.
3. Using the case study of the civil rights movement (beginning with Rosa Parks), show how that movement has gone through the various stages of social movements.
4. What are the implications of this chapter's thesis—that human beings construct and reconstruct society?

WEB RESOURCES

http://www.wsu.edu:8001/~amerstu/smc/smcframe.html
The Social Movements and Culture website offers a listing of some of the major historical and current social movements.

http://www.selfadvocacy.com/
This is a website for the disability rights organization Advocating Change Together. It is "run by and for people with developmental and other disabilities" and is "committed to freedom, equality, and justice for all people with disabilities."

http://www.glaad.org/org/index.php
The Gay and Lesbian Alliance against Defamation website offers news related to gays and lesbians and proactive ideas for creating visibility and awareness surrounding the gay and lesbian community.

http://www.colorlines.com/
Produced by the Applied Research Center, Color Lines is the "nation's leading magazine on race, culture, and organizing."

http://civilrights.org/
Civilrights.org's mission is to "empower the civil rights community to lead the fight for equality and social justice in the emerging digital society through the establishment of an online social justice network."

http://www.thp.org/index.html
The Hunger Project is committed to ending world hunger. The organization has projects in many parts of the world.

http://www.cuadp.org/index.html
Citizens United for Alternatives to the Death Penalty is a grassroots activist group with the goal of ending the death penalty in the United States.

http://members.aol.com/rasphila/linkspage.html
This site is a comprehensive list of peace-related websites. It includes links to activist groups advocating for peace, as well as alternative media sources.

Accommodation. Acceptance of one's position in a situation without struggle.

Achieved status. A position in a social organization attained through personal effort.

Age cohort. Individuals from the same generation and thus affected by similar societal events such as an economic depression or war.

Ageism. Discrimination against the elderly.

Aggregate. A collection of individuals who happen to be at the same place at the same time.

Alienation. An individual's feeling of separation from the surrounding society.

Altruistic suicide. The sacrificing of one's life for the good of the group.

Androgyny. Having the characteristics of both males and females.

Anomic suicide. Durkheim's term anomie indicates a social condition characterized by the absence of norms or conflicting norms. At the individual level, the person is not sure what the norms are, which leads to a relatively high probability of suicide.

Anomie. A social condition characterized by the absence of norms or conflicting norms.

Anticipatory socialization. Learning and acting out the beliefs, norms, and values of a group before joining it.

Argot. The specialized or secret language peculiar to a group.

Ascribed status. Social position based on factors such as age, race, and family over which the individual has no control.

Assimilation. The process by which individuals or groups voluntarily or involuntarily adopt the culture of another group, losing their original identity.

Baby boom. A term referring to a fifteen-year period in U.S. history following World War II in which an extraordinary number of babies were born.

Bias theories. An explanation that blames the prejudiced attitudes of majority members for the secondary status of the minority.

Blaming the victim. The belief that some individuals are poor, criminals, or school dropouts because they have a flaw within them.

Bourgeoisie. Karl Marx's term for the class of people that owns the means of production in a capitalist society.

Bureaucracy. A system of administration that is characterized by specialized roles, explicit rules, and a hierarchy of authority.

Bureaucratization. The trend toward greater use of the bureaucratic mode of organization and administration within society.

Capital flight. The investment choices that involve moving corporate monies from one investment to another (for example, investments in other countries, plant relocation, and mergers).

Capitalism. The economic system based on private ownership of property, guided by the pursuit of maximum profits.

Capitalist patriarchy. A condition of capitalism in which male supremacy keeps women in subordinate roles at work and in the home.

Case study. The research strategy that involves detailed and thorough analysis of a single event, community, or organization.

Caste system. The closed system of social stratification. Membership is fixed at birth and is permanent.

Caveat emptor. The Latin phrase that means "let the buyer beware."

Charisma. The extraordinary attributes of an individual that enable the possessor to lead and inspire without the legal authority to do so.

Charisma of office. Instead of charisma based on personal attributes, in some organizations, the holder of a particular position is believed to possess charisma.

Church. The highly organized, bureaucratic form of religious organization that accommodates itself to the larger society.

Civil disobedience. A public, nonviolent breach of the law with the purpose of calling attention to unfair laws or practices.

Civil religion. The set of religious beliefs, rituals, and symbols outside the church that legitimates the status quo.

Class. Ranking in a stratification system based on economic resources.

Class conflict. Karl Marx proposed that the owners of capital are locked in conflict with exploited workers.

Class consciousness. Karl Marx's term that refers to the recognition by people in a similar economic situation of a common interest.

Class segregation. Barriers that restrict social interaction to the members of a particular social class.

Cloning. The artificial production of genetically identical offspring.

Cohabitation. The practice of two people living together as a couple without being married.

Commune. A small, voluntary community characterized by cooperation and a common ideology.

Compulsory heterosexuality. The system of sexuality that imposes negative sanctions on those who are homosexual or bisexual.

Conflict model. A view of society that posits conflict as a normal feature of social life, influencing the distribution of power and the direction and magnitude of social change.

Consensus. Widely held agreement on the norms and values of society.

Conspicuous consumption. The purchase and obvious display of material goods to impress other people with one's wealth and assumed status.

Constraint. The state of being controlled by some force.

Contingent Employment. Work arrangement where employees work for employers as temporaries or as independent contractors.

Contingent workers. Those involved in an employment arrangement in which employees work for an employer as temporaries or as independent contractors.

Control group. A group of subjects in an experiment who are not exposed to the independent variable but are similar in all other respects to the group exposed to the independent variable.

Co-optation. The process by which representatives of a potentially destabilizing subgroup are incorporated into the leadership or management level of an organization to avert problems.

Corporate crime. The illegal and/or socially harmful behaviors that result from the deliberate decisions of corporate executives in accordance with corporate goals.

Correlation. The degree of relationship between two variables.

Counterculture. A subculture that fundamentally opposes the dominant culture.

Crime. An act that is prohibited by the law.

Cult. A religion with practices and teachings at odds with the dominant culture and religion.

Cultural deficiency theories. Explanations which argue that some flaw in a social group's way of life is responsible for its secondary status.

Cultural deprivation. An ethnocentric term implying that the culture of another group is not only deficient but also inferior.

Cultural diffusion. The spread of one culture's characteristics to another.

Cultural relativity. The belief that customs of another society must be viewed and evaluated by their standards, not by an outsider.

Cultural tyranny. The belief that the socialization process forces narrow behavioral and attitudinal traits on people.

Culture. The knowledge that the members of a social organization share.

Culture of poverty. The view that the poor are qualitatively different in values and lifestyles from the rest of society and that these cultural differences explain continued poverty.

Deferred gratification. The willingness to sacrifice in the present for expected future rewards.

Deficiency theories. Explanations that view the secondary status of minorities as the result of their own behaviors and cultural traits.

Deflation. The part of the economic cycle when the amount of money in circulation is down, resulting in low prices and unemployment.

Deindustrialization. The widespread, systematic diversion of capital (finance, plant, and equipment) from investment in the nation's basic industries into service and knowledge sectors of the economy or overseas.

Democracy. The form of government in which the citizens participate in government, characterized by competition for office, public officials being responsive to public opinion, and the citizenry having access to reliable information on which to make their electoral choices.

Demographics. The scientific study of the size, composition, and changes in human populations.

Dependency ratio. The relationship between old-age Social Security recipients and those workers paying Social Security taxes.

Dependent variable. A variable that is influenced by the effect of another variable (the independent variable).

Deprogramming. The process in which people believed to have been brainwashed by cults are abducted and retrained against their will.

Derogation. Discrimination in the form of words that put a minority down.

Determinism. The belief that human behavior is controlled by some force, whether genetic, economic, or political. Taken to the extreme, deterministic theories leave no room for human beings to adapt to and change social structures to meet their needs.

Deviance. Behavior that violates the expectations of society.

Dialectic. The clash between conflicting ideas and forces.

Differential association. The theory that a person becomes deviant because of an excess of definitions favorable to the violation of societal expectations over definitions supporting the norms and values.

Direct interlock. A type of interlocking directorate in which an individual serves on the board of directors of two companies.

Direct social control. Direct intervention by the agents of society to control the behavior of individuals and groups.

Discouraged workers. People who have not actively sought work for four weeks. They are not counted as unemployed by the Bureau of Labor Statistics.

Discrimination. To act toward a person or group with partiality, typically because they belong to a minority.

Disengagement. The process of removing oneself from society.

Division of labor. The specialization of economic roles resulting in an interdependent and efficient system.

Documentation generation. Also known as the *Millennial Generation*. This group has been heavily documented by themselves and others on the Internet.

Dogma. Positive statements not based in fact; doctrine.

Dominant class. Domhoff's mode of power, which posits that the very wealthy in society contribute a disproportionate number of people to the controlling institutions and key decision-making groups.

Downward mobility. Decline in socioeconomic status by an individual or family.

Dual-worker marriages. Marriages in which a husband and wife are both employed outside the home.

Dysfunctions. Consequences that are disruptive for the stability and cohesion of the social organization.

Economic inequality. The gap between the rich and the poor.

Economy. The institution that ensures the maintenance of society by producing and distributing the necessary goods and services.

Egalitarianism. Fundamental belief in equality.

Ego. According to Freud, the conscious, rational part of the self.

Egoistic suicide. Durkheim's finding that people lacking ties to social groups are more susceptible to suicide than are those with strong group attachments.

Elitist model of power. The assumption that power is concentrated in a few, rather than dispersed (the pluralist view).

Emoticon. A sequence of computer keyboard characters that is meant to convey emotions or other messages.

Environmental racism. The disproportionate exposure of some racial group to toxic substances.

Epistemology. The philosophical position that all reality is socially constructed.

Ethnic group. A social group with a common culture distinct from the culture of the majority because of race, religion, or national origin.

Ethnicity. Shared cultural heritage.

Ethnocentrism. The universal tendency to deprecate the ways of people from other societies as wrong, old-fashioned, or immoral and to think of the ways of one's own group as superior (as the only right way).

Ethnomethodology. The subdiscipline in sociology that studies the everyday living practices of people to discover the underlying bases for social behavior.

Eugenics. The attempt to improve the human race through the control of hereditary factors.

Experimental group. A group of subjects in an experiment who are exposed to the independent variable, in contrast to the control group, which is not.

Falling rate of profit. One of the contradictions of capitalism argued by Karl Marx. This refers to the propensity of employers to maximize profits by reducing labor expenses (using technology and paying the lowest possible wages). The result of this capitalist rationale, argued Marx, would actually be to reduce profits because the workers would be less and less able to purchase products.

False consciousness. In Marxian theory, the idea that the oppressed may hold beliefs damaging to their interests.

Family. Particular social construct whereby persons are related by ancestry, marriage, adoption, or choice.

Family values. The conservative term supporting the heterosexual two-parent family. The implication is that all other family arrangements are the source of social problems.

Feminist approach. An approach based on support for women's equality.

Feminization of poverty. A reference to the relatively large number of female-headed households living in poverty.

Feral children. Children reputedly raised by animals; they have the characteristics of their animal peers rather than of human beings.

Folkways. Relatively unimportant rules that if violated are not severely punished.

Function. Any consequence of a social arrangement that contributes to the overall stability of the system.

Functional integration. Unity among divergent elements of society resulting from specialized divisions of labor.

Functionalism. The theoretical perspective that emphasizes the order, harmony, and stability of social systems.

Gender. The cultural and social definitions of feminine and masculine. Differs from sex, which is the biological fact of femaleness or maleness.

Gender roles. The understanding of gender differences that emphasize the characteristics that individuals learn in the socialization process.

Gender segregation. The location of women and men in different job categories throughout the workforce.

Gender stratification. The differential ranking and rewarding of women's and men's roles.

Gender structure. Features of social organization that produce gender inequality.

Gendered. Behavior patterned as feminine or masculine.

Gendered institutions. Entire institutions that are patterned by gender.

Generalized other. Mead's concept that refers to the internalization of the expectations of the society.

Generation X. The generation cohort born 1956–1976.

Genetic engineering. The scientific effort to manipulate DNA molecules in plants and animals.

Glass ceiling. Invisible barriers that limit women's mobility in organizations.

Global culture. The diffusion of a single culture throughout the world.

Globalization. The economic, political, and social connections and interdependence among the societies in the world.

Glossolalia. The emotional religious experience involving the incoherent "speaking in tongues."

Goal displacement. When the original goals of an organization are displaced by the goals of maintaining the organization.

Group. A collection of two or more people who, because of sustained interaction, have evolved a common culture.

Hedonism. The pursuit of pleasure and self-indulgence.

Heterogeneous. Consisting of many different, diverse parts.

Hidden curriculum. That part of the school experience that has nothing to do with formal subjects but refers to the behaviors that schools expect of children (obedience to authority, remaining quiet and orderly, and so on).

Hierarchy. The arrangement of people or objects in order of importance.

Home-based work. Women working for pay in their homes.

Homeshoring or homesourcing. A form of contingent employment where individuals work at home-based jobs as independent contractors.

Homogeneous. Consisting of similar parts throughout.

Horizontal mobility. Changes in occupations or other situations without moving from one social class to another.

Household. A residential unit of unrelated individuals who pool resources and perform common tasks of production and consumption.

Human agency. When individuals, acting alone or with others, shape, resist, challenge, and sometimes change the social institutions that impinge on them.

Id. Freud's term for the collection of urges and drives people have for pleasure and aggression.

Ideal type. An abstraction constructed to show how some phenomenon would be characterized in its pure form.

Ideological social control. The efforts by social organizations to control members by controlling their minds. Societies accomplish this, typically, through the socialization process.

Ideology. A set of ideas that explain reality, provide guidelines for behavior, and express the interests of a group.

Immigration. The movement of people from one nation to another for permanent residence.

Income. The amount of money earned annually.

Independent variable. A variable that affects another variable (the dependent variable).

Indirect interlock. A type of interlocking directorate in which two companies each have a director on the board of a third company.

Individual racism. Overt acts by individuals of one race to harm a member or members of another race.

Inflation. The situation when too much money purchases too few goods, resulting in rising prices.

Institutional derogation. Occurs when the normal arrangements of society act to reinforce the negative stereotypes of minority groups.

Institutional discrimination. When the social arrangements and accepted ways of doing things in society disadvantage some social category.

Institutional process. The concept designating the forces that resist change, which emanate from the assumed human need for certainty and stability.

Institutional racism. Occurs when the social arrangements and accepted ways of doing things in society disadvantage a racial group.

Institutional sexism. Occurs when the social arrangements and accepted ways of doing things in society disadvantage females.

Institutional violence. Occurs when the normal workings of the society do harm to a social category.

Institutionalization. Occurs when a movement's beliefs are accepted by the larger society and its goals are achieved.

Institutions. Social arrangements that channel behavior in prescribed ways in the important areas of societal life.

Instrumental process. The search for technological solutions to human problems as an impetus for change.

Instrumentalist view. A view of power held by some Marxists that the ruling class controls political institutions through money and influence. Other Marxists accept the structuralist view of power.

Interest group. A group of like-minded persons who organize to influence public policy.

Intergenerational mobility. The difference in social class position between (typically) a son and his father.

Interlocking directorates. The linkages between corporations that result when an individual serves on the board of directors of two companies (a direct interlock) or when two companies each have a director on the board of a third company (an indirect interlock).

Internalization. In the process of socialization, society's demands become part of the individual, acting to control his or her behavior.

Intragenerational mobility. The movement by an individual from one social class to another.

"Iron cage" of rationality. The dehumanizing aspects of bureaucracy. Max Weber saw bureaucracies as cages with people trapped in them, denied of their basic humanity.

Labeling theory. The explanation of deviant behavior that stresses the importance of the society in defining what is illegal and in assigning deviant status to particular individuals, which in turn dominates their identities and behaviors.

Laissez-faire. The government policy of allowing the marketplace to operate unhindered.

Latent consequence. An unintended consequence of a social arrangement or social action.

Latent functions. Unintended or unanticipated consequences.

Life chances. Weber's term for the chances throughout one's life cycle to live and experience the good things in life.

Linguistic relativity. The language of a culture influences the way members of that society perceive reality.

Longitudinal survey. This type of survey collects information from the same people over many years.

Looking-glass self. Cooley's concept of the importance of how other people influence the way we see ourselves.

Macro level. The large-scale structures and processes of society, including the institutions and the system of stratification.

Male dominance. The beliefs, values, and cultural meanings that give higher value and prestige to masculinity than to femininity and that institutionalize male control of socially valued resources.

Manifest consequence. An intended consequence of a social arrangement or social action.

Manifest functions. The intended consequences of an activity or a social arrangement.

Marginality. The condition resulting from taking part in two distinct ways of life without belonging fully to either.

Master status. A status that has exceptional importance for social identity, overshadowing other statuses.

Material technology. Refers to the technical knowledge needed to use and make things.

Matriarchal family. A family structure in which the mother is dominant.

Matrix of domination. The intersections of the hierarchies of class, race, and gender in which each of us exists.

McDonaldization. George Ritzer's term for the process by which the principles of fast-food restaurants are coming to dominate more and more sectors of American society as well as the rest of the world.

Megachurches. A trend among evangelicals is toward very large churches. Their growth is fueled by entertaining church services, the provision of services, and specialized ministries for targeted groups.

Meritocracy. A system of stratification in which rank is based purely on achievement.

Micro level. The social organization and processes of small-scale social groups.

Millennial generation. Those born between 1977 and 1995.

Military-industrial complex. The term that refers to the direct and indirect relationships between the military establishment (the Pentagon) and the corporations.

Minority group. A social category composed of people who differ from the majority, are relatively powerless, and are the objects of discrimination.

Modal personality type. A distinct type of personality considered to be characteristic of the members of a particular society.

Model. The mental image a scientist has of the structure of society. This influences what scientists look for, what they see, and how phenomena are explained.

Modern family. The nuclear family that emerged in response to the requirements of an urban, industrial society. It consisted of an intact nuclear household unit with a male breadwinner, his full-time homemaker wife, and their dependent children.

Monogamy. The form of marriage in which an individual may not be married to more than one person at a time.

Monopolistic capitalism. The form of capitalism prevalent in the contemporary United States, where a few large corporations control the key industries, destroying competition and the market mechanisms that would ordinarily keep prices low and help consumers.

Monopoly. Occurs when a single firm dominates an industry.

Mores. Important norms, the violation of which results in severe punishment.

Mortality rate. The frequency of actual deaths in a population.

Myth of peaceful progress. The incorrect belief that throughout U.S. history, disadvantaged groups have gained their share of power, prosperity, and respectability without violence.

Myth of separate worlds. The belief that work and family roles operate independently of each other.

New immigration. Unlike previous waves of immigration in which the immigrants were primarily White and European, the latest wave of immigration is composed primarily of people of color (from Latin America and Asia).

New poor. The poor who are displaced by new technologies or whose jobs have moved away to the suburbs, to other regions of the country, or out of the country.

No Child Left Behind Act. Passed by Congress in 2001, this legislation is intended to improve United States academic standards and performance.

Nominalist position. A philosophical position that a group is nothing more than the sum of its parts.

Nonfamily household. People who live alone or with unrelated individuals.

Norms. Cultural rules that specify appropriate and inappropriate behavior (in other words, the shared expectations for behavior).

Nuclear family. A kinship unit composed of a husband, a wife, and children.

Offshoring. When a company moves its operations to another country.

Opiate of the masses. Karl Marx's term for religion's effect on society. In this view, religion inhibits societal change by making existing social arrangements seem right and inevitable. The dominant form of economics in society, the type of government, the law, and other social creations are given religious sanction.

Order model. The conception of society as a social system characterized by cohesion, consensus, cooperation, reciprocity, stability, and persistence.

Outsourcing. The practice of corporations of contracting work outside the company and its relatively well-paid (usually unionized) workers to companies inside and outside the United States where costs are cheaper.

Paradigm. The basic assumptions a scientist has of the structure of society (see Model).

Participant observation. A method in which researchers engage in the activities of the people they are observing.

Participatory socialization. The mode of socialization in which parents encourage their children to explore, experiment, and question.

Patriarchal family. A family structure in which the father is dominant.

Patriarchy. A form of social organization in which males dominate females.

Pay equity. Policies designed to bring the pay levels of women in closer alignment with those of men. Also called *comparable worth*.

Peer group. Friends usually of the same age and socioeconomic status.

Pluralism. A situation in which different groups live in mutual respect but retain their racial, religious, or ethnic identities.

Pluralist model of power. The diffuse distribution of power among various groups and interests.

Plutocracy. Government by or in the interest of the rich.

Political crime. Either crime against the state (the order model's view) or crime by the state (the conflict model's view).

Polity. The societal institution especially concerned with maintaining order.

Positivism. The scientific model for understanding reality.

Post–baby boomers. Those born between 1965 and 1976.

Postmodern families. Judith Stacey's term for the multiplicity of family and household arrangements that has emerged as a result of a number of social factors, such as women in the labor force, divorce, remarriage, and cohabitation arrangements.

Poverty. A standard of living below the minimum needed for the maintenance of adequate diet, health, and shelter.

Power. The ability to get what one wants from someone else.

Power elite. Mills' term for the coalition of the top echelon of the military, the executive branch of the federal government, and business.

Prestige. The respect of an individual or social category as a result of his or her social status.

Priestly role of religion. One role of the church and the clergy is to comfort individuals, helping them through difficult times. The church also celebrates the various important stages in life (birth, marriage, death). This role is conservative since it does not challenge the system.

Primary deviance. The original illegal act preceding the successful application of the deviant label.

Primary groups. Small groups characterized by intimate, face-to-face interaction.

Privilege. The distribution of goods and services, situations, and experiences that are highly valued and beneficial.

Progressive tax. A tax rate that escalates with the amount of income.

Proletariat. Marx's term for the industrial workers in a capitalistic society.

Prophetic role of religion. One function of the church is to challenge the existing system, leading the fight to right the inequities of society.

Protestant ethic. The religious beliefs, traced back to Martin Luther and John Calvin, that emphasize hard work and continual striving in order to prove by material success that one is saved.

Psychosurgery. A form of brain surgery used to change the behavior of the patient.

Race. A group socially defined on the basis of a presumed common genetic heritage resulting in distinguishing physical characteristics.

Racial-ethnic groups. Groups labeled as races by the wider society and bound together by their common social and economic conditions, resulting in distinctive cultural and ethnic characteristics.

Racial formation. The sociohistorical processes by which races are continually being shaped and transformed.

Racial profiling. The police practice of disproportionately stopping racial/ethnic minorities for traffic violations, then searching for evidence of criminal activity.

Racism. The domination of and discrimination against one racial group by the majority.

Radical nonintervention. Schur's term for the strategy of leaving juvenile delinquents alone as much as possible rather than processing (and labeling) them through the criminal justice system.

Random sample. The selection of a subset from a population so that every person has an equal chance of being selected.

Realist position. The philosophical position that a group is more than the sum of its parts (referring to the emergence of culture and mechanisms of social control that affect the behavior of members regardless of their personalities).

Recidivism. Reinvolvement in crime.

Reference groups. Groups to which one would like to belong and toward which one therefore orients her or his behavior.

Reform movements. Social movements that seek to alter a specific part of society.

Regressive tax. A tax rate that remains the same for all people rich or poor. The result is that poor people pay a larger proportion of their earned income than do affluent people.

Reliability. The degree to which a study yields similar results when repeated.

Religion. The social institution that encompasses beliefs and practices regarding the sacred.

Reserve army of the unemployed. Unemployed people who want to work. Their presence tends to depress the wages of workers and keeps those workers from making demands on employers for fear of being replaced.

Resistance movements. The organized attempt to reinforce the traditional system by preventing change.

Revolutionary movement. The collective attempt to bring about a radical transformation of society.

Rites of passage. The ritual whereby the society recognizes the adult status of a young member.

Ritual. Symbolic actions that reinforce the collective remembering of the group's shared meanings.

Role. The behavioral expectations and requirements attached to a position in a social organization.

Role conflict. Occurs when an individual cannot fulfill the expectations of one status without violating those of another.

Role performance (role behavior). The actual behavior of people occupying particular positions in a social organization.

Routinization of charisma. The process by which an organization attempts to transmit the special attributes of the former leader to a new one. This is done by various means, for example, laying on of hands and the old leader choosing a successor.

Sacred. That which inspires awe because of its believed supernatural qualities.

Sample. A representative part of a population.

Sanctions. Social rewards or punishments for approved or disapproved behavior.

Scientific management. Efforts by business managers to increase worker efficiency by breaking work down into very specialized tasks, standardizing tools and procedures, and speeding up repetitive work.

Second shift. Women's responsibilities for housework, child care, and home management that they must do in addition to their labor in the workforce.

Secondary deviance. Deviant behavior that is a consequence of the successful application of the deviant label.

Secondary groups. Large, impersonal, and formally organized groups.

Sect. A religious organization, in contrast to a church, that tends to be dogmatic, fundamentalistic, and in opposition to the world.

Secular. Of or pertaining to the world; the opposite of sacred.

Segmented labor market. The capitalist economy is divided into two distinct sectors, one in which production and working conditions are relatively stable and secure; the other is composed of marginal firms in which working conditions, wages, and job security are low.

Segregation. The separation of one group from another.

Self. George Herbert Mead's term for an individual's personality.

Self-esteem. The opinion of oneself.

Self-fulfilling prophecy. An event that occurs because it was predicted. The prophecy is confirmed because people alter their behavior to conform to the prediction.

Severely poor. Those at least 50 percent below the official poverty line.

Sex. Biological identity as male or female.

Sex-gender system. A system of stratification that ranks and rewards gender roles unequally.

Sex roles. The learned patterns of behavior expected of males and females by society.

Sexism. The individual actions and institutional arrangements that discriminate against women.

Sexual stratification. A hierarchical arrangement based on gender.

Sexuality. A way of organizing the social world based on sexual identity.

Shared monopoly. When four or fewer companies control 50 percent or more of an industry.

Significant others. Mead's term referring to people who are most important in determining a child's behavior.

Social class. A number of people who occupy the same relative economic rank in the stratification system.

Social construction of reality. The process by which individuals learn how to define reality from other people in interaction and by learning the culture.

Social control. The regulation of human behavior in any social group.

Social Darwinism. The belief that the principle of the survival of the fittest applies to human societies, especially the system of stratification.

Social determinism. The assumption that human behavior is explained exclusively by social factors.

Social differentiation. The process of categorizing people by some personal attribute.

Social facts. Durkheim's term referring to the forces outside individuals that constrain them in their behaviors.

Social group. Two or more people who identify with each other and who share a distinctive set of relationships.

Social inequality. The ranking of people by wealth, family background, race, ethnicity, or sex.

Social interaction. When individuals act toward or respond to each other.

Social location. One's position in society based on family background, race, socioeconomic status, religion, and other relevant social characteristics.

Social mobility. Movement by an individual from one social class or status group to another.

Social movement. A collective attempt to promote or resist change.

Social organization. The order of a social group as evidenced by the positions, roles, norms, and other constraints that control behavior and ensure predictability.

Social problems. There are two types of social problems: (1) societally induced conditions that cause psychic and material suffering for any segment of the population and (2) acts and conditions that violate the norms and values of society.

Social relationship. Occurs when two or more people engage in enduring social interaction.

Social roles. The expectations of what individuals should do in various statuses.

Social stratification. Occurs when people are ranked in a hierarchy that differentiates them as superior or inferior.

Social structure. The patterned and recurrent relationships among people and parts in a social organization.

Social system. A differentiated group whose parts are interrelated in an orderly arrangement, bounded in geographical space or membership.

Social technology. The knowledge necessary to establish, maintain, and operate the technical aspects of social organization.

Socialism. The economic system in which the means of production are owned by the people for their collective benefit.

Socialization. The process of learning cultural values, norms, and expectations.

Socialization agents. The individuals, groups, and institutions responsible for transmitting the culture of society to newcomers.

Society. The largest social organization to which individuals owe their allegiance. The entity is located geographically, has a common culture, and is relatively self-sufficient.

Socioeconomic status. The measure of social status that takes into account several prestige factors, such as income, education, and occupation.

Sociological imagination. The view that individual troubles are inextricably linked to social forces.

Sociological theory. A set of ideas that explain a range of human behavior and a variety of social and societal events.

Sociology. The scholarly discipline concerned with the systematic study of social organizations.

Spillover. Carrying over the concerns, responsibilities, and demands of one part of life to another (for example, the conditions of work that affect family life).

Status. A socially defined position in a social organization.

Status dropout rate. The percentage of sixteen- to twenty-four-year-olds that are not enrolled in school and have not earned a high school diploma or equivalency.

Status group. People of similar status. They view each other as social equals.

Status inconsistency. The situation in which a person ranks high on one status dimension and low on another.

Status withdrawal. The loss of status that occurs with downward mobility.

Stereotype. An exaggerated generalization about some social category.

Stigma. A label of social disgrace.

Structural approach to sexual inequality. The understanding of gender differences resulting from factors external to individuals.

Structural discrimination theories. Explanations that focus on the institutionalized patterns of discrimination as the sources of the secondary status of minorities.

Structural transformation of the economy. The shift to a new era evidenced by the move from a manufacturing to a service/information economy with microchip technology, the global economy, and the rapid movement of capital.

Structuralist view. A Marxian interpretation of power arguing that the ruling class gets its way because the political and economic institutions are biased in its favor. Other Marxists hold the instrumentalist view of power.

Structured social inequality. The patterns of superiority and inferiority, the distribution of rewards, and the belief systems that reinforce the inequities of society.

Student subculture. Students in a lower educational track may band together in a subculture that is antagonistic toward school.

Subculture. A relatively cohesive cultural system that varies in form and substance from the dominant culture.

Subsidy. Financial aid in the form of tax breaks or gifts granted by the government to an individual or commercial enterprise.

Suburb. A community adjacent to a city.

Sunrise industries. Industries characterized by increased output and employment.

Sunset industries. Industries declining in both output and employment.

Superego. Freud's term for the internalization of society's morals within the self.

Survey research. The research technique that selects a sample of people from a larger population in order to learn how they think, feel, or act.

Sweatshop. A substandard work environment in which workers are paid less than the minimum wage, workers are not paid overtime premiums, and other labor laws are violated.

Symbol. A thing that represents something else, such as a word, gesture, or physical object (cross, flag).

Synthesis. The blending of the parts into a new form.

Systemic imperatives. The economic and social constraints on the decision makers in an organization that promote the status quo.

Tax expenditures. Legal tax loopholes that permit certain individuals and corporations to pay lower taxes or no taxes at all.

Technology. The application of science to meet the needs of society.

Theodicy. The religious legitimation for a situation that might otherwise cause guilt or anger (such as defeat in a war or the existence of poverty among affluence).

Tracking. A practice of schools of grouping children according to their scores on IQ and other tests.

Transnational corporation. A corporation that operates in more than one country.

Underemployment. Being employed at a job below one's level of training and expertise.

Undocumented immigrants. Immigrants who have entered the United States illegally.

Urbanism. The ways in which city life characteristically affects how people feel, think, and interact with one another.

Urbanization. The movement of people from rural to urban areas.

Validity. The degree to which a scientific study measures what it attempts to measure.

Value neutrality. The attempt by scientists to be absolutely free of bias in their research.

Values. The shared criteria used in evaluating objects, ideas, acts, feelings, or events as to their relative desirability, merit, or correctness.

Variable. An attitude, a behavior, or a condition that can vary in magnitude from case to case (the opposite of a constant).

Vertical mobility. Movement upward or downward in social class.

Voluntary associations. Organizations that people join because they approve of their goals.

Wealth. A person's net worth (assets minus liabilities).

Wealthfare. Receipt by the affluent of financial aid and/or services from the government.

Welfare. Receipt of financial aid and/or services from the government.

Work–family interference. The ways in which the connections between jobs and family may be a source of tension for workers and family members.

Work–family role system. The traditional uneven division of labor in which men's work role takes priority over the family role, and women, even those who work outside the home, are to give priority to the family role.

REFERENCES

Acker, Joan. 1973. "Women and Stratification: A Case of Intellectual Sexism." *American Journal of Sociology* 78 (January):936–45.

———. 1990. "Hierarchies, Jobs, Bodies: A Theory of Gendered Organizations." *Gender and Society* 4:139–58.

———. 1992. "Gendered Institutions: From Sex Roles to Gendered Institutions." *Contemporary Sociology* 21 (September):575.

Acosta, R. Vivian, and Linda Jean Carpenter. 2009. "Are We There Yet? Thirty-Seven Years Later, Title IX Hasn't Fixed It All."*Academe* 95:22–24.

Adamson, Rebecca. 2009. "Foreword to Dedrick Muhammad." In *Challenges to Native American Advancement*. New York: Institute for Policy Studies, p. 5.

Adamuti-Trache, Maria, and Lesley Andres. 2007. "Embarking on and Persisting in Scientific Fields of Study: Cultural Capital, Gender, and Curriculum along the Science Pipeline." *International Journal of Science Education*:1–28.

Ahlburg, Dennis A., and Carol J. De Vita. 1992. "New Realities of the American Family." *Population Bulletin* 47 (August):entire issue.

Albelda, Randy. 1992. "Whose Values, Which Families?" *Dollars & Sense* 182 (December):6–9.

Albelda, Randy, and Chris Tilly. 1997. *Glass Ceilings and Bottomless Pits: Women's Work, Women's Poverty*. Boston, MA: South End Press.

Allegretto, Sylvia. 2006. "Economic Snapshots." *Economic Policy Institute* (August 23). Available online: http://www.epi.org/content/cfn/webfeatures_snapshots_20060823.

Allen, Walter R., and Angie Y. Chung. 2000. "Your Blues Ain't Like My Blues: Race, Ethnicity and Social Inequality in America."*Contemporary Sociology* 29 (November):796–805.

Alter, Jonathan. 2007. "The Other America: An Enduring Shame." In *Inequality: Social Class and Its Consequences*, D. Stanley Eitzen and Janis E. Johnston, eds. Boulder, CO: Paradigm Publishers.

Amato, Paul R., Alan Booth, David R. Johnson, and Stacy J. Rogers. 2007. *Alone Together: How Marriage in America Is Changing*. Cambridge, MA: Harvard University Press.

American Association of University Women (AAUW). 1992. "How Schools Shortchange Girls." *Executive Summary: AAUW Report*. Washington, DC: American Association of University Women Educational Foundation.

American Civil Liberties Union (ACLU). 2007. "The Persistence of Racial Profiling in Rhode Island: A Call for Action." (January). Available online: http://www.aclu.org/pdfs/racialjustice/riracialprofilingreport.pdf.

———. 2008a. "Charges Dismissed Against Reporter Who Was Victim of NYPD Racial Profiling as Figures Show Hundreds of Thousands of Innocent Black New Yorkers Were Stopped-and-Frisked in 2007." (February 13). Available online: http://www.aclu.org/racialjustice/racialprofiling/34288prs20080213.html.

———. 2008b. "Landmark Settlement Reached With Maryland State Police in 'Driving While Black' Case." (April 2). Available online: http://www.aclu.org/racialjustice/racialprofiling/34753prs20080402.html.

———. 2008c. "About the Campaign Against Racial Profiling." Available online: http://www.aclu.org/racialjustice/racialprofiling/34572res20080320.html.

American Society for Aesthetic Plastic Surgery. 2009. Available online: http://www.surgery.org.

American Sociological Association. 2003. *The Importance of Collecting Data and Doing Scientific Research on Race*. Washington, DC: American Sociological Association.

Amott, Teresa. 1993. *Caught in the Crisis: Women and the U.S. Economy Today*. New York: Monthly Review Press.

Amster, Randall. 2010. "Arizona Bans Ethnic Studies (Also Reason and Justice)." *CommonDreams.org* (December 29). Available online: http://www.commondreams.org/view/2010/12/29-2.

Andersen, Margaret L. 2009. *Thinking About Women*, 8th ed. Boston, MA: Allyn and Bacon.

———. 2011. *Thinking About Women: Sociological Perspectives on Sex and Gender*. Boston, MA: Pearson Education, Inc.

———. Forthcoming. "Whitewashing Race: A Critical Review Essay on 'Whiteness.'" In *Deconstructing Whiteness, Deconstructing White Supremacy*, Woody Doane and Eduardo Bonilla-Silva, eds. New York: Routledge.

Andersen, Margaret L., and Howard F. Taylor. 2000. *Sociology: Understanding a Diverse Society*. Belmont, CA: Wadsworth.

Anderson, Jack. 1983. "Plans to Test Adolescents Smack of 1984." *Rocky Mountain News* (October 13):106.

Angier, Natalie. 2000. "Scientists: DNA Shows Humans Are All One Race." *Denver Post* (August 22):2A, 5A.

Annie E. Casey Foundation. 2002. *Kids Count Pocket Guide*. Baltimore, MD: Annie E. Casey Foundation.

Appelbaum, Richard P., and William J. Chambliss. 1995. *Sociology*. New York: HarperCollins.

Archibald, Robert B., and David H. Feldman. 2010. *Forbes.com*. Available online: http://www.forbes.com/2010/08/01/rising-cost-education-opinion-best-colleges-10-feldman-archibald.html.

Armour, Stephanie. 2008. "Renters Can't Escape Housing Crisis." *USA Today* (April 2):1B–2B.

Armstrong, Karen. 2000. *The Battle for God*. New York: Ballantine Books.

Asch, Solomon E. 1958. "Effects of Group Pressure upon the Modification and Distortion of Judgments." In *Readings in*

441

Social Psychology, 3rd ed., Eleanor E. Maccoby, Theodore M. Newcomb, and Eugene L. Hartley, eds. New York: Holt, Rinehart and Winston, pp. 174–83.

Associated Press. 1976. "Jungle Boy Remains More Like Monkey." (May 15).

———. 2002. "FBI and Gov. Reagan Targeted 'Subversives.'" (June 14).

———. 2007. "Town Bans Pants That Sag Too Much." (June 14).

———. 2011. "For Minorities, New 'Digital Divide' Seen." (January 11).

Austin, Algernon. 2010. "Budget Cuts and Our Children's Future." *American Prospect* 21 (November):A18–A19.

Baca Zinn, Maxine, and Bonnie Thornton Dill. 1994. "Difference and Domination." In *Women of Color in U.S. Society*, Maxine Baca Zinn and Bonnie Thornton Dill, eds. Philadelphia, PA: Temple University Press, pp. 3–12.

Baca Zinn, Maxine, Stanley Eitzen D., and Barbara Wells. 2008. *Diversity in Families*, 8th ed. Boston, MA: Allyn and Bacon.

———. 2011. *Diversity in Families*, 9th ed. Boston, MA: Allyn and Bacon.

Baca Zinn, Maxine, Pierrette Hondagneu-Sotelo, and Michael A. Messner. 2010. *Gender Through the Prism of Difference*, 4th ed. New York: Oxford University Press.

Baca Zinn, Maxine, and Angela Y. H. Pok. 2002. "Tradition and Transition in Mexican-Origin Families." In *Minority Families in the United States: A Multicultural Perspective*, Ronald L. Taylor (ed.). Upper Saddle River, NJ: Prentice Hall, pp. 70–100.

Bacevich, Andrew J. 2010. "Unequal Sacrifice." *The Nation* (September 20):25–26.

Bales, Kevin. 1999. *Disposable People: New Slavery in the Global Economy*. Berkeley, CA: University of California Press.

Balswick, Jack, and Charles Peck. 1971. "The Inexpressive Male: A Tragedy of American Society." *Family Coordinator* 20:363–8.

Balswick, Jack, and James Lincoln Collier. 1976. "Why Husbands Can't Say 'I Love You.'" In *The Forty-Nine Percent Majority*, Deborah S. David and Robert Brannon, eds. Reading, MA: Addison-Wesley.

Baltzell, E. Digby. 1958. *Philadelphia Gentlemen: The Making of a National Upper Class*. New York: Free Press.

Bamshad, Michael J., and Steve E. Olson. 2003. "Does Race Exist?" *Scientific American* (December):78–85.

Bandura, Albert. 1977. *Social Learning Theory*. New York: General Learning Press.

———. 1986. *Social Foundations of Thought and Action: A Social Cognitive*. Englewood Cliffs, NJ: Prentice Hall.

Banfield, Edward C. 1974. *The Unheavenly City Revisited*. Boston, MA: Little, Brown.

Bannon, Lisa. 2000. "Gender-Specific Toy Marketing Irks Some." *Wall Street Journal* (February 17):7D.

Barber, Benjamin R. 1995. *Jihad vs. McWorld*. New York: Ballantine Books.

Barlett, Donald L., and James B. Steele. 2000. "Soaked by Congress." *Time* (May 15):64–75.

Barlow, Andrew L. 2003. *Between Fear and Hope: Globalization and Race in the United States*. Lanham, MD: Rowman and Littlefield Publishers, Inc.

Barnett, Rosalind, and Caryl Rivers. 2004. *Same Difference*. New York: Basic Books.

Barrera, Mario. 1979. *Race and Class in the Southwest: A Theory of Racial Inequality*. Notre Dame, IN: University of Notre Dame Press.

Barrett, Paul M. 2007. *American Islam: The Struggle for the Soul of a Religion*. New York: Farrar, Straus, and Giroux.

Barsamian, David. 1996. "Politics of the Christian Right: An Interview with Sara Diamond." *Z Magazine* 9 (June):36–41.

———. 1997. "Howard Zinn." *The Progressive* 61 (July): 37–40.

Baskir, Laurence M., and William A. Strauss. 1978. *The Draft, the War, and the Vietnam Generation*. New York: Knopf.

Basow, Susan. 1996. "Gender Stereotypes and Roles." In *The Meaning of Difference*, Karen E. Rosenblum and Toni-Michelle Travis, eds. New York: McGraw-Hill, pp. 81–96.

Battistoni, Alyssa. 2010. "The 'Culture of Poverty' Myth Returns." *Salon.com* (October 22). Available online: http://www.salon.com/politics/war_room/2010/10/22/culture_poverty_battistoni.html.

Bauman, Zygmunt. 1990. *Thinking Sociologically*. Cambridge, MA: Basil Blackwell.

Beall, Jackson. 2008. "Why Lobbyists Negatively Influence the U.S. Legislative Process." *Helium.com*. Available online: http://helium.com/items/195251-lobbyistsreal-lobbying-reform.

Bean, Frank D., Jennifer Lee, Jeanne Batalova, and Mark Leach. 2004. *Immigration and Fading Color Lines in America*. New York: Russell Sage Foundation and Population Reference Bureau.

Beck, Joan. 1995. "Preschool Can Help Close the Poverty Gap." *Denver Post* (January 19):7B.

Beck, Rachel. 2011. "Typical CEO Pay Is Up 24%." *Associated Press* (May 7).

Becker, Howard S. 1967. "Whose Side Are We on?" *Social Problems* 14 (Winter):239–47.

Beeghley, Leonard. 2008. *The Structure of Social Stratification in the United States*, 5th ed. Boston, MA: Allyn and Bacon.

Begley, Sharon. 1997. "The Science Wars." *Newsweek* (April 21):54–56.

Belkin, Lisa. 2009. "Public Displays of Disaffection." *New York Times Magazine* (July 12):9–10.

Bellah, Robert N. 1967. "Civil Religion in America." *Daedalus* 96 (Winter):1–21.

Belluck, Pam. 1998. "Hudson Foods Indicted in Meat Contamination." *New York Times* (December 20). Available online: http://nytimes.com.

Benokraitis, Nijole, and Joe R. Feagin. 1995. *Modern Sexism*, 2nd ed. Upper Saddle River, NJ: Prentice Hall.

Berger, Peter L. 1963. *Invitation to Sociology: A Humanistic Perspective*. Garden City, NY: Doubleday Anchor Books.

———. 1967a. "Religious Institutions." In *Sociology*, Neil J Smelser, ed. New York: Wiley.

———. 1967b. *The Sacred Canopy*. Garden City, NY: Doubleday.

Bernard, Jessie. 1972. *The Future of Marriage*. New York: Bantam.

Berry, Mary Frances. 1994. *Black Resistance, White Law*, Rev ed. New York: Penguin Books.

442

Bettelheim, Ruth. 2011. "America Can't Afford to Neglect Dementia Research." *USA Today* (March 16):9A.

Bianchi, Suzanne M. 1995. "Changing Economic Roles of Women and Men." In *State of the Union: America in the 1990s*, Vol. 1, Reynolds Farley, ed. New York: Sage, pp. 107–54.

Bianchi, Suzanne M., and Lynn M. Casper. 2000. "American Families." *Population Bulletin* 55 (December):entire edition.

Bianchi, Suzanne M., John P. Robinson, and Melissa A. Milike. 2006. *Changing Rhythms of American Family Life*. New York: Russell Sage Foundation.

Bierstedt, Robert. 1974. *The Social Order*, 4th ed. New York: McGraw-Hill.

Bilger, Burkhard. 2004. "God Doesn't Need Ole Anthony." *The New Yorker* (December 6):70–81.

Bilmes, Linda. 2008. "Another Year, Another $300 Billion." *Boston Globe* (March 16). Reprinted by *Common-Dreams.org*. Available online: http://www.common-dreams.org/archive/2008/03/16/7719.

Birnbaum, Norman. 1992. "One Cheer for Clinton." *The Nation* (September 28):318–20.

Blackman, Douglas A. 2008. *Slavery by Another Name: The Re-Enslavement of Black People in America from the Civil War to World War II*. New York: Doubleday.

Blau, Peter M., and Otis Dudley Duncan. 1967. *The American Occupational Structure*. New York: Wiley.

Blau, Peter M., and Scott W. Richard. 1962. *Formal Organizations: A Comparative Approach*. San Francisco, CA: Chandler.

Blauner, Robert. 1964. *Alienation and Freedom*. Chicago, IL: University of Chicago Press.

Block, Sandra. 2006. "Boomer Influences Shrink as Parents Live Longer, Health Costs Rise." *USA Today* (June 27):3B.

Block, Sandra. 2011. "Many Saw Net Worth Fall During Recession." *USA Today* (March 25):1B.

Bloom, Rhonda Bodfield. 2008. "Neighbor a Cheat? It's Easy to Tattle." *Arizona Daily Star* (January 6):1A, 1B.

Bloomsberg Business Week. 2011. "Joblessness, the Whole Nine Yards." (December/January 20/2):37.

Blumberg, Paul M., and Paul P. W. 1975. "Continuities and Discontinuities in Upper-Class Marriage." *Journal of Marriage and Family* 37 (February).

Blume, Howard. 2010. "Charter Schools' Growth Promoting Segregation, Studies Say." *LA Times* (February 5). Available online: http://latimes.com/news/local/la-me-charters5-1010feb05,0,3300930.story.

Blumer, Herbert. 1951. "Collective Behavior." In *Principles of Sociology*, 2nd ed., Alfred McClung Lee, ed. New York: Barnes & Noble, pp. 167–222.

Bobo, Lawrence D. 2009. "The Color Line, The Dilemma, and the Dream." In *Race and Ethnicity in Society*, Elizabeth Higginbotham and Margaret L. Andersen (eds.). Belmont, CA: Wadsworth, Cengage Learning, pp. 75–90.

Bonacich, Edna. 1992. "Class and Race." *Encyclopedia of Sociology*, Vol. 1. New York: Macmillan, pp. 204–8.

Bonilla-Silva, Eduardo. 1996. "Rethinking Racism: Toward a Structural Interpretation." *American Sociological Review* 62 (June):465–80.

———. 2003. *Racism Without Racists*. Lanham, MD: Rowman and Littlefield.

———. 2009. "Racism Without Racists." In *The Matrix Reader*, Aby Ferber, Andrea O'Reilly Herrera, Chrisitta M. Jimenez, and Dena R. Samuels, eds. New York: McGraw-Hill.

Booher-Jennings, Jennifer. 2008. "Learning to Label: Socialization, Gender, and the Hidden Curriculum of High-Stakes Testing." *British Journal of Society and Education* 29 (2):149–60.

Bowe, John. 2007. *Nobodies: Modern American Slave Labor and the Dark Side of the New Economy*. New York: Random House.

Boyle, D. Ellen, Nancy L. Marshall, and Wendy W. Robeson. 2003. "Gender at Play: Fourth-Grade Girls and Boys on the Playground." *The American Behavioral Scientist* 46 (10):1326–45.

Briggs, Xavier de Souza, ed. 2005. *The Geography of Opportunity: Race and Housing Choice in Metropolitan America*. Washington, DC: Brookings Institution Press.

Brodkin, Karen. 2009. "How Did Jews Become White Folks?" In *Race and Ethnicity in Society*, Elizabeth Higginbotham and Margaret L. Andersen (eds.). Belmont, CA: Wadsworth, Cengage Learning, pp. 59–66.

Brooks, David. 2011. "The Missing Fifth." *Hutchinson News* (May 13):A6.

Brouillette, John R., and Ronny E. Turner. 1992. "Creating the Sociological Imagination on the First Day of Class: The Social Construction of Deviance." *Teaching Sociology* 20 (October):276–9.

Brown, Chance. 2011. "KIPP (Knowledge in Power) Releases Their College Completion Report." (April 30). Available online: http://www.aboutgraduation.com/?p=827.

Brown, Dee. 1971. *Bury My Heart at Wounded Knee*. New York: Holt, Rinehart and Winston.

Brown, Jim. 2006. "Universities Continue Race-Based Admissions Despite Law." *OneNewsNow.com* (December 22). Available online: http://www.onenewsnow.com/2006/12/universities_continue_racebase.php.

Brown, Michael, and Wellman David. 2005. "Embedding the Color Line." *Dubois Review* 2 (2):187–207.

Brownlee, Kimberley. 2010. "Civil Disobedience." *Stanford Encyclopedia of Philosophy* (Spring). Available online: http://plato.stanford.edu/archives/spr2010/entries/civil-disobedience.

Broyles, William, Jr. 2004. "A War for Us, Fought by Them." *New York Times* (May 4):25A.

Buchanan, Patrick. 1994. "Is U.S. Culturally Superior?" *Denver Post* (May 19):B7.

Bukowski, William M., Brendgen Mara, and Vitaro Frank. 2007. "Peers and Socialization: Effects on Externalizing and Internalizing Problems." In *Handbook of Socialization*, Joan E. Grusec and Paul D. Hastings, eds. New York: The Guilford Press.

Bullard, Robert D. 2007. "Poverty and Pollution in the United States." In *Inequality: Social Class and Its Consequences*, D. Stanley Eitzen and Janis E. Johnston, eds. Boulder, CO: Paradigm Publishers.

Bullard, Robert D., and Wright Beverly. 2009. "The Color of Toxic Debris." *The American Prospect* 20 (March):A9–A11.

Bureau of Justice Statistics. 2010. Available online: http://bjs.ojp.usdoj.gov/.

Bureau of Labor Statistics. 2010. "Women in the Labor Force: A Databook." Available online: http://www.bls.gov/cps/wlf-databook2010.htm.

———. 2010. "Current Population Survey, Household Data Annual Averages." ftp://ftp.bls.gov/pub/special.requests/lf/aat10.txt

———. 2011. "Employment Situation Summary." Available online: http://www.bls.gov/news.release/empsit.t02.htm.

Buriel, Raymond, and Terri De Ment. 1997. "Immigration and Sociocultural Change in Mexican, Chinese, and Vietnamese American Families." In *Immigration and the Family*, Alan Booth, Ann C. Crouter, and Nancy Landale, eds. Mahwah, NJ: Erlbaum, pp. 165–200.

Burke, Daniel. 2009. "Survey: Number of Female Senior Pastors Doubles in 10 Years." *USA Today* (September 17). Available online: http://www.usatoday.com/news/religion/2009-09017-female-pastors_N.htm.

Burt, Keith B., and Jacqueline Scott. 2002. "Parent and Adolescent Gender Role Attitudes in 1990s Great Britian." *Sex Roles* 46 (7/8):239–45.

Burton, Linda, Eduardo Bonilla-Silva, Victor Ray, Rose Buckelew, and Elizabeth Hordge Freeman. 2010. "Critical Race Theories, Colorism, and the Decade's Research on Families of Color." *Journal of Marriage and Family* 72 (3):440–59.

BusinessWeek. 2008. "Flying in for a Tune-Up Overseas." (April 21):26–27.

Butz, William P., and Barbara Boyle Torrey. 2006. "Some Frontiers in Social Science." *Science* 312 (June):1898–9.

Bybee, Roger. 2010. "Which Side Are You On?" *In These Times* 34:1.

Byrnes, Nanette, and Christopher Palmeri. 2009. "Pensions Wade into Toxic Assets." *Business Week* (April 27):22.

Calefati, Jessica. 2010. "Arizona Bans Ethnic Studies." *Mother Jones* (May 12). Available online: http://motherjones.com/mojo/2010/05/ethnic-studies-banned-arizona.

Callahan, David. 2002. "Wal-Mart, Not Hi-Tech, Defines New Economy." *USA Today*. Available online: http://www.demos-usa.org/Pubs/Callahan/walmart/walmart.pdf.

Campbell, Frances A., and Craig T. Ramey. 1994. "Effects of Early Intervention on Intellectual and Academic Achievement: A Follow-Up Study of Children from Low-Income Families." *Child Development* 65 (April):684–98.

Campenni, C. Estelle. 1999. "Gender Stereotyping of Children's Toys: A Comparison of Parents and Nonparents." *Sex Roles* 40 (1/2):121–38.

Cannon, Angie. 1999. "DWB: Driving While Black." *U.S. News & World Report* (March 15):72.

Capellaro, Jennie. 1999. "Students for Sweat-Free Sweatshirts." *Progressive* 63 (April):16.

Carey, Kevin, and Marguerite Roza. 2008. "School Fundings Tragic Flaw." *Education Sector and the Center on Reinventing Public Education*. University of Washington. Available online: http://www.educationsector.org/sites/default/files/publications/tragic_flaw_may14_combo.pdf.

Carlton, Jim. 2011. "Hispanic Surge in California." *Wall Street Journal* (March 9):A2.

Carmichael, Stokely, and Charles V. Hamilton. 1967. *Black Power: The Politics of Liberation in America*. New York: Random House.

Carter, Michael J., and Susan Boslego Carter. 1981. "Women Get a Ticket to Ride after the Gravy Train Has Left the Station." *Feminist Studies* 7:477–504.

Carville, James. 1996. *We're Right, They're Wrong: A Handbook for Spirited Progressives*. New York: Random House.

Cassidy, John. 1997. "The Melting Pot Myth." *The New Yorker* (July 14):40–43.

Castro, April. 2010. "Texas Board of Education Approves Resolution to Limit Islam References." *Huffington Post* (September 24). Available online: http://www.huffingtonpost.com/2010/09/24/texas-board-of-education-islam-references_n_738930.html.

Cawthorne, Alexandra and Stephanie Gross. 2008. "Equal Benefits for Women." Center for American Progress (December 9). Available online: http://www.americanprogress.org/issues/200812/equal_benefits.html.

Center for American Women and Politics. 2011. Available online: http://www.cawp.rutgers.edu/.

Chafel, Judith A. 1997. "Societal Images of Poverty." *Youth and Society* 28 (June):432–63.

Chafetz, Janet Saltzman. 1997. "Feminist Theory and Sociology: Underutilized Contributions for Mainstream Theory." *Annual Review of Sociology* 23:97–120.

Chapin, Laura. 2010. "Supreme Court Ruling Empowers Corporations More than Labor Unions." *US News & World Report* (January 22). Available online: http://www.usnews.com/blogs/laura-chapin/2010/01/22.

Chen, David W. 2004. "What's a Life Worth?" *New York Times* (June 20):4w–k.

Cherlin, Andrew, and Frank F. Furstenberg, Jr. 1994. "The Modernization of Grandparenthood." In *Family in Transition*, 8th ed, Arlene S. Skolnick and Jerome H. Skolnick, eds. New York: HarperCollins, pp. 104–11.

Chicago Tribune. 2007. "Protection Money." (August 5): section 2.5.

Chideya, Farai. 1999. "A Nation of Minorities: America in 2050." *Civil Rights Digest* 4 (Fall):35–41.

Children's Defense Fund. 2004. "While Corporations and the Wealthy Benefit from Huge Tax Cuts, Poor Families Still Struggle." Press release (April 14).

———. 2005. *The State of American's Children 2005*. Washington, DC: Children's Defense Fund.

Child Trends. 2010. "Family Structure." (September). Available online: http://www.childtrendsdatabank.org/?Q=node/231.

———. 2011. "Illicit Drug Use: Differences by Race." Available online: http://www.childtrensdatabank.org/?Q-node/281.

Christian Chronicle. 2006. "Gallup Poll: Church of Christ Tops in Weekly Worship Attendance." (April 18). Available online: http://thetimehascom.wordpress.com/2006/04/18/gallup-poll-church.

Cleveland, Harlan. 1992. "The Age of People Power." *Futurist* 26 (January/February):14–18.

Coakley, Jay J. 2001. *Sport in Society: Issues and Controversies*, 7th ed. Boston, MA: Irwin McGraw-Hill.

———. 2007. *Sports in Society: Issues and Controversies*, 9th ed. New York: McGraw-Hill.

Coates, Joseph F. 2002. "What's Ahead for Families: Five Major Forces of Change." In *Annual Editions: The Family 2002/2003*, Kathleen Gilbert, ed. Sluice Dock, CT: Dushkin/McGraw-Hill.

Cockburn, Andrew. 2009. "21st Century Slaves." In D. Stanley Eitzen and Maxine Baca Zinn (eds.) *Globalization: The Transformation of Social Worlds*, 2nd ed. Belmont, CA: Wadsworth Cengage Learning, pp. 281–286.

Coffin, William Sloan. 2004. *Credo*. Louisville, KY: Westminster John Knox Press.

Cohen, Patricia. 2010. "'Culture of Poverty' Makes a Comeback." *New York Times* (October 17). Available online: http://www.nytimes.com/2010/10/18/us/18poverty.html.

Cohen, Robin, and Paul Kennedy. 2000. *Global Sociology*. New York: New York University Press.

Colarulli, Kate. 2011. "Big Oil's Free Ride." *Commondreams.org* (May 23). Available online: http://www.commondreams.org/view/2011/05/23-5.

Cole, David. 1994. "Five Myths about Immigration." *The Nation* (October 17):410–2.

———. 1999. "When the Reason Is Race." *The Nation* (March 15):22–24.

Coleman, Marilyn, and Lawrence H. Ganong. 1991. "Remarriage and Stepfamily Research in the 1980s: Increased Interest in an Old Family Form." In *Contemporary Families: Looking Forward, Looking Back*, Alan Booth, ed. Minneapolis, MN: National Council on Family Relations, pp. 192–207.

Colin, Chris. 2007. "Nobodies: Modern-Day Slavery in the United States." *SFGate.com* (October 1). Available online: http://www.sfgate.com/cgi-bin/article.cgi?ile=/g/a/2007/10/01/onthejob.DTL.

College Board. 2010. Available online: http://www.collegeboard.com.

Collins, Chris. 1998. "Hispanic Kids Less Likely to Be Enrolled in Medicaid." *USA Today* (April 27):3A.

Collins, Chuck. 2007. "Inequality Solutions: Don't Be Ridiculed." *Inequality.org* (June 13). Available online: http://www.demos.org/inequality/article.cfm?blogid=25278AEF-3FF4-6C82-5C36308C55.

———. 2011. "iHate Tax Dodgers Like Apple Computer." *Commondreams.org* (June 1). Available online: http://www.commondreams.org/view/2011/06/01.

Collins, Chuck, Betsy Leondar-Wright, and Holly Sklar. 1999. *Shifting Fortunes: The Perils of the Growing American Wealth Gap*. Boston, MA: United for a Fair Economy.

Collins, Patricia Hill. 1990. *Black Feminist Thought*. Cambridge, MA: Unwin Hyman.

Collins, Randall. 1988. "Women and Men in the Class Structure." *Journal of Family Issues* 9 (March):27–50.

———. 1992. *Sociological Insight: An Introduction to Non-Obvious Sociology*, 2nd ed. New York: Oxford University Press.

Coltrane, Scott. 1996. *Family Man: Fatherhood, Housework, and Gender Equity*. New York: Oxford University Press.

Comer, Lee. 1978. "Women and Class, the Question of Women and Class." *Women's Studies International Quarterly* 1:165–73.

Compete.com. 2010. Available online: http://www.compete.com/us/.

Conason, Joe. 2007. *It Can Happen Here: Authoritarian Peril in the Age of Bush*. New York: Thomas-Dunne Books.

Connell, Robert W. 1992. "A Very Straight Gay: Masculinity, Homosexual Experience, and the Dynamics of Gender." *American Sociological Review* 57:735–51.

———. 1998. "Masculinities and Globalization." *Men and Masculinities* 1 (July):3–23.

Consumer Reports. 2002. "Your Body, Your I.D.?" 67 (August):12–13.

Contemporary Sociology. 1995. "Symposium: The Bell Curve." 24 (March):149–61.

Cooley, Charles Horton. 1922. *Human Nature and the Social Order*. New York: Scribner.

Coontz, Stephanie. 1992. *The Way We Never Were*. New York: Basic Books.

———. 2005. *Marriage: A History*. New York: Viking.

———. 2007. "New Census Report on Marriage." *Council on Contemporary Families List Serve* (September 18). Available online: http://www.census.gov/population/www/socdemo/marr-div.html.

Corbett, Sara. 2001. "The Breast Offense." *New York Times* (June 6). Available online: http://www.nytimes.com/2001005/06/magazine/06NURSING.html.

Courier. 2009. "The Widening Gap Between Rich and Poor Countries." 12 (July–August).

Cox, Harvey. 1999. "The Market as God." *Atlantic Monthly* 283 (March):18–23.

Crabb, Peter, and Dawn Bielawski. 1994. "The Social Representation of Material Culture and Gender in Children's Books." *Sex Roles* 30 (1/2):69–79.

Cronin, John, Michael Daklin, Deborah Adkins, and Kingsbury G. Gage. 2007. "The Proficiency Illusion." *Thomas Fordham Institute* (October). Available online: http://www.edexcellence.net/doc/The_Proficiency_Illusion.pdf.

Crooks, Robert, and Karla Baur. 1987. *Our Sexuality*, 3rd ed. Menlo Park, CA: Benjamin Cummings.

Crowley, Sheila. 2002. "The National Low Income Housing Coalition." *Poverty and Race* 11 (January/February):24–26.

Curtis, John. 2011. "Persistent Inequity: Gender and Academic Employment." Presented at *New Voices in Pay Equity*, an Event for Equal Pay Day (April 11). Available online: http://www.aaup.org/aaup/issues/women/resources.htm.

Cutler, James E. 1905. *Lynch-Law: An Investigation into the History of Lynching in the United States*. New York: Longmans, Green.

Cuzzort, Raymond P. 1989. *Using Social Thought: The Nuclear Issue and Other Concerns*. Mountain View, CA: Mayfield.

Dahl, Robert. 1961. *Who Governs?* New Haven, CT: Yale University Press.

Dahrendorf, Ralf. 1959. *Class and Class Conflict in Industrial Society*. Stanford, CA: Stanford University Press.

———. 1968. "Out of Utopia: Toward a Reorientation of Sociological Analysis." *American Journal of Sociology* 64 (September).

Datnow, Amanda, and Robert Cooper. 2002. "Tracking." In *Education and Sociology: An Encyclopedia*, David L. Levinson, Peter W. Cookson Jr., and Alan R. Sadovnik, eds. New York: Routledge.

David, Deborah S., and Robert Brannon. 1980. "The Male Sex Role." In *Family in Transition: Rethinking Marriage, Sexuality, Child Rearing and Family Organization*, 3rd ed.,

Arlene S. Skolnick and Jerome H. Skolnick, eds. Boston, MA: Little, Brown.

Davidson, Paul. 2009. "Contract Workers Swelling Peaks." *USA Today* (December 7):1B.

Davidson, Paul, and Barbara Hansen. 2010. "Renters on the Ropes." *USA Today* (September 29):2B.

Davies, Karin. 1996. "Fat-Man Contest Trumpets Wealth." *Denver Post* (November 29):60A.

Davis, Kingsley. 1940. "Extreme Social Isolation of a Child." *American Journal of Sociology* 45 (January):554–64.

———. 1948. *Human Society*. New York: Macmillan.

Davis, Kingsley, and Wilbert E. Moore. 1945. "Some Principles of Stratification." *American Sociological Review* 10 (April):242–9.

Death Penalty Information Center. 2010. "Facts about the Death Penalty." (September 20). Available online: http://www.deathpenaltyinfo.org.

Delamont, S. 2001. *Changing Women, Unchanged Men?* Buckingham: Open University Press.

De Lone, Richard H. 1979. *Small Futures: Children, Inequality, and the Limits of Liberal Reform*. New York: Carnegie Council on Children.

DeParle, Jason. 2009. "Welfare Aid Isn't Growing as Economy Drops Off." *New York Times* (February 2). Available online: http://www.nytimes.com/2009/02//02/us/02welfare.html.

DeNavas-Walt, Carmen, Bernadette D. Proctor, and Jessica C. Smith. 2007. "Income, Poverty, and Health Coverage in the United States: 2006." U.S. Bureau of the Census, *Current Population Reports*, P60–233. Washington, DC: U.S. Government Printing Office.

DeNavas-Walt, Carmen, Bernadette D. Proctor, and Jessica C. Smith. 2011. *Income, Poverty, and Health Insurance Coverage in the United States: 2010*. U.S. Bureau of the Census, Current Population Reports, P60-239. Washington, DC: U.S. Government Printing Office.

De Parle, Jason. 1989. "Realizing the Rights of the Disabled." *New York Times* (December 17):1, 5 (section 4).

———. 2007. "The American Prison Nightmare." *New York Review of Books* (April 12). Available online: http://www.nybooks.com/article/20056.

Deresiewicz, William. 2011. "Faulty Towers." *The Nation* (May 21):27–34.

De Vita, Carol J. 1996. "The United States at Mid-Decade." *Population Bulletin* 50 (March): entire issue. p. 583.

di Leonardo, Micaela. 1992. "Boyz on the Hood." *The Nation* (August 17–24):178–86.

Doezema, Jo, and Kamala Kempadoo, eds. 1998. *Global Sex Workers: Rights, Resistance, and Redefinition*. New York: Routledge.

Dokoupil, Tony. 2011. "The Last Company Town." *Newsweek* (February 21):28–33.

Domhoff, G. William. 1970. *The Higher Circles: The Governing Class in America*. New York: Random House.

———. 1998. *Who Rules America? Power and Politics in the Year 2000*, 3rd ed. Mountain View, CA: Mayfield.

Donn, Jeff. 2004. "Insurers Paying Millions to Atone Fee Inflating Blacks' Policy Rates." *Associated Press* (October 10).

Draut, Tamara. 2008. "Economic State of Young America." *Demos* (Spring).

Drucker, Peter F. 1989. "The Rise and Fall of the Blue-Collar Worker." In *The Reshaping of America: Social Consequences of a Changing Economy*, D. Stanley Eitzen and Maxine Baca Zinn, eds. Englewood Cliffs, NJ: Prentice Hall, pp. 81–84.

———. 1993. *Post-Capitalist Society*. New York: HarperCollins.

Dubeck, Paula J., and Dana Dunn, eds. 2002. *Workplace/Women's Place: An Anthology*. Los Angeles, CA: Roxbury.

Dubow, Eric F., L. Rowell Huesmann, and Dara Greenwood. 2007. "Media and Youth Socialization." In *Handbook of Socialization*, Joan E. Grusec and Paul D. Hastings, eds. New York: The Guilford Press.

Duncan, Greg J. 1984. *Years of Poverty, Years of Plenty: The Changing Economic Fortunes of American Workers and Families*. Ann Arbor, MI: Institute of Social Research.

Duncan, Greg J., W. Jean Yeung, Jeanne Brooks-Gunn, and Judith R. Smith. 1998. "How Much Does Childhood Poverty Affect the Life Chances of Children?" *American Sociological Review* 63 (June):406–23.

Dunn, Andy. 2006. "The Other Domestic Spying." *Z Magazine* 19 (March):47–52.

Dunn, Dana. 1996. "Gender and Earnings." In *Women and Work: A Handbook*, Paula J. Dubeck and Kathryn Borman, eds. New York: Garland, pp. 61–63.

Durkheim, Emile. 1951. *Suicide*, reprinted ed. Glencoe, IL: Free Press.

———. 1958. *The Rules of Sociological Method*, 8th ed., Sarah A. Solovay and John H. Mueller, trans. Glencoe, IL: Free Press.

———. 1960. *The Division of Labor in Society*, George Simpson, trans. New York: Free Press.

———. 1965. *The Elementary Forms of Religious Life*, Joseph Ward Swain, trans. New York: Macmillan.

Dush, Claire M. Kemp, Catherine L. Cohan, and Paul R. Amato. 2003. "The Relationship between Cohabitation and Mental Quality and Stability: Change Across Cohorts? *Journal of Marriage and Family* 65 (August):539–49.

Dyer, Everett D. 1979. *The American Family: Variety and Change*. New York: McGraw-Hill.

Early, Frances H. 1983. "The French-Canadian Family Economy and Standard of Living in Lowell, Massachusetts, 1870." In *The American Family in Social Historical Perspective*, 3rd ed., Michael Gordon, ed. New York: St. Martin's Press, pp. 482–503.

Eaton, Joe, and M. B. Bell. 2010. "Lobbyists Swarm Capitol to Influence Health Reform." *Center for Public Integrity* (February 24). Available online: http://www.iwatchnews.org/2010/02/24/2725/lobbyists-swarm-capitol.html.

Eaton, Leslie. 2007. "In Mississippi, Poor Lag in Hurricane Aid." *New York Times* (November 16). Available online: http://www.nytimes.com/2007/n/16/us/I6mississippi.html?_r=1&hp=&ref=slogin&pa.

Ebony. 1995. "Amazing Grace: 50 Years of the Black Church." 50 (April):87–96.

Economist. 2006. "Migrants Remittances." (November 25):106.

———. 2007a. "O Come All Ye Faithful." (November 3):6–9.

———. 2007b. "Trouble in the Family." (March 3):40.

———. 2011. "Toddle to the Top." (May 7):32–33.

————. 2009. "Money in Misery." (February 7):21–24.

Education News. 2011. "Report Finds Number of Schools Failing to Make AYP Rising." (May 2). Available online: http://www.educationnews.org/ednews_today/155171.html.

Edwards, Renee, and Mark A. Hamilton. 2004. "You Need to Understand My Gender Role: An Empirical Test of Tannen's Model of Gender and Communication." *Sex Roles* 50 (7/8):491–504.

Edwards, Richard C., Michael Reich, and Thomas E. Weisskopf. 1978. "Sexism." In *The Capitalist System: A Radical Analysis of American Society*, 2nd ed. Englewood Cliffs, NJ: Prentice Hall.

Ehrenreich, Barbara. 1989. *Fear of Falling: The Inner Life of the Middle Class.* New York: Pantheon.

————. 1991. "Welfare: A White Secret." *Time* (December 16):84.

————. 2008. "Hell Is aGated Community." *The Progressive* 72 (February):12–13.

Ehrenreich, Barbara, and Dedrick Muhammad. 2009. "The Recession's Racial Divide." *New York Times* (September 13):17.

Eisenstein, Zillah. 1979. "Developing a Theory of Capitalist Patriarchy and Socialist Feminism." In *Capitalist Patriarchy and the Case for Socialist Feminism*, Zillah Eisenstein, ed. New York: Monthly Review Press, pp. 5–40.

Eitzen, D. Stanley. 2000. "Social Control and Sport." In *Handbook of Sport Studies*, Eric Dunning and Jay J. Coakley, eds. London: Sage.

————. 2009. *Fair and Foul: Beyond the Myths and Paradoxes of Sport*, 4th ed. Lanham, MD: Rowman & Littlefield.

————. 2011. "Tears, Snags, and Tangles in the Social Fabric of Society." Speech, University of the Incarnate Word, San Antonio, TX (April 19).

Eitzen, D. Stanley, and George H. Sage. 2009. *Sociology of North American Sport*, 8th ed. Boulder, CO: Paradigm Publishers.

Eitzen, D. Stanley, and Maxine Baca Zinn. 1989a. "The De-Athleticization of Women: The Naming and Gender Marking of Collegiate Sport Teams." *Sociology of Sport Journal* 6 (December):362–70.

————. 1998. "The Shrinking Welfare State: The New Welfare Legislation and Families." Paper presented at the annual meeting of the American Sociological Association, San Francisco (August 21–25).

Eitzen, D. Stanley, and George H. Sage. 2003. *The Sociology of North American Sport*, 7th ed. Madison, WI: Brown and Benchmark.

Eitzen, D. Stanley, and Kelly Eitzen Smith, eds. 2003. *Experiencing Poverty: Voices from the Bottom*. Belmont, CA: Wadsworth.

Eitzen, D. Stanley, Maxine Baca Zinn, and Barbara A. Wells. 2011. *Diversity in Families*, 9th ed. Boston, MA: Allyn and Bacon.

Eitzen, D. Stanley, Maxine Baca Zinn, and Kelly Eitzen Smith. 2011. *Social Problems*, 12th ed. Boston, MA: Allyn and Bacon.

Eitzen, D. Stanley, and Kenneth Stewart. 2007. *Solutions to Social Problems from the Bottom Up: Successful Social Movements*. Boston, MA: Allyn and Bacon.

Ekman, Paul, Wallace V. Friesen, and John Bear. 1984. "The International Language of Gestures." *Psychology Today* 18 (May):64–69.

Electronic Frontier Foundation. 2011. *Patterns of Misconduct: FBI Intelligence Violators from 2001-2008*, San Francisco.

Elliot, James R., and Jeremy Pais. 2006. "Race, Class, and Hurricane Katrina: Social Differences in Human Responses to Disaster." *Social Sciences Research* 35:295–321.

El Nasser, Haya. 2005. "Recent Arrivals Better Educated." *USA Today* (February 22):1A.

El Nasser, Haya, and Lorrie Grant. 2005. "Immigration Causes Age, Race Split." *USA Today* (June 9):1A.

England, Paula. 2010. "The Gender Revolution: Uneven and Stalled." *Gender and Society* 24 (2):149–66.

Epstein, Cynthia Fuchs. 1970. *Woman's Place*. Berkeley, CA: University of California Press.

Epstein, Joseph. 1997. "How Revolting: Why What Disgusts Us Defines Us." *The New Yorker* (July 14):78–82.

Eshleman, J. Ross. 1988. *The Family*, 5th ed. Boston, MA: Allyn and Bacon.

Espiritu, Yen Le. 1996. "Asian American Panethnicity." In *The Meaning of Difference*, Karen E. Rosenblum and Toni-Michelle Travis, eds. New York: McGraw-Hill, pp. 51–61.

Ettlinger, Steve. 2007. *Twinkie Deconstructed: My Journey to Discover How the Ingredients Found in Processed Foods Are Grown, Mined, and Manipulated into What America Eats*. New York, NY: Hudson Street Press.

Etzioni, Amitai. 1999. *The Limits of Privacy*. New York: Basic Books.

Everton, Terry. 2004. "Why School Sucks." *Z Magazine* 17 (November):54–56.

Fahim, Dareem. 2003. "The Moving Target." *Amnesty Now* 29 (Winter):6–9.

Falk, Erika. 2008. "Cutting Women Out." *In These Times* (March):20–23.

Faludi, Susan. 1991. *Backlash: The Undeclared War against Women*. New York: Crown.

Farley, John E., and Gregory D. Squires. 2009. "Fences and Neighbors: Segregation in 21st-Century America." In *Race and Ethnicity in Society*, Elizabeth Higginbotham and Margaret L. Andersen, eds. Belmont, CA: Wadsworth Cengage, p. 315.

————. 2012. "Fences and Neighbors: Segregation in 21st Century America." In *Race and Ethnicity in Society*, Elizabeth Higginbotham and Margaret L. Andersen, eds. Belmont, CA: Wadsworth, Cengage Learning, pp. 315–23.

Farr, Daniel. 2007. "Sissy Boy, Progressive Parents." In *Men's Lives*, 7th ed., Michael S. Kimmel and Michael A. Messner, eds. Boston, MA: Pearson Education, Inc.

Fausto-Sterling, Anne. 1992. *Myths of Gender: Biological Theories about Women and Men*. New York: Basic Books.

Feagin, Joe R. 2000. *Racist America*. New York: Routledge.

————. 2006. *Systemic Racism: A Theory of Oppression*. New York: Routledge.

Feagin, Joe R., and Clairece Booher Feagin. 1993. *Racial and Ethnic Relations*. Englewood Cliffs, NJ: Prentice Hall.

————. 1997. *Social Problems: A Critical Power-Conflict Perspective*, 5th ed. Upper Saddle River, NJ: Prentice Hall.

Feagin, Joe R., and Melvin P. Sikes. 1994. *Living with Racism: The Black Middle-Class Experience*. Boston, MA: Beacon Press.

Federal Bureau of Investigations. 2009. "2009 Hate Crime Statistics." Available online: *http://www2.fbi.gov/ucr/hc2009/data/table_10.html*.

Federal Bureau of Prisons. 2011. *U.S. Department of Justice*. Available online: *http://www.bop.gov/news/quick.jsp#2*.

Federal Interagency Forum on Aging-Related Statistics. 2010. *Older Americans 2010: Key Indicators of Well-Being*. Washington, DC: National Center for Health Statistics.

Feingold, Russ. 2001. "At the Debate of the Anti-Terrorism Bill, from the Senate Floor." (October 11). Available online: http://Feingold.senate.gov/~feingold/speeches/01/10/101101at.html.

Ferree, Myra Marx. 1991. "Feminism and Family Research." In *Contemporary Families: Looking Forward, Looking Back*, Alan Booth, ed. Minneapolis, MN: National Council on Family Relations, pp. 103–21.

———. 2006. "Globalization and Feminism: Opportunities and Obstacles for Activism in the Global Arena." In *Global Feminism: Transnational Women's Activism, Organizing, and Human Rights*, Myra Marx Ferree and Alli Marie Tripp, eds. New York: New York University Press.

Festinger, Leon, Henry W. Riecken, Jr., and Stanley Schachter. 1956. *When Prophecy Fails*. Minneapolis, MN: University of Minnesota Press.

Fields, Jason. 2004. "America's Families and Living Arrangements: 2003." *Current Population Reports*, P20–553 (November). Washington, DC: U.S. Bureau of the Census.

Fields, Jason, and Lynne M. Casper. 2001. "American Families and Living Arrangements." U.S. Bureau of the Census, *Current Population Reports*, P20–537. Washington, DC: U.S. Government printing office.

Filardo, Mary W., Jeffrey M. Vincent, Ping Sung, and Travis Stein. 2006. "Growth and Disparity: A Decade of U.S. Public School Construction." *Building Educational Success Together* [BEST]. Available online: http://www.21csf.org/csf.home/publications/BEST-Growth-Disparity-2006.pdf.

Fireside, Daniel. 2009. "Not Just Homeowners, but Renters Are Really Getting Screwed." *Dollars & Sense* (March 19).

Fischer, Claude S., Michael Hout, Martin Sanchez Jankowski, Samuel R. Lucas, Ann Swidler, and Kim Voss. 1996. *Inequality by Design: Cracking the Bell Curve Myth*. Princeton, NJ: Princeton University Press.

Fitzgerald, Frances. 1979. *America Revised: History Schoolbooks in the Twentieth Century*. Boston, MA: Atlantic/Little, Brown.

———. 2007. "Come One, Come All." *The New Yorker* (December 3):46–56.

Fletcher, Dan. 2010. "Facebook: Friends Without Borders." *Time* (May 31):30–39.

Forbes. 2009. "The Forbes 400." (October 19).

———. 2010a. "The Billionaire Issue." (March 28).

———. 2010b. "The Forbes Global 2000." (May 10).

Forden, Sara. 2011. "The Geek Who's Policing Our Privacy." *Bloomberg Business Week* (January 10/January 16):25–26.

Forrest, Christopher B., and Ellen-Marie Whelan. 2000. "Primary Care Safety-Net Delivery Sites in the United States: A Comparison of Community Health Centers, Hospital Outpatient Departments, and Physicians' Offices." *JAMA* 284, no.16 (October 25):2077–83.

Fost, Dan. 1991. "American Indians in the Nineties." *American Demographics* 13 (December):26–34.

Foster, John Bellamy, and Fred Magdoff. 2010. The Great Financial Crises—Three Years On." *Monthly Review* 62 (October).

Francis, Becky. 2010. "Gender, Toys, and Learning." *Oxford Review of Education* 36 (3):325–44.

Freeman, Jo. 1979. "The Women's Liberation Movement: Its Origins, Organizations, Activities, and Ideas." In *Women: A Feminist Perspective*, 2nd ed., Jo Freeman, ed. Palo Alto, CA: Mayfield, pp. 557–74.

Freepress.net. 2009. Available online: http://www.freepress.net.

Freud, Sigmund. 1946. *Civilization and Its Discontents*, Joan Riviére, trans. London: Hogarth Press.

Frey, William H. 2002. "Multilingual America." *American Demographics* 24 (July/August):20–23.

Friedan, Betty. 1963. *The Feminine Mystique*. New York: W. W. Norton.

Friedman, Thomas L. 2005. *The World Is Flat*. New York: Farrar, Straus, and Geroux.

Fuentes, Annette. 2007. "Segregation is Back in Class." *USA Today* (March 14):11A.

Fussell, Paul. 1983. *Class*. New York: Ballantine.

Galbraith, James K. 1998. "With Economic Inequality for All." *The Nation* (September 7):24–26.

Gallagher, Charles A. 2010. "Color Blind Privilege: The Social and Political Functions of Erasing the Color Line in Post Race America." In *Race, Class, and Gender*, 7th ed, Margaret L. Andersen and Patricia Hill Collins, eds. Belmont, CA: Wadsworth Cengage, p. 586.

———. 2012. "Color Blind Privilege: The Social and Political Functions of Erasing the Color Line in Post Race America." In *Race and Ethnicity in Society*, Elizabeth Higginbotham and Margaret L. Andersen, eds. Belmont, CA: Wadsworth, Cengage Learning, pp. 57–61.

Gallup Poll. 2010. "Religion." Available online: http://www.gallup.com/poll/1690/religion.aspx.

Gandel, Stephen, and Paul J. Lim. 2008. "What Do We Do Now?" *Money* (November):89–91.

Gans, Herbert J. 1962. *The Urban Villagers*. New York: Free Press.

———. 1971. "The Uses of Power: The Poor Pay All." *Social Policy* 2 (July–August):20–24.

———. 1990. "Second Generation Decline." *Ethnic Racial Studies* 15:173–92.

Garfinkel, Simson. 2000a. *Database Nation*. New York: O'Reilly.

Garrahy, Deborah A. 2001. "Three Third-Grade Teachers' Gender-Related Beliefs and Behavior." *The Elementary School Journal* 102 (1):81–94.

Garten, Jeffrey E. 1999. "Megamergers Are a Clear and Present Danger." *BusinessWeek* (January 25):28.

Gecas, Viktor, and Monica Seff. 1991. "Families and Adolescents." In *Contemporary Families: Looking Forward, Looking*

Back, Alan Booth, ed. Minneapolis, MN: National Council on Family Relations, pp. 208–25.

Gelles, Richard J. 1995. *Contemporary Families: A Sociological View*. Thousand Oaks, CA: Sage.

Gentry, Curt. 1991. *J. Edgar Hoover: The Man and His Secrets*. New York: W. W. Norton.

Gerrard, Nathan L. 1968. "The Serpent Handling Religions of West Virginia." *Transaction* 5 (May).

Gerson, Kathleen. 2010. *The Unfinished Revolution: How a New Generation is Reshaping Family, Work, and Gender in America*. New York: Oxford University Press.

Gerth, Hans, and C. Wright Mills. 1953. *Character and Social Structure: The Psychology of Social Institutions*. New York: Harcourt, Brace, & World.

Gibbs, Nancy. 2008. "College Confidential." *Time* (April 14):80.

Giddens, Anthony. 1991. *Introduction to Sociology*. New York: W. W. Norton.

Gilbert, Bil, and Nancy Williamson. 1973. "Sport Is Unfair to Women." *Sports Illustrated* (May 28):90–96.

Gilman, Richard. 1971. "Where Did It All Go Wrong?" *Life* (August 13).

Gilmore, Janet. 2004. "Modern Slavery Thriving in the U.S." University of California, Berkeley Press Release (September 23). Available online: http://berkeley.edu/news/media/releases/2004/09/03_16691.html.

Gobry, Pascal-Emmanuel. 2011. "Facebook Is Ramping Up Its Washington Lobbying." *Business Insider* (February 3). Available online: http://www.businessinsider.com/facebook-is-ramping-up-its-washingtong-lobbying.

Gold, David A., Clarence Y. H. Lo, and Erik Olin Wright. 1975. "Recent Developments in Marxist Theories of the Capitalist State." *Monthly Review* 27 (October):29–45.

Goldwert, Lindsay. 2010. "Constance McMillen, Mississippi Lesbian Teen Banned from Prom to Lead NYC Gay Pride Parade." *NY Daily News* (April 15). Available online: http://www.nydailynews.com/ny local/2010/04/15/2010-04-15_mississippi_lesbian_teen_banned_from_prom_to_lead_nyc_gay_pridede.html.

Goode, William J. 1966. "Social Class and Church Participation." *American Journal of Sociology* 72 (July).

———. 1984. "Idealization of the Recent Past: The United States." In *Family in Transition: Rethinking Marriage, Sexuality, Child Rearing, and Family Organization*, 4th ed., Arlene S. Skolnick and Jerome H. Skolnick, eds. Boston, MA: Little, Brown, pp. 43–53.

Goozner, Merrill. 2000. "The Price Isn't Right." *American Prospect* (September 11):25–29.

Gorman, Anna. 2007. "Immigrant Children Grow Fluent in English, Study Says." *Los Angeles Times* (November 30). Available online: http://www.latimes.com/news/local/la-me-english.30nov30,0,1163558.story?

Gould, Stephen Jay. 1994. "Curveball." *The New Yorker* (November 28):139–49.

———. 1998. "The Sharp-Eyed Lynx, Outfoxed by Nature." *Natural History* (May):16–21, 70–72.

Gouldner, Alvin W. 1962. "Anti-Minotaur: The Myth of Value-Free Sociology." *Social Problems* 9 (Winter).

Graham, Hugh Davis, and Ted Robert Gurr. 1969. *The History of Violence in America*. New York: Bantam Books.

Gramlich, John. 2010. "The Ever-Growing Sex Offender Registry." *Stateline* (April 12). Available online: http://www.stateline.org/live.

Graves, Lucia. 2007. "The Perils and Perks of Helicopter Parents." *US News and World Report* (December 18). Available online: http://www.usnes.com/education/articles/2007/12/18/the-perils-and-perks-of-helicopter-parents.

Greene, Jay P., and Marcus A. Winters. 2006. "Leaving Boys Behind: Public High School Graduation Rates." *Civic Report* (April). Available online: http://www.manhattan-institute.org/html/cr_48.htm.

Green, Mark. 2002. *Selling Out*. New York: HarperCollins.

Greenhouse, Steven. 2009. *The Big Squeeze: Tough Times for the American Worker*. New York: Anchor Books.

Greider, William. 1992. *Who Will Tell the People: The Betrayal of American Democracy*. New York: Simon & Schuster.

Greim, Lisa. 1998. "Working Women Protest Pay Gap." *Rocky Mountain News* (April 4):1B.

Gross, Daniel. 2008. "Today's 'Culture of Poverty.'" *Newsweek* (April 7):18.

Grossman, Cathy Lynn. 2011. "Number of U.S. Muslims Expected to Double." *USA Today* (January 27):1A.

Grossman, Lev. 2010/2011. "2010 Person of the Year: Mark Zuckerberg." *Time* (December/January 27/3):44–70.

Grunwald, Michael. 1999. "The HUD Chief Finds His Own Pulpit." *Washington Post National Weekly Edition* (June 7):29.

Grusec, Joan E., and Maayan Davidov. 2007. "Socialization in the Family: The Roles of Parents." In *Handbook of Socialization*, Joan E. Grusec and Paul D. Hastings, eds. New York: The Guilford Press.

Guastello, Denise D., and Stephen J. Guastello. 2003. "Androgyny, Gender Role Behavior, and Emotional Intelligence among College Students and Their Parents." *Sex Roles* 49 (1/2):663–73.

Hacker, Andrew. 1970. *The End of the American Era*. New York: Atheneum.

Hacker, Jacob S. 2006. *The Great Risk Shift*. New York: Oxford University Press.

Hall, M. Ann. 1985. "Knowledge and Gender: Epistemological Questions in the Social Analysis of Sport." *Sociology of Sport Journal* 2:25–42.

Hamburg, David A. 1993. "The American Family Transformed." *Society* 31 (January/February):60–69.

Hampson, Rick. 2011. "The Changing Face of American Jobs." *USA Today* (January 13):1A.

Hananel, Sam. 2010. "Layoffs Affect Union Ranks." *Associated Press* (January 23).

Hansen, Karen V. 2005. *Not So Nuclear Families: Class, Gender, and Networks of Care*. New Brunswick, NJ: Rutgers University Press.

Harding, Vincent. 1981. *There Is a River: The Black Struggle for Freedom in America*. New York: Harcourt Brace Jovanovich.

Harjo, Susan Shown. 1996. "Now and Then: Native Peoples in the United States." *Dissent* 43 (Summer):58–60.

Harrington, Michael. 1963. *The Other America: Poverty in the United States*. Baltimore, MD: Penguin.

———. 1979. "Social Retreat and Economic Stagnation." *Dissent* 26 (Spring):131–4.

———. 1985. *Taking Sides: The Education of a Militant Mind.* New York: Holt, Rinehart and Winston.

———. 1986. *The Next Left.* New York: Henry Holt.

Harris, Kathleen Mullan. 1996. "The Reforms Will Hurt, Not Help, Poor Women and Children." *Chronicle of Higher Education* (October 4):B7.

Harris, Marvin. 1974. *Cows, Pigs, Wars, and Witches: The Riddles of Culture.* New York: Random House.

———. 1978. "India's Sacred Cows." *Human Nature* 1 (February):28–36.

Harris, Roderick J., and Claudette Bennett. 1995. "Racial and Ethnic Diversity." In *State of the Union: America in the 1990s, Vol. 2:Social Trends,* Reynolds Farley, ed. New York: Sage, pp. 141–210.

Hartmann, Heidi I. 1976. "Capitalism, Patriarchy, and Job Segregation by Sex." *Signs* 1 (Spring):137–69.

Haynes, V. Dion. 2010. "U.S. Unemployment Rate for Blacks Projected to Hit 25-Year High." *Washington Post* (January 15).

Heilbroner, Robert L. 1974. *An Inquiry into the Human Prospect.* New York: W. W. Norton.

Helft, Miguel. 2010. "Facebook Wrestles With Free Speech and Civility." *New York Times* (December 12).

Henderson, Nell. 2006. "Winners and Losers in the Short Run." *Washington Post National Weekly Edition* (April 24):21.

Henneberger, Melinda, and Michael Marriott. 1993. "For Some, Youthful Courting Has Become a Game of Abuse." *New York Times* (July 11):1A, 14A.

Hennessy, Rosemary., and Chrys Ingraham, eds. 1997. *Materialist Feminism: A Reader in Class, Difference, and Women's Lives.* New York: Routledge.

Henslin, James M. 2008. *Sociology: A Down-to-Earth Approach,* 9th ed. Boston, MA: Allyn and Bacon.

Hermann, Andrew. 1994. "Muslims Plan Census to Chart Growth Here." *Chicago Sun-Times* (February 12):4.

Herrnstein, Richard. 1971. "I.Q." *Atlantic* 228 (September):43–64.

Herron, Janna. 2011. "Banks Repossess 1 Million Homes in 2010." *Denver Post* (January 13). Available online: http://www.denverpost.com/fdcp?294934685026.

Hess, Beth B., Elizabeth W. Markson, and Peter J. Stein. 1993. *Sociology,* 4th ed. New York: Macmillan.

Higginbotham, Elizabeth. 1994. "Black Professional Women: Job Ceilings and Employment Sectors." In *Women of Color in U.S. Society,* Maxine Baca Zinn and Bonnie Thornton Dill, eds. Philadelphia, PA: Temple University Press, pp. 113–31.

Higginbotham, Elizabeth, and Margaret L. Anderson. 2009. "Introduction, Race: Why It Matters." In *Race and Ethnicity in Society,* Elizabeth Higginbotham and Margaret L. Andersen, eds. Belmont, CA: Wadsworth. pp. 1–6.

———. 2012. *Race and Ethnicity in Society,* 3rd ed. Belmost, CA: Wadsworth Cengage Learning. pp. 7–10.

Hightower, Jim. 1987. "Where Greed, Unofficially Blessed by Reagan, Has Led." *New York Times* (June 21):25.

———. 1996. "Homeless Electorate." *Dollars & Sense* 206 (July/August):7.

———. 2007. "Subprime Loans=Primetime for Vampire Leaders." *Hightower Lowdown* (August 22).

———. 2011. "Playing With Economic Dynamite." *Progressive Populist* (February 1):3.

Hill, Shirley A., and Joey Sprague. 1999. "Parenting in Black and White Families: The Interaction of Gender with Race and Class." *Gender & Society* 13 (4):480–502.

Hill, Steven. 2002. *Fixing Elections: The Failure of America's Winner Take All Politics.* New York: Routledge.

Hindery, Leo, Jr., and Leo W. Gerard. 2009. "Our Jobless Recovery." *The Nation* (July 13):22–24.

Hoch, Paul. 1972. *Rip Off the Big Game.* New York: Doubleday.

Hochschild, Arlie, with Anne Machung. 1989. *The Second Shift.* New York: Viking Penguin.

Hodge, Robert W., Donald J. Treiman, and Peter H. Rossi. 1966. "A Comparative Study of Occupational Prestige." In *Class, Status, and Power,* 2nd ed., Reinhard Bendix and S. M. Lipset, eds. New York: Free Press, pp. 309–21.

Hodge, Robert W., Paul M. Seigel, and Peter H. Rossi. 1964. "Occupational Prestige in the United States, 1925-63." *American Journal of Sociology* 70 (November):286–302.

Hofferth, Sandra. 2002. "Did Welfare Reform Work? Implications for 2002 and Beyond." *Contexts: Understanding People in Their Social Worlds* 1 (2):45–51.

Hoffman, Matthew. 1996. "Electoral College Dropouts." *The Nation* (June 17):15–16.

Hole, Judith, and Ellen Levine. 1979. "The First Feminists." In *Women: A Feminist Perspective,* 2nd ed., Jo Freeman, ed. Palo Alto, CA: Mayfield.

Holmes, Stanley. 2002. "Boeing's High-Speed Flight." *BusinessWeek* (August 12):74–75.

Holstein, James A., and Jay Gubrium. 1999. "What Is Family? Further Thoughts on a Social Constructionist Approach." *Marriage and Family Review* 28 (3/4):3–20.

Homans, George. 1964. "Bringing Men Back In." *American Sociological Review* 29 (December):809–18.

Horne, Gerald. 1992–1993. "Race Backwards: Genes, Violence, Race, and Genocide." *Covert Action* (Winter):29–35.

Hosenball, Mark. 1999. "It Is Not the Act of a Few Bad Apples." *Newsweek* (May 17):34–35.

Huaco, George A. 1966. "The Functionalist Theory of Stratification: Two Decades of Controversy." *Inquiry* 9 (Autumn):215–40.

Hudson, Christopher G. 2005. "Socioeconomic Status and Mental Illness: Tests of the Social Causation and Selection Hypotheses." *American Journal of Orthopsychiatry* 75 (1). Available online: http:// www.apa.org/journals/releases/ort7513.pdf.

Huffington, Arianna. 2011. "Dear Class of 2011: Good Luck...You're Really Going to Need It!" *Huffington Post* (May 18). Available online: http://www.huffingtonpost.com/arianna-huffington/dear-class-of-2011.

Hughes, Diane, Ellen Gallinsky, and Anne Morris. 1992. "The Effect of Job Characteristics on Marital Quality." *Journal of Marriage and the Family* (February):31–42.

Humes, Karen R., Nicholas A. Jones, and Roberto R. Ramirez. 2011. "Overview of Race and Hispanic Origin 2010." *2010 Census Briefs* C201BR (March). Washington, DC: U.S. Census Bureau.

Hunt, Paula. 2007. "A Twinkie by Any Other Ingredient Wouldn't taste as Processed." *Chron.com.* Available online: http://www.chron.com/disp/story.mpl/life/4814243.html.

Hunter, Floyd. 1953. *Community Power Structure*. Chapel Hill, NC: University of North Carolina Press.

Huntington, Samuel P. 2005. *Who Are We? The Challenges to America's National Identity*. New York: Simon & Schuster.

Hurst, Charles E. 2001. *Social Inequality: Forms, Causes, and Consequences*, 4th ed. Boston, MA: Allyn and Bacon.

Hutchins, Robert M. 1976. "Is Democracy Possible?" *Center Magazine* 9 (January-February):2–6.

Hyman, Rebecca. 2008. "America's Frightening Alzheimer's Epidemic." *Alter Net* (May 16). Available online: http:www.alternet.org/story/85532.

Idle, Tracey, Eileen Wood, and Serge Desmarias. 1993. "Gender Role Socialization in Toy Play Situations: Mothers and Fathers with Their Sons and Daughters." *Sex Roles* 28 (11/12):679–91.

Intelligence Report. 2001. "Reevaluating the Net." *The Southern Poverty Law Center* 102 (Summer):54–55.

Internal Revenue Service Oversight Board. 2011. "2010 Taxpayer Attitude Survey." (January). Available online: http://www.treasury.gov/irsob/reports/2011/IRSOB%202010%20taxpayer%20attitude%20survey.pdf.

Internetstats.com. 2010.

ISR Newsletter. 1982. "Why Do Women Earn Less?" Institute for Social Research, University of Michigan (Spring/Summer).

Ivins, Molly. 2000. "Capitalism Gets a Really Bad Name." *Progressive Populist* (May 15):22–23.

Jackson, Jesse. 1998. "Market Rules and New Democracy." *Progressive Populist* 4 (June):19.

Jackson, Maggie. 2009. *Distracted: The Erosion of Attention and the Coming Dark Age*. Amherst, NY: Prometheus Books.

Jacobsen, Linda A., Mary Kent, Marlene Lee, and Mark Mather. 2011. "America's Aging Population." *Population Bulletin* 66 (February): entire issue.

Jacoby, Susan. 2011. "The Myth of Aging Gracefully." *Newsweek* (February 7):14.

James, Susan Donaldson. 2008. "Cheating Scandals Rock Three Top-Tier High Schools." *ABC News* (February 29). Available online: http://abcnews.go.com/US/story?id=4362510&page=1.

Janzen, David. 1974. "Love 'Em and Leave 'Em Alone." *Mennonite* (June 11):390.

Jarrett, Robin, and Linda Burton. 1999. "Dynamic Dimensions of Family Structure in Low-Income African American Families."*Journal of Comparative Family Studies* 30 (Spring):177–87.

Jaynes, Gerald David, and Robin M. Williams, Jr. 1989. *A Common Destiny: Blacks and American Society*. Washington, DC: National Academy Press.

Jayson, Sharon. 2005. "Budding Friendships Fill Out the Family Tree." *USA Today* (December 20):1A–2A.

———. 2010. "Catholic Church, and Religion in General, Losing Latinos in USA." *USA Today* (March 16). Available online: http://usatoday.com/news/religion/2010-03-16-latino-religion.

Jeffries, Vincent, and H. Edward Ransford. 1980. *Social Stratification: A Multiple Hierarchy Approach*. Boston, MA: Allyn and Bacon.

Jencks, Christopher, Marshall Smith, Henry Ackland, Mary Jo Bane, David Cohen, Herbert Gintis, et al. 1979. *Who Gets Ahead? The Determinants of Economic Success in America*. New York: Basic Books.

Jenkins, Philip. 2002. "The Next Christianity." *Atlantic Monthly* 290 (October):53–68.

Jensen, Arthur R. 1969. "How Much Can We Boost IQ and Scholastic Achievement?" *Harvard Educational Review* 39 (Winter):1–123.

———. 1980. *Bias in Mental Testing*. New York: Free Press.

Jervis, Rick. 2009. "Hispanic Worker Deaths Up 76%." *USA Today* (July 20):1A.

Jessop, Carolyn, with Laura Palmer. 2007. *Escape*. New York: Broadway Books.

Jhally, Sut. 1999. *Tough Guise: Violence, Media, and the Crisis in Masculinity*. Northampton, MA: Media Education Foundation, Inc.

Jimenez, Tomas R., and Laura Lopez-Sanders. 2011. "Unanticipated, Unintended, and Unadvised: The Effects of Public Policy on Unauthorized Immigration." *Pathways* (Winter):3–7.

Johnson, Charles S. 2011. "Lobbying Group Criticizes Subsidies For Oil and Gas Industry." *Billings Gazette* (May 19).

Johnson, Dirk. 2000. "Commandments Find Way into Schools." *Rocky Mountain News* (February 27):6A.

Johnson, Mary. 1991. "Disabled Americans Push for Access." *The Progressive* 55 (August):21–23.

Johnson, Tory. 2007. "Take Control: How to Negotiate Your Salary." *ABC Internet Ventures* (April 24). Available online: http://abcnews.go.com/print/id-3074877.

Johnson, Steven. 2010. "In Praise of Oversharing." *Time* (May 31):39.

Jones, J. H. 1981. *Bad Blood*. New York: Free Press.

Jones, Jeffrey M. 2009. "Majority of Americans Continue to Oppose Gay Marriage." *Gallup* (May 27). Available online: http://www.gallup.com/poll/118378/majority-americans-continue-oppose-gay-marriage.aspx.

Kadet, Anne. 2008. "Parents Spare No Expense in Children's Sports." *Smart Money Magazine* (June 27). Available online: http://www.smartmoney.com/spending/budgeting/parents-spare-no-expense-in-childrens-sports-23367.

Kahn, Joseph P. 2012. "Missed Connections" *Boston Sunday Globe* (April 15): A1, A6.

Kaiser Family Foundation. 2011. "Disparities & Public Opinion Data Note: The Digital Divide and Access to Health Information Online." April. Available online: http://www.kff.org.

Kalleberg, Arne L. 2009. "Precarious Work, Insecure Workers: Employment Relations in Transition." *American Sociological Review* 74 (February):11–22.

Kamau, Puis. 2001. "Educational Funding Unfair." *Denver Post* (April 8):81.

Kammeyer, Kenneth C. W., George Ritzer, and Norman R. Yetman. 1997. *Sociology*, 7th ed. Boston, MA: Allyn and Bacon.

Kanter, Rosabeth Moss. 1977. *Men and Women of the Corporation*. New York: Basic Books.

Karabell, Zachary. 2009. "The Case for Derivatives." *Newsweek* (February 2):35–36.

Kaufman, Gordon. 1997. "Mystery and God." *Mennonite Life* 52 (March):4–8.

Keating, Frank. 2002. "Dishwasher or Stockbroker: A Life Is a Life." *Fort Collins Coloradoan* (January 25):A10.

Keen, Judy. 2010. "On Front Lines of Homeless Crisis." *USA Today* (February 16).

———. 2011. "More Police Patrolling on Footage." *USA Today* (February 10):1A.

Keilholtz, Jeff. 2008. "The Megachurch Juggernaut." *Z Magazine* 21 (March):34–37.

Keller, Helen. 1954. *The Story of My Life*. Garden City, NY: Doubleday.

Kennedy, David. 1996. "Can We Still Afford to Be a Nation of Immigrants?" *Atlantic Monthly* (November):51–80.

Kennedy, Paul. 2001. "Introduction: Globalization and the Crisis of Identities." In *Globalization and National Identities: Crisis or Opportunity*, Paul Kennedy and Catherine J. Danks, eds. London: Pallgrave.

Kennickell, Arthur B. 2009. "Ponds and Streams: Wealth and Income in the U.S. 1989 to 2007." *Federal Reserve Board*. Working Paper. (January 7).

Kent, Mary M., Kelvin M. Pollard, John Haaga, and Mark Mather. 2001. "First Glimpses from the 2000 U.S. Census." *Population Bulletin* 56 (June): entire issue.

Kephart, William and William Zellner. 1990. *Extraordinary Groups*, 4th ed. New York: W. H. Freeman/Worth Publishers.

Kerbo, Harold R. 1983. *Social Stratification and Inequality: Class Conflict in the United States*. New York: McGraw-Hill.

Kerr, Jennifer. 1999. "A Kiss, a Promise and an Act of Defiance." *Rocky Mountain News* (January 17):37A.

Kesey, Ken. 1962. *One Flew Over the Cuckoo's Nest*. New York: Signet Books.

Kibria, Nazli. 1997. "The Concept of 'Bicultural Families' and Its Implications for Research on Immigrant and Ethnic Families." In *Immigration and the Family*, Alan Booth, Ann C. Crouter, and Nancy Landale, eds. Mahwah, NJ: Erlbaum, pp. 205–10.

Kids Count. 2009. "Data Across States: Kids in Single Parent Families." Available online: http://datacenter.kidscount.org/data/acrossstates/rankings.aspx?ind=106.

Kim, Marlene. 1998. "Are the Working Poor Lazy?" *Challenge* 41 (May/June):85–99.

Kimmel, Michael. 1992. "Reading Men, Masculinity, and Publishing." *Contemporary Sociology* 21 (March):162–71.

Kimmel, Michael, and Michael A. Messner. 2004. *The Gendered Society*, 2nd ed. New York: Oxford University Press.

———. 2007. *Men's Lives*, 7th ed. Boston, MA: Allyn and Bacon.

Kiser, Jim. 2005. "A Tattletale May Be Riding in Your Car." *Arizona Daily Star* (June 5):1H.

Kloos, Peter. 2000. "The Dialectics of Globalization and Localization." In *The Ends of Globalization*, Don Kalb, Marco van der Land, Richard Staring, Bart van Steenbergen, and Nico Wilterdink, eds. Lanham, MD: Rowman & Littlefield, pp. 281–98.

Knottnerus, J. David. 1987. "Status Attainment Research and Its Image of Society." *American Sociological Review* 52 (February): 113–21.

Kocieniewski, David. 2011. "G.E.'s Strategies Let It Avoid Taxes Altogether." *New York Times* (March 24). Available online: http://www.nytimes.com/2011/03/25/business/economy/25tax.html.

Konczal, Mike. 2011. "Cleaning Up the Aftermath of Subprime." *American Prospect* 22 (June): A16–A18.

Kozol, Jonathan. 2002. "Malign Neglect." *The Nation* (June 10):20–23.

———. 2005. "Still Separate, Still Unequal: America's Educational Apartheid." *Harper's Magazine* (September): 41–52.

Kramer, R. C. 1982. "Corporate Crime." In *White Collar and Economic Crime*, P. Wickman and T. Dailey, eds. New York: Lexington, pp. 75–94.

Krakauer, Jon. 2003. *Under the Banner of Heaven*. New York: Doubleday.

Kralis, Barbara. 2006. "Modern Day Slavery Flourishes." *Renew America* (July 19). Available online: http://www.renewamerica.us/column/kralis/060719.

Krantz, Matt. 2011. "214 Newly Minted Billionaires Land on 'Forbes' List." *USA Today* (March 10):1B.

Kriner, Douglas L., and Francis X. Shen. 2010. *The Casualty Gap: The Causes and Consequences of American Wartime Inequalities*. New York: Oxford University Press.

Kristof, Nicholas D. 2005. "Let Fathers Be Fathers." *New York Times* (April 10):wk13.

Kroeger, Brook. 1994. "The Road Less Rewarded." *Working Woman* (July):50–55.

Krugman, Paul. 2003. "Channels of Influence." *New York Times* (March 25). Available online: http://query.nytimes.com/gst/fullpage.html?res=9B0ZE1DD1230F9.

———. 2011. "Degrees and Dollars." *New York Times* (March 6). Available online: http://www.nytimes.com/2011/03/07/opinion/07krugman.html.

Kulik, Liat. 2002. "Like-Sex versus Opposite-Sex Effects in Transmissions of Gender Role Ideology from Parents of Adolescents in Israel." *Journal of Youth and Adolescence* 31 (6):451–7.

Kulman, Linda. 2004. "Our Consuming Interest." *U.S. News & World Report* (June 28/July 5):58–60.

Kuo, David. 2008. "Turning a Corner: The Religious Right Looks Beyond Bush." *Washington Post National Weekly Edition* (March 3–9):26.

Kuttner, Robert. 1996. "Fair Play for Female Athletes." *The Washington Post National Weekly Edition* (August 26–September 1):5.

———. 1998. "Toward Universal Coverage." *The Washington Post National Weekly Edition* (July 20):27.

Lacayo, Richard. 1991. "Death on the Shop Floor." *Time* (September 16):28–29.

Ladd, Gary W. 2007. "Social Learning in the Peer Context." In *Contemporary Perspectives on Socialization and Social Development in Early Childhood Education*, Olivia Saracho and Bernard Spodek, eds. Charlotte, NC: Information Age Publishing.

Ladner, Joyce A. 1971. *Tomorrow's Tomorrow*. New York: Doubleday.

Lane, Charles. 2006. "White House Fights Race-Based Admissions Policies." *Washington Post* (September 4):17A. Available online: http://www.washingtonpost.com/wp.dyn/content/article/2006/09/03/AR2006090300767_pf.html.

Lardner, James. 2005. "What's the Problem?" In *Inequality Matters*, James Lardner and David A. Smith, eds. New York: The New Press.

Lareau, Annette. 2003. *Unequal Childhoods: Class, Race, and Family Lives*. Berkeley, CA: University of California Press.

Lauer, Nancy Cook. 2002. "Studies Show Women's Role in Media Shrinking." Available online: www.equality2020.org/media.htm.

Lechner, Frank J. 1989. "Fundamentalism Revisited." *Society* 26 (January/February): 51–59.

Lee, Jennifer, and Frank D. Bean. 2004. "America's Changing Color Lines: Immigration, Race/Ethnicity, and Multiracial Identification."*Annual Review of Sociology* 30:221–42.

Lee, Sharon M. 1998. "Asian Americans: Diverse and Growing." *Population Bulletin* 53 (June):entire issue.

Lee, Valerie E., and David Burkam. 2002. *Inequality at the Starting Gate*. Washington, DC: Economic Policy Institute. Available online: http://www.epinet.org/books/starting_gate.html.

Leinwand, Donna. 1999. "Debate Rages on Remedies for Women's Pay Gap." *Denver Post* (October 11):15A.

Lekachman, Robert. 1979. "The Specter of Full Employment." In *Crisis in American Institutions*, 4th ed., Jerome H. Skolnick and Elliott Currie, eds. Boston, MA: Little, Brown, pp. 50–58.

Lemert, Edwin M. 1951. *Social Pathology: A Systematic Approach to the Theory of Sociopathic Behavior*. New York: McGraw-Hill.

Lenski, Gerhard. 1966. *Power and Privilege: A Theory of Social Stratification*. New York: McGraw-Hill.

Leondar-Wright, Betsy, Meizhu Lui, Gloribell Mota, Decrick Mohammad, and Mara Voukydis. 2005. *State of the Dream 2005: Disowned in the Ownership Society*. Boston, MA: United for a Fair Economy.

Leonhardt, David. 2011. "Is Your Religion Your Financial Destiny?" *New York Times* (May 11). Available online: http://www.nytimes.com/2001/05/15/magazine/is-your-religion-your-financial-destiny?

Levitan, Sar A., and Clifford M. Johnson. 1982. *Second Thoughts on Work*. Kalamazoo, MI: W. E. Upjohn Institute for Employment Research.

Levy, Steven. 2004. "A Future with Nowhere to Hide?" *Newsweek* (June 7):76.

Lewis, Amanda E., and Maria Kryson, eds. 2004. *The Changing Terrain of Race and Ethnicity*. New York: Russell Sage Foundation.

Liazos, Alexander. 1985. *Sociology: A Liberating Perspective*. Boston, MA: Allyn and Bacon.

Lichtenberg, Judith. 1992. "Racism in the Head, Racism in the World." *Report from the Institute for Philosophy and Public Policy* (University of Maryland) 12 (Spring/Summer):3–5.

Lichter, Daniel T., Diane K. McLaughlin, and David C. Ribar. 2002. "Economic Restructuring and the Retreat from Marriage."*Social Science Research* 31:230–56.

Lichter, Daniel T., and Zhenchao Qian. 2004. *Marriage and Family in a Multiracial Society*. Washington, DC: Russell Sage Foundation.

Liebow, Elliot. 1967. *Tally's Corner*. Boston, MA: Little, Brown.

Lindner, Eileen W., ed. 2011. *Yearbook of American and Canadian Churches*. New York: National Council of Churches.

Lipman-Blumen, Jean. 1984. *Gender Roles and Power*. Englewood Cliffs, NJ: Prentice Hall.

Livingston, Jay. 2011. "Tax Expenditures." *Montclair Socioblog* (March 16). Available online: http://monclair-soci.blogspot.com/2011/03/tax-expenditures.html.

Locke, John L. 1998. *The De-Voicing of Society: Why We Don't Talk to Each Other Anymore*. New York: Simon & Schuster.

Lockheed, Marlaine. 1985. "Sex Equity in the Classroom Organization and Climate." In *Handbook for Achieving Sex Equity Through Education*, Susan S. Klein, ed. Baltimore, MD: Johns Hopkins University Press, pp. 189–217.

Loewen, James W. 1995. *Lies My Teacher Told Me: Everything Your American History Textbook Got Wrong*. New York: Simon & Schuster.

Lopiano, Donna. 2008. "Pay Inequity in Athletics." Women's Sports Foundation. Available online: http://www.womenssports-foundation.org/cgi-bin/iowa/issues/disc/article.html?record=118.

Lorber, Judith. 1994. *Paradoxes of Gender*. New Haven, CT: Yale University Press.

———. 2005. *Gender Inequality: Feminist Theories and Politics*. Los Angeles, CA: Roxbury.

Lord, Walter. 1955. *A Night to Remember*. New York: Henry Holt.

Los Angeles Times. 2003. "A Formula for Inequity." (December 13). Available online: http://www.latimes.com/news/opinion/editorials/la-ed-schoolfund13d.

Lott, Juanita Tamayo, and Judy C. Felt. 1991. "Studying the Pan Asian Community." *Population Today* 19 (April 1):6–8.

Love, Alice Ann. 1998. "Gender Wage Gap Shrinks Slightly." *USA Today* (June 10):1A.

Lucal, Betsy. 1994. "Class Stratification in Introductory Textbooks: Relational or Distributional Models?" *Teaching Sociology* 22 (April):139–50.

———. 1996. "Oppression and Privilege: Toward a Relational Conceptualization of Race." *Teaching Sociology* 24 (July): 245–55.

Luker, Kristin. 1991. "Dubious Conceptions: The Controversy Over Teen Pregnancy." *American Prospect* 5 (Spring):73–83.

Mabry, J. Beth, Roseann Giarrusso, and Vern L. Bengston. 2004. "Generations, the Life Course, and Family Change." In Jacqueline Scott, Judith Teas, and Martin Richards (Eds.), The Blackwell Companion to the Sociology of Families. Malden, MA: Blackwell, p. 595.

Maccoby, Eleanor E. 2007. "Historical Overview of Socialization Research and Theory." In *Handbook of Socialization: Theory and Research*, Joan E. Grusec and Paul D. Hastings, eds. New York: The Guilford Press.

MacEwan, Arthur. 2001. "Ask Dr. Dollar." *Dollars & Sense* 233 (January/February): 40.

Madrick, Jeff. 2009. *The Case for Big Government*. Princeton, NJ: Princeton University Press.

Magdoff, Fred, and Harry Magdoff. 2004. "Disposable Workers: Today's Reserve Army of Labor." *Monthly Review* 55 (April):18–35.

Malec, Michael A. 1997. "Gender Equity in Athletics." In *Perspectives on Current Social Problems*, Gregg Lee Carter, ed. Boston, MA: Allyn and Bacon, pp. 209–18.

Malveaux, Julianne. 2002. *The Nation* (January 7/14):34–35.

Manning, Wendy, and Pamela J. Smock. 2002. "First Comes Cohabitation and Then Comes Marriage?" *Journal of Family Issues* 23 (November): 1065–86.

Marabel, Manning. 2006. "Inheritance, Wealth, and Race." (April). Available online: http://www.manningmarabel.net/works/pdf/apr06a.pdf.

Marger, Martin N. 1987. *Elites and Masses: An Introduction to Political Sociology*, 2nd ed. Belmont, CA: Wadsworth.

Marklein, Mary Beth. 2009. "SAT Scores Show Disparities by Race, Gender, Family Income." *USA Today* (August 26). Available online: http://www.usatoday.com/news/education/2009-08-25-SAT-scores_n.htm.

Marquardt, Katy and Kirk Shinkle. 2009. "Terrible Tale of the Tape." *U.S. News and World Report* (March):54.

Martin, Karen A. 2005. "William Wants a Doll: Can He Have One?" *Gender and Society* 19 (August):456–79.

Martin, Patricia Yancey. 2003. "Said and Done Versus Saying and Doing: Gendering Practices, Practicing Gender at Work." *Gender & Society* 17 (June): 342–66.

Martin, Philip, and Elizabeth Midgley. 1999. "Immigration to the United States." *Population Bulletin* 54 (June):entire issue.

———. 2006. "Immigration: Shaping and Reshaping America." *Population Bulletin* (December). Washington, DC: Population Reference Bureau.

Marx, Karl. 1967. *Capital: A Critique of Political Economy*, Vol. 1. New York: International.

Marx, Karl, and Friedrich Engels. 1947. *The German Ideology*. New York: International.

———. 1959. *Marx and Engels: Basic Writing on Politics and Philosophy*, Lewis S. Feuer, ed. Garden City, NY: Anchor Books.

Maschinot, Beth. 1995. "Behind the Curve." *In These Times* (February 6):31–34.

Massey, Douglas S. 1993. "Latino Poverty Research: An Agenda for the 1990s." *Items (Social Science Research Council)* 47 (March):7–11.

———. 1996. "Concentrating Poverty Breeds Violence." *Population Today* 24 (June/July): 5.

Mather, Mark. 2007. "Closing the Male-Female Labor Force Gap." *Population Reference Bureau*. Available online: http://www. prb.org/Articles/2007/Closingthemalefemalelaborforcegap.aspx?p=1.

Matthews, Jay. 2006. "Study Casts Doubt on the 'Boy Crisis.'" *Washington Post* (June 26):1A.

Mattingly, Marybeth J., and Liana Sayer. 2006. "Under Pressure: Gender Differences in the Relationship Between Free Time and Feeling Rushed." *Wiley.com*. Available online: http://onlinelibrary.wiley.com/doi/10.1111/j.1741-3737.2006.00242.x/abstract.

Matza, David. 1964. "Position and Behavior Patterns of Youth." In *Handbook of Modern Sociology*, Robert E. L. Faris, ed. Chicago, IL: Rand McNally.

McAdoo, John. 1988. "Changing Perspectives on the Role of the Black Father." In *Fatherhood Today: Men's Changing Role in the Family*, P. Bronstein and C. P. Cowan, eds. New York: Wiley, pp. 79–92.

McCabe, Janice, Emily Fairchild, Liz Graverholz, Bernice A. Pescosolido, and Daniel Trope. 2011. "Gender in Twentieth Century Children's Books: Patterns of Disparity in Titles and Central Characters." *Gender and Society* 25(2):197–226.

McCarthy, Sarah J. 1979. "Why Johnny Can't Disobey." *Humanist* (September–October).

McCormack, Richard. 2010. "The Plight of American Manufacturing." *American Prospect* 21 (Jan/Feb):A2–A5.

McGee, Reece. 1975. *Points of Departure: Basic Concepts in Sociology*, 2nd ed. Hinsdale, IL: Dryden Press.

McGrath, Kristin. 2010. "Status Update: Facebook Logs 500 Million Members." *USA Today* (July 22):3D.

McGuire, Meredith. 1992. *Religion: The Social Context*, 3rd ed. Belmont, CA: Wadsworth.

McIntosh, Peggy. 1992. "White Privilege and Male Privilege." In *Race, Class, and Gender: An Anthology*, Margaret L. Andersen and Patricia Hill Collins, eds. Belmont, CA: Wadsworth, pp. 70–81.

McKinley, Donald Gilbert. 1964. *Social Class and Family Life*. Glencoe, IL: Free Press.

McKinley, James C. 2010. "Texas Conservatives Win Curriculum Change." *New York Times* (March 15). Available online: http://www.nytimes.com/2010/03/13/education/13texas.html.

McManus, Doyle. 2011. "The Upward Mobility Gap." *Los Angeles Times* (January 2). Available online: http://latimes.com/news/opinion/commentary/la-oe-mcmanus-times-20110102,0,5332722.column.

———. 2011. "Sands Are Shifting in Religion and Politics." *Wichita Eagle* (June 11):15A.

McNamee, Stephen J., and Robert K. Miller, Jr. 2009. *The Meritocracy Myth*, 2nd ed. Lanham, MD: Rowman & Littlefield.

McPherson, Miller, Lynn Smith-Lovin, and Matthew E. Brashears. 2006. "Social Isolation in America: Changes in Core Discussion Networks Over Two Decades." *American Sociological Review* 71 (June): 353–75.

Mead, George Herbert. 1934. *Mind, Self, and Society*. Chicago, IL: University of Chicago Press.

Mead, Sara. 2006. "*The Truth and Boys and Girls*." Washington, DC: Education Sector. Available online: http://www.educationsector.org.

Media Report to Women. 2007. "Industry Statistics." Available online: www.mediareporttowomen.com/statistics.htm.

———. 2011. "Industry Statistics." Available online: http://www.mediareporttowomen.com/statistics.htm.

Merton, Robert K. 1957. *Social Theory and Social Structure*, 2nd ed. Glencoe, IL: Free Press.

Messner, Michael A. 1996. "Studying Up on Sex." *Sociology of Sport Journal* 13:221–37.

Metcalf, Stephen. 2002. "Reading Between the Lines." *The Nation* (January 28):18–22.

Meyerson, Harold. 2010. "The Politics of Industrial Renaissance." *American Prospect* 21 (January/February):A16–A18.

———. 2011. "GOPs Anti-Immigrant Stance Could Turn Texas Into a Blue State." *Washington Post* (March 2). Available online: http://www.washingtonpost.com/wp-dyn/content/article/2011/03/01/AR2011030105589.html.

Miller, David. 1991. "A Vision of Market Socialism." *Dissent* 38 (Summer): 406–14.

Miller, John. 2011. "No Fooling-Corporations Evade Taxes." *Dollars and Sense* 294 (May/June): 11–12.

Miller, Mark Crispin. 2002. "What's Wrong with This Picture." *The Nation* (January 7/14):18–22.

Mills, C. Wright. 1956. *The Power Elite.* New York: Oxford University Press.

———. 1959. *The Sociological Imagination.* Fair Lawn, NJ: Oxford University Press.

———. 1968. "The Power Elite." In *Reader in Political Sociology*, Frank Lindenfeld, ed. New York: Funk & Wagnalls, pp. 263–76.

Mishel, Lawrence, Jared Bernstein, and Sylvia Allegretto. 2007. *The State of Working America 2006/2007.* Washington, DC: The Economic Policy Institute.

Mitchell, George J. 2007. "Report to the Commissioner of Baseball of an Independent Investigation into the Illegal Use of Steroids and Other Performance Enhancing Substances by Players in Major League Baseball." Available online: http://files.mlb.com/mitchrpt.pdf.

Mohan, Geoffrey, and Ann M. Simmons. 2004. "Diversity Spoken in 39 Languages." *Los Angeles Times* (June 16). Available online: http://www.latimes.com/news/locak/la-me-multilingual16jun16,1,157.

Mokhiber, Russell. 2007. "Twenty Things You Should Know About Corporate Crime." *Alternet.org* (June 16). Available online: http://www.alternet.org/story/54093.

Mooney, Chris. 2006. "Some Like It Hot." *Mother Jones* (May/June):36–49.

Moore, Joan, and Raquel Pinderhughes, eds. 1994. *In the Barrios: Latinos and the Underclass Debate.* New York: Sage.

Moore, Wilbert E. 1969. "Social Structure and Behavior." In *The Handbook of Social Psychology*, 2nd ed., Vol. IV, Gardner Lindzey and Elliot Aronson, eds. Reading, MA: Addison-Wesley.

Morin, Richard. 1998. "Keeping the Faith." *Washington Post National Weekly Edition* (January 12):37.

Moser, Bob. 2008. "Who Would Jesus Vote For?" *The Nation* (March 24):11–16.

Moskos, Charles C., Jr. 1975. "The American Combat Soldier in Vietnam." *Journal of Social Issues* 31 (Fall): 25–37.

Moyers, Bill. 1996. "America's Religious Mosaic." *USA Weekend* (October 11):4–5.

———. 2005. "The Fight of Our Lives." In *Inequality Matters*, James Lardner and David A. Smith, eds. New York: The New Press.

Moyers, Bill, and Michael Winship. 2009. "Changing the Rules of the Blame Game." *Commondreams.org.* (April 8). Available online: http://www.commondreams.org/print/40559.

Muhammad, Dedrick. 2009. *Challenges to Native American Advancement: The Recession and Native America.* New York: Institute for Policy Studies. p. 597.

Mukhopadhyay, Carol, and Rosemary C. Henz. 2003. "How Real Is Race? Using Anthropology to Make Sense of Human Diversity." *Phi Delta Kappan* (May):669–78.

Murphy, Cait. 2000. "Are the Rich Cleaning Up?" *Fortune* (September 4):252–62.

Muwakkil, Salim. 1994. "Dangerous Curve." *In These Times* (November 28):22–24.

———. 1998a. "Movin' on Apart." *In These Times* (March 22):11–12.

———. 1998b. "Real Minority, Media Majority: TV News Needs to Root Out Stereotypes About Blacks and Crime." *In These Times* (June 28):18–19.

———. 2002. "Forgotten Freedoms." *In These Times* (January 7):17–18.

Myrdal, Gunnar. 1944. *An American Dilemma.* New York: Pantheon.

Nagano, Yuriko. 2010. "Device Gives Parents Their Child's Eye View." *New Scientist* (October 26). Available online: http://www.newscientist.com/article/dn19639-device-gives-parents-their-childs-eye-view.html.

Nagel, David. 2011. "What the Nation's Report Card Means for Science Education." *The Journal* (January 25). Available online: http://the journal.com/articles/2011/01/25/what-the-nations-report-card-means-for-science-education.aspx.

Naples, Nancy A. 1998. "Women's Community Activism and Feminist Action Research." In *Community Activism and Feminist Politics*, Nancy A. Naples, ed. New York: Routledge, pp. 1–27.

The Nation. 2007. "Time to Act on Inequality." (April 23):3.

National Assessment of Education Progress. 2009. "The Nation's Report Card: 2009." *National Center for Education Statistics.* Available online: http://nces.ed.gov/nationsreportcard.

National Center for Education Statistics. 2010. "The Condition of Education 2010." *U.S. Department of Education.* Available online: http://nces.edgov/programs/coe.

National Center for Science Education. 2006. "Defending the Teaching of Evolution in Public Schools." (February 19). Available online: http://www.ncseweb.org.

National Council of La Raza. 1999. "*The Mainstreaming of Hate: A Report on Latinos and Harassment, Hate Violence, and Law Enforcement Abuse in the '90s.*" (July). Washington, DC: National Council of La Raza.

National Council of State Legislatures (NCSL). 2011. "Same Sex Marriage, Civil Unions, and Domestic Partnerships." (June 27). Available online: http://www.ncsl.org/default.aspx?tabid=16430.

National Governors Association, Council of Chief State School Officers, and Achieve Inc. 2008. "Benchmarking for Success: Ensuring U.S. Students Receive a World Class Education." Available online: http://nga.org/files/pdf/0812benchmarking.pdf.

National Organization for Women. 2002. *Watch Out, Listen Up! 2002 Feminist Primetime Report.* Washington, DC: National Organization for Women.

National Women's Law Center. 2011. "Title IX Still Applies: Gender Equity in Athletics During Difficult Economic Times." (May 15). Available online: http://www.nwlc.org/resource/title-IX-still-applies-gender-equity-athletics.

Navarro, Lygia. 2011. "The Melting Pot." *The American Prospect* (April):A18–A20.

Nesdale, Drew. 2007. "The Development of Ethnic Prejudice in Early Childhood: Theories and Research." In

Contemporary Perspectives on Socialization and Social Development in Early Childhood Education, Olivia Saracho and Bernard Spodek, eds. Charlotte, NC: Information Age Publishing.

New America Foundation. 2009. "School Finance." Available online: http://febp.newamerica.net/background-analysis/school-finance.

Newman, Katherine S. 1988. *Falling from Grace: The Experience of Downward Mobility in the American Middle Class.* New York: Free Press.

Newman, Katherine S., and Victor Tan Chen. 2007. *The Missing Class: Portraits of the New Poor in America.* Boston, MA: Beacon Press.

Newsweek. 2010. "Exactly How Much Are the Times A-Changin'?" (July 26):56.

New York Times. 2000. "A Fix for the Broadcast Give-away." (October 11). Available online: http://nytimes.com/2000/10/11/opinion/11WED2.html.

———. 2003. "Fighting School Resegregation." (January 27). Available online: http://www.nytimes.com/2003/01/27/opinion/27MON1.html.

———. 2007. "Big Tobacco Defeats Sick Kids." (November 8). Available online: http://www.nytimes.com/2007/11/08/opinion/08thu4.html?ei=5070.

———. 2010. "The Court's Blow to Democracy." (January 22). Available online: http://www.nytimes.com/2010/01/02/opinion/22fril.html.

———. 2011. "Beyond the Happy Visuals." (January 19). Available online: http://www.nytimes.com/2011/01/20/opinion/20thu1.html.

Nicolaus, Martin. 1973. *Forword to Karl Marx, Grundrisse: Foundations of the Critique of Political Economy.* New York: Vintage Books.

Niebuhr, R. Gustav. 1998. "Doctrine Defines Wives' Roles." *Rocky Mountain News* (June 10):3A.

Nielsen. 2010. "U.S. Teen Mobile Report: Calling Yesterday, Texting Today, Using Apps Tomorrow." (October 14). Available online: http://blog.nielsen.com/nielsenwire/online_mobile/u-s-teen-mobile-report-calling-yesterday-texting-today-using-apps-tomorrow/.

Nielson, Joyce McCarl. 1990. *Sex and Gender in Society.* Prospect Heights, IL: Waveland Press.

Nilges, Lynda M., and Albert F. Spencer. 2002. "The Pictorial Representation in Notable Children's Picture Books: 1995-1999."*Sex Roles* 45 (1/2):89–101.

Nilsen, Alleen Pace. 2000. "Sexism in English: A 1990s Update." In *The Gender Reader*, 2nd ed., Evelyn Ashton-Jones, Gary A. Olson, and Merry G. Perry, eds. Boston, MA: Allyn and Bacon, pp. 301–13.

Nisbett, Richard E. 2007. "All Brains Are the Same Color." *New York Times* (December 9). Available online: http://www.nytimes.com/2007/12/09/opinion/09nisbett.html.

North, C. C., and Paul K. Hatt. 1947. "Jobs and Occupations: A Popular Evaluation." *Public Opinion News* 9 (September):3–13.

Nottingham, Elizabeth K. 1954. *Religion and Society.* New York: Random House.

Nuffield Council on Bioethics. 2005. "Genetics and Human Behavior." Available online: http://www.nufieldbioethics.org.

O'Dea, Thomas. 1966. *The Sociology of Religion.* Upper Saddle River, NJ: Prentice Hall.

Office of Minority Health and Health Disparities. 2011. "ATSDR Hispanic Health Program." Available online: http://www.cdc.gov/omhd/populations/hl/hhp/afsdr.htm.

Office of National Drug Control Policy. 2010. "Marijuana: Know the Facts." (October). Available online: http://www.whitehousedrugpolicy.gov/publications/pdf/marijuana.pdf.

O'Hare, William P. 1992. "America's Minorities: The Demographics of Diversity." *Population Bulletin* 47 (December):entire issue.

———. 1996. "A New Look at Poverty in America." *Population Bulletin* 51 (September):entire issue.

O'Kelly, Charlotte. 1980. *Women and Men in Society.* New York: Van Nostrand.

Oldenburg, Ray. 1997. *The Great Good Place.* New York: Marlowe.

Olinger, David, and Gwen Florio. 2002. "Fiery Debate Rages as Immigrants Pour In." *Denver Post* (October 17):1A, 26A.

Oliver, Melvin L., and Thomas M. Shapiro. 1995. *Black Wealth/White Wealth: A New Perspective on Racial Equality.* New York: Routledge.

Olsen, Marvin E. 1976. *The Process of Social Organization*, 2nd ed. New York: Holt, Rinehart and Winston.

Omi, Michael, and Howard Winant. 1986. *Racial Formation in the United States.* London: Routledge.

O'Neill, Tom. 2003. "Untouchable." *National Geographic* 203 (June):4–31.

Opensecrets.org. n.d. "Lobbying Database." Available online: http://www.opensecrets.org/lobbyists/index.asp.

Orenstein, Peggy. 2008. "Girls Will Be Girls." *New York Times* (February 28). Available online: http://www.nytimes.com/2008/02/10/magazine/10ww/n-1ede-t.html.

Orfield, Gary, and Chungmei Lee. 2010. "Historical Reversals, Accelerating Resegregation and the Need for New Integration Strategies." In *Race and Ethnicity in Society*, Elizabeth Higginbotham and Margaret L. Andersen, eds. Belmont, CA: Wadsworth Cengage, p. 331.

Orfield, Gary, and Chungmei Lee. 2012. "Historical Reversals, Accelerating Resegregation, and the Need for New Integration Strategies." In *Race and Ethnicity in Society*, Elizabeth Higginbotham and Margaret L. Andersen, eds. Wadsworth Cengage Learning, pp. 329–37.

Ortner, Sherry B. 1974. "Is Female to Male as Nature Is to Culture?" In *Woman, Culture, and Society*, Michelle Zimbalist Rosaldo and Louise Lamphere, eds. Stanford, CA: Stanford University Press, pp. 66–88.

Orwell, George. 1946. *Animal Farm.* New York: Harcourt Brace.

Oskamp, Stuart, Karen Kaufman, and Liannaa Atchison Wolterbeek. 1996. "Gender Role Portrayal in Preschool Books." *Journal of Social Behavior and Personality* 11 (5):27–39.

Oxford Analytica. 2007. "Anti-American Sentiment Grows Worldwide." *Forbes* (August 23). Available online: http://www.forbes.com/2007/08/22/bush-anti-americanism-cx_0823oxfordanalystic.html.

Page, Susan. 2009. "In One Year, 24 Million Slide from 'Thriving' to 'Struggling.'" *USA Today* (March 10):1A–2A.

Papper, Bob. 2010. "Number of Minority Journalists Down in 2009; Story Mixed for Female Journalists." *Radio-Television News Directors Association*. Available online: http://www.rtdna.org/pages/research/women-and-minorities.php.

Parenti, Christian. 2002. "DC's Virtual Panopticon." *The Nation* (June 3):24–26.

Parenti, Michael. 1978. *Power and the Powerless*, 2nd ed. New York: St. Martin's Press.

———. 1980. *Democracy for the Few*, 3rd ed. New York: St. Martin's Press.

———. 1986. *Inventing Reality: The Politics of the Mass Media*. New York: St. Martin's Press.

———. 1988. *Democracy for the Few*, 5th ed. New York: St. Martin's Press.

———. 1992. *Make-Believe Media: The Politics of Entertainment*. New York: St. Martin's Press.

———. 1994. *Land of Idols: Political Mythology in America*. New York: St. Martin's Press.

———. 1995. *Democracy for the Few*, 6th ed. New York: St. Martin's Press.

———. 2002. *Democracy for the Few*, 7th ed. New York: Bedford/St. Martin's Press.

———. 2008. *Democracy for the Few*, 8th ed. New York: St. Martin's Press.

———. 2010. *God and His Demons*. Amherst, NY: Prometheus Books.

Parents Television Council. 2008. "TV Bloodbath: Violence on Primetime Broadcast TV: A PTC State of the Television Industry Report." Available online: http://www.parentstv.org.

Parsons, Talcott, and Robert R. Bales. 1955. *Family, Socialization and Interaction Process*. Glencoe, IL: Free Press.

Patterson, Orlando. 2007. "The Root of the Problem." *Time* (May 7):58.

Paulson, Michael. 2000. "More Women Embracing the Study of Jewish Faith." *Boston Globe* (March 13):1B, 5B.

Pearce, Diana. 1978. "The Feminization of Poverty: Women, Work, and Welfare." *Urban and Social Change Review* II:28–36.

Pera, Gina. 1996. "School Sports: Girls Take the Field." *USA Weekend* (September 6):26.

Perman, Cindy. 2010. "New Homes Get Smaller as Homeowners Shift Priorities." *USA Today* (November 15):5B.

Perry, Bruce D. 2002. "Childhood Experience and the Expression of Genetic Potential: What Childhood Neglect Tells Us About Nature and Nurture." *The Child Trauma Academy*. Available online: http://www.feral-children.com/en/pager.php?df=perry2002.

Perry, Mark J. 2011. "The Truth About U.S. Manufacturing." *Wall Street Journal* (February 25):A13.

Peterson, Linda, and Elaine Enarson. 1974. "Blaming the Victim in the Sociology of Women: On the Misuse of the Concept of Socialization." Paper presented at the Pacific Sociological Association, San Jose, California (March).

Pew Center on the States. 2011. "*State of Recidivism: The Revolving Door of America's Prisons*." Washington, DC: The Pew Charitable Trusts.

Pew Research Center. 2010. "The Return of the Multi-Generational Family Household." Available online: http://pewsocialtrends.org/the-return-of-the-multi-generational-family-household.

Peyser, Marc. 1999. "Home of the Gray." *Newsweek* (March 1):50–53.

Phillips, Kevin. 2006. "God's Own." *Washington Post National Weekly Edition* (April 10–16):21.

Pierard, Richard V., and Robert D. Linder. 1988. *Civil Religion and the Presidency*. Grand Rapids, MI: Zondervan.

Pike, Jennifer J., and Nancy A. Jennings. 2005. "The Effects of Commercials on Children's Perceptions of Gender Appropriate Toy Use." *Sex Roles* 52 (1/2):83–91.

Pinsky, Mark I. 2006. "Meet the New Evangelicals." *Los Angeles Times* (September 16). Available online: http://www.latimes.com/news/opinion/la-oe-pinsky16sep16,0,6110112,print.story?coll=la.

Piven, Frances Fox. 1996. "Welfare and the Transformation of Electoral Politics." *Dissent* 43 (Fall):61–67.

Piven, Frances Fox, and Richard A. Cloward. 1971. "The Relief of Welfare." *Transaction* 8 (May).

———. 1993. *Regulating the Poor: The Functions of Public Welfare*, updated ed. New York: Vintage Books.

Pleck, Joseph. 1977. "The Work-Family Role System." *Social Problems* 24 (April):417–27.

Pogatchnik, Shawn. 2002. "Northern Ireland Tots Learn Hate." Associated Press (June 25).

Pollard, Kelvin M., and William P. O'Hare. 1999. "America's Racial and Ethnic Minorities." *Population Bulletin* 54, no. 3 (September). Washington, DC: Population Reference Bureau. p. 601.

Pollitt, Katha. 2010. "The Decade for Women: Forward, Backward, Sideways?" *The Nation* (January 15):10.

Pope, Liston. 1942. *Millhands and Preachers*. New Haven, CT: Yale University Press.

Port, Otis. 1999. "They're Listening to Your Calls." *BusinessWeek* (May 31):110–1.

Portes, Alejandro, and Min Zhou. 1993. "The New Second Generation: Segmental Assimilation and the Variants." *Annals of the American Academy of Political and Social Science* 530:74–96.

Potok, Mark. 2011. "The Year in Hate and Extremism, 2010." *Southern Poverty Law Center, Intelligence Report* 141 (Spring).

Poulantzas, Nicos. 1974. *Classes in Contemporary Capitalism*. London: New Left Books.

Powers, Kristen A. 2007. "Immigrants Become Target for All of Society's Ills." *USA Today* (August 29):13A.

Powledge, Fred. 1991. *Free at Last? The Civil Rights Movement and the People Who Made It*. Boston, MA: Little, Brown.

Prewitt, Kenneth. 2003. *Politics and Science in Census Taking*. New York: Russell Sage Foundation.

Public Broadcasting System (PBS). 2009. "Frontline: The Failure and Future of the Private Insurance Industry." (March 31).

Public Citizen. 2003. "The Other Drug War." (June 23). Available online: http://www.citizen.org/pressroom/release.dfm?ID=1469.

Putnam, Robert D., and David E. Campbell. 2010. *American Grace: How Religion Divides and Unites Us*. New York: Simon and Schuster.

———. 2010. "Walking Away from Church." *Los Angeles Times* (October 17). Available online: http://latimes.com/news/opinion/commentary/la-oe-1017-putnam-religion-20101017,0,6283320.story.

Pyke, Karen. 2004. "Immigrant Families in the U.S." In *The Blackwell Companion to the Sociology of Families*, Jacqueline Scott, Judith Treas, and Martin Richards (Eds.). Malden, MA: Blackwell, pp. 253–269.

Pyke, Karen. 2008. "Immigrant Families in the U.S." In *American Families: A Multicultural Reader*, 2nd ed., Stephanie Coontz, ed. New York: Routledge, pp. 210–21.

Quinney, Richard. 1970. *The Social Reality of Crime*. Boston, MA: Little, Brown.

———. 1973. *Critique of Legal Order: Crime Control in Capitalist Society*. Boston: Little, Brown.

———. 1974. *Criminal Justice in America: A Critical Understanding*. Boston, MA: Little, Brown.

Rai, Saritha. 2004. "Short on Priests, U.S. Catholics Outsource Prayers to Indian Clergy." *New York Times* (June 13):13.

Rampell, Catherine. 2011. "Dimming Optimism for Today's Youth." *New York Times* (May 2).

Rank, Mark R. 2011. "Rethinking American Poverty." *Contexts* 10 (Spring):16–21.

Rapp, Rayna. 1982. "Family and Class in Contemporary America." In *Rethinking the Family: Some Feminist Questions*, Barrie Thorne and Marilyn Yalom (eds.). New York: Longman, pp. 168–187.

Rawlings, Steve. 1995. "Households and Families: Population Profile of the United States: 1995." *Current Population Reports*, P23–189. Washington, DC: US Government Printing Office.

Reed, Adolph, Jr. 1990. "The Underclass as Myth and Symbol: The Poverty of Discourse About Poverty." *Radical America* 24 (January/March):21–40.

———. 1994. "Looking Backward." *The Nation* (November 28):654–62.

Reeves, Thomas C. 1996. *The Empty Church: The Suicide of Liberal Christianity*. New York: Free Press.

Reich, Robert. 1989. "Yes: Blame Election Funds." *New York Times* (October 12):A29.

———. 2002. *I'll Be Short: Essentials for a Decent Working Society*. Boston, MA: Beacon Press.

———. 2008. "Totally Spent." *New York Times* (February 13). Available online: http://www.nytimes.com/2008/02/13/opinion/13reich.html.

———. 2010. *Aftershock: The Next Economy and America's Future*. New York: Alfred A. Knopf.

Reilly, Sabrina L. 2006. "Transforming Aging: The Civic Engagement of Adults 55+." *Public Policy and Aging Report* 16:1, 3–7.

Reiman, Jeffrey H. 2007. *The Rich Get Richer and the Poor Get Prison: Ideology, Class, and Criminal Justice*, 8th ed. Boston, MA: Allyn and Bacon.

Religion News Service. 1995. "Vatican Declares 'Infallible' Its Ban on Women Priests."

Renzetti, Claire M., and Daniel J. Curran. 2003. *Women, Men, and Society*, 5th ed. Boston, MA: Allyn and Bacon.

Reskin, Barbara F. 1999. "Occupational Segregation by Race and Ethnicity Among Women Workers." In *Latinas and African American Women at Work: Race, Gender, and Economic Inequality*, Irene Browne, ed. New York: Russell Sage Foundation.

Reskin, Barbara F., and Patricia A. Roos. 1990. *Job Queues, Gender Queues*. Philadelphia, PA: Temple University Press.

Richmond, Julius B. 1994. "Give Children an Earlier Head Start." *USA Today* (April 12):13A.

Richmond-Abbott, Marie. 1992. *Masculine and Feminine: Sex Roles over the Life Cycle*, 2nd ed. New York: McGraw-Hill.

Ridgeway, Cecilia L. 1997. "Interaction and the Conservation of Gender Inequality: Considering Employment." *American Sociological Review* 62 (April):218–35.

Ridgeway, Cecilia L., and Lynn Smith-Lovin. 1999. "The General System and Interaction." *Annual Review of Sociology* 25:191–216.

Riesman, David. 1950. *The Lonely Crowd*. New Haven, CT: Yale University Press.

Rifkin, Jeremy. 1995. *The End of Work: The Decline of the Global Labor Force and the Dawn of the Post-Market Era*. New York: Putnam.

———. 1996. "Civil Society in the Information Age." *The Nation* (February 26):11–16.

Right Truth. 2010. "Mosques and Islamic Centers Across the U.S. and Those Who Object." (October 10). Available online: http://righttruth.typepad.com/right_truth/2010/10/mosques-and-islamic-centers.

Ritzer, George. 1996. *The McDonaldization of Society: An Investigation into the Changing Character of Contemporary Social Life*, rev. ed. Thousand Oaks, CA: Pine Forge Press.

———. 2000. *The McDonaldization of Society: New Century Edition*. Thousand Oaks, CA: Pine Forge Press.

Rivera, Amand, Brenda Colton-Escalera, and Anisha Desai. 2008. *Foreclosed: State of the Dream 2008*. Boston, MA: United for a Fair Economy.

Roberts, Russell. 2009. *The Price of Everything: A Parable of Possibility and Prosperity*. Princeton, NJ: Princeton University Press.

Roberts, Sam. 2008. "In a Generation, Minorities May Be U.S. Majority." *New York Times* (August 14). Available online: http://www.nytimes.com/2008/08/14/washington/14census.html.

Robins, Natalie. 1987. "The Defiling of Writers." *The Nation* (October 10):367–72.

———. 1992. "The Secret War Against American Writers." *Esquire* 117 (March):106–109, 158–160.

Robinson, Eugene. 2007. "Pulling Over for Prejudice." *The Washington Post National Weekly Edition* (May 7–13):31.

Rocky Mountain News. 2005. "Letterwriter Prefers the Rich, Not the Poor." (July 22):41A.

Roehling, Patricia, Phyllis Moen, and Rosalie Batt. 2003. "Spillover." In *It's About Time: Couples and Careers*, Phyllis Moen, ed. Ithaca, NY: Cornell University Press.

Rogers, Susan Carol. 1978. "Women's Place: A Critical Review of Anthropological Theory." *Comparative Studies in Society and History* 20 (1):123–62.

Romaine, Suzanne. 1999. *Communicating Gender*. Mahwah, NJ: Erlbaum.

Ropelato, Jerry. 2011. "Internet Pornography Sites." *Internet Filter Software Review*. Available online: http://internet-filter-review-toptenreviews.com/internet-pornography-statistics-html.

Rosaldo, Michelle Zimbalist. 1974. "Woman, Culture and Society: A Theoretical Overview." In *Woman, Culture, and Society*, Michelle Zimbalist Rosaldo and Louise Lamphere, eds. Stanford, CA: Stanford University Press, pp. 17–42.

———. 1980. "The Use and Abuse of Anthropology." *Signs* 5 (Spring):389–417.

Rosen, Ruth. 2000. "When Women Spied on Women." *The Nation* (September 4):18–25.

Rosenthal, Robert, and Lenore Jacobson. 1968. *Pygmalion in the Classroom: Teacher Expectations and Pupils' Intellectual Development*. New York: Holt, Rinehart and Winston.

Rotello, Gabriel. 1996. "To Have and to Hold: The Case for Gay Marriage." *The Nation* (June 24):11–18.

Rothfeder, Jeffrey. 1992. *Privacy for Sale: How Computerization Has Made Everyone's Life an Open Secret*. New York: Simon & Schuster.

Rothstein, Richard. 2007. "A Wider Lens on the Black-White Achievement Gap." In *Inequality: Social Class and Its Consequences*, D. Stanley Eitzen and Janis E. Johnston, eds. Boulder, CO: Paradigm Publishing.

Rubenstein, Richard E. 1970. *Rebels in Eden: Mass Political Violence in the United States*. Boston, MA: Little, Brown.

Rubin, Lillian B. 2006. "What Am I Going to Do with the Rest of My Life?" *Dissent* (Fall):88–94.

Rugh, Jacob S., and Douglas S. Massey. 2010. "Racial Segregation and the American Foreclosure Crisis." *American Sociological Review* 75 (5):629–51.

Russell, Jan Jarboe. 2003. "Religious Right Monkeying with Our Kids' Textbooks Again." *San Antonio Express News* (September 14):1H.

Russell, Marta. 1998. *Beyond Ramps: Disability at the End of the Social Contract*. Monroe, ME: Common Courage Press.

———. 2000. "The Political Economy of Disablement." *Dollars & Sense* 231 (September/October):13–15, 48–49.

Ryan, Joanna. 1972. "IQ–The Illusion of Objectivity." In *Race and Intelligence*, Ken Richardson and David Spears, eds. Baltimore, MD: Penguin.

Ryan, William. 1972. "Postscript: A Call to Action." *Social Policy* 3 (May–June).

———. 1976. *Blaming the Victim*, rev. ed. New York: Vintage Books.

Sacks, Karen. 1974. "Engels Revisited: Women, the Organization of Production, and Private Property." In *Woman, Culture, and Society*, Michelle Zimbalist Rosaldo and Louise Lamphere, eds. Stanford, CA: Stanford University Press, pp. 207–22.

Sadker, David. 2002. "An Educator's Primer on the Gender War." *Phi Delta Kappan* (November):235–44.

Sadker, Myra, and David Sadker. 1994. *Failing at Fairness: How America's Schools Cheat Girls*. New York: Scribner.

Saenz, Rogelio. 2005. "The Social and Economic Isolation of Urban African Americans." Population Reference Bureau. Available online: http://www.prb.org/Articles/2005/TheSocialandEconomicIsolationofUrbanAfricanAmericans.aspx.

Sage, George H. 2010. *Globalizing Sport*. Boulder, CO: Paradigm.

Sage, George H., and D. Stanley Eitzen. 2013. *Sociology of North American Sport*, 9th ed. New York: Oxford University Press.

Saldana, Dave. 2011. "Mega-mega-merger: Meet the New Media Monopoly." *CommonDreams.org* (January 24). Available online: http://www.commondreams.org/view/2011/01/24-10.

Salmon, Jacqueline L. 2008. "Protestant Churches Struggle to Diversify Flock." *Hutchinson News* (March 1):4B.

Samuelson, Paul Anthony, and William D. Nordhaus. 2005. *Economics*, 18th ed. New York: McGraw-Hill.

Sanderson, Stephen K. 1988. *Macrosociology: An Introduction to Human Societies*. New York: Harper & Row.

Sapiro, Virginia. 1999. *Women in American Society*, 4th ed. Mountain View, CA: Mayfield.

Sawhill, Isabel, and Sara McLanahan. 2006. "From Rags to Riches? Barriers to Achieving the American Dream." *Council on Contemporary Families* (October 11).

Scarpitti, Frank R., and Margaret Andersen. 1992. *Social Problems*, 2nd ed. New York: HarperCollins.

Schemo, Diana. 2007. "Failing Schools Strain to Meet U.S. Standard." *New York Times* (October 16). Available online: http://www.nytimes.com/2007/10/16/education/16child.html.

Schmit, Julie. 2011. "Rental Costs Rise with Economy." *USA Today* (May 5):1B.

Schneider, David M., and Raymond T. Smith. 1973. *Class Differences and Sex Roles in American Family and Kinship Structure*. Englewood Cliffs, NJ: Prentice Hall.

Schrag, Peter. 2007. "As California Goes . . ." *The Nation* (April 9):18–21.

Schumpeter, Joseph. 1950. *Capitalism, Socialism, and Democracy*, 3rd ed. New York: Harpers.

Schur, Edwin. 1973. *Radical Non-Intervention: Rethinking the Delinquency Problem*. Upper Saddle River, NJ: Prentice Hall.

Scott, Janny. 2005. "Life at the Top in America Isn't Just Better, It's Longer." *New York Times* (May 16). Available online: http://www.nytimes.com/2005/05/16/national/class/HEALTH-FINA.

Scott, Janny, and David Leonhardt. 2005. "Class in America: Shadowy Lines That Still Divide America." *New York Times* (May 15):15–18.

Sennett, Richard, and Jonathan Cobb. 1973. *The Hidden Injuries of Class*. New York: Random House Vintage.

Sesser, Stan. 1992. "A Nation of Contradictions." *The New Yorker* (January 13):37–68.

Shanker, Albert. 1991. "Improving Our Schools." *New York Times* (May 17):7E.

———. 1992. "How Far Have We Come?" *New York Times* (August 16):9E.

Shapiro, Joseph P. 1989. "Liberation Day for the Disabled." *U.S. News & World Report* (September 18):20–24.

Shapiro, Judith. 1981. "Anthropology and the Study of Gender." In *A Feminist Perspective in the Academy*, Elizabeth Langland and Walter Gove, eds. Chicago, IL: University of Chicago Press, pp. 110–29.

Shapiro, Thomas M. 2004. *Houses Divided: The Hidden Cost of Being African American*. New York: Oxford University Press.

Shaw-Taylor, Yoku. 2009. "The Changing Face of Black America." *Contexts* 8 (Fall):62–63.

Shelden, Randall G. 2004. "Resurrecting Radical Non-Intervention: Stop the War on Kids." *Center on Juvenile and Criminal Justice* (April). Available online: http://www.cjcj.org/pdf/radical.pdf.

Sheler, Jeffrey L. 1995. "The Era of Collective Repentance." *U.S. News & World Report* (July 3):10–11.

———. 2000. "The Mormon Moment." *U.S. News & World Report* (November 13):58–65.

Sherif, Muzafer. 1958. "Group Influences upon the Formation of Norms and Attitudes." In *Readings in Social Psychology*, 3rd ed., Eleanor E. Maccoby, Theodore M. Newcomb, and Eugene L. Hartley, eds. New York: Holt, Rinehart and Winston, pp. 219–32.

Sherif, Muzafer, and Carolyn W. Sherif. 1966. *Groups in Harmony and Tension*. New York: Farrar, Straus & Giroux.

Shils, Edward A., and Morris Janowitz. 1948. "Cohesion and Disintegration in the Wehrmacht in World War II." *Public Opinion Quarterly* 12 (Summer):280–315.

Sinderbrand, Rebecca. 2005. "A Shameful Little Secret." *Newsweek* (March 28):33.

Singer, Matt. 2006. "Overpaying for Jobs." *Progressive Populist* (August 1):6.

Skenazy, Lenore. 2008. "Why I Let My 9-Year-Old Ride the Subway Alone." *New York Sun* (April 1). Available online: http://www.nysun.com/editorials/why-i-let-my-9-year-old-ride-subway-alone.

———. 2009. "Traveling with (Virtual) Mom." *Creators.com*. Available online: http://www.creators.com/opinion/lenore-skenazy/traveling-with-virtual-mom.html.

Sklar, Holly. 1992. "Reaffirmative Action." *Z Magazine* 5 (May/June):9–15.

———. 2004a. "Break That Glass Ceiling." *Progressive Populist* (June 15):16.

———. 2004b. "Don't Get Duped Out of Your Social Security." *Knight Ridder/Tribune News Service* (March 8).

Sklaroff, Sara. 1999. "E-Mail." *U.S. News & World Report* (March 22):54–55.

Skolnick, Jerome. 1969. *The Politics of Protest*. New York: Ballantine Books.

Skolnick, Jerome, and Elliott Currie. 1970. "Approaches to Social Problems." In *Crisis in American Institutions*, Jerome H. Skolnick and Elliott Currie, eds. Boston, MA: Little, Brown.

Slevin, Peter. 2005. "The Anti-Evolution Revolution." *The Washington Post National Weekly Edition* (March 21–27):6.

Small, Maria Luis, David J. Harding, and Michele Lamont. 2010. "Reconsidering Culture and Poverty." *The Annals of the American Academy of Political and Social Sciences* 629 (6):6–27.

SmartMoney.com. 2008. "Long-Term Care." (September).

Smelser, Neil. 1962. *Theory of Collective Behavior*. New York: Free Press.

Smith, Elliot Blair. 2001. "Migrants Flex Muscles Back Home in Mexico." *USA Today* (June 28):9A.

Snipp, Matthew. 1996. "The First Americans: American Indians." In *Origins and Destinies: Immigration, Race, and Ethnicity in America*, Silvia Pedraza and Ruben G. Rumbaut, eds. Belmont, CA: Wadsworth, pp. 390–403.

Snyder, Eldon. 1972. "Athletic Dressing Room Slogans and Folklore." *International Review of Sport Sociology* 7:89–102.

Solis, Brian. 2010. "Influence Is Bliss: The Gender Divide of Influence on Twitter." (August 4). Available online: http://www.briansolis.com/2010/08/influence-is-bliss-the-gender-divide-of-influence-on-twitter.

Solove, Daniel. 2007. *The Future of Reputation: Gossip, Rumor, and Privacy on the Internet*. New Haven, CT: Yale University Press.

Southern Poverty Law Center [SPLC]. 2006. "Hate Group Numbers Top 800." *Southern Poverty Law Center Report* 36 (March):1.

———. 2007. "Hate Group Numbers Continue to Increase." *Southern Poverty Law Center Report* 37 (Spring):1.

———. 2010. "Injustice on Our Plates: Immigrant Women in the U.S. Food Industry." (November 20). Available online: http://www.splcenter.org/get-informed/publications/injustice/on-our-plates.

Spencer, Renée, Michelle V. Porche, and Deborah Tolman. 2003. "We've Come a Long Way–Maybe: New Challenges for Gender Equity in Education." *Teachers College Record* 105 (9):1774–1807.

Spong, John Shelby. 2005. *The Sins of Scripture: Exposing the Bible's Texts of Hate to Reveal the God of Love*. New York: Harper San Francisco.

Stacey, Judith. 1990. *Brave New Families: Stories of Domestic Upheaval in Late Twentieth-Century America*. New York: Basic Books.

———. 1991. "Backward toward the Postmodern Family: Reflections on Gender, Kinship, and Class in the Silicon Valley." In *America at Century's End*, Alan Wolfe, ed. Berkeley, CA: University of California Press, pp. 17–34.

Stack, Carol B. 1990. "Different Voices, Different Visions: Gender, Culture, and Moral Reasoning." In *Uncertain Terms: Negotiating Gender in American Culture*, Faye Ginsburg and Anna Lowenhaupt Tsing, eds. Boston, MA: Beacon Press, pp. 19–27.

Statzel, Sophie R. 2010. "Book Review: Cyber Racism: White Supremacy Online and the New Attack on Civil Rights." Available online: http://gas.sagepub.com/content/24/3/408.citation.

Stefanone, Michael A. 2011. "Study: Facebook Photo Sharing Reflects Focus on Female Appearance. What Affects Women's Self Worth Also Influences Their Social Networking Behavior." Available online: http://youtube.com/watch?v=TIGQHoLyS5Q&feature=relmfu.

Stein, Peter J., Judith Richman, and Natalie Hannon. 1977. *The Family: Functions, Conflicts, and Symbols*. Reading, MA: Addison-Wesley.

Steinberg, Stephen. 2011. "Culture Still Doesn't Explain Poverty." *Boston Review* (January 11):1–9.

Stivers, Richard. 1975. "Introduction to the Social and Cultural Control of Deviant Behavior." In *The Collective Definition of Violence*, F. James Davis and Richard Stivers, eds. New York: Free Press.

Stolberg, Sheryl Gay. 2002. "Minorities Got Inferior Care, Even if Insured, Study Finds." *New York Times* (March 21).

Stranahan, Susan Q. 2002. "The Clean Room's Dirty Secret." *Mother Jones* (March/April):44–49.

Strange, Mary Zeiss. 2010. "She Tackled the 'Male' God." *USA Today* (January 25):7A.

Street, Paul. 2007. "Corporate Money and the Democrats." *Z Magazine* (December 1).

Street, Paul. 2001. "Race, Prison, and Poverty." *Z Magazine* 14(May):25–31.

Sunstein, Cass R. 2009. *Going to Extremes: How Like Minds Unite and Divide*. New York: Oxford Press.

Sutherland, Edwin H., and Donald R. Cressey. 1966. *Principles of Criminology*, 7th ed. Philadelphia, PA: Lippincott.

Swartz, John. 2004. "Always on the Job, employees Pay with Health." *New York Times* (September 5):1, 23.

Swartz, Jon. 2011. "Facebook Changes Its Lobbying Status in Washington." *USA Today* (January 13). Available online: http://www.usatoday.com/money/industries/technology/2011-01-13facebook.html.

Symonds, William C. 2003. "College Admissions: The Real Barrier Is Class." *BusinessWeek* (April 14):66–67.

———. 2006. "Campus Revolutionary." *BusinessWeek* (February 27):65–70.

Szymanski, Albert. 1978. *The Capitalist State and the Politics of Class*. Cambridge, MA: Winthrop.

Takaki, Ronald. 1993. *A Different Mirror: A History of Multicultural America*. Boston, MA: Little, Brown.

Taylor, Marisa. 2011. "Overseas Call Records Fair Game, Says Memo." *McClatchy Newspapers* (February 12).

Teller-Elsberg, Jonathan, Nancy Folbre, and James Heintz. 2006. *Field Guide to the U.S. Economy*. New York: The New Press.

Terkel, Studs. 1975. *Working: People Talk About What They Do All Day and How They Feel About What They Do*. New York: Avon Books.

Thomas, Oliver. 2007. "Having Faith in Women." *USA Today* (April 9):13A.

Thornburgh, Nathan. 2006. "Dropout Nation." *Time* (April 17):29–40.

Thorne, Barrie. 1993. *Gender Play: Girls and Boys in School*. New Brunswick, NJ: Rutgers University Press.

Thornton, Russell. 1996. "North American Indians and the Demography of Contact." In *Origins and Destinies: Immigration, Race, and Ethnicity in America*, Silvia Pedraza and Ruben G. Rumbaut, eds. Belmont, CA: Wadsworth, pp. 43–59.

Thurow, Lester. 1995. "Companies Merge: Families Break Up." *New York Times* (September 3):11A.

Timmer, Doug A., D. Stanley Eitzen, and Kathryn D. Talley. 1994. *Paths to Homelessness: Extreme Poverty and the Urban Housing Crisis*. Boulder, CO: Westview Press.

Townsend, Nicholas W. 2002. *The Package Deal: Marriage, Work and Fatherhood in Men's Lives*. Philadelphia, PA: Temple University Press.

TRB. 1975. "The Case for More Planning." *Rocky Mountain News* (March 30):2.

Tribe, Lawrence H. 1996. "Toward a Less Perfect Union." *New York Times* (May 26):E11.

Troeltsch, Ernst. 1931. *The Social Teaching of the Christian Churches*, Olive Wyon, trans. New York: Macmillan.

Tumin, Melvin M. 1953. "Some Principles of Stratification." *American Sociological Review* 18 (August):387–93.

———. 1973. *Patterns of Society*. Boston, MA: Little, Brown.

Turkle, Sherry. 2011. *Alone Together: Why We Expect More from Technology and Less from Each Other*. New York: Basic Books.

Turse, Nick. 2009. "Younger and Hungrier in America." *TomDispatch.com* (March 9). Available online: http://www.commondreams.org/print/39230.

———. 2011. "From Two Breadwinners to One." *The Nation* (May 23):17–19.

Urban Institute. 2006. "A Decade of Welfare Reform: Facts and Figures." (June).

USA Today. 2000. "FBI Eavesdrops on E-mail, Crashes Privacy Barriers." (July 24):16A.

———. 2005. "FBI May Be Checking on You, but You Have No Way of Knowing." (November 19):14A.

———. 2010. "Myths Mar Efforts to Solve Nation's Immigration Woes." (July 30):7A.

U.S. Bureau of the Census. 2000. "Marital Status of People 15 Years and Over." Available online: www.census.gov/population/socdemo/hh-fam/p20-537/2000.

———. 2006. "America's Families and Living Arrangements, Detailed Tables." Table A1. Available online: http://www.census.gov.

———. 2009. "2008 American Community Survey." Available online: http://factfinder.census.gov.

———. 2010. "Census Shows America's Diversity." Available online: http://www.census.gov/newsroom/releases/archives/2010_cnesus/cb11-cn125.html.

Usdansky, Margaret L. 1992. "Middle Class Pulling Apart to Rich, Poor." *USA Today* (February 20):1A.

U.S. Department of Education, National Center for Education Statistics. 2006. "Digest of Education Statistics." (NCES 2006-030). Available online: http://nces.ed.gov.

U.S. Department of Health and Human Services. 2009. "HIV/AIDS Data Statistics." Available online: http://minorityhealth.hhs.gov/templates/browse.aspx?lvll=3&lvlio.

U.S. Department of Labor. 1965. *The Negro Family: The Case for National Action*. Washington, DC: Office of Policy Planning and Research.

U.S. State Department. 2007. "Human Trafficking and Modern Day Slavery." *Trafficking in Persons Report* (June 1). Available online: http://govnet.com/humantrafficking/USA.htm.

Valian, Virginia. 1998. "Running in Place." *Sciences* 38 (January/February):18–23.

Van Biema, David. 2004. "Rising Above the Stained-Glass Ceiling." Time (June 28):59–61.

van den Berghe, Pierre L. 1967. *Race and Racism: A Comparative Perspective*. New York: Wiley.

Vanneman, Reeve, and Lynn Weber Cannon. 1987. *The American Perception of Class*. Philadelphia, PA: Temple University Press.

Vecoli, Rudolph J. 1964. "Contadini in Chicago: A Critique of the Uprooted." *Journal of American History* 51:405–17.

Vernon, Mark. 2010. "Is True Friendship Dying Away?" *USA Today* (July 27):11A.

Vestal, Christine. 2009. "States Coping with Rising Homelessness." *Stateline.org* (March 18). Available online: http://www.stateline.org/live/details/story?contentid=385137.

Villano, Matt. 2009. "Reading, Writing, and Recession." *Time* (February 23):54–55.

Visher, Emily B., John S. Visher, and Kay Pasley. 2003. "Remarriage, Families, and Stepparenting." In *Normal Family Processes: Growing Diversity and Complexity*, 3rd ed., Froma Walsh, ed. New York: Guilford Press.

Von Drehle, David. 2007. "The Boys Are All Right." *Time* (August 6):40–42.

Waite, Linda J. 2000. "Trends in Men's and Women's Well-Being in Marriage." In *The Ties That Bind: Perspectives on Marriage and Cohabitation*, Linda Waite, ed. Hawthorne, NY: Aldine de Gruyter.

"The Wage Gap." 2003. Available online: http://www.infoplease.com/ipa10/7/6/1/7ao76317.phtml.

Waite, Linda, and Maggie Gallagher. 2000. *The Case for Marriage: Why Married People Are Happier, Healthier, and Better Off Financially*. New York: Doubleday.

Walby, Sylvia. 2000. "Gender, Globalization, and Democracy." *Gender and Development* 8 (March):20–28.

Wald, Matthew. 1996. "Royal Caribbean Cruise Line Indicted on Charges of Dumping Oil." *New York Times* (December 20). Available online: http://www.nytimes.com.

Wali, Alaka. 1992. "Multiculturalism: An Anthropological Perspective." Report from the *Institute for Philosophy and Public Policy* (University of Maryland)12 (Spring/Summer):6–8.

The Wall Street Journal. 2011. "Los U.S.A: Latino Population Grows Faster, Spreads Wider." (March 25):1A.

Walton, John. 1990. *Sociology and Critical Inquiry: The Work, Tradition, and Purpose*, 2nd ed. Belmont, CA: Wadsworth.

Warren, Mark. 2011. "The White Fight." *The American Prospect* (April):A20–A21.

Warren, Patricia, Donald Tomosakovic-Devey, William Smith, Matthew Zingraff, and Marcinda Mason. 2006. "Driving While Black: Bias Processes and Racial Disparity in Police Stops." *Criminology* 44 (3):709–38.

Warriner, Charles K. 1956. "Groups Are Real: A Reaffirmation." *American Sociological Review* 21 (October):549–54.

Waters, Mary C. 1996. "Optional Ethnicities: For Whites Only?" In *Origins and Destinies: Immigration, Race, and Ethnicity in America*, Silvia Pedraza and Ruben G. Rumbaut (eds.). Belmont, CA: Wadsworth, pp. 444–454.

Weber, Lynn. 2010. *Understanding Race, Class, Gender, and Sexuality*, 2nd ed. New York: Oxford University Press. pp. 444–454.

Weber, Max. 1947. *The Theory of Social and Economic Organization*, A. M. Henderson and Talcott Parsons, trans. New York: Free Press.

———. 1958. *The Protestant Ethic and the Spirit of Capitalism*, Talcott Parsons, trans. New York: Scribner.

———. 1963. *The Sociology of Religion*, Ephraim Fischoff, trans. Boston, MA: Beacon Press.

Wedekind, Jennifer. 2009. "Dying For Work." *Multinational Monitor* 30 (May/June):7–8.

Weisbrot, Mark. 2002. "Spying and Lying: The FBI's Dirty Secrets." *Progressive Populist* (July 1):14.

Weiss, Kenneth R. 2000. "More Rich Kids Get to Take Extra Time on SAT." *Denver Post* (January 9):2A.

Weitzman, Lenore J. 1985. *The Divorce Revolution: The Unexpected Social and Economic Consequences for Women and Children in America*. New York: Free Press.

Wellman, Barry. 2000. "Changing Connectivity: A Future History of Y2.03K." *Sociological Research Online* 4 (February):4.

Wellman, David T. 1977. *Portraits of White Racism*. Cambridge, England: Cambridge University Press.

West, Candace, and Don Zimmerman. 1987. "Doing Gender." *Gender and Society* 1:125–51.

West, Cornel. 1992. *Race Matters*. Boston, MA: Beacon Press.

West, Darrell M. 2010. "7 Myths That Have Clouded the Immigration Debate." *USA Today* (September 1):9A.

Westhues, Kenneth. 1982. *First Sociology*. New York: McGraw-Hill.

Wheatcroft, Geoffrey. 2007. "Who Made Her Queen?" *The Washington Post National Weekly Edition* (October 15–21):27.

Wheelis, Allen. 1958. *The Quest for Identity*. New York: W. W. Norton.

Whitehouse, Mark. 2011. "Number of the Week: Class of 2011, Most Indebted Ever." *Wall Street Journal* (May 7). Available online: http://blogs.wsj.com/economics/2011/05/07/number-of-work-classof2011.

Whyte, William Foote. 1956. *Street Corner Society: The Social Structure of an Italian Slum*, rev ed. Chicago, IL: University of Chicago Press.

———. 1988. *City: Rediscovering the Center*. New York: Doubleday.

Wikigender.org contributors. 2011. "Gender and Social Networking." Available online: http://wikigender.org/index.php?title=Gender_and_Social_Networking&oldid=17590.

Wilcox, Clyde. 2000. *Onward Christian Soldiers? The Religious Right in American Politics*, 2nd ed. Boulder, CO: Westview Press.

Wilkening, David. 2008. "Hotel Guests Believe In Taking It with Them." *Hotel Interactive* (February 14). Available online: http://www.hotelinteractive.com.

Will, George F. 2008. "Pencils and Politico." *Newsweek* (September 22):80.

Williams, Christine. 1992. "The Glass Escalator: Hidden Advantages for Men in the 'Female' Professions." *Social Problems* 39 (August):253–67.

———. 1995. *Still a Man's World: Men Who Do Women's Work*. Berkeley, CA: University of California Press.

Williams, David R. 1996. "The Health of the African American Population." In *Origins and Destinies: Immigration, Race, and Ethnicity in America*, Silvia Pedraza and Ruben G. Rumbaut, eds. Belmont, CA: Wadsworth, pp. 404–16.

Williamson, Elizabeth, Amy Schetz, and Geoffrey A. Fowler. 2011. "Facebook Seeking Friends in Beltway." *Wall Street Journal* (April 20). Available online: http://onlinewsj.com/article/SB100014240527487037891045762732.

Williamson, Thad. 2001. "The Real Y2K Crisis: Global Economic Inequality." *Dollars & Sense* 227 (January/February):42.

Willing, Richard. 2000. "Nader Finds 5% Goal Elusive." *USA Today* (November 8):9A.

Wilson, William J. 1987. *The Truly Disadvantaged: The Inner City, the Underclass, and Public Policy.* Chicago, IL: University of Chicago Press.

———. 1996. *When Work Disappears: The World of the New Urban Poor.* New York: Knopf.

———. 2010a. *More Than Just Race: Being Black and Poor in the Inner City.* New York: WW Norton & Co.

Wilson, William J., and Andrew J. Cherlin. 2001. The Real Test of Welfare Reform Still Lies Ahead. *New York Times* (July 13). Available online: www.nytimes.com/2001/07/13/opinion/13WILS.html.

Winant, Howard. 2009. Just Do It: Notes on Politics and Race at the Dawn of the Obama Presidency. *DuBois Review* 6 (1):49–70.

Witt, Susan. 1997. Parental Influence on Children's Socialization to Gender Roles. *Adolescence* 32 (126):253–9.

Woellert, Lorraine, and Dawn Kopecki. 2006. The Snooping Goes Beyond Phone Calls. *BusinessWeek* (May 29):38.

Wolf, Richard. 2007. Bush Signs Defense Bill but Balks at Cost of Domestic Plan. *USA Today* (November 14):6A.

———. 2010. Medicare to Swell with Boomer Onslaught. *USA Today* (December 30):5A.

Wolfe, Alan. 1999. The Power Elite Now. *American Prospect* 44 (May/June):90–96.

Wozniak, Abigail. 2011. The Negative Effects on Earnings for Workers Who Begin Careers During a Recession. *Journal of Human Resources* (Fall).

Wright, Erik Olin, David Hachen, Cynthia Costello, and Joey Sprague. 1982. The American Class Structure. *American Sociological Review* 47 (December):709–26.

Wright, Erik Olin, and Joel Rogers. 2011. *American Society: How It Really Works.* New York: W.W. Norton.

Yabroff, Jennie. 2008. Here's Looking at You, Kids. *Newsweek* (March 24):67–68.

Yen, Hope. 2009. Minority Kids in Majority by 2023. *Associated Press* (March 5).

Yinger, J. Milton. 1961. *Sociology Looks at Religion.* New York: Macmillan.

Yorburg, Betty. 1983. *Families and Societies: Survival or Extinction?* New York: Columbia University Press.

Young, Jeff. 2011. As Technology Evolves, New Forms of Online Racism Emerge. Available online: http://chronicle.com/blogs/wiredcampus/as-technology-evolves-new-forms-of-online-racism-emerge/30351.

Zaretsky, Eli. 1976. *Capitalism, the Family, and Personal Life.* New York: HarperColophon.

Zehr, Mary Ann. 2009. No Child Left Behind: Did Bush Get it Right? *Guardian Weekly* (February 6). Available online: http://www.guardian.co.uk/education/2009/feb/06/no-child-left-behind-english-learning.

Zeitlin, Maurice, Kenneth G. Lutterman, and James W. Russell. 1977. Death in Vietnam: Class, Poverty, and the Risks of War. In *American Society, Inc.*, 2nd ed., Maurice Zeitlin, ed. Chicago, IL: Rand McNally, pp. 143–55.

Zelizer, Gerald L. 1999. Year 2000 Looms . . . Or Is It 5760? 1421? *USA Today* (March 11):15A.

———. 2004. Time to Break the Stained Glass Ceiling. *USA Today* (September 16):1A.

Zeskind, Leonard. 2005. The New Nativism. *American Prospect* 16 (November):15A–18A.

Zhou, Min. 1997. Growing Up American: The Challenge Confronting Immigrant Children and Children of Immigrants. *Annual Review of Sociology* 23:63–95.

Zimbardo, Philip G. 1972. Pathology of Imprisonment. *Society* 9 (April).

Zinn, Howard. 1980. *A People's History of the United States.* New York: Harper & Row.

———. 2005. Against Discouragement. 2005 Commencement Address, Spelman College. (May 15).

Zuckerman, Mortimer B. 2005. Classroom Revolution. *U.S. News & World Report* (October 10):68.

Zvonkovic, Anisa M., Megan L. Notter, and Cheryl L. Peters. 2006. Family Studies: Situating Everyday Family Life at Work, in Time, and Across Contexts. In *The Work and Family Handbook: Multidisciplinary Perspectives and Approaches*, Marcie Pitt-Catsouphes, Ellen Ernst Kossek, and Stephen Sweet, eds. Mahwah, NJ: Lawrence Erlbaum, pp. 141–164.

PHOTO CREDITS

Chapter 1
p. 2: mainpicture/Alamy
p. 4: J.B. Handelsman/The New Yorker Collection/
    www.cartoonbank.com
p. 6: National Archives and Records Administration
p. 7: Pontino/Alamy
p. 11: Ron Cobb/Wild & Woolley
p. 13: Rocketclips, Inc./Shutterstock.com
p. 16: EdBockStock/Shutterstock.com
p. 18: Jeff Greenberg/Alamy

Chapter 2
p. 22: DENNIS VAN TINE/Landov
p. 25: Montgomery Martin/Alamy
p. 26: Luis Louro/Shutterstock.com
p. 29: Joy Brown/Shutterstock
p. 31: Rocketclips, Inc./Shutterstock.com
p. 32: Kirk Andersen
p. 33: Gary Oliver
p. 39: Yuri Arcurs/Shutterstock.com

Chapter 3
p. 42: Jim West/Alamy
p. 44: EdBockStock/Shutterstock.com
p. 45: Alex Gregory/The New Yorker Collection/
    www.cartoonbank.com
p. 47: Toddtaulma/Dreamstime.com
p. 52: MANDEL NGAN/AFP/Getty Images/Newscom
p. 54, 58: Rocketclips, Inc./Shutterstock.com
p. 55: Ron Cobb/Wild & Woolley
p. 60: Yuri Arcurs/Shutterstock.com

Chapter 4
p. 64: ZUMA Press/Newscom
pp. 68, 80: Rocketclips, Inc./Shutterstock.com
p. 69: Luis Louro/Shutterstock.com
p. 70: Catherine Karnow/Corbis
p. 73: Tom Cheney/The New Yorker Collection/
    www.cartoonbank.com
p. 74: Bob Krist/Corbis
p. 75: vario images GmbH & Co.KG/Alamy Limited
p. 79: The Image Works
p. 80: Courtesy of TLC/ABACAUSA.COM/Newscom
p. 85: AP Photo/Eric Gay
p. 85: Yuri Arcurs/Shutterstock.com

Chapter 5
p. 88: AP Photo/CHARLES DHARAPAK
p. 90: Buena Vista Pictures/courtesy Everett Collection
p. 93: Rocketclips, Inc./Shutterstock.com
p. 93: Lisa Eastman/Shutterstock.com

p. 96: Jeff Greenberg/Alamy
p. 96: Luis Louro/Shutterstock.com
p. 98: Jamaway/Alamy
p. 102: Pictorial Press Ltd/Alamy
p. 102: AF archive/Alamy
p. 102: Moviestore collection Ltd/Alamy
p. 102: AF archive/Alamy

Chapter 6
p. 106: A. Ramey/PhotoEdit
p. 109: Michael Newman/PhotoEdit
p. 110: Yuri Arcurs/Shutterstock.com
p. 114: Tom Cheney/The New Yorker Collection/
    www.cartoonbank.com
pp. 117, 122: Rocketclips, Inc./Shutterstock.com
p. 118: Robert Mankoff/The New Yorker Collection/
    www.cartoonbank.com
p. 121: SHANE T. MCCOY/AFP/Getty Images/Newscom
p. 125: Luis Louro/Shutterstock.com

Chapter 7
p. 128: Phakimata/Dreamstime.com
p. 131: Luis Louro/Shutterstock.com
p. 132: AP Photo/DAVID PELLERIN
p. 133: Paramount Pictures/Courtesy:
    Everett Collection
p. 137: Michael Maslin/The New Yorker Collection/
    www.cartoonbank.com
p. 139: Yuri Arcurs/Shutterstock.com
p. 144: AP Photo/Paul Sakuma
p. 144: Dariush M./Shutterstock.com

Chapter 8
p. 150: ArtPix/Alamy
p. 155: Rocketclips, Inc./Shutterstock.com
p. 156: Luis Louro/Shutterstock.com
pp. 153, 165: Lee Prince/Shutterstock.com
p. 157: Jeff Greenberg/PhotoEdit
p. 161: Yuri Arcurs/Shutterstock.com
p. 157: Kirk Andersen
p. 163: WALTRAUD GRUBITZSCH/DPA/Landov
p. 164: Gary Oliver
p. 177: Jim West/Alamy

Chapter 9
p. 182: Sally and Richard Greenhill/Alamy
p. 184: Rocketclips, Inc./Shutterstock.com
p. 185: Lee Prince/Shutterstock.com
p. 186: Fancy/Veer/Corbis/Glowimages.com
p. 191: Jake Lyell/Alamy
p. 197: Yuri Arcurs/Shutterstock.com

Achieve Inc., 367
Acker, Joan, 187, 188, 262, 280
Ackland, Henry, 220
Acosta, R. Vivian, 424
Adamson, Rebecca, 239
Adamuti-Trache, Maria, 267
Adkins, Deborah, 371
Ahlburg, Dennis A., 349
Albelda, Randy, 283, 345
Allegretto, Sylvia, 202, 219
Allen, Walter R., 255
Alter, Jonathan, 247
Amato, Paul R, 351, 355
American Association of University Women (AAUW), 267
American Civil Liberties Union (ACLU), 139
American Society for Aesthetic Plastic Surgery, 72
American Sociological Association, 16, 234, 249, 250
Amott, Teresa, 277, 278, 280
Amster, Randall, 68
Andersen, Margaret L., 7, 115, 233, 234, 243, 261, 267,
        272, 276, 279, 284
Anderson, Jack, 116
Andres, Lesley, 267
Angier, Natalie, 234
Annie E. Casey Foundation, 357
Appelbaum, Richard P., 74
April, Castro, 370
Archibald, Robert B., 219
Armour, Stephanie, 309
Armstrong, Karen, 76
Asch, Solomon E., 35
Associated Press, 71, 90, 120, 253
Austin, Algernon, 337

Baca Zinn, Maxine, 31, 187, 216, 237, 262, 351, 355, 358, 424
Bacevich, Andrew J, 217
Bales, Kevin, 183, 296
Bales, Robert R., 263
Balswick, Jack, 283
Baltzell, E. Digby, 209
Bamshad, Michael J, 234
Bandura, Albert, 94
Bane, Mary Jo, 220
Banfield, Edward C., 135, 194
Barber, Benjamin R., 75
Barlett, Donald L., 333
Barlow, Andrew L., 255
Barnett, Rosalind, 260, 267
Barrera, Mario, 190
Barrett, Paul M., 401

Barsamian, David, 14, 409
Baskir, Laurence M, 337
Basow, Susan, 260
Batalova, Jeanne, 234
Batt, Rosalie, 355
Battistoni, Alyssa, 194
Bauman, Zygmunt, 9
Baur, Karla, 403
Beall, Jackson, 331
Bean, Frank D., 234, 235
Bear, John, 69
Beck, Joan, 193
Beck, Rachel, 203
Becker, Howard S, 14
Beeghley, Leonard, 211
Begley, Sharon, 14
Belkin, Lisa, 30
Bell, M. B., 331
Bellah, Robert N., 393
Belluck, Pam, 146
Benokraitis, Nijole, 273
Berger, Peter L., 5, 7, 15, 38, 108, 389, 398, 415
Bernard, Jessie, 353
Bernstein, Jared, 202, 219
Berry, Mary Frances, 420
Bettelheim, Ruth, 176
Beverly, Wright, 251
Bianchi, Suzanne M., 275, 350, 359
Bielawski, Dawn, 265
Bierstedt, Robert, 92, 93
Bilger, Burkhard, 408
Bilmes, Linda, 338
Birnbaum, Norman, 300
Blackman, Douglas A., 422
Blau, Peter M., 23, 27, 219
Blauner, Robert, 296
Block, Sandra, 177, 308
Bloom, Rhonda Bodfield, 131
Bloomberg Business Week, 158
Blumberg, Paul M., 347
Blume, Howard, 369
Blumer, Herbert, 316
Bobo, Lawrence D., 241
Bonacich, Edna, 139
Bonilla-Silva, Eduardo, 235, 241, 244, 246, 252
Booher-Jennings, Jennifer, 267
Booth, Alan, 351, 355
Bowe, John, 183, 299
Boyle, D. Ellen, 266
Brannon, Robert, 264
Brashears, Matthew E., 26

Briggs, Xavier de Souza, 247
Brodkin, Karen, 236
Brooks, David, 306
Brooks-Gunn, Jeanne, 219
Brouillette, John R., 73
Brown, Chance, 205
Brown, Dee, 55
Brown, Jim, 381
Brown, Michael, 241, 242, 251
Brownlee, Kimberley, 144
Broyles, William, Jr., 337
Buchanan, Patrick, 68
Buckelew, Rose, 235
Bukowski, William M., 97
Bullard, Robert D., 251
Bureau of Justice Statistics, 137
Bureau of Labor Statistics, 158, 249, 250, 269, 273, 275,
     276, 278, 279, 298, 303
Buriel, Raymond, 169
Burkam, David, 378
Burke, Daniel, 402
Burt, Keith B., 265
Burton, Linda, 345
BusinessWeek, 154
Butz, William P., 18, 19
Bybee, Roger, 321
Byrnes, Nanette, 173

Calefati, Jessica, 68
Callahan, David, 287
Campbell, David E., 294, 387, 402, 404, 408
Campbell, Frances A., 193
Campenni, C. Estelle., 265, 266
Cannon, Angie, 140
Capellaro, Jennie, 419
Carey, Kevin, 377
Carlton, Jim, 161
Carmichael, Stokely, 243
Carpenter, Linda Jean, 424
Carter, Michael J., 280
Carter, Susan Boslego, 280
Carville, James, 16, 207
Casper, Lynn M., 350
Cassidy, John, 165, 167
Cawthorne, Alexandra, 175
Center for American Women and Politics, 274
Chafel, Judith A., 194
Chafetz, Janet Saltzman, 263
Chambliss, William J., 74
Chapin, Laura, 321
Chen, David W., 201
Cherlin, Andrew J., 228, 360
Chicago Tribune, 338
Chideya, Farai, 162
Child Trends, 15, 100
Children's Defense Fund., 204
Christian Chronicle., 404
Chung, Angie Y., 255
Chungmei Lee, 248
Claudette, Bennett, 251

Cleveland, Harlan, 420
Cloward, Richard A., 113, 114, 212, 334
Coakley, Jay J., 47, 73, 423
Coates, Joseph F., 363
Cobb, Jonathan, 61, 190
Cockburn, Andrew, 298
Coffin, William Sloan, 417
Cohen, David, 220
Cohen, Patricia, 194, 242
Cohen, Robin, 76
Cole, David, 139, 168
Coleman, Marilyn, 355
Colin, Chris, 299
College Board, 379
Collier, James Lincoln, 283
Collins, Chuck, 202, 246, 335
Collins, Patricia Hill, 188, 244
Collins, Randall, 108, 209, 212
Coltrane, Scott, 357
Comer, Lee, 187
Compete.com, 25
Conason, Joe, 122
Connell, Robert W., 262, 281
Consumer Reports, 127
Contemporary Sociology, 191, 241
Cooley, Charles Horton, 92, 93
Coontz, Stephanie, 343, 344, 345, 354
Cooper, Robert, 382
Corbett, Sara, 130
Costello, Cynthia, 209, 211, 213
Cotto-Escalera, Brenda, 306
Council of Chief State School Officers, 367
Courier, 185
Cox, Harvey, 113
Crabb, Peter, 265
Cronin, John, 371
Crooks, Robert, 403
Crowley, Sheila, 247
Curran, Daniel J., 266, 267, 275
Currie, Elliott, 39
Curtis, John, 269
Cutler, James E., 56
Cuzzort, Raymond P., 107

Dahl, Robert, 19
Dahrendorf, Ralf, 46, 50
Daklin, Michael, 371
Datnow, Amanda, 382
David, Deborah S., 264
Davidov, Maayan, 95
Davidson, Paul, 156, 307
Davies, Karin, 71
Davis, Kingsley, 90, 91, 189
De Lone, Richard H., 219
De Ment, Terri, 169
De Parle, Jason., 246, 418
De Vita, Carol J., 349, 351
Death Penalty Information Center, 140, 149
Delamont, S., 266
DeNavas-Walt, Carmen, 221

DeParle, Jason, 308
Deresiewicz, William, 309
Desai, Anisha, 306
Desmarias, Serge, 265
di Leonardo, Micaela, 241
Dill, Bonnie Thornton, 237
Doezema, Jo, 282
Dokoupil, Tony, 124, 274
Domhoff, G. William, 209, 323, 328
Donn, Jeff, 229
Draut, Tamara, 310
Drucker, Peter F., 151, 155
Dubeck, Paula J., 276, 278, 279
Dubow, Eric F., 97, 98
Duncan, Greg J., 195, 219
Duncan, Otis Dudley, 219
Dunn, Andy, 122
Dunn, Dana, 263, 276, 278, 279
Durkheim, Emile, 10, 34, 45
Dyer, Everett D., 347

Early, Frances H., 345
Eaton, Joe, 331
Eaton, Leslie, 338
Economist, 166, 260, 307, 309
Education News, 371
Edwards, Renee, 265
Edwards, Richard C., 282
Ehrenreich, Barbara, 207, 212, 250
Eisenstein, Zillah, 263
Eitzen, D. Stanley, 7, 15, 31, 47, 48, 50, 75, 81, 101, 107,
    110, 121, 208, 216, 222, 225, 226, 311, 351, 355,
    358, 418, 422, 424, 425, 426
Ekman, Paul, 69
El Nasser, Haya, 162
Electronic Frontier Foundation, 122
Elliot, James R., 242
Enarson, Elaine, 269
England, Paula, 266, 276
Epstein, Cynthia Fuchs, 281
Epstein, Joseph, 74
Eshleman, J. Ross, 211
Espiritu, Yen Le, 238
Ettlinger, Steve, 58
Etzioni, Amitai, 125, 126
Everton, Terry, 367

Fahim, Dareem, 253
Falk, Erika, 275
Faludi, Susan, 284
Farley, John E., 246, 247
Farr, Daniel, 97
Fausto-Sterling, Anne, 260
Feagin, Clairece Booher, 245
Feagin, Joe R., 187, 233, 244, 245, 246, 248, 273
Federal Bureau of Investigations, 127, 328
Federal Bureau of Prisons, 127, 140
Federal Interagency Forum on Aging-Related Statistics, 171
Feingold, Russ, 121
Feldman, David H., 219

Felt, Judy C., 238
Ferree, Myra Marx, 284, 345
Festinger, Leon, 35
Fields, Jason, 350
Fireside, Daniel, 307
Fischer, Claude S., 191, 220
Fitzgerald, Frances, 109, 407
Fletcher, Dan, 25
Florio, Gwen, 166
Forbes, 201, 292, 293
Forden, Sara, 125
Forrest, Christopher B., 251
Fost, Dan, 240
Foster, John Bellamy, 305, 306
Fowler, Geoffrey A., 334
Frank, Vitaro, 97
Freeman, Elizabeth Hordge, 235
Freeman, Jo., 284
Freepress.net., 98
Freud, Sigmund, 94
Frey, William H., 168
Friedan, Betty, 424
Friedman, Thomas L., 153
Friesen, Wallace V., 69
Fuentes, Annette, 380
Furstenberg, Frank F., Jr., 360
Fussell, Paul, 214

Gage, Kingsbury G., 371
Galbraith, James K., 207
Gallagher, Charles A., 244, 255
Gallagher, Maggie, 352
Gallinsky, Ellen, 355
Gallup Poll, 394, 405
Gandel, Stephen, 305
Ganong, Lawrence H., 355
Gans, Herbert J., 19, 169, 197
Garfinkel, Simson, 125
Garrahy, Deborah A., 268
Garten, Jeffrey E., 292
Gecas, Viktor, 358
Gelles, Richard J., 360
Gentry, Curt., 121
Gerard, Leo W., 154
Gerrard, Nathan L., 36
Gerson, Kathleen, 351
Gerth, Hans, 214
Gibbs, Nancy, 267
Giddens, Anthony, 415
Gilbert, Bil, 424
Gilman, Richard, 272
Gilmore, Janet, 299
Gintis, Herbert, 220
Gobry, Pascal-Emmanuel, 334
Gold, David A., 324
Goldwert, Lindsay, 71
Goode, William J., 344, 400
Goozner, Merrill., 335
Gorman, Anna, 168
Gould, Stephen Jay, 14, 191

Gouldner, Alvin W., 13
Graham, Hugh Davis, 53
Gramlich, John, 132
Grant, Lorrie, 162
Graves, Lucia, 96
Green, Mark, 322
Greene, Jay P., 373
Greenhouse, Steven, 153
Greenwood, Dara, 97, 98
Greider, William, 329
Greim, Lisa, 278
Gross, Daniel, 175
Gross, Stephanie, 175
Grossman, Cathy Lynn, 25, 26, 395
Grossman, Lev, 25, 26
Grunwald, Michael, 225
Grusec, Joan E., 95
Guastello, Denise D., 265
Guastello, Stephen J., 265
Gubrium, Jay, 345
Gurr, Ted Robert, 53

Haaga, John, 235
Hachen, David, 209, 211, 213
Hacker, Andrew, 313
Hacker, Jacob S., 158
Hall, M. Ann. 1985., 424
Hamburg, David A., 359
Hamilton, Charles V., 243
Hamilton, Mark A., 265
Hampson, Rick, 156
Hananel, Sam, 298
Hannon, Natalie, 347
Hansen, Karen V., 347
Harding, David J., 194, 241
Harding, Vincent, 420, 421, 422
Harjo, Susan Shown, 239
Harrington, Michael, 12, 44, 195, 312, 338
Harris, Kathleen Mullan, 227
Harris, Marvin, 73, 74, 251
Harris, Roderick J., 251
Hartmann, Heidi I., 302
Hatt, Paul K., 206
Haynes, V. Dion, 304
Heilbroner, Robert L., 313
Helft, Miguel, 25
Henderson, Nell, 163, 164
Henneberger, Melinda, 13
Hennessy, Rosemary, 282
Henslin, James M., 5
Henz, Rosemary C., 234, 237
Hermann, Andrew, 191
Herrnstein, Richard, 191
Herron, Janna, 307
Hess, Beth B., 420
Higginbotham, Elizabeth, 233, 234, 243, 250, 255
Hightower, Jim, 153, 160, 306, 317, 320
Hill, Shirley A., 267
Hill, Steven, 319
Hindery, Leo, Jr., 154

Hoch, Paul, 47
Hochschild, Arlie, 356
Hodge, Robert W., 206
Hoffman, Matthew, 319
Hole, Judith, 284
Holmes, Stanley, 153
Holstein, James A., 345
Homans, George, 24
Hondagneu-Sotelo, Pierrette, 262
Horne, Gerald, 115
Hosenball, Mark, 139
Hout, Michael, 220
Huaco, George A., 189
Hudson, Christopher G., 138
Huesmann, L. Rowell, 97, 98
Huffington, Arianna, 310
Hughes, Diane, 355
Humes, Karen R., 235
Hunt, Paula, 58
Hunter, Floyd, 19
Huntington, Samuel P., 241
Hurst, Charles E., 392
Hutchins, Robert M., 337, 339
Hyman, Rebecca, 176

Idle, Tracey, 265
Ingraham, Chrys, 282
Intelligence Report, 252
Internal Revenue Service Oversight Board, 129
Internetstats.com, 25
ISR Newsletter, 278
Ivins, Molly, 289

Jackson, Jesse, 288
Jackson, Maggie, 25, 26
Jacobsen, Linda A., 171, 172
Jacobson, Lenore, 382
Jacoby, Susan, 177
James, Susan Donaldson, 129
Jankowski, Martin Sanchez, 220
Janowitz, Morris, 32
Janzen, David, 139
Jarrett, Robin, 345
Jaynes, Gerald David, 401
Jayson, Sharon, 31, 401
Jeffries, Vincent, 188
Jencks, Christopher, 220
Jenkins, Philip, 390
Jennings, Nancy A., 266
Jensen, Arthur R., 190
Jervis, Rick, 297
Jessop, Carolyn, 85
Jhally, Sut, 102
Jimenez, Tomas R., 161
Johnson, Charles S., 317
Johnson, Clifford M., 296
Johnson, David R., 351, 355
Johnson, Dirk, 370
Johnson, Mary, 418
Johnson, Steven, 26

Jones, J. H., 146
Jones, Jeffrey M., 84

Kadet, Anne., 78
Kaiser Family Foundation, 253
Kalleberg, Arne L., 306
Kamau, Puis, 376
Kammeyer, Kenneth C. W., 12, 416
Kanter, Rosabeth Moss, 280
Karabell, Zachary, 306
Kaufman, Gordon, 388
Kaufman, Karen, 265
Keating, Frank, 201
Keen, Judy, 123, 309
Keilholtz, Jeff, 407
Keller, Helen, 91
Kempadoo, Kamala, 282
Kennedy, David, 162
Kennedy, Paul, 75, 76
Kennickell, Arthur B., 52
Kent, Mary M., 171, 172, 235
Kephart, William, 110
Kerbo, Harold R, 184, 186
Kerr, Jennifer, 403
Kesey, Ken, 142
Kibria, Nazli, 169
Kim, Marlene, 226
Kimmel, Michael, 259, 260, 262, 275
Kiser, Jim, 124
Kloos, Peter, 76
Knottnerus, J. David, 218
Kocieniewski, David, 336
Konczal, Mike, 307
Kopeck, Dawn, 122
Kozol, Jonathan, 377, 381
Krakauer, Jon, 389
Kralis, Barbara, 298
Kramer, R. C., 145
Krantz, Matt, 185
Kriner, Douglas L., 216
Kristof, Nicholas D., 405
Kroeger, Brook, 280
Krugman, Paul, 98, 156
Kryson, Maria, 233, 235, 246, 248, 252
Kulik, Liat, 265
Kulman, Linda, 82
Kuo, David, 409–410
Kuttner, Robert, 174, 176, 423, 424

Lacayo, Richard, 300
Ladd, Gary W., 97
Ladner, Joyce A., 267
Lamont, Michele, 194, 241
Lane, Charles, 381
Lardner, James, 205
Lareau, Annette, 358
Lauer, Nancy Cook, 271
Leach, Mark, 234
Lechner, Frank J., 406
Lee, Jennifer, 234, 235

Lee, Marlene, 171, 172
Lee, Sharon M., 238
Lee, Valerie E., 378
Leinwand, Donna, 278
Lekachman, Robert, 338
Lemert, Edwin M., 141
Lenski, Gerhard, 49
Leondar-Wright, Betsy, 246, 247, 249
Leonhardt, David, 219, 399
Levine, Ellen, 284
Levitan, Sar A., 296
Levy, Steven, 124
Lewis, Amanda E., 233, 235, 246, 248, 252
Liazos, Alexander, 209, 211
Lichtenberg, Judith, 243, 244
Lichter, Daniel T., 350, 353
Liebow, Elliot, 19, 23, 195
Lim, Paul J., 305
Linda, Burton, 235
Linder, Robert D., 393
Lindner, Eileen W., 405
Lipman-Blumen, Jean, 188
Livingston, Jay, 228
Lo, Clarence Y. H., 324
Locke, John L., 26
Lockheed, Marlaine, 268
Loewen, James W., 109
Lopez-Sanders, Laura, 161
Lopiano, Donna, 268–269
Lorber, Judith, 262, 281
Lord, Walter, 214
Lott, Juanita Tamayo, 238
Love, Alice Ann, 278
Lucal, Betsy, 209, 236
Lucas, Samuel R., 191, 220
Luker, Kristin, 16
Lutterman, Kenneth G., 337

Maccoby, Eleanor E., 95
MacEwan, Arthur, 336
Machung, Anne, 356
Madrick, Jeff, 50
Magdoff, Fred, 303, 305, 306
Magdoff, Harry, 303
Malec, Michael A., 423
Malveaux, Julianne, 99
Manning, Wendy, 353
Mara, Brendgen, 97
Marger, Martin N., 324, 325
Marklein, Mary Beth, 377
Markson, Elizabeth W., 420
Marquardt, Katy, 307
Marriott, Michael, 13
Marshall, Nancy L. 266
Martin, Karen A., 264, 265
Martin, Patricia Yancey, 270, 280
Martin, Philip, 163, 166, 168
Marx, Karl, 190, 291, 324
Maschinot, Beth, 193
Mason, Marcinda, 252

Massey, Douglas S., 225, 237, 238, 246, 254
Mather, Mark, 171, 172, 235
Matthews, Jay, 267
Mattingly, Marybeth J., 271
Matza, David., 111
McAdoo, John, 267
McCarthy, Sarah J., 109
McCormack, Richard, 154
McGee, Reece, 5
McGrath, Kristin, 25
McGuire, Meredith, 387, 388
McIntosh, Peggy, 236
McKinley, Donald Gilbert, 348
McKinley, James C., 370
McLanahan, Sara, 17
McLaughlin, Diane K., 353
McManus, Doyle, 218, 405
McNamee, Stephen J., 309
McPherson, Miller, 26
Mead, George Herbert, 92
Mead, Sara, 267, 373
Meizhu Lui, 247, 249
Merton, Robert K., 33, 134
Messner, Michael A., 259, 262, 275
Metcalf, Stephen, 372
Meyerson, Harold, 153, 162
Midgley, Elizabeth, 163, 166, 168
Milike, Melissa A., 359
Miller, David, 289
Miller, John, 336
Miller, Mark Crispin, 99
Miller, Robert K., Jr., 309
Mills, C. Wright, 7, 209, 214, 325, 326, 327
Min Zhou, 169
Mishel, Lawrence, 202, 219
Mitchell, George J., 81
Moen, Phyllis, 355
Mohan, Geoffrey, 162
Mokhiber, Russell, 145, 146
Mooney, Chris, 331
Moore, Joan, 254
Moore, Wilbert E., 37, 189
Morin, Richard, 405
Morris, Anne, 355
Moser, Bob, 410
Moskos, Charles C., 32
Mota, Gloribell, 247, 249
Moyers, Bill, 205, 306, 404
Muhammad, Dedrick, 239, 247, 249, 250
Mukhopadhyay, Carol, 234, 237
Murphy, Cait, 203
Muwakkil, Salim, 123, 192, 244, 246
Myrdal, Gunnar, 241

Nagano, Yuriko, 96
Nagel, David, 374
Naples, Nancy A., 284
National Assessment of Education Progress, 373
National Center for Education Statistics, 100, 205, 269, 369, 380, 385

National Center for Science Education, 370, 385
National Council of La Raza, 311
National Governors Association, 367
National Organization for Women, 272, 284, 424
National Women's Law Center, 426
Navarro, Lygia, 252
Nesdale, Drew, 67, 91
New America Foundation, 377
New York Times, 51, 205, 321, 331, 335, 380
Newman, Katherine S., 210, 348, 349
Newsweek, 25, 156
Nicholas A. Jones, 235
Nicolaus, Martin, 296
Niebuhr, R. Gustav, 407
Nielson, Joyce McCarl., 263
Nilges, Lynda M., 265
Nilsen, Alleen Pace, 91
Nisbett, Richard E., 191
North, C. C., 206
Notter, Megan L., 355
Nottingham, Elizabeth K., 388
Nuffield Council on Bioethics, 133

O'Dea, Thomas, 399
O'Hare, William P., 226–227, 234, 237, 238, 239, 245, 247, 248, 250
O'Kelly, Charlotte, 261
O'Neill, Tom, 184
Office of Minority Health and Health Disparities, 251
Office of National Drug Control Policy, 129
Oldenburg, Ray, 26
Olinger, David, 166
Oliver, Melvin L., 247
Olsen, Marvin E., 24
Olson, Steve E., 234
Omi, Michael, 244
Orenstein, Peggy, 266
Orfield, Gary, 248
Ortner, Sherry B., 262
Orwell, George, 202
Oskamp, Stuart, 265
Oxford Analytica, 75

Page, Susan, 308
Pais, Jeremy, 242
Palmeri, Christopher, 173
Papper, Bob, 271
Parenti, Christian, 120
Parenti, Michael, 51, 112, 113, 114, 119, 120, 159, 190, 294, 297, 311, 329, 330, 332, 333, 334, 339, 389, 393, 398, 407
Parents Television Council, 101
Parsons, Talcott, 263
Pasley, Kay, 354
Patterson, Orlando, 243
Paul P. W., 347
Paulson, Michael, 272, 273
Pearce, Diana, 283
Peck, Charles, 283

Pera, Gina, 425
Perman, Cindy, 310
Perry, Bruce D., 90, 91
Perry, Mark J., 158
Peters, Cheryl L., 355
Peterson, Linda, 269
Pew Center on the States, 136
Pew Research Center, 360
Peyser, Marc, 169
Phillips, Kevin, 409
Pierard, Richard V., 393
Pike, Jennifer J., 266
Pinderhughes, Raquel, 254
Pinsky, Mark I., 410
Piven, Frances Fox, 113, 114, 212, 334, 430
Pleck, Joseph, 355
Pogatchnik, Shawn, 89
Pollard, Kelvin M., 235, 237, 238, 239, 245, 248, 250
Pope, Liston, 398
Porche, Michelle V., 268
Port, Otis, 120
Portes, Alejandro, 169
Potok, Mark, 167, 252
Poulantzas, Nicos, 212
Powers, Kristen A., 168
Powledge, Fred, 420
Prewitt, Kenneth, 235
Proctor, Bernadette D., 221
Public Broadcasting System (PBS), 308
Public Citizen, 336
Putnam, Robert D., 294, 387, 402, 404, 408
Pyke, Karen, 168

Qian, Zhenchao, 353
Quinney, Richard, 118–119

Rai, Saritha, 396
Ramey, Craig T., 193
Ramirez, Roberto R., 235
Rampell, Catherine, 310
Rank, Mark R., 17
Ransford, H. Edward, 188
Rapp, Rayna, 345, 346, 347
Rawlings, Steve, 350
Ray, Victor, 235
Reed, Adolph, Jr., 191, 241
Reeves, Thomas C., 405
Reich, Michael, 282
Reich, Robert, 52, 158, 204, 207, 212, 322
Reilly, Sabrina L., 178
Reiman, Jeffrey H., 141
Renzetti, Claire M., 266, 267, 275
Reskin, Barbara F., 279, 280
Ribar, David C., 353
Richard, Scott W., 23, 27
Richman, Judith, 347
Richmond, Julius B., 193
Richmond-Abbott, Marie, 270
Ridgeway, Cecilia L., 262, 263, 270, 280, 281

Riecken, Henry W., Jr., 35
Riesman, David, 323
Rifkin, Jeremy, 155
Ritzer, George, 12, 33, 295, 416
Rivera, Amand, 306
Rivers, Caryl, 260, 267
Roberts, Russell, 58
Roberts, Sam, 58, 162
Robeson, Wendy W., 266
Robins, Natalie, 119
Robinson, Eugene, 252
Robinson, John P., 359
Roehling, Patricia, 355
Rogers, Joel, 27, 58, 211
Rogers, Stacy J., 351, 355
Rogers, Susan Carol, 262
Romaine, Suzanne, 270
Roos, Patricia A., 280
Ropelato, Jerry, 130
Rosaldo, Michelle Zimbalist, 262, 263
Rosen, Ruth, 119, 120
Rosenthal, Robert, 382
Rossi, Peter H., 206
Rotello, Gabriel, 39
Rothfeder, Jeffrey, 124
Rothstein, Richard, 248
Roza, Marguerite, 377
Rubenstein, Richard E., 53
Rubin, Lillian B., 177, 178
Rugh, Jacob S., 246
Russell, James W., 337
Russell, Jan Jarboe, 370
Russell, Marta, 418
Ryan, Joanna, 192
Ryan, William, 15, 48, 192

Sacks, Karen, 263
Sadker, David, 267, 373
Sadker, Myra, 373
Saenz, Rogelio, 254
Sage, George H., 47, 81, 268, 419, 425
Saldana, Dave, 98
Salmon, Jacqueline L., 389
Samuelson, Paul Anthony, 203
Sanderson, Stephen K., 209
Sapiro, Virginia, 263, 270, 271, 272
Sawhill, Isabel, 17
Scarpitti, Frank R., 115
Schachter, Stanley, 35
Schemo, Diana, 371
Schetz, Amy, 334
Schmit, Julie, 307
Schneider, David M., 347
Schrag, Peter, 161
Schumpeter, Joseph, 154
Schur, Edwin, 142
Scott, Jacqueline, 265
Scott, Janny, 216, 219
Seff, Monica, 358
Seigel, Paul M., 206

Sennett, Richard, 61, 190
Sesser, Stan, 117
Shanker, Albert, 300, 371
Shapiro, Joseph P., 418
Shapiro, Judith, 262
Shapiro, Thomas M., 247
Shaw-Taylor, Yoku, 237
Shelden, Randall G., 142–143
Sheler, Jeffrey L., 390, 400
Shen, Francis X., 216
Sherif, Carolyn W., 23
Sherif, Muzafer, 23, 35
Shils, Edward A., 32
Shinkle, Kirk, 307
Sikes, Melvin P., 246
Simmons, Ann M., 162
Sinderbrand, Rebecca, 115
Singer, Matt, 335
Skenazy, Lenore, 96
Sklar, Holly, 174, 227, 246, 274, 278
Sklaroff, Sara, 26
Skolnick, Jerome, 39, 43, 53
Slevin, Peter, 370
Small, Maria Luis, 194, 241
Smelser, Neil, 416
Smith, Jessica C., 221
Smith, Judith R., 219
Smith, Kelly Eitzen, 7, 48, 101, 121, 311, 418
Smith, Marshall, 220
Smith, Raymond T., 347
Smith, William, 252
Smith-Lovin, Lynn, 26, 270
Smock, Pamela J., 353
Snipp, Matthew, 239, 240
Snyder, Eldon, 111
Solis, Brian, 271
Solove, Daniel, 131
Spencer, Albert F., 265
Spencer, Renée, 268
Spong, John Shelby, 412
Sprague, Joey, 209, 211, 213, 267
Squires, Gregory D., 246, 247
Stacey, Judith, 349
Stack, Carol B., 267
Statzel, Sophie R., 253
Steele, James B., 333
Stefanone, Michael A., 271
Stein, Peter J., 347, 420
Steinberg, Stephen, 194, 242
Stewart, Kenneth, 422
Stivers, Richard, 108
Stolberg, Sheryl Gay, 251
Stranahan, Susan Q., 297
Strauss, William A. 337
Street, Paul, 116, 331
Sunstein, Cass R., 51
Sutherland, Edwin H., 134
Swartz, Jon, 334
Swidler, Ann, 220
Symonds, William C., 217, 218, 379
Szymanski, Albert, 109

Takaki, Ronald, 236, 237
Talley, Kathryn D., 15, 222, 225
Taylor, Howard F., 7
Taylor, Marisa, 123
Teller-Elsberg, Jonathan, 292
Terkel, Studs, 296
The Wage Gap, 278
Thomas, Oliver, 272, 273
Thornburgh, Nathan, 368, 375
Thorne, Barrie, 264, 266
Thornton, Russell, 239
Thurow, Lester, 207
Tilly, Chris, 283
Timmer, Doug A., 15, 222, 225
Tolman, Deborah, 268
Tomosakovic-Devey, Donald, 252
Torrey, Barbara Boyle, 18, 19
Townsend, Nicholas W., 357
Treiman, Donald J., 206
Tribe, Lawrence H., 39
Troeltsch, Ernst, 396
Tumin, Melvin M., 186, 189
Turkle, Sherry, 95, 96, 360
Turner, Ronny E., 73
Turse, Nick, 309

U.S. Bureau of the Census, 221, 235, 237, 238, 239, 246, 247, 248, 250, 357, 368
U.S. Department of Labor, 241
U.S. State Department, 299
Urban Institute, 228
USA Today, 17, 120, 122
Usdansky, Margaret L., 346

Valian, Virginia, 264, 265
Van Biema, David, 273, 405
van den Berghe, Pierre L., 49, 389
Vanneman, Reeve, 209, 211, 212, 213
Vecoli, Rudolph J., 345
Vernon, Mark, 25
Vestal, Christine, 309
Villano, Matt, 376
Visher, Emily B., 354
Visher, John S., 354
Von Drehle, David, 267
Voss, Kim, 220
Voukydis, Mara, 247, 249

Waite, Linda J., 352–353
Walby, Sylvia, 281
Wald, Matthew, 145
Wali, Alaka, 236
The Wall Street Journal, 163
Walton, John, 4, 9, 45
Warren, Mark, 246
Warren, Patricia, 252
Warriner, Charles K., 24
Waters, Mary C., 236
Weber, Lynn, 236, 244

Weber, Max, 11, 32, 397, 398
Wedekind, Jennifer, 297
Weisbrot, Mark, 120
Weiss, Kenneth R., 378
Weisskopf, Thomas E., 282
Weitzman, Lenore J., 265
Wellman David T., 241, 242, 251
Wellman, Barry, 26
Wells, Barbara A., 31, 187, 351, 355, 358
West, Candace, 270
West, Cornel, 139
West, Darrell M., 165
Westhues, Kenneth, 103
Wheatcroft, Geoffrey, 275
Wheelis, Allen, 49
Whelan, Ellen-Marie, 251
Whitehouse, Mark, 310
Whyte, William Foote, 19, 23
Wikigender.org contributors, 271
Wilcox, Clyde, 393
Wilkening, David, 129
Will, George F., 58
Williams, Christine, 280, 281, 401
Williams, Robin M. Jr., 401
Williamson, Elizabeth, 334
Williamson, Nancy, 424
Williamson, Thad, 185
Willing, Richard, 320
Wilson, William J., 228, 241, 242, 254
Winant, Howard, 243, 244
Winship, Michael, 306
Winters, Marcus A., 373

Witt, Susan, 264, 265
Woellert, Lorraine, 122
Wolf, Richard, 175, 338
Wolfe, Alan, 327
Wolterbeek, Liannaa Atchison, 265
Wood, Eileen, 265
Wozniak, Abigail, 310
Wright, Erik Olin, 27, 58, 209, 211, 213, 324

Yabroff, Jennie, 101
Yen, Hope, 162
Yetman, Norman R., 12, 416
Yeung, Jean W., 219
Yinger, Milton J.
Yorburg, Betty, 187
Young, Jeff, 253

Zaretsky, Eli, 362
Zehr, Mary Ann, 380
Zeitlin, Maurice, 337
Zelizer, Gerald L., 65, 273
Zellner, William, 110
Zeskind, Leonard, 52, 167
Zhou, Min, 169
Zimbardo, Philip G., 29, 30
Zimmerman, Don, 270
Zingraff, Matthew, 252
Zinn, Howard, 319, 420, 421, 427
Zuckerman, Mortimer B., 368
Zvonkovic, Anisa M., 355

Abecedarian Project, 193
Aborigines (Australian), religion of, 390
Achievement
   individual, 78–79
Adherence to the rules, 33
Adolescents, 357–359
The Adonis Complex (Pope), 93
Advertising, 94
AFCD (Aid to Families with Dependent Children), 16
African-Americans
   culture-of-poverty hypothesis and, 193, 194
   death penalty and, 140, 141
   discrimination against, 245–251
      education and, 248–249
      employment type and, 249–250
      health and, 250–251
      income and, 246–248
      segregation, 237
      unemployment and, 249
   income, education and, 377, 380
   IQ tests and, 191, 192
   labor disputes, 57
   myths/stereotypes, 15
   as new poor, 159–160
   in prison, 137
   religion and, 400–401
   subprime crisis and, 306
   unemployment rates, 158
   in United States population, 161, 162, 167, 237
   as victims, 136
   women, earnings gap and, 278
African tribes, 73
Age/aging. *See also* Elderly
   families and, 346
   as long-term trend, 170
   of U.S. population, 170
Age cohort, 101
Agency. *See* Human agency
Aggregate, 23–24
Agriculture, jobs in, 154, 155
Aid to Families with Dependent Children (AFDC), 16, 226
Alienation, 296
Altruistic suicide, 34
Alzheimer's disease, 176
American Dream, 78
American Revolutionary War, 55
American Society of Plastic Surgeons, 93
Americans with Disabilities Act, 418
Amish religious sect
   selection of new ministers, 29
   shunning of sinners, 30
   social control and, 110

Androgyny, 265
Animal Farm (Orwell), 202
Anomic suicide, 34
Anomie, 34
Anti-immigration movement, 165, 167
Aphorisms, 17
Ascribed status, 72
Asian Americans
   income, education and, 375
   in United States, 166
   in United States population, 166, 238–239
Assimilation, 168–169
Australian aborigines, religion of, 390
Authority, sources of, 18
Automation, loss of blue-collar jobs and, 154–156

Baby boomers, 101
Balkanization of America, 167
"Ban," 110
Behavior
   aphorisms/proverbs, 17
   culture and, 66–67
   discrepancy with values, 83
   good, teaching, 95
   group effects on, 36–37
   patterned, 186
   prediction of, 8
   similar, differential treatment for, 130
   status-related expectations of, 28
   when alone *vs.* with people, 24
Belief systems, culture and, 66
The Bell Curve (Herrnstein & Murray), 191, 241
Bias
   minimizing, 16
   racial profiling and, 139–140
   value neutrality and, 13–14
Bias of the system theory, 330–332
Bias theories, of racial/ethnic inequality, 241–243
Biculturalism, 169
Bill of Rights, 83
Biological deficiency theory, of racial/ethnic inequality, 241
Biological inferiority, 190–193
Biological theories, of deviance, 133
Bipartisan Campaign Reform Act (McCain-Feingold law),
      320–321
Blacks. *See* African-Americans
Blaming the victim hypothesis
   deviance and, 135–137
   gender socialization as, 269
Blue-collar jobs, 154–156
Body image, 93
Boeing corporation, 153

"Boy crisis," 267
Brazil
    abolishment of slavery in, 183
    Aimore tribe in, 73
    soybean crop in, 3
Brown v. Board of Education, 205
Buddhism, 390
Bureaucracy, 32–33
Business world, dishonesty in, 80

CAFTA (Central American Free Trade Agreement), 152
California, population changes in, 162–163
Capital flight, 151
Capitalism, 154, 155, 288–289
    competition and, 288
    in crisis, 305–313
    families in, 344–345
    inequality and, 293–294
    negative consequences, 311–312
    values of, 82
Capitalist patriarchy, 263
Caste system, 54, 183, 184
Caste violence, in India, 54
Catcher in the Rye (Salinger), 370
Catholic religion, 34, 89
Cause-and-effect relationships, 19
Censorship, in Singapore, 117
Central American Free Trade Agreement (CAFTA), 152
CEOs (chief executive officers), 203
Charisma, 11, 397
Charisma of office, 397
Chief executive officers (CEOs), 203
Children
    feral, 89
    gender learning
        formal education and, 267–269
        at home, 264–265
        at play, 266–267
    poverty and, 357–358
    socialization of, 89
Christian calendar, 65
Christian fundamentalism, 406–407
Christian fundamentalists, 75
Church, 396
CISPES (Committee in Solidarity with the People of El Salvador), 119
Civil disobedience, 144
Civil religion, 392–394
Civil Rights Movement, 119, 420–423
Class
    administration of justice, 217
    conflict model conception of, 211–213
    consequences of, 207–209
    definition of, 187
    deviance and, 135
    draft, 216–217
    education, 204–206, 215, 217–218
    family instability, 216
    fighting the nation's wars, 216–217
    health, 214–216

intersection with race and gender, 188–189
    IQ and, 191
    media selective perception of, 60
    near poor, 210
    order model conception of, 209–210
    privilege and, 187
    religion, relationship, 399–400
    social stratification and, 38
Class conflict, 11
Class consciousness, 11
Coinciding interests, of power elite, 327
COINTELPRO, 119
COLA (Cost of Living Adjustment), 176
Collective belonging, socialism and, 289
College, Homeland Security tactics, 122
College access, inequalities in, 378
College campuses, racial tensions, 248
College students, United Students against Sweatshop, 419
Color-blind racism, 255
Committee in Solidarity with the People of El Salvador (CISPES), 119
Communicative contact, 90–91
Comparative questions, 12
Competition, 79–81, 288
Compulsory heterosexuality, 262
Concentrated power, consequences of, 333–339
Conflict model, 383
    deviance and, 143–147
    families and, 362–363
    gender stratification and, 264
    vs. order model, 46, 61–62
    power distribution and, 339–340
    racial stratification and, 244
    religion and, 391–392, 411–412
    social classes and, 211–213
    social control and, 126
    socialization and, 103
    social problems and, 48
    social stratification and, 189–190
    of society, 45, 47, 61
    sport and, 47–48
    synthesis with order model, 48–50
    values and, 86
Confucian fundamentalisms, 75–76
Contingent employment, 156
Control group, 19
Convictions, group affects on, 35
Cooperation, socialism and, 289
Co-optation, 61
Corporate crime, 145–147
    consequences of labeling, 141–142
    labeling and, 138, 139
    racial profiling, 139–140
Corporate wealth, concentration of, 293
Corporation-dominated economy, 290–293
Corporations
    global free market mobility for, 164–165
    large, subsidies for, 335–336
    transnational, 160
Cost of Living Adjustment (COLA), 176
Counterculture, 84

Couvade, 71
Cow worship, in India, 73–74
"Creative destruction," 154, 155
Criminal justice system, 116
    consequences of labeling, 141–142
    labeling and, 138, 139
    racial profiling and, 139–140, 252
Criminals, recidivism and, 136
Cub Scouts, 80
Cult, 398
Cultural control, 108. *See also* Socialization
Cultural deficiency theory, of racial!
    ethnic inequality, 245
Cultural deprivation, 136, 377
Cultural diffusion, 75
Cultural diversity, 83–84
Cultural inferiority, 193–195
Cultural relativity, 73–74
Cultural transmission, of deviant behavior, 134
Culture, 65–86
    boundary maintenance, 67–68
    as channel for human behavior, 66–67
    characteristics, 66–68
    definition of, 23
    as emergent process, 66
    globalization of, 74–76
    as learned, 66
    of poverty, 135, 193–195
    social construction of reality and, 72–73
    social organization and, 26–27
    of society, 38
    types of shared knowledge and, 69–72
    values, 76–86
Curriculum, 371, 372

Data
    collection, problems in, 12–18
    existing, 19
    sources, 18–19
DEA (Drug Enforcement Administration), 120
Death penalty, race and, 140, 141
Death rates, work-related, 297
Declaration of Independence, 55, 59, 77, 83, 116
Defense of Marriage Act, 39
Deficiency theories
    of racial/ethnic inequality, 245
    of social stratification, 190–195
Democracy, 207, 318
    pay-to-play mentality and, 322
    structural barriers to, 319–320
Democratization, socialism and, 289–290
Demographic change, 160, 163, 169, 173
Department of Homeland Security, 122
Dependency ratio, 175
Dependency ratio, demographic factor, 175
Dependent variables, 19
Determinism, 415
Deviance, 129–148
    characteristics of, 129–132
    conflict model, 147

conflict theory, 143–147
    as socially constructed, 130
    solutions, from labeling perspective, 142–143
    source of
        individual as, 133–138
        society as, 138–147
    traditional theories, 133–147
        biological, 133
        blaming-the-victim critique, 135–138
        psychological, 133–134
        sociological, 134–135
*The De-Voicing of Society: Why We Don't Talk to Each Other
    Anymore* (Locke), 26
Dialectic, 49
Differential opportunities, deviance and, 134–135
Direct interlock, 292
Direct social control
    agents of, 113–123
    definition of, 113
    government, 116–123
    medicine, 114–116
    science, 114–116
    welfare, 113–114
Discouraged workers, 303
Discrimination, workplace, 301–303
Disengagement, 178
Dissident groups, targeting, 122
Diversity
    cultural, 83–84
    demographic transition in U.S., 160
Divorce
    generalizations about, 354
    grounds for, 71
    rates, 12, 31
Documentation Generation, 101
Dominant group, 233
Drug Enforcement Administration (DEA), 120
Dual labor market theory, 280
Durkheim, Emile, 10, 33, 34, 45, 47, 131, 132, 391
Dysfunctions, 62
Dyslexia, 133

Echelon, 120
Economic crisis, 305–306
Economic determinism, 10–11
Economic inequality, 54
Economic planning, lack of, 312–313
Economic violence, in India, 54
Economy, 287–313
    changing nature of job, 154–157
    corporation-dominated, 290–293
    families and, 348–349
    global, gender in, 281, 282
    globalization of, 152
    structural transformation of, 154–156
Education, 367–383
    academic performance, 375, 378
    as agent of ideological social control, 109
    competitive nature of, 372
    conflict model and, 383

as conserving force, 367
curriculum, standardized, lack of, 371, 372
in curriculum, inequalities, 373–376
in foreign countries, 367
formal, gender learning in, 267–269
  curriculum, 267
  female role models, 269
  sports, 268–269
  teacher–student interactions, 268
fragmented system of, 369–370
future payoffs, 382–383
inequalities, 204–205, 373–376
  in college access, 367
  in curriculum, 371–372
  income and, 373
  racial minorities in higher education, 380
local control of, 369–370
mass, 368
preoccupation with order and control, 368
race/ethnicity and, 248
segregation and, 380–381
social class and, 214
social mobility and, 218–221
teacher's expectations and, 381–382
tracking, 381–382
trends in, 100
Education Amendments Act, Title IX, 267
Egalitarianism, socialism and, 289
Ego, 94
Egoistic suicide, 34
Elderly
  demographics trends, 171
  human agency and, 177–178
  paying for health care, 176–177
  poverty and, 223–224
  problems of, 174
  racial/ethnic minorities, 159, 162, 173
  social security, 174–176
The Elementary Forms of Religious Life (Durkheim), 391
Elitist model of power, 318
Elitist models, 324–332
E-mail, isolating effects of, 26
Emoticon, 69
Employment
  increase in working poor, 159
  insecurity of, 157–158
  social security, 174–176
  types, race/ethnicity and, 249–250
  unemployment, race/ethnicity and, 249
Environment, cognitive development and, 192, 193
Environmental racism, 250
Equality of people, 83
Ethnic group, 236–237
Ethnic identity, *vs.* assimilation, 168–169
Ethnicity, 187–188
  religion and, 401
Ethnic minorities, 234–235
  contemporary trends/issues in United States, 234
  definition of, 234
  education and, 248
  employment type and, 249–250

health and, 250–251
income, education and, 381
income and, 246–248
inequality, explanations of, 234
minority groups (*See* Ethnic minorities)
vs. racial groups, 236, 237
racial tensions and, 159
social stratification and, 187–188
unemployment and, 249
in U.S. population, aging of, 162
violence and, 56
Ethnic prejudice, 91
Ethnic violence, in India, 54
Ethnocentrism, 67–68, 74
Ethnomethodology, 70
Eugenics, 115
Evangelical message, Savvy marketing, 407–408
Exiguus, Dionysius, 65
Experimental group, 19
Experiments, 19
Extortion, 295

Factual questions, 13
Falling rate of profit, 312
False consciousness, 10, 61
Family/families, 343–364
  as agent of ideological social control, 108–109
  in capitalism, 344–345
  characteristics of, 346
  children/adolescents in, 357–359
  declining significance of, 31
  definition of, 345
  diversity of, 349–351, 350–351
  economic resources, educational attainment and, 377–379
  economic transformation and, 348–349
  elderly members, 360, 361
  forms, changes in, 99–100
  in future, 363
  instability social class and, 216
  myths about, 343–344
  order and conflict perspectives, 362–363
  roles in, work and, 355–357
  as socialization agent, 95
  violence in, 360–361
Farmers, exploited, 55
FBI, 121, 122
Female role models, 269
The Feminine Mystique (Friedan), 424
Feminist approach, 259
Feminist movement, in United States, 283–284
Feminization of poverty, 223
Feral children, 89
FLDS (Fundamentalist Church of Jesus Christ of Latter Day Saints), 85
Folkways, 27, 71
Foreign policy, for corporate benefit, 339
Freedom, individual, 82–83
Free market system, 165
Functional integration, 57, 58

Functionalism. *See* Order model
Fundamentalist Church of Jesus Christ of Latter Day Saints
    (FLDS), 85
The Future of Reputation (Solove)

Game stage, of personality development, 93
GATT (General Agreement on Tariffs and Trade), 152
Gay marriage, 39, 353–354
Gay rights, 30
Gender
  biological bases for, 260–261
  definition of, 259
  equity in sports, 423–426
  in global economy, 281
  intersection with class and race, 188–189
  learning, 264–267, 283
  poverty and, 223
  power and, 262
  religion and, 401–402
  social bases for, 261
  social stratification and, 188
Gendered institutions, 262
Gendered men, 259
Gender inequality, 259–285
  fighting, 283–284
  individual costs of, 283
  occupational distribution and, 275–278, 277
  structured, 275, 276, 277
    earnings gap and, 278
  workplace, 303
Gender roles
  biological bases for, 260, 261
  changes in, 103
  definition of, 188
  social bases for, 261
Gender socialization, 264
Gender stratification, 259
Gender structure, 264
General Agreement on Tariffs and Trade
    (GATT), 152
Generalizations, faulty, 15
Generalized other, 94
Generation cohorts, changes in, 101
Generation X, 101
Geographic distribution, 172
Ghettoization, 280
Glass ceiling, 281
Global culture, 75
Globalization
  of economy, 151–160
  of religion, 390–391
Global warming, 152
Goal displacement, 420
Governing class theory, 328–330, 329
Government
  as agent of ideological social control, 113
  direct social control and, 116–123
The Grapes of Wrath (John Steinbeck), 370
Gratz v Bollinger, 381
Great Recession, 305, 309–311

Group/groups
  definition of, 24
  ethnic (*See* Ethnic minorities)
  as integrative factor, 59
  status and, 28

Habits, teaching, 95
Health
  group effects on, 35–36
  race/ethnicity and, 250–251
  social class and, 214–216
Health care, paying for, 176–177
Heterogeneous, 99
Hidden curriculum, 383
Hierarchy, 28
Hinduism, 390
Hindu-Muslim riots, 54
Hindu religion, caste system and, 184
Hispanics, use of term, 234. *See also* Latinos (Hispanics)
Historical questions, 13
History, turning points in, 151
Holy water, 73
Homeland security, 122
Homeless persons, myths/stereotypes, 15
Home-schooling, 100
Homeshoring, 156
Homesourcing, 156
Homogeneous, 99
Homosexuality, same-sex marriage and, 353–354
Hopi language, 72
Horizontal mobility, 218
Households
  definition of, 345
  diversity of, 349–351, 350–352
Housing, cheaper, new migrants and, 161
Housing woes, 307
Human agency, 414–431
  elderly population and, 177–178
  immigration and, 167–168
  social change and, 420–429
  social movements (*See* Social movements)
  social structure and, 415–416
Human capital theory, 280
Humans
  as social beings, 5
  social determination of, 5–6, 138

Id, 94
Ideological social control
  agents of, 108–113
  definition of, 108
  education, 109
  family, 108–109
  government, 113
  media, 111–112
  religion, 109
  sport, 110–111
Ideology
  cultural, 70
  defined, 416

Imitation stage, of personality
  development, 92
Immigrants
  black, 237
  ethnic minority, 56
  illegal, 165
  race/privilege and, 242–243
  religion and, 401
  settlement patterns of, 161
  white, 245
Immigration
  agency and, 167–168
  consequences of, 163–167
  definition of, 160
  global economy and, 152, 165, 177
  increasing diversity and, 162–163
  new, 160–169
  patterns, 160–162
  racial-ethnic tensions and, 166–167
  society's resources and, 164–166
  waves of, 160, 168
Immigration Act amendments of 1965, 160
Income
  definition of, 202
  educational attainment and, 373
  inequalities in, 207
  private, concentration of, 293–294
  productivity and, 154, 158
  race/ethnicity and, 246–248, 247
Independent variables, 19
India
  caste system in, 183, 184
  cow worship in, 73–74
  violence and division in, 54
Indirect interlock, 292
Individualism, 47, 82–83
Individual racism, 243
Individuals, autonomous, 24
Industrial revolution, 151
Inequality
  capitalism and, 293–294
  dimensions of, 202–209
  in education, 204–205, 373–376, 374
  income and, 373, 377, 379
  in occupation, 206–207
  racial/ethnic, explanations of, 233–234
  societal consequences of, 207–209
Inequality gap, 52
Instability, family, social class and, 216
Institutional discrimination, 195–196
Institutionalization, 419
Institutional process, 49
Institutional racism, 243
Institutional violence, 43
Institutions, 38
  diminishing trust in, 51–52
  types of, 39, 40
Instrumentalist view, 324
Instrumental process, 49
Integration
  functional, 57, 58
  planned, 61

Integrity, in social research, 16
Intergenerational mobility, 218
Interlocking directorates, 292
Internalization, 66, 95
Internal Revenue Code, 321
Internal Revenue Service (IRS), 119
International competition and conflict, 59
Internet
  deviance and, 129–132
  globalization of culture and, 74
  privacy rights and, 125
  public shame and, 131
  workplace transformations and, 163
Interpersonal behavior, in reinforcing male dominance, 270
Intragenerational mobility, 218
IQ tests, 191–192
Irish Catholic immigrants, 56
"Iron cage" of rationality, 33
IRS (Internal Revenue Service), 119
Islam, 390, 395

Jensen-Herrnstein-Murray thesis, 192, 193
"Jihad vs. McDonaldization," 75
Job insecurity, 157–158
Jobs, low-skilled, 287
Judeo-Christian ethic, 77
Judiasm, 390
Justice, administration of, social class and, 217

Kamikaze attacks, by Japanese pilots, 34
Kentucky River cases, 299
Ku Klux Klan, 243, 252

Labeling theory, 138–143
  consequences of labeling, 141
  deficiencies of, 143
  definition of, 142
  racial profiling and, 139–140
  solutions for deviance and, 142
  strengths of, 143
Labor disputes, 56–57
Labor market, segmented, 301–302
Labor unions, 298, 299
Laissez-faire, 288
Language, 90–91
  California, 161
  cultural factors in, 72–73
  in reinforcing male dominance, 270
  socialization and, 91
Latch-key children, 101
Latent consequence, 45
Latent functions, 82
Latinos (Hispanics)
  discrimination against, 245–251
    education and, 248–249
    employment type and, 249–250
    health and, 250–251
    income and, 246–248
    segregation, 237
    unemployment and, 249

Hispanic category, use of, 238
  income, education and, 380
  as new poor, 159–160
  subprime crisis for, 306
  surname count on U.S. Census, 162
  unemployment rates, 158
  in United States population, 162, 167, 170
  work-related death rates, 297
Law
  administration of, 145
  breaking, common examples of, 139
  discriminatory, 144
  in reinforcing male dominance, 273–274
Law enforcement, 117, 120, 121, 123
Learning, gender, 264–269
Lesbians, same-sex marriage and, 353–354
Liberal democratic theory, 118
Life, group effects on, 35–36
Life chances, 186–188
Linguistic relativity, 72
Linguistic violence, in India, 54
Loans, sub-prime, 306
Lobbying, 331
Longitudinal surveys, 18
Looking-glass self, 92, 93
Lower-lower class, 210
Lower-middle class, 210
Lower-upper class, 210

Mainline churches, role of, 410–411
Mainline denominations, church, 405–406
Majority, determination of deviance and, 131
Make-Believe Media: The Politics of Entertainment
      (Parenti), 112
Male dominance
  definition of, 269
  interpersonal behavior and, 270
  language and, 270
  law and, 273–274
  mass media and, 270–272
  politics and, 274–275
  reinforcing, 269–275
  religion and, 272–273
  at work, 302–303
Maltreatment, racial/ethnic, 252–253
Manifest consequence, 45
Manifest functions, 82
Manufacturing
  blue-collar jobs, 154–156
  in United States, 154
Marriage, 351–355
  remarriage, 354–355
  same-sex, 130, 353–354
  social and individual benefits of, 352–353
Marx, Karl, 391–392
Marxism, 118
Mass media. See Media
Master status, 28
Material progress, 82
Material technology, 69
Matrix of domination, 188

McCain-Feingold law, 320–321
McDonaldization, 32–33
Media
  as agent of ideological social control, 111–112
  body image and, 93
  consolidation, 99
  images, changes in, 101–102
  as integrative force, 60
  in reinforcing male dominance, 270–272
  selective perception of race and class, 60
  as socialization agent, 97–99
Medicare, 165, 177
Medicine, direct social control and, 114–116
Megachurches, 407
Megamergers, 291–292
Meidung, 110
Men
  biological differences from women, 260
  gender stratification and (See Gender stratification)
Men and Women of the Corporation (Kanter), 280
Mennonites, 30, 110. See also Ethnic minorities
Meritocracy, 191
Migration, effects on immigrants, 168–169
Military draft, social class and, 216, 217
Millennial Generation, 101
Minority groups. See also Ethnic minorities; specific minority
      groups
  definition of, 234
  in United States population, 173
Misery, concentration of, 294
Mistresses, 71
Mob violence, contemporary, 56
Modal personality, 99
Model, 45
Modern family, 349
Monopolistic capitalism, 291–292
Mores, 27, 71
Motherhood, unwed, 16
Muli men, of Papua, New Guinea, 74
Murder, 130, 132, 140
Muslim suicide bombers, 34
Myth of peaceful progress, 53, 55

NAFTA (North American Free Trade Agreement), 152
National Assessment of Educational Progress (NAEP), 375
National Lawyers Guild, 120
National power structure, models of, 318–332
National Security Agency, 119, 120, 121
Nations, inequality in, 185
Native Americans
  income, education and, 374
  in United States, 239–240
  violence and, 55, 57
Nazi Germany, eugenics and, 115
Near poor, 210
Neolithic agricultural revolution, 151
New immigration, 160–169
New poor, 159–160
1984 (Orwell), 123, 125
No Child Left Behind Act, 371
Nominalist position, 24

Nonfamily household, 350
Norms
    definition of, 26–27
    violation of (*See* Deviance)
North American Free Trade Agreement (NAFTA), 152

Objectivity, in social research, 16
Observation, 19
Occupation
    distribution, gender inequality in, 275–278
    inequalities in, 206–207
Occupational Safety & Health Association (OSHA), 297
Oedipal conflict, 133
Offshoring, 153
Opiate of the masses, 392
Order model
    social stratification and, 189
Order model (functionalism)
    vs. conflict model, 46, 61–62
    description of, 44–45, 46
    deviance and, 147
    families and, 362–363
    gender stratification and, 262–264
    power distribution and, 339–340
    of racial stratification, 244–245
    of religion, 391, 411–412
    of social classes, 209–210
    social control and, 126
    socialization and, 103
    of social problems, 48
    of sport, 47–48
    synthesis with conflict model (*See* Synthesis model)
    use of, 61–62
    values and, 86
Organization of society, synthesis model and, 49
OSHA (Occupational Safety & Health
        Association), 297
Outsourcing, 153, 154
Outsourcing prayer, 396

Pacific Islanders. *See* Asian Americans
Pakistan, 5, 71
Parents, transmission of beliefs to offsprings, 5
Parole, race and, 140
Partisan violence, in India, 54
Patriarchy, 188, 262, 402
Patriot Act of 2001, 121
Pay-to-play mentality, 322
Peers, as socialization agents, 97
Perceptions, group affects on, 35
Personal bankruptcies, 308
Personal bias, minimizing, 16
Personality
    behavioral variations and, 28
    development stages, 92–94
    as social product, 91–92
Personal Responsibility and Work Opportunity
        Reconciliation Act, 226
Philippines, private schooling in, 207
Planned integration, 61

Planning
    economic, lack of, 312–313
    socialism and, 290
Play
    gender learning and, 264–269
    role in personality development, 93
Pluralism, 318, 320–324
Pluralist models of power, 318–324
Plutocracy, 323
Political crime, 145, 146
Political economy, of society, 196
Politics, 317–341
    contemporary Christianity and, 408–411
    pay-to-play mentality, 322
    two-party system, 319, 322
    in United States, 8–9
Positivism, 10
Post–baby boomers, 101
Postmodern families, 349
Poverty
    benefiting from, 196
    blaming the poor and, 192
    causes of, 185
    families and, 346
    increase in working poor, 159
    inevitability of, 192
    institutional discrimination and, 195–196
    myths about, 226–229
        refusal to work, 226
        special advantages for the poor, 228–229
        welfare dependency and, 226–228
    poor people
        coping strategies of, 222
        new poor, 159–160
        severely poor, 225
    in United States, 221–225
        children and, 222, 224
        elderly and, 223–224
        gender and, 223
        geography of, 224–225
        nativity and, 223
        racial minorities and, 222
Poverty line, 202, 217
Power, 317–341
    concentrated, consequences of, 333–339
    deviance and, 130, 135, 145
    foreign policy for corporate benefit, 339
    gender and, 262
    perspectives on distribution, 339–340
    pluralist models of, 318–324
    powerless bear the burden, 337–338
    subsidies to big business, 335–336
    trickle-down economics and, 336–337
Power elite, 325–332
Powerless bear the burden, 337–338
Power play, 266
Presidential Commissions on Civil Disorders and
        Violence, 57
Primary deviance, 141
Primary groups, 31
Principles of American Way of life, 77

Prison life, impact on guards and prisoners, 29
Privacy rights, violations of, 124–126
Private sector, social control in, 124–126
Privilege, 186, 187
Productivity, wages, total compensation and, 158–159
Professional-managerial class, 211
Profiling, 252–253
Progress, 81–82
Property, private, 82–83
Protestant ethic, 77
The Protestant Ethic and the Spirit of Capitalism (Weber), 11, 77, 392
Protestant religion, suicide and, 34
Protestants, 89
Proverbs, 17
Psychoanalytic view, 94
Psychological similarity, power elite and, 327
Psychological theories, of deviance, 133–134
Psychosurgery, 115
Public ownership, socialism and, 289
Public temper, 131
Public welfare, direct social control and, 113–114
Pyramid of power, 318, 325–326, 330

Questions, sociological, 9, 11–12

Race
    contemporary trends/issues in United States, 251–255
    death penalty and, 140
    defining, growing difficulty with, 251–252
    demographic changes in United States and, 101
    education and, 248–249
    employment type and, 249–250
    ethnic tensions and, 166–167
    families and, 346
    health and, 250–251
    income, education and, 374, 381
    income and, 246–248
    inequality, explanations of, 240–245
    intersection with class and gender, 188–189
    media selective perception of, 60
    myths/stereotypes, 15–16
    and religion, 400–401
    social isolation in U.S. cities and, 253–254
    social stratification and, 187–188
    unemployment and, 249
    of United States population, 161–162, 167, 170
Racial-ethnic groups, 237–240
Racial formation, 235
Racial inequality, 233–255
Racially-based groups/activities, 252
Racial minorities, 56, 141, 234–240
    higher education and, 380
    poverty and, 222
    racial groups, *vs.* ethnic groups, 236–237
    in U.S. population, aging of, 161–162, 167, 170
Racial profiling, 139–140, 252–253
Racial stratification
    definition of, 244
    from order and conflict perspectives, 244–245

Racial tensions
    on college campuses, 253
    contemporary, 251–255
Radical nonintervention, 142
Radical Non-Intervention: Rethinking the Delinquency Problem (Shur), 142
Realist position, 24
Reality, social interpretation of, 73
Reality television, body image and, 93
Recidivism, 136
Reference groups, 67
Reform movements, 417
Regressive tax, 229
Religion, 387–413
    as agent of ideological social control, 109
    conflict model perspective of, 391–392, 411–412
    and ethnicity, 401
    fundamentalist, 75
    and gender, 401–402
    globalization of, 390–391
    order model perspective of, 391, 411–412
    and Race, 400–401
    in reinforcing male dominance, 272–273
    and sexuality, 402–403
    and social change, 392
    social class, relationship, 399–400
Religious right, 408–410
Religious sects
    affects on health, 36
Religious trends, 404–408
Religious violence, in India, 54
Remarriage, 354–355
Research
    bias in, 13–14
    standards for objectivity and integrity, 16
Reserve army of the unemployed, 304
Resistance movements, 416
Resources, new immigration and, 163–166
Revolutionary movement, 417
Reward-punishment system, 76–77
Ritual, 388
Roe v. Wade, 273–274
Role conflict, 410–411
Roles
    cultural, 72
    expectations from, 28
Routinization of charisma, 397
Rules, adherence to, 33
Ruling class, 211

Same-sex marriage, 39, 130, 353–354
Sample, 18
Sanctions, 30–31
SAT (Scholastic Aptitude Test), 373
Scholastic Aptitude Test (SAT), 373
Schools
    educational trends, 100
    sifting/sorting function of, 372
    as socialization agents, 95, 97
    sports in, 110–111

Science
    direct social control and, 114–116
Scientific management, 295
Scientists
    political, cultural and social influences on, 14
Secondary deviance, 141
Secondary groups, 31
Sect, 396–397
Segmented labor market, 301–302
Segregation, 246–248, 380–381
Self, 92
Self-fulfilling prophecy, 134, 136, 140, 143, 382
Self-reliance, 83
September 11, 2001 terrorist attacks
    airlines industry after, 153
    government control after, 121–123
    repression of decent before, 119–120
    victims, government compensation for, 213
Severely poor, 225
Sex, definition of, 259
Sex discrimination, 283, 284
Sex-gender system, 188, 196
Sexism, costs/consequences of, 282–283
Sex roles, 8, 188
Sex trafficking, 282
Sexual behavior, group effects on, 36
Sexual intercourse, 130
Sexuality, religion and, 402–403
Sexual orientation, 53
Sex work, industrialization of, 282
Shame, Internet and, 130–131
Shared monopoly, 291
Shunning, 110
Significant others, 94
Singapore, 117
Slaveholders, 56
Slavery
    historical perspective, 6, 201
    modern day, 299
Small-business owners, 212
Smoking, 130, 146
Snake handling, poisonous, 36
Social boundaries, maintenance, culture and, 67–68
Social change, 50
Social change, religion and, 392
Social class. See Class
Social cognitive theory, 94
Social construction of reality, 72–74
Social control, 30–31, 107–126
    conflict model and, 126
    definition of, 107
    direct, 113–123
        agents of, 113–123
        definition of, 113
    ideological
        agents of, 108–113
        definition of, 108
    order model and, 126
    in private sector, 124–126
Social Darwinism, 137, 190, 191
Social determinism, 5–6, 191

Social differentiation, 185
Social facts, 10
Social forms, 6
Social groups, 31
    convictions and, 35
    health and life effects, 35–36
    perceptions and, 35
    power of, 33–37
    societal or macro level, 37–39, 40
    suicide probability and, 33–35
Social inequality, 186, 189. See also Social stratification
Social institutions, 39, 40
Social integration (social bond), 10, 77–83
Social interactions
    definition of, 24
    of power elite, 327
    social media, through, 25–26
    transitory vs. enduring, 24
Socialism, principles of, 289–290
Social isolation, of racial/ethnic groups US. cities, 253–254
Socialization
    in changing social landscape, 99–103
    definition of, 66, 89
    family, 95
    language and, 91
    looking-glass self and, 92
    media, 97–99
    peers, 97
    personality and, 91–92
    school, 95, 97
    societal agents, 95–99
    taking the role of the other, 92–94
Social life, duality of, 46–47
Social mobility, 218–221
Social movements, 416–420
    life course, 417–420
    types, 416–417
Social order, 59
Social organization
    culture and, 26–27
    definition of, 23
    process of, 23, 36
    social control and, 107
    sources, values as, 77–83
Social problems
    from order and conflict perspectives, 48
    person-blame approach, 137
Social relationship, 24
Social scientists, values and, 44
Social Security Administration poverty line, 221
Social security system, 174–175
Social stratification, 38, 183–198
    biological inferiority, 190–193
    caste system, 183, 184
    by class, 187
    conflict theory and, 189–190
    cultural inferiority, 193–195
    deficiency theories, 190–195
    definition of, 38
    by ethnicity, 187–188
    by gender, 188

hierarchies, 186–188
  intersection of class, race and gender, 188–189
  order theory and, 189
  by race, 187–188
  social differentiation and, 185
  structural theories, 195–198
Social structure
  agency and, 415–416
  role and, 28–29
  social interaction and, 24–25
  status and, 27–28
Social systems
  conflict model and, 45–46
  definition of, 37
  order model and, 44–45
  society as, 49
Social technology, 70
Societal goals, deviance and, 134–135
Societal norms, 70–72
Societal problems, institutions and, 39, 40
Societal values, consensus on, 58–59
Society
  aging (*See also* Elderly)
    demographics of, 169–171
    problems of, 174–177
  complementary interests of, 49–50
  culture of, 38
  definition of, 37
  division in, 50–53
  healthy, deviant behavior and, 131
  integrative forces in, 57–61
  political economy of, 196
  as social system, 37–38, 49
  as source of deviance, 133–138
  structural transformations, 178–179
Sociological imagination, 7
Sociological perspective
  assumptions of, 4–6
  personal level, 4
  problems with, 7–9
Sociological theory
  definition of, 12
  of deviance, 133
Sociology
  data collection problems, 12–18
  definition of, 4
  historical development of, 9–11
  methods, 11–19
  questions, 11–12
  subversive nature of, 9
Soft money, 320–321
Software tools, for spying, 125
Soviet Union, 59
Spillover, 355
Sports
  as agent of ideological social control, 110–111
  cheating in, 81
  conflict model and, 47–48
  gender equity in, 423–426
  gender learning in, 268–269
  order model and, 47–48

Status, 27–30
Status dropout rate, 375
Stereotypes, 15, 28
Stigma, 382
Stratification, of families in U.S., 345–348, 346
Structural discrimination theories, 243–244
Structuralist view, 325
Structural theories, of social stratification, 195–198
Structural transformation of economy, 151–160
Students, college, Homeland Security
    tactics and, 122
Student subculture, 383
Subculture
  definition of, 84
  differences, deviance and, 136, 143
Subsidies, for big businesses, 335–336
Success (individual achievement), 375, 376
  culture and, 78–79
Sudan, unmarried Dinka men of, 71–72
Suicide
  probability, group affects on, 33–35
  types of, 34
Suicide (Durkheim), 10
Sunrise industries, 155
Sunset industries, 154
Superego, 94
Surveillance, government, 123
Sweatshops, 298
Symbols, cultural, 69
Synthesis model, assumptions of, 48–50
System-blame approach, to deviance, 138

Taxes, 289, 290
Tax expenditures, 227
Taylorization, 295
Teacher-student interactions, gender learning in, 268
Technology
  material, 69
  for monitoring employees, 295
  progress and, 81–82
  social, 70
Television
  as socialization agent, 97–98
  violence on, 101–102
Terrorism. *See also* September 11, 2001 terrorist attacks
  domestic, 121–123
Theodicy, 398
Theoretical questions, 13
Title IX, Education Amendments Act, 267
Tough Guise: Violence, Media, and the Crisis in Masculinity
    (Jhally), 102
Toys, in gender learning, 266
Tracking, 381–382
Tradition
  acceptance of, 8
  culture and, 84
Traffic violations, racial profiling and, 139, 140
Transnational corporations, 153, 160, 178, 292–293
Trickle-down economics and, 336–337
Two-party system, 319, 322

Unemployment, 303–304
    race/ethnicity and, 249
    rates, 158
Unions, 298–301
United States
    changing nature of, 154–157
    competition in, 79–81
    consensus on societal values, 58–59
    contemporary racial and ethnic relations, 251–255
    demographic change, 160, 163, 167, 179
    demographics of, 160, 161
    domestic policy, 337–338
    elderly (See Elderly)
    families, historical perspective, 344–351
        capitalist economy and, 344–345
        economic transformation and, 348–349
        stratification and, 345–348, 346
    foreign-born, 160, 161, 163
    government, 116–123
    by Hispanic origin, 163
    liberal democratic theory, 118
    popular surnames in, 161
    population demographics, changes in, 101
    principles, historical factors and, 77
    by race, 160, 162, 163, 166
    racial classification in, 234
    racial/ethnic clusters, 166
    religion, distinctive features of, 392–398
    religious beliefs, variety of, 394, 396
    religious organization, 396–398
    repression of dissent
        after September 11, 2001, 121–123
        prior to September 11, 2001, 119–120
    rural-urban differences, 84
    sending overseas, 153
    societal principles of, 77
    work in, 294–304
        problems with, 295–301
United States army draft, social class and, 216–217
United States Census Bureau, popular surnames in United
        States, 162
United States Constitution, 58–59
United States economoy, 37
United States Patriot Act of 2001, 121
United Students against Sweatshops (USAS), 419
Unnithan, N.Prabha, 54
Upper-lower class, 210
Upper-middle class, 210
Upper-upper class, 209
USAS (United Students against Sweatshops), 419
U.S. education, characteristics of, 367–373
US. Steel, 154, 155

Value neutrality, 13
Values
    cultural, 72, 76–86
    discrepancy with behavior, 83
    evaluation techniques, 76
    media and, 112
    from order and conflict perspective, 86
    social problems, 77–84

    social scientists and, 44
    sports and, 111
Variables, 18
Vertical mobility, 218
Veto groups, 323–324
Violence, 53–57
    description of, 43
    in families, 360–361
    in India, 54
    myth of peaceful progress and, 53, 55
    on television, 101–102
Voting, elderly population and, 178
Vouchers, educational, 369

Wages, 152–153, 158–159, 312
Want, concentration of, 294
War, paying for, 338
War on terror, 120, 121, 122
WASP Supremacists, 56
Wealth
concentration, inequalities in, 202
    corporate, concentration of, 293
    definition of, 202
    private, concentration of, 293–294
Wealthfare, 227
Welfare
    definition of, 226–228
    direct social control and, 113–114
    myths/stereotypes, 15
    poor people and, 221, 222
Western culture, secular, 75
WIC (Women, Infants, Children), 229
Winning, 79–81
Women
    biological differences from men, 260
    gender stratification of (See Gender stratification)
Women, Infants, Children (WIC), 229
Women's movement. See Feminist movement, in United
        States
Work, family roles and, 355–357
Workers
    control of, 295
    discouraged, 303
Workers compensation, 158–159
    Work–family interference, 355
Working (Terkel), 296
Working class, 159, 168, 212
Working conditions, dangerous, 297–298
Working poor, 159
Workplace
    discrimination, 301–303
    inequality, 279–281
    intersection of race and gender in, 279
    male dominance in, 302–303
Writers, U.S., 119

XYY syndrome, 133

Zero tolerance, 142